A History of Sanskrit Literature

A History of Sanskrit Literature

A. Berriedale Keith

MOTILAL BANARSIDASS PUBLISHERS
PRIVATE LIMITED • DELHI

Reprint: Delhi, 1996, 2001, ***2007***
First Indian Edition: Delhi, 1993

ISBN: 978-81-208-0979-6 (Cloth)
ISBN: 978-81-208-1100-3 (Paper)

MOTILAL BANARSIDASS
41 U.A. Bungalow Road, Jawahar Nagar, Delhi 110 007
8 Mahalaxmi Chamber, 22 Bhulabhai Desai Road, Mumbai 400 026
203 Royapettah High Road, Mylapore, Chennai 600 004
236, 9th Main III Block, Jayanagar, Bangalore 560 011
Sanas Plaza, 1302 Baji Rao Road, Pune 411 002
8 Camac Street, Kolkata 700 017
Ashok Rajpath, Patna 800 004
Chowk, Varanasi 221 001

PRINTED IN INDIA
BY JAINENDRA PRAKASH JAIN AT SHRI JAINENDRA PRESS,
A-45 NARAINA, PHASE-I, NEW DELHI 110 028
AND PUBLISHED BY NARENDRA PRAKASH JAIN FOR
MOTILAL BANARSIDASS PUBLISHERS PRIVATE LIMITED,
BUNGALOW ROAD, DELHI 110 007

IN MEMORIAM FRATRIS
ALAN DAVIDSON KEITH

(1885–1928)

PREFACE

TAKEN in conjunction with my *Sanskrit Drama*, published in 1924, this work covers the field of Classical Sanskrit Literature, as opposed to the Vedic Literature, the epics, and the Purāṇas. To bring the subject-matter within the limits of a single volume has rendered it necessary to treat the scientific literature briefly, and to avoid discussions of its subject-matter which appertain rather to the historian of grammar, philosophy, law, medicine, astronomy, or mathematics, than to the literary historian. This mode of treatment has rendered it possible, for the first time in any treatise in English on Sanskrit Literature, to pay due attention to the literary qualities of the Kāvya. Though it was to Englishmen, such as Sir William Jones and H. T. Colebrooke, that our earliest knowledge of Sanskrit poetry was due, no English poet shared Goethe's marvellous appreciation of the merits of works known to him only through the distorting medium of translations, and attention in England has usually been limited to the Vedic literature, as a source for comparative philology, the history of religion, or Indo-European antiquities; to the mysticism and monism of Sanskrit philosophy; and to the fables and fairy-tales in their relations to western parallels.

The neglect of Sanskrit Kāvya is doubtless natural. The great poets of India wrote for audiences of experts; they were masters of the learning of their day, long trained in the use of language, and they aim to please by subtlety, not simplicity of effect. They had at their disposal a singularly beautiful speech, and they commanded elaborate and most effective metres. Under these circumstances it was inevitable that their works should be difficult, but of those who on that score pass them by it may fairly be said *ardua dum metuunt amittunt vera viai*. It is in the great writers of Kāvya alone, headed by Kālidāsa, that we find depth of feeling for life and nature matched with perfection of expression and rhythm. The Kāvya literature includes some of the great poetry of the world, but it can never expect to attain wide popularity in the West, for it is essentially untranslatable;

German poets like Rückert can, indeed, base excellent work on Sanskrit originals, but the effects produced are achieved by wholly different means, while English efforts at verse translations fall invariably below a tolerable mediocrity, their diffuse tepidity contrasting painfully with the brilliant condensation of style, the elegance of metre, and the close adaptation of sound to sense of the originals. I have, therefore, as in my *Sanskrit Drama*, illustrated the merits of the poets by Sanskrit extracts, adding merely a literal English version, in which no note is taken of variations of text or renderings. To save space I have in the main dealt only with works earlier than A.D. 1200, though especially in the case of the scientific literature important books of later date are briefly noticed.

This book was sent in, completed for the press, in January 1926, but pressure of work at the University Press precluded printing until the summer of 1927, when it was deemed best, in order not to delay progress, to assign to this preface the notice of such new discoveries and theories of 1926 and 1927 as might have permanent interest.

On the early development of the Kāvya welcome light has been thrown by Professor H. Lüders's edition [1] of the fragments found in Central Asia of the *Kalpanāmaṇḍitikā* of Kumāralāta, which is the true description of the work hitherto known to us through a Chinese translation as the *Sūtrālaṁkāra* of Açvaghoṣa. That work, it is suggested, was very different in character from Kumāralāta's. It may have been an exposition in verse, possibly with prose additions, of the Canon of the Sarvāstivādins, and it may be represented by fragments still extant; this suggestion can be supported by Asaṅga's choice of title, *Mahāyānasūtrālaṁkāra*, for his exposition of Mahāyāna tenets. But that is still merely a conjecture, and even less proved is the view that Subandhu's famous allusion [2] *Bauddhasaṁgatim ivālaṁkārabhūṣitām* is to such a text as that ascribed to Açvaghoṣa. Kumāralāta may well have been a younger contemporary of Açvaghoṣa, who lived after the death of Kaniṣka, a fact which explains an old crux, the difficulty of ascribing to Açvaghoṣa the references

---

[1] *Bruchstücke der Kalpanāmaṇḍitikā des Kumāralāta*, Leipzig, 1926.

[2] Below, p. 308. Lévi (*Sūtrālaṁkāra*, ii. 15 f.) reads *saṁgītim* very plausibly, and holds that a work of Asaṅga is meant.

in the *Sūtrālaṁkāra* which seemed inconsistent with the traditional relation of the patriarch and that king. How the Chinese version of the *Kalpanāmaṇḍitikā*, 'that which is adorned by poetic invention', came to bear the style *Sūtrālaṁkāra*, remains an unexplained problem.

The fragments shed a very interesting light on the development of the style of prose mingled with verses which appears in a more elaborate form in the *Jātakamālā*. The narratives, eighty in number, which, with ten parables, make up the work, begin with the enunciation of some doctrine, which is then established by means of an appropriate narrative; unlike the *Jātakamālā*, the text does not follow a stereotyped plan of drawing out at the close of each tale the moral which it inculcates. The stanzas used are normally portions of the speeches of the dramatis personae; there is a complete breach with the tradition of the canonical texts which introduce such verses by the term *bhāṣām bhāṣate*; but of course this does not mean that Kumāralāta, or Ārya Çūra who follows this plan in the *Jātakamālā*, is the author of all the verses used; doubtless he often adopts or adapts current maxims. Narrative[1] or descriptive stanzas are rare, and they are marked out for the benefit of the reciter by the words *vaksyate hi*. Ārya Çūra, on the other hand, shows a distinct advance; he uses descriptive or narrative stanzas to the extent of over a fifth of his total number of verses, and omits any introduction, inserting them freely to beautify his prose narration. The parables take a different form: in them a prose parable (*dṛṣṭānta*) is simply followed by a prose exposition (*artha*). The language shows the same adherence to correct Sanskrit, with occasional lapses, as in Açvaghoṣa, and there is a rich variety of metres, including the earliest Āryās in Kāvya so far datable with reasonable certainty; the Çloka, Upajāti, Vasantatilaka, and Çārdūlavikrīḍita are affected. Very important is the fact that Prākrit lyric written in the Prākrit of the grammarians (Middle Prākrit) is preluded in two Prākrit Āryās, written in Old Çaurasenī, which already manifest that affection for long compounds which is carried to excess in the *Gaüḍavaha*.

[1] Cf. below, pp. 244, 256, 332. The evidence of slow development of use of narrative stanzas is clear. For the priority of Ārya Çūra to the *Vessantara Jātaka*, see R. Fick, *Festgabe Jacobi*, pp. 145–59.

Kālidāsa has suffered from attempts [1] to defy style by placing him before Açvaghoṣa, and to ignore [2] the use of his works in Vatsabhaṭṭi by ascribing him to the period 525–75, when no great Empire existed, on the strength of his picture of India in the *Raghuvança*. Much more ingenious is an effort [3] to fix his home in Kashmir, and to trace in his poetry an adumbration of the Pratyabhijñāçāstra of that land, with its doctrine of recognition of the unity of the divine love. Kālidāsa would thus be a master of suggestion, which later was definitely developed in Kashmir as the essence of poetry by the Dhvanikāra, who was doubtless not Ānandavardhana. Use by Kālidāsa of the *Padma Purāṇa* has been suggested but is not plausible. His possible relation to the Vākāṭakas has been investigated, and use has been made of Kṣemendra's ascription to him of a *Kunteçvaradautya*, but all is mere hypothesis.[4]

Discussion of the migration of fables and other literature has failed to achieve decisive results. Some stress has lately been laid on the evidence of connexions between Egypt and India contained in the *Oxyrhynchus Papyri*,[5] but it is difficult to believe seriously that Isis was worshipped in India as Maia,[6] as asserted with complete vagueness in the Isis litany,[7] and Professor Hultzsch's effort [8] to find Kanarese explanations for certain terms in the farce regarding Charition's adventures on the coast of a country bordering the Indian Ocean, are as little plausible as those of Sir G. Grierson to discover Sanskrit. It seems prima facie absurd to suppose that any Greek farce writer would trouble to embody passages in foreign speeches which would be utterly unintelligible to his audience.[9]

[1] Kshetreśachandra Chaṭṭopādhyāya, *Allahabad Univ. Stud.*, ii. 80 ff.; K. G. Śankar, IHQ. i. 309 ff. But contrast IHQ. ii. 660 for Açvaghoṣa's influence on Kālidāsa's grammar.

[2] D. R. Bhandarkar, ABI. viii. 202–4.

[3] Lachhmi Dhar Kalla, *Delhi University Publications*, no. 1.

[4] See POCM. 1924, p. 6.

[5] In ii. no. 300 a woman Indike appears.

[6] xi. no. 1380. That Māyā is meant is not probable.

[7] iii. no. 413.

[8] JRAS. 1904, pp. 399 ff.

[9] Pischel's view that mixture of language is Indian specifically is disproved by Reich, DLZ. 1915, p. 591. India was known in Egypt, but there is not the slightest ground to believe that any one knew Kanarese or Sanskrit well enough to reproduce either of them in a farce.

It is indeed probable that no assured results can be expected regarding borrowing of tales; Sir Richard Temple's ingenious suggestions [1] as to non-Aryan origins of certain *motifs*, with which may be compared those of Professor Przyluski [2] regarding the influence of Austro-Asiatic peoples on early Indian thought and speech, are inconclusive, nor is it clear that, as Dr. Gaster [3] inclines to hold, we owe to India the ideas of fallen angels, genii who return to earth, or legends of asceticism carried to ludicrous extremes. Dr. Gaster, however, rightly stresses the impossibility of assuming that India gave only and did not borrow, and insists on the importance of investigating the possibility of a literary origin for many fairy tales current among the people. Moreover, parallelism should often, it appears to me, be admitted in literary development. It is instructive, for instance, to compare the scheme of development of the practice of emboxing tales within tales given below (p. 320) for India with that suggested by Schissel von Fleschenberg [4] for Greek literature: the simple tale passes through stages illustrated by the *Milesiaka* of Aristeides, the work of Antonius Diogenes, the *Golden Ass* of Apuleius, and the romance of Petronius, to the complete outcome in later romance. The many *motifs* found in the *Kathāsaritsāgara*, for which parallels are adduced by the learned editor [5] of a new edition of Tawney's excellent version from western literature, suggest likewise that much may be said for the doctrine of parallelism.

On Çivadāsa's version of the *Vetālapañcaviṅçatikā* much light has been thrown by Hertel's researches.[6] He establishes that Çivadāsa used a version in verse, whence some stanzas of merit, including those cited below (p. 290), are taken; the many verse fragments found in his prose are explained by the origin of his work. Similar features are not rare in late texts, such as

[1] *Ocean of Story*, i. pp. xiv ff.

[2] For other possibilities (Sumerian connexions) cf. Przyluski, BSL. xxvii. 218–29.

[3] *Ocean of Story*, iii. pp. ix ff.

[4] *Entwickelungsgeschichte des griechischen Romans im Altertum*, and *Die griechische Novelle*; cf. Reich, DLZ. 1915, pp. 543 f. For the parallel development of the Helen and Sītā legends, see Printz, *Festgabe Jacobi*, pp. 103 ff.

[5] N. M. Penzer, *Ocean of Story*, ten vols., 1924–8. For elaborate notes on *motifs* see references in Indexes in each volume.

[6] *Streitberg Festgabe*, pp. 135 ff. He places him not much before A. D. 1487.

Meghavijaya's *Pañcākhyānoddhāra*, the *textus simplicior* of the *Çukasaptati*, the *Madanarekhākathā*, the *Kusumasārakathā*, the *Aghaṭakumārakathā*,[1] and that version of the *Vetālapañcaviṅçatikā* which goes back to Kṣemendra's verse rendering. This, however, does not decide the question of the original form of the *Vetālapañcaviṅçatikā*; the common source of Kṣemendra and Somadeva may have been in prose or prose and verse; we have not sufficient evidence to show which. Hertel proves by comparison of texts that Çivadāsa was deeply influenced in vocabulary and syntax by Old Gujarātī, and concludes that he was a man of small education, belonging to the class who did not use Sanskrit as their 'Hochsprache', but understood it *tant bien que mal*, and endeavoured to express themselves in it.

The question of the authenticity of the dramas ascribed to Bhāsa by the late T. Gaṇapati Çāstrī has been frequently discussed since my *Sanskrit Drama* appeared, but without results of value, largely because the true issues have been misunderstood and effort has been devoted to proof of the obvious. It is true that it is not a matter of much importance whether the dramas be ascribed to Bhāsa or to an unknown poet, but it is important to consider whether (1) they are all by one hand, and (2) by a writer earlier than Kālidāsa and the *Mṛcchakaṭikā*. Both these propositions seem to me clearly established, for, though some Indian and, less excusably, some European [2] scholars still seem not to have weighed the evidence adduced by Dr. Morgenstierne, the English protagonist against T. Gaṇapati Çāstrī's theory recognizes that the *Cārudatta* must be placed before the *Mṛcchakaṭikā*. Priority to Kālidāsa seems established by evidence of use by that poet, and of greater antiquity in technique, style, diction, metre, and forms of Prākrit; it is significant that Kālidāsa has Māhārāṣṭrī, unknown to Bhāsa. Moreover, it is perfectly clear that Bhāsa's Prākrits, as revealed by the manuscripts of his plays, occupy a position intermediate between the Prākrits of Açvaghoṣa and of Kālidāsa as shown by European critical [3] editions. It is no reply to this fact to point out that manuscripts

[1] Trans. Ch. Krause, *Ind. Erz.*, iv.

[2] Nobel, ZII. v. 141 f. He sets Çūdraka and the *Mṛcchakaṭikā* before Kālidāsa.

[3] Indian editions, e.g. that of the *Āçcaryacūḍāmaṇi*, have not even the value of a MS. in this connexion.

of Kālidāsa's works of similar provenance to those of Bhāsa's dramas show Prākrit forms similar to those of Bhāsa's plays, for the obviously correct explanation is that Kālidāsa's works in these southern manuscripts have been affected by the usage of Bhāsā. It is clear that quite late dramas use forms of the Prākrits of Bhāsa, doubtless as a result of his great influence, just as the dramas recently published from southern manuscripts show frequent signs of borrowing of ideas and style from Bhāsa, as in the case of the *Dāmakaprahasana* absurdly ascribed to him.[1] Moreover, it must be noted that the most searching criticism has failed yet to find any proof of borrowing by Bhāsa from Kālidāsa, or references to matters later than that poet. The effort to turn the term *rājasiṅhaḥ*—a mere variant of *rājā*—into a proper name has found no general acceptance, and the identification of the *Nyāyaçāstra* of Medhātithi, mentioned in the *Pratimānāṭaka*, with Medhātithi's commentary on Manu is clearly due to forgetfulness that Medhātithi is obviously Gautama, the famous author of the *Nyāya Sūtra*. Unity of authorship is proved by style, a consideration which unfortunately seems often to be ignored, as when, for instance, it seems seriously to be suggested [3] that the author of the *Āçcaryacūḍāmaṇi*,[4] Çaktibhadra, who obviously imitated Bhāsa, might be the author of the works. This evinces the same curious lack of discrimination which ascribes to Daṇḍin the *Avantisundarīkathā*, credits Bāṇa with the *Pārvatīpariṇaya*, and would rob Kālidāsa of the *Ṛtusaṁhāra*.

The ascription of these old plays specifically to Bhāsa rests primarily on the testimony of Rājaçekhara, doubtless the critic and dramatist of *c*. A.D. 900, who tells us that the *Svapnavāsavadatta* of Bhāsa survived exposure to the fire of criticism, when his dramas were exposed to that ordeal by experts. It would indeed be a curious coincidence if an unknown dramatist had written like Bhāsa a number of dramas, of which the *Svapnavāsavadattā* stands out in the judgement of many critics as unques-

[1] See Jolly's disproof, *Festgabe Garbe*, pp. 115–21.

[2] See Keith, BSOS. iii. 623–5. A like lapse has converted the *Priyadarçikā* into the *Ratnāvalī* (JRAS. 1927, p. 862, n. 1) and found the Oḍras in the *Taittirīya Araṇyaka* in lieu of the *Trikāṇḍaçeṣa*, ii. 1. 11 (*Cambridge Hist. of India*, i. 601). Quandoque bonus dormitat Homerus!

[3] MASI. xxviii. 10; IHQ. iii. 222.

[4] Of uncertain, but not early date, and of modest literary value.

tionably the finest, and in any case is so admirable that it may easily have won general acceptance in Rājaçekhara's circle as the finest of the works. Add to this the facts that Kālidāsa himself, who seems from internal evidence to have sought to vie with these dramas, recognizes ruefully the great difficulty a young poet must have in contending with Bhāsa, and that the author of these works is assuredly a greater dramatist than any other Sanskrit writer than Kālidāsa, and Rājaçekhara's testimony is strongly confirmed. Again, from the vast mass of confused conjecture on the mode of beginning dramas, the fact emerges that Bāṇa's reference to Bhāsa's dramas as introduced by the Sūtradhāra corresponds precisely with the manner of introducing these dramas, and, when all is said and done, is most simply and naturally explained by the obvious view that he is referring to them.

One argument against the validity of Rājaçekhara's evidence should be noted. It is claimed [1] that in the context of the passage Rājaçekhara ascribes the authorship of the *Priyadarçikā*, *Ratnāvalī*, and *Nāgānanda* to Bhāsa and, therefore, must be untrustworthy. It is deplorable that this argument should ever have been adduced; the alleged context is plainly and indubitably a recent forgery,[2] and it would be idle to attach any value to other arguments adduced by a critic who has not the capacity to avoid being deceived, and unfortunately deceiving others, by such evidence. It must, however, be admitted that the forgery is so gross and palpable that it was presumably never intended to be taken seriously, and other Indian scholars have been prompt to repudiate it.

The ascription suggested by the evidence given above has recently been confirmed in the most gratifying manner by the discovery of fresh references in works on poetics and dramaturgy, inaccessible in Europe. The *Çṛṅgāraprakāça* of Bhoja in the eleventh century A.D. attests the currency of a drama in essentials as regards substance in accord with Act V of the *Svapnavāsava-*

[1] K. R. Pisharoti, IHQ. i. 105. The same writer makes an error of six centuries in Kulaçekhara's date, and numerous other serious blunders, in which others have followed him, including a complete failure to understand the issues as to Prākrit.

[2] K. G. Sesha Aiyar, IHQ. i. 361; G. Harihar Sastri, *ibid.*, 370–8. Dr. Sukthankar's acceptance of this foolish and obvious forgery is regrettably uncritical, as is his following of Mr. Pisharoti as to the Prākrits.

dattā; the *Bhāvaprakāça* of Çāradātanaya (13th century), knew a work not merely very similar in structure, but actually containing a verse found in the Trivandrum text. Sāgaranandin in the *Nāṭakalakṣaṇaratnakoça* ascribes to the *Svapnavāsavadattā* a passage which undoubtedly, as T. Gaṇapati Çāstrī shows, is a paraphrase of a passage at the beginning of our text, not a citation from a variant text as Professor Lévi suggested.[1] I agree also with T. Gaṇapati Çāstrī that the passage cited by Rāmacandra and Guṇacandra in the *Nāṭyadarpaṇa* from Bhāsa's *Svapnavāsavadattā* could easily have found a place in our text, while in any event it is clear that that play contained a scene parallel with one in our play. The most that can be made out from these facts against the ascription to Bhāsa is simply that there were probably varying recensions of the plays. That, of course, may be taken for granted; it was the fate of every much-studied and used play, and we have it exemplified to perfection in the case of Kālidāsa,[2] the variations regarding whose works seem to have been unknown to or forgotten by those who refuse to recognize Bhāsa's authorship of these dramas. There is no evidence at all to show that any of the versions of the *Çakuntalā* can be credited with any greater fidelity to the original of Kālidāsa than is possessed by the Trivandrum *Svapnavāsavadattā* in relation to Bhāsa's original. Moreover, it seems too often to be forgotten that variants may be due to the dramatist himself, who can hardly be supposed to have given his dramas a single perfectly definite text. It is, of course, tempting to adopt with Hermann Weller[3] the belief that the actors of Kerala have the responsibility for mangling our texts, and to accept the view that Bhāsa is preserved to us in a deteriorated form, and that, for example, the *Pratijñāyaugandharāyaṇa* and the *Svapnavāsavadattā* made up a single piece. But I am satisfied that to accept this view is uncritical and is to substitute our preferences for reality; the pedestrian character of some of Bhāsa's stanzas can far better be explained by the simple fact of his early date; Kālidāsa exhibits the influence of increased refinement of style in his dramas, just

[1] JA. cciii. 193 ff., followed in the very uncritical MASI. xxviii. 11.

[2] Cf. also the recensions of the *Uttararāmacarita*, Belvalkar, JAOS. xxxiv. 428 ff.

[3] Trans. of *Svapnavāsavadattā*, p. 8. The same theory applies, of course, to the *Çakuntalā*.

as in his epics he normally avoids the pedestrian traits which are easily to be found in the epics of his forerunner Açvaghoṣa. The dramatic defects of Bhāsa need not be ascribed to actors, for Kālidāsa himself in any version of even the *Çakuntalā* is far from perfect, and Shakespeare's flaws are notorious. On the other hand, we owe a very considerable debt to Hermann Weller [1] for showing in detail, with true insight into the nature of Bhāsa's poetic talent,[2] that six of the stanzas which by the anthologies are attributed to Bhāsa bear remarkable resemblance to the style of stanzas in our dramas. We may dismiss as far-fetched the suggestion that the makers of anthologies ascribed them to him because they felt in them the spirit of his poetry; it is common sense to assume that the ascriptions are correct, and that they add one more link to the chain of evidence which ascribes the dramas to Bhāsa, and vindicates the suggestion of a great Indian scholar.

The effort [3] to strengthen the case for dating Daṇḍin later than Bhāmaha by using the evidence of the *Avantisundarīkathā* and its *Sāra* is clearly a complete mistake. The Kathā should never have been published from one mutilated manuscript, whose readings, even if correctly stated, have already been proved wrong by other manuscript evidence.[4] Even, however, from the mutilated text it was clear that Bhāravi was not made out to be the great-grandfather of Daṇḍin, who is given as Dāmodara. But, as Dr. Dé [5] has pointed out, even the most careless reader of the Kathā and the *Daçakumāracarita* should have been struck by the extraordinary difference of style between the two works, the Kathā rivalling unsuccessfully the worst mannerisms of the *Harṣacarita* and the *Kādambarī*. If a Daṇḍin wrote the work, he was assuredly not the author of the *Daçakumāracarita,* and its date may be centuries later than the great Daṇḍin, for there is no reason to accept the suggestion [6] that the writer of the Kathā lived sufficiently soon after the famous Daṇḍin to be familiar

[1] *Festgabe Jacobi*, pp. 114–25.

[2] Cf. Garbe's emphatic testimony, *Festgabe Jacobi*, p. 126, in contrast with ZII. ii 250; ABA. viii. 17 ff.

[3] J. Nobel, ZII. v. 136–52.

[4] G. Harihar Sastri, IHQ. iii. 169–71.

[5] IHQ. iii. 395 ff. As Daṇḍin wrote according to Bhoja's *Çṛṅgāraprakāça* (BSOS. iii. 282) a *Dvisaṁdhānakāvya*, this may be his third work (cf. below, p. 296).

[6] *Ibid.*, p. 403.

with his genealogy and to work it into his story. It may be added that the effort [1] to find in v. 17 of the Kathā an allusion to *kāvyatraya* of Kālidāsa, thus confirming the denial to him of the *Ṛtusaṁhāra*, is wholly impossible and has not even the authority of the editor. It is very difficult to say whether we can derive from the Kathā any assurance as to Bhāravi's connexion with Viṣṇuvardhana or identify the latter with the prince who became Eastern Cālukya king in A.D. 615 and was the brother of that Pulakeçin, whose Aihole inscription (A.D. 634) mentions Bhāravi's fame, but at least there is no flagrant anachronism, though we know already of one literary forgery [2] which ascribes to Durvinīta of Koñgaṇi a commentary on *Kirātārjunīya* xv.

Of Abhinavagupta's important commentary on the *Nāṭya Çāstra* we have now the beginning of an edition, which, unhappily, is fundamentally uncritical,[3] while a new effort [4] has been made to assign their precise shares in the *Kāvyaprakāça* to its two authors, but without any convincing result; in cases of this sort it is probably hopeless *a priori* to expect to find any conclusive evidence; an editor who has to fill out lacunae is certain to adapt the whole more or less to his own style and to render restoration of the original and his additions almost impossible.[5]

The curious scepticism which has marked the attitude of Indian and some European scholars towards Bhāsa has not been shown in recent work on the *Kauṭilīya Arthaçāstra*, on which I have written in the Patna memorial volume in honour of that great Indian, Sir Asutosh Mookerjee. The only ground of this differentiation of treatment appears to be the sanctity ascribed to the written word: because the work in an obviously later appended verse assures us it was written by Viṣṇugupta, i. e. Kauṭilya—the reading Kauṭalya is clearly [6] of no value—therefore it

[1] ZII. v. 143.

[2] *Ep. Carn.*, iii. 107. It is noteworthy that a Durvinīta appears in the Kathā.

[3] *Gaekwad Oriental Series* 36, 1926 (i–vii); cf. S. K. Dé, IHQ. iii. 859–68.

[4] H. R. Divekar, JRAS. 1927, pp. 505–20; he assigns all the commentary to Alaṭa as well as the Kārikās from that on Parikara.

[5] The effort of Dr. Dé to ascribe Vallabhadeva's *Subhāṣitāvali* to the 12th cent. has been discussed in a note to appear in BSOS. iv. (1928). As regards Kavirāja's date (below, p. 137), Achyutacharan Chaudhuri ascribes him to the 11th cent. as protégé of a king Kāmadeva of Jaintia; see IHQ. iii. 848 f.

[6] Cf. P. V. Kane, ABI. vii. 89; Jolly, ZII. v. 216–21. Bhandarkar's theory (ABI. vii. 65–84) of a verse original known to Daṇḍin is incapable of demonstration.

must be so, although it seems patently absurd that the minister of an Emperor should confine his work to a moderate-sized kingdom, and should not once by word or allusion betray the name of the country for which and in which he was writing. Nevertheless there is nothing too fantastic to find defenders, though it is difficult not to feel that it is a very misplaced patriotism which asks us to admire the *Arthaçāstra* as representing the fine flower of Indian political thought. It would, indeed, be melancholy if this were the best that India could show as against the *Republic* of Plato or the *Politics* of Aristotle, or even the common-sense and worldly wisdom of the author of the tract on the constitution of Athens, formerly ascribed falsely to Xenophon. Certainly fantastic is the elaborate theory worked out by J. J. Meyer in his translation, and in his treatise *Über das Wesen der indischen Rechtsschriften und ihr Verhältnis zu einander und zu Kauṭilya* (1927). These works, produced in great difficulties, contain, amid much that is unsound and despite disconcerting changes of view, valuable contributions to our understanding of Kauṭilya, and throw light on many of the obscure sides of Indian life. But the main thesis of the author, who seeks to distinguish two sharply severed streams of literature, the one Brahmanical, essentially concerned with magic, the other of the people, practical and legal, is clearly based on a false foundation. The effort to regard the Brahmins as something apart in Indian life is one of those delusions which may find sympathy in the non-Brahmanical classes in India and in Europe, but which run counter to all that we know of Indian thought, which owes its life and strength to the Brahmins, not to warriors or rulers, still less to the commonalty. The efforts of the author[1] to establish that the *Arthaçāstra* was used by *Yājñavalkya* are certainly without weight; the evidence tends far more to show that the borrowing was the other way. Not a single passage referred to really favours the priority of the *Arthaçāstra*, but in several passages the obscurities of the

W. Ruben's defence of Jacobi's date (*Festgabe Jacobi*, pp. 346 ff.) is ineffective. For Kālidāsa's relation to the *Arthaçāstra*, cf. K. Balasubrahmanya Ayyar, POCM. 1924, pp. 2–16.

[1] pp. 65, 69, 70, 71, 77, 121, 130, 133, 158–79, 179–90, 213, 216, 284, 290, 294, 299, 300.

Arthaçāstra can be readily understood by realizing that it was drawing from *Yājñavalkya*. Nor does Meyer attempt systematically[1] to prove that *Manu* is later than the *Arthaçāstra*, though on his theory of dates that text is more than a hundred years at least posterior to the *Arthaçāstra*. He has been as unable as the Indian supporters of Cāṇakya's[2] authorship to explain the silence which the *Arthaçāstra* observes regarding everything imperial and its absolute ignoring of the facts as to Pāṭaliputra. His further effort[3] to prove the late date of the *Gautama Dharmaçāstra* is in itself less open to objection, but his contentions are largely inconclusive[4] and do little more than prove, what has always been admitted, that our text of that Dharmaçāstra has been considerably worked over. The main principles of the development of the legal literature remain as they were formulated by Max Müller and Bühler, and further established by Oldenberg and Jolly. Indeed, Meyer's own view at present[5]—his conclusions lack admittedly any great fixity—is that *Baudhāyana* and *Āpastamba* are pre-Buddhist, *Vāsiṣṭha* belongs to the fourth century B. C., and *Manu* may be ascribed rather nearer to 200 B. C. than to A. D. 200; there is, however, no tolerable proof of *Vāsiṣṭha's* posteriority to *Āpastamba*, still less that *Āpastamba* is pre-Buddhist in date. Still less convincing again are Meyer's efforts[6] to assign *Nārada* to a period anterior to *Manu* and *Yājñavalkya*; if we take our present texts as the basis of argument, this is certainly out of the question; if we reconstruct originals for all three, we lose ourselves in idle conjectures which, like all guesses, merely obscure knowledge. For *Yājñavalkya* there may be noted an interesting effort[7] to reconstruct the original Smṛti on the basis of comparison with parallel texts in the *Agni* and the *Garuḍa Purāṇas*. It is very possible that

[1] What is said, e. g. p. 112, is quite inconclusive; contrast IHQ. iii. 812.

[2] Jacobi (IHQ. iii. 669-75) holds that Cāṇakya and Viṣṇugupta were distinct persons later confused with Kauṭilya. Cāṇikya may be original, not Cāṇakya.

[3] See references at pp. 417, 418.

[4] For a further argument as to Gautama's later date, see Bata Krishna Ghosh, IHQ. iii. 607-11.

[5] *Altind. Rechtsschriften*, p. vii.

[6] Ibid., pp. 82-114.

[7] Hans Losch, *Die Yājñavalkyasmṛti* (1927). The *Garuḍa* has a version of the Nidānasthāna of the *Aṣṭāṅgahṛdaya* and *Aṣṭāṅgasaṁhitā*; *Festgabe Garbe*, pp. 102 ff.

the parts of the text dealing with Rājadharma and Vyavahāra have been amalgamated with a text dealing with the topics of the Gṛhyasūtras; but it is very dubious if it is possible to recover the original form of the Smṛti. It is, of course, easy to eliminate certain obviously late passages, such as those dealing with the Vināyaka- and Graha-çānti and the anatomical matter in Book iii, but the more radical analysis suggested is far less satisfactorily made out.

Of auxiliary sciences architecture has at last received expert treatment from Professor Prasanna Kumar Acharya in his *Dictionary of Hindu Architecture* and *Indian Architecture*,[1] based on a new text and rendering of the *Mānasāra*, for which the period of A. D. 500–700 is suggested. Striking similarities between the prescriptions of the *Mānasāra* and Vitruvius are unquestionably established. Unhappily, the deplorable condition of the text of the *Samarāṅgaṇasūtradhāra*[2] of Bhoja adds to the difficulty of valuing his remarks on architecture, town-planning, engineering, and the construction of remarkable machines, probably akin to the mechanical toys of the Middle Ages.[3] The *Principles of Indian Śilpa Śāstra*, with the text of the *Mayaśāstra*, by Phanindra Nath Bose, is also of value.[4] Hawking figures in a *Çyainikaçāstra* by Rudradeva.

On the early development of logic an interesting light has been thrown by Professor O. Strauss's demonstration from the *Mahābhāṣya*[5] that Patañjali was well acquainted with the doctrine of the causes familiar from the *Sāṁkhyakārikā*[6] why things in themselves visible are sometimes not seen, and also had some knowledge of the theory of the syllogism—how much, is not altogether certain. The evidence, however, is useful as supporting the view that our philosophical Sūtras are essentially the outcome of a long period of development, and, whatever their date as we have them, contain doctrines much earlier in point of time. The effort to distinguish strata, though energetically pursued, leads to little that is certain. For instance, while we may readily believe

[1] Oxford, 1927 ff. [2] GOS. 1924-5.

[3] *Ocean of Story*, iii. 56 ff.

[4] A text and trans. of a *Çilpa Çāstra* are in print.

[5] *Festgabe Garbe*, pp. 84-94. See also Prabhat Chandra Chakravarti, IHQ. ii. 478 ff.

[6] Verse 7; cf. Caraka, Sūtrasthāna, ix. 8.

that the *Pūrvamīmāṅsā* and the *Vedānta Sūtras* represent a long period of working over, it is by no means clear that we can deduce[1] from a remark of so late a writer as Sureçvara that Jaimini, the author of the *Pūrvamīmāṅsā*, also wrote a more philosophical *Çārīraka Sūtra*, the first two Sūtras of which correspond with those of the extant *Vedānta Sūtra*. The fact that in these two *Sūtras*, *Pūrvamīmāṅsā* and *Vedānta*, references are made both to Jaimini and Bādarāyaṇa is best explained, not by assuming a number of Jaiminis and Bādarāyaṇas, but simply by recognizing that each text represents a long scholastic development and that the use of the names may not represent the views of the authors in question any more accurately than do, for instance, those of the Christian Fathers or the Scholastics the doctrines of Aristotle, or those of the neo-Platonists those of Plato. Nothing, of course, conclusive can be adduced against the belief in many Jaiminis or Bādarāyaṇas, and recourse has recently been had[2] to the same device to explain the fact that Prabhākara sometimes appears in tradition as later than Kumārila, while his work as known to us shows no certain trace of such a relation. In this case the suggestion is probably needless. The much discussed question of Dignāga's place in the history of Indian logic, in special his relation to Praçastapāda, has been furthered by Dr. Randle's edition of Dignāga's fragments[3]; it appears to me that Dignāga's priority is still the more probable view, but this issue, as well as the important contributions to our knowledge of Indian philosophy by Professor M. Walleser, Th. Stcherbatsky, Louis de la Vallée Poussin, S. Radhakrishnan, Das Gupta, O. Strauss, Masson Oursel, J. W. Hauer, Ryukan Kimura, Kokileswar Sastri, Mahendranath Sircar, and others, must be reserved for discussion elsewhere. Y. Kanakura[4] has shown that the alleged interpolations in Çaṅkara's Bhāṣya are known to Vācaspati Miçra, while the date adopted by me[5] for Çaṅkara is supported by Jinavijaya's proof that Haribhadra, whom Çaṅkara

[1] S. K. Belvalkar, *Festgabe Garbe*, pp. 162–70; *Ind. Phil. Rev.*, ii. 141–5. *Contra*, Nilakantha Sastri, IA. l. 172.

[2] Stcherbatsky, *Festgabe Jacobi*, p. 372. What is said in POCM. 1924, pp. 475 ff., 523 ff. is inconclusive.

[3] The *Nyāyapraveça* is now published in GOS. 32 (vol. ii).

[4] *Festgabe Jacobi*, pp. 381–5; on Ānandajñāna, cf. p. 382, n. 1.

[5] IOC. ii. 612.

used, falls in the period A. D. 700–770. Mention, however, should be made of the controversy which has raged over the authorship of the *Nyāyapraveça*, which is ascribed with equal confidence to Dignāga[1] and to Çaṅkarasvāmin[2]; a final judgement is difficult, and the matter has been dealt with by me at length in an article to appear elsewhere.[3] It should also be noted that Professor Jacobi[4] has now admitted that the *Nyāya Sūtra* knows the Vijñānavāda system, on the ground that the Sūtra in iv. 2. 26 deals with a Vijñānavāda tenet found in the *Laṅkāvatāra*; I have already dealt with this suggestion,[5] and pointed out that it possesses no cogency. Professor Jacobi's further suggestion that Vātsyāyana knew Vasubandhu and may be placed *c.* 400 accords with the results adopted by me[6] on the score of other evidence. He criticizes the well-known attempt of S. C. Vidyabhusana to prove that Uddyotakara and Dharmakīrti were contemporaries, on the ground that (1) Uddyotakara must have flourished a generation before Bāṇa since he was known to Subandhu, and (2) Dharmakīrti cannot have attained literary fame before Hiuen Tsang's stay in India, since he ignores him as an author of standing. These arguments are not conclusive, and it is quite possible that Subandhu, Bāṇa, Uddyotakara, and Dharmakīrti were more or less contemporaries; this issue also will be dealt with elsewhere. But Professor Jacobi renders it very probable that Dignāga, perhaps even Dharmakīrti, was known to the well-known *Maṇimēkhalai* in Tamil.[7]

On the interesting issue of the effect of Indian philosophy on Schopenhauer and of the present importance of that philosophy for western thought reference may be made to the *Fünfzehntes Jahrbuch der Schopenhauer-Gesellschaft*, 1928. An energetic polemic against the view of early influence of Indian on Greek philosophy has been delivered by Th. Hopfner,[8] which at least

[1] Vidhushekhara Bhattacharya, IHQ. iii. 152–60.

[2] Tubianski, *Bulletin de l'Académie de l'USSR*. 1926, pp. 975 ff.

[3] IHQ. 1928.

[4] ZII. v. 305 f.

[5] *Indian Logic and Atomism*, pp. 23 f.

[6] Ibid., pp. 27 f.

[7] ZII. v. 305; the *Nyāyapraveça* was used in the *Maṇimēkhalai* (p. 309). On the vexed date of the Çangam literature, cf. K. G. Śankar, JRAS. 1924, pp. 664–7.

[8] *Orient und griechische Philosophie* (1925). For a probably forged reference to Apollonius of Tyana in a Sanskrit text, see M. Hiriyanna, IHQ. ii. 415.

has the merit of showing the precariousness of the assumptions of such influence. Part of the argument for Indian influence rests on the belief in early dates for the Indian schools of thought, and it is clear that there is great difficulty in arriving at definite conclusions on this issue. Thus Professor Das Gupta [1] places the *Laṅkāvatāra* before Açvaghoṣa, but the text we have seems to know the Vijñānavāda school and the barbarian inroads of *c*. A. D. 500. Much stress has of late been laid on the Sāṁkhya philosophy,[2] as it is presented in the Saṁhitā of Caraka, but it seems to be overlooked that we have not the slightest proof that this or any special part of the text is really Caraka's.[3]

Some light has been thrown by the discoveries of manuscripts in East Turkestan on the *Bheḍa Saṁhitā*.[4] A paper manuscript with a fragment of the text, which can be assigned to the ninth century A. D., suggests strongly that the text published from a single Telugu MS. presents a version of the Saṁhitā which has suffered alteration, a chapter on *raktapitta* in the Nidānasthāna having been replaced by one on *kāsa*. Another manuscript fragment, written on leather, from South Turkestan or Northern India, dating probably from the end of the second century A. D., say a hundred years before the manuscript of the *Kalpanāmaṇḍitikā* and fifty years after the manuscript of Açvaghoṣa's plays, is of interest, as it preserves a tradition of a doctrine of eight or ten *rasas* as opposed to the six which Caraka and Suçruta recognize, and which are generally accepted in Indian medicine. It is possible that we here have a trace of an older medical system, which was ultimately superseded by the system of Ātreya, on which the work of Caraka is based.

The vexed issue of the indebtedness of Arabia and Europe to India for the numerical system has been reconsidered by Sukumar Ranjan Das,[5] who has dealt at length with Dr. Kaye's views.

[1] *Hist. of Indian Phil.*, i. 280.

[2] *Ibid.*, i. 280 f., 312 ff.

[3] Cf. Hoernle, *Archiv f. Gesch. d. Medizin*, i. 30 ff.; Jolly, *Munich Catal.*, p. 48. The list of Tantrayuktis in viii is, of course, by Dṛḍhabala, who again used the Uttaratantra of Suçruta; Ruben, *Festgabe Jacobi*, pp. 354–7.

[4] H. Lüders, *Festgabe Garbe*, pp. 148 ff.; for the doubtful character of Caraka's text, see also pp. 154 f.

[5] IHQ. ii. 97–120; iii. 356–75. See also D. E. Smith, *Hist. of Math.*, vol. ii, ch. ii.

Some of the evidence adduced is clearly inconclusive. The *Arthaçāstra* knows (ii. 7) an elaborate system of keeping accounts, but its date cannot be assumed as the fourth century B.C., nor does in any case the keeping of accounts imply any definite system of the use of numerals similar to that attested for the sixth century A.D.[1] References to boys learning reckoning (*saṁkhyāna*)[2] are equally inconclusive, and the date of the *Lalitavistara* is very uncertain. But the use of *çūnya* in the *Chandassūtra* of Piñgala[3] must be accorded due weight, and the Indian hypothesis has gained strength from the new investigations accorded to it. But certainty is unattainable, and it may be observed that, while the identification of Puliça with Paulus of Alexandria is merely conjectural, it is not sufficient to dispose of it by pointing out that Puliça was an authority on astronomy, Paulus on astrology, for we have nothing to show that the latter did not deal with astronomy, as would be natural enough in a professed astrologer.[4]

On the question of the origin of Sanskrit no conclusive evidence has been recently adduced. Professor Hertel's conviction of the late date of the *Ṛgveda* and of Zoroaster is not likely to secure general acceptance, despite its ingenuity,[5] nor is a recent and not less ingenious effort[6] to show that the Aryans lived for a time together under strong Mitanni influences and only turned definitely east, to break up into Indians and Iranians, after the Mitanni *débâcle* in the middle of the fourteenth century B.C. The deductions drawn from certain terms, and from the similarity of Çiva to the Himmels-und Wettergott of Asia Minor, whose name in Mitanni was Tešup, and of Pārvatī to the Great Mother of Asia Minor, Hepa in Mitanni, and from the syllabic Brāhmī script, are all suggestive, but without probative force. Very interesting and worthy of serious consideration in the field of

[1] The Sumerians (*c.* 3000 B.C.) and the Egyptians had elaborate systems of account-keeping; see D. E. Smith, *Hist. of Math.*, i. 37 ff.

[2] *Arthaçāstra*, i. 5; *Lalitavistara*, x. 15.

[3] viii. 29 f.; Weber, IS. viii. 169, 444 ff. It must be noted that this part is not probably early, and is not to be assigned to the 2nd cent. B.C. (IHQ. iii. 374).

[4] On the *ketus* and their influence on men's fates, see Ballālasena's *Adbhutasāgara* (12th cent.), and J. von Negelein, *Festgabe Jacobi*, pp. 440 ff.; *Festgabe Garbe*, pp. 47–53.

[5] On Zoroaster's date cf. Keith, IHQ. iii. 683–9.

[6] W. Porzig, ZII. v. 265–80.

comparative philology are the arguments recently adduced by Professor Max Walleser[1] to refute the at present accepted theory regarding the merger in Sanskrit of the three vowels *a e o* into *a*, and to show that Sanskrit preserved as late as the seventh century A. D. the labio-velar consonants. One point is of special interest, as it confirms a view in which I differ from Professor Liebich,[2] the question of the priority of the *Taittirīya Prātiçākhya* to Pāṇini; it is made most probable that the distinction between *ā* and *a* as connected with the openness of the former and the closed character of the latter vowel was not noted by the *Ṛk* or *Taittirīya Prātiçākhyas* but by the *Atharva Prātiçākhya*, the *Vājasaneyi Prātiçākhya*, and Pāṇini. Liebich's argument against the priority of the *Taittirīya Prātiçākhya* to Pāṇini rests merely on the identity of certain Sūtras in both texts and the use of *pragraha* for *pragṛhya*. The latter appears to give no possible indication of relative position in time; it may be a local variant, which accords with other evidence as to the provenance of the text; the former fact is most naturally explained by the certainty that Pāṇini's work embodies much earlier material, which was made use of also by the Prātiçākhya, unless Pāṇini simply is the debtor to the Prātiçākhya.

In an exhaustive analysis of Yāska's etymologies[3] Dr. Hannes Sköld has suggested that certain of the suggested derivations are only explicable on the ground that Yāska was familiar with and used a Middle Indian (Prākrit) speech. Beside this suggestion may be placed the opinion recently expressed by Professor H. Lüders,[4] that the language of Açoka's Chancery was 'eine Art Hochsprache', while the actually spoken speech was much further advanced and probably had reached the stage represented in the literary Prākrits, though it is candidly admitted that the latter point cannot be said yet to have been established. Nor, it may be added, are Sköld's proofs regarding Yāska free from much doubt. But the more important issue is whether the matter is really to be viewed in the light suggested, of a contrast between actually spoken language and a Hochsprache. It is rather, it appears to me, a matter of class speeches; Yāska spoke Sanskrit

[1] ZII. v. 193–202; *Zur Aussprache des Sanskrit und Tibetischen* (1926).
[2] *Zur Einführung in die indische einheimische Sprachwissenschaft*, ii. 47.
[3] *The Nirukta*, pp. 128 ff.
[4] ZII. v. 259.

much as he wrote it, and the officials of Açoka equally conversed in a speech essentially similar to that in which they wrote, while contemporaneously lower classes of the population spoke in dialects which were far further advanced in phonetic change. It is clear that the Aryan invaders succeeded in imposing their speech on many of the earlier inhabitants of the country, and there is no cogent argument to refute the natural belief that strange Prākritic forms, such as we find sporadically even in the *Ṛgveda*, when not mere later corruptions are often loan-words from class dialects with which the speakers of the more conservative form of speech were in contact. The influence of lower speech-forms was doubtless of increasing importance, since it evoked the elaborate grammatical studies summed up in the *Aṣṭādhyāyī*, testifying to the anxiety of the priests to preserve the Bhāṣā from corruption, and Patañjali's insistence [1] on the evils of barbarisms doubtless proves their occurrence. But there seems no ground for conceiving of the position as one in which the priests used a formal language only in their business, and discarded it for a true vernacular in daily life. There seems a very fair analogy with the standard English of the higher classes of society in this country; the East-end curate's true vernacular is standard English, though he ought to be able to adapt his speech to the comprehension of the dockers if he works at a mission, and a landowner's true vernacular is that which he habitually uses in his own circle, not that in which he talks familiarly to his farm workers or villagers of the old type, whose dialect often is as different from standard English as an old Prākrit from Sanskrit. The presence of many Sanskritized versions of Prākrit terms, to which Zachariae [2] has suggested an interesting addition in the term *protha*,[3] is a perfectly natural phenomenon where higher and lower speeches exist contemporaneously in the same community, apart altogether from the further possibilities of speech mixture due to the development

[1] So already Kātyāyana, Vārttika 12 on Pāṇini, i. 3. 1. Sköld's effort (IA. lv. 181 ff.) to prove Pāṇini older than the *Ṛk Prātiçākhya* cannot be accepted, for the reasons given by B. Liebich, *Zur Einführung in die ind. einheim. Sprachwissenschaft*, ii. 30 f.

[2] ZII. v. 228–31.

[3] A variant for *pāntham* in the verse cited (from Bhāṣya on Pāṇini, i. 4. 56) below, p. 46. For the idea cf. *Çakuntalā*, iv. (ed. Cappeller), p. 48.

of local as well as class dialects. At any rate arguments used to deny vernacular character to Sanskrit are quite adequate to prove the same hypothesis of standard English, which unquestionably is a true vernacular.[1]

Moreover, the fact that Sanskrit was thus regularly used in conversation by the upper classes, court circles eventually following the example of the Brahmins in this regard, helps to explain the constant influence exercised by the higher form of speech on the vernaculars which reveals itself *inter alia* in the constant influx of Tatsamas, words whose phonetic state runs counter to the tendencies of the vernacular. It is quite impossible to explain this phenomenon adequately by the theory of borrowing from literature only; those who adapted the vernaculars for the purpose of writing in any form or literary composition were doubtless in constant touch with circles in which Sanskrit was actually in living use. Doubtless, important changes to the disadvantage of Sanskrit as a spoken language resulted from the Mahomedan invasions, which culminated in the substitution of a new speech in official use at the courts of Mahomedan rulers, but for the period from A. D. 300 up to 1200, dealt with in this work, there is little evidence of any fundamental change in the extent or character of the use of Sanskrit; the same impression is given by the *Kāmasūtra*, perhaps *c.* 400, the *Kāvyamīmāṅsā* of Rājaçekhara (*c.* 900), and Bilhaṇa (*c.* 1100).

On the vital chronological issue of Kaniṣka's date certainty has not yet been achieved; a case for A. D. 128–9 as the initial year of his era[2] has been made out, while his death in Khotan is assigned to 152.[3] This places him half a century after A. D. 78, and it can only be said at present that the new dating, while it has many merits, none the less leaves unexplained difficulties.

[1] An interesting loan-word is suggested in *kampana* or *kampanā* (below, p. 170) by B. Liebich (*Festgabe Streitberg*, pp. 230–2) who sees in it a derivative of *campus*. Liebich has a most amusing note (ZII. v. 153–63) showing how in *Pañcatantra*, i. 7 (below, p. 257) the original version has a bug, not a flea, but the latter was introduced by Burzōe's version. Burzōe's alleged narrative is suspected by Sir E. Denison Ross (*Ocean of Story*, v. pp. v ff.; BSOS. iii. 443), but the existence of a Pahlavi rendering, which alone is of importance to Indologists, is not questioned.

[2] W. E. van Wijk, *Acta Orientalia*, v. 168 ff.

[3] S. Konow, IHQ. iii. 851–6. The conclusions of this article are far from certain.

The affairs of Harṣa have recently been considered once more,[1] with the usual indecisive results.

The necessity of economy of space, no less than the meagre resources of the Library of a University perforce incurious of Oriental Letters, has necessitated the reduction of bibliographical references to a minimum, but I have, I trust, passed over nothing of permanent value; as in my *Religion and Philosophy of the Veda and Upanishads*, I have omitted such work as seems to display mere ingenuity or unscientifically to revive ancient errors. Specific acknowledgements will be found in the notes; a more general debt is due to the historians of literature and the editors of anthologies, and I tender grateful thanks to Professors Macdonell, Peterson, Thomas, Weber, Oldenberg, von Schroeder, and Winternitz. By devoting special attention to matters of style and literary form I have endeavoured to avoid dealing at length with issues already effectively discussed by my predecessors. In my short sketch of *Classical Sanskrit Literature*, written in 1922 for The Heritage of India Series, I have anticipated many of the views which here are set out in detail and supported by further argument.

I have to express my most sincere appreciation of the willingness of the Delegates of the Press to publish this work as well as my *Sanskrit Drama*, and of the great assistance rendered to me in preparing it by my wife.

A. BERRIEDALE KEITH.

UNIVERSITY OF EDINBURGH,
February 1928.

[1] Nihar Ranjan Ray, IHQ. iii. 769-92. Congratulations are due to the editor, Dr. Narendra Nath Law, of this most interesting Quarterly, in which there has already appeared much useful and suggestive work on a wide range of topics.

CONTENTS

PREFACE	vii
Kumāralāta and the early Kāvya, Sanskrit, and Prākrit	viii
Kālidāsa's Date and Place of Birth	x
Greek and Indian Fables	x
The Dramas of Bhāsa	xii
Daṇḍin and the *Avantisundarīkathā*	xvi
The Authenticity of the *Arthaçāstra*	xvii
The Dates of the Philosophical Systems	xx
Medical Fragments from Turkestan	xxiii
The Indian Origin of the Numerals	xxiii
Sanskrit as a vernacular	xxiv

PART I. THE LANGUAGE

I. Sanskrit, Prākrit, and Apabhrança.	?
1. The Origin of Sanskrit	3
2. The Character and Extent of the Use of Sanskrit	8
3. The Characteristics and Development of Sanskrit in Literature	17
4. The Prākrits	26
5. Apabhrança	32

PART II. BELLES-LETTRES AND POETICS

II. The Origin and Development of Kāvya Literature	39
1. The Sources of the Kāvya	39
2. The Testimony of the Rāmāyaṇa	42
3. The Evidence of Patañjali and Piṅgala	45
4. Kāvya in Inscriptions	48
5. The Kāmasūtra and the Poet's Milieu	51
III. Açvaghoṣa and Early Buddhist Kāvya	55
1. Açvaghoṣa's Works	55
2. Açvaghoṣa's Style and Language	59
3. The Avadānas	64
4. Ārya Çūra and later Poetry	67
IV. Kālidāsa and the Guptas	74
1. The Guptas and the Brahmin Revival	74
2. Hariṣeṇa and Vatsabhaṭṭi	77

3. Kālidāsa's Life 79
4. The Ṛtusaṁhāra 82
5. The Meghadūta 84
6. The Kumārasambhava 87
7. The Raghuvañça 92
8. Kālidāsa's Thought 98
9. Kālidāsa's Style and Metre . . . 101

V. Bhāravi, Bhaṭṭi, Kumāradāsa, and Māgha . . 109
1. Bhāravi 109
2. Bhaṭṭi 116
3. Kumāradāsa 119
4. Māgha 124

VI. The Lesser Epic Poets 132

VII. Historical Kāvya 144
1. Indian Historical Writing . . . 144
2. The Beginnings of History . . . 147
3. Bilhaṇa 153
4. Kalhaṇa's Life and Times . . . 158
5. The Rājataraṅgiṇī and its Sources . . 161
6. Kalhaṇa as a Historian . . . 164
7. Kalhaṇa's Style 169
8. Minor Historical Kāvya 172

VIII. Bhartṛhari, Amaru, Bilhaṇa, and Jayadeva . . 175
1. Bhartṛhari 175
2. Amaru 183
3. Bilhaṇa 188
4. Jayadeva 190

IX. Lyric Poetry and the Anthologies . . . 199
1. Secular Poetry 199
2. Religious Poetry 210
3. The Anthologies 222
4. Prākrit Lyrics 223

X. Gnomic and Didactic Poetry 227
1. Gnomic Poetry 227
2. Didactic Poetry 236

XI. The Didactic Fable 242
1. The Origin of the Fable 242
2. The Reconstruction of the Pañcatantra and its Origin 246
3. The Subject-matter of the Pañcatantra . . 248
4. The Style and Language of the Pañcatantra . 255
5. The Derivative Forms of the Pañcatantra . 259
6. The Hitopadeça 263
XII. The Bṛhatkathā and its Descendants . . 266
1. Guṇāḍhya and the Bṛhatkathā . . . 266
2. The Bṛhatkathāçlokasaṁgraha of Budhasvāmin . 272
3. The Kashmirian Bṛhatkathā . . . 275
4. Kṣemendra's Bṛhatkathāmañjarī . . . 276
5. Somadeva's Kathāsaritsāgara . . . 281
XIII. The Romantic and the Didactic Tale . . 288
1. The Romantic Tale 288
2. The Didactic Tale 293
XIV. The Great Romances 296
1. The Age and Works of Daṇḍin . . . 296
2. The Daçakumāracarita 297
3. The Content and Style of the Daçakumāracarita 299
4. Subandhu 307
5. The Vāsavadattā 308
6. Bāṇa's Life and Works 314
7. The Harṣacarita 316
8. The Kādambarī 319
9. Bāṇa's Style 326
XV. The later Romances and the Campūs . . 331
1. The Romances 331
2. The Campūs 332
XVI. The Aims and Achievement of Sanskrit Poetry . 338
1. The Aims and Training of the Poet . . 338
2. The Achievement 344
XVII. The West and Indian Literature . . . 352
1. The Fables and Märchen of Greece and India . 352
2. The Translations of the Pañcatantra . . 357
3. The Çukasaptati 359
4. Other Cases of Contact between East and West . 359

5. The Romance in Greece and India . . 365
6. The Hexameter and Indian Metre . . 370
XVIII. Theories of Poetry 372
1. The Beginnings of Theory on Poetry . . 372
2. The Early Schools of Poetics . . . 375
3. The Doctrine of Dhvani . . . 386
4. The Critics and Supporters of the Doctrine of Dhvani 391

PART III. SCIENTIFIC LITERATURE

XIX. The Origin and Characteristics of the Scientific Literature 403
1. The Origin of the Çāstras . . . 403
2. The Characteristics of the Scientific Literature 406
XX. Lexicography and Metrics . . . 412
1. The Origin and Characteristics of Sanskrit Lexicography 412
2. The Extant Lexica 413
3. Treatises on Metre 415
4. The Metres of Classical Poetry . . . 417
XXI. Grammar 422
1. The Beginnings of Grammatical Study . 422
2. Pāṇini and his Followers . . . 423
3. The Later Schools 431
4. Grammars of Prākrit 433
XXII. Civil and Religious Law (Dharmaçāstra) . . 437
1. The Origin of the Dharmaçāstras . . 437
2. The Smṛti of Manu 439
3. The Later Smṛtis 445
4. The Digests of Law 448
XXIII. The Science of Politics and Practical Life (Arthaçāstra, Nītiçāstra) 450
1. The Origin of the Arthaçāstra . . . 450
2. The Content and Form of the Kauṭilīya Arthaçāstra 452
3. The Authenticity of the Arthaçāstra . . 458
4. Later Treatises 462
5. Ancillary Sciences 464

XXIV. The Science of Love (Kāmaçāstra) . . 467
XXV. Philosophy and Religion 471
1. The Beginnings of Indian Philosophy . . 471
2. The Pūrvamīmāṅsā 472
3. The Vedānta 474
(*a*) The Doctrine of Non-duality and Illusion 475
(*b*) Rāmānuja 478
(*c*) Other Commentators . . . 479
4. Theology and Mysticism . . . 479
5. Logic and Atomism 482
6. The Sāṁkhya and Yoga Schools . . 487
7. Buddhism 491
8. Jainism 497
9. Cārvākas or Lokāyatas 498
10. Historians of Philosophy . . . 499
11. Greece and Indian Philosophy . . . 500
XXVI. Medicine 505
1. The Development of Indian Medicine . . 505
2. The Older Saṁhitās 506
3. The Medical Tracts in the Bower MS. . 509
4. Later Medical Works 510
5. Greece and Indian Medicine . . . 513
XXVII. Astronomy, Astrology, and Mathematics . 516
1. The pre-scientific Period . . . 516
2. The Period of the Siddhāntas . . . 517
3. Āryabhaṭa and later Astronomers . . 521
4. Āryabhaṭa and later Mathematicians . . 523
5. Greece and Indian Mathematics . . 525
6. Varāhamihira and early Astrologers . . 528
7. Greece and Indian Astrology . . . 530
8. Varāhamihira's Poetry 532
9. Later Works on Astrology . . . 534
English Index 537
Sanskrit Index 559

ABBREVIATIONS

ABA. Abhandlungen der Berliner Akademie der Wissenschaften, philol.-histor. Klasse.
ABayA. Abhandlungen der Bayerischen Akademie der Wissenschaften, phil. Klasse.
ABI. Annals of the Bhandarkar Institute.
AGGW. Abhandlungen der königl. Gesellschaft der Wissenschaften zu Göttingen, philol.-histor. Klasse.
AKM. Abhandlungen für die Kunde des Morgenlandes.
AMG. Annales du Musée Guimet.
AMJV. Sir Asutosh Mookerjee Silver Jubilee Volumes.
ĀnSS. Ānandāçrama Sanskrit Series, Poona.
ASGW. Abhandlungen der philol.-histor. Klasse der königl. Sächs. Gesellschaft der Wissenschaften.
BB. Bibliotheca Buddhica, St. Petersburg.
BBeitr. Beiträge zur Kunde der indogermanischen Sprachen, herausgeb. von A. Bezzenberger.
BEFEO. Bulletin de l'école française d'Extrême Orient.
BenSS. Benares Sanskrit Series.
BI. Bibliotheca Indica, Calcutta.
BSGW. Berichte über die Verhandlungen der königl. Sächs. Gesellschaft der Wissenschaften zu Leipzig, philol.-histor. Klasse.
BSL. Bulletin de la Société de Linguistique de Paris.
BSOS. Bulletin of the School of Oriental Studies, London Institution.
BSS. Bombay Sanskrit Series.
ChSS. Chowkhambā Sanskrit Series, Benares.
DLZ. Deutsche Literaturzeitung.
EHI. Early History of India, by V. A. Smith, 4th ed., Oxford, 1924.
EHR. English Historical Review.
EI. Epigraphia Indica.
ERE. Encyclopaedia of Religion and Ethics.
GGA. Göttinger gelehrte Anzeigen.
GIL. Geschichte der indischen Litteratur, by M. Winternitz.
GN. Nachrichten von der königl. Gesellschaft der Wissenschaften zu Göttingen, philol.-histor. Klasse.
GSAI. Giornale della Società Asiatica Italiana.
Haeberlin. Kāvyasaṁgraha, by J. Haeberlin, Calcutta, 1847.
Haraprasād, Report I, II. Report on the Search for Sanskrit MSS., 1895-1900, 1901-6.
HOS. Harvard Oriental Studies, ed. Charles Lanman.
IA. Indian Antiquary.

IF.	Indogermanische Forschungen.
IHQ.	Indian Historical Quarterly.
IOC.	India Office Catalogue of Sanskrit Manuscripts.
IS.	Indische Studien, ed. A. Weber.
IT.	Indian Thought, Allahabad.
JA.	Journal asiatique.
JAOS.	Journal of the American Oriental Society.
JBRAS.	Journal of the Bombay Branch of the Royal Asiatic Society.
JPASB.	Journal and Proceedings of the Asiatic Society of Bengal.
JRAS.	Journal of the Royal Asiatic Society.
KM.	Kāvyamālā, Bombay.
KZ.	Zeitschrift für vergleichende Sprachforschung.
MASI.	Memoirs of the Archaeological Survey of India.
MSL.	Mémoires de la Société de Linguistique de Paris.
NSP.	Nirṇaya Sāgara Press, Bombay.
OC.	Orientalistenkongresse.
POCM.	Proceedings of the Third Oriental Congress, Madras, 1924.
POCP.	Proceedings and Transactions of the First Oriental Congress, Poona, 1919.
RHR.	Revue de l'histoire des religions, Paris.
RSO.	Rivista degli studi orientali, Rome.
SBA.	Sitzungsberichte der Berliner Akademie der Wissenschaften.
SBayA.	Sitzungsberichte der Bayerischen Akademie der Wissenschaften, philol.-histor. Klasse.
SBE.	Sacred Books of the East, Oxford.
SBH.	Sacred Books of the Hindus.
SIFI.	Studi Italiani di Filologia Indo-Iranica.
SWA.	Sitzungsberichte der Wiener Akademie der Wissenschaften.
TSS.	Trivandrum Sanskrit Series, ed. T. Gaṇapati Śāstrī.
VizSS.	Vizianagram Sanskrit Series.
WZKM.	Wiener Zeitschrift für die Kunde des Morgenlandes.
ZDMG.	Zeitschrift der Deutschen Morgenländischen Gesellschaft.
ZII.	Zeitschrift für Indologie und Iranistik.

PART I

THE LANGUAGE

I

SANSKRIT, PRĀKRIT, AND APABHRAṄÇA

1. *The Origin of Sanskrit*

SOMETIME in the course of the second millennium B.C. Indo-European tribes occupied, in varying degrees of completeness, vast areas in Iran, Asia Minor, and north-west India.[1] The problems of their movements and affiliations are still far from solution, but on linguistic grounds we postulate a group conveniently styled Aryan, whose speech can be regarded as the ancestor of the speeches of India and Iran. Of these Indian speeches[2] our oldest evidence is the *Ṛgveda*, and the language of this great collection of hymns is obviously a hieratic and conventional one. It testifies to the cultivation of sacred poetry by rival families of priests among many distinct tribes during a considerable period of time, and in various localities. Some of the hymns were doubtless composed in the Punjāb, others in the region which in the Brāhmaṇas is recognized as the home of the Kurus and Pañcālas, tribes representing the consolidation of units familiar to us in the *Ṛgveda*. It is even claimed that Book vi is the poetry of the period before the tribes entered India proper, though the contention is still implausible. That, under these circumstances, the speech of the *Ṛgveda* should show dialectic mixture is only to be expected, and, despite the great difficulties involving the attempt to discriminate, some progress is possible towards determining the characteristics of the dialect which lies at the basis of the *Ṛgveda*. It was marked by the open pronunciation of intervocalic *dh*, *bh*, *ḍ*, and *ḍh* as *h*, *ḷ*, and *ḷh*; by the change of *l* into *r*; and by the intrusion of the pronominal instrumental plural termination *ebhis* into the

[1] Cf. Keith, *Religion and Philosophy of the Veda*, Chap. I.

[2] Cf. Wackernagel, *Altind. Gramm.*, i, pp. ix ff.; H. Reichelt, *Festschrift Streitberg* (1924), pp. 238 ff.; Macdonell, *Vedic Grammar* (1910); Meillet, IF. xxxi. 120 ff.; JA. 1910, ii. 184 ff.; *Mélanges Lévi*, p. 20; Grammont, MSL. xix. 254 ff.; Bloch, *Formation de la langue marathe* (1920); S. K. Chatterji, *Bengali* (1926).

nominal declension. Borrowings from other dialects can here and there be confidently asserted; in some cases the forms thus found may be regarded as of equal age with those of the *Ṛgveda*, as in the case of words in *l* and *jajjhatī*, with *jjh* in lieu of *kṣ* for Aryan *gžh*, but in other instances we find forms[1] which are phonetically more advanced than those normal in the *Ṛgveda*, and attest loans either from tribes whose speech had undergone more rapid change, perhaps as the result of greater admixture with non-Aryan elements, or from lower classes of the population. Thus we have irregular cerebrals as in *kaṭa* beside *kṛta*, *kāṭa* beside *karta*; *ch* for *ps* in *kṛchra*; *jy* for *dy* in *jyotis*; *i* for *ṛ* in *çithira*; *busa* for *bṛça*, and many other anomalous forms. To localize these dialects is in the main impossible; the rhotacism of the *Ṛgveda* accords with its western origin, for the same phenomenon is Iranian. The use of *l* is later a sign of eastern connexion, and in one stereotyped phrase, *sūre duhitā*, we perhaps find *e* for *az*, as in the eastern Prākrit.

From the language of the *Ṛgveda* we can trace a steady development to Classical Sanskrit, through the later Saṁhitās and the Brāhmaṇas. The development, however, is of a special kind; it is not the spontaneous growth of a popular speech unhampered by tradition and unregulated by grammatical studies. The language of the tribes whose priests cherished the hymns of the *Ṛgveda* was subject doubtless to all the normal causes of speech change, accentuated in all likelihood by the gradual addition to the community of non-Aryan elements as the earlier inhabitants of the north, Muṇḍā or Dravidian tribes, fell under their control.[2] But, at least in the upper classes of the population, alteration was opposed by the constant use of the sacred language and by the study devoted to it. Parallels to such restricted evolution are not hard to find; the history of the Greek Koine, of Latin from its fixation in the first century B.C., and of modern English, attests the power of literature to stereotype. In India

[1] In some cases, no doubt, forms have been altered in transmission.

[2] Cf. W. Petersen, JAOS. xxxii. 414–28; Michelson, JAOS. xxxiii. 145–9; Keith, *Camb. Hist. India*, i. 109 ff. Common sense renders Dravidian and Muṇḍā influences inevitable, though proof may be difficult; Przyluski, MSL. xxii. 205 ff.; BSL. xxiv. 120, 255 ff., xxv. 66 ff.; Bloch, xxv. 1 ff.; Lévi, JA. cciii. 1–56. Przyluski endeavours to prove Austroasiatic influence on culture; JA. ccv. 101 ff.; ccviii. 1 ff.; BSL. xxvi. 98 ff. Cf. Poussin, *Indo-européens*, pp. 198 ff.; Chatterji, i. 170 ff., 199.

the process was accentuated by the remarkable achievements of her early grammarians whose analytical skill far surpassed anything achieved until much later in the western world. In the normal life of language a constant round of destruction and reconstruction takes place; old modes of expression disappear but new are invented; old distinctions of declension and conjugation are wiped out, but new differentiations emerge. In Sanskrit the grammarians accepted and carried even farther than did contemporary vernaculars the process of the removal of irregularities and the disuse of variant forms, but they sanctioned hardly any new formations, producing a form of expression well ordered and purified, worthy of the name Sanskrit which the *Rāmāyaṇa* first accords to it. The importance of the part played by religion in preserving accuracy of speech is shown by the existence of a special form of sacrifice, the Sarasvatī, which was destined to expiate errors of speech during the sacrifice, and in the *Mahābhāṣya* of Patañjali (150 B.C.) it is recorded that there were at one time seers of great knowledge who in their ordinary speech were guilty of using the inaccurate *yar vā ṇas tar vā ṇaḥ* for *yad vā nas tad vā naḥ*, but who, while sacrificing, were scrupulously exact.

The influence of the grammarians, whose results were summed up in Pāṇini's *Aṣṭādhyāyī*, probably in the fourth century B.C., is seen in the rigid scheme of euphonic combination of the words within the sentence or line of verse. This is clearly artificial, converting a natural speech tendency into something impossibly rigid, and, as applied to the text of the *Ṛgveda*, often ruining the metrical effect. Similar rigidity is seen in the process which substitutes in many cases *y* and *v* for the *iy* and *uv* of the earlier speech. Dialectic influence may be traced in the recognition of *l* in many words in lieu of *r*, and a certain distinction between the dialect which underlies the *Ṛgveda* and that of Pāṇini is revealed by the absolute ignoring by the latter of the substitution of *ḷ* and *ḷh* for *ḍ* and *ḍh*.[1] Otherwise the chief mark of progress is the growth of the tendency to cerebralization, possibly under Dravidian influence.

In morphology there was elimination of double forms; *ā* as a variant for *ena* in the instrumental singular of *a* stems disappeared,

[1] Cf. Lüders, *Festschrift Wackernagel*, pp. 294 ff.

a and *ā* yielded to *au* in the dual, *āsas* to *ās*, *ā* to *āni*, *ebhis* to *ais*, *ām* to *ānām* in the plural; *ni* alone is permissible in the locative singular of *an* stems; the effective distinction of root and derivative stems in *ī* disappears; the intrusion of weak forms into the place of strong and vice versa is banished; the irregular *vas* of the vocative of *vant* stems is abandoned, and by eliminating the nominative *yuvam* and ablative *yuvat* the pronominal declension is harmonized with the simplicity of the three forms of the nominal. Similarly, in verbal forms the variant *masi* in the first plural active is laid aside, the *e* of the third singular middle yields to *te*, *dhva* in the second plural to *dhvam*, and forms in *r* in the third plural are confined to the perfect and the root *çī*; in the imperative *dhvāt* is dropped, and *dhi* is no longer permitted to rival *hi* in the second person. Far more important is the laying aside of the subjunctive, whose functions were felt to be adequately performed by the optative, save in so far as a complete set of forms was made up for the imperative by utilizing the first persons. Even in the optative the wealth of forms is seriously diminished, only the present and a specialized precative being allowed. The rich variety of infinitives is steadily lessened; the final result allows only that in *tum*, while of the gerunds that in *tvā* supersedes *tvī* and *tvāya*. Against these losses can be set little more than the development of two forms of periphrasis, the future middle in *tāhe*, and the perfect [1] composed of a nominal accusative form with the auxiliaries *kṛ*, *bhū*, or *ās*, the extended use of gerundives in *tavya* and *anīya*, the creation of a perfect active participle in *tavant*, the invention of a new third singular aorist passive as in *adāyiṣi*, and the development of tertiary verbal forms.

In some of these losses Sanskrit keeps pace with popular speech, but the evidence is conclusive against ascribing too much weight to this fact. While such categories as the dual of noun and verb alike, the middle, and the past tenses, practically vanished from popular speech, Sanskrit rigidly retains them. On the other hand it rejects irregularities which popular speech permitted to survive, such as the *ā* of the instrumental singular and nominative plural neuter of *a* stems, the *āsas* of the masculine plural, the

[1] On changes in the use of verbal forms see L. Renou, *La valeur du parfait dans les hymnes védiques* (1925), pp. 88 ff., 188 ff.

form *gonām*, the pronominal plurals *asme* and *yuṣme*, the short forms *yāt* and *tāt*, and verbal forms in *r*. Traces of the subjunctive, the infinitive in *tave*, the aorist *akar*, the instrumental in *ebhis* exist in Prākrit, but are banned in Sanskrit. On the other hand, although Pānini recognizes fully the Vedic accent, it can hardly be doubted that already by his time in actual speech in many regions it had yielded in part to an expiratory accent. The tendency to such a result is already visible in the *Ṛgveda*, where *duhitā* by the testimony of the metre must at times be read *dhitā*, comparable with Pāli *dhītā*;[1] the weakening of *bh* and *dh* to *h* occurs there normally after unaccented syllables,[2] and the curious mode of notation of the accent in the *Çatapatha Brāhmaṇa* has with some ground been ascribed to a stage of transition from the musical to the expiratory accent.[3]

We must not, however, exaggerate the activity of the grammarians to the extent of suggesting with some writers that Classical Sanskrit is an artificial creation, a product[4] of the Brahmins when they sought to counteract the Buddhist creation of an artistic literature in Pāli by recasting their own Prākritic speech with the aid of the Vedic language. It is, in point of fact, perfectly obvious that there is a steady progress through the later Saṃhitās, the Brāhmaṇas, and the Āraṇyakas and Upaniṣads, and that the Bhāṣā, the spoken language of Pāṇini's grammar, is closely related to, though not identic with, the language of the Brāhmaṇas and the older Upaniṣads. Nor in point of fact does Classical Sanskrit present the appearance of an artificial product; simplified as it is in comparison with the redundant luxury of the Vedic texts, it yet presents no artificial symmetry, but rather admits exceptions in bewildering profusion, showing that the grammarians were not creators, but were engaged in a serious struggle to bring into handier shape a rather intractable material.

1 Lüders, KZ. xlix. 236 f.

2 Wackernagel, *Altind. Gramm.*, i. 252 f.

3 Leumann, KZ. xxxi. 22 f.

4 Hoernle and Grierson, *Bihārī Dict.*, pp. 33 ff.; Senart, JA. sér. 8, viii. 318 ff. Contrast Franke, *B. Beitr.*, xvii. 86; Boxwell, *Trans. Phil. Soc.* 1885–7, pp. 656 ff. Poussin (*Indo-européens*, pp. 191 ff.) stresses the literary character of Sanskrit.

2. *The Character and Extent of the Use of Sanskrit*

We have seen that the Sanskrit of the grammarians is essentially a legitimate development from the Vedic speech; it remains to consider the extent of its use, in the time of Pāṇini and later. In examining the matter it is essential to remember the social conditions of India. In Britain to-day the varieties of English spoken and written are complex and numerous; in India, where caste, clan, and racial distinctions were far more prominent and important, linguistic facts were far more complicated still. What is clear[1] is that Sanskrit represents the language of Brahmanical civilization, and the extent of that civilization was ever increasing, though the Brahmanical religion had to face competition from new faiths, in special Buddhism and Jainism, from the fifth century B.C. The Buddhist texts themselves afford the most convincing evidence of all of the predominance of Brahmanism; the Buddha is represented as attempting not to overthrow the ideal of Brahmanism, but to change its content by substituting merit in place of birth as the hall-mark of the true Brahmin. The public religious rites and the domestic ritual were recorded and carried out in Sanskrit, and education was in Brahmin hands. The Buddhist texts repeatedly confirm the Brahmanical principle that instruction of the people (*lokapakti*) was the duty of Brahmins, and the tales of the Jātakas[2] show young men of all classes, not merely Brahmins but boys of the ruling class, Kṣatriyas, and children of the people, Vaiçyas, seeking instruction in the north from Brahmin teachers. Sanskrit was the language of science, not merely grammar, prosody, astronomy, phonetics, etymology, but doubtless also of more magic arts, such as the physiognomy and demonology recorded in the Buddhist texts and confirmed by the inclusion of magic, Sarpajanavidyā, and Devajanavidyā in the list of the subjects taught by the Brahmin to the people given in the *Çatapatha Brāhmaṇa*.[3] The same text[4] mentions also

[1] Thomas, JRAS. 1904, pp. 465 ff.

[2] Fick, *Sociale Gliederung*, p. 131.

[3] xiii. 4. 3. 9 ff.

[4] xi. 5. 6. 8. Cf. *Bṛhadāraṇyaka Upaniṣad*, ii. 4. 10; iv. 1. 2; 5. 11; *Chāndogya*, vii. 1. 2; Faddegon, *Act. Or.* iv. 4 ff., 133. Vākovākya perhaps denotes the dialogues which develop into philosophy.

Anuçāsanas, Vidyās, Vākovākya, Itihāsa, Purāṇa, Gāthās, and Nārāçaṅsīs, and the continuity of tradition is attested by the *Mahābhāṣya*[1] which includes under the range of Sanskrit speech the four Vedas with their Aṅgas and Rahasyas, the Vākovākya, Itihāsa, Purāṇa, medicine. The *Āçvalāyana Gṛhyasūtra*,[2] probably not far removed from Pāṇini in date, repeats in the main the list of the *Çatapatha*, but adds Sūtras, Bhāṣyas, *Bhārata*, *Mahābhārata*, and the works of the Dharmācāryas. Other sciences such as those of the bow, music, architecture, and politics are recorded in the *Mahābhārata*,[3] and, so far as they were in the hands of the Brahmins, we need not doubt that Sanskrit here also had its place.

These facts are not in dispute, and the predominance of Sanskrit in the sphere in question remained unchallenged until the Mahomedan invasions brought a new literary language into prominence. The evidence indicates clearly that Sanskrit must have been in constant use as a means of teaching and performing religious duties among the Brahmins at least. It has been denied that it was really even their vernacular in the time of Pāṇini, and *a fortiori* later, but the evidence for this view is unsatisfactory. Pāṇini has rules[4] which are meaningless for anything but a vernacular, apart from the fact that the term Bhāṣā which he applies to the speech he teaches has the natural sense of a spoken language. Thus the doubling of consonants is expressly forbidden in passionate speech, as in the term of abuse *putrādinī* applied to a cruel mother; he prescribes the use of prolongation in the case of calling from a distance, in greeting, question, and reply; he gives information on the terminology of dicing and the speech of herdsmen; he cites expressions redolent of real daily life. Indeed, it is the grammarians alone who preserve for us such usages as the repetition of the second person imperative followed by the present indicative to express intense action: *khāda khādeti khādati*, 'eagerly he eats', whence we have in colloquial Marāṭhī *khā khā khāto*; other popular uses are *udarapūram bhuṅkte*, 'he eats filling his belly'; *daṇḍādaṇḍi keçākeçi*, 'a struggle in which sticks are brandished and hair is

[1] i. 9.
[2] iii. 3. 1; 4. 1. Cf. Utgikar, POCP. 1919, ii. 46 ff.
[3] Hopkins, *Great Epic*, pp. 11 ff.
[4] Wackernagel, i, p. xliii; Bhandarkar, JBRAS. xvi. 330.

pulled'; *atra khādatamodatā vartate*, 'eat and enjoy' is the rule here; *jahistambo 'yam*, 'he is one who says "strike the sheaves of corn"'. They record also the parenthetical use[1] of *manye*, 'I think'; the humorous *apacasi*, 'you're no cook'; and authorize such quaint forms[2] as *yāmaki*, 'I go'. The elaborate rules regarding the accent reflect also actual speech.

Confirmatory evidence can also be adduced from the references of Yāska,[3] Pāṇini, and Kātyāyana to particular usages of the northerners and the eastern peoples; Kātyāyana also recognizes as a matter of notoriety the existence of local variations, which Patañjali illustrates by reference to the practice of the Kambojas, Surāṣṭras, Prācyamadhyas, &c. Here too may be mentioned the references of Kātyāyana and Patañjali to changes in usage after Pāṇini's time, as when the former[4] finds fault with Pāṇini for not giving *nāma* as well as *nāman* as the vocative, for not mentioning that pronominal forms are permitted in the masculine as well as in the feminine singular of *dvitīya* and *tṛtīya*, and for allowing only the feminines *upādhyāyī*, *āryā*, *kṣatriyā*, and *mātulānī*. Patañjali shows us that in his time participial phrases had superseded the second person perfects such as *tera*, *ūṣa*, *peca*, a fact specially characteristic of a genuine living speech.[5]

Further information of a precise character is incidentally given us by Patañjali.[6] He insists that grammar does not exist to create words, but to make clear what are correct uses; in ordinary life (*loke*) a man thinks of a thing and uses the appropriate word without going to a grammar; the words of Sanskrit are of ordinary life (*laukika*). We find a grammarian and a charioteer (*sūta*) engaged in a discussion conducted in Sanskrit, and the latter has decided opinions of his own on the etymology of his designation and on that of the term *prājitṛ*, driver. The norm of speech is that of the Çiṣṭas, and these are people who speak correct Sanskrit without special tuition; the purpose of grammar is to enable us to recognize who are Çiṣṭas, and thus to

[1] As in Pāli; Franke, ZDMG. xlvi. 311 f.

[2] Keith, JRAS. 1915, pp. 502 ff.

[3] *Nirukta*, ii. 2; v. 5, *Mahābhāṣya*, i. 9; v. 8 on vii. 3. 45.

[4] Bhandarkar, JBRAS. xvi. 273. Cf. Macdonell, *Vedic Grammar*, p. 307, n. 2.

[5] Bloch, MSL. xiv. 97; L. Renou, *La valeur du parfait*, p. 189.

[6] vi. 3. 109; Bhandarkar, JBRAS. xvi. 334 ff. Grierson (JRAS. 1904, pp. 479 ff.) misunderstands the passage to mean that Çiṣṭas require to be taught Sanskrit.

apply to them to find the correct form of such terms as *pṛṣodara*, which do not fall under the ordinary rules of grammar. The Çiṣṭas are further defined as Brahmins of Āryāvarta, the region south of the Himālayas, north of Pāriyātra, east of the Ādarça, west of the Kālakavana, who are not greedy, who do good disinterestedly, and who store only so much grain as a pot can hold. Other persons may make errors; thus they may pronounce *ṣaṣa* for *çaça*, *palāṣa* for *palāça*, *mañjaka* for *mañcaka*; or they may commit graver errors by using incorrect forms (*apaçabda*) such as *kasi* for *kṛṣi*, *disi* for *dṛçi*, *gāvī*, *goṇī*, *gotā*, *gopotālikā* for *gaus*, or even verbal forms such as *āṇapayati*[1] for *ājñāpayati*, *vaṭṭati* for *vartate*, and *vaḍḍhati* for *vardhate*. But from the Çiṣṭas they could acquire the accurate forms. This suggests a close parallel to modern conditions in England, where an upper educated class sets the norm to all those in lower social classes; the speech of that class is clearly a living language, and Sanskrit was so in much the same sense. The standard comparison of Latin in the Middle Ages is somewhat unsatisfactory; in the earlier period of the use of Sanskrit it is clear that it was much more closely similar to the speech of the lower classes in its numerous varieties than was Latin in medieval Europe. Comparison of Sanskrit with the dialects of the inscriptions of Açoka is significant in this regard; their differences are not essential nor such as to hinder mutual comprehension, and could easily be paralleled in English speech to-day.

Moreover, the conclusions thus attained are directly supported by the evidence of the drama, in which Brahmins and kings and other persons of high station and education use Sanskrit, while inferior characters employ some form of Prākrit. It has been attempted to argue against this view on the score that the drama was originally in Prākrit, and that Sanskrit was introduced only when it became essentially the general language of culture. But this contention ignores the fact that on one side at least the drama is closely connected with the epic in Sanskrit; Bhāsa, indeed, has one drama without Prākrit, and there is little of it in his other dramas based on the epic. Nor was the Sanskrit

[1] So Açoka's Brahmagiri inscr. I; *vaḍhati* (the usual single consonant is merely graphic; CII. i, p. lix; Grierson's argument (JRAS. 1925, p. 228) from the writing of other conjuncts is clearly untenable) occurs in Delhi-Toprā, iv. 20.

unintelligible in early times at least to the audience, which might be one including persons of quite humble rank; the *Nāṭyaçāstra* expressly lays it down that the Sanskrit is to be such as is easily intelligible to every one. The denial that realism was ever aimed at in the use of language by the characters in the drama is negatived by the facts; the Prākrits used by the dramatists show a steady advance from those of Açvaghoṣa through those of Bhāsa to the dialects of Kālidāsa, who introduced to the stage the Māhārāṣṭrī which, earlier unimportant, had won fame in India as the medium of erotic lyric.[1] The evidence of Açvaghoṣa is of special value, for it attests the fact that about A. D. 100 the stage tradition was so firmly in favour of the use of Sanskrit by the persons of the highest rank that he adopted it in his plays despite their Buddhist theme, and despite the fact that the Buddha himself, according to tradition, had forbidden the employment of Sanskrit as the medium for preserving his sayings.[2]

The extent to which Sanskrit was used or understood is further attested by the epics. It is perhaps hardly necessary now to do more than mention the implausible conjecture[3] which ascribes the writing of the epics in Sanskrit to some period after the Christian era and sees in them translations from some Prākrit. The silence of antiquity on this vast undertaking is inexplicable, and it is incredible that the translation should have taken place at a period when Buddhism was triumphant and Brahminism comparatively depressed. The language itself has a distinctive character which renders the idea of translation absurd;[4] we have in Buddhist literature of the so-called Gāthā type abundant evidence of the results produced by efforts to Sanskritize, and the arguments which are adduced to establish the reality of translation would suffice to prove that Vedic texts were likewise translations. Moreover, there is conclusive evidence that Pāṇini[5] knew a *Mahābhārata* or at least a Bhāratan epic in Sanskrit, and that the bulk of the *Rāmāyaṇa*[6] was composed

[1] Keith, *Sanskrit Drama*, pp. 72 ff., 85 ff., 121 f., 140, 155.
[2] *Cullavagga*, v. 33. 1; Keith, IHQ. i. 501.
[3] Grierson, IA. xxiii. 52; Barth, RHR. xxvii. 288.
[4] Jacobi, *Rāmāyaṇa*, p. 117; ZDMG. xlviii. 407 ff.; Keith, JRAS. 1906, pp. 2 ff.
[5] Hopkins, *Great Epic*, p. 385.
[6] Keith, JRAS. 1915, pp. 318 ff.

long before Açoka. Now, though the Brahmins made the epics largely their own, they were not the earliest composers of this form of literature, and the fact is attested in the simpler, more careless, language which shows indifference to many of the refinements of Brahmanical speech. Pāṇini ignores these deviations from his norm; it was no part of his aim to deal with the speech current outside the hieratic circle, and in the epic speech we have doubtless the form of language used by the Kṣatriyas and the better educated of the Vaiçyas during the period when the poems took shape. Both the *Mahābhārata* and the *Rāmāyaṇa* are, it must be remembered, essentially aristocratic; they correspond to the *Iliad* and the *Odyssey*, and like them became the objects of the deep interest of wider circles. In recent times, no doubt, the epics have been unintelligible to the audience, to whom interpretation has been requisite, though delight is still felt in the sound of the sacred language. But this doubtless was not the case in older times; we must postulate a long period when the epic was fairly easily intelligible to large sections of the people.

Doubtless, as time went on, the gulf between Sanskrit and the languages of the day became more and more marked; even between the epic language and that of the Brahmin schools there were differences to which express reference is made in the *Rāmāyaṇa*,[1] and both the practice of the dramas and such passages as that in Kālidāsa's *Kumārasambhava*,[2] in which Sarasvatī addresses Çiva and his bride, the one in Sanskrit, the other in Prākrit, attest dialectic differences based on rank, sex, and locality. In a sense doubtless Sanskrit came more and more to resemble Latin in the Middle Ages, but, like Latin, its vitality as the learned speech of the educated classes was unimpaired, and it won victories even in fields which were at first hostile to it.[3] The medical textbook current under the name of Caraka tells us that Sanskrit was used in discussions in the medical schools of the day. A work of very different character, the *Kāmasūtra* of Vātsyāyana, bids its man of fashion in his con-

[1] v. 30. 17 f.; iv. 3. 28 f.; ii. 91. 22; vii. 36. 44; Jacobi, *Rāmāyaṇa*, p. 115. Cf. Hopkins, *Great Epic*, p. 364.

[2] vii. 87.

[3] Cf. Jacobi, *Scientia*, xiv. 251 ff.; Oldenberg, *Das Mahābhārata*, pp. 129 ff.

versation in polite society use both Sanskrit and the vernacular of his country (*deçabhāṣā*). Hiuen Tsang tells us in the seventh century that Buddhist disputants used officially Sanskrit in their debates; in his *Upamitibhavaprapañcakathā* the Jain Siddharṣi (A. D. 906) gives as his reason for preferring Sanskrit for this allegory of human life that persons of culture despise any other form of speech, and claims that his Sanskrit is so simple as to be understood even by those who preferred Prākrit. The writing of Sanskrit poems which even women and children—of course of the higher classes—can understand is contemplated by Bhāmaha in his treatise on poetics (*c.* A. D. 700). Bilhaṇa (A. D. 1060) would have us believe that the women even of his homeland, Kashmir, were able to appreciate Sanskrit and Prākrit as well as their mother tongue (*janmabhāṣā*). The famous collection of tales known as the *Pañcatantra* owes its origin in theory in part, according to one later version, to the importance of instructing princes in Sanskrit as well as in the conduct of affairs.

There were, of course, spheres in which Sanskrit was at first rejected, beyond all in the early literatures of Jainism and Buddhism, which were probably couched in an old form of what became known as Ardhamāgadhī Prākrit. As has been shown,[1] however, the question was early raised, if we may trust the Buddhist tradition, whether Sanskrit should not serve as the medium to preserve the Master's instruction, a notice which bears emphatic testimony to the predominance of Sanskrit as a literary medium. In both cases, however, Sanskrit finally won its way, and first Buddhists, then Jains, rendered great services both to Sanskrit literature and grammar.

The Buddhist revolt against Sanskrit had, however, one important result. The edicts of Açoka, in which he impressed on his subjects throughout his vast realm the duty of practising virtue, were inevitably couched in Prākrit, not Sanskrit, and the epigraphic tradition thus established died hard. But it had to contend with facts; inscriptions were intended to be intelligible, and in the long run it proved that Sanskrit was the speech which had the best chance of appealing to those who could read inscriptions. In the second century B. C. traces of the influence

[1] Keith, IHQ. i. 501 f.

of Sanskrit are apparent; in the next century on one view[1] is found the first inscription which on the whole may be called Sanskrit, and Sanskritisms are on the increase.[2] In the first century A. D. Prākrit still prevails, but, though it is prominent also in the next century, we find the great Sanskrit inscription of Rudradāman which displays clearly the existence of an elaborate Sanskrit literature. In the next century Sanskrit and Prākrit contend, in the fourth Prākrit becomes rare with the Brahmanical revival under the Gupta dynasty, and from the fifth it almost disappears in Northern India. A parallel process was going on in literature; in such Buddhist works as the *Lalitavistara* and the *Mahāvastu* we find the results of an effort to convert a Prākrit into Sanskrit, and similar results are to be found in other fields, as in the medical treatises of the Bower manuscript. From this the Buddhists soon advanced to the stage in which Sanskrit proper was used, as in the *Divyāvadāna*, perhaps of the second century A. D.[3] The Jains showed more conservatism, but even they ultimately accepted the use of Sanskrit as legitimate. Serious competition with Sanskrit as the language of literature again arose when the Mahomedan conquests brought Persian into play, and when the vernaculars in the period shortly after A. D. 1000 began first to influence Sanskrit and then to develop into literary languages.

The true home of the Çiṣṭas is given by Patañjali as Āryāvarta, but even in his time the Dekhan was a home of Sanskrit; Kātyāyana himself seems to have lived there in the third century B. C. Yāska[4] (*c.* 500 B. C.) already mentions a southern use of the Vedic word *vijāmātṛ*, and Patañjali records the love in the south for derivative formations and the use of *sarasī*, large pond. Even in Southern India, despite the existence of a vigorous Kanarese and Tamil literature, Sanskrit inscriptions appear from

[1] On sacrificial post at Īsāpur, 24th year of Vāsiṣka, 33 B. C. acc. Fleet, JRAS. 1910, pp. 1315 ff.; Hoernle, *Bower MS.*, p. 65; *Ann. Rep. A. S., India*, 1910–11, pp. 39 ff. It is much more probably of the second century A. D. (? A. D. 102); an inscr. of Huviṣka shows almost correct Sanskrit; JRAS. 1924, pp. 400 ff.

[2] Franke, *Pāli und Sanskrit*, pp. 13, 58; Rapson, JRAS. 1904, p. 449.

[3] Przyluski (*La légende de l'empereur Açoka*, pp. 14 ff.) ascribes much to the influence of Mathurā and its Sarvāstivādin school, and places its use of Sanskrit in the *Açokāvadāna* at least in the second century B. C. (cf. pp. 166 ff.).

[4] vi. 9. Cf. Bühler, WZKM. i. 3. For Āryāvarta, see IA. xxxiv. 179 (Madhyadeça) and *Kāvyamīmāṅsā*, p. xxiv.

the sixth century onwards, often mixed with Dravidian phrases, attesting the tendency of Sanskrit to become a Koine, and Sanskrit left a deep impression even on the virile Dravidian languages. Ceylon fell under its influence, and Sinhalese shows marked traces of its operation on it. It reached the Sunda Islands, Borneo, the Philippines, and in Java produced a remarkable development in the shape of the Kavi speech and literature. Adventurers of high rank founded kingdoms in Further India, where Indian names are already recorded by the geographer Ptolemy in the second century A. D. The Sanskrit inscriptions of Campā begin perhaps in that century, those of Cambodia before A. D. 600, and they bear testimony to the energetic study of Sanskrit grammar and literature. Of greater importance still was the passage of Sanskrit texts to Central Asia and their influence on China, Tibet, and Japan.

It is characteristic of the status of Sanskrit as the speech of men of education that in one sphere of use it only slowly came to be widely employed. Coins were meant for humble practical uses, and even Western Kṣatrapas, like Rudradāman, who used Sanskrit for their inscriptions, were contented with Prākrit for coin legends; but even in this sphere Sanskrit gradually prevailed.[1]

The results which we have attained are in accord with the evidence afforded by Greek renderings of Indian terms.[2] These are neither wholly based on Sanskrit forms nor on Prākrit. Derived doubtless from the speech now of the upper, now of the lower classes, they remind us of the salient fact that at any given moment in India there were in active use several forms of speech varying according to the class of society. The denial of the vernacular character of Sanskrit[3] rests largely on a failure to realize the true point at issue, on a confusion between the earlier period when Sanskrit was far more close to the speech of the lower classes and later times, or on the fallacious view that the only speech which deserves the style of a vernacular must be

[1] Bloch, *Mélanges Lévi*, p. 16.

[2] Lévi, BSL. viii, pp. viii, x, xvii; Franke, ZDMG. xlvii. 596 ff.; Bloch, *Mélanges Lévi*, pp. 1 ff.

[3] Grierson, JRAS. 1904, p. 481. On this view standard English would not be a vernacular.

the language of the lower classes of the population. Still less plausible is the suggestion[1] that Sanskrit as a vernacular was preserved in Kashmir during its eclipse in India generally, a view which has no support either in tradition or in the form of the Kashmirian vernacular. What we do find is that the Buddhism which penetrated Kashmir was strongly influenced by Mathurā, where the new faith had fallen into the hands of men trained in the Brahmanical schools, who applied their own language to the propagation of the faith. We have in this one more proof of the hold which Sanskrit had in Brahmanical circles, and of the obvious fact that it was far better fitted as a language of theology and philosophy than Ardhamāgadhī or any similar dialect.

3. *The Characteristics and Development of Sanskrit in Literature*

It is a characteristic feature of Sanskrit, intimately connected with its true vitality, that, unlike Medieval Latin, it undergoes important changes in the course of its prolonged literary existence, which even to-day is far from ended. Moreover, we must note the existence of two streams of movement, the Sanskrit of the Brahmanical schools as summed up in the grammar of Pāṇini, and the less formal language of the ruling class and the Brahmins in their entourage as shown in the epics. The works of Classical Sanskrit literature show the clearest evidence of influence in both directions; the Brahmins, to whom or to whose influence and tradition we owe most of the literature, were schooled in grammar and were anxious to avoid solecisms, but they were also under the literary influence of the epics, and in special of the *Rāmāyaṇa*, and it was not possible for them to avoid assimilating their language in great measure to that of their model.

Hence it follows that much of what is taught by Pāṇini and his followers has no representation in the literature. As we have seen, Kātyāyana and Patañjali recognize the disuse of certain verbal forms; there disappear also many idioms,[2] such as *anvāje-* or *upāje-kṛ*, strengthen, *nivacane-kṛ*, be silent, *mano-* or *kaṇe-*

[1] Franke, *Pāli und Sanskrit*, pp. 87 ff.

[2] Bhandarkar, JBRAS. xvi. 272; Speijer, *Sansk. Synt.*, pp. 39, 45, 61 f., 65 f., 72, 89 f., 108.

han, fulfil one's longing, *celaknopaṁ vṛṣṭaḥ*, 'rained until the clothes were wet'; many words are no longer used, such as *anvavasarga*, allowing one his own way, *niravasita*, excommunicated, *abhividhi*, including, *utsañjana*, throwing up, *abhreṣa*, equitableness. The pronominal base *tya* disappears; in the verb the infinitive *tavai* is lost, many formations such as *jajanti* disappear, and the perfect participle middle in *āna* is disused. The adverbial form in *trā*, as in *devatrā*, and the old word *parut* are lost. Many nominal derivatives are not exemplified, and the use of such phrases as *çuklīsyāt* disappears. Many syntactical rules are obsolete, such as the use of the accusative with adjectives in *uka*; the instrumental with *saṁjñā* or *saṁprayam*; the dative with *çlāgh* and *sthā*; *tṛṇaṁ man* or *çune* or *çvānaṁ man*; the ablative with words denoting far or near; the genitive with verbs of remembering other than *smṛ*, with *nāth*, hope, with *jas* and other verbs denoting injury, and impersonally with expressions of illness, *caurasya rujati*; the instrumental with *prasita* and *utsuka*; *uta* in simple interrogations, and many other usages.

It is, however, true that beside this feature we have the deliberate employment by poets of usages, prescribed in the grammar, but so rare as to reveal themselves as purely learned reminiscences. From Açvaghoṣa on, the great authors are fond of displaying their erudition; Kālidāsa has *anugiram*, 'on the mountain', though this is given by Pāṇini[1] merely as an optional form, and *sausnātaka*, 'asking if one has bathed well', from a Vārttika.[2] Māgha is adept in these niceties; he has *khalu* with the gerund to denote prohibition; *mā jīvan*, 'let him not live'; he distinguishes *vi-ṣvan*, eat noisily, and *vi-svan*, howl; he affects the passive use of the perfect, revives aorist forms and gerunds in *am*, including *vastraknopam*, and uses *klam* as a finite verb. Çrīharṣa, author of the *Naiṣadhīya*, is responsible for the solitary example of the first person periphrastic future middle, *darçayitāhe*, yet cited.[3] The case is still more extreme with Bhaṭṭi, whose epic is at once a poem and an illustration of the rules of grammar and rhetoric, and who has imitators in Bhaumaka's *Rāvaṇārjunīya* and Halāyudha's *Kavirahasya* (10th cent.). Even in writers of the folk-tale knowledge of grammar sometimes

[1] v. 4. 112 (Senaka). [2] iv. 4. 1, v. 3.
[3] Cf. grammatical similes; Walter, *Indica*, iii 38.

is exhibited quite unexpectedly in the shape of recondite forms culled from Pāṇini or his successors. So serious a philosopher as Çaṅkara resorts to the use of the negative with finite verbs—which originally must have been merely a comic use—and he is guilty also of the employment of the comparative of a verb, *upapadye-tarām*, a linguistic monstrosity of the worst kind.

The influence of the grammarians explains also the free use of the aorist in the writers of elaborate prose; Bāṇa and Daṇḍin, moreover, observe the precise rule for the use of the perfect in narration prescribed by the grammarians. It has been suggested that this may be explained by the derivation of prose from a different tradition than poetry, but the suggestion appears needless.[1] Subandhu ignores the rule as to the perfect, and the simple explanation of the accuracy of the other writers is the desire to display their skill in grammar, which was naturally facilitated by the absence of metrical restrictions. The same liberty explains their practice in postponing the verb to the end of the sentence, unquestionably its traditional resting-place, but one impossible to observe in verse.

Very different was the effect on Classical poetry of the influence of the epics.[2] They show, with special frequency in the case of the *Mahābhārata*,[3] the tendency of uncultivated speech to ignore fine distinctions and by analogical formations to simplify grammar. Thus rules of euphonic combination are not rarely ignored; in the noun the distinction of weak and strong case-forms is here and there forgotten; there is confusion of stems in *i* and *in*; by analogy *pūṣāṇam* replaces the older *pūṣaṇam*; there is confusion in the use of cases, especially in the pronoun; in the verb primary and secondary endings are sometimes confused; active and middle are often employed for metrical reasons in place of each other; even the passive is found with active terminations; the delicate rules affecting the use of the intermediate *i* are violated at every turn; the feminine of the present participle active is formed indifferently by *antī* or *atī*; the

[1] Speijer, *Sansk. Synt.*, §§ 328 ff.; Renou, *La valeur du parfait*, pp. 86 ff.

[2] For the *Rāmāyaṇa* cf. Böhtlingk, BSGW. 1887, pp. 213 ff.; ZDMG. xliii. 53 ff.; Roussel, *Muséon*, 1911, pp. 89 ff.; 1912, pp. 25 ff., 201 ff.; JA. 1910, i. 1–69; Keith, JRAS. 1910, pp. 468 ff., 1321 ff.

[3] Holtzmann, *Gramm. aus d. M.* (1884).

middle participle of causatives and denominatives is often formed by *āna*, partly doubtless on grounds of metrical convenience; the rule that the gerund is formed by *tvā* in simple, in *ya* in compound, verbs is constantly disregarded; minutiae such as the substitution of *dhāvati* for the present of *sṛ* are habitually neglected. The tendency to prefer *a* bases is seen in the verb and the noun alike, giving such forms as *diçā* and *duhitā*.

It was inevitable that so distinguished models as the *Mahābhārata* and the *Rāmāyaṇa* should deeply affect later poets, and Patañjali, in citing an epic fragment containing the irregular term *priyākhya* in lieu of *priyākhyāya*, expressly asserts that poets commit such irregularities (*chandovat kavayaḥ kurvanti*). We find, therefore, occasional errors such as the confusion of *antī* and *atī*, of *tvā* and *ya*, of active and middle, as well as regular disregard of the specific sense of the past tenses as laid down by the grammarians but ignored in the epic. As in the epic, the perfect and imperfect freely interchange as tenses of simple narration without nuance of any kind. Even Kālidāsa permits himself *sarati* and *āsa* for *babhūva*, and Çrīharṣa with the *Rāmāyaṇa* uses *kavāṭa* for the *kapāṭa* of Pāṇini. Lesser poets, especially the poetasters who turned out inscriptions, are naturally greater sinners by far against grammatical rules, especially when they can plead metrical difficulties as excuse.

Neither the epic nor the grammarians, however, are responsible for the fundamental change which gradually besets the Kāvya style, in the worst form in prose, but in varying degree even in verse. This is the change from the verbal to the nominal style, as Bhandarkar [1] not inaptly termed it. In the main, Vedic and epic Sanskrit show a form of speech closely akin to Greek and Latin; verbal forms are freely used, and relative clauses and clauses introduced by conjunctions are in regular employment. The essential feature of the new style is the substitution of the use of compounds for the older forms.[2] In its simplest form, of course, the practice is unobjectionable and tends to conciseness; *hataputra*

[1] JBRAS. xvi. 266 ff.; cf. Bloch, MSL. xiv. 27 ff.; Renou, *La valeur du parfait*, pp. 90 ff.; Stchoupak, MSL. xxi. 1 ff.; Jacobi, IF. xiv. 236 ff.

[2] Jacobi (*Compositum und Nebensatz*, pp. 25, 91 ff.) points out that they are properly used for ornamental description, not for important qualifications, and also suggests poetic convenience as a cause of popularity; cf. Chap. II, § 4. See also Wackernagel, *Altind. Gramm.*, II. i. 25, 27, 159; Whitney, *Sansk. Gramm.*, § 1246.

is less cumbrous than 'whose sons have been slain'. But when new members are added there are soon lost the advantages of an inflective language with its due syntactical union of formed words into sentences; brevity is attained at a fatal cost in clearness. A compound like *jalāntaçcandracapala*, 'fickle as the moon reflected in the water', is comparatively innocuous, but even a stylist like Kālidāsa permits himself such a phrase as *vīcikṣobha-stanitavihagaçreṇikāñcīguṇā*, 'whose girdle-string is a row of birds loquacious through the agitation of the waves'. True, in such a case there is no real doubt as to the sense, but often this is not the case, and in point of fact it is one of the delights of the later poets to compose compounds which contain a double entendre, since they can be read in two ways; of such monstrosities Subandhu is a master. Moreover, the nominal forms of the verb are given a marked preference; the expression of past time is regularly carried out by a past participle passive in form of an intransitive verb, such as *gatas*, he went, or if the verb is active the subject is put into the instrumental and the past participle passive is employed, as in *mṛgeṇoktam*, the deer said. Or an active past participle is created by adding *vant* to the passive participle, *kṛtavān*, he did; a distant parallel in the grammarians has been seen in the sanction by Pāṇini of the use of such forms as *dāçvāṅs* in lieu of a finite verb. Or the use of any save a verb of colourless kind may be avoided by substituting such an expression as *pakvaṁ karoti* for *pacati*, he cooks, or *pakvo bhavati*, it is cooked, for *pacyate*. Similarly the periphrastic future is preferred to the finite verb. Or the verb may wholly disappear as when for *ayaṁ māṅsam bhakṣayati* we have *māṅsabhojako 'yam*, he is a meat eater. In harmony with this is the tendency to lay great stress on case relations as expressing meaning, a practice which in the later style in philosophy, exegesis, and dialectics results in the occurrence of sentences passim with no verb and practically only the nominative and ablative cases of abstract nouns. Frequent, and indeed in some forms of composition, such as the folk tale, tedious in its reiteration, is the use of gerunds in lieu of subordinate clauses.

We are reduced to conjecture as to the cause of this tendency. The desire for brevity is already seen in the style of the Vedic

Sūtras, and the grammarians carried it to excess; their works furnish abundant instances of insistence on using cases in a pregnant sense and in affecting compounds; gerunds are frequent in the ritual texts. It has been suggested that the love for participial forms is partly explained by Dravidian influence;[1] the periphrastic future in both Sanskrit and Dravidian uses the auxiliary verb only in the first and second persons; the type *kṛtavān* has a parallel in *çeydavan*; the rule of the order of words in which the governed word precedes and the verb is placed at the end of the sentence is Dravidian. Unhappily, the arguments are inconclusive;[2] the omission of the auxiliary in the third person is natural, for in that person in any sentence whatever it is commonly omitted as easily understood; the order of words in Sanskrit has parallels in many other languages than Dravidian and rests on general rules of thought.

Beside the correct or comparatively correct Sanskrit of the poetic literature we find, especially in technical and non-Brahmanical works, abundant evidence of a popular Sanskrit or mixed Sanskrit in various forms. Generically it can be regarded as the result of men who were not wont to use Sanskrit trying to write in that language, but there are different aspects. Thus the early Buddhist writers who decided to adapt to the more learned language the Buddhist traditions probably current in Ardhamāgadhī were hampered by the desire not to depart unduly in verse at least from their models, a fact which explains the peculiar forms found especially in Gāthās, but also in prose in such a text as the *Mahāvastu*.[3] Traces of this influence persist even in much more polished Buddhist writers such as Açvaghoṣa, and much of it may be seen in the *Divyāvadāna*, though that work

[1] Konow, LSI. iv. 279 ff.; Grierson, BSOS. I. iii. 72; Carnoy, JAOS. xxxix. 117 ff.; Chatterji, i. 174 ff.

[2] Cf. R. Swaminatha Aiyar, POCP. 1919, i, pp. lxxi ff., who legitimately points out that the evidence of Dravidian is very late in date, and these languages probably borrowed from Aryan. K. G. Śankar (JRAS. 1924, pp. 664 ff.) points out that the *Tol-kāppiyam*, the oldest Tamil work, must be after 400 A. D. as it refers to the *Poruḷadhikāraṁsūtra*, horary astrology, and that the Moriyas of the Sangam are the Mauryas of the Koṅkaṇa, who date after 494 A. D.

[3] Cf. Senart, i, pp. iv, xiii ff.; Wackernagel, *Altind. Gramm.*, i, p. xxxix. Contrast F. W. Thomas, JRAS. 1904, p. 469, who regards the mixed Sanskrit as representing middle-class speech. Poussin (*Indo-européens*, p. 205) stresses convention as stereotyping usage.

marks in part a successful attempt to adapt Sanskrit prose, as known at Mathurā and elsewhere, to Buddhist use. The degree of cultivation of those who endeavoured to write in Sanskrit might vary greatly; thus the Sanskritization of the treatises in the Bower Manuscript, perhaps of the fourth century A.D., is comparatively good in the case of those on medicine, and decidedly poor in those on divination and incantation. In part the deviation from Sanskrit as laid down in the grammars is purely a case of Prākritic forms intruding scarcely disguised into the texts, but in other instances popular influence reveals itself in a Sanskrit which ignores delicate distinctions and confuses forms. The distinction between Prākritisms and careless Sanskrit is not absolute, but it is convenient and legitimate.

Thus we have in the phonology of this popular Sanskrit as seen in the Bower MS. some confusion of *ṛ* and *ri*, of *n* and *ṇ*, of *ç*, *ṣ*, and *s*; metrical lengthening and shortening of vowels is not rare; *ml* becomes *mbl*, and rarely *a* is prefixed as in *alatā*. In Sandhi hiatus and hyper-Sandhi, even to the extent of an elided consonant (*açvibhyānumataḥ*), are known, while *ā* is occasionally elided when initial. In declension we find *īs* and reversely *ū* as feminine nominatives for *ī* and *ūs*; *īs* is often replaced by *yas* as the accusative feminine, and *in* stems are treated as *i* stems, as in *pittīnām* for *pittinām*. In the verb we have simplification in class, as in *lihet* for *lihyāt*, *pīṣet* for *piṅsyāt*; and, as in the epic, very free interchange of active and middle forms; the gerunds in *tvā* and *yā* are confused. Stem formation shows frequently the mixture of bases in *a*, *i*, or *u* for those in *as*, *is*, or *us*, and, rarely, such a base as *hantāra* from the accusative of *hantṛ*; there is confusion in feminine suffixes, as in *ghnā* for *ghnī*, *caturthā* for *caturthī*, while ordinals in composition are sometimes replaced by cardinals. Very characteristic is confusion of gender, especially between masculine and neuter, more rarely between masculine and feminine or feminine and neuter. Case confusion is common, as is non-observation of rules of concord and confusion of numbers, while the interpolation of particles within compounds or sentences, absolute constructions, and very loosely compacted clauses are common.

Existing as it did side by side with Prākrit dialects, it was inevitable that there should be frequent borrowings on either side,[1] despite the objections raised from time to time by grammarians and sticklers for purity in the use of the sacred language in sacrificial matters.[2] Thus, though Classical Sanskrit lost many of the words and roots recorded in the *Gaṇapāṭha* and the *Dhātupāṭha* associated with Pāṇini's grammar, it was enriched by numerous additions, some easy, others difficult, of detection. In many cases the Prākrit forms were taken over with only the necessary changes requisite to make them seem to have terminations allowed in Sanskrit. It appears as if even Pāṇini [3] recognized this practice, since he allows eastern place-names to pass as correct though having the Prākrit *e* and *o* for the regular *ai* and *au* which his rules require. In other cases the retention of the Prākrit form was aided by the possibility of regarding the form as genuine Sanskrit; thus the poetic technical term *vicchitti*, really from *vikṣipti*,[4] in all likelihood seemed to be derivable from *vi-chid*; Kṛṣṇa's epithet Govinda, perhaps Prākrit for *gopendra*, was felt as *go-vinda*, winner of cows; in late texts *bhadanta*, from the phrase of greeting *bhadraṁ te*, is defended as from *bhad* with the suffix *anta*, and *uttṛ* is not recognized as from *avatṛ* through Prākrit *otarati*; *duruttara*, hard to overcome, really from Prākrit *duttara* for *duṣṭara*, was felt as *dur-uttara*. In many cases, doubtless, Prākrit words were correctly rendered into good Sanskrit equivalents, in which case borrowing cannot now be established. In others, however, the process is betrayed by false forms; thus Prākrit *mārisa*, friend, where *s* stands for *ç*, was mechanically made into *māriṣa*; *guccha*, for the lost *gṛpsa*, became *gutsa*, cluster; *masiṇa*, Sanskrit *mṛtsna*, reappeared as *masṛṇa*, soft; *rukkha*,[5] for *rukṣa* or rather *vṛkṣa*, *rūkṣa*, tree; and *heṭṭhā*, from *adhastāt*, gave by reconstruction *heṣṭa*. A common formation in Jain texts is *vidhyai*, go out, which is based on Prākrit *vijjhai*, from Sanskrit *vikṣai*; similarly *vikurv*, produce by magic, is traced through *viuvvai*, *viuvvae* to *vikṛ*. Later there are borrowings from vernaculars such as Gujarātī or Marāṭhī or

[1] Zachariae, *Beitr. z. Lexikogr.*, pp. 53 ff.

[2] See Çabarasvāmin and Kumārila on *Mīmāṅsā Sūtra*, i. 3, 24 ff.; *Sarasvatī-kaṇṭhābhāraṇa*, i. 16; *Mahābhāṣya*, i. 5.

[3] i. 1. 75.

[4] Zachariae, *B. Beitr.*, xiii. 93; cf. *argala* (IA. xix. 59) through *aggala* for *agralaka*; Kielhorn, GN. 1903, p. 308.

[5] See Hultzsch, CII. i, pp. lxx ff., *contra* Turner, JRAS. 1925, p. 177. I agree with Oldenberg that in RV. vi. 3. 7 *rukṣa* is not = *vṛkṣa*.

Hindī.[1] Often, of course, the Sanskrit version has been ingeniously made to appear valid in itself, as when *pabbhāra* is metamorphosed into *prāgbhāra*, though *prahvāra* is its origin.

Occasionally we find the process of Sanskritization applied to what was really Sanskrit ; probably thus are to be explained *prasabham*, violently, from *pra-sah* ; Naghuṣa for the older proper name Nahuṣa, *varṣābhū*, frog, for *varṣāhū*.

From foreign sources borrowings also occurred naturally enough in those cases where, as in the Dekhan or Further India, Sanskrit was used side by side with a native speech. Kumārila permits the incorporation of Dravidian terms, provided that they are given Sanskrit terminations, and names especially such as Sāyaṇa were freely thus Sanskritized. The *ḷ* which marks South Indian texts [2] in lieu of the *ḍ* and *l* of the north is doubtless in part due to Dravidian influence. On the other hand, invasions from the north brought early and late Iranian words such as *lipi*, writing, Old Persian *dipi*,[3] *kṣatrapa*, satrap, and perhaps *mudrā*, seal,[4] or *divira*, scribe, *mihira*, Mithra, *bahādura*, *sāha*, and *sāhi*. The Greek invasions in the north left little trace in the language, but probably later India borrowed *suruṅgā* from syrinx in the technical sense of an underground passage, and a large number of terms of astrology. Many of these they ingeniously altered to seem true Sanskrit, as when for hydrochoos we find *hṛdroga*, or *jāmitra* for diametron. With similar ingenuity the useful camel was metamorphosed into *kramela*,[5] suggesting connexion with *kram*, go. The Mahomedan invasion brought with it Arabic and Turkish terms, and the European powers have contributed occasional additions to the modern Sanskrit vocabulary, testifying to its capacity of assimilation. The scientific literature in special has shown its willingness to appropriate the terms used by those from whom knowledge has been acquired, together with considerable skill in disguising the loan.

[1] Cf. Bloomfield, *Festschrift Wackernagel*, pp. 220–30 ; Hertel, HOS. xii. 29 f.

[2] Lüders, *Festschrift Wackernagel*, p. 295.

[3] Bühler, *Ind. Stud.*, iii. 21 ff. ; Hultzsch, CII. i, p. xlii.

[4] Franke, ZDMG. xlvi. 731 ff. Hāla has *vandī*, captive. Cf. Weber, *Monatsber. Berl. Ak.*, 1879, pp. 810 ff.

[5] Lévi (*De Graecis vet. Ind. Mon.*, p. 56) doubts this, but the word is late ; *lopāka* (ἀλώπηξ) is different, as *lopāça* is Vedic. Hāla has *kalama* (κάλαμος) and *maragaa* (σμάραγδος).

As the passage of time made Sanskrit more and more a language of culture, it reveals in increasing measure a lack of delicate sensibility to idiomatic use of words, such as is engendered by usage in a living speech more closely in touch with ordinary life. The defect, however, is sometimes exaggerated, for it must not be forgotten that poets of all times are apt, through considerations of metre or desire for effect,[1] to adopt unusual senses of words and to strain meanings; Pindar and Propertius illustrate a tendency which is found more or less markedly throughout classical literature, while the Alexandrian Lykophron is guilty of as distinct linguistic monstrosities as any Indian poet. The tendency in their case was accentuated by the growing love for paronomasias, and the tendency to study poetic dictionaries which gave lists of synonyms, ignoring the fact that in reality two terms are practically never really coextensive in sense. The grammatical knowledge of the poets also led them into inventing terms or using terms in senses etymologically unexceptionable but not sanctioned by usage.

4. *The Prākrits*

The most widely accepted etymology of Prākrit current in India treats the name as denoting derivative, the prime source (*prakṛti*) being Sanskrit. Another view reverses the position; Prākrit is what comes at once from nature, what all people without special instruction can easily understand and use.[2] It is impossible to decide what was the process which led to the use of the term; perhaps speeches other than Sanskrit received the name from being the common or vulgar speech, the language of the humble man as opposed to him of education who could talk the pure language. In the grammarians and writers on poetics the term more especially denotes a number of distinctly artificial literary dialects, which as they stand were certainly not vernaculars; but it is customary to use the term to apply to Indian vernaculars prior to the period when the modern vernaculars became fixed. An even wider sense is given by Sir George Grierson, who classifies Prākrits in three great stages:

[1] Catullus' curious compounds in the *Attis* illustrate this theme.

[2] Pischel, *Grammatik der Prakrit-Sprachen* (1900), §§ 1, 16.

Primary Prākrits, of which the Vedic language and its successor Sanskrit are literary forms; Secondary Prākrits, represented in literature by Pāli, by the Prākrits of the grammarians, of the drama and literature generally, and by the Apabhrançças of the grammarians; and Tertiary Prākrits, the modern vernaculars. It may be doubted whether the terminology has sufficient merit to render it desirable to give it currency, because it obscures the constant process of change and suggests that there are greater distinctions between the periods than do exist, while it does not allow a special place to a fundamental innovation which occurs with the period designed as Secondary Prākrit.

Apart from conclusions drawn from odd forms in the Vedic literature, our first real knowledge of the Prākrits is derived from the inscriptions of Açoka,[1] from which can be deduced with certainty the existence of three dialects,[2] that of the east, used in the capital and intended to be the lingua franca of the Empire, that of the north-west, and that of the west. Of these the north-west preserves the most ancient aspect, for it retains the *r* element of the *ṛ* vowel and *r* in consonantal groups, while the western dialect has *a* for *ṛ* and assimilates, as in *mago* for *mṛgas*, *a*(*t*)*tha* for *artha*, and the eastern dialect has *i* or *u* for *ṛ* as well as *a*, and assimilates with cerebralization, as in *a*(*ṭ*)*ṭha* for *artha*, *va*(*ḍ*)*ḍhita* for *vardhita*, while in *kaṭa* or *kiṭa* for *kṛta* it shows cerebralization, suggesting an eastern origin for Sanskrit words with unusual cerebralization. The north-west dialect again preserves all three sibilants, though with departures from the norm due to assimilation, as in *çaçana* for *çāsana*, or dissimilation, as in *suçruṣa* for *çuçrūṣā*; the eastern has *s* and so also the western, but in this case there are traces that the distinction longer prevailed, since *rç* in such a word as *darçana* seems to have been transformed to *darṣana*, in which condition it cerebralized the *n*, before assimilating *rṣ* to *ss*.[3] The authors of the Bhaṭṭiprōḷu inscriptions in South-east India, seemingly colonists from the west, had a sound intermediate between *ç* and *ṣ* indicating the manner of the change. The north-west and the west again

[1] New ed. E. Hultzsch (1925); on dialects see Chaps. VI–XI.

[2] Michelson, AJP. xxx. 284 ff., 416 ff.; xxxi. 55 ff.; JAOS. xxx. 77 ff.; xxxi. 233 ff.; xxxvi. 210 f.

[3] Michelson, JAOS. xxxi. 236 f.; Lüders, SBA. 1912, pp. 806 ff.; 1914, p. 843.

agree against the east in assimilating *ty* to *cc* and *kṣ* to *cch*, against the representation of *ty* as *tiy* and the assimilation to *kkh*; the east again is marked by the use of *e* for primitive *az* as against *o*, and by its rejection of *r* in favour of *l*. This eastern dialect may fairly be regarded as a forerunner of the Ardhamāgadhī of the grammatical tradition, though that language has been largely affected by western influences in its later form. An inscription in a cave on the Rāmgarh hill, probably of the second century B.C., reveals to us the precursor of the later Māgadhī, since it shows its characteristics, *e* for *o*, *l* for *r*, *kkh* for *kṣ*, and *ç* for *s*.

Our next information of a definite character regarding the dialects is afforded not so much by the various inscriptions of the post-Açokan period as by the dramas of Açvaghoṣa, which may be regarded as good testimony for the period *c.* A.D. 100. Here we find dialects which may justly be styled Old Ardhamāgadhī, Old Çaurasenī, and Old Māgadhī; of these the former may well have been the dialect in which, as tradition asserts, Mahāvīra preached his doctrines and established Jainism, and in which Buddhist teachers carried on their work.[1] The early Jain scriptures, however, have admittedly perished, and the actual canon of the Çvetāmbaras now extant is redacted in a form strongly influenced by the later south-western speech Māhārāṣṭrī, while later texts are written in what has been fairly called Jain Māhārāṣṭrī, and the Digambaras adopted under western influence what has been styled Jain Çaurasenī. The canonical language of Buddhism, on the other hand, is more ancient; it is not, however, Ardhamāgadhī, but is distinctly of a western type, perhaps more closely connected with Avantī or Kauçāmbī than any other region. To the group of old Prākrits belongs also the mysterious Paiçācī, in which the famous *Bṛhatkathā* of Guṇāḍhya was written; its home is still uncertain; it has been connected by Sir G. Grierson[2] with the north-western dialect of the Açokan inscriptions on the one side and the modern languages of the north-west, which with dubious accuracy he has styled Piçāca; against this may be set, *inter alia*, the fact that the north-western

[1] Cf. Keith, IHQ. i. 501 ff.

[2] *Pisāca Lang.*, pp. 1 ff.; ZDMG. lxvi. 49 ff.; JRAS. 1921, pp. 424 ff.; IA. xlix. 114; AMJV. i. 119 ff.

dialect of Açokan times kept the three sibilants which Paiçācī reduces to one, although the Gipsy dialect and the dialects of the Hindu Kush distinguish still between *s* and *ṣ* on the one hand and *ç* on the other.[1] The possession by Paiçācī of the letters *ḷ* and *l*, and the use of one nasal *n* only, have been adduced by Konow[2] as proof of location in addition to its close connexion with Pāli, and, as these features were preserved in modern Mālvī, and its hardening of soft consonants is probably due to Dravidian influence, Paiçācī has been located in accord with Indian tradition in the Vindhya region. Inscriptions suggest also that south of the Narmadā there was a measure of independent development, adding a south-western to the three great groups already known; thus in the south we have *duhutuya*, *dhūā* in the later Māhārāṣṭrī, pointing to the source of Ardhamāgadhī *dhūyā*, as opposed to the *dhitā* of the northern inscriptions, Pāli *dhītā*, Çaurasenī (beside *duhidā*) and Māgadhī *dhīdā*, Vedic *dhitā* beside the normal *duhitā*.[3]

The characteristics of these Old Prākrits are simple.[4] They include the loss of the vowels *ṛ* and *ḷ*, and of the diphthongs *ai* and *au*; reduction in the number of sibilants and nasals; and the assimilation of consonants. They show also the operation of the substitution of the expiratory for the musical accent, a feature which is obvious in Sanskrit during the same period. Further, they are subject to a most important law which reduces each syllable to the form either of a vowel, short or long, a short vowel followed by one or two consonants, or a long vowel followed by a single consonant; the resulting changes of form are intensified by the confusion which results from substituting a long vowel with a single consonant for an originally short vowel with two consonants, or the use of a nasal vowel in lieu of

[1] Reichelt, *Festschrift Streitberg*, p. 245.

[2] ZDMG. lxiv. 95; JRAS. 1921, pp. 244 ff.; cf. Ranganathaswami Aryavaraguru, IA. xlviii. 211 f. Przyluski (*La légende de l'empereur Açoka*, p. 72) holds that Pāli may have had relations with Kauçāmbī.

[3] Lüders, KZ. xlix. 233 f.

[4] Lüders, *Bruchstücke buddh. Dramen*, pp. 29 ff.; Keith, *Sanskrit Drama*, pp. 72 ff. 85 ff., 121 ff. Contrast Michelson, AJP. xli. 265 ff.; Bloch, JA. 1911, ii. 167. In a Prākrit of the Western Panjāb is composed the *Dhammapada* of the Dutreuil de Rhins MS.; Konow, *Festschrift Windisch*, pp. 85 ff. (1st cent. A. D.); Lüders, SBA 1914, pp. 101 ff. (3rd cent. A. D.).

a long vowel, or a short vowel and a consonant, when another consonant follows.

It is probable enough that literature of a secular character was composed in these Old Prākrits until the second century A. D., but about that date we have clear evidence of the fundamental changes which mark what may be called the Middle Prākrit of the grammarians and of most of the extant literature. This consists in the softening or disappearance of intervocalic consonants, carried to the furthest in Māhārāṣṭrī in the dominions of the Çātavāhanas of the south-west, but noteworthy also in the other Prākrits recognized by the grammarians, Māgadhī, and Çaurasenī. We see in the dramas of Bhāsa, as compared with those of Açvaghoṣa on the one hand and of Kālidāsa on the other, clear evidence of transition, the omission of intervocalic consonants, the softening of surds to sonants, the reduction of aspirates to *h*, the change of *y* into *j*, the substitution of *ṇ* for *n*, the simplification of double consonants with compensatory lengthening. The evidence of inscriptions supports the view which assigns the loss of intervocalic consonants to the second century A. D.,[1] in which century Māhārāṣṭrī lyric began its successful career, made known to us in the anthology of Hāla. Once stereotyped by the grammarians at an uncertain date, the Prākrits rapidly lost in importance as they became more and more divorced from current speech, while they did not possess the traditional sanctity of Sanskrit or its clarity of structure and beauty of form.

Of the Prākrits Māhārāṣṭrī held pre-eminence by its use in drama, whence it was introduced perhaps by Kālidāsa from lyric poetry, and by its adoption for epic poetry. Çaurasenī was normally the prose Prākrit, though it appears to have been occasionally used in verse; its employment in prose outside the drama was probably once much wider than was later the case when the Jains used a form of Māhārāṣṭrī for prose as well as for verse, though the presence of Çaurasenī forms in prose suggests that Māhārāṣṭrī is here intrusive.[2] Çaurasenī was markedly more

[1] Bloch, *Mélanges Lévi*, pp. 12 ff. (*kamāra*, however, is from *karmāra*). As regards lingualization cf. Turner, JRAS. 1924, pp. 555 ff., 582 ff. (*daṇḍa*, however, is not for *dandra*; see Lidén, *Stud. z. altind. und vergl. Sprachg.*, p. 80).

[2] Jacobi, *Bhavisatta Kaha*, pp. 88 ff.; RSO. ii. 231 ff.

closely akin to Sanskrit than Māhārāṣṭrī; its place of origin was within the sphere of the strongest influence of Sanskrit, and it remained in specially close relation with it both in morphology, syntax, and vocabulary. Hence it was appropriately used for persons of good position in the drama. Māgadhī, on the other hand, was reserved for those of low rank, and, though tales[1] were composed in it, it was of comparatively minor importance. The *Nāṭyaçāstra*, perhaps in the third century A.D., enumerates other dramatic dialects (*vibhāṣās*) which are clearly of no real popular origin; such are Dākṣiṇātyā, Prācyā, Āvantī, and Ḍhākkī or Ṭākkī, which are mere varieties of Çaurasenī, while Cāṇḍāli and Çākārī are species of Māgadhī.[2] Paiçācī, though practically unknown in the extant dramas, enjoyed, it appears, a considerable vogue in the popular tale, as a result, doubtless, of the fame of the *Bṛhatkathā*.

The comparatively late date at which Māhārāṣṭrī appears to have come into fame, as indicated by its exclusion until late from the drama, suggests that some other Prākrit was employed for poetry before its rise into repute. Jacobi has found traces of such a Prākrit in the verses cited in the *Nāṭyaçāstra*;[3] it was marked by the facultative retention or change or loss of intervocalic consonants, and was akin on the one hand to Çaurasenī, for example in such forms as *sadisa* for *sadṛça* and the gerund in *iya*, while it shared with Māhārāṣṭrī the locative in *ammi* and the gerund in *ūṇa*; from these local indications he suggests that it had its centre in Ujjayinī. It was, he holds, from this dialect that the softening of *t* to *d* passed into Çaurasenī, which in Açvaghoṣa hardly shows any trace of it, and also in the dialect, otherwise similar to Jain Māhārāṣṭrī, which on this account Pischel[4] named Jain Çaurasenī. This poetic Prākṛit, like Çaurasenī, is essentially closely akin to Sanskrit.

[1] Probably in verse, like Māhārāṣṭrī and Apabhrança tales; Daṇḍin, i. 38; Rudraṭa, xvi. 26. Daṇḍin's Gauḍī Prākrit may be Māgadhī; he mentions also Lāṭī.

[2] Cf. Keith, *Sanskrit Drama*, pp. 140 ff., 337; Gawroński, KZ. xliv. 247 ff. Iranian traits in Çākārī are not proved (JRAS. 1925, pp. 237 ff.); the points adduced all are essentially Māgadhī (cf. *ibid.*, pp. 218 ff.).

[3] *Bhavisatta Kaha*, pp. 84 ff. He does not touch on its relation to Pāli.

[4] *Op. cit.*, § 21.

5. *Apabhraṅça*

Pischel[1] and Sir G. Grierson[2] have given currency to the view that the term Apabhraṅça denotes the true vernaculars as opposed to literary Prākrits, and the latter has constructed a scheme for the derivation of modern vernaculars from the various local Apabhraṅças; thus from Çaurasena (or Nāgara) Apabhraṅça came Western Hindī, Rājasthānī, and Gujarātī; from Māhārāṣṭra Apabhraṅça Marāṭhī; from Māgadha Bengālī, Bihārī, Assamese, and Oṛiyā; from Ardhamāgadha Eastern Hindī; from Vrācaḍa Sindhī; and from Kaikeya Lahndā. Unfortunately this theoretical scheme will not stand investigation, for the evidence of texts and even of the literature proves clearly that Apabhraṅça has a different signification.[3]

The essential fact regarding Apabhraṅça is that it is the collective term employed to denote literary languages not Sanskrit or Prākrit. Bhāmaha[4] expressly gives this threefold division, and Daṇḍin[5] expressly says that Apabhraṅça is the term applied to the idioms of the Ābhīras, &c., when they appear in poetry. Guhasena of Valabhī, whose inscriptions have dates from A.D. 559–69, is declared to have composed poems in the three languages, Sanskrit, Prākrit, and Apabhraṅça. Rudraṭa,[6] in the ninth century, asserts that Apabhraṅça is manifold through the difference of lands, doubtless in agreement with Daṇḍin. Hemacandra also does not identify Apabhraṅça with the vernaculars. The vernacular (*deçabhāṣā*) is a different thing; hetairai are required to be skilled in the eighteen vernaculars according to the Jain canon; the *Kāmasūtra*, in enumerating their sixty-four accomplishments, includes knowledge of vernaculars as well as of literary speeches (*kāvyakriyā*); moreover, it preserves the

[1] *Gramm. der Prakrit-Sprachen*, § 4.

[2] BSOS. I. iii. 62 ff.; cf. IA. li. 13 ff.

[3] Jacobi, *Bhavisatta Kaha*, pp. 53 ff.; *Sanatkumāracaritam*, pp. xviii ff.; *Festschrift Wackernagel*, pp. 124 ff.

[4] i. 16.

[5] i. 32. Nobel's effort (*Indian Poetry*, pp. 132, 159) to distinguish between Bhāmaha's and Daṇḍin's use of Apabhraṅça is a failure.

[6] ii. 12.

interesting notice that a man of taste would mingle his vernacular with Sanskrit, as is the way with modern vernaculars, not with Apabhrañça. The identification of the vernaculars and Apabhrañça is given as the opinion of some authorities by the commentator of the *Prākṛta Piṅgala*, and other late authorities adopt this view. But the oldest authority who has been cited[1] for it is the Kashmirian Kṣemendra (11th cent.), and it is extremely doubtful whether he meant anything of the sort when he refers to poems in vernacular; it is as likely as not that in Kashmir, as probably in the case of Mahārāṣṭra, Apabhrañça was never a literary language, vernacular poems supervening directly on Prākrit poetry.

The first actual remnants of Apabhrañça preserved occur in a citation in Ānandavardhana, in the *Devīçataka*, and in Rudraṭa. By preserving *ṛ* and *r* it is clear that these verses belong to the species of Prākrit styled by the eastern school of grammarians (Kramadīçvara, Mārkaṇḍeya, Rāma Tarkavāgīça) Vrācaṭa, which also is styled the speech of the Ābhīras. This tribe appears to have entered India some time before 150 B.C., when it is mentioned by Patañjali. Its early home was Sindhudeça, by which is meant[2] not Sindh but the Peshāwar district of the Rāwalpindi division, where they had as eastern neighbours the Gurjaras.[3] Later both tribes spread; the Gurjaras are found as Gūjars in the United Provinces; in the main, however, they went south and occupied Gujarāt. The Ābhīras are recorded in the *Mahābhārata* as in the Panjāb, later they are heard of in Kurukṣetra, and their descendants, the Ahirs, range as far east as Bihar; some went south and settled on the coast to the west of Gujarāt; they won considerable fame, and an Ābhīra dynasty is stated in the *Viṣṇu Purāṇa* to have succeeded the Andhrabhṛtyas. Both Ābhīras and Gurjaras were probably of the Dardic branch of the Indian race, to judge at least from the strong Dardic

[1] Jacobi, *Bhavisatta Kaha*, p. 69, corrected p. 214.

[2] Jacobi, *Festschrift Wackernagel*, p. 124, n. 2; cf. *Raghuvança*, xv. 87, 89. See *Mahābhāṣya*, i. 2. 72, v. 6.

[3] See references in EHI. pp. 427 ff.; R. C. Majumdar, *The Gurjara-Pratīhāras* (1923). The view of them as Khazars or Huns is unproved, and their earliest date unknown, but Alexander did not find them in the Panjāb. Cf. Grierson, IA. xliii. 141 ff., 159 ff.

element in Lahndā, the speech of the western Panjāb. As they grew in civilization, they must have sought to create a literature; whether they attempted it in their own dialect at first and later produced Apabhraṅça must remain uncertain; what is clear is that Apabhraṅça originally was an effort to infuse into Prākrit a measure of their vernacular.

The effort to make Prākrit more readily intelligible to the people was not new; in the earliest epic in Jain Māhārāṣṭrī known to us, the *Paumacariya*[1] of Vimala Sūri, probably not before A. D. 300, we find the free use of what the grammarians style Deçīçabdas, words for which no derivation from Sanskrit is obvious or normally possible; similarly it seems that Pādalipta's *Taraṅgavatī*, mentioned in the *Anuyogadvāra* (5th cent.), though written in Prākrit, contained very many of such words. The large number of Deçī terms preserved in the *Deçīnāmamālā* of Hemacandra, some four thousand in all, testifies to the prevalence at one time of this practice, which, however, failed to retain favour. The reason for this may easily be conjectured; the words taken from the vernaculars were a barrier to comprehension in a wide circle, and with the rapid change of the vernaculars became obscure even in the poet's own land, so that poets who desired permanence of repute and wide circles of readers preferred to content themselves with those terms which had general currency. In Apabhraṅça, however, the effort was made to simplify Prākrit by adopting as the base of the grammar the vernacular, while using in the main the Prākrit vocabulary, and to some extent also Prākrit inflexions. There is a certain parallel with modern vernaculars which borrow freely from Sanskrit as opposed to Prākrit, but they do not use Sanskrit inflexions at all.

The Prākrit used as the base of early Apabhraṅça seems to have been often Māhārāṣṭrī, but sometimes also Çaurasenī. But once Apabhraṅça had become popular, perhaps through the activity of the Ābhīra and Gurjara princes, it spread beyond the west and various local Apabhraṅças arose, as is recognized by Rudraṭa; in these, we may assume, the special characteristics of the Vrācaṭa or Vrājaḍa Apabhraṅça were refined. We find this

[1] Jacobi, ERE. vii. 467.

confused condition reflected in the grammarians. Hemacandra, who belonged to the western school which goes back to the *Vālmīki Sūtras*, describes one kind of Apabhrañça, but alludes to others; in the eastern school we find a division as Vrācaṭa, Nāgara, and Upanāgara, in all of which *r* after consonants is kept while in the first *r* before consonants also. Faint traces of the observance of this rule may be found in a few verses cited by Hemacandra; the great poems, *Bhavisattakaha* and *Nemināhacariu* assimilate *r*, and thus belong to a later type of Apabhrañça. In Bengal we find a type of Apabhrañça long in use in Buddhist texts, and a much degraded form, Avahaṭṭhā, is evidenced in the *Prākṛta Piñgala* (14th cent.), but the basis even of this Apabhrañça is Māhārāṣṭrī, not Māgadhī, testifying to its ultimate western origin.

From the nature of Apabhrañça it follows naturally that in Old Gujarātī we find a considerable amount of resemblance in inflexion to Apabhrañça, as was to be expected from the fact that the vernacular is a descendant in considerable measure of that vernacular which was applied to Prākrit to form the early Apabhrañça. In other cases we could not expect to find any such important coincidences; thus in Bengal the Apabhrañça used was not formed by applying vernacular inflexions to the local Prākrit; at most some local colour was given to a speech which came from the west, and the same remark clearly applies in other cases. Sir G. Grierson's efforts[1] to establish a Māhārāṣṭra Apabhrañça as a connecting link between Prākrit and Marāṭhī are clearly unsuccessful. Nor indeed, it must be added, is there yet any adequate proof even of the relations suggested by him between the Prākrits and the vernaculars;[2] thus traces of Māgadhī in Bengālī are extremely difficult to establish with any cogency.[3]

There is no reason to suppose that Apabhrañça formed a necessary step towards composition in vernaculars, and in Mahārāṣṭra and Kashmir Apabhrañça appears to have been

[1] BSOS. I. iii. 63.

[2] E.g. his view (JRAS. 1925, pp. 228 ff.) as to single consonants in the North-West Prākrit is clearly improbable.

[3] M. Shahidullah, IHQ. i. 433 ff. Bloch (*Formation de la langue marathe*; JA. 1912, i. 336) insists that the modern dialects presuppose a Prākrit koine.

unknown, while in the latter region vernacular poetry appears to have been practised in the eleventh century. Literary evidence of compositions in the vernaculars is fragmentary, but at least from the twelfth century there was a Hindī literature, from the thirteenth one in Marāṭhī, and probably enough still earlier dates may be assigned to the adaptation of vernaculars to literary uses.[1]

[1] For Bengal see Dinesh Chandra Sen, *Hist. of Bengal Lang. and Lit.* (1911) and S. K. Chatterji, i. 129 ff.

PART II

BELLES-LETTRES AND POETICS

II

THE ORIGIN AND DEVELOPMENT OF KĀVYA LITERATURE

1. *The Sources of the Kāvya*

INDIA produced no historian of her Sanskrit literature, and, naturally enough, the appearance of great poets of the calibre of Kālidāsa, Bhāravi, and Māgha so eclipsed earlier efforts that their works and even their names passed into oblivion. Natural causes helped the result; it was difficult to multiply manuscripts, difficult to preserve them, and it is not surprising that the lesser poets should have passed from recollection. On the other hand, the absence of literary remains for the centuries just before and after the Christian era, and the fact that foreign invasions, Greeks, Parthians, and Çakas, and Yueh-chi deeply affected the north-west of India, gave an appearance of reason to Max Müller's famous suggestion[1] that there was a comparative cessation of literary activity in India until in the sixth century a great renaissance began with Kālidāsa and his contemporaries. The theory is now wholly discredited in the form in which it was put forward, if for no other reason than that it ignored the Brahmanical revival of the Gupta empire at the beginning of the fourth century A. D. But it lingers on in the form of the suggestion[2] that in the period up to that revival Sanskrit was little used for secular poetry, which was composed in Prākrit, until the reviving power of the Brahmins resulted in their creating the epic by translation from Prākrit originals, developed a lyric poetry to replace the simpler Prākrit songs of the people, and transformed the popular beast-fable and fairy-tale.

For this theory of a Prākrit period of Indian literature preced-

[1] *India* (1883), pp. 281 ff. Contrast Lassen, *Ind. Alt.*, ii.[2] 1159 ff.

[2] Bhandarkar, *Early Hist. of India* (1920), pp. 70 ff., who admits the existence of some Sanskrit literature, but places Açvaghoṣa under Kaniṣka *c.* A. D. 300. But as early as 185 B. C. there was a Brahmanical revival under Puṣyamitra; EIII. pp. 208 ff.; Przyluski, *La légende de l'empereur Açoka*, pp. 90 ff.

ing the Sanskrit period there is no evidence of value. The suggestion of the translation of the epic may be dismissed as absurd, but the case with other forms of literature is more worthy of consideration. The fairy-tale is a thing which readily circulates among the people long before it is dignified by literary treatment by the higher classes of society, and in point of fact there is a strong tradition to the effect that it was in a Prākrit dialect, though one closely allied to Sanskrit, that the great collection of such tales, which powerfully affected Sanskrit literature, as the *Bṛhatkathā* of Guṇāḍhya, was composed. Guṇāḍhya's work, however, is of very complex art and uncertain date, and in all probability came into being at a time when we have abundant evidence of the existence of Sanskrit literature, so that this instance is irrelevant to the contention in favour of a Prākrit period of literature. Equally little value attaches to the argument for the priority of Prākrit lyric. It was founded on a wholly misleading view of the antiquity of the anthology of Hāla, who was placed in the first century A. D. Against this view must be set the form of Māhārāṣṭrī Prākrit, which shows a development in the language such as cannot be dated before the latter part of the second century A.D., if regard be paid to the evidence of the inscriptions and of the Prākrits of the dramas of Açvaghoṣa.[1] It is true that Vararuci's Prākrit grammar recognizes Māhārāṣṭrī of the type of the anthology, but there is no evidence that Vararuci is early in date, for his identification by later tradition with the Kātyāyana who criticized Pāṇini is without serious value. Jacobi,[2] on the other hand, has identified Hāla with the Sātavāhana under whom Jain tradition records a change in the Church calendar in A.D. 467. There is no cogent reason to accept or deny this date; what is clear is that so far as the evidence goes there is nothing to suggest great antiquity for Prākrit lyric. Lüders, who finds traces of its existence about the second century B.C. in the short inscriptions of the Sītābengā and Jogīmārā caves on the Rāmgarh hill, and who assigns to the same

[1] *Bruchstücke buddh. Dramen*, pp. 61 ff. On the Sītābengā inscr. cf. Boyer, *Mélanges Lévi*, pp. 121 ff. Khāravela's date is still disputed.

[2] *Ausg. Erzählungen in Mâhârâshṭrî*, p. xvii; cf. *Bhavisatta Kaha*, p. 83. The *Paumacariya* of Vimala Sūri, the oldest Māhārāṣṭrī epic, is not before A. D. 300 and may be much later (cf. *ibid.*, p. 59).

century the Hāthigumphā inscription of Khāravela of Kaliṅga, which displays, though faintly, some of the characteristics of Sanskrit prose Kāvya, makes no claim for the priority of Prākrit to Sanskrit in these literary uses; on the contrary he acknowledges fully the coexistence of a Sanskrit literature.

Still less can be said for the priority of Prākrit in the sphere of the beast-fable. Such fables are readily current among the people, and the *Mahābhārata* shows their popularity in the circles to whom the epic appealed. The Jātaka tales of the Buddhists show likewise the skill by which they could be turned to the service of that faith, but of an early Prākrit fable literature we know little or nothing. On the other hand, the Sanskrit literature is marked by the fact that it adopts the fable to a definite purpose, the teaching to young princes and their entourage the practical conduct of life, and thus constitutes a new literary genre.

The causes of the rise of Sanskrit literature are in fact obvious, and there was no need for writers in Prākrit to set an example. It would indeed have been surprising if the simplicity of the earlier epic had not gradually yielded to greater art. The Upaniṣads show us kings patronizing discussions between rival philosophers and rewarding richly the successful; we need not doubt that they were no less eager to listen to panegyrics of themselves or their race and to bestow guerdon not less lavishly. We have indeed in the Vedic lists of forms of literature references to the Nārāçansīs, encomia,[1] which candour admitted to be full of lies, and we have actually preserved a few verses from which we can guess the high praise promiscuously bestowed on their patrons by the singers. Into the *Ṛgveda* itself have been admitted hymns which contrive to flatter patrons as well as extol the gods, and added verses, styled praises of gifts (*dānastutis*), recount the enormous rewards which a clever singer might obtain. We cannot doubt that from such contests must have sprung the desire to achieve ever-increasing perfection of literary form as compared with the more pedestrian style of the mere narrative of the epic.

In yet another sphere such heightening of style must have

[1] Macdonell and Keith, *Vedic Index*, i. 445 f.

been striven after. The Vedic poets, who can compare[1] the goddess Dawn to a fair dancer, to a maiden who unveils her bosom to a lover, cannot have been incapable of producing love poetry for secular use. Nor is it doubtful that it was the early writers of the love lyric who enriched Sanskrit with a vast abundance of elaborate metres; for the flow of epic narrative such metrical forms were wholly unsuited; on the other hand, the limited theme of love demanded variety of expression if it were to be worthily developed. The gnomic utterance of which the *Aitareya Brāhmaṇa* has preserved some Vedic specimens naturally shared in the cultivation of the lyric, and the elaboration of verse doubtless reacted on prose style, inducing writers to seek to reproduce in that medium something of the elegance after which poets now habitually strove. There is, then, no justification for presuming a breach in literary continuity, and, despite the fact that so much has perished, we have indisputable proofs of the active cultivation of Sanskrit literature during the period from 200 B.C. to A.D. 200, when on one theory it had not yet come into being, and secular literature was composed in Prākrit.

2. *The Testimony of the Rāmāyaṇa*

The validity of the *Rāmāyaṇa* as evidence of the growth of the Kāvya has been disputed on the score that the poem was, even if in large measure early in date,[2] still under constant revision, so that those features in it which foreshadow the later Kāvya and justify its own claim to that title as the first of Kāvyas may be dismissed as interpolations. The argument, however, is clearly unsatisfactory, and does not establish the result at which it aims. We may readily agree that some part at least of the elegancies of style [3] which mark the poem is a later addition, but there is no ground whatever to admit that these additions fall later than the second century B.C., and they may

[1] Hirzel, *Gleichnisse und Metaphern im Ṛgveda* (1908). For the early, which is also the later, ideal of feminine beauty, see *Çatapatha Brāhmaṇa*, i. 2. 5. 16; iii. 5. 1. 11; the love charms of the *Atharva* attest the beginnings of erotic poetry (IS. v. 218 ff.).

[2] Keith, JRAS. 1915, pp. 318 ff.

[3] Jacobi, *Rāmāyaṇa*, pp. 119 ff. The *Rāmāyaṇa* also shows the development of the Çloka metre almost to its classic state; cf. SIFI. VIII. ii. 38 ff. See also Krishnamachariar, *Raghuvaṅçavimarça* (1908).

be earlier in date. The *Rāmāyaṇa* in fact, as we have it, affords an illustration of the process of refinement which style was undergoing, but it is essential to realize that even in its original form the poem must have shown a distinct tendency to conscious ornament. The mere theme, the blending together of two distinct legends, the court intrigues of Ayodhyā and the legend of Rāma's war on Rāvaṇa for the rape of Sītā—in ultimate origin a nature myth—is the work of an artist, and the same trait is revealed in the uniformity of the language and the delicate perfection of the metre, when compared with the simpler and less polished *Mahābhārata*. Vālmīki and those who improved on him, probably in the period 400–200 B.C., are clearly the legitimate ancestors of the court epic.

Ānandavardhana[1] has not inaptly contrasted the object of the court epic with that of the legend (*itihāsa*); the latter is content to narrate what has happened, the former is essentially dependent on form. The *Rāmāyaṇa* occupies an intermediate place, and its formal merits are not slight. But in any case it essentially anticipates the means by which the later poets seek to lend distinction and charm to their subject-matter; as they drew deeply upon it for their themes, so they found in it the models for the ornaments of their style. If the city of Ayodhyā appears in human form to the king in Kālidāsa's *Raghuvaṅça*, Vālmīki has set the example in his vision of Lankā in the Sundarakāṇḍa. The action in the later Kāvya is all but obstructed by the wealth of the poet's descriptive powers; Vālmīki's followers have described with no less than twenty-nine similes the woes of Sītā in her captivity, with sixteen the sad plight of Ayodhyā bereft of Rāma.[2] Descriptions of the seasons, of mountains and rivers, bulk largely in the Kāvya, but Vālmīki has set the example in his elaborate accounts of the rainy season and autumn, of the winter, of Mount Citrakūṭa, and of the river Mandākinī.[3] Metaphors of beauty abound in the Kāvya side by side with those of strained taste and pointless wit; the *Rāmāyaṇa* is guilty of

viṣādanakrādhyuṣite paritrāsormimālini
kim māṁ na trāyase magnāṁ vipule çokasāgare?

[1] *Dhvanyāloka*, p. 148.

[2] ii. 19 and 114.

[3] iv. 28; iii. 16; ii. 94, 95. There is a brilliant picture of the sound of the sea: *parvasūdīrṇavegasya sāgarasyeva niḥsvanaḥ*.

'Why dost thou not save me that am sunk in a broad ocean of woe, whose coronal of waves is horror, and in which dwell the crocodiles of despondency?'

Much happier is the famous simile:

sāgaraṁ cāmbaraprakhyam ambaraṁ sāgaropamam
Rāmarāvaṇayor yuddhaṁ Rāmarāvaṇayor iva.

'Ocean peer of sky, sky ocean's counterpart; Rāma and Rāvaṇa alone could match their mortal combat.' A later commonplace is foreshadowed in:

tvāṁ kṛtvoparato manye rūpakartā sa viçvakṛt
na hi rūpopamā hy anyā tavāsti çubhadarçane.

'When he had made thee, I ween, the All-maker stayed from his making of lovely forms, for there is no beauty on earth to match thine, o fair-faced one.' As later, we find as prognostications of good the wind that blows free from dust, the clear skies, the flowers that are rained down to earth, and the resonance of the drums of the gods. Indra's banner, erected and then taken down at the festival in his honour, affords material for similes; eyes expand with joy (*harṣotphullanayana*); men drink in faces with their eyes (*locanābhyām pibann iva*); breasts are like golden bowls (*kucau suvarṇakalaçopamau*); before men's wondering eyes the host stands as if in a picture; the Ganges shows her white teeth as she smiles in the foam of her waves (*phenanirmalahāsinī*); winds blow with fragrant coolness; the clouds rumble with deep and pleasant sound (*snigdhagambhīraghoṣa*); the action of the fool is like that of the moth that flies into the flame; man leaves his worn frame as the snake its old skin. The love of alliteration is already present, as in *dakṣiṇā dakṣiṇaṁ tīram*; we find even an example of the figure, concise expression (*samāsokti*), in which the dawn is treated on the analogy of a loving maiden:

cañcaccandrakarasparçaharṣonmīlitatārakā
aho rāgavatī saṁdhyā jahātu svayam ambaram.

'Ah that the enamoured twilight should lay aside her garment of sky, now that the stars are quickened to life by the touch of the rays of the dancing moon.' The *Rāmāyaṇa* is not given to erotic descriptions; its tone is serious and grave, but such passages[1] as the description of the vision by Hanumant of the sleeping wives of Rāvaṇa mark the beginning of a tradition which Açvaghoṣa handed on to his successors. Imitation in detail of the *Rāmāyaṇa* is frequent and patent, and its language and verse technique deeply affected the whole of the history of the Kāvya.

The content of the *Mahābhārata* naturally afforded to later poets an inexhaustible material for their labours, but save in its later additions the great epic suffered little elaboration of style, and affords no evidence comparable to that of the *Rāmāyaṇa* attesting the development of the Kāvya style.

3. *The Evidence of Patañjali and Piṅgala*

Direct and conclusive evidence of the production of secular Sanskrit literature before 150 B.C. is afforded by the testimony of the *Mahābhāṣya*.[2] Much earlier evidence from the point of view of grammar would be available, if we could believe the assertion[3] of Rājaçekhara—perhaps the dramatist—that Pāṇini was the author not merely of the grammar but also of the *Jāmbavatīvijaya*; that epic and apparently another, the *Pātālavijaya*, are ascribed to him by anthologies which cite verses from them. The fact, however, that grammatical errors occur in a verse from the latter work renders the ascription implausible, even if epic excuse can be alleged, and we may reasonably accept the existence of two or more Pāṇinis, despite the rarity of the name.

The testimony of the *Mahābhāṣya*, however, is quite clear, and its value is all the greater because it is given incidentally and by accident in the discussion of disputed rules of the master. Patañjali, of course, knows the Bhāratan epic, but he refers also to dramatic recitals of epic legends—perhaps to actual dramatic performances—and the topics mentioned include the slaying by Kṛṣṇa of his wicked uncle Kaṅsa and the binding of Bali by the god Viṣṇu. We are told of rhapsodes who tell their tales until the day dawns, and stories were current which dealt with the

[1] Not probably by Vālmīki. For Vedic precedents in alliteration and Yamakas see Hillebrandt, *Kālidāsa*, pp. 161 ff.; for the epic, Hopkins, *Great Epic*, pp. 200 ff.

[2] Cf. Weber, IS. xiii. 356 ff., 477 ff.; Kielhorn, IA. xiv. 326 f.; Bühler, *Die indischen Inschriften*, p. 72; Bhandarkar, IA. iii. 14.

[3] See Thomas, *Kavīndravacanasamuccaya*, pp. 51 ff.

legends of Yavakrīta, Yayāti, Priyaṅgu, Vāsavadattā, Sumanottarā, and Bhīmaratha. A Vāraruca Kāvya is actually mentioned, though unfortunately we know no more of it. We have, however, invaluable help in appreciating the growth of Kāvya in the incidental citation of stanzas clearly taken from poems of the classical type. Many are tantalizing in their brevity; we hear of a maiden bought with a price who was dearer to her lord than his life (*sā hi tasya dhanakrītā prāṇebhyo 'pi garīyasī*). The verse *varatanu sampravadanti kukkuṭāḥ*, 'O fair one, the cocks proclaim together', has afforded later authors an opportunity of exhibiting skill in filling up the missing three verses (*samasyāpūraṇa*).[1] Erotic verse is attested also by *priyām mayūraḥ pratinarnṛtīti*, 'The peacock danceth towards his beloved', perhaps also by *ā vanāntād odakāntāt priyam pāntham anuvrajet*, 'Let her follow the wanderer she loveth to the end of the woods, to the end of the waters'. Epic or panegyric is found in the address *prathate tvayā patimatī pṛthivī*, 'The earth with thee as lord maketh true its name as wide'; so also *asidvitīyo 'nusāra Pāṇḍavam*, 'With sword as mate he attacked Pāṇḍu's son', *jaghāna Kaṅsaṁ kila Vāsudevaḥ*, 'Vāsudeva slew Kaṅsa.' Brief as it is, there is pathos in

yasmin daça sahasrāṇi putre jāte gavāṁ dadau
brāhmaṇebhyaḥ priyākhyebhyaḥ so 'yam uñchena jīvati.

'On his scanty gleaning now he liveth, he for whose birth were given ten thousand kine to the Brahmins who brought the good tidings.'

Gnomic poetry is also strongly represented:

tapaḥ çrutaṁ ca yoniç cety etad brāhmaṇakārakam
tapaḥçrutābhyāṁ yo hīno jātibrāhmaṇa eva saḥ.

'Asceticism, learning, birth, these make the Brahmin; he who lacks asceticism and learning is a Brahmin by birth alone.' Or again, *bubhukṣitaṁ na pratibhāti kiṁcit*, 'Nothing seems right to a hungry man.' Solomon's maxim regarding the education of children has a worthy parallel:

sāmṛtaiḥ pāṇibhir ghnanti guravo na viṣokṣitaiḥ
lāḍanāçrayiṇo[2] *doṣās tāḍanāçrayiṇo guṇāḥ.*

[1] See Chap. IX, § 1.
[2] Cf. the forms in *Festschrift Wackernagel*, p. 303.

'Fraught with life, not with poison, are the blows that teachers give; vice grows by indulgence, virtue prospers by reproof.' The inevitability of death is recorded:

ahar ahar nayamāno gām açvam puruṣam paçum
Vaivasvato na tṛpyati surayā iva durmadī.

'Though day by day he takes his toll in cattle, horses, men, and beasts, Vivasvant's son is sated never, as a drunkard is never wearied of brandy.' A maxim of political wisdom may be seen in

kṣeme subhikṣe kṛtasaṁcayāni: purāṇi rājñāṁ vinayanti kopam.

'Citadels well stored in peace and abundance calm the wrath of kings.'

Noteworthy also is the fact that in the scanty number of verses there occur specimens of such ornate metres as the Mālatī, the Praharṣiṇī, the Pramitākṣarā, and the Vasantatilaka, beside the normal Çloka and Triṣṭubh. These new metres lead us into a different sphere from the Vedic metres, and striking light on this development is afforded by the metre of the Kārikās,[1] mostly, if not all, written probably by predecessors of Patañjali, which deal with disputed points of grammar. Among these are besides the Çloka and Vaktra, Indravajrā, Upajāti, Çālinī, Vaṅçasthā, all later usual, and the much less common metres, Samānī, consisting of four verses each of four trochees, Vidyunmālā, similarly made up of spondees, the anapaestic Toṭaka, and the Dodhaka, in which the verse has three dactyls and a spondee. This richness and elaboration of metre, in striking contrast to the comparative freedom of Vedic and epic literature, must certainly have arisen from poetical use; it cannot have been invented for grammatical memorial verses, for which a simple metre might better suffice. The names Toṭaka and Dodhaka have been suspected of Prākritic origin, and the latter of ultimate Greek origin, but these are unproved hypotheses without literary or other support.

In addition to the clear indications thus given of the existence of epic, lyric, and gnomic verse, we may deduce from other hints the existence of the material whence later developed the beast-

[1] Cf. Kielhorn, IA. xv. 229 ff.; Jacobi, *Festschrift Wackernagel*, p. 127.

fable. We have allusions [1] to such proverbial tales as that of the goat and the razor (*ajākṛpāṇīya*), of the crow and the palm fruit (*kākatālīya*), and to the hereditary enmity of the snake and the ichneumon, and of the crow and the owl, later famous as the theme of a book of the *Pañcatantra.*

Corroboration of the evidence of Patañjali can be obtained from the *Chandassūtra* of Piñgala, which ranks as a Vedāñga but is mainly devoted to the exposition of secular prosody. Piñgala ranks as an ancient sage, being sometimes identified with Patañjali; the aspect of his work suggests considerable age, and many of the metres which he describes are certainly not derived from the Kāvya literature which has come down to us. They suggest a period of transition in which the authors of the erotic lyric [2] were trying experiment after experiment in metrical effect. The names of the metres can often most plausibly be explained as epithets of the beloved; the stanzas may have been so styled because the word in question occurred in them. Thus we have the metre Kāntotpīḍā, the plague of her lovers, Kuṭilagati, she of crooked gait, Cañcalākṣikā, she of the glancing eyes, Tanumadhyā, she of the slender waist, Cāruhāsinī, the sweet-smiling one, and Vasantatilakā, the pride of spring. Other names suggest poetic observation of animal life; thus we have Açvalalita, the gait of the horse, Kokilaka, the cry of the cuckoo, Sinhonnatā, tall as a lion, Çārdūlavikrīḍita, the tiger's play. The plant world gives others as Mañjarī, the cluster, Mālā, the garland. That a strong school of lyric poetry existed about the Christian era and probably much earlier we cannot seriously doubt; to its influence we may with reason ascribe the appearance and bloom of the Māhārāṣṭrī lyric about A.D. 200.

4. *Kāvya in Inscriptions*

Chance has preserved for us certain evidence in the early inscriptions [3] which disposes definitely of the theory of the dormancy of Sanskrit during the period of foreign invasions in India. An inscription at Girnār [4] dated about A.D. 150–2 under the Mahā-

[1] *Mahābhāṣya*, ii. 1. 3; v. 3. 106; IS. xiii. 486.

[2] Jacobi, ZDMG. xxxviii. 615 f.

[3] Bühler, *Die indischen Inschriften und das Alter der indischen Kunstpoesie* (1890).

[4] EI. viii. 36 ff.; EHI. pp. 139 f.; IA. xlviii. 145 f.

kṣatrapa Rudradāman, grandson of the Kṣatrapa Caṣṭana, known to Ptolemy as Tiastanes of Ozene, Ujjayinī, is written in prose (*gadyaṁ kāvyam*) and shows in a most interesting manner the development from the simple epic style to that of the Kāvya. Grammar is obeyed, but epic licence is found ; *patinā*, for *patyā*, is thus explained and *vīçaduttarāṇi* is a Prākritism for *viṅcad-*, which the epic, though not the grammar, permits ; epic again is the pleonasm in *Parjanyena ekārṇabhūtāyām iva pṛthivyāṁ kṛtāyām*, 'when the storm had turned as it were all earth to ocean'. But in *anyatra saṁgrāmeṣu*, 'save in battles', we have a pure error. From the epic style a distinct departure is made in the use of compounds ; Daṇḍin, doubtless following earlier authority, bids them be used freely in prose, and approves of their being long. The inscription prefers compounds to simple words, and at the beginning presents us with a compound of nine words with twenty-three syllables ; the description of the king produces even a finer effort of seventeen words of forty syllables. The length of the sentences vies with that of the compounds ; one attains twenty-three Granthas, each of thirty-two syllables. Of the figures of sound (*çabdālaṁkāras*) alliteration is freely used as in *abhyastanāmno Rudradāmno*, sometimes with real effect. Of figures of sense (*arthālaṁkāras*) one simile compares in the later manner the curtain wall of a reservoir to a mountain spur in the Kāvya phrase *parvatapratisparddhi*. The description, if never of a very high order, displays some merit, especially in the vivid picture of the destruction by flooding of the dam of the reservoir. But what is far more important is that the author thinks it fit to ascribe to the king the writing of poems in both prose and verse ; flattery or not, it was obviously not absurd to ascribe to a Kṣatrapa, of foreign extraction, skill in Sanskrit poetry. Moreover, the poems are qualified by a string of epithets as adorned by the qualities of simplicity, clearness, sweetness, variety, beauty, and elevation arising from the use of conventional poetic terminology (*sphuṭalaghumadhuracitrakānta-çabdasamayodārālaṁkṛta*). The term *alaṁkṛta* points unmistakably to the author's acquaintance with a science of poetics prescribing the ornaments of poetry, and a comparison with the merits ascribed by Daṇḍin[1] to the Vaidarbha style which he

[1] *Kāvyādarça*, i. 40 ff. See below, chap. xviii, § 2.

admires is decidedly instructive. Simplicity and clearness may well be equivalent to the *arthavyakti* and *prasāda* which he mentions; sweetness is his *mādhurya* which includes richness in tasteful sound and sense (*rasavat*); variety is probably akin to the strength or force (*ojas*) prescribed by Daṇḍin, and he recognizes that in the view of some authorities elevation was induced by the use of the stock terms of poets such as *krīḍāsaras*, a lake for sport.

The evidence of this inscription is confirmed and strengthened by that derivable from a record[1] of Siri Puḷumāyi at Nāsik, written in Prākrit prose. There can be no doubt of the familiarity of the writer with Sanskrit; it is even possible that he wrote his text in that language and then, in order to comply with the usage of the day, rendered it into Prākrit for purposes of publication. Siri Puḷumāyi may be identified with Siro-Polemaios of Baithana, Pratiṣṭhāna on the Godāvarī, of Ptolemy and the date of the inscription is not far removed from that of the Girnār record. It begins with an enormous sentence of eight and a half lines, long compounds fill lines 2–6, then a brief rest is given by the insertion of short words, and the whole ends with a compound of sixteen words and forty-three syllables. This is deliberate art, however little we may admire it, and the same technique is found in Bāṇa, used perhaps with greater skill. Alliteration is freely used; the queen is *mahādevī mahārājamātā mahārājapatāmahī*. What, however, is specially interesting is the appearance of mannerisms of the later Kāvya, used in a way which implies current familiarity with the themes. Thus the king is of like strength with the mountains Himavant, Meru, and Mandara, a brief allusion to the view that the king, like the Himālaya, possesses abundant treasures, like Meru is the centre of the world and overshadows it with his might, and, like Mandara, which the gods used as their churning stick when they churned the ocean, can produce and preserve Lakṣmī, the *fortuna regum*. The king again is compared with the heroes of the epic in a manner which preludes the frequent use of this theme made by Subandhu and Bāṇa. Finally, he is described as winning

[1] EI. viii. 60 ff.; S. Lévi, *Cinquantenaire de l'école pratique des Hautes Études* (1921), pp. 91 ff., who holds that its hero Gotamīputa's, death in victory is described.

victory in a battle in which in wondrous wise the Wind, Garuḍa, Siddhas, Yakṣas, Rākṣasas, Vidyādharas, Bhūtas, Gandharvas, Cāraṇas, the sun, the moon, the Nakṣatras, and the planets take part. Thus early we find that confusion of the mortal and the supernatural which induces an alleged historian like Bilhaṇa to allow Çiva to intervene when needed in the fate of his patron.

There can be no doubt from these inscriptions of the existence of Sanskrit Kāvya, and doubtless also of a science of poetics among the Brahmins.[1] It is, therefore, accident only which has preserved Buddhist works like those of Açvaghoṣa as the earliest specimens of the Kāvya. Moreover there is a simple explanation of the accident; Açvaghoṣa was one of the great names of Buddhism; no one arose to surpass his achievement in depicting the life of the Buddha, whereas the glory of earlier poets was eclipsed by that of Kālidāsa. Nor is this mere theory; we know in fact that of the predecessors in drama enumerated by Kālidāsa himself the works of all save one are lost, apparently irretrievably.

5. *The Kāmasūtra and the Poet's Milieu.*

Vātsyāyana's *Kāmasūtra*[2] is of uncertain date, but it is not improbably older than Kālidāsa, and in any case it represents the concentrated essence of earlier treatises on the Ars Amoris. There is no question of the importance of knowledge of this topic for the writers of erotic poetry, and there is abundant proof that the *Kāmasūtra* was studied as eagerly by would-be poets as were grammar, poetics, and lexicography. To Vātsyāyana we owe a vivid conception of the Indian parallel to the man about town (*nāgaraka*) whose existence was due to the growing elaboration of Indian life, and whose interest the poet was anxious to propitiate. We see him,[3] opulent, a denizen of the town which lends him his name, or, if compelled by adverse fortune to vegetate in

[1] The use of compounds in ornamental epithets appears to have been much promoted by their convenience in eulogies of kings, places, &c., in inscriptions, just as in Jain texts they are heaped up in stock descriptions.

[2] See below, chap. xxiv; cf. Haraprasād, *Magadhan Literature*, chap. iv. On the arts, Kalās, sixty-four in number at least, of early India, see A. Venkatasubbiah and E. Müller, JRAS. 1914, pp. 355–67.

[3] The comm. allows him to be of any caste.

the country, seeking, like Martial in his retreat from Rome, to find congenial society with which to continue the pleasures of his town life. His home boasts all the luxury of the age, soft couches, a summer house in a park, seats strewn with flowers, and swings to amuse the ladies who share and lend zest to his leisure moments. Much of his time is devoted to his toilet; he must bathe, be anointed, perfumed, and garlanded; then he can teach the cage birds which surround him to speak, or enjoy the brutal spectacle of ram or cock fights, both favourite amusements of the gilded youth of the period. Or, in the company of ladies of the demi-monde, he may visit the parks outside the town, returning home crowned with the flowers which they have plucked. There are concerts to be attended, ballets and theatrical spectacles to be visited; he has a lute beside him so that he may make music when he will, and a book to read at leisure. Boon companions and hangers-on of various ranks, the Viṭas, Pīṭhamardas, and Vidūṣakas of the texts, are essential to his happiness, and drinking parties are not unknown, but the ideal forbids mere rude licence; even in his enjoyments the man about town aims at elegance, moderation, and a measure of dignity. He condescends to the use of the vernacular, but blends it with Sanskrit, thus indicating his fine culture. Hetairai are essential to him, but they also are not without accomplishments; indeed the *Kāmasūtra* demands from them knowledge encyclopaedic, including poetic taste. The most famous of them achieved great riches, as we learn from the description of the palace of the heroine in the *Mṛcchakaṭikā* and, as in the Athens of Perikles, discussions on literature, music, and art, must often have afforded the participants a pleasure which could not be expected from their own wives, from whom they demanded children and care for their homes.

An atmosphere of this kind is unquestionably favourable, if not to the highest poetry, at least to the production of elaborate verse, and the care demanded from those who are exposed to keen criticism cannot but produce excellent results in the case of men naturally gifted, though on the other hand it leads to exaggerated love of style with inevitable tasteless extravagance. If under such a system Maecenases produce few Vergils, they are responsible for a plentiful crop of Valerii Flacci, and to the kings of India[1] we unquestionably owe most of the poets of repute; patronage by the king was at once the reward of skill in panegyric and the means of obtaining the leisure for serious composition and a measure of publicity for the works produced. It was the duty of the king to bridge the gulf between wealth and poetic talent, of the poet to save his patron from the night of oblivion which else must assuredly settle on him when his mortal life closed. At the royal courts poets vied in eager rivalry with one another; probably in quite early times there were practised such arts as the composition of verses to complete a stanza when one verse was given, and the production of extempore poems on a given topic. The festival of Sarasvatī each month afforded opportunities for displays in honour of the patroness of poetry and the arts. Fortunately, too, for the poets, kings were willing to claim renown for skill in poetry; we have seen that his panegyrist thought well to ascribe fame in this sphere to Rudradāman and we shall see that the great Gupta Emperor Samudragupta strove for renown as a man of letters.[2] Harṣa not only patronized Bāṇa, but claimed the authorship of dramas and poems, though unkind hints were prevalent that others were the true begetters of his literary offspring.[3] Four hundred years later Bhoja of Dhārā was more fortunate, for we have no real knowledge to disprove his claim to polymathy exhibited in a large variety of works. In the twelfth century[4] the court of Lakṣmaṇasena revived the glory of Harṣa's patronage, for besides the famous Jayadeva, other poets such as Umāpatidhara, Dhoī, and Govardhana wrote with acceptance. The kings of Kashmir often distinguished themselves by generosity to their laureates, (*kavirāja*) and to such enlightened activity we owe Somadeva's

[1] Rājaçekhara (*Kāvyamīmāṅsā*, p. 55) gives Vāsudeva (? the Kāṇva or the Kuṣaṇa), Sātavāhana, Çūdraka, and Sāhasāñka (? Candragupta II; Pischel, GN. 1901, pp. 485–7) as famous patrons.

[2] Minor royal authors include the dramatists Mahendravikramavarman (*c.* 675); Yaçovarman, patron of Bhavabhūti (*c.* 735), the Kalacuri Māyurāja (*c.* 800), and Vigrahārājadeva (1153). We have stanzas of a Nepalese king (8th cent.), of Amoghavarṣa (815–77), of Muñja (975–95), and Arjunavarman's comm. on Amaru (13th cent.). Cf. Jackson, *Priyadarśikā*, pp. xxxvii ff.

[3] Cf. Keith, *Sanskrit Drama*, pp. 170 ff.

[4] Smith, EHI. pp. 419 ff., 432 wishes to place this king about fifty years before the usual date, but ignores important evidence; see R. C. Majumdar, JPASB. 1921, pp. 7 ff.; C. V. Vaidya, IHQ. i. 126 ff.; C. Chakravarti, iii. 186 ff.

Kathāsaritsāgara. Yet it is worth remembering that we cannot prove any royal patron for Kālidāsa, greatest of Indian poets, or even for Kalhaṇa, the one historian of real merit in Sanskrit literature. Nor, of course, was royal generosity confined to Sanskrit poetry; to a king, Hāla or Sātavāhana, is ascribed the anthology of Māhārāṣṭrī verse, and Vākpatirāja wrote his epic, *Gaüḍavaha*, for Yaçovarman of Kanauj, thus assuring him an immortality to survive his defeat at the hands of Lalitāditya of Kashmir. So, too, if we believe tradition, it was perhaps the patronage of Kaniṣka which produced the first great work of the court epic preserved to us, the *Buddhacarita* of Açvaghoṣa.

III

AÇVAGHOṢA AND EARLY BUDDHIST KĀVYA

1. *Açvaghoṣa's Works.*

THE deplorable darkness which still envelops early India renders it impossible to establish with certainty the date of Açvaghoṣa, famous alike as a poet and as a philosopher. Tradition unquestionably makes him a protégé of the famous Kaniṣka, but the matter is complicated by the fact that if the *Sūtrālaṁkāra*[1] is his, he tells two stories in which Kaniṣka's reign seems to be referred to as in the past; this may be explained either on the theory that Kaniṣka died before him, which does not accord with tradition, or on the view that the stories are interpolated in whole or as regards the name, or that there was an earlier Kaniṣka; again an inscription[2] held to belong to the time of Kaniṣka mentions an Açvaghoṣarāja who has been temerariously identified with the poet. Assuming the validity of the tradition despite these difficulties, the date of Açvaghoṣa would fall to be determined by that of Kaniṣka, for whom *c.* A.D. 100[3] still seems a just estimate. Tradition also tells that he was originally a Brahmin, that he first adhered to the Sarvāstivāda school of Buddhism, but was attracted by the doctrine of the saving grace of faith in the Buddha, and became one of the forerunners of the Mahāyāna school. I-tsing, who travelled in India in A.D. 671–95, refers to him as one of the great teachers of the past, and asserts that a collection of his works was still studied in his time. From the colophons of his own works we learn that his mother was named Suvarṇākṣī and that his home was Sāketa, while he is given the style of Ācārya and Bhadanta.

[1] Nos. 14 and 31 (Huber's trans., Paris, 1908). Cf. Lévi, JA. 1896, ii. 444 ff.; Kimura, IHQ. i. 417. Kumāralāta (*c.* 150) is more probable.

[2] EI. viii. 171; S. Ch. Vidy bhusana (POCP. 1919, I. xxxiii ff.) puts Kaniṣka, patron of Açvaghoṣa, about A. D. 320.

[3] Cf. Smith, EHI. pp. 272 ff.; Foucher, *L'Art Gréco-Bouddhique*, ii. 484 ff., 506 ff., who finds in the Çaka epoch merely the beginning of the fifth century of the Maurya epoch, placing Kaniṣka *c.* A. D. 81. Cf. D. R. Sahni, JRAS. 1924, pp. 399 ff.

Whether the *Mahāyānaçraddhotpāda*, a famous text-book of early Mahāyāna views, or the *Vajrasūcī*, an able and bitter attack on the Brahmanical caste system, are rightly ascribed to Açvaghoṣa need not be discussed, and his dramas are preserved only in fragments, which reveal little of his poetic skill.[1] Of the songs for which he was renowned the *Gaṇḍīstotragāthā*[2] displays great metrical skill and attests his comprehension of the power of music ; it is an effort to describe in words the religious message carried to the hearts of men by the sounds produced by beating a long strip of wood with a short club. Of later authorship is the *Sūtrālaṁkāra* or *Kalpanāmaṇḍitikā*, which unhappily is preserved only in a fragmentary condition in Sanskrit, though Huber has translated into French the Chinese version of A.D. 405. The wide culture of the writer displays itself in his allusion to the Bhāratan epic[3] and the *Rāmāyaṇa*, the Sāṁkhya and Vaiçeṣika philosophies, and Jain tenets, while in the tales he exhibits himself as a fervent believer in the doctrine of the saving power of worship of the Buddha. The collection is made up of tales, in the main already current in literature still preserved, inculcating the Buddhist faith; many are attractive, even pathetic, but the doctrine of devotion carries the author to strange results, as in the tale of the sinner who never in his life did one good deed, but because in deadly terror of his life from attack by a tiger he uttered the salutation, 'Homage to the Buddha', is granted entrance to the order and straightway proceeds to sainthood. From the literary point of view the essential fact is that the tales are written in prose and verse, clearly of the classical type. We need not doubt that this combination was taken over by the author direct from the contemporary Jātakas current in Pāli, even if no strict proof of this view is possible.

The *Sūtrālaṁkāra* mentions a *Buddhacarita*, perhaps Açvaghoṣa's work, and there is reason to suppose that that epic was later than the *Saundarananda*.[4] At the close of that work Açvaghoṣa frankly declares the purpose which led to his adopting the Kāvya

[1] Cf. Keith, *Buddh. Phil.*, pp. 252 ff. ; *Sanskrit Drama*, pp. 80 ff.

[2] Ed. BB. 15, 1913.

[3] We find two verses from the *Harivaṅça* in the *Vajrasūcī*.

[4] Ed. Haraprasād Śāstrī, BI. 1910. Cf. Baston, JA. 1912, i. 79 ff. ; Hultzsch, ZDMG. lxxii–lxxiv ; Gawroński, *Studies about the Sansk. Buddh. Lit.*, pp. 56 ff.

form ; he recognizes that men rejoice in the delight of the world and seek not salvation, and therefore he sets out the truth which leads to enlightenment in attractive garb, in the hope that men attracted by it may realize the aim and extract from his work the gold alone. As he makes no allusion to an earlier poem, we may conclude that the *Saundarananda* was his first attempt. The topic of the poem is the legend of the conversion of the reluctant Nanda, his half-brother, by the Buddha, a story recounted in the *Mahāvagga* and the *Nidānakathā*, but Açvaghoṣa deals with it in the approved manner of the later Kāvya. He begins with an account of the foundation of Kapilavāstu, which gives him occasion to display his knowledge of heroic tales and mythology (Canto i). There follows the description of the king, Çuddhodana, and briefly an account of the birth of Sarvārthasiddha and his half-brother Nanda. The Buddha is described in full in the next Canto (iii) ; then we hear of Sundarī's beauty and the perfection of her union with Nanda as of the night with the moon. Reluctantly Nanda leaves her (iv), and the Buddha hastens to secure his ordination as a monk, much against his inclination (v). Bitter is Sundarī's grief (vi), and Nanda himself seeks by a long list of legendary parallels to defend his desire to cling to his beloved ; kings of yore have laid aside the hermit's garb and returned to the world of joy and life (vii). In vain are the demerits of women, the flattery on their lips, the treachery in their hearts, pointed out (viii) ; in vain is he warned of the evils of pride illustrated by the fate of heroes of the past (ix). The Buddha determines on a bolder plan ; he carries him to heaven and shows him on the way in the Himālaya a one-eyed ape of hideous form, asking him if Sundarī is fairer than it. Nanda energetically asserts his wife's loveliness, but on the sight of the heavenly Apsarases must admit that their beauty raises them as far above Sundarī as she is above the ape ; with fickle faith he resolves to win an Apsaras as bride, but is warned that he must win heaven by good works, if he is to obtain this end (x). Returned to earth he strives for this end, but Ānanda warns him, adducing a wealth of examples, that the joys of heaven are fleeting and that, when man's merit is exhausted, he must return to earth again (xi). Nanda is thus induced to lay aside all thought of heavenly joys and to seek and obtain instruction from the Buddha; he becomes not merely a saint, but on the Buddha's bidding determines on the nobler course of seeking salvation not for himself alone, but of preaching it to others (xii–xviii).

The *Buddhacarita*[1] deals with the greater theme of the life of the Buddha, and it is a misfortune that as we have it the poem contains but seventeen Cantos and of these only the first thirteen —with certain exceptions—are genuine, the remainder being an addition made a century ago by Amṛtānanda who records that he did so because he could not find a manuscript of the rest of the text. The poem now ends with the conversions made at Benares, but the Chinese version, made between A.D. 414 and 421, and the Tibetan, have twenty-eight Cantos, and I-tsing still knew of this number. The exact source which influenced Açvaghoṣa in his choice of incident is unknown, for it is not proved that the *Lalitavistara* existed in his time in anything like its present form. In any case the contrast between the two works is remarkable; the *Lalitavistara* is written in the main in Sanskrit prose of the plain type, intermingled with ballads in mixed Sanskrit of the so-called Gāthā style; at best it is confused, at worst incoherent. Açvaghoṣa's poem is essentially the work of an artist; in choice of incident and arrangement he seeks to produce the maximum effect, and, though he does not vary in essentials the tradition, he renders vivid and affecting the scenes which he describes. The prince's fatal journeying forth from the palace which brings him into contact with the hateful spectacle of age, is preceded by the account of the fair women who crowd to watch his exit; the poet again shows his skill in depicting the loving ruses by which the ladies of the harem seek to divert his mind from the desire to renounce the vanities of the world, and in describing the famous scene when the prince gazing on them in their sleep resolves to abandon the palace. Nor is he skilled in the Kāmaçāstra alone; he adduces the arguments by which the family priests, fortified by the precepts of political science, seeks to deter the prince from his resolution to abandon

[1] Ed. E. B. Cowell, Oxford, 1893; trans. SBE. 46; Formichi, Bari, 1912. See also Hultzsch, ZDMG. lxxii. 145 ff.; Cappeller, ZII. ii. 1 ff.; Speyer, JRAS. 1914, pp. 105 ff.; Gawroński, *Rocznik Oryentalistyczny*, i. 1 ff.; i–v ed. and trans. K. M. Joglekar, Bombay, 1912. On Buddhist Sanskrit Literature cf. G. K. Nariman, *Sanskrit Buddhism* (1923).

secular life with its duties, and true to the rule which requires a description of a battle he provides a spirited picture of the contest of Buddha against the demon Māra and his monstrous hosts.

There is not the slightest doubt of one of the sources of Açvaghoṣa. Though Cowell was unable to find decisive proof of his knowledge of the *Rāmāyaṇa* as opposed merely to the legend of Rāma, the fact is put beyond doubt, apart from a mention of the poem in the *Sūtrālaṁkāra*, by careful study of the references in the *Buddhacarita* itself[1]; when the people of the town see that Siddhārtha has not returned they weep as aforetime when the chariot of Daçaratha's son returned without him; Çuddhodana compares himself to Daçaratha, bereft of Rāma, whose death he envies, and in these and many other passages there is clear knowledge by Açvaghoṣa of the wording of our present text. It was natural that the parallel should deeply affect Açvaghoṣa, and the broad structure of the episode of the return of Sumantra to Ayodhyā without Rāma and of Chandaka to Kapilavāstu without Siddhārtha is unmistakable; the charioteer leaves his master, and returns to the city now sadly changed; the eager citizens rush out to greet him, learn his news, and are filled with lamentation; the women throng the windows and then withdraw in deep depression to their inner chambers; the charioteer enters the presence of the king. Similarly again, Yaçodharā's lament for the sufferings of the prince in his new life of hardship is modelled on Sītā's sorrow for her husband's sufferings in the forest. Nor does it seem reasonable to deny that the description of the aspect of the women of the harem in sleep is based on the portraiture of Rāvaṇa's harem.[2]

2. *Açvaghoṣa's Style and Language.*

Daṇḍin[3] draws a vital distinction between two styles as prevalent in his day, the Gauḍa and the Vaidarbha, eastern and southern, and from his account and other evidence we gather that

[1] Gawroński, *Studies about the Sansk. Buddh. Lit.*, pp. 27 ff.

[2] v. 9–11, which Winternitz (GIL. i. 417) asserts to be based on Açvaghoṣa. But see Walter, *Indica*, iii. 13.

[3] *Kāvyādarça*, i. 40 ff.

among the characteristics of the former was the love of long compounds not merely in prose, where they were accepted even by the Vaidarbha, but in verse also; love of alliteration and of harsh sound effects; the use of recondite etymologizing phraseology, and a desire for strength resulting often in bombast and affectation. It has been suggested by Jacobi [1] that the contrast of styles has a historical basis; Sanskrit poetry was practised, it is argued, eagerly in the east and Sanskrit poetry there had developed the evil effects of old age, before the art became current in the west and south. The simpler style of the south was also on this view influenced by the freshness of the lyric of Mahārāṣṭra born of close contact with the people. It is already a serious objection to such a conclusion that in the *Nāṭyaçāstra* we find the qualities which Daṇḍin ascribes as characteristic of the Vaidarbha ascribed to the Kāvya style in general; this is a strong suggestion that at the time of the *Nāṭyaçāstra* there had not developed those characteristics of the Gauḍa style, and that they emerged gradually with the development of poetry at the courts of princes of Bengal. This view gains support from the fact that, though Daṇḍin praises the Vaidarbha style, and evidently disapproves of the Gauḍa, in practice poets of later date often affect the Gauḍa manner. Açvaghoṣa, however, affords a more convincing proof still of the early character of the Vaidarbha; his style unmistakably is of the Vaidarbha type; as Bāṇa later says of the western poets, it aims at sense rather than mere ornament; it is his aim to narrate, to describe, to preach his curious but not unattractive philosophy of renunciation of selfish desire and universal active benevolence and effort for the good, and by the clarity, vividness, and elegance of his diction to attract the minds of those to whom blunt truths and pedestrian statements would not appeal. This project left no room for mere elegance or for deliberate straining after effect, and thus it results that Açvaghoṣa's works attain a high measure of attractiveness, especially when we make the necessary allowance for the decidedly bad condition of the text tradition of both epics. Simple, of course, in the sense in which it can be applied to English poetry, is an inappropriate epithet as regards any Sanskrit Kāvya, but relatively to the later standard, even in some measure to Kālidāsa,

[1] *Ausgewählte Erzählungen in Mâhârâshṭrî*, pp. xvi f.

Açvaghoṣa's style is simple. Nor may we deny it the epithets of sensuous and passionate; the picture of the pleasures of love drawn by Açvaghoṣa is already marked by that wealth of intimate detail which appeals to all Indian poets, but proves a grave stumbling block to critics who find matter for offence even in the charming picture of the deceiving Zeus in the *Iliad* and reprobate in the author of the *Odyssey* the episode of the amour of Ares and Aphrodite. But still more sincere is the burning enthusiasm of the poet for his own ideal, not the Arhat, contented to seek his own freedom from rebirth in this world of misery, but the Bodhisattva, the Buddha to be, who delays, however, his entering into Nirvāṇa until he has accomplished his view of freeing all other creatures from the delusion which makes them cling throughout the ages to mortal life and its woes. This is a new note in Sanskrit poetry; Vālmīki has majesty and a calm seriousness, but he is free from passion like his hero, who though he experiences viçissitudes yet stands apart from them, and of whose ultimate success we never doubt. Nanda's rejection of Sundarī may seem to us heartless enough; his transference of his fickle affection to the Apsarases has its comic side, but in the end he seeks the welfare of others, even as does the Buddha; Rāma on the contrary in his rejection of Sītā after the long agony of separation from him has no warmer motive than obedience to the doctrine that Caesar's wife must be above suspicion.

As Çuddhodana reminds us of Daçaratha, so Sundarī has traces of Sītā, but with a vehemence of passion unknown to that queen, and without her dignity and steadfast courage. Nor is it in theme and character-drawing alone that Vālmīki is laid under contribution; the metaphors and similes of the *Rāmāyaṇa*[1] appear in more refined form; the king, hearing of his son's final resolve, falls, smitten by sorrow as Indra's banner is lowered when the festival is over (*Çacīpater vṛtta ivotsave dhvajaḥ*); the maidens stand drinking in the prince's beauty with eyes that stay wide open in joy (*niçcalaiḥ prītivikacaiḥ pibantya iva locanaiḥ*); they display their bosoms that are like bowls of gold (*suvarṇakalaçaprakhyān darçayantyaḥ payodharān*). The epic speaks of the ocean laughing with the foam of its waves, the poet embodies the idea in the picture of a sleeping beauty of the

[1] Cf. Walter, *Indica*, iii. 11 ff.

harem, with a daintiness of elaboration which is far removed from the epic:

vibabhau karalagnaveṇur anyā: stanavisrastasitāṅçukā çayānā
ṛjuṣaṭpadapaṅktijuṣṭapadmā: jalaphenaprahasattaṭā nadīva.

'And one lay resplendent, holding a flute in her hand, while her white garment slipt from her bosom, like unto a river whose banks laugh with the foam [1] of her waves, and in whose lotuses long rows of bees delight.' Açvaghoṣa unquestionably is at his best in simple and elegant description by which a clear picture is presented to the eyes:

tathāpi pāpīyasi nirjite gate: diçaḥ praseduḥ prababhau niçākaraḥ
divo nipetur bhuvi puṣpavṛṣṭayo: rarāja yoṣeva vikalmaṣā niçā.

'So when the evil one had retired worsted, the sky became calm, the moon shone forth, flowers fell in rain from heaven on the earth; night shone clear like a maiden free from stain.' When the charioteer returns:

punaḥ kumāro vinivṛtta ity atho: gavākṣamālāḥ pratipedire 'ṅganāḥ
viviktapṛṣṭhaṁ ca niçamya vājinam: punar gavākṣāṇi pidhāya cukruçuḥ.

'"'Tis the prince returned", said the women and rushed to their windows, but, seeing the steed's back bereft of its master, closed them again and wailed aloud.' Yaçodharā, who is more akin to Sītā than Sundarī, laments her husband's new lot:

çucau çayitvā çayane hiraṇmaye: prabodhyamāno niçi turyanisvanaiḥ
katham bata svapsyati so 'dya me vratī: paṭaikadeçāntarite mahītale.

'How can he sleep to-night, my faithful one, on one poor mat covering the bare earth, he who hath slept aforetime on a couch of gold undefiled, and whom music hath aroused from his slumbers?' Açvaghoṣa is also a master of simple pathos:

mahatyā tṛṣṇayā duḥkhair garbheṇāsmi yayā dhṛtaḥ
tasyā niṣphalayatnāyāḥ kvāham mātuḥ kva sā mama.

[1] Cf. *Meghadūta*, 50.

'With deep longing and many a pain did she bear me in her womb; all her effort hath come to nought; why was she mother, why was I her son?' As often the idea has a prototype in the *Rāmāyaṇa*,[1] but Açvaghoṣa has heightened by his delicate touch the effect of the whole.

Sanskrit poetry, which does not aim at rhyme, nevertheless is fond of the repetition of the same syllables in close relation, especially if the meaning thus conveyed is altered, and instances of Yamakas, as they are styled, are not rare in Açvaghoṣa as in *pranaṣṭavatsām iva vatsalāṁ gām*, 'like a loving cow which hath lost its calf', a clear refinement on the *vivatsā vatsalā kṛtā* of the epic; a more elaborate effect is produced in Canto i where stanzas 14–16 approximate to rhyme as in *udārasaṁkhyaiḥ sacivair asaṁkhyaiḥ*, 'with countless ministers of noble counsels' and *samagradevīnivahāgradevī*, 'queen supreme of all the host of queens', but such effects are rarely [2] sought. Occasionally a phrase is overworked as in *tapaḥpraçāntaṁ sa vanaṁ viveça*, 'he entered the penance grove where penance had ceased', and now and then the poet errs in his display of his culture,[3] as when he derives a simile from the use of the verbal form *asti* as a particle, though his successors equally delight to prove by recondite allusions that they are masters of the works of Pāṇini. His own skill is shown especially in Canto ii of the *Saundarananda* where he exhibits his knowledge of aorist forms, and he evidently felt pleasure in the skill which uses *mīyate* as the passive of the three verbs *mā*, *mi*, and *mī*, *ajījipat* as the aorist of *jap* and *ji*, and *adīdipat* as that of *dā* and *do*. On the other hand we find forms which, if excusable, are so only on the ground of the epic, as in the gerunds *gṛhya* and *vivardhayitvā*; beside the common *niçamya*, hearing, we find *niçāmya*, observing, and, while the derivative form *daiçika* is regularly used *sudeçika* stands beside it. The periphrastic future as *aham praveṣṭā* replaces *praveṣṭāsmi*, and in the use of particles Açvaghoṣa permits himself irregularities which are not rare in Buddhist Sanskrit; thus

[1] ii. 53. 20.

[2] *hariturагaturaṅgavatturaṅgaḥ*, *Buddhacarita*, v. 87, is not a success.

[3] The poet shows in a simile his knowledge of the new art of Gandhāra. His use of the technical terms *bhāva* and *hāva* (iv. 12) proves his knowledge of Alaṁkāra, and he fully employs Yathāsaṁkhya, v. 42; ix. 16. For artistic parallels see Foucher, *L'Art Gréco-Bouddhique du Gandhāra*, i. 321, 339 ff.

kim bata and *prāg eva* denote 'how much more'; *saced* is used for *ced*; and, as in the epic, some pleonasm of particles is allowed; we find, unless we amend, *api* repeated, *hi* and *tu* combined in one sentence and even *na jaharṣa na cāpi cānutepe*. Some Buddhist terms occur, such as *pratīvedha*, *iñjita*, *praçrabdhi*, and *praverita*, while *maitrā*, for the wonted *maitrī*, is based on Pāli *mettā*; moreover it is impossible to defend some of Açvaghoṣa's genders. But these are minor blemishes in a Sanskrit which is normally grammatically correct.

Nor is there any real doubt as to Açvaghoṣa's metrical skill, though the manuscripts do undoubtedly present a text in which metrical deficiencies are not rarely present. In addition to the more easy metres he adopts the Udgatā for Canto iii of the *Saundarananda*, an example followed in Canto xii of the *Kirātārjunīya* and Canto xv of the *Çiçupālavadha*, while the Suvadanā and the Vardhamāna species of the Upasthitapracupita [1] are also found.

3. *The Avadānas.*

Connected with Açvaghoṣa, sometimes identified with him by tradition, is a mysterious Mātṛceṭa,[2] of whose numerous works fragments alone, from his *Çatapañcāçatikastotra*,[3] exist in Sanskrit. These show a fairly elegant style of religious lyric devotion. The taste of the time, however, seems to have preferred the telling of tales dealing with the endless theme of the fruits of man's deeds. Moreover the view of the Buddhists who loved these Avadānas[4]—tales of great acts or perhaps of the causes of man's future[5]—was not a narrowly moral one. They were not content to exemplify the somewhat cold doctrine of the due reward of a man's actions regarded merely from the moral point of view. They were frankly Buddha worshippers and

[1] *Saund.* ii. 65; cf. Jacobi, ZDMG. xxxviii. 603; SIFI. VIII. ii. 113.

[2] Cf. Thomas, ERE. viii. 495.

[3] Lévi, JA. 1910, ii. 433–56; Poussin, JRAS. 1911, pp. 759–77. For his *Varṇanārhavarṇana* see Thomas, IA. xxxiv. 145 ff.

[4] Przyluski (*La légende de l'empereur Açoka* (1923), pp. viii f., 214) holds that there were two Vinayas of the Sarvāstivādins, one of Mathurā with Avadānas or Jātakas, one of Kashmir without them; the *Divyāvadāna* may all be derived from the first of these Vinayas; Lévi, *T'oung Pao*, viii. 105–22; JA. 1914, ii. 494.

[5] Zimmer, ZII. iii. 203 ff.

believed wholeheartedly in the efficacy of any act of devotion to the Buddha or his followers as having the power to influence indefinitely for good the life of man; equally they held that an insult to the Buddha was certain to bear appalling fruit. Of the Avadāna texts preserved the oldest may be the *Avadānaçataka*,[1] which is stated to have been rendered into Chinese in the first half of the third century A.D., and which, as containing the term *dīnāra*, can hardly belong to any period earlier than A.D. 100. Artistically the work has scanty merit; its arrangement in ten decades each according to subject-matter is schematic; the tales open with set formulae, contain set formulae of description, as of the laughter of the Buddha, and of moral exhortation; exaggeration and long-windedness mark the whole, and beauty of form is sacrificed to the desire to be edifying. From this point of view, indeed, the tales often reveal thoughts of some beauty; Maitrakanyaka, condemned for wrongs done to his mother to endure in hell the punishment of bearing on his head a wheel of red-hot iron for 66,000 years until another who has committed a like sin comes to relieve him of his burden, resolves that rather will he for ever and ever endure the pain, and is rewarded forthwith by the disappearance of the instrument of torment. Çrīmatī, wife of Bimbisāra, pays homage to the relics of the Buddha which the king had enclosed in a Stūpa for worship by the ladies of his harem; the parricide Ajātaçatru forbids such homage on pain of death, but Çrīmatī disobeys, and, slain by the king's order, is born again in the world of the gods.

Far more interesting as literature is the *Divyāvadāna*,[2] a collection of legends which draws, like the *Avadānaçataka*, largely on the *Vinayapiṭaka* of the Sarvāstivādin school of Buddhism. Its date is uncertain; its origin is complex; one section is definitely described as a Mahāyāna Sūtra, while the body of the work is still of the Hīnayāna school. The term *dīnāra* occurs, and one famous tale, the Çārdūlakarṇāvadāna, was rendered into Chinese in A.D. 265. It tells how the Buddha by his skill in persuasion converted to the faith the maiden Prakṛti, who had conceived a deep love for the beloved disciple Ānanda and would have won him from his vows, had he not at the moment of his greatest

[1] Ed. J. S. Speyer, BB. 3, 1902–9; trans. L. Feer, AMG. 18, 1891.
[2] Ed. E. B. Cowell and R. A. Neil, Cambridge, 1886.

danger sought refuge in his master's strength. The gem of the collection is doubtless the pathetic legend of Kunāla, son of Açoka,[1] whose false stepmother succeeds in poisoning his father's mind against him and in having him blinded without his permitting himself either hate or reproach. We find, however, also a still more gruesome and to us repellent theme in the tale of Rūpavatī, who severs her own breasts in order to feed a hungry mother when on the point of eating her own child; Rūpavatī is extolled as a pattern of the Bodhisattva who seeks to save the whole world, and is accorded the somewhat quaint honour of being reborn as a prince, Rūpavata.

The style of the book is very uneven, as a result of the diversity of its sources. Besides ordinary simple Sanskrit prose, intermingled here and there with Gāthās, we find here and there passages in elaborate metres and prose with the long compounds approved by writers on poetics. Thus Avadāna xxxviii is a version in elaborate style of the story of Maitrakanyaka in the form found in the *Avadānaçataka*. More interesting to us is the preservation, as part of the cycle of legends of Açoka (xxvi–xxix), of the dramatic episode of the conversion of the demon Māra by the virtuous Upagupta. The idea, ingenious in itself, is carried out with spirit and imagination; Māra is converted and Upagupta, who desires to see with his eyes the Buddha long since dead, asks him to appear before him in the Buddha's form. Māra obeys, and the devotee falls down in worship before the wondrous apparition of the master he loved. We can recognize here, without question, borrowing from Açvaghoṣa in manner, as in substance from the *Sūtrālaṁkāra*; style and metre are of the classical type which his poems display. Moreover, we can trace[2] in this section of the work clear instances of knowledge of the *Buddhacarita* and even of the less popular *Saundarananda*; thus Gupta's son is described as beautiful beyond men but yet inferior to the gods (*atikrānto mānuṣavarṇaṁ asamprāptaç ca divyavarṇam*), and this somewhat clumsy expression can hardly be derived from any source other than Açvaghoṣa's elegant *atītya martyān anupetya devān*.

[1] The original *Açokāvadāna*, according to Przyluski, *La légende de l'empereur Açoka* (1923), was composed by a monk of Mathurā about two centuries before Kaniṣka (between 150–100 B.C.).

[2] Gawroński, *Studies about the Sansk. Buddh. Lit.*, pp. 49 ff.

Similarly, both xxii and xxxviii contain reminiscences of the *Buddhacarita* both in the polish of their style and in actual verbal similarities; in the latter we have:

> *tṛṣṇānilaiḥ çokaçikhāpracaṇḍaiç: cittāni dagdhāni bahuprakāram*
> *āçāvatāṁ sapraṇayābhirāmair: dānāmbuṣekaiḥ çamayāmbabhūva.*

'The flames of desire, kindled by sorrow, in the minds of those full of longing were extinguished by the torrents of his generosity, made beautiful by his courtesy.'

In the less polished parts of the collection we find many curious specimens of the influence of Pāli or Prākrit on the writers. Thus we have forms like *sarpi* for *sarpis*, *parvaḥ* for *parva*, *yam* for *yat*, *tāvanta* for *tāvant*, *pīthi* for *vīthi*. The use of particles often deviates from Sanskrit practice: thus *api . . . api* serves as equivalent to *et . . . et*; *apy eva* means perhaps, *prāg eva* often, *yāvat quippe*; the favourite Buddhist form of denoting place, *yena . . . tena*, is common; and *yataḥ*, *yadbhūyasā*, *tatprathamataḥ*, and *yat khalu* are common as conjunctions. As prepositions we find *sarvānte*, after, *sakāmam*, to please, *sthāpayitvā*, except. Rare words and meanings abound, as *āpatti*, sin, *kola*, raft, *gulma*, custom-house, *uddhava*, cheerfulness, *paribhāṣ*, abuse, *niçritya*, going to, *pragharati*, ooze forth (*prakṣar-*),[1] *vyatisārayati kathām*, converse, *anyatara*, *anyatama*, any one, *bhūyasyā mātrayā*, still more.

4. *Ārya Çūra and later Poetry*

The influence of Açvaghoṣa is unquestionably to be traced in the elegant and interesting collection of lectures or sermons in the form of edifying anecdotes of the Buddha's action in former births produced by Ārya Çūra under the style of *Jātakamālā*.[2] The mere fact that the tales appear in Sanskrit of the Kāvya

[1] The Vedic *ghṛ* may be the origin of this formation, if it is not itself a Prākritism; cf. Geiger, *Pāli*, p. 67.

[2] Ed. H. Kern, HOS. i, 1891; trans. J. S. Speyer, London, 1895. Cf. Lüders, GN. 1902, pp. 758 ff.; F. W. Thomas, *Album Kern*, pp. 405 ff.; on the Chinese version, Ivanovski, RHR. xlvii. 298 ff.; cf. E. Wohlgemuth, *Über die chinesische Version von Aśvaghoṣa's Buddhacarita* (Leipzig, 1916).

type is sufficient proof of the spread of the use of that language for purposes of literature and discussion in the courtly circles in which, we may safely assume, Ārya Çūra moved and lived. The material of the tales was doubtless ready to hand; nearly all of them are extant in the Pāli Jātaka book,[1] and twelve of them are also found in the Pāli *Cariyāpiṭaka*. Moreover, as in that book, the tales are told with the definite purpose of illustrating the various perfections (*pāramitās*) ascribed by Buddhist theory to the Buddha to be. Their chief defect to modern taste is the extravagance which refuses to recognize the Aristotelian mean. The very first tale, which is not in the Jātaka book, tells of the extraordinary benevolence of the Bodhisattva who insists on sacrificing his life in order to feed a hungry tigress, whom he finds on the point of devouring the young whom she can no longer feed, and the other narratives are no less inhuman in the disproportion between the worth of the object sacrificed and that for whose sake the sacrifice is made. But these defects were deemed rather merits by contemporary and later taste. I-tsing mentions the *Jātakamālā* as one of the popular works among Buddhists of his day, and the frescoes of Ajaṇṭā include both pictures and verses, proving the existence then of the text. The date of this evidence, unfortunately, is not certain, but the style of writing suggests the sixth century, and with this accords the fact that a Chinese rendering of another work of Ārya Çūra was made in A. D. 434. The author may then have written in the third, or more probably the fourth, century.

Ārya Çūra's style is classical, showing command of the resources of his art, but restrained and saved from exaggeration by good taste. His prose and verse alike are careful and polished, and, though he is not averse to the use of fairly long compounds, especially in prose, he employs them naturally and is seldom obscure. His good taste is conspicuous in the lines put in the mouth of the son whose father in his insensate generosity has given away his wife and children; the child speaks in simple but pathetic words:

naivedaṁ me tathā duḥkhaṁ yad ayaṁ hanti māṁ dvijaḥ
nāpaçyam ambāṁ yat tv adya tad vidārayatīva mām

[1] GN. 1918, pp. 464 ff.

rodiṣyati ciraṁ nūnam ambā çūnye tapovane
putraçokena kṛpaṇā hataçāveva cātakī.
asmadarthe samāhṛtya vanān mūlaphalam bahu
bhaviṣyati kathaṁ nv ambā dṛṣṭvā çūnyaṁ tapovanam?
ime nāv açvakās tāta hastikā rathakāç ca ye
ato 'rdhaṁ deyam ambāyai çokaṁ tena vineṣyati.

''Tis not so much that the Brahmin beats me that causes me sorrow, but that I have not seen my mother to-day pierces my heart. Long will my mother weep in the penance grove, now lonely, sorrowing for the woes of her children, like a cuckoo whose young are slain. She has gathered for our sake many a fruit and root from the forest; how then will she feel when she sees the penance grove left lonely? Here, daddy, are our toy horses, our elephants, our cars; give a half to mother; thus will she assuage her grief.' But he is equally happy in more elaborate themes, as in the description of the rule of the just king:

samaprabhāvā svajane jane ca: dharmānugā tasya hi daṇḍa-nītiḥ
adharmyam āvṛtya janasya mārgaṁ: sopānamāleva divo babhūva.

'Impartial to kin and stranger alike, his rule followed in the steps of righteousness; blocking the path of unrighteousness to men, it was as a ladder to raise them to the sky.' No doubt in his language there are traces here and there of Pālicisms,[1] but these do not seriously detract from Ārya Çūra's claim to correctness of language, and his metrical skill is considerable.

The form of his tales as composed of prose with verses intermingled, now singly, now in larger numbers, is of historical interest. It is not, of course, an invention of Ārya Çūra, who followed Kumāralāta and doubtless many others in the employment of this style. But its origin is disputed. Oldenberg[2] developed with his usual skill the thesis that the original form of literature in India, as perhaps elsewhere, was prose, with verses interposed at those points where the primitive mind naturally tends to give utterance to its feelings in verse form, as when

[1] He is praised in the *Saduktikarṇāmṛta*, ZDMG. xxxvi. 365. For his Pālicisms see Franke, IF. v. Anz. 31.

[2] GGA. 1909, pp. 66 ff.; GN. 1911, pp. 459 ff.; 1919, pp. 79 ff. Cf. Winternitz, WZKM. xxiii. 102 ff.

a god is invoked, a curse is pronounced, a benediction uttered, a prayer put up, in short at any point where emotion is let free and the pedestrian prose is inadequate as an expression of the feeling. He has found proofs of the existence of literature of this kind in the *Ṛgveda*, the Brāhmaṇas, the epic, and in Pāli texts, including the Jātakas. In principle the verses alone were preserved in fixed form, and they only received skill and care, the prose being supplied by those who told the tales. The process of development which followed was, on the one hand, the elimination of the prose by substituting verse, and it has been suggested that a remnant of the old condition is to be found in the *Mahābhārata*, where the speakers in case of dialogue are given in prose, while in the more finished *Rāmāyaṇa* such devices are unknown, the poet, like the authors of the *Iliad* and *Odyssey*, working into verse the name of the spokesman. On the other hand, the step was taken of applying to the prose the artistic polish which marked the verse, and Oldenberg[1] claims that, apart from an exceptional case like the *Kuṇāla Jātaka* of the Pāli Jātaka book, where the verses are accompanied by an ornate prose, the *Jātakamālā* and the *Pañcatantra* or *Tantrākhyāyika* are among the earliest examples of this form.

It seems clear for reasons elsewhere adduced[2] that the theory is not substantiated by Vedic evidence, and that it must stand or fall according as other considerations may appear to render it credible. The evidence of comparative literature is still quite inadequate to support it, and from the Indian point of view matters can much more simply be explained. The earliest form of prose with verse intermingled which we find in Indian literature appears to be that in which gnomic verse is cited to illustrate

[1] *Altind. Prosa*, pp. 82 ff. What is true is that elaboration of prose style is later than and based on development of verse; cf. Jacobi, *Compositum und Nebensatz*, p. 93, who cites the symmetrical Varṇakas of the Jain canon and their long compounds (cf. IS. xvii. 389 ff.).

[2] Keith, JRAS. 1911, pp. 979 ff.; 1912, pp. 429 ff.; HOS. xxv. 43 ff. There are cases of intermixture of prose and verse in other languages, e. g. Latin (Varro's *Saturae Menippeae*, Petronius, Martianus Capella (*c.* A. D. 400), Boethius (480–524), and two novels, Julius Valerius (*c.* 300) and *Historia Apollonii Tyrii*; Teuffel-Schwabe, *Rom. Lit.*, §§ 28, 165, 305, 399, 452, 478, and 489); Norse; Mediaeval Irish (Windisch, *Irische Texte*, iii. 447 ff.); Chinese; Old Picard, *Aucassin et Nicolett*; Boccaccio's *L'Ameto*; Sa'dī's *Gulistān*; Basutos and Eskimos (MacCulloch, *Childhood of Fiction*, pp. 480 ff.); Gray, *Vāsavadattā*, p. 32.

what is stated in the prose; this is akin to the practice of the Brāhmaṇas to adduce occasionally Yajñagāthās, verses on sacrificial points, in their discussions, and to the habit of the Dharmasūtras to enforce the rules which they lay down with verse citations. Here and there in the Upaniṣads we find similar cases, verses being cited in illustration and explanation of a doctrine stated in prose; in these cases it is made quite clear that the verses are quotations, from which, no doubt, it was an easy step to the writer composing verses of his own to enliven his theme or summarize his moral. The Kārikās found in the *Mahābhāṣya* prove that grammarians recognized the convenience of thus putting on record in easily remembered and accurate form their observations on disputed points. In the case of narrative the evidence seems clearly to indicate that originally in India prose and verse were used independently; if so, it is easy to understand how they could come to be combined, especially as in the other instances adduced above there already existed examples of the combination of verse and prose in one literary form. The few cases in the epic of prose and verse combined seem to be distinctly instances of contamination, not remnants of an older form of composition. How far models in Pāli were available for the author of the *Jātakamālā* or Kumāralāta we cannot, of course, prove, for the Jātaka book in Pāli as we have it presents grave problems which are yet unsolved. But the *Kuṇāla Jātaka* at any rate suggests that it would be unwise to claim that the transition first took place in Sanskrit versions of Jātaka tales.

Other Buddhist writers contributed much less to literature than to philosophy. The mysterious Nāgārjuna, perhaps of the latter part of the second century A.D., in his *Madhyamakakārikās* shows a perverse ability to develop paradoxes, while Ārya Deva (*c.* A.D. 250) in his *Catuḥçatikā*[1] shows considerable power of irony in his onslaught on the Brahmanical practice of bathing in the Ganges to remove sin and acquire merit. The *Çiṣyalekhadharmakāvya*[2] of Candragomin, in which instruction is given in the form of a letter to a pupil dealing with the essential facts of the

[1] Ed. Calcutta, 1914. On his *Hastavālaprakaraṇavṛtti*, cf. Thomas and Ui, JRAS. 1918, pp. 267 ff. Cf. P. L. Vaidya, *Études sur Āryadeva* (Paris, 1923).
[2] Ed. I. P. Minayeff, *Zapiski*, iv.

Buddhist faith, has a predecessor in the *Suhṛllekha*[1] of Nāgārjuna, in which he summarizes Buddhist doctrine for a king, unhappily unidentified. The *Subhāṣitāvali* cites a verse actually found in the letter, though omitted in the Tibetan version:

> *viṣasya viṣayāṇāṁ ca dūram atyantam antaram*
> *upabhuktaṁ viṣaṁ hanti viṣayāḥ smaraṇād api.*

'Vast indeed the difference between poison and objects of sense; poison slays only when tasted, but the things of sense by mere thought thereof.' The name of the author is given in the text as Candragopin, but on the whole it is improbable that he is to be distinguished from Candragomin, and we may place him in the seventh century A.D., as his grammar was used in the *Kāçikā Vṛtti*, while he seems to have been alive as late as the time of I-tsing, though his reference is not free from doubt. As might be expected from a grammarian, the poem is written in correct and fluent Sanskrit, but without special distinction.

The case is other with Çāntideva, author of the laborious compendium of Buddhist dogmatics of the Mahāyāna school, the *Çikṣāsamuccaya*, in his *Bodhicaryāvatāra*,[2] in which he sketches the career of him who seeks to attain Buddhahood as opposed to the narrow Hīnayāna ideal of saintship. Çāntideva, who lived in the seventh century and whom tradition alleges to have been the son of a king who was induced by the goddess Tārā to lay aside royal state, disclaims any literary pretension; he writes for himself only and for those of nature akin to his. His poem is a strange blend of passionate devotion to the aim of aiding men to achieve freedom from the miseries of life coupled with the utter negativism of the Mahāyāna philosophy. There is nothing real, nothing can be gained or lost, none honoured or despised; joy and sorrow, love and hate, all are idle names, without reality; search as you will, nothing can be found that is. None the less Çāntideva seems to be intoxicated with the nobility of the aim of seeking to be a saviour of mankind; the good we do in our efforts is a joy to the Buddhas and Bodhisattvas; we are allied with them in the struggle to attain the end. It is a delusion by

[1] Trans. H. Wenzel, JPTS. 1886, pp. 1 ff.; for the king Sātavāhana, cf. Vidyabhusana, POCP. 1919, ii. 125.

[2] Ed. de la Vallée Poussin, BI. 1901 ff.; trans. Paris, 1907.

which we treat our own bodies as something essentially our own; we must realise that the grief of another is our own, the joy of another not alien to us. The poetic power of the author stands out brilliantly when contrasted with the uninspired verses in which his predecessors Vasubandhu and his brother Asañga, probably in the fourth century, preached their doctrines. Of the latter we have the *Mahāyānasūtrālaṁkāra*, written in correct but undistinguished Sanskrit, utterly overloaded with technicalities, and, despite its great length and the obvious efforts of the author to express himself effectively, deplorably obscure. But the poem is of literary interest as proving how fully Buddhist teachers had adopted Sanskrit as their literary medium.

IV

KĀLIDĀSA AND THE GUPTAS

1. *The Guptas and the Brahmin Revival*

UTTER obscurity attends the decline of the power of the followers of Kaniṣka in India,[1] but it is certain that in A.D. 320 Candragupta founded, as a result of a matrimonial alliance with a Licchavi princess, a dynasty with head-quarters at Pāṭaliputra, which under his son, Samudragupta (*c.* A.D. 330–75), stood out as the paramount power in northern India, while his grandson, Candragupta II, completed its success by overthrowing the Kṣatrapas and adding Mālwā, Gujarāt, and Kāṭhiāwār to the empire. His son and successor, Kumāragupta (A.D. 413–55), seems to have reigned in unbroken prosperity, and Skandagupta, his son, shortly after his reign began, won a decided success over the Hūṇa invaders who were advancing from the north-west and menacing India. But between A.D. 465 and 470 the Hūṇa advance seems to have become irresistible, and at any rate after the death of Skandagupta about 480 the greatness of the empire was irretrievably departed, though the dynasty continued to rule sadly diminished dominions for several generations. By 499 Toramāṇa, leader of the Hūṇas, was established as ruler of Mālwā, while his successor, Mihiragula, had his capital at Siālkōṭ in the Panjāb. The expulsion of the Huns seems to have been the result about 528 of a victory won by Yaçodharman, a ruler of central India, and the Gupta Bālāditya of Magadha, but the records are curiously unsatisfactory. At any rate Mihiragula retreated to Kashmir, where he won an unenviable reputation,[2] and shortly after 550 the Turks conquered the Hun kingdom on the Oxus.

There can be no doubt that the Gupta empire signified a distinct revival of Brahmanism and a reassertion of Indian

[1] Smith, EHI. chaps. x and xi; Bhandarkar, *Early History of India*, pp. 47 ff.

[2] To him is ascribed the ruin of Gandhāra and its art; Foucher, *L'Art Gréco-Bouddhique*, ii. 588 ff.

nationality as opposed to the somewhat cosmopolitan Kushan régime, under which Buddhism was decidedly in chief favour, though Brahmanism and Jainism must have been widespread. The art of the period is of a high order, reflecting a national spirit reacting to the impulse of Greek inspiration,[1] although the architecture of the period has largely disappeared, owing doubtless to the appalling destruction wrought by the Mahomedan invaders of north India. The sculpture, however, exhibits an unusual beauty of figure, dignity of pose, and restraint and refinement of treatment in detail. The coinage, often of merit, shows clear traces of intercourse with the Roman world, also attested by records of missions to Rome and Constantinople in 361 and 530. Mathematics, astronomy, and astrology flourished, taking new life under Greek influence, as is abundantly established by the *Pañcasiddhāntikā* of Varāhamihira (*c.* 550) and by the works of Āryabhaṭa (born 476). Relations with China were maintained by visits of Buddhists from and to India. Fa-hien (401–10) gives us a most favourable picture of India under Candragupta II. There was freedom of movement throughout mid-India; justice was dispensed with mercy, fines being normally inflicted, capital punishment being disused, and mutilation restricted to rebels or brigands; the revenues of the crown were derived mainly from land, and the royal officers and servants received regular salaries. Among Buddhists at least—and they still were very numerous—the rule of refraining from animal food or taking life was widely observed, and in many places butchers' shops and distilleries were unknown. What is of special interest is that he alone records a very significant proof of the revival of Brahmanism; the Caṇḍālas or outcasts were obliged to live apart, and, when they approached a town or bazaar, to strike a piece of wood as a warning of their presence, in order that others might avoid pollution by contact with them. The emperors were clearly devotees of Viṣṇu and attached to the Bhāgavata faith, but religious toleration was still the order of the day, and the signs of the decadence of Buddhism were concealed from Fa-hien's eyes. Nor is this surprising, for it is probable that Samudragupta himself was a friend of Vasubandhu when that Buddhist sage attended his father's court.[2] Samudra-

[1] Foucher, ii. 756 ff.

[2] Cf. Vāmana's evidence; Smith, EHI. pp. 346 ff.

gupta, however, was careful to assert his devotion to Brahmanical ideals; thus he renewed the ancient horse sacrifice as a sign of his paramount sway, and Kumāragupta appears to have followed his example. The centre of Gupta power, originally fixed at Pāṭaliputra, seems clearly to have shifted during the reign of Candragupta II to Ujjayinī, doubtless in order to secure the steadfast adherence to the empire of the newly acquired lands.

That such princes should favour poetry and fine arts was inevitable. Samudragupta was proud of his skill with the lute, and a coin depicts him playing that instrument. But a more secure support for his claims is afforded by the assertions of the panegyrist Hariṣeṇa (*c.* 350), who assures us that his patron had a poetic style which was worth study and wrote poems which increased the poet's spiritual treasure, and again that his title of king of poets, Kavirāja, was well grounded through his composition of many poems deserving imitation by others. He delighted also in the society of the earnest students of literature, was interested in the explanation and defence of holy scripture, and devoted to music. Moreover, he won fame by removing the discrepancy between the poet's art and riches, doubtless his chief merit in the eyes of many of his flatterers. Of his great son Candragupta we know that he adopted the title Vikramāditya, reminiscent of the legendary Vikramāditya of Ujjayinī, and it is certainly plausible to suggest that the fame of Vikramāditya as the patron of poets, attested in the late and in itself worthless legend of the Nine Jewels,[1] was due to the literary distinction of Candragupta's court. The list of Jewels runs Dhanvantari, Kṣapaṇaka, Amarasiṅha, Çaṅku, Vetāla Bhaṭṭa, Ghaṭakarpara, Kālidāsa, Varāhamihira, and Vararuci. Of these Dhanvantari, as the author of a medical glossary, is older than Amarasiṅha, who also used Kālidāsa; the fourth and fifth are mere names; Varāhamihira definitely lived in the sixth century, and the dates of Kṣapaṇaka as a lexicographer and of Vararuci are unknown. But we have a distinct corroboration of the idea of Candragupta as a patron of poets in the fact that his minister of external affairs, Vīrasena Kautsa Çāba, was interested in poetry. Probably the succeeding emperors manifested equal concern in poetry.

[1] Weber, ZDMG. xxii. 708 ff.; Zachariae, *Die indischen Wörterbücher*, pp. 18 ff.; Fleet, IA. xxx. 3 f.

Nor is there any doubt that the drama must have flourished under their patronage; indeed it has been suggested that Candragupta's epithet *rūpakṛtin* denotes maker of plays, which would make the king a predecessor of Harṣa as a dramatist; the accuracy of the rendering is not, however, beyond cavil. What, however, is certain is that Sanskrit was essentially the language of the court and of learned men; even Buddhists such as Vasubandhu and Asañga resorted to it as a matter of course as the means of securing a respectful hearing for their doctrines. The disputes between the rival schools were probably friendly enough; the Sāṁkhya philosophy as expounded in the *Kārikā* of Īçvarakṛṣṇa seems to have been the object of special attack by Vasubandhu, and Samudragupta's interest in these matters may have been aroused by that teacher.

2. *Hariṣeṇa and Vatsabhaṭṭi*

Fortune has enabled us to obtain an interesting insight into the poetry of the Gupta epoch by the preservation of two Praçastis, separated by about a century in time, the panegyric of Samudragupta inscribed on a pillar at Allahabad and composed by Hariṣeṇa, perhaps in 345,[1] and Vatsabhaṭṭi's inscription in the temple of the sun at Mandasor, written in 473–4. These inscriptions alone would suffice to prove abundantly the existence of a developed Kāvya poetry during the whole period of the Gupta power, and in the first case we actually find a poet of distinct power, though he was foreign minister and general of the king.

Hariṣeṇa's poem bears expressly the title Kāvya, though it consists both of prose and verse. Its structure is similar to the delineation of kings adopted in the prose romances of Subandhu and Bāṇa, in which all is crowded into a single long sentence, made up of relative clauses and adjectives and appositions heaped upon one another. In this case the whole poem is one sentence, including first eight stanzas of poetry, then a long prose sentence, and finally a concluding stanza. The thought is no less complex than the form, for the poet's ingenuity has been equal to the effort to connect the pillar with the emperor's fame. That, as

[1] Cf. Gawroński, *Festschrift Windisch*, pp. 170 ff.; *The Digvijaya of Raghu* (1915); Bühler, *Die indischen Inschriften* (1890); Smith, EHI. pp. 298 ff.

usual in the Kāvya, is personified as feminine and is regarded as having embraced the whole world so that no more room for it remains on earth. It passes therefore by the way of the pillar up to the abode of the gods. There it appears as the Ganges, and, pure as that stream, it overflows on heaven, atmosphere, and earth. The metre is no less elaborate than the thought; of seven verses preserved there are four metres, Sragdharā, Çārdūlavikrīḍita, Mandākrāntā, and Pṛthvī. The style is markedly and undeniably of the Vaidarbha or southern manner; the verse eschews long compounds while the prose delights in them, one having no less than 120 syllables, though it is but fair to say that on the whole they are not difficult to understand. Of figures of sound alliteration is used, but sparingly; metaphors are most used of the figures of sense, rarely similes and *double entendres* as in Samudragupta's epithet *sādhvasādhūdayapralayahetupuruṣasyācintyasya*, 'a hero unfathomable, the cause of the elevation of the good and the destruction of the bad (and thus a counterpart of the unfathomable absolute, which is the cause of the origin and the destruction of the world, and in which good and bad have their being)'. But Hariṣeṇa spares us much of this; he shows his skill rather by new turns of ingenious thought, and by the care with which his long compounds are relieved by the interposition of short words to give the reciter time to recover breath and the hearer to understand the sense, and by the cunning arrangement of words in the compounds themselves in order to produce the maximum of metrical effect. His choice of words and care in their arrangement are no less seen in his verses, of which one certainly has the right to be ranked as among the most perfect effects of Indian miniature word pictures, the description of the scene when before his rivals and the court Candragupta in his old age designated Samudragupta as his successor:

āryo hīty upaguhya bhāvapiçunair utkarṇitai romabhiḥ
sabhyeṣūcchvasiteṣu tulyakulajamlānānanodvīkṣitaḥ
snehavyālulitena bāṣpaguruṇā tattvekṣiṇā cakṣuṣā
yaḥ pitrābhihito nirīkṣya nikhilām pāhy evam urvīm iti.

'"He is noble", with these words he embraced him, tremors of joy betraying his emotion; he gazed on him with tear-filled eyes, following his every movement, and weighing his worth—the courtiers sighed in relief and gloomy were the faces of his kinsfolk—and said to him, "Do thou protect all this earth".'

Very different is the work of Vatsabhaṭṭi,[1] no minister of an emperor but a humble local poet, glad to earn a fee by writing for the guild of silk-weavers of a provincial town. What is interesting in him is his testimony to the prevalence of the Kāvya in his time; the adjective *pūrvā*, above, is used as sufficient description of his poem, the missing *praçasti*, eulogy, being so naturally supplied by those familiar with current verse. He asserts that his work was done with effort or care (*yatnena*), and there is every evidence of the truth. In obedience to the laws of poetics he inserts in his forty-four stanzas descriptions both of Lāṭa and of the town Daçapura, of the seasons, winter and spring, and shows by the use of twelve metres his skill in versification, though the effect is marred by his inability to bring off his results without free use of the weak caesura. His style is the eastern or Gauḍa, as is clearly proved by his love of long compounds in verse, and by the way in which in one stanza he has fitted the sound of the verses to the altering sentiment, advancing from soft harmonious sounds in describing the gentleness of his hero to discords when proclaiming him *dviṭdṛptapakṣakṣapaṇaikadakṣaḥ*, 'peerless in destroying the proud hosts of the foe'. His alliterations, similes, and metaphors all are of types abundant in the Kāvya, but his skill is small, and his poem is disfigured by tautologies as in *tulyopamānāni*, the use of verse-fillers or needless particles as in *tatas tu*, or prefixes as in *abhivibhāti*, or words as in *samudrānta*, while *spṛçanniva* for the necessary neuter and *nyavasanta* are offences against grammar. But his panegyric is invaluable testimony to the widespread cultivation of Sanskrit poetry and it helps definitely to aid us in determining the date of India's greatest poet.

3. *Kālidāsa's Life*

We know nothing whatever of value from later sources regarding the life and character of Kālidāsa.[2] Anecdotes are told

[1] Bühler, *Die indischen Inschriften*, pp. 31 ff.

[2] On his date see Liebich, IF. xxxi. 198 ff.; Keith, *Sanskrit Drama*, pp. 143 ff.; Hillebrandt, *Kālidāsa* (1921). S. Ray (POCP. 1919, i, p. lix) held him to be Agnimitra's court poet (*c.* 150 B.C.), but K. G. Sankar (IHQ. i. 309 ff.) puts him between 75 and 25 B.C.

asserting that he was originally extremely stupid, and won skill in poetry by the favour of Kālī, an obvious deduction from his name, slave of Kālī. He is alleged also to have shown remarkable skill in the ready manufacture of verses to order, either to describe a given situation or to complete an imperfect stanza, and a more circumstantial legend[1] tells of his murder in Ceylon while a guest of King Kumāradāsa at the hands of a greedy hetaira. There is not the slightest ground to accept the suggestion, still less to find in it an indication of date, Kālidāsa's visit to Ceylon on this view being due to the Hun inroads. His own poems, on the other hand, and especially the description of Raghu's conquests, prove him intimately acquainted with many Indian scenes, the sandal of Kashmir, the pearl fisheries of the Tāmraparṇī, the deodars of the Himālayas, the betel and coco-palms of Kaliñga, the sand of the Indus, but it would be hazardous to claim for him any part in the great expedition of Samudragupta when he won his right to perform the horse sacrifice as a sign of his paramount power in India.

Nonetheless it is difficult to dissociate Kālidāsa from the great moments of the Gupta power. He was later than Açvaghoṣa and than the dramatist Bhāsa; he knew Greek terms, as his use of *jāmitra* proves, the Prākrit of his dramas is decidedly later than Açvaghoṣa's and Bhāsa's, and he cannot be put before the Gupta age. His complete acceptance of the Brahmanical system, the sense of sharing in a world of prosperity and power, the mention of the horse sacrifice in the *Mālavikāgnimitra*, Raghu's conquests in the *Raghuvañça*, seem best explicable as the outcome of the enjoyment of the protection of a great Gupta ruler, and we must remember that Candragupta II had the style of Vikramāditya, with whose name tradition consistently connects Kālidāsa. Nor is it absurd to see in the title *Kumārasambhava* a hint at the young Kumāragupta, the heir apparent, or even in *Vikramorvaçī* an allusion to the title Vikramāditya. It has been attempted to refer Kālidāsa to the sixth century by making the Vikramāditya of tradition the Yaçodharman[2] who defeated the

[1] Geiger, *Lit. und Sprache der Singhalesen*, pp. 3 ff.; Rhys-Davids, JRAS. 1888 pp. 148 ff.; Bendall, p. 440; Nandargikar, *Kumāradāsa*, pp. v ff.; Vidyabhusana, POCP. 1919, i, p. clxxii.

[2] Hoernle, JRAS. 1909, pp. 89 ff.

Huns, but this theory is no longer in repute. More favour[1] has been shown to the view that Kālidāsa lived under Kumāragupta and Skandagupta, mainly on the score that Mallinātha and Dakṣiṇāvartanātha ascribe to him in v. 14 of the *Meghadūta* a *double entendre* referring to Dignāga, the Buddhist logician, as a hostile critic, and that his own reference to the Hūṇas and the river Vañkṣū in the *Raghuvañça* alludes to the time when these warriors were still in the Oxus valley just before their defeat by Skandagupta. The first argument is invalidated by the grave improbability of the tasteless reference in the *Meghadūta* and by the fact that, even if it were real, Dignāga's date need not be later than 400. The second imputes to Kālidāsa a desire to achieve historic realism quite out of keeping with his poetic aim, and irreconcilable with his mention of the Greeks as on the north-west frontier as well as the Pārasīkas, Kāmbojas and Hūṇas.[2] That Kālidāsa lived to see the Hūṇa victories is most implausible, while his evident affection for Ujjayinī suggests that he spent much of his time there under Candragupta's favour.

This conclusion is strongly supported by evidence culled from Vatsabhaṭṭi. Two of his verses run:

calatpatākāny abalāsanāthāny : atyarthaçuklāny adhikonnatāni
taḍillatācitrasitābhrakūṭa- : tulyopamānāni gṛhāṇi yatra.
Kailāsatuñgaçikharapratimāni cānyāny : ābhānti dīrghavalabhīni savedikāni
gāndharvaçabdamukharāṇi niviṣṭacitra- : karmāṇi lolakadalīvanaçobhitāni.

'The houses there, dazzling white and towering high, with their waving banners and tender maidens, are rivals of the cloud-pinnacles, snow-white, but stained by the lightning-creeper. Yet others match Kailāsa's lofty peaks, with their long balconies and seats of stone, as they resound with music, are decked with pictures, and are adorned with groves of waving plantains.'

[1] Gawroński, *The Digvijaya of Raghu*, pp. 1 ff.; Smith, EHI. p. 321, n. 1.

[2] The term found in the epic was perhaps first used of the Hiung-nu of the 2nd cent. B. C.

These stanzas can hardly be deemed other than an attempt to improve on v. 65 of the *Meghadūta*:

vidyutvantaṁ lalitavanitāḥ sendracāpaṁ sacitrāḥ
saṁgītāya prahatamurajāḥ snigdhagambhīraghoṣam
antastoyam maṇimayabhuvas tuṅgam abhraṁlihāgrāḥ
prāsādās tvāṁ tulayitum alaṁ yatra tais tair viçeṣaiḥ.

'There the palaces can vie with thee at every point: their fair maidens rival thy lightning, their paintings thy rainbow, their drums beaten in concert thy lovely deep thundering, their jewelled floors thy water, their peaks that touch the sky thy height.' To suppose that Kālidāsa knew these clumsy verses of an obscure poetaster and turned them into the simple elegance of his verse is absurd; to hold that a local poet appropriated and tried to improve on a verse of the great poet of Ujjayinī is natural and simple, and, if confirmation were needed, it is supplied by the fact[1] that v. 31 of the inscription deals similarly with vv. 2 and 3 of Canto v of the *Ṛtusaṁhāra*. Kālidāsa then lived before A. D. 472, and probably at a considerable distance, so that to place him about A. D. 400 seems completely justified.[2]

4. *The Ṛtusaṁhāra*

The opinion of India which makes the *Ṛtusaṁhāra*, cycle of the seasons, a youthful work of Kālidāsa, has recently[3] been assailed on many grounds. Thus it has been complained that the poem lacks Kālidāsa's ethical quality, that it is too simple and uniform, too easy to understand. The obvious reply is that there is all the difference between the youth and the maturity of a poet, that there is as much discrepancy between the youthful work of Virgil, Ovid, Tennyson, or Goethe, and the poems of their manhood as between Kālidāsa's primitiae and the rest

[1] Kielhorn, GN. 1890, pp. 251 ff.

[2] On the later emperors, see R. C. Majumdar, JPASB. 1921, pp. 249 ff.

[3] Walter, *Indica*, iii. 6 ff.; Nobel, ZDMG. lxvi. 275 ff.; JRAS. 1913, pp. 401 ff.; Hari Chand, *Kālidāsa*, pp. 240 ff. *Contra* Keith, JRAS. 1912, pp. 1066 ff.; 1913, pp. 410 ff.; Hillebrandt, *Kālidāsa*, pp. 66 ff. Kielhorn, Bühler, Hultzsch, Macdonell, von Schroeder, among others, accept Kālidāsa's authorship; often ed., e. g. Gajendragadkar, 1916.

of his work. Nor is it the slightest use to argue that Sanskrit poets differed from other poets since they were essentially learned and artificial; the poets mentioned are precisely of the analogous type, men who worked steadily at their art until at their prime they could create structures which make their youthful attempts seem childish folly. In point of fact the *Ṛtusaṁhāra* is far from unworthy of Kālidāsa, and, if the poem were denied him, his reputation would suffer real loss. The contention that Mallinātha commented on the other three of his poems but not on this is met effectively by the consideration that its simplicity rendered it poor game for the very learned commentator to deal with. The fact that the writers on poetics do not cite from the poem has an obvious explanation in the same fact; these authors never exhibit the slightest trace of liking what is simple, and they could find in the later poems abundant material to use as illustration. More deplorable still are some of the æsthetical arguments adduced; complaint is made that the poet begins with the summer, whereas the spring was the usual beginning of the year, forgetting that Kālidāsa was not composing an almanac or writing a *Shepheard's Calendar*. Again, heat or its derivatives (*tap*) is found seven times in Canto i, as if this did not accord with summer, as does eagerness (*samutsukatva*) with the rains and longing (*utkaṇṭh*) with autumn. The poet is censured for asserting that the swans excel maidens in beauty of gait and the branches rob their arms of loveliness; later, he was not guilty of such discourtesy. He mixes a metaphor in speaking of clouds as having the lightning as creeper; as we have seen, Vatsabhaṭṭi borrows the phrase, and exploits two other verses of the poem, proving its antiquity and rendering most probable its authorship. It is objected that he uses here only the construction *ā mūlataḥ*, in lieu of the ablative, though equally once only in the *Kumārasambhava* he has *āmekhalam*; the freshness and liveliness of the seven verbal forms (ii. 19) is unparalleled and, therefore, not by Kālidāsa. Even the lack of developed use of figures of speech is adduced against him, and the use of *saṁhāra* in the title has been questioned as unique. Poets happily do not feel themselves bound to be parrots.[1]

[1] His developed style is seen in his pictures of spring (*Kumāras.* iii; *Ragh.* ix), and summer (*Ragh.* xvi).

The poem is far from a mere description of the seasons in their outward aspect, though Kālidāsa exhibits delicate observation and that loving sympathy with nature which seems innate in Indian poets. Throughout he insists on the relation of the diverse moods of the year to the loves of man and maiden or husband and wife. Though the days of summer are a burden, the nights are the more delightful, when the moon is bright and coolness refreshes the earth; at midnight the young delight in song and dance and wine; the moon in jealousy of youthful love retires in sorrow. The rainy season comes in kingly guise, the clouds the elephants which bear him, the lightning his standard, the thunder his drum. The emotion of love is awakened by the sight of the clouds which bend down to kiss the peaks of the mountains. Autumn comes like a young bride, clad in a garment of sugar cane, girdled with ripening rice, and with face of lotus blooms. Winter's cold makes all the more welcome, all the more close and tender, the embraces of lovers. In the cool season the nights are cold, the moon shines chill, the lovers close the window of their chamber, wrap themselves warmly in their garments, and enjoy every moment of the still feeble rays of the sun, or rest beside the fire. But spring brings to them and to all nature new life and joy; we see now why the poet begins with summer; it enables him to end with the season in which young love, in harmony with the birth of a new year, is made perfect. The poem in every line reveals youth; the lack of the ethic touch[1] is in perfect accord with the outlook of the young, and though Kālidāsa was to write much finer poetry, he was also to lose that perfect lucidity which is one of the charms of the poem to modern taste, even if it did not appeal to writers on poetics.

5. *The Meghadūta*

In distinction to the *Ṛtusaṁhāra* the *Meghadūta*[2] is unquestionably a work of Kālidāsa's maturity; the mere fact that he adopts for it and maintains throughout with only occasional

[1] Stenzler, ZDMG. xliv. 33, n. 3.

[2] Ed. E. Hultzsch, London, 1911 (with Vallabhadeva's comm.); ed. and trans. Pathak, Poona, 1916; ed. TSS. 54, 1919.

harshness a metre so elaborate as the Mandākrāntā is conclusive proof that he was no novice, though we may admit the possibility that he desired by this metrical *tour de force* to establish his capacity once and for all, and to exhibit himself as a great poet. Suggestions for the subject-matter may have been taken from the *Rāmāyaṇa*,[1] where Rāma's deep longing for his lost Sītā offers an obvious prototype for the Yakṣa's sorrow for the wife from whom he is severed, and the description of the rainy season in iv. 28 has some points of similarity. But the idea is carried out with marked originality and beauty. A Yakṣa banished for a year by Çiva his master, because of failure of duty, is reminded by the approach of the rainy season of his wife, lamenting him in their abode at Alakā, and begs a passing cloud to bear to his beloved the news of his welfare and the assurance of his devotion. From Rāmagiri, his place of exile, the cloud is bidden go, in the company of the cranes and the royal swans *en route* for Lake Mānasa, to the region of Māla and to mount Āmrakūṭa. Thereafter it is to seek the Daçārṇa country with its city of Vidiçā, and then must drink the waters of the Vetravatī before proceeding to visit Ujjayinī, after crossing the Nirvindhyā and the Sindhu. The shrine of Mahākāla must be visited, the Carmaṇv-tī crossed, and the holy Brahmāvarta after passing Daçapura; there the cloud will visit the field of Kurukṣetra, the scene of Arjuna's great deeds, and drink the water of the Sarasvatī, for which Balarāma, who fought not for love of his kin, abandoned his beloved wine. Thence it must go to where the Ganges descends from the Himālaya near mount Kanakhala, and then to Kailāsa, passing through the gap of mount Krauñca which Paraçurāma made as a path to the south. Then the water of lake Mānasa will refresh the cloud, and on the top of the mountain is Alakā where the beloved of the Yakṣa dwells. The delights of the divine city are fully depicted, and the poet then describes to the cloud the home he is to seek out; it can be seen from afar off through its archway; in the garden is a coral tree, its mistress's pet, and a flight of emerald steps leads to a well in which golden lotuses grow, and the swans, delighted, think no more even of their beloved Mānasa. There is the beloved, sorrowful, and blighted by separation, emaciated,

[1] There is in the *Kāmavilāpa Jātaka* (ii. 443) a very distant parallel.

seeking by many a device to while away the long days until her husband's return. Gently she is to be wakened from her slumber by the cloud, which is to give her a message of tender love from her husband, and an assurance of his faith and certainty of reunion.

At first sight the effect of the poem seems to be marred by an element of unreality in the longing of the Yakṣa, whose separation is but temporary and who as an attendant of Çiva cannot in truth fear either death or even injury for his beloved from his absence. The message would have read very differently had it been sent, as in Schiller's *Maria Stuart*, by a helpless captive awaiting in resignation or despair an ineluctable doom. But to understand the poem aright we must remember that the poet doubtless felt that it was, as later writers expressly allege, the duty of the poet to suggest rather than to say outright; the loves of the two immortals is a symbol of human love; perhaps[1] Kālidāsa had some experience of his own which the poem indicates, for the vivid colours in which he describes the Yakṣa's abode seem to be drawn from real life. Certainty is wholly unattainable, but in any event it is difficult to praise too highly either the brilliance of the description of the cloud's progress or the pathos of the picture of the wife sorrowful and alone. Indian criticism has ranked it highest among Kālidāsa's poems for brevity of expression, richness of content, and power to elicit sentiment, and the praise is not undeserved.

Popularity has had the penalty of many interpolations of the text. There is a remarkable mass of evidence available; in the eighth century Jinasena, applying the art of Sạmasyāpūraṇa, worked the whole of the text of 120 verses as he knew it into an account of the life of the Jaina saint Pārçvanātha;[2] it exists in a Tibetan[3] version in the Tanjur, and in a Sinhalese rendering; many stanzas are quoted in works on poetics; it was repeatedly[4] imitated from the *Pavanadūta* of Dhoī in the twelfth century onwards; we have from that century and later many com-

[1] Bhau Dāji, *Lit. Rem.*, pp. 50 f.

[2] Pathak's ed. (1916) rests on this. A *Nemidūta* of Vikrama in 125 verses ends each with a line from a rather interpolated text.

[3] H. Beckh, *Ein Beitrag zur Textkritik des Kālidāsas Meghadūta* (1907); G. Huth, SBA. 1895, pp. 268 ff., 281 ff.; date 13th cent.

[4] Aufrecht, ZDMG. liv. 616, mentions other imitations; cf. IHQ. iii. 273 ff.

mentaries, including that of Vallabhadeva,[1] who gives 111 verses, of Dakṣiṇāvartanātha (*c.* 1200), who has 110, and of Mallinātha,[2] who has 118.

Inevitably many other lyric poems were ascribed to Kālidāsa, including two of some merit, the *Ghaṭakarpara* and the *Çṛṅgāra-tilaka*, but there is no real probability of proving them his.

6. *The Kumārasambhava*

High as Indian opinion ranks the *Meghadūta*, which won also the commendation of Goethe,[3] to modern taste the *Kumārasambhava*[4] appeals more deeply by reason of its richer variety, the brilliance of its fancy, and the greater warmth of its feeling. The *Meghadūta* has, with reason, been ascribed the merit of approaching more closely than any other Indian poem to the rank of an elegy; the *Kumārasambhava* varies from the loveliness of the spring and the delights of married love to the utter desolation induced by the death of the beloved. The subject is unquestionably a daring one, the events which bring about the marriage of the highest god Çiva to Umā and the birth of Skanda, the war god, and Ānandavardhana[5] tells us that there were critics who deemed it wrong to depict the amour of two deities. Still less permissible does the subject naturally appear to modern taste, unless we realize that as in the *Meghadūta* we must see the poet's power of suggestion; the wedlock of Çiva and Umā is no mere sport, no episode of light love such as that of Zeus with Danae or many another. From this union springs a power destined to perform the slaying of the demon Tāraka, who menaces the world with destruction; moreover, their nuptials and their love serve as the prototype for human marriage and human love, and sanctify with divine precedent the forces which make the home and carry on the race of men.

[1] Hultzsch places him in the 10th cent., but see Pathak's ed., pp. xiv ff. He knew Bilhaṇa and Hemacandra, but is cited in 1140 A. D.

[2] This famous commentator, who also explained the epics of Kālidāsa, Bhāravi, Bhaṭṭi, and Māgha, and Vidyādhara's *Ekāvalī* (see ed., pp. xxiv ff.) lived *c.* 1400. A comm. on the *Nalodaya* is given, *Madras Catal.*, xx. 7923.

[3] Cf. von Schroeder, *Indiens Lit. und Cultur*, p. 548.

[4] Ed. NSP. 1906; i–viii, TSS. 1913–14; i–vii, trans. R. H. Griffith, London, 1879.

[5] iii. 6, p. 137. Mammaṭa disagrees.

The poem begins with a brilliant piece of description of the Himālaya, the abode of Çiva. Kālidāsa, unlike many a classical and even modern poet, had no hatred of mountains; his fancy makes them the dwelling of merry sprites who play in their caves, round which eddy the clouds, affording welcome screens for the maidens when they undress; the wind, wet with the drops of the streams of the Ganges as it descends from heaven, beats on the trunks of the deodars, and bends the peacock feathers, the scanty dress of the gnomes who chase the antelope. In marked contrast to this innocent frolic sits Çiva, sunk in deepest meditation, and on him with other maidens waits Umā, born of the mountain god himself, plucking flowers to offer to him, and fetching water and grass for his service. Canto ii shows us the gods in deep distress, for a demon Tāraka has arisen to menace them, and Brahman himself can afford no aid, for he has accorded him his protection, and even a poison tree cannot be cut down, if one has reared it oneself. Only Çiva can aid, Çiva who surpasses Brahman and Viṣṇu in glory, and, if Umā can win him, from them will spring a deliverer. Indra then seeks the aid of Kāma, god of love, to win Çiva's heart for Umā. The next Canto shows Kāma ready and willing to effect the end desired if Spring will be his comrade as well as his dear wife Rati. There follows a brilliant picture of the new life and love awakened in nature by the advent of Spring with Kāma, but the sight of Çiva seated still as a flame when no wind blows, a cloud without rain, daunts even Kāma's heart and he quails. But Umā with her friends appears, and Çiva is begged to hearken to their devotions; he feels himself strangely moved, and glancing sees Kāma on the point of discharging at him his deadly arrow. One fiery glance from the god's eye reduces him to ashes. Then follows (iv) a brilliant and touchingly pathetic picture of the lament of Rati for her dead husband; she will not accept the consolation urged on her by Spring; instead she bids him heap the pyre so that she may follow him in death. But her fatal purpose is stayed by a voice from on high, which assures her of reunion with her beloved when Çiva shall have relented and taken Umā to spouse. In sorrowful hope Rati continues her life.

The first throw has failed and Umā is bitterly disappointed, bitterly ashamed. She determines, despite all protests, to perform asceticism until she wins her desire; in summer she exposes herself to the appalling heat and smoke of four fires, in winter lies in icy water, in the rains sleeps on the naked rock. As she is engaged in these acts a hermit appears before her and questions her; from her sighs he learns that she loves, and from her maids who that lover is. He proceeds to depict in appalling colours the god of her desire, but she fiercely and bitterly rebukes his attacks; delighted he reveals himself as Çiva incarnate (v). All now is ripe for the wedding, but Kālidāsa detains us with a gay picture of the solemn scenes which lead up to it. The Seven Seers themselves with Arundhatī come as wooers from Çiva to seek the maiden's hand; she stands, eyes downcast, counting the leaves on the lotus in her hand, at her father's side, while his eyes wander to the face of his consort, for in matters affecting their daughters householders are wont to obey their wives' desires (vi). The wedding follows, described, doubtless from the model of imperial ceremonies, with rich abundance of detail; the mother, in her excitement between joy and sorrow, cannot see to place correctly the painted mark on her daughter's forehead, and misplaces the woollen marriage thread which the nurse, more calm and practical, sets aright.

With this ends the poem in many manuscripts; others add ten cantos. Of these Canto viii describes, according to the principles of the Kāmaçāstra, the joys of the wedded pair; doubtless such frankness is abhorrent to western taste, but the doubts of its genuineness which have been expressed are clearly groundless; it seems certainly[1] to have been known to Bhāravi, to Kumāradāsa, and to Māgha, and quotations from it occur in the writers on poetics. Nor in poetic skill is it in the least inferior to Kālidāsa's work. The case[2] is other with the following cantos. They tell of Agni's approach, first in dove shape, then in his proper person, to Çiva as he prolongs for centuries the joys of dalliance, begging his aid. From the seed of Çiva, cast in the

[1] See Walter, *Indica*, iii. 21, 25 f., who suggests use of viii. 63 in *Vikramorvaçī*, iii. 6.

[2] Jacobi, OC.V. ii, 2. 133 ff. i–viii are used in the *Çaṅkarasaṁhitā* of the *Skanda Purāṇa*, but it in ix–xvii; Weber, ZDMG. xxvii. 179 ff., 190 ff.; *Pandit*, iii. 19 ff., 85 ff.

Ganges and shared by the six Kṛttikās, Pleiades, Kumāra is miraculously born, and grows up delighting his parents by his childish play. But the gods are in terror, the city of the gods is dismayed through Tāraka; Indra comes to demand help; Çiva grants his prayer and assigns Kumāra to the task. The great host of Tāraka is described in Canto xiv, then the portents which warn him not to war (xv). Blinded by pride he refuses, bids his young opponent go back to his father and mother rather than fight, assails him with his whirlwinds and magic fire, until pierced to the heart he falls dead. The poem thus goes far beyond the birth of Kumāra as its title promises, and the inferiority of the new cantos is obvious on every ground. The metre is carelessly handled; in five cases caesura is neglected at the end of the first and third verses of the Çloka, a negligence quite foreign to Kālidāsa; the same carelessness is seen six times in Upajāti stanzas, where too weak caesuras—at the end of a compound, not of a word—are used far more often than by Kālidāsa. In order to manage his metres the poet has to resort to versefillers, abhorred of really good writers; *su* is repeatedly thus used, as well as *sadyaḥ* and *alam*; the constant use of periphrasis is doubtless due to the same cause: the writer expends much ingenuity in coining new designations for his characters, and is so fond of the superfluous *anta* at the end of compounds—which we have seen in Vatsabhaṭṭi—that Jacobi has conjectured that he was a Marāṭha, in view of the Marāṭhī locative *āṁt*. In the later manner is the free use of prepositional compounds and the impersonal passive with subject in the instrumental; the former use just appears in Kālidāsa, the latter is common from Bhāravi onwards. Moreover, save occasionally, as in the battle scene, the poetical value of the cantos is small, and in confirmation of the internal evidence it may be added that neither commentators nor writers on poetics cite them nor are imitations found in later poets.

Of Kālidāsa's model for his poem we know nothing, but we can trace in it the influence of Vālmīki. In the *Rāmāyaṇa*[1] we have a brilliant picture of the contrast of the beauty of spring in the Kiṣkindhā forest as contrasted with the ceaseless sorrow of Rāma, bereft of Sītā, nor can we doubt that this has influenced

[1] iv. 1.

Kālidāsa to draw the wonderful picture of Spring's advent and the revival of the youth and life of the world. There is a parallel too for Rati's despair[1]; when Vālin falls Tārā addresses him with words not less sincere because they bear the stamp of the classic style: 'Why dost thus speak no more to thy beloved? Arise and share this fair couch with me; the best of men lie not, as thou, on the ground. Too dear dost thou hold, o lord, the earth even in death, since me thou dost leave alone and her hast clasped in thine embrace. Ended our days of joy together in the fair forest; sunken am I in a deep sea of sorrow, without joy, without sustenance, since thus hast departed. Hard my heart that it can see thee stretched on the ground and yet not break from sorrow.' Hints too for the demon Tāraka are clearly taken from the description of Rāvaṇa in the *Rāmāyaṇa*.[2] There are doubtless reminders here and there of Açvaghoṣa,[3] as in the description of the actions[4] of the women of the city on the advent of Çiva and Pārvatī, which has a prototype in the description in the *Buddhacarita*[5] of the entrance of the prince, and which is taken up again in the description in the *Raghuvaṅça*[6] of the entry of Aja and Indumatī.

The problem why the poem was never finished by its author remains insoluble. The loss of the last pages of a solitary manuscript may be the explanation, but it is far more likely that the poet, deterred either by contemporary criticism of his treatment of the divine pair, or by the feeling that the legend of the birth with its strangeness and miracles was not a true theme for poetry, abandoned the purpose and left his work unfinished. It can hardly be claimed that death intervened, for there can be no doubt that the *Raghuvaṅça* is a later work. This shows itself both in the graver tone, in the references to the Yoga philosophy and the less personal conception of the universe as compared with the magnification of Çiva in the *Kumārasambhava*, and in the growing pedantry seen in the use of similes derived from grammar, of which we have only modest suggestions in the *Kumārasambhava*.[7] Thus Rāma's army follows him to serve

[1] iv. 23; cf. vi. 111 (of Rāvaṇa).
[2] Cf. also *Rām.* vi. 124. 45 with xiii. 36.
[3] Cf. Walter, *Indica*, iii. 11 ff.
[4] vii. 56–69.
[5] iii. 13–24.
[6] vii. 5–16.
[7] ii. 27; vii. 69; *Raghuvaṅça*, xii. 58; xi. 56; i. 1; xv. 7, 9.

his purpose as the prefix *adhi* is followed by the root *i* to make the word *adhyayana*; Sugrīva is put in Vālin's place as king as a substitute replaces the root, and husband and wife are theme and suffix. Moreover, in the constant parallels between the two poems, as in the description of the marriage rites, the priority seems to belong to the *Kumārasambhava*; it is curious that Kālidāsa shows a distinct love of using the same metre for the same theme; thus in both we have the Çloka used in prayers,[1] death is described in the Viyoginī,[2] a ruined state in the Upajāti.[3]

7. *The Raghuvança*

Though inferior in some slight degree to the *Kumārasambhava,* the *Raghuvança* may rightly be ranked as the finest Indian specimen of the Mahākāvya as defined by writers on poetics. Daṇḍin[4] lays down that the subject should be taken from old narratives or traditions, not therefore invented; the hero should be noble and clever; there should be descriptions of towns, oceans, mountains, seasons, the rising and setting of the sun and the moon, sport in parks or the sea, drinking, love-feasts, separations, marriages, the production of a son, meeting of councils, embassies, campaigns, battles, and the triumph of the hero, though his rival's merits may be exalted. It should not be too compressed, and it should be replete with sentiments (*rasa*) and the emotions which underlie them (*bhāva*). It should have effective transitions (*sandhi*), an allusion to the five stages of action recognized by the writers on drama, by which from its opening the movement advances after a halt to the central moment, pauses, and reaches the *dénouement*. The metres must be charming, and each Canto, which should not be too long, should end with a change of metre. The poem should begin with a prayer, paying homage or in addition invoking a blessing, or an indication of the subject-matter. It should promote the ends of Dharma, conduct, Artha, worldly success, Mokṣa, final release, and Kāma, love.

1 *Kum.* ii. 4–16; *Ragh.* x. 16–32.
2 *Kum.* iv; *Ragh.* vii.
3 *Kum.* xiii; *Ragh.* xvi.
4 i. 23 ff.

The *Raghuvaṅça*[1] is true to the type, for the central figure is Rāma, though in accord with the title the poem first sketches the history of the dynasty of the sun-born kings, descendants of the Ikṣvāku whose name occurs in the *Ṛgveda*, and whose family is renowned in the epic and the Purāṇas. This wide theme gives the poet full space to exercise his power of description; war and the coronation of a king, the choosing of her mate by a young princess at a Svayaṁvara, the marriage rite, the loss of a darling life and the grief of the bereaved husband, town and country, the seasons, the incidents of a great Digvijaya, the triumphal progress of a king who seeks to conquer the earth, all form occasions for the poet's skill. The poem carries us at once into an atmosphere strange to us; Dilīpa is king but childless; he learns that by chance when returning from a visit to Indra he has failed to show reverence to his sacred cow, who has cursed him; to make amends he determines to follow in worship the movements of her daughter, Nandinī, on earth; dutifully he carries out his vow, saves her from a lion by offering his own body in exchange, and Nandinī accords him the wish of his heart. Soon the father gazes, with eyes as still as lotus blossoms shielded from the wind, on the lovely face of his son, his heart overflows as the sea at the sight of the moon. The young Raghu waxes fast, is given the rank of Crown Prince and bidden guard the horse that must wander for a year before his father can perform the sacred horse sacrifice; the steed disappears, but with Nandinī's aid Raghu's eyes are opened until he can see where in the east Indra has taken the horse. Vainly he strives against the god, but pleased by his valour he accords him every wish save the return of the horse, and the gallant youth demands that his father shall have the full fruit of the sacrifice. The offering performed, Dilīpa gives to his son the white parasol, emblem of sovereignty, and, true to his family's rule, retires to the life of an ascetic in the forest (i–iii). Canto iv recounts the knightly adventures of Raghu as conqueror of India; he advances against the Suhmas, defeats the princes of Bengal, and erects pillars of victory on the islands of the Ganges; neither the elephants nor the arrow hail of Kaliṅga stay his course, Ma-

[1] Ed. S. P. Pandit, BSS. 1869–74; Nandargikar, Bombay, 1897; trans. Walter, Munich, 1914.

hendra yields, the Kāverī is crossed, the south invaded, the Pāṇḍyas pay tribute of pearls. Thence the hero bends his path north, through the Malaya and Dardura hills, the sea of his host covers the long slopes of the Sahya mountain, the dust of the army clings to the hair of the ladies of Kerala, the Muralā river, the Trikūṭa hill witness his fame. Thence by land, as a pious king, not by the polluting sea, he advances against the Persians and the Yavanas, Greeks; the dust of the conflict hides the warring hosts whose presence is revealed by the twang of their bows alone, the bearded foemen cover thick the ground, those who escape death cast off their helms in token of submission; the victors wearied slake their thirst with wine. Next Raghu bids his steeds roll in the Indus—a variant has Oxus—sands, overthrows Hūṇas and Kāmbojas; the winds of the Himālaya set the reeds hymning his victories. The mountain folk feel his power, fire flashes from the mountain-sides beneath the rain of spears and arrows, and the folk of the Utsavas lose for ever their joy in festivals (*utsava*). The Lauhityā is crossed, Prāgjyotisa subdued, and Kāmarūpa yields tribute of wild elephants.

In this spirited and martial narrative we may justly see the reflex in the poet's mind of Samudragupta's great conquests,[1] and with customary skill the subject changes in Canto v to a very different theme. Raghu's generosity impoverishes him; when a Brahmin Kautsa begs him to aid him to meet the vast demands of his teacher, he resolves to storm the treasure-house of Kubera, god of wealth, but a rain of gold saves him from impiety. The Brahmin's gratitude secures him a son, Aja, who soon equals his father. Bidden to take part in the Svayaṁvara, at which the sister of a kingly neighbour will choose her mate, he sets forth; on the way he boldly attacks a monstrous wild elephant, which under his stroke changes to a Gandharva, condemned by a curse to wear this shape until released by the blow of an Ikṣvākuid's arrow, who gives him in reward a magic weapon. Canto vi presents us with a brilliant picture of the Svayaṁvara; the princess, with her companion Sunandā beside her, passes by prince after prince as they stand eager before her;

[1] This fact renders it far more probable that his Açvamedha is that present to Kālidāsa's mind than that of Kumāragupta, of whom we have no record of great military achievements.

none please her, one is a dicer, therefore bad as a man; in vain Sunandā presses on her Añga's lord; he has all merits, but tastes vary. In revenge she bids Indumatī pass on, when she notes that her heart is won by Aja, but the maiden lays shame aside, and accords to him the coronal which marks him as her spouse. The marriage ceremony is performed, the young pair set out home, but the shamed princes have planned revenge, and resolved to take away by force the princess. Aja wages fierce battle with them, in the end the Gandharva's gift prevails, and he takes from his foes their honour, though he spares their lives (vii). His reign is fortunate; while Raghu as a hermit tames the senses, Aja destroys the foes of his realm, and, when Raghu dies, he pays him all the honours of a Yogin's funeral. But a fatal misfortune awaits him; a garland from the sky blown by the wind falls on Indumatī's breast and slays her, though in truth for her death means release from her mortal bondage imposed on her, in reality an Apsaras, through a curse. No consolation is this thought to Aja; in vain is he reminded of the folly of mourning for the dead who are burnt by the tears of the living; in vain every consolation regarding the shortness of life and the duty of kings is urged on him; broken-hearted, he dies and Dilīpa reigns in his place. Of him Canto ix has no concrete facts to tell us, until after a brilliant description of spring we are told of the fatal hunt, when, after displaying equal prowess and pity, Dilīpa in pursuit of an elephant mortally wounds a Brahmin boy; he bears the dying youth to his aged parents, and hears the curse of a like doom. In Canto x we leave the realities of life to learn of the magic incarnation of Viṣṇu in the sons born to Dilīpa; in xi Rāma's youth, his visit to Viçvāmitra's hermitage where he slays the demon Tāḍakā, his journey to Janaka's court, where he wins at the Svayamvara the hand of Sītā, and his overthrow of Paraçurāma, who recognizes in him the godhead, are rapidly recounted. The banishment of Rāma by Kaikeyī's device, the life of Rāma and Sītā in the forest, her capture by Rāvaṇa, the search for Lañkā,[1] the crossing of the ocean with the monkey horde, and the great battle between Rāma and Rāvaṇa, described in vivid colours, bring us to Canto xii in which Kālidāsa's descriptive

[1] Cf. for its situation M. V. Kibe, *Rawana's Lanka Discovered* (1920). Hopkins (*Great Epic*, p. 80) appears to accept Ceylon as Lañkā.

powers find congenial subject-matter in describing the sights of India as seen from the aerial car on which Rāma and Sītā return to Ayodhyā.

Then follows a series of brilliant sketches; Rāma and Sītā visit the widows of the king, who scarce can see them for their tears, which speedily change to joy. Sītā alone weeps for the trouble her beauty has brought her husband, a foreboding of woe. For the moment all is brightness; the glorious ceremonial of the royal consecration follows. But disaster is at hand; malicious voices reproach the king whose one wife has stayed so long in Rāvaṇa's home. Rāma places duty above love; he bids Lakṣmaṇa take Sītā—now pregnant—to Vālmīki's hermitage, and there break to her the truth of her fate; overwhelmed, she deplores her lot but utters no reproach. Rāma rules in solitude, her sculptured form his companion in his sacrifices (xiv). From his sorrow he is awakened to overthrow demon foes on the Yamunā banks, while in the hermitage Sītā bears two boys who, taught by Vālmīki the tale of their father's deed, console her sorrowing heart by reciting it. The day comes when Rāma determines to perform the horse sacrifice; he rests in a hut beside the golden statue of his wife; he hears from the boys the song of his deeds; the people, Rāma himself recognize them for his own, Vālmīki begs reinstatement for the queen. Rāma asks only that her stainless purity be made clear; she comes before him, swears to her truth as she drinks the holy water; the earth goddess appears and takes her in her bosom to bear her to the realm below. Rāma transfers to his sons the burdens of the state, saddened by the restoration of Sītā only to be lost forthwith; in due course, followed by all the people, he goes forth from the town and is caught up in a heavenly chariot.

The effective and pathetic picture of Sītā's end and the return to heaven of Rāma might well have closed the poem, but Canto xvi is not without merit. Kuça, Rāma's son, reigns at Kuçāvatī; in a dream Ayodhyā appears to him in the guise of a woman whose husband is afar, reproaches him with her fallen condition, and bids him return. Kuça obeys, Ayodhyā once more is glorious, and a description of the delights of summer rivals, but fails to equal, that of spring in Canto ix. For the rest the poem sinks in interest, as Kālidāsa has nothing to tell us but names of worthless kings whose harems supplied their sole interest in life. We cannot deny [1] his authorship of Cantos xviii and xix; no ancient authority questions them, and they are cited, if rarely, by writers on poetics. But their brevity and the utter abruptness of the end, when the widow of Agnivarman, a worthless debauchee, is awaiting the birth of her child, suggest that we have no more than a rough draft. Yet we would gladly assign to a poetaster meaningless puns on names of kings, as when Pāriyātra is merely said to have exceeded in height the Pāriyātra mountains, or the incredible tastelessness of the action of a king who hangs his foot out of the window for the people to kiss.

Vālmīki, of course, is the chief creditor [2] of Kālidāsa in this poem. Here and there one certainly surpasses the other; though normally the advantage lies with the younger poet, yet there are exceptions. Fine as is Kālidāsa's picture of Rāma's meeting with the sons who know him not, it yet is still more affecting in the leisurely march of the epic, and Kālidāsa has failed to improve on the scene of Sītā's vindication. But his merit shines out in such cases as his description of the return to Ayodhyā; future poets were to imitate it, but not one to equal it.

No other epic of Kālidāsa has come down to us, and the relation in time of his epics to his dramas is insoluble. The suggestion that he is responsible for the *Setubandha*,[3] which relates the tale of Rāma from the advance against Rāvaṇa and the building of the bridge to Lañkā down to Rāvaṇa's death, is excluded by the style, with its innumerable plays on words, alliterations, recondite similes, exaggeration, and its enormous compounds. Its date is uncertain, as of Pravarasena of Kashmir [4] its author or patron we know nothing definite. Still more ludicrous is the suggestion that the *Nalodaya* [5] is his; that rimed poem of

[1] As does Hillebrandt, *Kālidāsa*, pp. 42 f. They seem known to the Aihole inscr. (EI. vi. 8 f.) of Ravikīrti who boasts his rivalry with Kālidāsa and Bhāravi. For unevenness in great poets cf. *Aeneid* v as criticized by Tyrrell, *Latin Poetry*, pp. 153 f.

[2] On alleged use of the *Padma Purāṇa*, see H. Śarmā, *Calc. Or. Series*, 17.

[3] Ed. and trans. S. Goldschmidt, 1880–4. Date before Bāṇa, perhaps late 6th cent., Stein, *Rājataraṅgiṇī*, i. 66, 84 f.

[4] That the Vākāṭaka Pravarasena had anything to do with the poem seems quite unproved.

[5] Ed. and trans. W. Yates, Calcutta, 1844; Bhandarkar, *Report*, 1883–4, p. 16; A. R. S. Ayyar, JRAS. 1925, pp. 263 ff., who ascribes Vāsudeva as author also of the

intolerable affectation is perhaps not the production of Ravideva, author of the *Rākṣasakāvya*, of equal demerit, before the seventeenth century, but the work of Vāsudeva, protégé of Kulaçekhara and Rāma.

8. *Kālidāsa's Thought*

As Sophokles seems to have found his perfect *milieu* in the Athens of Perikles' happy days, so Kālidāsa appears to us as the embodiment in his poems, as in his dramas, of the Brahmanical ideal of the age of the Guptas, when order had been restored to a troubled earth, foreigners assimilated or reduced, and prosperity broadcast.[1] Ingenuity[2] has traced in the history of the first five of the rulers in the *Raghuvança* an exemplar of the exploits of the first five of the Gupta kings; granted that Kālidāsa may have known and profited by the literary activity of Hariṣeṇa, which doubtless extended far beyond the one inscription which has come down to us, still we may safely doubt any such parallelism. But Kālidāsa does represent, if we may judge from his poetry, the complete carrying out of the rule of life laid down for a Brahmin or a warrior or clansman. Youth, in this view, is the time for study under a teacher, then follows the period of manhood with its happy wedlock, then in stages that of the hermit whose mind is set on things eternal. The scheme is in many ways perfectly adapted to Indian life; it starves no side of man's life; four aims of existence are recognized by Kālidāsa himself, who finds them embodied in the sons of Dilīpa, themselves reflexes of Viṣṇu himself. They are duty, governing man's whole life; the pursuit of wealth and of love, the occupations of his manhood; and release, the fruit of his meditations in old age. We may not share the affection of Indian and even of a section of modern taste for the erotic scenes of the last cantos of the *Raghuvança*, but we must not regard them as the outpourings of a sensual mind. The sages of the Upaniṣads themselves deemed marriage obligatory and the *Bṛhadāraṇyaka* gives the

Yudhiṣṭhiravijaya, *Tripuradahana*, and *Çaurikathodaya*, all rimed, to the 9th cent. The date is improbable; ZII. iv. 226 f.

[1] Cf. M. T. Narasimhiengar, IA. xxxix. 236 ff. with Hillebrandt, *Kālidāsa*, pp. 137 ff.

[2] A. Gawroński, *The Digvijaya of Raghu* (1915).

spell to obtain a male son; the saintly Çvetaketu is deemed an authority on the *Kāmasūtra*, and Kālidāsa expressly claims the divine precedent of Çiva and Umā as sanction for the most passionate married love. Statecraft again is essentially part of the material ends of life, and not only does he paint in Rāma an ideal ruler, but throughout the *Raghuvança* we are reminded of the duties of kings to the subjects. Let us grant that his vision was Brahmanical; he deliberately repeats the condemnation of the *Rāmāyaṇa* on the Çūdra who threatens the security of established order by venturing to expose himself, head downwards, hanging from a tree to fire, in order by penance to acquire merit. This reminds us of Fa-hien's[1] emphatic testimony of the degradation of the Caṇḍālas in the Gupta realm.

Youth and manhood are no time for deep philosophic views, and the Kālidāsa of the *Ṛtusaṁhāra*, *Meghadūta*, and *Kumārasambhava* remains within narrower limits. We feel, however, a growing sense of the greatness and glory of Çiva; the remote figure of the *Meghadūta* is definitely brought nearer to us in the *Kumārasambhava*. Even Brahman and Viṣṇu are less than he, and the term Lord, Īçvara, is his *par excellence*; moreover, despite his all-embracing majesty, he is intensely personal. Yet neither Brahman nor Viṣṇu is forgotten; to Brahman in the *Kumārasambhava* itself, to Viṣṇu in the *Raghuvança* two noble prayers are addressed in which in the true spirit of kathenotheism either appears as the greatest of gods, as more than the world, as beyond all comprehension. The inconsistency, however, is rather apparent than real; it is possible to ascertain with fair certainty the view Kālidāsa took of the universe, and this affords a reconciliation of his diverse views.

Both epics, but especially the *Raghuvança*, show that Kālidāsa accepted Sāṁkhya and Yoga views of the nature of the universe. The three constituents of nature, goodness, passion, and dullness, in their ethical aspect afford themes for simile; the Brahman sea as the source of the Sarayū is like the unmanifested (*avyakta*) whence springs intelligence. Yoga practices are recognized; the aged king practises concentration (*dhāraṇā*) as he sits on Kuça grass; the difficult posture known as Vīrāsana of ascetics is compared to trees standing motionless; Sītā by asceticism

[1] Smith, EHI. p. 314; Foucher. *L'Art Gréco-Bouddhique du Gandhāra*, ii. 8.

seeks to secure reunion in her next life with her spouse; the power to pass through closed doors may be won, and the Yogin needs not cremation, but like Raghu is buried in mother earth. But we cannot hold that the godhead envisaged by Kālidāsa is the pale Īçvara of the Yoga; in Brahman we are told are united both matter and spirit as they are known in the Sāṁkhya, and this we may fairly take as indicating that to Kālidāsa, as to the author of the *Kaṭha Upaniṣad*, over the spirits and matter stood the absolute, who to Kālidāsa takes specially the form of Çiva but who is also Brahman and Viṣṇu, the spirit that perishes not beyond the darkness. With this absolute man is merged on death if he has attained enlightenment, for this is the sense of *brahmabhūyaṁ gatim ājagāma* in the *Raghuvaṅça*. If enlightenment is not his but good deeds, he has heaven for his share, for knowledge alone burns up man's deeds which else force him to life after life. We need have the less hesitation to accept this view in that it is essentially the standpoint of popular Vedāntism and that it afforded to a man of thought and good sense an effective means of reconciling belief in the three great gods. What is clear is that in his advancing years Kālidāsa's mind turned more and more to the conception of the all-embracing character of the godhead and of the efficacy of Yoga practices to attain union with him.

From such a philosophy it would be idle to seek any solution for essential conflicts in the heart of man, or to demand any independent criticism of man's aims and fate. India knew atheists enough, but their works have all but perished, and we must rather be grateful that we have preserved in such perfection the poetic reflex of the Brahmanical ideal both in its strength and in its weakness. Nor, let us remember, does such an ideal shut out deep human feeling such as we may suspect in the longing of the *Meghadūta*, the lament of Aja over the dead Indumatī, of Rati for Kāma slain. But it does demand resignation, and if in perfection of form Kālidāsa's poems proclaim him the Virgil of India, we may admit that he was incapable of the vision and imagery of the sixth book of the *Aeneid*.

9. *Kālidāsa's Style and Metre.*

In Kālidāsa we have unquestionably the finest master of Indian poetic style, superior to Açvaghoṣa by the perfection and polish of his work,[1] and all but completely free from the extravagances which disfigure the later great writers of Kāvya. Daṇḍin ascribes to his favourite style, the Vaidarbha, qualities which we may fairly sum up as firmness and evenness of sound, avoiding harsh transitions and preferring gentle harmonies; the use of words in their ordinary sense and clearness of meaning; the power to convey sentiment; beauty, elevation, and the employment of metaphorical expressions. He assures longevity to a poem which, in addition to conforming to the rules for a Mahākāvya, is rich in ornaments (*alaṁkāra*), and Kālidāsa is not sparing in his use of these means of adding grace to his work. But he has the fundamental merit that he prefers suggestion to elaboration; his successors too often thought that they could only prove their capacity by showing all of what it was capable; he was content to produce a definite effect, and to leave well alone; his was the golden mean of Virgil between rustic simplicity and clumsiness and that over-refinement which is specially fatal.[2] Thus it results that his miniature-painting in its polished elegance often attains relative perfection.

The truth of his delineation is seen in the picture of the sorrowing bride in the *Meghadūta*:

utsañge vā malinavasane saumya nikṣipya vīṇām
madgotrāñkaṁ viracitapadaṁ geyam udgātukāmā

[1] The critics occasionally find fault, e.g. in the *Vyaktiviveka* (p. 66) *Raghuvaṅça* xvi. 33 is censured for the position of *tadīye*, but they cite him repeatedly as a master, first of Mahākavis; *Dhvanyāloka*, pp. 29, 207; *Kāvyaprakāça*, p. 2. Bhāmaha's assertion that a cloud is not suitable as a messenger must refer to the *Meghadūta* and may be put beside his attack on Bhāsa's *Pratijñāyaugandharāyaṇa*, proved by T. Gaṇapati Śāstrī; cf. Thomas, JRAS. 1925, p. 103, who (pp. 100 ff.) deals effectively with the attacks on the authenticity of Bhāsa's dramas. His verse (*Subhāṣitāvali*, 1353) is imitated in *Ragh.* viii. 66; GIL. iii. 159, n. 1.

[2] His improvements on Açvaghoṣa are numerous and undeniable; cf. the passages in Nandargikar, *Raghuvaṅça* (ed. 3), pp. 161 ff.; Formichi, *Aśvaghoṣa*, p. 350; cf. also *Saund.* iv. 42 with *Kum.* v. 45. The parallel *Kum.* vii. 56 ff.; *Ragh.* vii. 5 ff. with *Buddh.* iii. 13 ff. is conclusive and Hillebrandt's doubts (pp. 102 f.) are hypercritical.

tantrīm ārdrām nayanasalilaiḥ sārayitvā kathaṁcit
bhūyo bhūyaḥ svayam api kṛtām mūrcchanāṁ vismarantī.

'Or perhaps, placing her lute on her lap, whose dark garment proclaims her grief, she will seek to sing a song wherein she has worked my name, but, scarce able to move the string which her tears have bedewed, she will forget the air which she herself hath made.' Or, again:

tvāṁ ālikhya praṇayakupitāṁ dhāturāgaiḥ çilāyām
ātmānaṁ te caraṇapatitaṁ yāvad icchāmi kartum
asrais tāvan muhur upacitair dṛṣṭir ālupyate me
krūras tasminn api na sahate saṁgamaṁ nau kṛtāntaḥ.

'When I have portrayed thee in love's anger on the rock with my colours and seek to add myself lying at thy feet, my tears well up and ever blot out my sight; cruel the fate which even thus will not permit our union.' There is a brilliant picture of Umā's confusion and of her joy when Çiva reveals himself:

adya prabhṛty avanatāṅgi tavāsmi dāsaḥ
krītas tapobhir iti vādini candramaulau
ahnāya sā niyamajaṁ klamam utsasarja
kleçaḥ phalena hi punar navatāṁ vidhatte.

'"From this moment, o drooping maiden, I am thy slave, bought by thy penance," so spake he whose crest is the moon, and straightway all the fatigue of her self-torment vanished, so true is it that fruitful toil is as if it had never been.' There is perfect simplicity of passionate longing in Rati's address to the dead Kāma:

kṛtavān asi vipriyaṁ na me: pratikūlaṁ na ca te mayā kṛtam
kim akāraṇam eva darçanaṁ: vilapantyai rataye na dīyate?

'Thou hast never displeased me; thee I never have wronged; why then, without cause, dost thou hide thyself from thy weeping Rati?' The timid shyness of the new-made bride and her lover's ruses are delicately drawn:

vyāhṛtā prativaco na saṁdadhe: gantum aicchad avalambitāñçukā
sevate sma çayanam parāñmukhī: sā tathāpi rataye pinākinaḥ.

'Addressed she could not answer; when he touched her gown she sought to leave him; with head averted she clung to her couch; yet none the less did she delight the lord of the trident.'

ātmānam ālokya ca çobhamānam: ādarçabimbe stimitāyatākṣī
Haropayāne tvaritā babhūva: strīṇām priyālokaphalo hi veçaḥ.

'When with her long eyes fixed on her mirror she saw the reflection of her radiant loveliness, swift she hastened to seek Çiva, for the fruit of woman's raiment is the light in the lover's eyes.' Equally complete in its own effectiveness is the description of the tragic shock received by Rati:

tīvrābhiṣañgaprabhaveṇa vṛttim: mohena saṁstambhayatendriyāṇām
ajñātabhartṛvyasanā muhūrtaṁ: kṛtopakāreva Ratir babhūva.

'The bitterness of the blow cast Rati into a faint which dulled her senses and for the moment with true kindness robbed her of memory of her husband's ruin.'

Aja's tears have their excuse in nature itself:

vilalāpa sabāṣpagadgadaṁ: sahajām apy apahāya dhīratām
abhitaptam ayo'pi mārdavam: bhajate kaiva kathā çarīriṣu?

'He wailed aloud, his voice broken by sobs, forgetting the high courage that was his; iron in the fire yieldeth its strength; how much more feeble mortals?' He feels that his wife has doubted his love:

dhruvam asmi çaṭhaḥ çucismite: viditaḥ kaitavavatsalas tava
paralokam asaṁnivṛttaye: yad anāpṛcchya gatāsi mām itaḥ.

'Surely, sweet smiling one, thou hast judged me traitor whose love was feigned that thou hast gone from me to the world whence there is no return and hast not bidden me even a word of farewell.' No woman could desire a more perfect eulogy:

gṛhiṇī sacivaḥ sakhī mithaḥ: priyaçiṣyā lalite kalāvidhau
karuṇāvimukhena mṛtyunā: haratā tvāṁ vada kiṁ na me hṛtam?

'Wife, counsellor, companion, dearest disciple in every loving art; in taking thee tell me what of me hath not pitiless Death taken.' The fatal blow is depicted:

kṣaṇamātrasakhīṁ sujātayoḥ. stanayos tām avalokya vihvalā
nimimīla narottamapriyā: hṛtacandrā tamaseva kaumudī.

'For a moment she gazed on the garland as it lay on her rounded breasts, then closed her eyes in unconsciousness, like the moonlight when the darkness obscures the moon.' There is humour, on the contrary, in Indumatī's rejection of the Añga prince:

athāñgarājād avatārya cakṣur: yāhīti janyām avadat kumārī
nāsau na kāmyo na ca veda samyag: draṣṭuṁ na sā bhinnarucir hi lokaḥ.

'But the princess turned away from Añga's lord her gaze, and bade her maiden proceed; it was not that he had not beauty nor that she could not see it, but folk have different tastes.' This has the same graceful ease as often in the *Ṛtusaṁhāra*:

vivasvatā tīkṣṇatarāñçumālinā: sapañkatoyāt saraso 'bhitāpitaḥ
utplutya bhekas tṛṣitasya bhoginaḥ: phaṇātapatrasya tale niṣīdati.

'As the sun's garland of rays grows ever hotter, the frog sore tormented leaps up from the muddy water of the lake only to fall into the mouth of the thirsty snake, who spreads his hood to shade him from the glare.' There is a pretty picture of girlish haste:

ālokamārgaṁ sahasā vrajantyā: kayācid udveṣṭanavāntamālyaḥ
baddhuṁ na sambhāvita eva tāvat: kareṇa ruddho 'pi ca keçapāçaḥ.

'As she rushed to the window, her garlands fell from their place, and she did not even trouble to knot the abundant hair which she caught together in her hand.'

The structure of each of these cameos is simple; throughout

it is normal to have each verse complete in itself, a single verb serving to support a number of adjectives and appositions, though relative clauses with verb expressed or implied are not rare. The compounds are normally restricted in length, but this is less closely observed in the Mandākrāntā metre, though even then clearness is aimed at and normally achieved. The order of words is very free, partly no doubt by reason of metrical necessity. Of the figures those of sound are employed not rarely but usually with skill. Beside the ordinary forms of alliteration as in *nirmame nirmamo 'rtheṣu*, we find the more important Yamaka, in which the same syllables are repeated, in the same or inverted order,[1] but with different sense. There is a certain liberality in the process; thus Kālidāsa is able to match *bhujalatām* with *jaḍatām*, for *l* and *ḍ*, like *r* and *l*, *b* and *v*, are admitted as similar, and the same principle is clearly to be seen in

cakāra sā mattacakoranetrā : lajjāvatī lājavisargam agnau.

'She with the eyes of the intoxicated Cakora, in modesty (*lajjā*) made offering of fried rice (*lāja*) in the fire.' In Canto ix of the *Raghuvaṅça* Kālidāsa deliberately shows his skill in Yamakas; there is no doubt that this offends the sound rule of Ānandavardhana that to seek deliberately such a result destroys the function of poetry which is to suggest—or express—not merely to exhibit form, and we can only conjecture that in this canto, which also is marked out by the amazing number of metres employed, Kālidāsa was seeking to prove that he could vie with any rival in these niceties. In Canto xviii also, Yamakas are superabundant. Throughout, however, we feel Kālidāsa seeking for the matching of sound and sense, to which the Indian ear was clearly more susceptible than our own.

Of figures of sense Kālidāsa excels in Indian opinion in the simile, and the praise is just. The Indian love of simile appears freely in the *Ṛgveda*, and is attested by the elaborate subdivisions of Indian poetics. The width of Kālidāsa's knowledge and the depth of his observation of nature and life are here shown to the highest advantage. But his world is not ours, and doubtless at

[1] As distinct from alliteration the repetition should be in corresponding parts of the verse (Jacobi, ZDMG. lxii. 303, n. 1).

times his figures[1] seem grotesque to our taste, as when the king comes from his bath and plays with his harem like an elephant on whose shoulder still clings a shoot of the lotus sporting with the females of his herd. But often there can be only admiration; the chariot of the prince is so covered by the arrows of his foes that only by the point of its standard can it be discerned, as the morning wrapped in mist by the feeble rays of the sun; the wound torn by the arrow is the door of death; with joyful eyes the women of the city follow the prince as the nights with the clear stars of autumn the polar star. Characteristic is the love of elaboration of a comparison; the reader is not to be contented with a mere hint, the comparison must be drawn out in full. The Pāṇḍya king is peer of the lord of mountains, for the necklaces which hang over his shoulders are its foaming cascades, and the sandal that reddens his limbs the young sun which colours its peaks. Or again, the princes who hide their jealousy under the semblance of joy are compared to the pool in whose calm depths lurk deadly crocodiles. Or again, the ruined city, with towers broken, terraces laid down and houses destroyed, is like the evening when the sun sets behind the mountains and a mighty wind scatters the clouds.

To us, no doubt, both similes and metaphors sometimes seem far-fetched; those from grammar leave us cold, but there is wit in the assertion that the wearing by Rāma of the royal dress when the ascetic's garb revealed already his fairness is equivalent to the vice of repetition (*punarukta*). The bowmen whose arrows strike one another are like disputants whose words conflict. The king seeks to subdue the Persians as an ascetic his senses through the knowledge of truth. Kālidāsa is rich also in plays of fancy which present a vivid picture (*utprekṣā*); it is natural to him to think vividly, to attribute to the mountains, the winds, the streams the cares, sorrows, joys, and thoughts of men. He loves also the figure corroboration (*arthāntaranyāsa*); indeed, its careless use reveals the hand of the forger of the last cantos of the *Kumārasambhava*. But the *double entendre* is rare indeed; the instances of it are very few, and they lend no

[1] Cf. Hillebrandt, *Kālidāsa*, pp. 112–20. For the *Çakuntalā*, cf. P. K. Gode, POCP. 1919, ii. 205 ff. A very interesting comparison is afforded by Lucan's similes (Heitland in Haskins' *Lucan*, pp. lxxxiv ff.).

credit whatever to the suggestion that v. 14 of the *Meghadūta* is an attempt obliquely to praise Nicula and damn Dignāga. Of the former we know nothing, and it was doubtless the later love for Çleṣas which bade men find them in Kālidāsa, where not one elaborate case even can be proved to exist.[1]

Kālidāsa's metrical skill is undoubted. In the *Ṛtusaṁhāra* he used normally the Indravajrā and Vaṅçasthā types, with Vasantatilaka and Mālinī; one stanza only in Çārdūlavikrīḍita occurs. The *Meghadūta* shows the more elaborate Mandākrāntā used without variation; a few slight roughnesses as regards caesura may be adduced as proof of the relatively early date of the poem, but the evidence is too slight to weigh seriously in itself. In the *Kumārasambhava* we find the normal rule that the canto is written in a single metre with change, as the writers on poetics require, at the close. Thus i, iii, and vii are written in the Indravajrā; ii and vi in the Çloka, iv in the Vaitālīya, and v in the Vaṅçasthā, while viii is in the Rathoddhatā. The closing changes are furnished by Puṣpitāgrā, Mālinī, and Vasantatilaka. The *Raghuvaṅça* follows on the whole this principle, but exhibits greater variety, suggesting later date. The Indravajrā type serves for ii, v–vii, xiii, xiv, xvi, and xviii; the Çloka for i, iv, x, xii, xv, and xvii; the Vaitālīya for viii, and the Rathoddhatā for xi and xix. Canto ix is orthodox up to v. 54, being in Drutavilambita, then it deliberately displays the poet's skill in new metres, each with a verse or so, Aupacchandasika, Puṣpitāgrā, Praharṣiṇī, Mañjubhāṣiṇī, Mattamayūra, Vasantatilaka, which is also used for 11 verses in v, Vaitālīya, Çālinī, and Svāgatā. There occur also odd verses in Toṭaka, Mandākrāntā, Mahāmālikā, and iii is written in Vaṅçasthā, with a concluding verse in Hariṇī. There are thus nineteen metres in all to eight in the earlier epic. Detailed efforts to find some sign of development in any of the metres in respect of caesuras &c. have failed to yield any results worthy of credence.[2]

In the Çloka the rules had already been established by epic

[1] In *Meghadūta* 10 *āçābandha* may have a double sense; 28 *rasa*; *Kumārasambhava*, viii. 22; *Raghuvaṅça*, xi. 20. But in v. 14 Nicula is to be a poet friend, elsewhere utterly unknown.

[2] Huth, *Die Zeit des Kālidāsa* (1890), App.; Hillebrandt, *Kālidāsa*, p. 157. Cf. SIFI. VIII. ii. 40 ff.

practice, and Kālidāsa observes them carefully. Of the four Vipulā forms he uses the last once only; the figures[1] for the other three out of 1410 half-stanzas in the epics are 46, 27, and 41, or 8·15 per cent., showing that the third Vipulā was Kālidāsa's favourite. It is interesting to note that in the form of the syllables preceding the first Vipulā Kālidāsa shows special care to select that form (⏓ ⏓ – –) which is not allowed in the second Vipulā as against that (⏓ – ⏑ –) which is permitted in both. The *Kumārasambhava* has 11 cases of the first to 3 of the second form, the *Raghuvaṅça* 31 to 1; this doubtless indicates increasing care to secure elegance, and it accords with this that in the *Kumārasambhava* alone is the fourth Vipulā found.[2]

[1] For the *Raghuvaṅça* they are 32, 18, 27 out of 1096; Jacobi's figures (IS. xvii. 444 f.) are corrected from SIFI. *l.c.* The percentage in Bhāravi is 9·6; Māgha 27·15; Bilhaṇa 8·64; Çrīharṣa 0·53; Kumāradāsa 2·35.

[2] *Raghuvaṅça*, xii. 71, should perhaps be read *dvitīyahemaprākāram.* In *Kumārasambhava*, vii. 11 on one reading position is neglected as in *Çiçupālavadha*, x. 60, both dubious (SIFI. VIII. ii. 7). For the schemes of the metres see chap. xx, § 4.

V

BHĀRAVI, BHAṬṬI, KUMĀRADĀSA, AND MĀGHA

1. *Bhāravi*

OF Bhāravi's life we know nothing whatever, though he ranks as second in magnitude among the constellations of the Kāvya. External evidence proves that he was older than A.D. 634 when he is mentioned with Kālidāsa in the Aihole inscription, and he is cited in the *Kāçikā Vṛtti*; on the other hand he manifestly is influenced by Kālidāsa, while he strongly affected Māgha.[1] Bāṇa ignores him, so that he can hardly have preceded him long enough for his fame to compel recognition. It is, therefore, wiser to place him *c.* A.D. 550 than as early as A.D. 500.

His *Kirātārjunīya*[2] is based, as usual, on the epic. The *Mahābhārata*[3] tells us how, when the Pāṇḍavas with their wife Draupadī have retired under their vow of twelve years' banishment to the Dvaita forest, Draupadī, with truly feminine faithlessness, urges the heroes to break their pledge. A council is held; Yudhiṣṭhira pleads for the bond; Bhīma controverts his contentions. Vyāsa counsels retirement from the Dvaita forest, and the brothers go to the Kāmyaka wood, where Yudhiṣṭhira takes the prudent course of bidding Arjuna, as a preliminary to war, to secure from Çiva divine weapons. Arjuna obeys, practises in the Himālaya severe penances, meets and struggles with a Kirāta, who proves to be Çiva himself; he grants the boon desired, to which the other gods add further largesse. This theme Bhāravi has chosen to expand and illustrate with all the resources of a refined and elaborate art. The opening shows at once the hand of the artist; in the epic the discussion of the brothers arises merely from the dreary plight in which they are

[1] Cf. Jacobi, WZKM. iii. 121 ff.

[2] Ed. NSP. 1907; trans. C. Cappeller, HOS. 15, 1912; i–iii, with Citrabhānu's comm., TSS. 63.

[3] iii. 27–41.

placed; Bhāravi begins instead with the return of a spy whom Yudhiṣṭhira has sent to report on the deeds of Suyodhana—as he is always styled; he bears the unwelcome tidings that the king is walking in the ways of virtue and charming the hearts of the people. Hence, naturally, Draupadī, anxious for the future, taunts Yudhiṣṭhira with his inglorious plight and urges swift battle (i). Bhima adds his support; Yudhiṣṭhira, the unready, has scruples of honour (ii), but seeks counsel from Vyāsa, and the sage admits that war must be, but, since the foe is so strong, urges that Arjuna should by penance in the Himālaya win Indra's aid. He vanishes, but a Yakṣa appears to lead Arjuna on his way, and they depart, cheered by the good wishes of the remainder of the party (iii). At this point the poet's invention displays itself in elaboration; just before, by omitting all mention of the move to the Kāmyaka wood, he had shortened the narrative, improving greatly the effect; now he takes the opportunity to display the poet's command of language. In Canto iv the Yakṣa leads Arjuna on; and a brilliant picture is drawn of the autumnal scene, partly in narrative, partly in the mouth of the Yakṣa. Then follows (v) the description of the Himālaya itself, the Yakṣa lays stress on the mystery which guards it and on its close kinship with Çiva and Pārvatī, and vanishes after bidding Arjuna do penance on Indrakīla. The penance of Arjuna terrifies the Guhyakas, the spirits who haunt Indrakīla; they appeal to Indra to aid them, and he sends Gandharvas and Apsarases to disturb the asceticism which menaces the quiet of his mountain (vi). The heavenly host speeds through the air to Indrakīla and makes there its camp; their elephants merit special description (vii). The Apsarases now leave their palaces, just made by their magic power, and wander in the woods to pluck the flowers; then the Ganges invites them to the bath, and the bathing scene is described with much charm and beauty (viii). Evening comes, the sun sets, the moon arises—the banal theme wins new effect through the poet's skill; the nymphs and their lovers drink and seek the pleasures of love; the day dawns (ix). The Apsarases now turn their minds to their task; aided by the seasons who now appear six in number to second their efforts, they expend, but in vain, all their charms on the young ascetic (x). Seeing his minions thus foiled through Arjuna's constancy, Indra appears himself in the guise of a sage, admires the fervour of the penance, but contends that to bear arms and practise asceticism are inconsistent; Arjuna admits the logic of the censure, but asserts that he will do all to save his family's honour. Indra is touched, reveals himself, and bids him win the favour of Çiva (xi). Here ends the poet's invention, and we again find the epic as his source. Arjuna continues his penance in order that Çiva may bless him; the seers in distress appeal to the great god, who expounds to them Arjuna's divine nature as an incorporation of Nara, a part of the primeval spirit; a demon Mūka in boar form plans to slay him; therefore Çiva bids his host follow him to guard the prince (xii). The boar appears to Arjuna; it falls pierced by his own and Çiva's dart; the prince advances to recover his arrow, but is challenged by a Kirāta who claims it in his master's name (xiii). Arjuna rejects the demand in a long speech; the Kirāta returns, and Çiva launches, but in vain, his host against Arjuna, who endures unscathed the shower of their arrows (xiv). The host is rallied from flight by Skanda and Çiva himself, who then begins a deadly battle of arrows with Arjuna (xv). The two then strive with magic weapons, the hero is beaten (xvi), but grasps again his bow, and with sword, mighty rocks, and the trunks of great trees assails the god, but all in vain (xvii). They box, at last they wrestle; Çiva reveals his true form, and the hero, humbled at last, praises the greatness of the god and begs him for strength and victory; the god and the world guardians, who come to the scene, accept his devotion and give him the magic weapons that he craves.

The introduction of Çiva's host, of its struggles under Skanda's leadership with the hero, and the whole episode of the contest with magic weapons are the fruit of the poet's imagination. One difficulty is obvious; it is made necessary to duplicate the episode of the force of the penance causing fear and evoking divine intervention, and the prolongation of the conflict results in some repetition of ideas. Duplication also results from the description of the amours of the nymphs with the Gandharvas and their attempts on the prince. The poet's skill led him, we must confess, to exhibit it too freely, and the introduction of magic weapons leaves us cold. In this regard Vālmīki has a fatal influence on Sanskrit poetry; the mythical background of the

Rāma legend produced the unreality of his combats, which every epic poet felt bound to copy. Another influence seen strongly in the first two Cantos is that of the political principles of the day, which have ample opportunity of illustration in the record of Suyodhana's rule and in the arguments by which Yudhiṣṭhira seeks to justify the keeping of their faith by his brothers.

There is no doubt of the power of Bhāravi in description; his style at its best has a calm dignity which is certainly attractive, while he excels also in the observation and record of the beauties of nature and of maidens. The former quality is revealed repeatedly in the first Canto, the very first line of which strikes the true note of high policy; then follows:

kṛtapramāṇasya mahīm mahībhuje: jitāṁ sapatnena nivedayiṣyataḥ
na vivyathe mano na hi priyam: pravaktum icchanti mṛṣā hitaiṣiṇaḥ.

'When he bent low in homage his mind wavered not, though he had to tell the king that his realm had been won by his foe, for men who seek one's good care not to speak flattering words.' In the same strain Suyodhana is praised:

na tena sajyaṁ kvacid udyataṁ dhanuḥ: kṛtaṁ na vā tena vijihmam ānanam
guṇānurāgeṇa çirobhir uhyate: narādhipair mālyam ivāsya çāsanam.

'Never has he raised his bow to shoot, never has a frown distorted his face; loving his virtues the kings bear as a garland on their heads his royal orders.' The setting sun and the rising moon are happily portrayed:

aṅçupāṇibhir atīva pipāsuḥ: paṅkajam madhu bhṛçaṁ rasayitvā
klībatām iva gataḥ kṣitim eṣyaṅl: lohitaṁ vapur uvāha pataṅgaḥ.

'Ruddy glowed the sun as he hastened to rest, as though overdeep he had drunken with his rays, in his thirst, the sweetness of the lotus.'

saṁvidhātum abhiṣekam udāse: Manmathasya lasadañçu-
jalaughaḥ
yāminīvanitayā tatacihnaḥ: sotpalo rajatakumbha ivenduḥ.

'For Love's consecration the lady night raised aloft the moon with its shimmering sea of beams and its spots full in view, like a silver chalice decked with lotuses.' The advent of the cool season is thus greeted:

katipayasahakārapuṣparamyas: tanutuhino 'lpavinidrasin-
duvāraḥ
surabhimukhahimāgamāntaçaṅsī: samupayayau çiçiraḥ sma-
raikabandhuḥ.

'Then came the cool season, Love's one friend, lovely with its mango blooms here and there, when frost is rare and but a few Sinduvāras awake from sleep, the harbinger of the end of winter and the coming of spring.' The bathing scene is rich in prettinesses:

tirohitāntāni nitāntam ākulair: apāṁ vigāhād alakaiḥ
prasāribhiḥ
yayur vadhūnāṁ vadanāni tulyatāṁ: dvirephavṛndāntari-
taiḥ saroruhaiḥ.

'Hidden by their long hair in utter disorder through plunging in the water, the maidens' faces seemed like lotuses covered with swarms of bees.'

priye 'parā yacchati vācam unmukhī: nibaddhadṛṣṭiḥ çithi-
lākuloccayā
samādadhe nāñçukam āhitaṁ vṛthā: viveda puṣpeṣu na pāṇi-
pallavam.

'Yet another, face upturned and eyes fixed on her lover as he spoke, gathered not together her garment, though the knot slipped and fell, nor realized that her tender hand had missed the flowers it sought.' Characteristically, the same idea is varied later in the canto:

vihasya pāṇau vidhṛte dhṛtāmbhasi: priyeṇa vadhvā ma-
danārdracetasaḥ
sakhīva kāñcī payasā ghanīkṛtā: babhāra vītoccayabandham
añçukam.

'As her hand, full of water, was laughingly grasped by her lover, 'twas her kindly girdle which the water had stiffened that saved from falling the garment of the loving maiden, for the knot that held it had slipped.' His play of fancy is constant and extensive; he acquired the style of parasol-Bhāravi from his comparison (v. 39) of the lotus dust driven by the winds to the goddess Lakṣmī mirrored in a golden parasol. Still less attractive to our taste is a simile [1] based on the mute letter (*anubandha*) between stem and ending in grammar.

Bhāravi, however, is guilty of errors of taste from which Kālidāsa is free. Especially in Canto xv he sets himself to try *tours de force* of the most foolish kind, redolent of the excesses of the Alexandrian poets. Thus one verse has the first and third, second and fourth lines identical; in another all four are identical; one has practically only *c* and *r*, another only the letters *s*, *ç*, *y*, and *l*; in other stanzas each line reads backwards the same way as the next, or the whole stanza read backwards gives the next; one stanza has three senses; two no labial letters; or each verse can be read backwards and forwards unchanged. One sample must serve:

na nonanunno nunnono nānā nānānanā nanu
nunno 'nunno nanunneno nānenā nunnanunnanut.

'No man is he who is wounded by a low man; no man is the man who wounds a low man, o ye of diverse aspect; the wounded is not wounded if his master is unwounded; not guiltless is he who wounds one sore wounded.' But at least he eschews long compounds, and, taken all in all, is not essentially obscure.

Bhāravi sets a bad example in his fondness for showing his skill in grammar, and he is in many ways the beginner of mannerisms in the later poets. The ridiculously frequent use of the root *tan* begins with him; [2] he is fond of passive perfect forms, including the impersonal use; the adverbial use of prepositional compounds is a favourite form of his; many of Pāṇini's rules of rare type [3] are illustrated by him, as *çās* with double accusative,

[1] xiii. 19; cf. xvii. 6. Cf. Māgha, ii. 47, 95, 112; x. 15; xiv. 66; xvi. 80; xix. 75.

[2] Walter, *Indica*, iii. 34 f.

[3] Cappeller, pp. 153 ff. On the perfect cf. Renou, *La valeur du parfait*, p. 87.

darçayate in the same use, *anujīvisātkṛta*, *stanopapīḍam*, the double negative as a positive, and *na* compounded as in *nanivṛtam*; it occurs also with the imperative. Most interesting in his elaborate care in the use of the narrative tenses, which Kālidāsa and the other poets treat indifferently. In Bhāravi the imperfect and the aorist are not tenses of narrative use; they occur only in dealing with what the speaker has himself experienced (*aparokṣe*), and the imperfect denotes what happened in the more remote past (*anadyatane*), the aorist the immediate past (*adyatane*), exceptions being minimal; the aorist hence is extremely rare, occurring only ten times to 272 times in Māgha. The perfect is the tense of narrative, save in the case of the present perfects *āha* and *veda*. The present occurs with *sma* not rarely in narrative as a past; the participle in *tavant* is used in speeches only, that in *ta* in both. Both the imperative and the aorist with *mā* are found in interrogations beside their normal uses, and *labdhā* is used in the passive, the periphrastic future having always its precise sense of a distant event. Errors in grammar are few, but *ājaghne* seems indefensible.

In metrical form Bhāravi is as developed as he is in the use of the figures of speech, of which scores can be illustrated from his poem. Only once does he condescend to use a single difficult metre, the Udgatā, for a whole canto (xii), a single Praharṣiṇī terminating it. In v he uses sixteen, in xviii also sixteen different forms. The Upajāti of Indravajrā type predominates in iii, xvi, and xvii; Vaṅçasthā in i, iv, and xiv; Vaitālīya in ii; Drutavilambita in xviii; Pramitākṣarā in vi; Praharṣiṇī in vii; Svāgatā in ix; Puṣpitāgrā in x; Çloka in xi and xv; Aupacchandasika in xiii. Of the other metres few save Vasantatilaka [1] have much use; Aparavaktra, Jaloddhatagati, Jaladharamālā occur, like Candrikā, Mattamayūra, Kuṭila, and Vaṅçapattrapatita, once only. The Rathoddhatā is a good deal used in xiii; but Çālinī, Mālinī, Prabhā, and Çikhariṇī are all rare.[2]

In the Çloka Bhāravi conforms in general to the same rules as Kālidāsa. But he never uses the fourth Vipulā form, and in his 250 half-stanzas he uses the first three Vipulās respectively fifteen,

[1] The final syllable is ⏑ in three cases in line *a*, in one case in line *c*.

[2] Thus Bhāravi has eleven or twelve principal metres to six of Kālidāsa and sixteen of Māgha.

eight, and two times; Kālidāsa, on the contrary, likes best the third Vipulā.

2. *Bhaṭṭi*

Bhaṭṭi, the author of the *Rāvaṇavadha*,[1] more usually simply styled *Bhaṭṭikāvya*, tells us that he wrote in Valabhī under Çrīdharasena. But four kings of this name are known, the last of whom died in A.D. 641, so that we remain with nothing more secure than that as a *terminus ad quem*. The suggestion[2] that he is to be identified with Vatsabhaṭṭi of the Mandasor inscription lacks all plausibility, if only for the reason that Vatsabhaṭṭi commits errors in grammar. The name Bhaṭṭi is Prākritized from Bhartṛ, and it is not surprising that in tradition he has been either identified with Bhartṛhari or made a son or half-brother of that famed poet. There is, however, nothing but the name to support the suggestion. We know, however, that he was imitated by Māgha, and it is a perfectly legitimate suggestion that his work gave Māgha the impetus to show his skill in grammar to the extent that he does. More important still is the plain fact that he was known to Bhāmaha. In ending his poem he boasts that it needs a comment:

vyākhyāgamyam idaṁ kāvyam utsavaḥ sudhiyām alam
hatā durmedhasaç cāsmin vidvatpriyatayā mayā.

'This poem can be understood only by a comment; it suffices that it is a feast for the clever and that the stupid come to grief in it as a result of my love of learning.' Bhāmaha rather clumsily repeats in almost identical terms this verse. The list of Alaṁkāras given by Bhaṭṭi is in a certain measure original, when compared with those of Daṇḍin and Bhāmaha; its source is still unknown.

Bhaṭṭi's poem, a lamp in the hands of those whose eye is grammar, but a mirror in the hands of the blind for others, is esssentially intended to serve the double plan of describing Rāma's history and of illustrating the rules of grammar. In the latter aspect its twenty-two cantos fall into four sections; the first

[1] Ed. with Jayamañgala's comm., Bombay, 1887; with Mallinātha, BSS. 1898; i–iv ed. and trans. V. G. Pradhan, Poona, 1897. Cf. Hultzsch, EI. i. 92; Keith, JRAS. 1909, p. 435.

[2] B. C. Mazumdar, JRAS. 1904, pp. 395–7; 1909, p. 759.

four cantos illustrate miscellaneous rules; v–ix the leading rules, x–xiii [1] are given to illustration of the ornaments of poetry, the names of the figures unfortunately being supplied merely in the commentary or the manuscripts, and the rest of the poem illustrates the use of the moods and tenses. The combination of pleasure and profit is by no means ill devised, and Indian opinion gives Bhaṭṭi without hesitation rank as a Mahākavi. It is dubious if any sound taste can justify this position; what is true is that, considering the appalling nature of the obstacle set and the rather hackneyed theme adopted, Bhaṭṭi contrives to produce some fairly interesting and, at its best, both lively and effective verse. His aim in some degree helps his style, as it prevents the adoption of long compounds or too recondite allusions or ideas.

His style may best be judged by a fragment of the scene where Rāvaṇa in his need turns to Kumbhakarṇa for aid, and airs his aorists:

nājñāsīs tvaṁ sukhī Rāmo yad akārṣīt sa rākṣasān
udatārīd udanvantam puraṁ naḥ parito 'rudhat
vyajyotiṣṭa raṇe çastrair anaiṣīd rākṣasān kṣayam.
na prāvocam ahaṁ kiṁcit priyaṁ yāvad ajīviṣam
bandhus tvam arcitaḥ snehān mā dviṣo na vadhīr mama.
vīryam mā na dadarças tvaṁ mā na trāsthāḥ kṣatām puram.
tavādrākṣma vayaṁ vīryaṁ tvam ajaiṣīḥ purā surān.

'Hast thou not known in thy happiness what Rāma hath done to the Rākṣasas? He hath crossed the ocean, and completely hemmed in our city. He hath warred brilliantly and his weapons have brought death to the Rākṣasas. Never in all my life have I spoken one word of flattery; thou hast been honoured by me from love of kin; do not fail to slay my foes. Fail not to show thy might, fail not to guard our smitten town; thy might have we beheld, thou didst aforetime conquer the gods.' The flow of the narrative is, it will be seen, simple and limpid, but it lacks fire and colour, and the task of illustrating the figures of speech proves extremely wearisome to all but the commentators, whose joy the poet was. Some, no doubt, of the passages are happy enough; in one we find a proverb known from the *Vikramorvaçī*: [2]

[1] x is on figures; xi on the quality of sweetness; xii on Bhāvika, vivid description; xiii gives verses which can be read as Sanskrit or Prākrit.

[2] ii. 16 (ed. Pandit).

Rāmo 'pi dārāharaṇena tapto: vayaṁ hatair bandhubhir ātmatulyaiḥ
taptena taptasya yathāyaso naḥ: sandhiḥ pareṇāstu vimuñca Sītām.

'Rāma is aflame through Sītā's rape, we through the death of kinsfolk dear as ourselves; let us make compact with our foe as flaming iron with flaming iron; let Sītā go free.' Another example[1] describes Rāvaṇa's advent:

jalada iva taḍitvān prājyaratnaprabhābhiḥ: pratikakubham udasyan nisvanaṁ dhīramandram
çikharam iva Sumeror āsanaṁ haimam uccair: vividhamaṇivicitram pronnataḥ so 'dhyatiṣṭhat.

'Like a lightning cloud through the rays sparkling from his jewels, and emitting like it on all sides a deep dull resonance, the lofty prince sat him on a high golden throne, radiant with many a gem, as the cloud clings to a pinnacle of mount Sumeru.' The use of *viçāla*, broad, in the next example illustrates the straits into which a poet may be driven, even if he is a grammarian:[2]

kva strīviṣahyāḥ karajāḥ kva vakṣo: daityasya çailendraçilāviçālam
sampaçyataitad dyuṣadāṁ sunītam: bibheda tais tan narasiṅhamūrtiḥ.

'What can finger-nails meet for maidens' breasts avail against the bosom of the demon, that is broad as a rock of the lord of mountains? Nay, consider this cunning scheme of the immortals; with these in his shape as man and lion (Viṣṇu) clove this bosom.'

The chief metre used by Bhaṭṭi is the Çloka, which is used in Cantos iv–ix and xiv–xxii. Upajāti of the Indravajrā type prevails in i–ii, xi and xii. The Gīti form of Āryā prevails in xiii, and x is largely in Puṣpitāgrā; no other metre has any currency of importance. Only Praharṣiṇī. Mālinī, Aupacchandasika, Vaṅçasthā, and Vaitālīya occur six times or more; Açvalalita, Nandana, Pṛthvī, Rucirā, and Narkuṭaka occur only once each; others used are Tanumadhyā, Toṭaka, Drutavilambita, Pramitākṣarā, Praharaṇakalikā, Mandākrāntā, Çārdūlavikrīḍita, and Sragdharā. The

[1] xi. 47; imitated by Māgha, i. 19.
[2] xii. 59; Māgha, i. 47 (below, § 4).

absence of the longer metres in frequent use explains, of course, the comparative ease of the style, for the larger stanzas encourage development both of thought and expression.

3. *Kumāradāsa*

Fate was long unkind to the *Jānakīharaṇa*[1] of Kumāradāsa, since it left the poem preserved only in a Sinhalese word-for-word translation, though, since first published from this source, it has come to light in southern India, where Sanskrit literature has often found preservation denied in the north. Ceylonese tradition of no early date or value asserts the identity of the author with a king of Ceylon (A.D. 517–26) who is connected, as we have seen, in tradition with the death of Kālidāsa. What is certain is that Kumāradāsa was a zealous admirer of Kālidāsa and very freely imitates him in manner as well as in general treatment of the subject, as comparison of Canto xii of the *Raghuvaṅça* with the relevant portions of the *Jānakīharaṇa* establishes beyond cavil. On the other hand, it is really beyond question that he knew the *Kāçikā Vṛtti* (*c.* A.D. 650), while on the other hand he must have been known to Vāmana (*c.* A.D. 800) who censures the use of *khalu* as first word, found in Kumāradāsa, and cites a stanza which in content and form proclaims itself as unquestionably a citation from the lost part of the *Jānakīharaṇa*. Finally, he was probably earlier than Māgha, who seems to echo a verse of his. Rājaçekhara, the poet (*c.* A.D. 900), asserts his fame:[2]

Jānakīharaṇaṁ kartuṁ Raghuvaṅçe sthite sati
kaviḥ Kumāradāsaç ca Rāvaṇaç ca yadi kṣamaḥ.

'No poet save Kumāradāsa could dare to sing the rape of Sītā when the *Raghuvaṅça* was current, even as none but Rāvaṇa could perform the deed, when Raghu's line remained on earth.'

The *Jānakīharaṇa* suffers, of course, from the trite theme; Sanskrit poetry affords us a very vivid explanation of the com-

[1] Ed. Ceylon, 1891; i–x, Bombay, 1907; xvi, BSOS. iv. 285 ff. See Leumann, WZKM. vii. 226 ff.; Thomas, JRAS. 1901, pp. 253 ff.; Keith, *ibid.*, 578 ff.

[2] In the *Kāvyamīmāṅsā* he mentions his blindness, as also that of Medhāvirudra (p. 12).

plaint of a great poet: *cui non dictus Hylas puer et Latonia Delos*, for we actually have so many poems on the same theme preserved for us. Still, it is fair to say that Kumāradāsa does very well indeed in handling his story; his invention is negligible, but he uses effectively the innumerable opportunities for description which the theme offers. Thus we have poetic pictures of Daçaratha and his wives as well as of Ayodhyā (i); in ii Bṛhaspati, in appealing to Viṣṇu for aid, sketches the exploits of Rāvaṇa; in iii he revels in his themes; the king and his wives disport in the garden, then, as in Bhāravi, we have the king's own description of the scene; the poet then describes the sports in the water, the king the sunset, then night and morning are sketched. Cantos iv and v carry on the narrative, the one from the birth of Daçaratha's sons to the slaying of the Rākṣasī who plagues the hermitage, the other to the close of the defeat of the Rākṣasa host. In vi the scene shifts to Mithilā where Viçvāmitra and Janaka exchange greetings. In vii Sītā and Rāma meet; he describes her beauty, the poet their love and marriage. Then follows the picture of the joys of their union ending with a fine description of sunset and night (viii). The next canto brings us to Ayodhyā, and in x the poet shows his command of the maxims of politics by giving us a lecture from Daçaratha, who proposes to crown Rāma, on the duties of the sovereign. Events are crowded together, and Sītā is stolen before the canto closes. With equal haste are related the reception of the news by Rāma, his alliance with Hanumant who fights Vāli; the poet then turns to the more graceful theme of the rainy season, which he first himself and then through Rāma describes with considerable beauty. Canto xii matches the description of spring (iii) with a picture of autumn; then policy once more has its turn, for Sugrīva tenders ill counsel and Lakṣmaṇa rebukes him. Rāma is dejected, and to cheer him Sugrīva describes the mountain, while in xiv we have first a picture of the monkeys as they build the causeway, then Rāma's impression of the scene, after which the poet resumes the description and presents a lively impression of the crossing of the host. Canto xv gives us the mission of Añgada as envoy to Rāvaṇa; Canto xvi the revels of the Rākṣasas; xvii–xx Rāma's triumph.

Kālidāsa influenced Kumāradāsa in style as well as subject;

he adopts the Vaidarbha form,[1] and he develops in a marked degree the love of alliteration, though he never carries it to the point of affectation, as in the efforts of such poets as Māgha to produce effects by the constant repetition of a single letter. Nor is he fond of the Yamaka form to any undue degree: a good example is:

atanunātanunā ghanadārubhiḥ: smarahitaṁ rahitaṁ pradidhakṣuṇā
rucirabhācirabhāsitavartmanā: prakhacitā khacitā na na dīpitā.

'Strong love, eager to burn the lover deserted, kindled with cloud-logs the sky refulgent and irradiated with the lightning.' Prettiness is, perhaps, the chief characteristic of Kumāradāsa; he abounds in dainty conceits expressed with a felicity of diction and a charm of sound and metre which no language but Sanskrit can produce. Thus we have a pretty picture of the naughty Rāma as a child:

na sa Γāma iha kva yāta ity: anuyukto vanitābhir agrataḥ
nijahastapuṭāvṛtānano: vidadhe 'līkanilīnam arbhakaḥ.

'"Rāma is not here; where has he gone?" the women called as they searched for him, but the child, covering his face with his clasped hands, played hide-and-seek with them.' Though flagrant imitations of Kālidāsa, these stanzas are not unworthy of that poet:

puṣparatnavibhavair yathepsitaṁ: sā vibhūṣayati rājanandane
darpaṇaṁ tu na cakāṅkṣa yoṣitāṁ: svāmisammadaphalaṁ hi maṇḍanam.

'With richness of jewels and flowers she adorned herself before the prince as was his will; but she sought not a mirror, for woman's tiring hath its guerdon in her lord's delight.'

[1] Nandargikar (*Kumāradāsa*, p. xxiv) asserts that he uses the Gauḍī, but this exaggerates, though he may have known Māgha. The reverse is probable; cf. *Jān.* iii. 34 f. with Māgha, v. 29; below, § 4. Walter (*Indica*, iii. 34, 36) claims that Bhāravi borrows the use of *tan* and perfect impersonal passives from him, but this is doubtless the reverse of the truth.

kaitavena kalaheṣu suptayā: sa kṣipan vasanam āttasādhvasaḥ
cora ity uditahāsavibhramaṁ: sapragalbham avakhaṇḍito 'dhare.

'In their dalliance she feigned to fall asleep; then as he touched her robe in diffidence, "Thief!" she exclaimed in laughing confusion, and boldly kissed him on the lips.' Another verse, describing love-weariness, proves use of Canto viii of the *Kumārasambhava*: [1]

tasya hastam abalā vyapohitum: mekhalāguṇasamīpasaṅginam
mandaçaktir aratiṁ nyavedayal: lolanetragalitena vāriṇā.

'Though in her weariness she had not strength to push away the hand that sought to loosen her girdle, still she showed her indifference by the tears that fell from her glancing eyes.' A famous crux in the creation of woman's beauty is posed:

paçyan hato manmathabāṇapātaiḥ: çakto vidhātuṁ na mimīla cakṣuḥ
ūrū vidhātrā hi kṛtau kathaṁ tāv: ity āsa tasyāṁ sumater vitarkaḥ.

'If he looked, then love's darts must have pierced his heart; if he closed his eyes, he could not have seen to create; how then did the creator fashion the beauty of her limbs? Thus even the wisest was at fault.' Love and nature are inseparably blended:

prāleyakālapriyaviprayoga-: glāneva rātriḥ kṣayam āsasāda
jagāma mandaṁ divaso vasanta-: krūrātapaçrānta iva krameṇa.

'Night perished, as a maiden fadeth through severance from her lover in winter's cold, and in her place slow came the day, as though wearied by the fierce spring heat.'

In another stanza we may have a reminiscence of Bhāravi: [2]

vāsantikasyāñçucayena bhānor: hemantam ālokya hataprabhāvam
saroruhām uddhṛtakaṇṭakena: prītyeva ramyaṁ jahase vanena.

[1] viii. 14 is copied in Kumāradāsa, viii. 8 and 24.
[2] x. 36 compared with *Jānakīharaṇa*, iii. 9; cf. ix. 21 with i. 4.

'Seeing that winter's prowess had been quelled by the army of the rays of the spring sun, sweetly laughed the forest in its joy that the tormenter of the lotuses had been banished.'

Though not a pedant, Kumāradāsa was a keen student of grammar, and there is no doubt that he must rank as an authority of some weight in judging the correctness of disputed forms. He himself sneers in a paronomasia at bad poets who spoil their compositions by the use of such particles [1] as *tu*, *hi*, *na*, by incorrect employment of roots, and by hiding their meaning through wrong words, and doubtless he had authority for such formations as *halacarma*, furrow, where *carma* is clearly from *car*, go, and *maruta*, a by-form of *marut*. He borrows from the *Kāçikā* the rare forms *vitūst-*, to comb one's top-knot, *marmāvidh*, piercing the vitals, *satyāp-*, declare truth, and such aorists as *acakamata*; other rare terms from the grammarians are *anyataredyus*, one day, *āyaḥçūlikatā*, violence, *ikṣuçākaṭa*, field of sugar cane, *jampatī*, husband and wife, *nīçāra*, covering, *paçyatohara*, robber in broad daylight, *pravara*, covering, *bhidelima*, fit to be broken, *muṣṭiṁdhaya*, fist-sucking baby, *çāyikā*, sloth, and *saukharātrika*, asking if one has slept well. Of constructions he has very freely adverbial prepositional compounds, the impersonal use of the perfect passive, and the weird passive *muninā joṣam abhūyata*, 'the sage rejoiced'. The accusative with *sarvatas* and *ubhayatas* is grammatical; *kālasya kasyacit* has a similar origin, but *samāḥ sahasrāṇi* seems careless and *doṣā* as instrumental of *doṣan* is unparalleled; the use of *khalu* and *iva* at the beginning of lines is quite wrong, and censured by Vāmana as regards *khalu*.[2] From Vālmīki he has *tanucchada*, feather, from Kālidāsa *avarṇa*, shame, and *ajarya*, friendship. His love of periphrasis is remarkable: he styles himself even Kumāraparicāraka.

Kumāradāsa's use of metre is skilled, but he follows in the main the manner of Kālidāsa without seeking the elaboration of the use of many shifting metres as in Bhāravi. The Çloka [3] is

[1] Already in *Vāsavadattā* (p. 134); see *Jān.* i. 89; viii. 29.

[2] xiii. 39. In Māgha, ii. 70 the use is correct, as *khalu* there equals *alam*. Nandargikar (pp. xii f.) gives some dubious words, *klamathu*, *āsa* as perfect, *tapasyadbhavanam*, *jayamānam* as middle, *ātmasu* as plural.

[3] In 424 half-stanzas in ii, vi, and x there are only 10 Vipulās, 8 first, 1 second (irregular ◡ — — — beginning), 1 third; 4 fourth Vipulās in Nandargikar's ed. must be false readings. Before the first Vipulā the first foot is 6 times ⏑̄ — — — or ⏑̄ ◡ — — as against 2 ⏑̄ — ◡ —, a phenomenon like the facts in Kālidāsa.

dominant in Cantos ii, vi, and x; Drutavilambita in xi; Pramitākṣarā in xiii; Upajāti of Indravajrā type in i, iii, and vii; Vaṅçasthā in v, ix, xii, and iii. 64–76; Vaitālīya in iv; and Rathoddhatā in viii. The minor metres are Çārdūlavikrīḍita, Çikhariṇī, Sragdharā, Puṣpitāgrā (xvi), Praharṣiṇī, Vasantatilaka, Avitatha, Mandākrāntā, and Mālinī.

4. *Māgha*

All that Māgha tells us of himself is the fact that his father was Dattaka Sarvāçraya, and his grandfather, Suprabhadeva, was the minister of a king whose name is variously read by the manuscripts as Varmalākhya, Varmalāta, &c. Now an inscription[1] exists of a certain king Varmalāta of A.D. 625, and it is plausible to hold that thus we can date Māgha somewhere in the later part of the seventh century. This accords satisfactorily with the fact that he is clearly later than Bhāravi, who in a sense was his model, than Bhaṭṭi, whose *mumuhur muhuḥ* he trumps with his *kim u muhur mumuhur gatabhartṛkāḥ*, 'ever and again they fainted, their spouses gone', and probably than Kumāradāsa. Nor is there really any doubt that Māgha knew the *Kāçikā Vṛtti.* What is more important is that in ii. 112 the only natural interpretation of the verse is that we have a reference to the Nyāsakāra, a commentator on the *Kāçikā*, Jinendrabuddhi, whose date must be *c.* A.D. 700. It is much wiser to accept this date, and to place Māgha about that time than to endeavour to explain the passage away, and there is no reason whatever to think the date too late. He certainly knew the *Nāgānanda* of Harṣa, and the effort to prove that he was used by Subandhu, though very ingenious, is unconvincing. It is simplest to recognize that the similarities between the two writers, if not due to their working in the same field with similar models, is due to Māgha's knowledge of the romance of *Vāsavadattā.*[2]

Māgha's theme is borrowed like that of Bhāravi from the *Mahābhārata*,[3] but, while Bhāravi magnifies Çiva, Māgha's

[1] Kielhorn, GN. 1906, pp. 143 f.; JRAS. 1908, p. 499. Cf. Jacobi, WZKM. iv. 236 ff.; Bhandarkar, EI. ix. 187 ff.; Hultzsch, ZDMG. lxxii. 147; Walter, *Indica*, iii. 32 (Māgha, xx. 47, *Jānakīharaṇa*, i. 4).

[2] The text is ed. NSP. 1923. Trans. up to xi. 25 by C. Schütz, Bielefeld, 1843; extracts Cappeller, *Bālamāgha* (1915), and as a whole by Hultzsch, *Asia Major*, ii.

[3] ii. 33–45.

favourite god is Viṣṇu ; the contrast is doubtless deliberate, just as in Cantos iv and xix he sets himself out to vie with Cantos iv and xv of the *Kirātārjunīya* as studies in variety of metre and curiosities of form respectively. The epic tale is simple ; Kṛṣṇa encourages Yudhiṣṭhira to perform his royal consecration. The rite proceeds, and Bhīṣma's counsel results in the award to Kṛṣṇa of the present of honour. Çiçupāla, king of Cedi, is wroth and leaves the hall ; Yudhiṣṭhira would follow him and appease him, but Bhīṣma extols Kṛṣṇa and restrains him. Çiçupāla stirs up revolt and seeks to destroy the sacrifice. Yudhiṣṭhira seeks Bhīṣma's counsel as usual ; he is advised to trust Kṛṣṇa and defy the king. The latter insults Bhīṣma who retorts by a denunciation of him, and explains that Kṛṣṇa has been under a promise to the king's mother to endure a hundred deeds of evil of her son. Çiçupāla then transfers his vituperation to Kṛṣṇa, who replies, evoking a fresh onslaught of words, including a reproach for Kṛṣṇa's theft of his affianced bride. Kṛṣṇa replies that he has now fulfilled his pledge, and with his discus severs the head of his foe. Māgha shows decided originality in touching up this theme ; in Canto i we have a new *motif* ; the sage Nārada appears in the house of Vasudeva where Kṛṣṇa lives, and in the name of Indra bids the hero dispose of the Cedi king whose hostility menaces men and gods. This affords Māgha the opportunity of displaying his skill in politics ; Kṛṣṇa takes counsel with Balarāma and Uddhava ; the former advises immediate war, the latter acceptance of the invitation to Yudhiṣṭhira's consecration. Then, imitating Bhāravi in Cantos iv–xi, he leaves his original entirely and proceeds to exhibit his skill in a longer series of descriptions. Kṛṣṇa leaves Dvārakā for Indraprastha, not without a fine picture of his capital (iii). Mount Raivataka is reached, and Dāruka, his charioteer, expatiates to Kṛṣṇa on its loveliness (iv). The army encamps, enabling Māgha to air his knowledge of campaigns as they should be conducted in poetry (v) ; needless to say the women are not forgotten : the queens accompany the host in litters, their ladies ride on horses or the humble ass, the hetairai swarm and make their toilets for their masters ; soldiers, elephants, and women alike must enjoy the bath. Kṛṣṇa himself must have pleasure ; so the six seasons as fair maidens appear to give one more opportunity of picturing love (vi). No wonder that the Yādavas imitate him; with fair ladies they wander in the woods (vii), and share the bath (viii). The sun, charmed by the appearance of these heroes, desires to imitate them and bathe in the waters of the western ocean; thus we have a very elaborate and often happy picture of the sunset and the rising of the moon, which waken again love in the hearts of the women, who send their eyes and their invitations to their lovers (ix). They are only too eager to accept them, and after drinking together they indulge in the joys of love (x). Day dawns (xi), the army awakens to its duties, and the Yamunā is crossed (xii), Kṛṣṇa enters Indraprastha and is welcomed by Yudhiṣṭhira; the poet remembers to vie with Açvaghoṣa and Kālidāsa in describing the feelings of the women who crowd to see him enter. We now return to the narrative of the epic, but in more polished form. The ceremony is performed, Kṛṣṇa receives the gift of honour (xiv). Çiçupāla protests, Bhīṣma challenges him, he leaves the hall and prepares his army for battle (xv). A *tour de force* follows; Çiçupāla's envoy brings a message of set ambiguity, either a defiance or a submission; Sātyaki answers it, and the envoy replies haughtily (xvi). The two armies move forward to battle (xvii); their contest is described at length, not without ability, though, like nearly every Sanskrit writer, he gives the impression of painting his picture from books, not life and death. In the end the two rivals meet, fight with their arrows, then with supernatural weapons, until Kṛṣṇa slays his foe, whose power passes over to the victor.

The changes made in the epic narrative are not inconsiderable. One great improvement is the shortening of the rival speeches, though even so they remain long. The picture of the sacrifice replaces the single line given to it in the epic, and the preliminaries of the contest are carried on not by the the rivals but by envoys. More important is the imitation of Bhāravi's procedure in making a struggle between rival armies precede the duel.

Admitting that these stories taken over from the epic gave little scope for the highest qualities of poetry, and that, as in Bhāravi, plot and characterization are of no great account, Māgha unquestionably has no mean poetical merits, though we need not accept the eulogies of later critics who claimed that he united the merits of his greatest rivals. If he lacks the conciseness, the calm serenity and dignity of Bhāravi at his best, he possesses much luxuriance of expression and imagination, and in the many love passages of his epic sweetness and prettinesses abound. He admits directly his indebtedness to the *Kāmasūtra* and exhibits intimate knowledge of its details in a manner which western taste finds tedious, while Indian opinion—*homo sum, humani nil a me alienum puto*—accepts it with admiration. The worst of his sins is his deplorable exhibition in xix of his power of twisting language. He actually compares the array of the army to the appearance of a Mahākāvya when verses are put in the form of the figures Sarvatobhadra, Cakra, Gomūtrikā, &c., and such figures he illustrates in his poem. No doubt we hear in the Alexandrian age, as in later Roman poetry,[1] of such things as Sotadean verses to be read backwards, of Simmias making poems, *technopaignia*, in the form of an axe, or a nightingale's egg, of Dosiadas's similar feat with an altar, and so on. It may be that these tricks arose from the practice of writing inscriptions on swords or leaves, but in any case Māgha shows himself devoid of taste; so also in the construction of such a stanza as xix. 3 where the first line has no consonant but *j*, the second only *t*, the third *bh*, and the last *r* with a final Visarga. More clever is the speech of the envoy in xv which begins:

abhidhāya tadā tad apriyaṁ: Çiçupālo 'nuçayam paraṁ gataḥ
bhavato 'bhimānaḥ samīhate: saruṣaḥ kartum upetya mānanam.

'Çiçupala, having merited your displeasure, in deep regret (in high anger) seeks eagerly (fearlessly) to come before you and pay due homage (slay you).' These *double entendres* are beloved in India, and Bhāravi has a fair number, but it is impossible, while admitting their cleverness, to cultivate a real taste for such tricks. Moreover they have a fatal effect on language; if a double sense is to be expressed, it is impossible for the best of poets to avoid straining meanings, constructions, and word order. The effort leads to constant ransacking of the poetical lexicons extant and turns the pursuit of poetry into an intellectual exercise of no high value to the utter ruin of emotion and thought.

Happily there is much in Māgha to make up for his demerits.

[1] Cf. Martial, ii. 86. 9 f.: turpe est difficiles habere nugas
et stultus labor est ineptiarum.

He can imitate the good sense and simplicity of Bhāravi's moral sentiments :

nālambate daiṣṭikatāṁ na niṣīdati pauruṣe
çabdārthau satkavir iva dvayaṁ vidvān apekṣate.

'He relies not on fate, he depends not on human power alone ; as a good poet has regard to sound and sense alike, so he cultivates both.' Or again :

saṁpadā susthirammanyo bhavati svalpayāpi yaḥ
kṛtakṛtyo vidhir manye na vardhayati tasya tām.

'If a man think himself established securely by a slight success, then, I ween, Fate, having accomplished all he seeks, affords him no further blessing.' In more elaborate style, with a distinct aim at suiting sense and sound, he vies with Bhaṭṭi [1] and echoes perhaps a phrase of K māradāsa : [2]

saṭāchaṭābhinnaghanena bibhratā : nṛsiṅha saiṅhīm atanuṁ
tanuṁ tvayā
sa mugdhakāntastanasaṅgabhaṅgurair : urovidāram prati-
caskare nakhaiḥ.

'O man-lion, when thou didst assume that mighty lion form and cleft with thy tawny mane the clouds, thou didst tear him to pieces, rending asunder his breast with those nails which bend so gently on a loving maiden's bosom.' There is a martial tone in :

āyāntīnām aviratarayaṁ rājakānīkinīnām
itthaṁ sainyaiḥ samam alaghubhiḥ çrīpater ūrmimadbhiḥ
āsīd oghair muhur iva mahad vāridher āpagānāṁ
dolāyuddhaṁ kṛtagurutaradhvānam auddhatyabhājām.

'As the hosts of the king with unbroken flow, with unceasing clamour in their proud onslaught, advanced against the vast armies of Kṛṣṇa, there arose a battle swaying to and fro as when the waters of the streams mingle with the foaming waves of ocean.' More commonplace but neatly phrased is :

sajalāmbudharāravānukārī : dhvanir āpūritadiṅmukho ra-
thasya
praguṇīkṛtakekam ūrdhvakaṇṭhaiḥ : çitikaṇṭhair upakar-
ṇayāmbabhūva.

[1] xii. 59 ; Māgha, i. 47.

[2] xi. 45.

'The roar of the chariot, matching the thunder of the rain-cloud and filling the air, was eagerly echoed by the peacocks, who stretched out their necks and redoubled their loud calls.' There is real strength in this vignette of the battle:

tūryārāvair āhitottālatālair: gāyantībhiḥ kāhalaṁ kāhalābhiḥ
nṛtte cakṣuḥçūnyahastaprayogaṁ: kāye kūjan kambur uccair jahāsa.

'Over a corpse that danced blindly moving its hands midst the loud roll of the drums and the trumpet's clangour, the conch rang shrill as it laughed aloud.'

Extremely characteristic is the plan of blending the emotion of love with war; we have two strange pictures of a stricken field, wholly Indian in spirit:

kaçcin mūrchām etya gāḍhaprahāraḥ: siktaḥ çītaiḥ çīkarair vāraṇasya
ucchaçvāsa prasthitā taṁ jighṛkṣur: vyarthākūtā nākanārī mumūrcha.

'One, sore smitten, fainted; then drenched with cool water from his elephant's trunk breathed again, and the heavenly nymph, who had started to seize him, her purpose foiled, fell back fainting.'

tyaktaprāṇaṁ saṁyuge hastinīsthā: vīkṣya premṇā tatkṣaṇād udgatāsuḥ
prāpyākhaṇḍaṁ devabhūyaṁ satītvād: āçiçleṣa svaiva kaṁcit puraṁdhrī.

'One lady who seated on an elephant had seen her beloved slain in the battle and on the spot died from grief, winning by her faith complete divinity, embraced once more in heaven her husband.' Māgha, however, is capable of very effective strength and simplicity, especially in the speeches of his heroes, as in Çiçupāla's dignified protest against the honour paid by Yudhiṣṭhira to Kṛṣṇa:

yad apūpujas tvam iha Pārtha: Murajitam apūjitaṁ satām
prema vilasati mahad tad aho: dayitaṁ janaḥ khalu guṇīti manyate.

anṛtāṁ giraṁ na gadasīti: jagati paṭahair vighuṣyase
nindyam atha ca Harim arcayatas: tava karmaṇaiva vikasaty asatyatā.

'That thou hast honoured, o king, the slayer of Mura, unhonoured by the good, doth prove thy partiality; one, forsooth, deemeth virtuous him whom he loveth. "Thou sayst no word of falsehood", so art thou proclaimed with beat of drum throughout the world; yet by having honour paid to the worthless Hari, thou dost blazon abroad thy falsity.' We prefer this eloquence to the ingenuity which won him the sobriquet of bell-Māgha, because of his cleverness [1] in comparing a mountain, on one side of which the sun set, while on the other the moon rose, to an elephant from whose back two bells hung, one on either side. His use of figures is free and often, as may be seen above, happy; his alliterations usually have point and effect.

Māgha is an adept in language and affords abundant exemplification of grammatical rules,[2] very possibly under Bhaṭṭi's influence. His periphrastic perfects passive such as *bibharāmbabhūve* are frequent; rare uses are *madhyesamudram* and *pārejalam*; *vairāyitāras* is from the denominative *vairāyate*; *aghaṭate*, *niṣedivān*, and *nyadhāyiṣātām* are recondite forms; purely borrowed from Pāṇini are the unique use in i. 51 of the imperative to express repeated action, and of the future in lieu of the imperfect after a verb of remembering.

As regards metre Māgha's chief feat is his accomplishment in Canto iv when he manages to use twenty-two as opposed to the mere sixteen of Bhāravi's corresponding *tour de force*. The Çloka is the most common, being the basis of Cantos ii and xix; Upajāti of Vaṅçasthā type prevails in i and xii; the Indravajrā type [3] in iii; the Udgatā in xv; the Aupacchandasika in xx; the Drutavilambita in vi; the Puṣpitāgrā in vii; the Pramitākṣarā in ix; the Praharṣiṇī in viii; the Mañjubhāṣiṇī in xiii; the Mālinī in xi; the Rathoddhatā in xiv, and the Rucirā, Vasantatilaka,[3]

[1] iv. 20; Peterson, OC. VI, III. ii. 339.

[2] Cappeller, *Bālamāgha*, pp. 187 f.

[3] In these metres occasionally *a* and *c* end in ◡, a licence as a rule permissible only in the even lines; cf. Vāmana, v. 1. 2 f.; *Sāhityadarpaṇa* 575. He uses a short final thrice in the first, once in the second Vipulā; Bhāravi never permits this, and Kālidāsa only once, doubtfully, has ◡ in the first Vipulā.

Vaitālīya, and Çālinī in xvii, v, xvi, and xviii respectively, an enumeration which shows how proud was Māgha of his skill in varying the metre of the cantos. The Svāgatā in x was doubtless borrowed from Bhāravi, and Bilhaṇa in his turn freely uses this rare form. The Gīti form of Āryā occurs twice, while there is but one stanza each of the Utsara, Kalahaṅsa, Citralekhā, Jaladharamālā, Jaloddhatagati, Toṭaka, Dodhaka, Dhṛtaçrī, Pṛthvī, Prabhā, Pramadā, Bhramaravilasita, Mañjarī, Mahāmālikā, Vaṅçapattrapatita, Vaiçvadevī, Çikhariṇī, Sragdharā, Sragviṇī, and Hariṇī. The Mattamayūra, Mandākrāntā, and Çārdūlavikrīḍita have two, three, and four stanzas apiece.

In his use of the Çloka Māgha has out of 464 half-stanzas 125 cases of Vipulā forms, 47 of the first, 44 of the second, and 34 of the third, no case of the fourth being allowed.[1] This frequency of use is in striking contrast to that of Kālidāsa and Bhāravi, for he has one Vipulā in every three or four verses while in the others the proportions range from one to twelve or fourteen. Kālidāsa again prefers the third to the second Vipulā, while Bhāravi hardly has the third, and Māgha treats them equally. Māgha is not quite so polished a writer as Bhāravi, for he allows the weak caesura in *manāg abhyāvṛttyā vā*, and in xi. 18 and 22 omits this caesura entirely, without the excuse of recondite forms of xix. 52 and 108. A further sign of decline in feeling is the almost equal use in the case of the first Vipulā of the form ⏓ – ⏑ – for the first foot as opposed to ⏓ ⏓ – –, the figures being twenty-one to twenty-six; Māgha evidently did not appreciate the desirability of differentiating between the treatment of the first and second Vipulās. From his frequent employment of Vipulās Jacobi[2] suggests a western origin for the poet, having regard to the similar fact in the case of Hemacandra, and the poet's knowledge of the Vindhya, but this conclusion must be deemed uncertain.

[1] In SIFI. VIII. ii. 55 the figures are given as 45, 45, 33, and 3, different readings being followed.

[2] IS. xvii. 444. His style, however, is Gauḍa, not Vaidarbha. Tradition makes him a native of Çrīmāla, and this place may have been under Varmalāta's rule.

VI

THE LESSER EPIC POETS

NO other of the epic poets who have come down to us stands on the level of those whom we have reviewed, and of the early epic poets whose works are now lost we have far too little to be able to form any judgement of their true merit. Of Meṇṭha, or Bhartṛmeṇṭha, also called Hastipaka, Kalhaṇa[1] tells us that the king Mātṛgupta, himself a poet, found his *Hayagrīvavadha* so charming that he rewarded the poet by giving him a golden dish to place below it when it was being bound, lest the flavour should escape; delighted with this sign of appreciation the poet felt the reward needless. Mātṛgupta was according to Kalhaṇa a predecessor of Pravarasena, and his personality has suffered a confusion with Kālidāsa by unwise conjecture. His date must remain doubtful, but he is credited with a comment on the *Nāṭyaçāstra* of Bharata of which quotations remain. Kalhaṇa cites textually two stanzas, the former of which is heavy and laboured, the latter deserves citation:

nākāram udvahasi naiva vikatthase tvaṁ: ditsāṁ na sūcayasi muñcasi satphalāni
niḥçabdavarṣaṇam ivāmbudharasya rājan: saṁlakṣyate phalata eva tava prasādaḥ.

'Thou dost display no emotion, nor dost thou boast; thou dost not reveal thy intention to give, but dost yield thy fair fruits; as when the cloud sheds its rain without a sound, so from its fruit alone, o king, is thy favour revealed.' Meṇṭha receives the compliment, such as it is, of being placed second in the spiritual lineage of Vālmīki, Meṇṭha, Bhavabhūti and Rājaçekhara, while Mañkha places him beside Subandhu, Bhāravi, and Bāṇa. Some pretty verses are cited from him in the anthologies, as usual with dubious correctness, but one may be quoted:

[1] iii. 125 ff., 260 ff. Cf. Peterson, *Subh.*, pp. 92 ff., 117 ff.; Aufrecht, ZDMG. xxvii. 51; xxxvi. 368. Thomas (*Kavīndravacanasamuccaya*) gives references to anthology verses for these poets.

tathāpy akṛtakottālahāsapallavitādharam
mukhaṁ grāmavilāsinyāḥ sakalaṁ rājyam arhati.

'None the less the face of the village maiden, when her lower lip blossoms in an unfeigned loud laughter, is worth a whole kingdom.' If we trust such evidence as there is regarding the date of Pravarasena,[1] successor of Mātṛgupta on the throne of Kashmir, we may set Menṭha towards the latter part of the sixth century, and make him a contemporary of the author of the *Setubandha.*

Not much later falls the *Rāvaṇārjunīya* [2] or *Ārjunarāvaṇīya* of Bhaumaka, also styled Bhīma, Bhūma, or Bhūmaka, who won fame in Kashmir. The epic in twenty-seven cantos tells the tale, found in the *Rāmāyaṇa*, of the strife between Arjuna Kārtavīrya and Rāvaṇa, but as in the case of Bhaṭṭi, whose example may have been followed, though the dates are indecisive, the aim is to illustrate rules of grammar. The pedantic side predominates in the later work, *Kavirahasya* [3] of Halāyudha, which is really meant to illustrate the modes of formation of the present tense of Sanskrit roots, but incidentally serves as a eulogy of the Rāṣṭrakūṭa king Kṛṣṇa III (*c.* A.D. 940–56).

Kashmir under Avantivarman before the close of the ninth century gives us a Buddhist epic of some interest, the *Kapphaṇābhyudaya*,[4] which is based on a tale in the *Avadānaçataka* of the conversion of a king of the south who had harboured evil designs against the king of Çrāvastī. This topic is treated by Çivasvāmin in the full epic manner, manifestly under the influence of Māgha and of Bhāravi, for the structure of the poem is manifestly based on that of the *Kirātārjunīya* as well as of the *Çiçupālavadha.* The poem opens with a description of Kapphaṇa and Līlāvatī, his royal capital (i). A spy bears the news of the pride of Prasenajit and of his just rule, as in *Kirātārjunīya* i. The princes at the court are in confusion at the news (iii); there is held a council of war (iv), and an envoy is dispatched to bear the threat of war to Prasenajit (v). Then occurs the usual digression; the king is

[1] Cf. Stein, *Rājatar.*, i. 83 f.

[2] Ed. KM. 68, 1900. Cf. Trivedī, *Bhaṭṭikāvya*, i. pp. x f.

[3] Ed. Greifswald, 1900. A *Yudhiṣṭhiravijaya* with a continuation, *Dhātukāvya*, dealing with the Bhārata story and grammar and roots (KM. x. 52–231) is ascribed to a Vāsudeva; cf. possibly the Vāsudeva of the rimed poems (JRAS. 1925, pp. 264 ff.).

[4] Śeshagiri, *Report*, 1893–4, pp. 49 ff.; Aufrecht, ZDMG. xxvii. 92 f.; Thomas, *Kavīndravacanasamuccaya*, pp. 111 ff.; Mitra, *Nep. Buddh. Lit.*, p. 38 (Kapphiṇa of the Dakṣiṇāpatha).

induced by a Vidyādhara to visit with him the Malaya mountain in order there to devise a plan of campaign (vi), in reality to allow of the time-honoured descriptions, in which he vies as regards figures of sound with *Çiçupālavadha* iv and *Kirātārjunīya* v. Then are fully developed the encampment of the host (vii), the seasons which unite on the mountain in order to permit of the poet describing them all in one canto (viii), the sports of the army with its women in the water (ix), then their amusements in roaming the woods and picking flowers (x). Sunset is now due (xi), and the moon must rise (xii), to excite the damsels to join with their unwarlike swains in a drinking bout (xiii), and then in the mysteries of love in the best manner of the Kāmaçāstra (xiv). The end of the night and daybreak are now inevitable (xv). The host, refreshed and encouraged by its debaucheries, marches (xvi), and a long drawn out conflict (xvii–xix) results in the conversion of Kapphaṇa (xx). The anthologies have some quite pretty verses, but all is very much at second hand, and in this case the master is decidedly superior to the pupil. The author clearly was well read in Sanskrit literature, and, very naturally for a Buddhist, he has a reference to the *Nāgānanda* of Harṣa in an allusion to the piles of bones of Nāgas slain by Garuḍa heaped up on the seashore beyond the Malaya mountains.

Māgha's great influence is seen also in the *Haravijaya*,[1] the work of another Kashmirian, Ratnākara with the styles Rājānaka and Vāgīçvara, who flourished under Bṛhaspati or Cippaṭa Jayāpīḍa and Avantivarman, and was thus in his prime about A.D. 850. The theme is of the lightest, the slaying of the demon Andhaka, born of Çiva when Pārvatī playfully covered his eyes with her hands. The child thus unhappily born blind grows up, by austerities wins sight, and becomes master of the three worlds until, as usual, Çiva finds it necessary to kill him. The plan is the same scheme we have seen already; Çiva's capital must be described (i), then his Tāṇḍava dance (ii), the seasons (iii), and mount Mandara (iv, v). Then comes in the *motif* of the appeal of the seasons, headed by spring, to Çiva for protection against the new conqueror. Çiva's counsellors now debate, and the poet has

[1] Ed. with Alaka's comm., KM. 22, 1890. For anthology verses see Peterson, *Subhāṣitāvali*, pp. 96 ff.; Aufrecht, ZDMG. xxxvi. 372 ff. For imitation of Māgha, cf. Jacobi, WZKM. iv. 240 f.; Dhruva, v. 25.

up to Canto xvi to display his perfection in the art of politics. After all the talk an envoy is dispatched to the demon to bid him retire from the realms he has usurped. Here is the moment for the usual digression, and we have thirteen cantos of the sports of the retinue of Çiva, precisely of the same sort already recorded, including sunrise, sunset, the stormy sea, and a very careful exposition of the practice of the Kāmaçāstra in xxix. The envoy at last reaches the demon's kingdom in heaven, which necessarily must be described at length (xxxi). The exchange of speeches which follows requires seven cantos. The envoy naturally returns without having accomplished anything save a prodigious amount of bad rhetoric; the forces of Çiva take four cantos to be made ready for battle—for which their amorous sports would seem to render them dubiously fitted. They prove somewhat mediocre warriors, but after Canto xlvii has been variegated by the insertion of a hymn to the dread goddess Caṇḍī, the poem is allowed to close at Canto l with the death of the miscreant. The poet claims to have imitated Bāṇa, and some notice is taken of him in the anthologies, but, though he is doubtless responsible for some good stanzas, and Kṣemendra attests his skill in the Vasantatilaka metre, his poem is a hopeless blunder and his fondness for Yamakas adds to its inherent dreariness. No more striking instance exists than this of the utter lack of proportion which can afflict the minds of poets with considerable technical facility and abundant knowledge.

To the same century and Kashmir belongs Abhinanda, son of Jayanta Bhaṭṭa, the logician, who wrote an epitome in epic form of the *Kādambarī* of Bāṇa, styled the *Kādambarīkathāsāra*,[1] and who mentions Rājaçekhara as a contemporary. The date of his namesake, son of Çatānanda, author of a *Rāmacarita*, which deals with the history of Rāma from the rape of Sītā, is unknown, and equally uncertain is it to which of these worthies is ascribed by an unknown hand[2] comparison with Kālidāsa. What is certain is that neither deserves it in the slightest. Kashmir again in the eleventh century produced a writer of the most unflinching industry and often dreariness,[3] the polymath Kṣemendra. In

[1] Cf. Thomas, *Kavīndravacanasamuccaya*, p. 20; Bühler, IA. ii. 102 f.

[2] *Çārṅgadhara*, viii. 5, where Acala and Amala are added.

[3] Cf. Lévi, JA. 1885, ii. 420.

1037 he wrote his *Bhāratamañjarī*,[1] in 1066 a *Daçāvatāracarita*,[2] in which each of the ten incarnations of Viṣṇu is described, the ninth being the Buddha thus definitely adopted into the Hindu pantheon. Of early date no doubt is his *Rāmāyaṇamañjarī*,[3] an epitome of the epic, which like that of the *Bhārata* is correct and important for the history of the text but poetically worthless. He turned the *Kādambarī* also into verse in the *Padya-Kādambarī*.

Kashmir again in the twelfth century produced an interesting writer in Mañkha, pupil of Ruyyaka, who mentions in his *Alaṁkārasarvasva* his epic, the *Çrīkaṇṭhacarita*,[4] which in twenty-five cantos tells the tale of the overthrow by Çiva of the demon Tripura. The form is the stereotyped one with a few variations; thus in Canto i prayers and benedictions occupy a considerable space, in ii and iii we have some ethical matter in the form of descriptions of the good and the bad, &c. But by iv we are back to a description of Kailāsa, of its master (v), the spring (vi), and then of the usual sports, swinging, plucking flowers in the woods, mixed bathing (vii–ix). Then follow the equally usual descriptions of the dusk, the rising of the moon, and allied topics until in xviii–xxi we have a return to more martial exploits; after the usual confusion the hosts of Çiva are marshalled and got under way. The Daityas are confounded (xxii), the battle is fought in the stereotyped way (xxiii), and Tripura burned. Then by a happy transition Mañkha gives us in xxv the only part of the poem worth reading. He depicts a durbar of learned men held by his brother Alaṁkāra, minister of Jayasiṅha (1129–50). Here we have a picture from the real life of the persons who made up this learned society, their special capacities and interests, the occasion for the gathering being his completion of his poem and his declamation of it to his friends. We learn much of interest, including the fact that he was one of four brothers who all were writers and officials of the court. Doubtless such a Sabhā must have represented with great accuracy the meetings common in the days of Kālidāsa and earlier; the similarity to those

[1] Ed. KM. 65, 1898.
[2] Ed. KM. 26, 1891.
[3] Ed. KM. 83, 1903. Cf. Jacobi, *Rāmāyaṇa*, p. 15.
[4] Ed. KM. 3, 1887. Cf. Bühler, *Report*, pp. 50 ff. On his use of the Udgatā metre cf. Jacobi, ZDMG. xliii. 467.

familiar to us from Statius, Juvenal, Martial, and Pliny is striking and interesting. No such excursion into the realms of real life enlivens the *Haracaritacintāmaṇi*[1] of the Kashmirian Jayaratha in the same century, which, however, has some value for religion as at once a storehouse of Çaiva myths and of evidence of Çaiva practices and beliefs.

As is well known, the Jains sought steadily to take over all Brahmanical myths and make them their own. To Amaracandra (*c.* 1250) we owe a *Bālabhārata*,[2] which is distinguished in metre but in no other respect. Apparently about 1050 Lolimbarāja wrote his *Harivilāsa*[3] which in Canto iii gives the usual description of the seasons and in iv of Kṛṣṇa. But little religious poetry aimed at Kāvya style; the influence of the Purāṇas resulted in the great mass of Jain work, for instance, being cast in an unpretentious and pedestrian Sanskrit.

But a triumph of misplaced ingenuity was attained in the twelfth century by three writers. The first perhaps in time was Sandhyākara Nandin, whose *Rāmapālacarita*[4] is intended to refer in each stanza to the history of Rāma and also to the king Rāmapāla, who flourished at the close of the eleventh century in Bengal. The second was apparently the Jain writer Dhanaṁjaya,[5] perhaps called Çrutakīrti, a Digambara, who wrote between 1123 and 1140; the third Kavirāja,[6] styled also Sūri or Paṇḍita, whose real name was perhaps Mādhava Bhaṭṭa, and whose patron, as he obligingly tells us, was Kāmadeva, probably the Kādamba king (1182–97). Both these authors perpetrated poems styled *Rāghavapāṇḍavīya* in which we are told simultaneously the stories of the *Rāmāyaṇa* and the *Mahābhārata*. The feat, which at first sight appears incredible, is explained without special difficulty by the nature of Sanskrit. Treating each line of verse as a unit, it is possible to break it up very variously into words by grouping

[1] Ed. KM. 61, 1897. Cf. Bühler, *Report*, p. 61.

[2] Ed. KM. 45, 1894. Cf. Weber, ZDMG. xxvii. 170 ff.; he uses the Lalitā and Svāgatā.

[3] Ed. KM. xi. 94–133.

[4] Ed. MASB. iii. 1–56.

[5] Ed. KM. 49, 1895 (18 cantos). Cf. Bhandarkar, *Report*, 1884–7, pp. 19 f.; Pathak, JBRAS. xxi. 1 ff.; Fleet, IA. xxxiii. 279.

[6] Ed. KM. 62. The date, *c.* 1000, ascribed by Bhandarkar, p. 20, is dealt with by Pischel (*Die Hofdichter des Lakṣmaṇasena*, pp. 37 f.). Cf. Fleet, *Bombay Gaz.*, i. 2. 563.

together the syllables. Then the meaning of compounds is often vitally affected by the mode in which the relations between the words composing them are conceived, even when the words are understood in the same sense and the compound is analysed into the same terms. Further, and this is of special importance, the Sanskrit lexica allow to words a very large variety of meanings and they supply a considerable number of very strange words which have a remarkable appearance of being more or less manufactured, in the sense that the meaning or form ascribed may have been derived from some mere misunderstanding or in some cases from a mere misreading. The way for such works as these two poems was paved by the *double entendres* of Subandhu and Bāṇa, and Kavirāja expressly states that he claims to be unrivalled by any but these two in the use of twisted language (*vakrokti*). The *Rāghavanaiṣadhīya* of Haradatta Sūri, of unknown date, performs the same feat for the tale of Rāma and Nala, and a doubtless quite late *Rāghavapāṇḍavīyayādavīya* by Cidambara adds the absurdity of telling three stories, the third being the legend of the *Bhāgavata Purāṇa*.[1] The deplorable folly of such works is obvious, but it remains true that Kavirāja at least shows some very fair talent and might have written something worthy of consideration if his taste had not led him to this extravagance.

A couple of stanzas from the second canto may serve to indicate the devices by which two stories are told simultaneously:

> *nṛpeṇa kanyāṁ janakena ditsitām: ayonijāṁ lambhayituṁ svayaṁvare*
> *dvijaprakarṣeṇa sa dharmanandanaḥ: sahānujas tām bhuvam apy anīyata.*

'(Rāma), who gladdened righteousness, was conducted, together with his younger brother, by that best of sages (Viçvāmitra) to the place of the Svayaṁvara, in order that he might be made to win the daughter born of no mortal womb, whom king Janaka was fain to give in wedlock.' According to the *Mahābhārata* version this runs: 'The son of Dharma (Yudhiṣṭhira) was conducted, together with his younger brothers, by (order of) that

[1] Veṅkaṭādhvarin's *Yādavarāghavīya* in 30 stanzas tells Rāma's story, while read backwards it gives Kṛṣṇa's (*Madras Catal.*, xx. 7956).

best of sages (Vyāsa) to the place of the Svayaṁvara (Pañcāla), in order that he might be made to win the daughter born of no mortal womb whom her royal father (Drupada) was fain to give in wedlock.' Sītā was born from the ploughshare, Draupadī from the sacrificial altar.

mārgeṣv atho dīrghatamaḥsutasya : kalatrakṛsrapratimokṣaṇena
aṅgāravarṇasya jitātmano 'sau : cakāra toṣaṁ naradevajanmā.

'Then, as he fared along, the son of the king of men delighted the heart of (the sage) of flaming hue and senses controlled, son of Dīrghatamas (Gotama) by releasing his spouse from her misfortune (of being reduced to a stone).' In the case of the *Mahābhārata* we must read *tamaḥsu tasya*, and render : 'Then, as he fared on ways where darkness long lingers (near the Ganges), the son of the king of men delighted the heart of (the Gandharva) Aṅgāravarṇa, whom he defeated, by releasing him at the prayer of his wife from peril of death.' The commentator adds ingenuously that there is a variant of Aṅgāraparṇa in the *Bhārata* whence the tale alluded to is derived, and in that case suggests a different rendering for the term as applied to the *Rāmāyaṇa*.

The result thus achieved is, of course, ultimately nothing more than the systematic development of the love of paronomasias which is seen to such perfection in Subandhu and Bāṇa. We find a similar result achieved in the curious *Rasikarañjana* [1] of Rāmacandra, son of Lakṣmaṇa Bhaṭṭa who wrote in 1542 at Ayodhyā, for the verses of that work, read one way, give an erotic poem, in another, a eulogy of asceticism. L. H. Gray [2] has noted a western parallel in the elegy of Leon of Medina on his teacher Moses Bassola, which can be read either as Italian or as Hebrew.[3]

An interesting and characteristic figure of the latest stage of classical Kāvya is Çrīharṣa, son of Hīra and Māmalladevī, author of the *Naiṣadhacarita* [4] or *Naiṣadhīya*, who wrote probably under Vijayacandra and Jayacandra of Kanauj in the second half of the

[1] Ed. and trans. R. Schmidt, Stuttgart, 1896.

[2] *Vāsavadattā*, p. 32, n. 1.

[3] Vidyāmādhava, author of a treatise on horary astrology (ed. *Bibl. Sansk.* 63) and a comm. on Bhāravi, cites Bāṇa, Subandhu, and himself with Kavirāja as masters ; his *Pārvatīrukmiṇīya* describes the marriages of Çiva and Pārvatī, Kṛṣṇa and Rukmiṇī. He wrote under Somadeva of the Culukya line (*Madras Catal.*, xx. 7778 f.).

[4] Ed. BI. 1836 and 1855 (two parts) and NSP. 1894.

twelfth century,[1] though this date has not passed unquestioned.[2] He was also author of other works, including the *Khaṇḍanakhaṇḍakhādya* in which he establishes the reasonableness of the Vedānta by showing that all attempts at obtaining certainty are fallacious. The *Naiṣadhīya* unquestionably has a definite interest in the history of Sanskrit literature, for it exhibits the application to the charming episode of the *Mahābhārata*, familiar to all students as the *Nala*, of the full resources of a master of diction and metre, possessed of a high degree of skill in the difficult art of playing on words, and capable of both delicate observation of nature and of effective expression of the impressions thence derived. Indian taste shows its appreciation of him beyond question in naming him a Mahākavi as the successor of Kālidāsa, Bhāravi, and Māgha, nor need we doubt that to any of these critics the *Nala* would have seemed insufferably tame compared to the work of Çrīharṣa. As one enthusiast of modern times[3] says, 'all mythology is at his fingers' ends. Rhetoric he rides over. He sees no end to the flow of his description,' and the same author, in recounting a tradition that the work counted when complete 60 or 120 cantos expresses the hope that the missing portion may be discovered in some collection of manuscripts. It is happily incredible that even Çrīharṣa should have thought it worth while further elaborating his theme. As it is, the long poem carries us only to a description of the married bliss of Nala and Damayantī, leaving off with a description of the moon carried out in a dialogue between the amorous pair. Needless to say, Çrīharṣa, in dealing with the theme of the wedding, shows that his logical studies had in no way prevented him becoming an expert of great skill in all the complexities of the *Kāmasūtra*. We could wish that there was some respectable authority for an anecdote once current regarding Harṣa; he was, this tale runs, the nephew of Mammaṭa, the famous author of the *Kāvyaprakāça*, to whom in pride he exhibited his poem. His uncle, in lieu of rejoicing, expressed only profound regret that he had not seen it before he wrote the chapter on faults in poetry in that treatise, since it would have saved him all the labour to which he had

[1] Bühler, JBRAS. x. 31 ff.; xi. 279 ff. [2] R. P. Chanda, IA. xlii. 83 f., 286 f.

[3] Krishnamacharya, *Sanskr. Lit.*, p. 45. Nilakamala Bhattacharya (*Naiṣadha and Śrī Harṣa*) argues that he was a Bengali.

been put in searching books to find illustrations of the mistakes which he censured.

Yet it is fair to admit Çrīharṣa's cleverness; his power of *double entendre* receives perfectly fair use in the recast of the famous scene in which Damayantī sees before her five men apparently exactly alike and cannot decide which is her lover. Sarasvatī, in Çrīharṣa's version, presents the five to her and describes each in words which on one reading do express his true identity, but on the other apply to Nala, thus setting the poor girl a still more distracting task. It is a consolation to reflect that, even had she known Sanskrit, she would not have been able without a comment to understand what was said by the goddess. Nor, again, is it possible to deny that the transition in the last canto from the description of night to that of the moon is gracefully effected; Nala exclaims that the moon has grown red with anger at the too prolonged celebration of the beauties of his friend, and then to appease his wrath he straightway hails the appearance of the moon rising in ruddy splendour.[1]

Çrīharṣa uses only nineteen metres, a comparatively small number. Of these, the favourite is Upajāti of the Indravajrā type, which is predominant in seven cantos; the Vaṅçasthā type prevails in four cantos and is the chief metre in Canto xii, in which after the model of Bhāravi and Māgha the poet goes out of his way to vary his metres. The Çloka,[2] Vasantatilaka, and Svāgatā are each the main metre of two cantos, while one canto each is found of Drutavilambita, Rathoddhatā, Vaitālīya, and Hariṇī. There is only one stanza in each of Acaladhṛti, Toṭaka, Dodhaka, and Pṛthvī, and five in Mandākrāntā. More frequent yet limited use is made of Puṣpitāgrā, Mālinī, Çikhariṇī, and Sragdharā.

Though on the whole we must condemn the elaboration of Çrīharṣa and his excessive use of Yamakas and rime, he was certainly capable of elegance and skill in the use of language, as in his famous description of the rising of the moon:

[1] The *Suprabhātastotra* (Thomas, JRAS. 1903, pp. 703–22) ascribed to him is also claimed for Harṣavardhana (Jackson, *Priyadarśikā*, p. xlv). An *Uttaranaiṣadhīya* in sixteen cantos was written by Vandāru Bhaṭṭa (*Madras Catal.*, xx. 7692).

[2] He rarely has Vipulās (only four in 752 half-stanzas in xvii and xx); SIFI. VIII. ii. 54. In xvii. 199 a line ends with a caesura in Sandhi.

paçyāvṛto 'py eṣa nimeṣam adrer : adhītyakābhūmitiraskariṇyā
pravarṣati preyasi candrikābhiç : cakoracañcūculukam pratīnduḥ.

'See, darling, how, for a moment hidden though it be by the curtain of the summit of the mountain, the moon doth spare the rain of its moonbeams to quench the thirst of the Cakora birds.'

dhvāntadrumāntān abhisārikās tvaṁ : çaṅkasva saṁketaniketam āptāḥ
chāyāchalād ujjhitanīlacelā : jyotsnānukūlaiç calitā dukūlaiḥ.

'Just fancy that these beams are maidens which have sought at the foot of the trees in the dusk secret meeting with their lovers; now laying aside their dark garments as though they were the shadow, they move in raiment that matches the moonlight.'

tvadāsyalakṣmīmukuraṁ cakoraiḥ : svakaumudīm ādayamānam indum
dṛçā niçendīvaracārubhāsā : piboru rambhātarupīvaroru.

'Drink thou deep with thine eyes, that are fair as the night lotus, the moon that doth serve to mirror the loveliness of thy face, and that doth make the Cakoras feed on its light, o lady whose thighs are fair as the young plantain shoots.'

The Jains naturally enough aimed at vying with the classical epic, and we have in the *Yaçodharacarita*[1] of Kanakasena Vādirāja, a resident in the Draviḍa country, whose pupil Çrīvijaya flourished about A.D. 950, a Kāvya in four cantos with 296 verses. Its contents agree with the *Yaçastilaka* of the slightly later Somadeva, showing that the tale must have been then current; the two versions differ slightly in content but not in spirit. Another version of the legend is that of Māṇikya Sūri whose *Yaçodharacaritra*[2] belongs probably to the eleventh century at latest. It represents the work of a Çvetāmbara Jain of Gujarāt, as opposed to the Digambara version of Vādirāja, but the two accounts are independent. To the period between 1160 and 1172 belongs the enormous work of Hemacandra (1088–1172),

[1] Ed. 1910; see Hertel, *Pāla und Gopāla*, pp. 91 ff., 146 ff.
[2] Ed. Tanjore, 1912; Hertel, pp. 81 ff., 139 ff.

the *Trişaṣṭiçalākāpuruṣacarita*,[1] which in ten Parvans handles the lives of the sixty-three best men of the Jain faith, the twenty-four Jinas, twelve Cakravartins, nine Vāsudevas, nine Baladevas, and nine Viṣṇudviṣas. The epic is long and wearisome, though the language is simple and not elaborate; the last Parvan, which deals with the life of Mahāvīra, comes nearer to sober history in that it gives us some definite information regarding the life of this worthy, if prolix, monk, who succeeded in converting to Jainism Kumārapāla of Gujarāt. Of unknown date is Haricandra, author of the *Dharmaçarmābhyudaya*,[2] in twenty-one cantos, on the life of the fifteenth Tīrthakara, Dharmanātha. Nemināṭha's life is the subject of a Kāvya [3] in fifteen cantos by the writer on poetics Vāgbhaṭa, probably in the twelfth century. There may be mentioned as having some claim to consideration the *Pāṇḍavacaritra* and *Mṛgāvatīcaritra* [4] of Devaprabha Sūri of the school of Maladhārin in the thirteenth century, and Cāritrasundara Gaṇin's *Mahīpālacaritra*,[5] which claims to be a Mahākāvya in fourteen cantos of 1159 verses. These works, however, have value rather for their tales than for their literary merit. Of much higher merit in this regard, though it deals with a trite theme and the author evidently knew both Açvaghoṣa and Kālidāsa's works well, is the Mahākāvya *Padyacūḍāmaṇi* [6] ascribed to a Buddhaghoṣācārya. That this is the work of the famous Pāli scholar Buddhaghoṣa can hardly be seriously affirmed; the silence of our records of that able man would be inexplicable, and, if the attribution is not a case of false ascription, it remains that there must have lived a scholar of the same name, whose date at present evades definite determination.

[1] Ed. Bombay, 1905. See Bühler, *Über das Leben des Jaina-Mönches Hemachandra* (1889); Jacobi, ERE. vi. 591.

[2] Ed. KM. 1888. Cf. Peterson, *Report*, ii, pp. 77 ff. He perhaps wrote the *Jīvandharacampū*, and uses Māgha and Vākpati (WZKM. iii. 136 ff.). His father was a Kāyastha, Ārdradeva.

[3] *Neminirvāṇa*, ed. KM. 56, 1896. The identity of the author is not certain. In *Madras Catal.*, xx. 7754 he is son of Dāhaṭa (? Bāhaṭa), of the Prāgvādi family.

[4] Ed. 1909; Hertel, pp. 105 ff., 150 ff. Cf. Peterson, *Report*, iii, pp. 273 ff.

[5] Ed. 1909; Hertel, pp. 72 ff., 138 ff.

[6] Ed. Madras, 1921.

VII

HISTORICAL KĀVYA

1. *Indian Historical Writing*

TO the old complaint that India has no historians and no historical sense it has recently been objected, doubtless with a measure of truth, that there is a certain amount of writing and a number of facts attesting a degree of sense for history. In view of the antiquity and the developed character of Indian civilization it would indeed be ridiculous to expect to find India destitute of historical sense, but what is really essential is the fact that, despite the abundance of its literature, history is so miserably represented, and that in the whole of the great period of Sanskrit literature there is not one writer who can be seriously regarded as a critical historian. We have as the nearest approach to a true historian a poet of no mean ability, much industry, and a desire to tell the truth, who had for recent history very fair sources of information, but the most ardent admirer of Kalhaṇa would not for a moment claim for him that he could be matched even with Herodotos, and it must be remembered that no other writer approaches even remotely the achievement of Kalhaṇa.

The causes of this phenomenon must lie in peculiarities of Indian psychology aided by environment and the course of events, and it is idle to hope to give any explanation which will be entirely satisfying. We may remember that India produced no oratory, despite the distinct power often displayed both in the epics and in Classical Kāvya of the rhetorical presentment of a case by opposing disputants. Oratory doubtless, as history proves, has flourished best where there has been political freedom; Athens is as celebrated for oratory as Sparta was deficient in it, and Rome produced its best orators when there still was a Republic in which certain classes at least had effective political rights. It may be that India failed to produce historians because the great political events which affected her during the period up to A.D. 1200 did not call forth popular action in the sense in which the repulse of the Persian attacks on Greece evoked the history of Herodotos.[1] The national feeling, which is at least a powerful aid to the writing of history, was not evoked in India in the same manner as it was when democratic states formed the most serious element of resistance to the Persian attack at a time when more oligarchic governments were apparently far less deeply moved by any sentiment of nationalism.[2]

It may be admitted that the foreign attacks on India in the period of the first four centuries B.C. were probably not such as to excite deep national feeling. Alexander's invasion was followed by the early loss of the most Indian of the territories won to Candragupta, apparently without any such struggle as would induce a sense of national danger and national triumph. The Greek, Parthian, Çaka, and Kuṣaṇa successes were possible in large measure because such a sentiment did not exist, and the process of assimilation went on so steadily that, when the Gupta revival came, it can hardly have been felt as a national revival, however much it seems so to us *ex post facto*. Thereafter, until the eleventh century, the wars of India were merely struggles between rival dynasties, wars of crows and kites, in which no deep signification could lie.[3] The Mahomedan invaders found India without any real national feeling; their successes were rendered possible largely because the chiefs disliked one another far more than they did the Mleccha. It is characteristic that even in the ballads evoked by the struggle the sense of nationality is only in process of development.

From the standpoint of psychology it is not difficult to understand that the view that history had any meaning or value was one unlikely to receive acceptance in India. The prevailing doctrines told distinctly against any such estimate of events. In

[1] Another side of Greek mentality, the criticism of tradition, is seen in Hekataios of Miletos, whose patriotism, like his history, was marked by caution and weighing of evidence. Cf. J. B. Bury, *Ancient Greek Historians* (1909).

[2] Stein, *Rājataraṅgiṇī*, i. 28 ff.; Oldenberg, *Aus dem alten Indien*, pp. 65 ff.

[3] Contrast Lucan's prophetic words (vii. 432 f.):

> quod fugiens civile nefas redituraque nunquam
> Libertas ultra Tigrim Rhenumque recessit.

the strict logical sense of the doctrine of Karman all men's actions were the outcome of actions done in previous births; they were, therefore, wholly uncalculable, for no one could tell what deed in the remotest past might not spring up to work out its inevitable end. Beside this belief, and evidently in full strength in many minds, was the view that all things were brought about by fate, working in a manner wholly unintelligible and beyond all foresight. To these more rational views, which might be combined and even reconciled by exercise of a little ingenuity, was added the acceptance by the Indian mind of the miraculous in the shape of divine intervention, magic, and witchcraft.[1] The scientific attitude of mind which seeks to find natural causes for events of nature is not normal in India, and the conception that nature is not capable of being affected by divine or demoniac instrumentalities would have seemed ludicrous to the vast majority of its people; Buddhists and Jains were as little inclined to abandon popular superstitions as were Brahmins. Nay, all three religions favoured the belief in the habit of sages by asceticism to attain magic powers; the doctrine that these powers can be acquired by regular forms of process is inculcated in their philosophies, and persons who were able to achieve these results were capable of affecting the processes of nature, so that to ascribe similar powers to superhuman beings was perfectly natural. Moreover, the philosophies of every kind taught that there was no progress in our sense in the world; things had happened age after age in precisely the same way; the doctrine of the periodical creation and destruction of the world of the Brahmanical post-Vedic texts is on the same plane as the theory of the Buddhists of the existence of innumerable earlier Buddhas and the long line of Jain Tīrthakaras.

Nor were the Indians without what seemed to them an excellent substitute for history in our sense. To the average Indian now, and doubtless of centuries ago, the heroes of the past and those historical kings who had been converted by their imagination into heroic figures were quite as real as, if not more real than, their local princes of the present time. Nor was it merely that they were as real; they possessed the great advantage of being recognized and admired over wide areas of India. It is

[1] Cf. Lucan on the Thessalian witches, vi. 415 ff.

hardly wonderful, therefore, that even those chronicles and panegyrics which were composed in honour of contemporary princes were soon no longer copied by scribes or studied, preference being accorded in lieu to works like the epics, which were certain to be of abiding interest. It has been well remarked [1] that, while the Paṇḍits have copied and commented with eagerness on the *Naiṣadhīya* of Çrīharṣa, they have allowed to sink into oblivion the *Navasāhasāñkacarita*, which he wrote to celebrate the deeds of his patron.

Something too must be allowed for the tendency of the Indian mind to prefer the general to the particular, which is shown in widely different spheres of knowledge. We hear, for instance, in Buddhist texts of certain definite heresies, but we are equally faced with schematic lists of unsound philosophical views which are asserted to have been held by others, but which in large measure are obviously mere inventions. Throughout the history of Indian philosophy the same thing is seen; no one seems to be in the least interested in the history of doctrines, no one writes a history of philosophy as contrasted with summaries of opposing doctrines; no one even attempts a real history of politics or medicine. What interests writers is not questions of the opinions of predecessors as individuals, but the discussion of divergencies of doctrine all imagined as having arisen *ex initio*. The names of some great authorities may be preserved, as in the case of the schools of philosophy, but nothing whatever with any taint of actuality is recorded regarding their personalities, and we are left to grope for dates. This indifference to chronology is seen everywhere in India, and must be definitely connected, in the ultimate issue, with the quite secondary character ascribed to time by the philosophies.

2. *The Beginnings of History*

The Purāṇas, as we have them, contain amidst vast masses of other matter, religious and social, some traces of the activity of court poets who made genealogies, but the value of these notices is of the most limited description; the lists of names and dates alone which is what they normally contribute are regularly,

[1] Bühler, *Vikramāñkadevacarita*, p. 2. His other panegyrics are lost, and we are not certain of his patron.

when compared with our more reliable evidence, hopelessly inaccurate, showing that at the time when th y came into being the interest of genealogists was rather edification by constructing pleasing ancestries than accurate record of facts. It may indeed be doubted whether with the most critical care anything could be retrieved of substantial value additional to other sources of information; hitherto they have been treated only without critical judgement or acumen.[1] Beside them may be put the lists of teachers which occasionally are recorded in later Vedic texts, but which are anything but free from suspicion of interpolation and exaggeration, though they prove, what was hardly dubious in any event, that there prevailed the practice of remembering series of teachers and pupils. The Buddhists made some more serious approach to history in their legends of the Buddha, but, valuable as is the matter which they have preserved, it remains clear, from their greatest creation,[2] the *Mahāvaṅsa* of Mahānāman in the fifth century A. D., that during the passage of the centuries the monks had not acquired any real historical sense. A king like Açoka was, of course, a model of pious deeds, but not the slightest attempt is made to treat his life and efforts in an historical spirit; instead, we learn of the courteous action of the wild beasts and birds who come to the royal kitchen and die there, to prevent the sin of slaying them for food, of miracle-performing snakes, and sages who come down to earth to cleanse the community of heretics. Even in contemporary times the poet is untrustworthy; all is looked at merely from the point of view of the attitude of the king for the time being towards the special community of monks among whom the author lived. Still less, of course, do we find history among the Jains; their Paṭṭāvalis, kept doubtless from early times but only recorded rather late, preserve lists of pontiffs, they had a stereotyped life of their Tīrthakaras, and endeavoured to attach Jain legends to such names as that of Candragupta,[3] but serious history was repugnant to them. Eulogies of saints are common to the sects, but serious historical work is quite unknown.

[1] To ascribe authority for the period 1000–500 B. C. to works that know nothing of the 3rd cent. A. D. is foolish. See Keith, EHR. 1922, pp. 607 f.

[2] Geiger, *Dīpavaṃsa und Mahāvaṃsa*; Oldenberg, *Aus dem alten Indien*, pp. 77 ff.

[3] Smith's acceptance (EHI. p. 154) of the legend of his resignation is quite unconvincing.

Poetic merit of a modest kind, however, may be found from time to time in the inscriptions which are the most substantial early contribution to Indian history. The most valuable in this regard are the encomia, Praçastis, of which we have already noted specimens of the Gupta age. The typical Praçasti[1] is simple in structure; after a benediction, it proceeds to describe the donor, and, when the two are not identical, the reigning prince, giving in either case some genealogical information, then it sets out the donation and enumerates any conditions or privileges accompanying it, such as freedom from interference by the royal officers or remission of taxation, invokes the favour of heaven for the maintenance of the memorial, utters imprecations on any person interfering with the donation, and sets out the name of the architect who constructed it, the priest who consecrated it, the poet, and the scribe who engraved the letters, with in many cases the date. The form, of course, varies with the nature of the object on which it is engraved, temple, public building, copper plate, memorial of the dead, &c., but the historically interesting part is normally the genealogy and account, if any, of the deeds of the dedicator, if a king. These Praçastis may be quite short, ten or twelve lines, or they may even exceed a hundred lines, and their value as history and poetry differs enormously. What is fairly certain is that the genealogies are frequently 'faked'; the kings for whom they were composed desired to be connected either with fabled heroes and royal lines of old, or, especially in the south, desired to make out that they were scions of the great royal houses of the north. As poetry they do not normally merit admiration, for they are decidedly elaborate in form, if at all pretentious, and we are not favourably impressed by the self-confidence of that Rāma who in the eighth century calls himself Kavīçvara, lord of poets, and asserts that the goddess of eloquence dwelt in his childish mouth ere he had forgotten the taste of his mother's milk. His skill is of the type admired in India but less attractive to western taste; he composes a Stotra, hymn of praise, in which each of the fourteen stanzas applies equally well to Pārvatī as to

[1] See Bühler, WZKM. ii. 86 ff.; EI. i. 97 ff. Their form as a blend of prose and poetry is recognized in the later writers on poetics as a Biruda; *Sāhityadarpaṇa*, vi. 570. For a collection see *Prācīnalekhamālā*, KM. 34, 64, 80.

her consort Çiva, and he exhibits by his choice of recondite constructions and rare words that he had studied diligently both grammar and lexica. The same curious device of including a Stotra in an inscription is seen in the case of Lalitasuradeva in the ninth century.[1] It is fair to say that not rarely there is found a poetical idea happily expressed in a panegyric both early and late, but in the main they are rather dreary and hackneyed documents.[2] And, what is vital, they represent merely a first step towards history.

We can hardly say that we are carried further into the region of history by the *Harṣacarita* of Bāṇa, for, beyond a very few facts about his immediate predecessors, we are given merely a confused glimpse of a very small part of the deeds of Harṣa of Thānesar, and the work may best be treated as a romance, which it is in all essentials. As a nearer approach to history may be ranked the *Gaüḍavaha*[3] of Vākpatirāja, which was written to celebrate the defeat of a Gauḍa prince by the poet's patron, Yaçovarman of Kanauj, who himself, however, was overthrown and killed not much later (*c.* 740) by Lalitāditya of Kashmir. Possibly this fact explains the curious condition of the poem, which contains as little history as possible, but expatiates instead in the wonted Kāvya manner in descriptions of scenery and the seasons, and of the amusements of kings, and does not scruple to relate myths. It may be that the poet, after his patron's death, left unfinished the poem which thus is merely a torso. The alternative is to suppose that we have in it as it stands a series of excerpts dealing with those topics which Paṇḍits liked, omitting tedious historical details. No certainty is possible; it may be that the poem is all that Vākpati ever intended to write. It is in Māhārāṣṭrī Prākrit, and, though it does not aim at plays on words and double meanings, it affects far too long compounds in the Gauḍa manner, nor does it normally reach any high standard of merit, though it contains some vivid pictures of village life—Māhārāṣṭrī poetry has always clung close to the soil—and the description of a southern temple of Kālī where

1 IA. xxv. 177 f.

2 Harṣa has some spirited lines; Jackson, *Priyadarśikā*, pp. xliii f.

3 Ed. S. P. Pandit, BSS. 34, 1887; cf. Bühler, WZKM. i. 324 ff.; ii. 328 ff.; Smith, JRAS. 1908, pp. 765–93. Hertel's views (*Asia Major*, i) on Bhavabhūti and Vākpati carry no conviction.

human sacrifices are offered has the grim horror which attracts Indian taste. Uncertainty attends its date; it is characteristic of the poem that we do not even hear the name of the Gauḍa king; if written after Yaçovarman's fall it may be placed about A.D. 750.

We are still far from serious history in the *Navasāhasāñka-carita*[1] of Padmagupta, also called Parimala, whose work, in eighteen cantos, was written about 1005. It relates the mythical theme of the winning of the princess Çaçiprabhā, but is intended at the same time to allude to the history of king Sindhurāja Navasāhasāñka of Mālava; we have by the hand of Bilhaṇa a similar example of this curious treatment in the drama *Karṇasundarī* in which he celebrates, under the guise of the marriage of a Caulukya prince to the daughter of a Vidyādhara king, an actual wedding of his patron to a princess. Obviously the method does not tend towards historical treatment or results. But the poet is by no means without the power of graceful expression, however impossible it may be to treat seriously his poem as a whole. Thus he has quite a happy conception in:

citravartiny api nṛpe tattvaveçena cetasi
vrīḍārdhavalitaṁ cakre mukhendum avaçaiva sā.

'As the truth pierced the soul of the king, though 'twas only his picture, the maiden made his moon-like forehead half-wrinkled with shame.'

āhāraṁ na karoti nāmbu pibati straiṇaṁ na saṁsevate
çete yat sikatāsu muktaviṣayaç caṇḍātapaṁ sevate
tvatpādābjarajaḥprasādakaṇikālābhonmukhas tan marau
manye Mālavasiṅha Gūrjarapatis tīvraṁ tapas tapyate.

'He eats not nor drinks water; women he frequents not; he lies on the sand, indifferent to things of sense he courts the burning heat; surely, o Lion of Mālava, the lord of Gūrjara performs thus a dread penance there in the desert that he may become worthy to be honoured by touching the dust of thy lotus feet.' Pretty is the following:

[1] Ed. V. S. Islāmpurkar, BSS. 53, 1895; G. Bühler and Th. Zachariae, *Über das Navasāhasāñkacharita* (1888). On his use of the Udgatā metre see Jacobi, ZDMG. xliii. 467; SIFI. VIII. ii. 110.

tatra sthitaṁ sthitimatā varadeva daivād: bhṛtyena te cakitacittam iyanty ahāni
utkampini stanataṭe hariṇekṣaṇānāṁ: hārān pranartayati yatra bhavatpratāpaḥ.

'There, my noble liege, as fate willed, thy servant won a footing and abode for many days with troubled heart, where thy valour makes to dance the necklaces on the quivering breasts of the deer-eyed ladies.' A more elaborate effort to depict the plight of the Gūrjara queen in her husband's defeat is less successful:

magnāni dviṣatāṁ kulāni samare tvatkhaḍgadhārākule
nāthāsminn iti vandivāci bahuço deva çrutāyām purā
mugdhā Gūrjarabhūmipālamahiṣī pratyāçayā pāthasaḥ
kāntāre cakitā vimuñcati muhuḥ patyuḥ kṛpāṇe dṛçau.

'As she wanders in terror in the forest, o King, the simple queen of Gūrjara's lord gazes ever at her husband's blade in her craving for water; has she not heard many a time the minstrels chant, "The hosts of the foe, o lord, have been drowned in the whirlpool of battle raised by the torrent of thy glaive"?' The unfortunate lady is misled by the ambiguity of the term *magnāni* and of *dhārā*, which means both torrent and edge of a sword.

We have only the name of Çañkuka, who wrote the *Bhuvanābhyudaya*, in which Kalhaṇa[1] tells us he described the dread battle of Mamma and Utpala (*c.* A. D. 850)

ruddhapravāhā yatrāsīd Vitastā subhaṭair hataiḥ

'where the current of the Vitastā was stemmed by the bodies of the slain.' The anthologies ascribe to a Çañkuka certain verses, but it is quite uncertain whether he is to be identified with this author; in the case of one verse the ascription is to Çañkuka Mayūra's son, and it has been conjectured that the Mayūra meant may be the contemporary of Bāṇa (*c.* A. D. 630), though this is mere surmise. A Çañku figures in the list of jewels of Vikramāditya's court; he may represent the tradition of one or other of these poets, if indeed they are to be identified.

[1] iv. 704 f. Cf. Peterson, *Subhāṣitāvali*, p. 127; Quackenbos, *The Sanskrit Poems of Mayūra*, pp. 50–2.

3. *Bilhaṇa*

It is to Kashmir that we must look for the first more serious contribution to history, for Bilhaṇa—the form of name is Kashmirian—was born there, though he left his home perhaps under Kalaça's reign and wandered far and wide visiting Mathurā, Kanauj, Prayāga, and Kāçī, and staying for a time at the court of a prince Karṇa of Ḍāhala,[1] perhaps also with the Caulukya Karṇadeva Trailokyamalla (1064–94) of Aṇhilvāḍ, before he was received as Vidyāpati, master of the sciences, by Vikramāditya VI, Cālukya king of Kalyāṇa (1076–1127), who bestowed upon him the gifts of a blue parasol and an elephant and chained him to his court. When at Karṇa's capital, he defeated in a literary competition the poet Gañgādhara and appears to have written a poem on Rāma, and he hints that the famous Bhoja of Dhārā [2] would have been glad to welcome him to his court. At any rate he rewarded his patron by composing in his honour his epic in eighteen cantos, the *Vikramāñkadevacarita*.[3] The date of that work appears to fall before 1088, because it passes in silence the great expedition of the king to the south which took place then, and because it mentions as prince, not king, Harṣadeva of Kashmir who became king only in that year, and we know from Kalhaṇa [4] that Bilhaṇa actually lived to hear of Harṣadeva's accession. Of his parentage we know that his immediate ancestors Muktikalaça, Rājakalaça, and Jyeṣṭhakalaça, his father, were Brahmins, students of the Veda, who performed the Vedic Agnihotra (fire-oblation) sacrifice; his mother was Nāgadevī, his brothers were Iṣṭarāma and Ānanda, both scholars and poets, while he himself was taught the Veda, grammar up to the *Mahābhāṣya*, and poetics.

The *Vikramāñkadevacarita* is essentially an application of the normal recipe for making an epic to a historical theme, and it begins, therefore, with the usual application, in this case to

[1] Presumably of Cedi, and different from the Karṇa of the *Karṇasundarī* (Konow, *Das indische Drama*, p. 112). The Cedi king was seemingly of long life and many vicissitudes (Duff, *Chronology*, pp. 120, 121, 135).

[2] This suggests that Bhoja was alive later than 1060; so also Kalhaṇa, vii. 259, treats him as alive in 1062.

[3] Ed. G. Bühler, BSS. 14, 1875. Cf. A. V. V. Ayyar, IA. xlviii. 114 ff., 133 ff.

[4] vii. 936–8.

Brahman, to create a hero for the safety of the world; the god agreed, and from his waterpot (*culuka*) sprang the founder of the Cālukya dynasty, whose first home in Ayodhyā was abandoned by later kings who extended their conquests to the betel palms of the south, 'where the hooves of their horses wrote the record of their victories on the sands of the ocean shore which witnesses the secrets of the Colas.' This purely imaginary origin for the family is followed by a long break in the tradition, and Bilhaṇa passes to Tailapa (973–97) whose victory over the Rāṣṭrakūṭas is recorded but not his defeat by the king of Mālava. The kings following are, with one exception, mentioned, and then the poet concentrates on Āhavamalla (1040–69), the father of his hero. This victorious king has no son; he and his wife serve humbly in Çiva's temple, and he is promised in reward by the god two sons as the reward of his penance, but one more as a special boon. Three sons are born, Someçvara, Vikramāditya, and Jayasiṅha, the birth of the second being preceded by remarkable portents presaging his future greatness. When the boys grew up, Āhavamalla pressed on Vikramāditya the duty of fulfilling the purpose of Çiva and accepting the heir-apparentship, but the virtuous prince declined to oust his brother. He proceeded, however, to win many victories which greatly delighted his father, but in the midst of his rejoicing he was attacked by a malignant fever. Greatly distressed, he decided to end his life, and, his ministers giving reluctant consent, journeyed to the Tuṅgabhadrā, the Ganges of the south, and there perished in the water, setting his heart on Çiva. Vikramāditya was deeply distressed by the news, was with difficulty induced to remain alive, but ultimately returned to the capital where his brother for a time lived peaceably with him. But suspicions arose between the two, and Vikramāditya retired with his brother Jayasiṅha, and took up a position on the Tuṅgabhadrā. He effected then an alliance with the Cola king, but after his ally's death the throne, despite efforts on his part, fell into the hands of Rājiga, who concerted an alliance with Someçvara against Vikramāditya. The result, however, was fatal to the allies; Çiva urged the reluctant Vikramāditya to do battle, and, when he had captured his brother, angrily compelled him to abandon his intention of allowing his brother to resume the royal power. He then made Jayasiṅha viceroy in Vanavāsa and effected more conquests. At this point the poet introduces the usual diversion from serious matters. The king hears of the Svayaṁvara of a Rājput princess, Candaladevī, and wins her as his bride; this gives Bilhaṇa the opportunity of describing the effect of the spring on the passions, and the beauties of the maiden in minute detail (viii). The wedding over, the king and his bride disport themselves; he swings her with his own hand, they pluck flowers, bathe together, and a carousal at which the Rājput ladies drink deep follows (ix–xi). The king now returns to Kalyāṇa, but merely to occupy a canto with fresh bathing scenes (xii) and an ode to the breaking of the monsoon (xiii). Jayasiṅha, however, gave trouble; he had to be overcome but pardoned (xiv, xv), and the king then engaged in hunting, slaying lions, hunting boars with dogs, and shooting arrows at deer (xvi). Sons were born to him, and he built a city Vikramapura, and erected a temple to Viṣṇu Kamalāvilāsin. But the Colas, having apparently been defeated rather in the poet's imagination than in reality, gave more trouble. Vikrama has to defeat them again and occupy for a time Kāñcī. The last canto is refreshingly interesting, for it gives an account of Bilhaṇa's own family and his life as a wandering Paṇḍit, attesting a practice which prevailed down to the most recent times.

It is difficult to say much for Bilhaṇa as a historian. We may justly suspect his impartiality; Çiva intervenes in the affairs of his hero with suspicious promptitude, and the impression conveyed is certainly that the poet is trying by stressing the supernatural intervention in his favour to explain away the awkward fact that he fought with both his brothers. We have no real character-drawing, but merely the reflex of the epic; Āhavamalla and Vikramāditya are as heroes necessarily paragons of virtue, the others vicious. It is quite in keeping with the epic manner that the Colas, so often rooted out, are at the end of the poem still perfectly capable of worrying the ruler. Again, the artificial style leaves often difficulty as to the precise sense; it is not even certain whether while at Karṇa's court Bilhaṇa wrote a poem on Rāma or made a journey to Ayodhyā. Chronology is utterly lacking, as it is in Bāṇa; 'after some days' or 'after many days' are expressions quite worthless, and while the inscriptions generally confirm Bilhaṇa's narrative, there remain much vagueness and inaccuracy, or at least exaggeration as in the case of his alleged Gauḍa conquests. An irritating but epic vagueness prevails; there is dubiety about the identity of the two Karṇas whom he mentions,[1] and he frequently leaves out the names of minor personages, leaving us to guess their identity. The descriptions of the usual pleasures of a royal court are doubtless generically true, but they are clearly out of place, and the Svayaṁvara is too obviously based on Kālidāsa to give us any confidence in its existence, in anything like the form in which it is pictured, though we know that Rājputs long kept up the practice. There is also only too much ground for accepting as true to life the scene of drunkenness, for the Rājputs have long found delight in romping, equivoke, debauchery, and drinking.

Bilhaṇa, however, is more satisfactory as a poet. He affects the Vaidarbha style and avoids long compounds; his language is normally simple and clear, and he does not overdo alliterations or plays on words. His masterpiece is admittedly the picture of the death of Ahavamalla in Canto iv; it is a fine piece of simple pathos, and the dignity and courage of the dying king are effectively portrayed. Nor is Bilhaṇa without skill in more elaborate effects, as in his plea for poets:

svecchābhaṅgurabhāgyameghataḍitaḥ çakyā na roddhuṁ çriyaḥ
prāṇānāṁ satatam prayāṇapaṭahaçraddhā na viçrāmyati
trāṇaṁ ye 'tra yaçomaye vapuṣi vaḥ kurvanti kāvyāmṛtais
tān ārādhya gurūn vidhatta sukavīn nirgarvam urvīçvarāḥ.

'Ye lords of earth, prosperity, the lightning of the cloud of fate that moves at its own will, cannot be chained; ever soundeth the drum that doth proclaim the hour of man's departure; honour, therefore, and take as your guides, laying aside all pride, those skilled poets whose poems provide the drink of immortality to your bodies of fame.'

he rājānas tyajata sukavipremabandhe virodhaṁ
çuddhā kīrtiḥ sphurati bhavatāṁ nūnam etatprasādāt
tuṣṭair baddhaṁ tad alaghu Raghusvāminaḥ sac caritraṁ
kruddhair nītas tribhuvanajayī hāsyamārgaṁ daçāsyaḥ.

'O kings, cease to obstruct the true poet's attachment; it is to

[1] i. 102 f.; xviii. 93.

them that is due the refulgence of your pure fame; by them in gratitude was composed the great, the noble tale of Rāma, by them in anger was Rāvaṇa, conqueror of the universe, made a laughing-stock.' The advent of winter is depicted quite prettily:

çaratkālātapaklāntakāntavakrenduvallabhaḥ
athājagāma hemantaḥ sāmantaḥ smarabhūpateḥ.

'Then came the winter, feudatory of our Lord, Love, himself beloved by the crescent moon dear to those aweary of autumn's heat.' Pretty is the description of Khonamukha, his ancestral home:

brūmas tasya prathamavasater adbhutānāṁ kathānāṁ
kiṁ çrīkaṇṭhaçvaçuraçikharikroḍakīlālalāmnaḥ
eko bhāgaḥ prakṛtisubhagaṁ kuṅkumaṁ yasya sūte
drākṣām anyaḥ sarasasarayūpuṇḍrakacchedapāṇḍum.

'What shall I sing of that spot, the fountain-head of wonder-tales, that shone as a playful embellishment on the crest of the mountain god, Çiva's father-in-law? One part bears the saffron in its natural perfection, the other the grape, pale as a slice of juicy sugar-cane from Sarayū's banks.' We may suggest that the reference to wonder-tales is an effort to ascribe to his native place the honour of being the source of works like the *Bṛhatkathā*. Āhavamalla's last words are perfect in their elegant simplicity:

jānāmi karikarṇāntacañcalaṁ hatajīvitam
mama nānyatra viçvāsaḥ Pārvatījīviteçvarāt.
utsañge Tuñgabhadrāyās tad eṣa Çivacintayā
vāñchāmy ahaṁ nirākartuṁ dehagrahaviḍambanām.

'I know that my life, tremulous as the tip of an elephant's ear, is gone; no other hope have I save in the lord of Pārvatī's life. In the bosom of Tuñgabhadrā I desire to lay aside this deception of human life, my heart set fast on Çiva.'

Bilhaṇa's diction is normally accurate, and for his occasional lapses he can plead precedent. Metrically he is simple; six cantos are of Indravajrā type, three of Vaṅçasthā, two of Çloka[1] and Rathoddhatā; one in Mandākrāntā, one in Puṣpitāgrā, and

[1] He has Vipulās I–III 20, 10, and 7 times respectively, and a weak caesura in Sandhi in Vipulā III in iv. 93 (IS. xvii. 444) in 428 half-stanzas.

one in Svāgatā. Çārdūlavikrīḍita and Vasantatilaka are not rare as change metres; Mālinī is occasional, and Aupacchandasika, Pṛthvī, Çikhariṇī, Sragdharā, and Hariṇī are just used, while Vaitālīya dominates Canto xv.

4. *Kalhaṇa's Life and Times*

Kalhaṇa of Kashmir [1] is not merely the one great Indian chronicler who has come down to us; but, though we have little direct information about him, we can gather from his poems a far more definite impression of his personal character than is usual with Indian poets; compared with Kālidāsa, who is a mere name, the subject of anecdotes clever and stupid, Kalhaṇa stands out as a very definite and rather attractive personality. We owe his activity as a chronicler in all probability to the internal struggles of Kashmir. His father Caṇpaka, doubtless a Brahmin, was a faithful adherent of king Harṣa (1089–1101); he remained, unlike the average Kashmirian, true to his sovereign in adversity, and was on an important mission entrusted to him by the king when the latter was assassinated; the details of the murder are known to us because Mukta, one of his servants, was with the king at the last, escaping in a manner which the poet fully relates. Caṇpaka seems to have lived long after his master's death, but seemingly he ceased to take active part in political affairs, for which, if we accept his loyalty, he can hardly have been well fitted, and thus young Kalhaṇa, who may have been born about 1100, was cut off from the possibility of ministerial office and political life. His uncle, Kanaka, was also deeply attached to Harṣa, who rewarded his complaisance in taking singing lessons from the music-loving king by presenting him with a lakh of gold coins. He restrained the king in his madness from destroying the image of the Buddha at Parihāsapura, probably the home of Kalhaṇa's family, and retired to Benares on his patron's death. Like his father, Kalhaṇa was a devotee of Çiva, but though he knew and respected the Çaivaçāstra, the recondite system of Çaiva philosophy for which Kashmir was famous, he seems to have had a poor opinion of the devotees of the Tantric rites of Çaivism. But he is markedly respectful in his attitude to

[1] M. A. Stein, *Kalhaṇa's Chronicle of Kaśmīr* (1900), and ed. (1892).

Buddhism, and approves the practice of non-destruction of life (*ahiṅsā*) enjoined and enforced by some kings. Buddhism, it is clear from his account, had long since accommodated itself to Hinduism ; Kṣemendra had celebrated the Buddha as an Avatār of Viṣṇu, and married monks were known long before Kalhaṇa's day.

Debarred from politics, Kalhaṇa must have conceived the idea of rewriting the chronicles of Kashmir, perhaps at the instigation of Alakadatta, the patron of whom we hear only from the *Çrīkaṇṭhacarita*[1] of Mañkha, who mentions him under his more elegant appellation of Kalyāṇa, of which his name is a vernacular equivalent. It is clear that he studied deeply the great poems of the past, such as the *Raghuvañça* and *Meghadūta* of Kālidāsa, and naturally the *Harṣacarita* of Bāṇa, as a model of romance based on a historical kernel. Bilhaṇa he knew well and used his work, and Mañkha expressly tells us that Kalhaṇa's style had become so polished that it could reflect as in a mirror the whole perfection of Bilhaṇa's muse. But he studied also deeply the epics, as his constant references to the heroes of the *Mahābhārata* and his familiarity with the *Rāmāyaṇa* prove. He was naturally interested in literary history, and studied the science of astrology, as his references to Varāhamihira's *Bṛhatsaṁhitā* attest.

Contemporary history was stormy and bloody. Harṣa's death left his foes Uccala and Sussala to divide the kingdom ; Sussala received the territory of Lohara. Uccala had to keep in power by playing off one of the turbulent Ḍāmaras, a feudal body of landholders, against another, Gargacandra of Lahara proving his chief support. In 1111 he was assassinated by a plot of his officials, one of whom, Raḍḍa, occupied the throne for a day. Gargacandra then ruled through a *roi fainéant* for four months, but Sussala patched up friendship with him and became king. His reign was one mass of trouble ; the Ḍāmaras, when Gargacandra was removed by murder, rose under Bhikṣācara, a grandson of Harṣa who ruled from 1120 to 1121, but Sussala regained power, and civil war raged until he was murdered in 1128 as the result of a plot he had contrived to assassinate his rival. His son Jayasiṅha succeeded and kept the throne, not by his father's reckless valour, but by cultivating the feudal grandees and by

[1] xxv. 78–80.

Machiavellian diplomacy. Bhikṣācara was murdered two years later, but a new pretender appeared, and, although there was peace for a time after 1135, a new trouble arose in 1143, when prince Bhoja supported by the Dard tribes rose in revolt. Diplomacy at last quelled this outbreak, and in 1149 Kalhaṇa began and in the next year finished his great poem. He had clearly stood apart from the struggle; though he wrote under Jayasiṅha, his remarks regarding him are utterly opposed to the wholesale panegyric of the normal court poet; he condemns severely the deeds of Sussala, and is equally severe to Loṭhana and Mallārjuna, the earlier pretenders of Jayasiṅha's reign. His account of Bhikṣācara is more favourable, and that this was not induced by personal motives is established by the fact that his record shows clearly that he and his family gained nothing by the brief period of that prince's power. Bhoja he evidently both knew and liked, and much of his information regarding the tedious negotiations and manœuvres which preceded his reconciliation with the king in 1145 must have been derived from him personally, when with the other pretenders he was living in amity at Jayasiṅha's court.

Kalhaṇa's detachment enabled him to envisage dispassionately the demerits of his own countrymen, and his testimony is abundantly confirmed by history. Fair and false and fickle is a perfect description of the Kashmirian as seen by Kalhaṇa. The disorderly and cowardly soldiery receives his wholehearted contempt; they are prepared to fly at a rumour, and, if a few resolute men murder the king, a *sauve qui peut* of guards, attendants, and courtiers follows at once. Fidelity is unknown to the vast majority of the court, and Kalhaṇa notes it with special care, even when its object is a rebel. Contrasted with this is the courage and loyalty of the Rājaputras and other foreign mercenaries on whom the kings had largely to rely for serious fighting. The city populace is presented as idle, pleasure-loving, and utterly callous, acclaiming a king to-day and welcoming another to-morrow, and their passions raise disdain in the aristocratic Brahmin's mind. Against the Ḍāmaras he is extremely bitter; his family had doubtless suffered greatly at the hands of these cruel and brutal men, who oppressed the peasants and plundered when they could the estates of the officials and the

Brahmins of the capital; their boorishness and crudeness, traces of their humble origin, are also a source of offence. But he has no illusions regarding the official classes; their greed, peculations, oppressions, and disloyalty are frankly exposed. The priests are not spared; Kashmir was cursed then by activities of the Purohitas, who, in possession of costly endowments, sought by their solemn fasts (*prāyopaveça*), intended to proceed to death if their demands were not granted, to influence the progress of events. Kalhaṇa ridicules their ignorance of affairs and their arrogance in intervention in matters beyond their skill. He is not, however, all compact of dislikes; he mentions appreciatively the minister Rilhaṇa and Alaṁkāra, whom we know from Mañkha as a patron of poets; Mañkha himself is only mentioned as a minister, not as a poet; for Udaya, commander of the frontier defences, he seems to have had a warm regard, and personal relations are obvious both with Bhoja and with Rājavadana, another of the pretenders who attacked Jayasiṅha. All that we have points, therefore, to a mind very busily in contact with reality, observing intently the process of current events in lieu of becoming a mere book-worm, and endeavouring to find satisfaction for a keen intellect in recording the events around him and those of earlier days in lieu of the participation in affairs traditional in his family and congenial to his tastes.

5. *The Rājataraṅgiṇī and its Sources*

Kalhaṇa tells us himself that he was not the first to seek to write a chronicle of the kings of Kashmir from the earliest days; it appears that extensive works of ancient date contained the royal chronicles, but these had apparently disappeared in his time through the energy of one Suvrata in composing a poem embodying them, evidently written in the Kāvya style, and, therefore, difficult to follow. He consulted also, he says, eleven works of former scholars as well as the still extant *Nīlamatapurāṇa*. The polymath Kṣemendra had written a *Nṛpāvali* which Kalhaṇa censures for want of care, but which probably was a careful summary of his sources and, therefore, is a real loss. From Padmamihira Kalhaṇa took eight kings beginning with Lava who come first after the gap of thirty-five lost kings in Book I; Padmamihira's source was a certain Pāçupata Helārāja whose work must have been extensive but which Kalhaṇa did not know. From Chavillākara, whose text he cites, he derived some really historical information in the shape of Açoka's name and his devotion to Buddhism. If the other authorities he used carried their work from the beginnings to their own times, or were mere chronicles of recent events, we do not know. Kalhaṇa probably used some writers of this kind, as he emphatically disclaims this sort of work as worthy of him, and insists on covering the whole history of Kashmir so far as his sources allow.

But Kalhaṇa used much more original sources to check his literary authorities. He tells us that he inspected inscriptions of various kinds, those envisaged recording the construction of temples, memorials, or palaces, records of land grants or privileges (usually on copper plates), Praçastis, eulogies engraved on temples and other buildings, and manuscripts of literary works, which often record names of rulers and dates. The claim is borne out by the precise details of facts as to the foundation of sacred edifices, land grants, &c., which abound in his text, and by his precise assertions as to literary history, which are of great value. He studied also coins and inspected buildings, while he was clearly a master of the topography of the valley. Further, he used freely local traditions of all kinds, and family records, while from his own knowledge and from that of his father and many others he culled the minute details which mark his treatment of the events of the fifty years preceding the date of his work.

Kalhaṇa frankly admits that the first fifty-two kings, evidently a traditional number, whom he recognizes were not recorded by his predecessors as chroniclers; the first four he took from the *Nīlamata*, the next eight from Helārāja frankly come after a gap of thirty-five kings, then follow five from Chavillākara. The first king Gonanda is of special importance because he is made to have come to the throne in the same year 653 of the Kali era in which Yudhiṣṭhira was crowned, and on this absolutely groundless synchronism is built up the whole fabric of Kalhaṇa's chronology. Gonanda is made to attack Kṛṣṇa in Mathurā and to be slain by Balabhadra, Kṛṣṇa's brother. His son Dāmodara I sought to avenge him, but perished, Kṛṣṇa placing his wife, then pregnant, on the throne, so that Gonanda II, his son, was a babe who could take no part in the great war. It must be noted that in Book III we find Gonanda III virtually treated as the real head of the dynasty, nor can we deny that these fabulous kings were merely invented by a pious fraud to give Kashmir a place in the heroic legends of India. Of the other kings recorded in Book I Açoka is given a son Jalauka, elsewhere unknown, and a reminiscence of the Kuṣaṇas is seen in the names Huṣka, Juṣka, and Kaniṣka, recognized as Buddhists, though their order is exactly the reverse of the historical. They were followed by a Brahmanical Abhimanyu, who is stated to have favoured the study of the *Mahābhāṣya*, but whose historical character is unverifiable. Under him a pious Brahmin with the aid of Nīlanāga purifies Kashmir from Buddhist contagion and saves the land from snow, the tale being a mere *réchauffé* of the legend of the *Nīlamata* which makes Piçācas the sinners. The line of Gonanda kings after Gonanda III has little appearance of authenticity, and in Book II we find a new line of kings, unconnected with the old, and apparently with no claims to historicity. Book III gives the history of the restored Gonanda dynasty under Meghavāhana. In the new list Mātṛgupta's short reign figures, and possibly in him and his patron Vikramāditya Harṣa we have a reference to Çīlāditya [1] of Mālava, giving us a date in the sixth century. As a member of the Gonanda line figures Toramāṇa, who can hardly be other than the Hūṇa king of that name, and it is not enough to discount the fact that his father Mihirakula is given at a date 700 years earlier, for Kalhaṇa recognizes a reign of 300 years for Raṇāditya, who was the third last king of the dynasty and whose date would fall in quite historical times. A romantic tale ends the dynasty; the last king, Bālāditya, in order to avoid the fulfilment of a prophecy that his son-in-law would succeed him, married his daughter to a minor official Durlabhavardhana, but the son-in-law became a favourite of the king, and, having the wisdom if not the honour to pardon the minister Khañkha for an intrigue with his wife, was on the king's death elevated to the throne as first of the Kārkoṭa dynasty, the name being explained as due to the fact that he was really the son of a Nāga Kārkoṭa. With this dynasty in Book IV we approach historical reality in

[1] Cf. EHI. p. 344.

the seventh century A.D., as Durlabhavardhana may have been the king who ruled contemporaneously with the Chinese pilgrim Hiuen Tsang. The first date in the Laukika era of Kashmir (3076–5 B.C.) is given in the case of Cippaṭa Jayāpīḍa or Bṛhaspati, whom he assigns to A.D. 801–13, but this can definitely be proved wrong from the fact that the poet Ratnākara, author of the *Haravijaya*, distinctly tells us that he wrote under the patronage of that prince, while Kalhaṇa assures us that he was prominent under Avantivarman, who certainly began to reign in 855. There is clearly an error of at least twenty-five or even fifty years. The dynasty ended in usurpation by Avantivarman, son of Sukhavarman and grandson of Utpala, an able man of humble origin who had become virtual ruler of the realm. With Avantivarman we are in the full light of history; Book V carries the dynasty down to 939, and Book VI completes it to the death of queen Diddā in 1003 and the peaceful accession of her nephew, the first prince of the Lohara dynasty. Book VII ends with the tragedy of the death of Harṣa, and Book VIII deals at great length (3449 stanzas) with the events of the half-century from the accession of Uccala. One curious omission of importance can be proved; Kalhaṇa records in an interesting manner the aid sent vainly under Tuñga to the Çāhi king Trilocanapāla in his effort to stay the Mahomedan invasion under Maḥmūd Ghaznī, the Hammīra of the Indian texts; but he does not mention the actual onslaught about 1015 of the Mahomedan forces directed against Kashmir, which was stayed by the resolute resistance of the castle of Lohara, and as a result of the narrow outlook of the people of Kashmir in their inaccessible valley he appreciates hardly at all the significance of the new storm bursting over India.

6. *Kalhaṇa as a Historian*

To understand Kalhaṇa's outlook on history we must not, of course, think of Thucydides or Polybios; we must, as has been well said, remember that, with these great works before them, Roman opinion was still content to see in history the opportunity for displaying command of rhetoric and of inculcating moral maxims. Kalhaṇa's aim is to produce a work which shall conform to the demands not of rhetoricians—of whom India had none—but of writers on poetics, and at the same time to impress on his readers moral maxims. The first of his aims he frankly admits at the outset: 'Worthy of praise is the strange power of true poets which surpasses in value even the drink of immortality, since by it not only their own bodies of glory, but also those of others, are sustained. It is the creative genius of the poet alone which by its power of the production of beauty can place past times before the eye of men.' He admits [1] the difficulty which he has to face; the amplitude of his task forbids the development of attractive variety (*vaicitrya*), which means that, having so much to narrate, he could not follow Bhāravi and Māgha in filling up his poem with descriptions of the poet's stock-in-trade. There are indeed digressions but modest in kind, and it is only in them that we find the constant occurrence of the ornaments which mark the true poetic style. Nothing, however, shows his self-imposed moderation better than comparison with Bāṇa's *Harṣacarita* or Bilhaṇa's poem.

The influence of the epic combines with that of poetics to produce the second mark of Kalhaṇa's chronicle, its didactic tendency. Poetics requires that each poem should have a dominant sentiment, and that of the *Rājataraṅgiṇī* is resignation; [2] it is definitely so asserted, and based on the impression produced on the mind by the sudden appearance of human beings who last for a moment alone. It is reinforced by insistence on the tales of kings who by renunciation or otherwise come to a pathetic end, and Books I–III and VII are deliberately brought to a close with the occurrence of such episodes. Stress is ever laid on the impermanence of power and riches, the transient character of all earthly fame and glory, and the retribution which reaches doers of evil in this or a future life; the deeds of kings and ministers are reviewed and censured or commended by the rules of the Dharmaçāstra or Nītiçāstra, but always with a distinct moral bias. In this we certainly see the influence of the *Mahābhārata* in its vast didactic portions and its general tendency to inculcate morality, but we cannot say whether it was original in Kalhaṇa or had already been noted in the works of one or more of his predecessors.

Kalhaṇa, therefore, makes no claim to be a scientific investigator,

[1] i. 6. [2] i. 23.

and in complete harmony with this tells us nothing of the divergences in his authorities. It is, in fact, clear that down to the middle of the ninth century with the advent of the Utpala dynasty he had no trustworthy materials to go upon. But, in lieu of sifting what he had and confessing his ignorance, he chose instead to patch up a continuous narrative. The results have already been seen; his chronology for the older period is hopelessly absurd and Kalhaṇa is quite unable to recognize the absurdity. Moreover, he is exactly on the same level as his average fellow-countryman in his attitude to heroic legend and to fact; he accepts without hesitation the ancient legends of the epic as just as real as things of his day; some sceptics went so far as to doubt the magic feats of Meghavāhana and other kings, but Kalhaṇa will have none of them;[1] indeed he takes occasion, when recounting the acts done by Harṣa in his madness, to observe that future generations may on that account doubt their truth as they do the tales of Meghavāhana, apparently wholly unconscious of the vast difference in the character of the two kinds of stories. Inevitably, too, Kalhaṇa's outlook was dimmed by the narrow limits of his home and its isolation; hence we do not find in him any real appreciation of the relations of Kashmir to the outer world; the invasions of the Kuṣaṇas and Hūṇas are confused and misunderstood. A further Kashmirian trait reveals itself throughout his work; the land was known to Marco Polo[2] as famous for sorcery and 'devilries of enchantment', and Kalhaṇa quite cheerfully accepts witchcraft as a legitimate cause of deaths;[3] we may remember the Roman[4] and medieval acceptance of poison as a natural cause of the dooms of princes. The deplorable chronology was doubtless not invented by Kalhaṇa, but he took it over and never realized its flagrant absurdities and its ludicrously long reigns, though contemporary experience would have shown how absurd they were.

We must, however, realize that Kalhaṇa was completely under the dominion of Indian views of life, which rendered doubt on

[1] vii. 1137 ff.

[2] Yule, i. 175; cf. Bühler, *Report*, p. 24.

[3] So the *Arthaçāstra* seriously commends this expedient against foes.

[4] e.g. Tacitus, *Ann.*, iii. 17; Pliny, *H.N.*, xxix. 20; Mayor on Juvenal, xiv. 252 ff.

such topics idle. The current theory of the ages of the world told him that he was living in the Kali age, when things were far declined from their ancient glory; it was, then, idle to mete the past by the present. Again, to seek for rational explanations of human action by merely stressing the motives of the present day would be idle, for man's deeds are the outcome of ancient acts, looming up from a forgotten past which may at any time bring forth deeds incalculable and utterly at variance with the character of their performer. Yet fate ranks also as a cause of action, nor does Kalhaṇa take care to show that it can be reconciled with the doctrine of Karman. It is fate [1] which drives Harṣa at the close of his life to disregard wisdom and policy, though it is clear from the poet's own account that the unhappy prince was a madman. Fate again is blamed for the ingratitude shown by recipients of the royal favour. But if all these explanations fail to satisfy Indian credulity avails, for it admits possession by demons, and Kalhaṇa actually himself ascribes [2] to this cause an obvious political murder. He accepts also the power of the man who starves himself to death to bring about terrible effects, though he hated the Brahmanical employment of this device to influence royal policy. The desecration of shrines naturally evokes the wrath of the gods, and Harṣa and Sussala pay for their evil acts by death. The anger of Nāgas, spirits of Kashmir's springs, is specially frequent and deadly, while omens and portents are accepted as of unquestionable validity. We need not wonder, therefore, when we find Kalhaṇa solemnly recording and believing in the resurrection by witches of Sandhimati, impaled by his jealous king, and his attainment of the royal power.

We are in a more normal world when we find Kalhaṇa concerned to prove to us that evil deeds meet retribution, by an enumeration [3] of the cases in which the avarice of kings resulted in the alienation of their subjects, though as a true Brahmin he admits that the use made of evil gains may sanctify the means, as when they are bestowed on Brahmins. But beyond this Kalhaṇa does not advance to any philosophy of history; he only exercises a criticism of individual actions on the basis of established rules of the Çāstras. Thus Kamalavardhana's folly in seeking to attain by diplomacy what could only be won by the sword is

[1] vii. 1455 ff. [2] viii. 2241. [3] v. 183 ff., 208 f.

shrewdly commented on,[1] and Jayasiṅha's fiasco in the Kiṣangaṅgā valley is explained [2] as due to the folly of attack without adequate information, and undue deliberation in the face of the foe. His own contribution to an art of governing Kashmir is placed in the mouth of Lalitāditya [3] and is very much in the spirit of the *Kautilīya Arthaçāstra,* but with the great advantage of reference to particular conditions, as is indicated by the distinctly Kashmirian flavour of the advice given. The border tribes are never to be left in peace, even if they give no offence, lest they acquire wealth and plunder the country. The peasants are not to be allowed to keep more than one year's consumption of grain or more oxen than essential for working their land. The maxim is clearly aimed at the Ḍāmaras, whose exactions from the peasants were the source of the turbulence which plagued the country and won them from the poet the sobriquet of robbers (*dasyus*). Border forts are to be guarded securely, and high offices are to be shared among the great families, so as to prevent ill feeling and conspiracies; above all, no faith is to be put in the loyalty of the changeable and untrustworthy people.

We need not doubt that Kalhaṇa endeavoured to attain his own ideal—'that noble-minded poet alone merits praise whose word, like the sentence of a judge, keeps free from love or hatred in recording the past.' His treatment of Harṣa supports this impression, for his father had been a trusted minister and evidently fell with his patron, but Kalhaṇa does not ignore the appalling cruelties of this Indian Nero, however much he pities his end. His description of incidents in recent history appears to achieve a high standard of accuracy, and is filled with those small touches which imply personal knowledge or acceptance of the testimony of eye-witnesses, as when he recounts the details of the self-immolation of Sūryamatī or of Sussala's murder.[4] The popular sayings and anecdotes which he records bear the stamp of being taken from life. Excellent also is his delineation of character, and the change from the manner of the earlier to that of the later books is significant. The former give but the typical poetical description of heroes such as Tuñjīna and Pravarasena, the latter present vivid personalities such as Tuṅga, Ananta,

[1] v. 456 ff. [2] viii. 2521 ff. [3] iv. 344 ff.
[4] vii. 463 ff.; viii. 1287 ff.

Harṣa and Sussala; there is nothing like this in Bāṇa, Padmagupta, or Bilhaṇa. In the minor figures his humour, sometimes Rabelaisian, has full play, as in his picture of his contemporary Kularāja, whose abilities had raised him from the rank of a bravo to that of city prefect. His accuracy in genealogical information is conspicuous, and his topography most favourably distinguishes him from such a historian as Livy, who apparently never looked at one of the battlefields he described.

7. *Kalhaṇa's Style*

We need not regret that Kalhaṇa was not permitted by his subject to indulge in the Kāvya style of description; we have sufficient examples of it in such pictures as that of Yudhiṣṭhira's departure into exile and Sussala's entry into the capital to realize that we have lost nothing of value in being spared more of these stereotyped and colourless imitations.[1] Much, indeed, of the rest of the poem is mere versified prose, comparable, but for the beauty of the language itself, to medieval chronicles, but the true poetic power of the author is revealed in many episodes. The account of Bhoja's terrible journey over the snow-clad mountains in A.D. 1144 to the Dards,[2] the funeral of Ananta and Sūryamatī's Satī, the dialogue between the Brahmins whom he has injured and Jayāpīḍa who is to perish by their curse, above all, the tragic tale of Harṣa's isolation and misery, redeemed from sordidness by the courage of his last defence and the magnanimity which spared the life of one of his murderers, are all conclusive instances of Kalhaṇa's power of simple, yet deeply affecting narrative. The use of dialogues or set speeches lends not merely variety but dramatic power; thus Uccala is made to expound his claim to the throne and Harṣa to defend his political conduct.[3] Or the situation is brought vividly before us, as in the dialogue of Ananta and Sūryamatī before her suicide; or the feelings of the bystanders, as in the comments of the soldiers and the Ḍāmaras on Bhikṣācara's fall.[4] On the other hand must be set an unquestionable obscurity, arising in part from the metaphorical

[1] Cf. i. 368 ff.; v. 341 ff.; viii. 947 ff.; 1744 ff. He imitates Bāṇa rather freely.

[2] viii. 2710–14. Stein compares Claudian, *de bello Getico*, 340 ff.

[3] vii. 1281 ff., 1416 ff.

[4] vii. 423 ff.; 1704 ff., 1725 ff.

expressions which take the place of plain statements of fact, in part from the poet's indifference to the ignorance of posterity of the exact conditions of Kashmir in his own day. This leads him to assume our knowledge of situations which, therefore, are referred to in terms conveying now no clear impression, and to the use of words in technical senses without any explanation, as *kampana*, army, command in chief; *dvāra*, frontier watch station, command of the frontiers; *pādāgra*, high revenue office; and *parṣad,* corporation of Purohitas. Another source of trouble is the use of varying forms of the same name, as Losṭhaka, Loṭhaka, and Loṭhana, and the mention of individuals either by the title of their office, or by the title of an office no longer held.

Kalhaṇa is fond of diversifying the flow of the narrative by ingenious similes, by antitheses, by occasional plays on words, and by the expedient of varying the simplicity of the Çloka metre by interposing more ornate stanzas of moral or didactic content, in which the language is more intricate, but often graceful and elegant, while the ideas, if not original, are not rarely just and weighty. The value of poetry strikes him forcibly and happily in:

bhujataruvanacchāyām̐ yeṣām̐ niṣevya mahaujasām̐
jaladhiraçanā mediny āsīd asāv akutobhayā
smṛtim api na te yānti kṣmāpā vinā yadanugraham
prakṛtimahate kurmas tasmai namaḥ kavikarmaṇe.

'Homage we pay to the innate wonder of the poet's art, without whose favour are forgotten even those mighty kings in the shadow of whose strong arms the earth, girdled by the ocean, lay secure as under the forest trees.' Or in different form:

ye 'py āsann ibhakumbhaçāyitapadā ye 'pi çriyam̐ lebhire
yeṣām̐ apy avasan purā yuvatayo geheṣv ahaçcandrikāḥ
tām̐l loko 'yam avaiti lokatilakān svapne 'py ajatān iva
bhrātaḥ satkavikṛtya kim̐ stutiçatair andham̐ jagat tvām̐ vinā.

'Without thee, o brother, the craft of true poets, the world would not even dream of those ornaments of the world who rested their feet on the foreheads of elephants, who attained riches, and in whose halls dwelt maidens, moons of the day;

without thee, I say, this world is blind; not hundreds of eulogies could extol thee becomingly.' The evil deeds of Tārāpīḍa ended in his attacking Brahmins and death:

yo yaṁ janāpakaraṇāya sṛjaty upāyaṁ: tenaiva tasya niyamena bhaved vināçaḥ
dhūmam prasauti nayanāndhyakaraṁ yam agnir: bhūtvāmbudaḥ sa çamayet salilais tam eva.

'The man who devises a plot shall assuredly perish thereby; the smoke that the fire sends up to blind the eyes, turning into a cloud, quenches with its water the fire itself.' The goddess Bhramaravāsinī, whose shrine was guarded by bees, who reduced to bones the mortal who sought it, appears in lovely form:

bhāsvadbimbādharā kṛṣṇakeçī sitakarānanā
harimadhyā çivākārā sarvadevamayīva sā.

'Her lip was red as the Bimba, black her hair, moonlike her face, lionlike her waist, gracious her aspect: so seemed she to unite all the gods in one.' Here the epithets suggest the gods Sūrya, Kṛṣṇa, Soma, Hari, and Çiva. A biting attack on women's conduct as opposed to their beauty runs:

avakāçaḥ suvṛttānāṁ hṛdaye 'ntar na yoṣitām
itīva vidadhe dhātā suvṛttau tadbahiḥ kucau.

'Since in women's hearts there is no room for good conduct, the creator in his mercy hath guarded them with their rounded breasts.' The wise king recognized the transitory character of prosperity:

gobhujāṁ vallabhā lakṣmīr mātaṅgotsaṅgalālitā
seyaṁ spṛhāṁ samutpādya dūṣayaty unnatātmanaḥ.

'Fortune, the beloved of kings, who dallies on the back of her elephant (in the arms of one of low degree) creates eager desires and brings to ruin the man of high mind.' The flatterers of kings are effectively denounced:

karṇe tat kathayanti dundubhiravai rāṣṭre yad udghoṣitaṁ
tan namrāṅgatayā vadanti karuṇaṁ yasmāt trapāvān bhavet
çlāghante yad udīryate 'riṇāpy ugraṁ na marmāntakṛd
ye ke cin nanu çāṭhyamaugdhyanidhayas te bhūbhṛtāṁ rañjakāḥ.

'They whisper in his ear what is proclaimed in the town with beat of drum; with body bent, dolorously they tell what makes him ashamed; boastfully they say cruel things, cutting to the quick, such as no foe would say; whoever are embodiments of falsity and foolishness, they are the flatterers of princes.'

8. *Minor Historical Kāvya*

India has nothing comparable to set beside the work of Kalhaṇa, and a brief mention is all that the remaining epics deserve. Another Kashmirian, Jalhaṇa, mentioned by Mañkha as a member of the Sabhā of Alaṁkāra, wrote an account of the life of the king of Rājapurī, Somapālavilāsa, who was conquered by Sussala, in his *Somapālavilāsa*.[1] The virtuous but extremely dreary Jain monk Hemacandra (1088–1172) wrote while the Caulukya king of Aṇhilvāḍ, Kumārapala, was still alive and at the height of his fame, about 1163 his *Kumārapālacarita*[2] or *Dvyāçrayakāvya* in his honour. The poem owes its second name to the fact that it consists of two parts, one of twenty cantos in Sanskrit and one of eight in Prākrit, and it has, besides its historical, a definitely grammatical purpose, being intended to afford illustrations of the rules of Sanskrit and Prākrit grammar taught in his own grammar. The poem, of course, includes some account of the predecessors of his hero, and it has a distinct value for the history of the Caulukyas. But Hemacandra was an earnest Jain; he saw things distorted by his devotion to his religion, of which he was a zealous propagandist. His success in this regard is proved by the fact that the cantos (xvi–xx) of the poem celebrating Kumārapāla's rule seem to be true to fact, in substance at any rate, in representing the king as a loyal follower of the principles of Jainism who forbade the slaughter of animals under the severest penalty, erected freely Jain temples, and pursued a definitely pro-Jain policy.

Fate unfortunately has left only one fragmentary and defective manuscript of a poem of some historical interest, the *Pṛthvīrājavijaya*,[3] an account of the victories of the Cāhamāna king of

[1] Cf. *Rājataraṅgiṇī*, viii. 621 f.
[2] Ed. BSS. 60, 69, 76, 1900–21; Bühler, *Hemachandra*, pp. 18 f., 43.
[3] Har Bilas Sarda, JRAS. 1913, pp. 259 ff.; ed. BI. 1914–22.

Ajmir and Delhi, Pṛthvīrāja, who won a great victory over Sultan Shihāb-ud-dīn Ghorī in 1191, though he was shortly afterwards ruined and slain. The poem seems to have been written in the lifetime of the king probably just after that victory, though as it is unfinished this is a mere conjecture. The name of the author is unknown, but he may have been a Kashmirian, as is suggested by his imitation of Bilhaṇa's style; his form of exordium, in which he mentions Bhāsa; and the fact that he is mentioned by Jayarath in the *Alaṁkāravimarçinī* (*c.* 1200), and is commented on by Jonarāja (*c.* 1448) of Kashmir.

A minister of the princes of Gujarāt, the Vāghelās, Lavaṇaprasāda and Vīradhavala, is responsible for the writing of two panegyrics. The first is the *Kīrtikaumudi*[1] of Someçvaradatta (1179–1262), author of various inscriptions in which verses from his poem occur; the eulogy of Vastupāla, who was clearly a generous man, and very probably an excellent minister of a type well known in Indian history, is of moderate poetic worth, but it throws a good deal of light on various aspects of Indian social and political life. The *Surathotsava*[2] in fifteen cantos by the same author is on the face of it mythical, but it is possible that it is a political allegory, as it ends with an account of the poet's own history, a phenomenon which is noteworthy in the *Harṣacarita* of Bāṇa and in Bilhaṇa, and it alludes again to Vastupāla. A direct panegyric is the *Sukṛtasaṁkīrtana*[3] of Arisiṅha, also of the thirteenth century, in eleven cantos, which is useful historically as affording a check on Someçvaradeva. It is not until a century later that we have in the *Jagaḍūcarita*[4] of Sarvāṇanda a panegyric of a pious Jain layman who aided his townsfolk by building new walls and affording them great support in the terrible famine of 1256–8 in Gujarāt. It is interesting to find in this poem of seven cantos the usual miracles and legends told in respect of a simple merchant, but as poetry the work is worthless, and in language and metre alike it is no better than the contemporary Jain verse legends.

Of some importance as giving details of historical events else-

[1] Ed. A. V. Kathvate, BSS. 25, 1883.

[2] Ed. KM. 73, 1902.

[3] G. Bühler, *Das Sukṛtasaṃkīrtana des Arisiṃha* (1889).

[4] G. Bühler, *Indian Studies*, i (1892).

where more vaguely recorded is the *Rāmapālacarita*[1] of Sandhyākara Nandin, who described the feats of the powerful king Rāmapāla of Bengal, who recovered his ancestral throne from an usurper, Bhīma, and conquered Mithilā, reigning *c.* 1084–1130. The *Rājendrakarṇapūra*[2] of Çambhu is a panegyric of Harṣadeva of Kashmir at whose court he wrote the *Anyoktimuktālatāçataka*. The poem is of no great merit.

Finally there may be noted the work of the Kashmir writers who continued the *Rājataraṅgiṇī*.[3] Jonarāja, who died in 1459, carried it on under the same style to the reign of Sultan Zainu-l-'ābidīn; his pupil Çrīvara covered in the *Jaina-Rājataraṅgiṇī* in four books the period 1459–86, while Prājya Bhaṭṭa and his pupil Çuka in the *Rājāvalipatākā* carried on the tale to some years after the annexation of Kashmir by Akbar. The work of these writers is devoid of originality or merit; Çrīvara shamelessly borrows from Kalhaṇa, and, despite the length of the period with which they deal, the total of their work is not more than half that of the *Rājataraṅgiṇī*; they waste space in episodic descriptions, and they are far less accurate in matters of topography than Kalhaṇa.

[1] Ed. Haraprasāda Sāstrī, *A. S. B. Memoirs*, III. i (1910). Cf. EI. ix. 321; EHI. p. 416; above, p. 137.

[2] Ed. KM. i. 22 ff.

[3] Ed. Calcutta, 1835; Bühler, *Report*, p. 61; Stein, *Rājataraṅgiṇī*, ii. 373.

VIII

BHARTṚHARI, AMARU, BILHAṆA, AND JAYADEVA

1. *Bhartṛhari*

A HISTORY of Sanskrit lyric [1] and gnomic verse is impossible in the absence of any chronology, and, apart from minor poems which will be discussed later, our first great monument after Kālidāsa of these kinds of verse, in which Indian poets admittedly excel, is to be found in the Çatakas of Bhartṛhari. As we have them, they are handed down as three collections each theoretically of a hundred stanzas, in varied metres, of pictures of love, *Çṛṅgāraçataka*, of indifference to things of sense, *Vairāgya*, and of wise conduct, *Nīti*. It is obvious that a form like this allows of interpolation and addition, and the task of arriving at a definitive text which we can reasonably assert to be original is probably beyond our means of accomplishment. What we can say is that for a considerable number of stanzas in each of the Çatakas the concurrence of manuscript evidence renders reference to the original extremely probable. A perplexing fact is that the collections contain stanzas from well-known works such as the *Tantrākhāyika*, the *Çakuntalā* of Kālidāsa, the *Mudrārākṣasa* of Viçākhadatta, and stanzas which in the anthologies are ascribed to authors other than Bhartṛhari. If the anthologies were trustworthy, it would be possible to deduce important results from these facts, but, as they are full of errors and frequently contradict themselves, it is hopeless to draw any chronological conclusions or to derive from these references or the stanzas from other works actually included any support for the theory that the collections are really an early anthology.[2]

Indian tradition, none of it early, unquestionably sets down

[1] Cf. P. E. Pavolini, *Poeti d'amore nell' India* (Florence, 1900).

[2] Cf. Peterson, *Subhāṣitāvali*, pp. 74 f.; Aufrecht, *Leipzig Catal.*, No. 417; Hertel, WZKM. xvi. 202 ff.; Pathak, JBRAS. xviii. 348.

the Çatakas as the work of one man, and does not consider them anthologies. Of this man unfortunately no clear memory remained, but, as this applies equally even to Kālidāsa, the only conclusion which can be drawn is that like that writer he belonged to a fairly early date, before authors became sufficiently self-conscious to ensure the handing down of their memory by embodying references to themselves in their poems. But we do learn from the Buddhist pilgrim I-tsing that about forty years before he wrote, therefore about 651, there died in India a grammarian, Bhartṛhari, certainly the author of the *Vākyapadīya*, the last independent contribution to Indian grammatical science. Of him I-tsing[1] tells the tale that he ever wavered between the monastic and the lay life, moving seven times between the cloister and the world in the manner permitted to Buddhists. On one occasion, when entering the monastery, he bade a student have a chariot ready for him without, that he might depart in it if worldly longings overcame his hard-won resolution. I-tsing also cites a verse in which Bhartṛhari reproaches himself for his inability to decide between the attractions of the two lives. It is natural, therefore, to accept the suggestion of Max Müller[2] that we have here a reference to the author of the Çatakas, though it is certain that I-tsing does not actually refer to them, for the vague terms in which he alludes to his writing on the principles of human life cannot well be treated as a real allusion to the Çatakas. It is also clear that Bhartṛhari in the Çatakas is not a Buddhist, though he, like Buddhists, arrives at counsels of freedom from desire and resignation, but a Çaiva of the Vedānta type, to whom Çiva appears as the most perfect presentation of the final reality, the Brahman. We may, of course, suppose that Bhartṛhari was once a courtier—as his reflections on the miseries of serving the great attest—and a Çaiva, and that in old age he became a Buddhist, and that I-tsing either did not learn of his Çatakas or deliberately ignored them. Or he may even have composed the Çatakas after his investigation of Buddhism had decided him upon abandoning that faith; such a fact I-tsing would not record with any pleasure, even if he knew of it. Or, if

[1] *Records of the Buddhist Religion*, pp. 178 ff.; cf. Erm. La Terza, OC. XII, i. 201 f.

[2] *India* (1883), pp. 347 ff.

he were a mere compiler, the difficulty would disappear. It must, however, be said that it is not probable that we are to explain the notices as a confusion on the part of I-tsing of two Bhartṛharis, one older, the poet, and the grammarian, for it has been shown by very substantial evidence[1] that Bhartṛhari the grammarian was actually a Buddhist, a fact which explains in large measure the neglect accorded to his work. On the whole it seems most probable that Max Müller's conjecture may stand.

The question of compilation is more difficult still, and it seems unnecessary to exclude the probability that in his collections Bhartṛhari may have included work not his own, as well as verses composed by himself. Indeed, it would be difficult to find any convincing ground for suggesting that this is not the case with the *Nīti* and *Vairāgya Çatakas*.[2] The case of the *Çṛñgāra-çataka*[3] is different, for unquestionably there is a definite structure which may be, of course, the work of a skilled compiler, but which more naturally suggests the product of a creative mind. The Çataka opens with pictures of the beauty of women and the passion of love as it varies with the changing seasons of the year, and the joys of its fruition. We pass thence to stanzas in which the joys of dalliance are contrasted with the abiding peace brought to man by penance and wisdom, and finally the poet reaches the conviction that beauty is a delusion and a snare, that woman is sweet but poisonous as a snake on man's way in life, that love leads only to worldly attachment, and that the true end of man lies in renunciation and in God, Çiva or Brahman. We may, therefore, adopt with moderate certainty the view that in this Çataka we have much more individual work than in the other two, though we need not suppose that Bhartṛhari held any views—quite foreign to Indian poets—which would have prevented him from including in his poem a predecessor's work, and still less, of course, a slightly improved edition of such work. Some weight must certainly be allowed to the fact that the Indian tradition is consistent, and that it cannot be explained as in the case of the *Cāṇakya Nītiçāstra* by the fame of a name, for Bhartṛhari stands isolated.

[1] Pathak, JBRAS. xviii. 341 ff.
[2] Ed. K. T. Telang, BSS. 11, 1885.
[3] Ed. P. von Bohlen, Berlin, 1833; NSP. 1914. Cf. Winternitz, GIL. iii. 139 f.

Nothing for history or chronology can be derived from the legends which make him out to have been a brother of the famed Vikramāditya, and the attempted identification of him with Bhaṭṭi, author of the *Bhaṭṭikāvya*, has no plausibility.

Bhartṛhari's poetry exhibits Sanskrit to the best advantage. The epics unquestionably lack life and action, their characters are stereotyped, and their descriptions, admirable in detail, tend to be over-elaborate and to lose force by this very fact. In Bhartṛhari each stanza normally can stand by itself and serves to express one idea, be it a sentiment of love, of resignation, or of policy, in complete and daintily finished form. The extraordinary power of compression which Sanskrit possesses is seen here at its best; the effect on the mind is that of a perfect whole in which the parts coalesce by inner necessity, and the impression thus created on the mind cannot be reproduced in an analytical speech like English, in which it is necessary to convey the same content, not in a single sentence syntactically merged into a whole, like the idea which it expresses, but in a series of loosely connected predications. The effect which the best stanzas of the lyric and gnomic poets achieve is essentially synthetic, as opposed to the analytic methods of modern poetry, and it follows inevitably that a series of stanzas of this kind is too heavy a burden for the mind; considered, however, each in itself, as they should be, these stanzas, like those of the Greek anthology,[1] present us with an almost infinite number of brilliant poems in miniature, on which it would often be hard to improve. It must be remembered that the use of the longer metres gives a Sanskrit poet the opportunity of compressing into a single stanza material sufficient to fill a compact English sonnet, so that there is no need to restrict within too narrow limits either the thought or the expression.

Bhartṛhari speaks in many tones; his picture of the magnanimous man is:

vipadi dhairyaṁ athābhyudaye kṣamā: sadasi vākpaṭutā yudhi vikramaḥ
yaçasi cābhirucir vyasanaṁ çrutau: prakṛtisiddham idaṁ hi mahātmanām.

[1] Cf. J. W. Mackail, *Select Epigrams from the Greek Anthology* (1906).

'Constancy in misfortune, gentleness in prosperity, in the council-chamber eloquence, in battle valour, delight in glory, love of holy writ: these are innate in the noble man.' His picture of the stages of life is impressive:

āyur varṣaçataṁ nṛṇāṁ rātrau tadardhaṁ gataṁ
tasyārdhasya parasya cārdham aparam bālatvavṛddhatvayoḥ
çeṣaṁ vyādhiviyogaduḥkhasahitaṁ sevādibhir nīyate
jīve vāritarañgabudbudasame saukhyaṁ kutaḥ prāṇinām?

'To man is allotted a span of a hundred years; half of that passes in sleep; of the other half, one-half is spent in childhood and old age; the rest is passed in service with illness, separation, and pain as companions. How can mortals find joy in life that is like the bubbles on the waves of the sea?' The acts of man's life are finely depicted in a manner in its own way as finished as Shakespeare's:

kṣaṇam bālo bhūtvā kṣaṇam api yuvā kāmarasikaḥ
kṣaṇaṁ vittair hīnaḥ kṣaṇam api ca sampūrṇavibhavaḥ
jarājīrṇair añgair naṭa iva valīmaṇḍitatanur
naraḥ saṁsārānte viçati yamadhānīyavanikām.

'For a moment man is a boy, for a moment a lovesick youth, for a moment bereft of wealth, for a moment in the height of prosperity; then at life's end with limbs worn out by old age and wrinkles adorning his face, like an actor, he retires behind the curtain of death.' The utter unsatisfactoriness of life is insisted upon:

ākrāntam maraṇena janma jarasā yāty uttamaṁ yauvanam
saṁtoṣo dhanalipsayā çamasukham prauḍhāñganāvibhramaiḥ
lokair matsaribhir guṇā vanabhuvo vyālair nṛpā durjanair
asthairyeṇa vibhūtayo 'py upahatā grastaṁ na kiṁ kena vā?

'By death is life assailed; by old age the delight of youth departeth, by greed contentment, the calm of inner joy through the coquetries of forward ladies; envy attacks our virtues, snakes trees, villains kings; all power is transient. What is there that another doth not overwhelm or it another?' The might of time to obliterate all is sadly recognized:

sā ramyā nagarī mahān sa nṛpatiḥ sāmantacakraṁ ca tat
pārçve tasya ca sā vidagdhapariṣat tāç candrabimbānanāḥ
udvṛttaḥ sa ca rājaputranivahas te bandinas tāḥ kathāḥ
sarvaṁ yasya vaçād agāt smṛtipathaṁ kālāya tasmai namaḥ.

'That fair city, that mighty king, the circle of vassal princes at his side, that assembly of learned men, those maidens with faces like the moon or the Bimba, that haughty ring of princes of the blood, those minstrels and their ballads—all are but memories, and to time, who hath wrought this deed, let us pay homage due.' Yet men are blind to the fate that awaits them:

ādityasya gatāgatair aharahaḥ saṁkṣīyate jīvitaṁ
vyāpārair bahukāryabhāragurubhiḥ kālo na vijñāyate
dṛṣṭvā janmajarāvipattimaraṇaṁ trāsaç ca notpadyate
pītvā mohamayīm pramādamadirām unmattabhūtaṁ jagat.

'With the rising and the setting of the sun man's life day by day wears away; struggling beneath the burden of active toil we note not the passing of time; birth, age, misfortune, death we see and tremble not; the world is maddened by drinking too deep of the draught of carelessness and confusion.' The ascetic's life is compared with that of the king greatly to its advantage, and a touch of quiet humour enlightens the picture of the old age for which the poet pines:

Gaṅgātīre himagiriçilābaddhapadmāsanasya
brahmadhyānābhyasanavidhinā yoganidrāṁ gatasya
kiṁ tair bhāvyam mama sudivasair yeṣu te nirviçaṅkāḥ
kaṇḍūyante jaṭharahariṇāḥ çṛṅgam aṅge madīye.

'When will those days come when I can take my seat on Ganges' bank on a rock of the snowy mountain, and fixing my thoughts for ever on Brahman fall into the deep sleep of contemplation, while the old deer fearlessly rub their horns on my limbs?' The end is union and merger in the highest spirit, the absolute:

mātar medini tāta māruta sakhe jyotiḥ subandho jala
bhrātar vyoma nibaddha eṣa bhavatām antyaḥ praṇāmāñjaliḥ
yuṣmatsaṅgavaçopajātasukṛtodrekasphurannirmala-
jñānāpāstasamastamohamahimā līye pare brahmaṇi.

'O mother earth, father wind, friend fire, loved kinsman water, brother ether, for the last time I clasp my hands before you in homage. I now merge in the highest Brahman, since through my abundance of good deeds, born of union with you, I have won pure and brilliant knowledge and thus have cast aside all the power of confusion.'

Thus speaks the old man in Bhartṛhari; a very different note is struck in the stanzas which celebrate love without *arrière-pensée* or thought of the to-morrow:

adarçane darçanamātrakāmā : dṛṣṭau pariṣvañgarasaikalolāḥ
āliñgitāyām punar āyatākṣyām : āçāsmahe vigrahayor abhedam.

'When we see not our loved one, we are content to long to gaze upon her; seen, our one aim is the joy of close embraces; embraced, our one prayer is that her body and our own may be made one.' Every act, every emotion, in the beloved has its charm:

smitena bhāvena ca lajjayā bhiyā : parāñmukhair ardhaka-ṭākṣavīkṣaṇaiḥ
vacobhir īrṣyākalahena līlayā : samastabhāvaiḥ khalu bandhanaṁ striyaḥ.

'Smiles, sentiment, shame, fear, glances averted, half-turned towards us, and side-long looks, loving words, jealousy, disputes, and play: all these are the weapons by which women bind us.' It is absurd to call maidens by that name (*abalā*, feeble):

nūnaṁ hi te kavivarā viparītabodhā
ye nityam āhur abalā iti kāminīnām
yābhir vilolataratārakadṛṣṭipātaiḥ
Çakrādayo 'pi vijitās tv abalāḥ kathaṁ tāḥ?

'Feeble-minded indeed those great poets who ever say that loving maids are weak (women); how can they be deemed weak whose flashing star-like glances have laid low Çakra and other gods?' Another graceful play on words extols love's archery:

mugdhe dhanuṣmattā keyam apūrvā tava dṛçyate
yayā vidhyasi cetāṅsi guṇair eva na sāyakaiḥ.

'Without parallel, o fair one, assuredly is thy marksmanship. With thy bowstrings (charms), not thine arrows, thou dost pierce our hearts.' A pretty picture shows us the beloved in the forest:

viçramya viçramya vane drumāṇāṁ: chāyāsu tanvī vicacāra kācit
stanottarīyeṇa karoddhṛtena: nivārayantī çaçino mayūkhān.

'With many a pause midst the shade of the forest trees moved the slender girl, shielding herself from the moonbeams by raising from her bosom her outer robe.' Two views of women are possible, as helps or hindrances:

saṁsāre 'sminn asāre kunṛpatibhavanadvārasevākalaṅka-vyāsaṅgadhvastadhairyāḥ katham amaladhiyo mānasaṁ saṁvidadhyuḥ
yady etāḥ prodyadindudyutinicayabhṛto na syur ambhojanetrāḥ preṅkhatkāñcīkalāpāḥ stanabharavinamanmadhyabhāgās taruṇyaḥ.

'In this unhappy world, where high courage is overwhelmed by the shame brought by waiting in the ante-chambers of evil kings, how could noble men find comfort in their hearts, were it not for the tender maidens, with the beauty of the rising moon, with lotus eyes, whose girdle-bells tinkle as their slender waists bend beneath the burden of their breasts?'

saṁsārodadhinistārapadavī na davīyasī
antarā dustarā na syur yadi nāryo mahāpagāḥ.

'The path across the ocean of life would not be long, were it not that women, those mighty unfordable streams, hinder the passage.'

kāminīkāyakāntāre kucaparvatadurgame
mā saṁcara manaḥpāntha tatrāste smarataskaraḥ.

'O wandering heart, stray not in the forest of woman's fair body, nor in the steeps which are her breasts, for there lurks Love, the highwayman.'

The predominant metre of Bhartṛhari is the Çārdūlavikrīḍita, which in Böhlen's edition[1] is found in 101 verses; then comes the Çikhariṇī in 48, the Çloka in 37, the Vasantatilaka in 35; the Sragdharā and the Āryā each occur 18 times, while the Gīti

[1] Stanzler, ZDMG. xliv. 34 f.; Gray, JAOS. xx. 157 ff.

variety of the Āryā type is found twice, in one case in an unusual form. Other metres are sporadic; they include the Indravajrā type, Mālinī, Hariṇī, Mandākrāntā, Pṛthvī, Drutavilambita, Vaṅçasthā—in one stanza an Indravajrā line is included—and Çālinī; Rathoddhatā and Vaitālīya each occur twice, while there is a single example of each of the Dodhaka, Puṣpitāgrā, and Mātrāsamaka of 16 *morae*.

2. *Amaru*

Like Bhartṛhari, Amaru or Amaruka—the quantity of the *u* varies—is a person of mystery. His century of stanzas,[1] like those of Bhartṛhari, is presented to us in a very different condition in the manuscripts, which have from 90 to 115 verses. Of the four recensions[2] which have been distinguished only fifty-one stanzas are common to all, and there is much variation in order. Moreover, some of the stanzas in the Çataka are attributed by the anthologies to other writers, while conversely they ascribe to Amaru verses not found therein. Various efforts have been made to decide the original form of the text, but the suggestion that only Çārdūlavikrīḍita verses should be admitted as genuine lacks any proof, incidentally leaving us with only sixty-one such verses to make up the century; there is more plausibility in suggesting the superior value of the text as recognized by the oldest commentator Arjunavarman (*c.* 1215), but no certainty is possible.

It is equally impossible to decide the date of the author. We know that the Çataka was recognized by Ānandavardhana (*c.* 850) as a work of high repute, for he cites it as a proof that a poet can in single stanzas convey so much sentiment that each appears like a poem in miniature. Further, Vāmana (*c.* 800) cites, without naming the author, three stanzas. These citations establish certainly that the Çataka dates before 750, but it is a long step from this to the conclusion that the work is of the period of Kālidāsa, and, therefore, older than Bhartṛhari. From the elaboration and perfection of the technique it seems much more probable that the poet wrote after rather than before 650.

[1] See R. Simon, *Das Amaruçataka* (Kiel, 1893); ZDMG. xlix. 577 ff.

[2] South Indian (comm. Vemabhūpāla); Bengal (Ravicandra); that used by Arjunavarman; and a mixed recension (Rāmarudra, Rudramadeva).

Unfortunately the only tradition recorded is absolutely foolish; the great sage Çañkara is alleged to have animated for a period the body of a king of Kashmir in order to obtain knowledge of the pleasures of love, and the Çataka is the record of his experiences with the hundred ladies of the harem. The commentator Ravicandra carries this out to the extent of finding a theosophic sub-meaning in the stanzas. Other commentators have different views. Vemabhūpāla (14th cent.), commentator of the first recension, following up the description of the poem as having as its purpose the exposition of the sentiment of love, contained in the manuscripts, seeks to show for each stanza that it describes the condition of a Nāyikā, or heroine according to the description of the text-books of poetics. Others content themselves with explaining the forms of rhetorical figures found therein. We may, however, dismiss the idea that the work was intended, like Rudra Bhaṭṭa's *Çṛṅgāratilaka*, to illustrate types of anything, whether figures or heroines.[1] The Çataka is essentially a collection of pictures of love, and it differs from the work of Bhartṛhari in that, while Bhartṛhari deals rather with general aspects of love and women as factors in life, Amaru paints the relation of lovers, and takes no thought of other aspects of life. Possibly, if the reference to the purpose in the title in the manuscripts has any value, he may have planned illustrating other sides of life, but that is idle conjecture, and we have sufficient cause to be grateful to him for what he has given us without seeking more.

The love which Amaru likes is gay and high-spirited, delighting in tiny tiffs and lovers' quarrels, but ending in smiles; the poet hardly ever contemplates the utter disappearance of love; the maiden may be angry, but she will relent, and she is angry indeed when her lover takes her too seriously:

katham api sakhi krīḍākopād vrajeti mayodite
kaṭhinahṛdayas tyaktvā çayyāṁ balād gata eva saḥ
iti sarabhasadhvastapremṇi vyapetaghṛṇe spṛhām
punar api hatavrīḍaṁ cetaḥ karoti karomi kim?

'In feigned anger, dear friend, I said to my beloved, "Depart", and straightway the hard-hearted one sprang from our couch and

[1] See Pischel's ed. of Rudra, pp. 9–11.

left me. Now my shameless heart yearns for that cruel one who so hastily broke off our love, and what can I do?' Means to win back the errant one may be devised by a kind confidante:

datto 'syāḥ praṇayas tvayaiva bhavatā seyaṁ ciraṁ lālitā
daivād adya kila tvam eva kṛtavān asyā navaṁ vipriyam
manyur duḥsaha eṣa yāty upaçamaṁ no sāntvavādaiḥ sphuṭaṁ
he nistriṅca vimuktakaṇṭhakaruṇaṁ tāvat sakhī roditu.

'"Thou didst give her thy love; long hast thou cherished her; fate has decreed that to-day thou hast caused her fresh displeasure; her anger is hard to bear and words of comfort cannot stay it, o thou heartless man," let this her friend say to melt his heart in tones that he can hear.' The hard-hearted maiden herself is warned:

likhann āste bhūmim bahir avanataḥ prāṇadayito
nirāhārāḥ sakhyaḥ satataruditocchūnanayanāḥ
parityaktaṁ sarvaṁ hasitapaṭhitam pañjaraçukais
tavāvasthā ceyaṁ visṛja kaṭhine mānam adhunā.

'The beloved of thy life standeth without, his head bowed down drawing figures on the ground; thy friends can eat nothing, their eyes are swollen with constant weeping; the parrots in their cages no more laugh or speak, and thine own state is this! Ah, lay aside thine anger, o hard-hearted maiden.' And the punishment of the peccant lover is often sheer joy to both of them and her friends:

kopāt komalalolabāhulatikāpāçena baddhvā dṛḍhaṁ
nītvā mohanamandiraṁ dayitayā svairaṁ sakhīnām puraḥ
bhūyo 'py evam iti skhalanmṛdugirā saṁsūcya duçceṣṭitaṁ
dhanyo hanyata eva nihnutiparaḥ preyān rudatyā hasan.

'Happy the lover whom his enraged darling binds firm in the supple embrace of her arms and bears before her friends into love's abode, to denounce his misdeeds in a soft voice that trembles as she says, "Yet once more he wronged me", while he keeps on denying everything and laughing as she cries and pummels him.' But the picture may be more serious if the lover will insist on going despite all:

yātāḥ kiṁ na milanti sundari punaç cintā tvayā matkṛte
no kāryā nitarāṁ kṛçāsi kathayaty evaṁ sabāṣpe mayi
lajjāmantharatārakeṇa nipatatpītāçruṇā cakṣuṣā
dṛṣṭvā māṁ hasitena bhāvimaraṇotsāhas tayā sūcitaḥ.

'"Do travellers never return? Thou must not, fair one, vex thyself on my account; thou art all too thin." So said I midst tears, but, though she laughed, her eyes filled with tears, their pupils dull with shame, betrayed her rash purpose of death to come.' But more common is the light-hearted treatment of lovers' quarrels:

ekasmiñ çayane vipakṣaramaṇīnāmagrahe mugdhayā
sadyaḥ kopaparāñmukhaglapitayā cāṭūni kurvann api
āvegād avadhīritaḥ priyatamas tūṣṇīṁ sthitas tatkṣaṇam
mā bhūt supta ivety amandavalitagrīvam punar vīkṣitaḥ.

'As they lay together the fair maiden, hearing her rival's name, averted her head in anger and vehemently repulsed her lover despite his flatteries. But when he stayed still, straightway she turned her neck fearing he had fallen asleep.' A lively dialogue is compressed into the following stanza, which is a marvel of brevity:

bāle nātha vimuñca mānini ruṣaṁ rosān mayā kiṁ kṛtaṁ
khedo 'smāsu na me 'parādhyati bhavān sarve 'parādhā mayi
tat kiṁ rodiṣi gadgadena vacasā kasyāgrato rudyate
nanv etan mama kā tavāsmi dayitā nāsmīty ato rudyate.

'"Dear girl." "My lord." "Stay thine anger, dearest." "What anger have I shown?" "I am sorry." "No blame is thine, all the fault is mine." "Then why dost thou weep and why doth thy voice tremble?" "Before whom do I weep?" "Surely before me." "What am I to thee?" "My beloved." "Not that am I, and so I weep."' A more serious note still may be struck:

dṛṣṭas kātaranetrayā cirataram baddhvāñjaliṁ yācitaḥ
paçcād añçukapallave ca vidhṛto nirvyājam āliṅgitaḥ
ity ākṣipya samastam evam aghṛṇo gantum pravṛttaḥ çaṭhaḥ
pūrvam prāṇaparigraho dayitayā muktas tato vallabhaḥ.

'Long she gazed on him with timid eyes, then entreated him with folded hands, then grasped the hem of his garment, next frankly embraced him; but all her advances he rejected and started to leave her, cruel deceiver; then first she abandoned her life for love, and last her beloved.' Contrast is afforded by a pretty idea:

kva prasthitāsi karabhoru ghane niçīthe: prāṇeçvaro vasati yatra manaḥpriyo me
ekākinī vada kathaṁ na bibheṣi bāle: nanv asti puṅkhitaçaro madanaḥ sahāyaḥ.

'"Whither away, o fair-limbed one, in this dark night?" "Where the lord of my life, my heart's love dwelleth." "But tell me, lady, dost not fear to go alone?" "Is not Love with his feathered arrows my companion?"' Very pretty is the fancy:

mugdhe mugdhatayaiva netum akhilaṁ kālaṁ kim ārabhyate
mānaṁ dhatsva dhṛtim badhāna ṛjutāṁ dūre kuru preyasi
sakhyaivam pratibodhitā prativacas tām āha bhītānanā
nīcaiḥ çaṅsa hṛdi sthito hi nanu me prāṇeçvaraḥ çroṣyati.

'"Foolish one, dost mean to spend all thy time in simple faith? Show proper pride, take courage, heed not loyalty to thy loved one." So did her friend advise; but she all afraid made reply, "Speak low, for my beloved dwells in my heart and he will hear you."' Sly humour, reminding us a little of the homelier style of the poets of Mahārāṣṭra whose work is preserved in Hāla's anthology, may be found in:

dampatyor niçi jalpator gṛhaçukenākarṇitaṁ yad vacas
tat prātar gurusaṁnidhau nigadatas tasyātimātraṁ vadhūḥ
karṇālambitapadmarāgaçakalaṁ vinyasya cañcūpuṭe
vrīḍārtā vidadhāti dāḍimaphalavyājena vāgbandhanam.

'The house parrot overheard at night some dalliance of the young pair and in the morning began to repeat it unduly before their elders; so the young wife in shame stays his speech by putting in his beak a fragment of ruby from her earring, on the pretext of giving him a pomegranate fruit.'

The stanzas cited show adequately the elegance and precision of Amaru's style, his avoidance of unduly long or difficult compounds, and the effectiveness of his verse. His normal metre is the Çārdūlavikrīḍita; but the Hariṇī, Vasantatilaka, Çikhariṇī, and Sragdharā occur fairly often, while the Çloka, Drutavilambita, Mālinī, and Mandākrāntā are sporadically employed.

3. *Bilhaṇa*

The author of the *Vikramāñkadevacarita* has left us a much more interesting relic in the shape of the poem often called *Caurapañcāçikā*,[1] perhaps more correctly *Caurīsuratapañcāçikā*, fifty stanzas on a secret love. In two of the versions in which it is found, that of Kashmir[2] and that of South India,[3] it is embedded in a poem styled *Bilhaṇakāvya*, in which, as also by the commentators, the poem is asserted to have been composed to record a secret intrigue with a princess. Discovered by the king, the poet was sentenced to death and led out for this purpose, but his recitation of the glowing verses, in which he called to his memory for the last time the joys of their secret union, induced the king to relent and permit his marriage to the princess. Thus far there is agreement, but the Kashmir version asserts that the princess was Candralekhā, daughter of Vīrasiṅha of Mahilapattana, while the southern version makes her Yāminīpūrṇatilakā, daughter of Madanābhirāma of Pañcāla. The commentator Rāma Tarkavāgīça (1798) insists[4] that the poem is an appeal to Kālikā by the prince Sundara of Caurapallī when condemned to death by Vīrasiṅha for his intrigue with Vidyā, while the title has been explained as indicating that the poet was Caura, of whom indeed verses are extant. It is quite clear from Bilhaṇa's autobiography in his epic that he made no claim to royal intrigues, and common sense suggests that he portrayed the love of a robber chief and a princess, placing the robber in the delicate situation to which tradition assigned himself. The poem as a matter of fact merely makes it clear that the heroine was a princess; it refers to the poet's hour of death only in a probably spurious stanza, and the two stanzas prefixed to it in the Kashmir recension, even assuming their genuineness, are hard to interpret satisfactorily. The popularity of the text has rendered it most uncertain, but, as the author was a Kashmirian, and lived at a southern court, there is doubtless some reason for accepting as

[1] Ed. Haeberlin, 227 ff.; KM. xiii. 145–69.

[2] Ed. W. Solf, Kiel, 1886.

[3] Ed. J. Ariel, JA. s. 4, xi. 469 ff. Cf. *Madras Catal.*, xx. 8004 ff. (ascribed to Corakavi).

[4] So in Bhāratacandra's *Vidyāsundara* (18th cent.); D. C. Sen, *Bengali Lang. and Lit.*, pp. 650 f.; *I. O. Catal.*, i. 1524.

genuine the thirty-four stanzas vouched for by both these recensions. That from northern India agrees with both the others in seven stanzas only.

The Vasantatilaka stanzas depict with minute and often charming detail the past scenes of happy love, and possess an elegance which is not exhibited in the *Vikramāñkadevacarita*, though with that poem the *Pañcāçikā* agrees in its simplicity of style, which has the great advantage of being in harmony with the tone of the poem and the feigned occasion of its recital. Nor can it be termed too long; there is sufficient variety in the ideas to prevent it becoming wearisome:

adyāpi tāṁ aviganayya kṛtāparādham: māṁ pādamūlapatitaṁ sahasā galantīm
vastrāñcalam mama karān nijam ākṣipantīm: mā meti roṣaparuṣam bruvatīṁ smarāmi.

'Even to-day do I see her, as, heedless of my falling at her feet to expiate my offence, she rushed away, flung off my hand from the hem of her garment, and in anger cried out, "No, never!"'

adyāpi tāṁ rahasi darpaṇam īkṣamāṇāṁ: saṁkrāntamatpratinibham mayi pṛṣṭhalīne
paçyāmi vepathumatīṁ ca sasambhramāṁ ca: lajjākulāṁ samadanāṁ ca savibhramāṁ ca.

'Even to-day I do see her secretly gazing at the mirror in which I was pictured while I stood behind her, all atremble and confused, utterly shamed between love and distraction.'

adyāpi tām mayi samīpakavāṭalīne: manmārgamuktadṛçam ānanadattahastām
madgotraliṅgitapadam mṛdukākalībhiḥ: kiṁcic ca gātumanasam manasā smarāmi.

'Even to-day do I see her, as, head resting on her hand and eyes fixed on my path—though in truth I was hidden behind the door near by—she sought to sing in sweet tones a verse into which she had woven my name.' The imitation of the *Meghadūta* is obvious, but elegant and attractive.

adyāpi tām bhujalatārpitakaṇṭhapāçāṁ: vakṣaḥsthalam mama pidhāya payodharābhyām
īṣannimīlitasalīlavilocanāntām: paçyāmi mugdhavadanāṁ vadanam pibantīm.

'Even to-day do I see the fair arms that encircled my neck, when she clasped me close to her breast, and pressed her dear face against my own in a kiss, while her playful eyes half closed in ecstasy.'

adyāpi me varatanor madhurāṇi tasyā: yāny arthavanti na ca yāni nirarthakāni
nidrānimīlitadṛco madamantharāyās: tāny akṣarāṇi hṛdaye kim api dhvananti.

'Even to-day here echo in my heart the words—sweet whether they bore meaning or not—of my fair one, when her eyes were shut in sleep and she was heavy with our love-play.' It seems as if there were deliberate purpose in mentioning the princess's rank in a verse with a distinct touch of humour, alluding as it does to the Indian fashion of addressing a man who sneezed with the words 'Live on':

adyāpi tan manasi samparivartate me: rātrau mayi kṣutavati kṣitipālaputryā
jīveti maṅgalavacaḥ parihṛtya kopāt: karṇe kṛtaṁ kanakapattram anālapantyā.

'Even to-day do I think how, when I sneezed at night, the princess would not wish me the wonted blessing of "Live on", but in silence placed on my ear an ornament of gold.' The gold brings life, and thus served in lieu of the benediction.

adyāpi tām praṇayinīm mṛgaçābakākṣīm: pīyūṣavarṇakucakumbhayugaṁ vahantīm
paçyāmy ahaṁ yadi punar divasāvasāne: svargāpavargavararājyasukhaṁ tyajāmi.

'Could I but see at the close of day once more my love with the eyes of a fawn, and milk-white rounded breasts, gladly would I sacrifice the highest joys of here and hereafter.'

4. *Jayadeva*

To the reign of Lakṣmaṇasena[1] in Bengal belongs the last great name in Sanskrit poetry, Jayadeva, son of Bhojadeva of Kindubilva, and with Govardhana, Dhoī, Çaraṇa, and Umāpati-

[1] Cf. EHI. pp. 419 ff., 431 ff.; M. Chakravarti, JPASB. 1906, pp. 163 ff.; R. C Majumdar, JPASB. 1921, pp. 7 ff. (1175–1200); above, p. 53 n. 4.

dhara, one of the five jewels which adorned the court. We have preserved of him one tiny Hindī poem, a eulogy of Hari Govind, claimed to be the oldest in the *Ādi Granth* of the Sikhs, and many legends are told in the *Bhakt Mālā* of his devotion to Kṛṣṇa, who himself aided him to describe the loveliness of Rādhā when his mortal powers failed. It is strange that we should have nothing else from a man so talented, but at any rate he achieved in its own way a perfect and very novel work of art in the *Gītagovindakāvyam*, or *Gītagovinda*,[1] the poem in which Govinda, Kṛṣṇa as lord of the herdsmen and their wives, is sung. The fame of the author is attested by the fact that in his honour for centuries there was held each year at his birthplace a festival, in which during the night the songs of his poem were sung. Pratāparudradeva in 1499 ordered that the dancers and Vaiṣṇava singers should learn his songs only, and an inscription of 1292 already cites a verse. Hence his own claim that he is over-king of poets (*kavirājarāja*) has been justified in his own land, while even through the distorting medium of Sir William Jones's version his high qualities attracted the praise which Goethe[2] also lavished on Kālidāsa's *Meghadūta* and *Çakuntalā*.

The form of the poem is extremely original, and has led to the belief that we have in the poem a little pastoral drama, as Jones called it, or a lyric drama, as Lassen styled it, or a refined Yātrā, as von Schroeder preferred to term it. Pischel and Lévi, on the other hand, placed it in the category between song and drama, on the ground *inter alia* that it is already removed from the Yātrā type of dramatic performance by the fact that the transition verses are put in definite form and not left to improvisation, but Pischel also styles it a melodrama. The facts are, however, satisfactorily clear and allow of greater precision of statement. The poet divides the poem into cantos, which is a clear sign that he recognized it to belong to the generic type Kāvya, and that he did not mean it to be a dramatic performance with the division into acts, interludes, and so forth. On the other hand, he had before his mind when he wrote the Yātrās of Bengal, where in honour of Kṛṣṇa in a primitive form of drama dances

[1] Ed. C. Lassen (1836); NSP. 1923; trans. F. Rückert, ZKM. i. 128 ff.; G. Courtillier, Paris, 1904.

[2] *Werke*, xxxvii. 210 f.

accompanied by music and song were performed, and in inserting as the most vital element in his poem such songs he doubtless foresaw the use that would be made of them both in the temples and at festivals. The songs are given to us in the manuscripts with precise indication by technical terms of the melody (*rāga*) and time (*tāla*) of the music[1] and dance which they were to accompany, and the poet definitely bids us think of songs as being performed in this way before our mental eyes. To conceive of writing such a poem was a remarkable piece of originality, for it was an immense step from the popular songs of the Yātrās to produce so remarkably beautiful and finished a work.

The art of the poet displays itself effectively in the mode in which song and recitative are blended and the skill with which monotony of form is avoided by not restricting the recitative to mere introductory verses explaining the situation, while the songs express in their turn the feelings of the personnel of the poem, Kṛṣṇa, his favourite Rādhā, and the faithful friend, who is the essential confidante of every Indian heroine. Recitative is used for occasional narrative verses to explain the situation, but also in brief descriptions, and, as a mode of securing variety, in speeches which serve as an alternative to songs as the mode of intimating the sentiments of the characters. There is thus no stereotyped form; the recitative and the song, narrative, description, and speeches are cunningly interwoven, all with deliberate purpose. The first canto, which contains four of the twenty-four Prabandhas, songs, into which the poem is also divided, exhibits in perfection the complex structure. The poet begins with four verses, in the last of which he celebrates himself and his fellow-poets; then the first Prabandha begins, consisting of a hymn in eleven stanzas sung in honour of the ten incarnations of Viṣṇu, and ending with a mention of the author, whose hymn Kṛṣṇa is entreated to hear; each stanza ends with the refrain, 'Conquer, o lord of the world, o Hari.' This closes the Prabandha, and a single stanza, doubtless recited, follows, in which the poet sums up the forms of Viṣṇu which the hymn has glorified. Prabandha ii opens with another hymn in nine stanzas sung in honour of the god, each ending with the refrain, 'Conquer, conquer, o god,

[1] Soma, son of Mudgala, in his *Rāgavibodha* gives the music for the songs; cf. S. M. Tagore, *Hindu Music* (1875), i. 159.

o Hari.' At the close of the Prabandha and before the next is a recited stanza invoking a benediction from Kṛṣṇa. Prabandha iii consists of a recited verse telling how Rādhā's friend spoke to her in the spring and then sings in eight stanzas [1] how Kṛṣṇa is dancing with the cowherdesses in the groves. Three stanzas in recitative follow, describing the spring, and ending with the statement that Rādhā's friend once more addressed her, and Prabandha iv consists of a song in eight stanzas in which she describes how the loving maidens flock to Kṛṣṇa and embrace him in their passion. Then three stanzas of recitative follow, the first two descriptive, the last a benediction. Canto ii tells us first of Rādhā's dejection and gives her song of complaint against her lover (Prabandha v), followed by a stanza of recitative, introducing another song (vi) in which she expresses her deep longing for the god. Then in two recited stanzas she celebrates the god, while the poet in the last stanza invokes the usual benediction.

In Canto iii Kṛṣṇa appears in person; remorse and longing for Rādhā have seized him; two recited verses describe his state, and Prabandha vii gives his song of love. This is followed by recited verses addressed by him, first to the god of love, and then to Rādhā herself, and the poet closes the canto with a prayer to Kṛṣṇa as the lover of Rādhā to confer fortune and happiness on the hearers. In Canto iv Rādhā s friend addresses Kṛṣṇa and in two songs (viii and ix) depicts the yearnings of her mistress and her deep sorrow at separation from her beloved. A benediction ends the canto. In the next two we find Rādhā's friend urging in three fine songs (x–xii) reconciliation of her mistress with Kṛṣṇa. But in Canto vii we find that the faithless god has not come, and the moon's rising heightens Rādhā's love, to which she gives expression in four passionate songs (xiii–xvi). He appears, but she addresses him again in a song (xvii) expressing her resentment, followed by recitative in the same sense (viii). Her companion seeks by a song (xviii) to console her (ix), and Kṛṣṇa himself appears and sings (xix) to her (x). There still remains Rādhā's reluctance and shyness to be overcome in three songs by her friend (xi); but all is secure at last, and the poem closes with songs in which Kṛṣṇa addresses his beloved and she replies.

[1] This is the normal number, and hence the poem figures as *Aṣṭapadī* in the south Cf. Śeshagiri, *Report*, 1893–4, pp. 60 ff.

The poet invokes the usual benediction, and extols his own knowledge of music, his devotion to Viṣṇu, his delicate discrimination of sentiments, and his poetical charm and grace.

Efforts have been made to establish that the poem has a mystical significance and to interpret it in this sense. The desire in part at least has been prompted by the feeling that the loves of Kṛṣṇa and Rādhā are too essentially of the body rather than of the mind, and that to ascribe them to the divinity is unworthy. But this is to misunderstand Indian feeling. The classical poets one and all see no harm in the love-adventures of the greatest deities, and what Kālidāsa did in the *Kumārasambhava* was repeated by all his successors in one form or another. But, on the other hand, it must not be forgotten that the religion of Jayadeva was the fervent Kṛṣṇa worship which found in the god the power which is ever concerned with all the wishes, the hopes and fears of men, which, if in essence infinite and ineffable, yet expresses itself in the form of Kṛṣṇa, and which sanctions in his amours the loves of mankind. In this sense Jayadeva's work is deeply touched with the spirit of religion, and stands like the *Bakchai* of Euripides utterly apart from the attitude of the Alexandrine poets or Propertius and Ovid in their treatment of the legends of the gods. To Kallimachos as much as to his Roman imitators the gods and goddesses were no more than names, at best elegant symbols of a higher reality, but without real life of their own. Roman poets could here and there catch the tone of seriousness as in the atheist Lucretius' famous exordium to the mother of the Aeneidae, darling of gods and men, increase-giving Venus, and still more in Catullus' extraordinary if repellent picture of the adorer of Cybele who becomes as Attis. But neither Lucretius nor Catullus was himself a believer, and all doubt, all scepticism are far from Jayadeva, to whom alike in his play with others and in his more abiding love for Rādhā Kṛṣṇa remained not merely divine, but the embodiment of the highest of gods.

Jayadeva's work is a masterpiece, and it surpasses in its completeness of effect any other Indian poem. It has all the perfection of the miniature word-pictures which are so common in Sanskrit poetry, with the beauty which arises as Aristotle asserts from magnitude and arrangement. All the sides of love, save that of utter despair and final separation, are brilliantly described; all the emotions of longing, of awakened hope, of disappointment, of hot anger against the unfaithful one, of reconciliation, are portrayed by the actors themselves or Rādhā's friend in songs which are perfect in metrical form and display at its highest point the sheer beauty of words of which Sanskrit is pre-eminently capable. There can be no doubt that in their wider range of interests, in which love plays a part important indeed but not paramount in human affairs, Aischylos, Sophokles, and Euripides can attain in their choruses effects more appealing to our minds than Jayadeva, but their medium is not capable of producing so complete a harmony of sound and sense. We are apt to regard with impatience the insistence of the writers on poetics on classing styles largely by the sounds preferred by different writers, but there is no doubt that the effects of different sounds were more keenly appreciated in India than they are by us, and in the case of the *Gītagovinda* the art of wedding sound and meaning is carried out with such success that it cannot fail to be appreciated even by ears far less sensitive than those of Indian writers on poetics. The result, however, of this achievement is to render any translation useless as a substitute for the original; if to be untranslatable is a proof of the attainment of the highest poetry Jayadeva has certainly claim to that rank.

The poet's effects are not produced by any apparently elaborate effort, nor is he guilty of straining language; his compounds are often fairly long but they are not obscure; in poems which were to be sung and to be used at popular festivals artificiality was obviously out of place, and, though they can never have been intelligible to the mass of their admirers without the readily given aid of vernacular interpretations, the songs are such as, once explained, would doubtless easily be comprehended and learned. Canto ix exhibits the poet's effective simplicity:

Harir abhisarati vahati madhupavane: kiṁ aparam adhikasukhaṁ sakhi bhavane
Mādhave mā kuru mānini mānam aye.
tālaphalād api gurum atisarasam: kiṁ viphalīkuruṣe kucakalasam: Mādhave
kati na kathitam idam anupadam aciram: mā parihara Harim atiçayaruciram: Mādhave

kim iti viṣīdasi rodiṣi vikalā: vihasati yuvatisabhā tava sakalā: Mādhave
mṛdunalinīdalaçītalaçayane: Harim avalokaya saphalaya nayane: Mādhave
janayasi manasi kim iti gurukhedam: çṛṇu mama vacanam anīhitabhedam: Mādhave
Harir upayātu vadatu bahumadhuram: kim iti karoṣi hṛdayam atividhuram: Mādhave
çrījayadevabhaṇitam atilalitam: sukhayatu rasikajanaṁ Haricaritam: Mādhave

'Hari cometh, as the spring wind bloweth; what joy more perfect hast thou in thy home, dear one? Noble one, be not wroth with Mādhava. Why dost thou waste the fairness of thy bosom, lovelier far than the palm fruit? Noble one, be not wroth with Mādhava. How often have I not told thee, at every moment? Reject not Hari who is exceeding fair. Noble one, be not wroth with Mādhava. Why art despondent, tearful and dejected? All the young company doth make mock of thee. Noble one, be not wroth with Mādhava. On the couch cooled by the soft lotus petals gaze upon Hari, give thine eyes their fruition. Noble one, be not wroth with Mādhava. Why dost kindle in thy mind deep sorrow? Hearken to my warning that seeketh not to part you. Noble one, be not wroth with Mādhava. Let Hari come and speak to thee long and tenderly. Why dost thou so harden thy heart against him? Noble one, be not wroth with Mādhava. May this tale of Hari, spoken by Jayadeva, by its sweetness delight all men of taste. Noble one, be not wroth with Mādhava.'

Not less pretty is the invitation to Rādhā by her companion to enter into the grove where Kṛṣṇa, pining for reconciliation and the fruition of his love, awaits her:

mañjutarakuñjatalakelisadane: praviça Rādhe Mādhavasamīpam iha
vilasa ratirabhasahasitavadane.
navabhavadaçokadalaçayanasāre: praviça Rādhe Mādhavasamīpam iha
vilasa kucakalasataralahāre.
kusumacayaracitaçucivāsagehe: praviça Rādhe Mādhavasamīpam iha
vilasa kusumasukumāradehe.

'In his playground neath the lovely thicket, come, o Rādhā, to Mādhava, thy face all smiling with the eagerness of love. In his grove with young Açoka shoots as thy couch, come, o Rādhā, to Mādhava, play with him, as thy necklet quivers on the cups of thy bosom. In this bright home wrought of many a flower, come, o Rādhā, to Mādhava, play with him, thou whose body is tender as a flower.' Equally brilliant is the picture drawn by her friend of the delights of Kṛṣṇa with his loving maidens around him in the grove, though the effect is produced by the accumulation of long compounds:

candanacarcitanīlakalevarapītavasanavanamālī
kelicalanmaṇikuṇḍalamaṇḍitagaṇḍayugasmitaçālī
Harir iha mugdhavadhūnikare: vilasini vilasati kelipare.
pīnapayodharabhārabhareṇa Harim parirabhya sarāgam
gopavadhūr anugāyati kācid udañcitapañcamarāgam: Harir
kāpi vilāsavilolavilocanakhelanajanitamanojam
dhyāyati gopavadhūr adhikam Madhusūdanavadanasarojam:
Harir

'His black body sandal-bedecked, clad in yellow, begarlanded, with his earrings dancing on his cheeks as he sporteth, smiling ever, Hari here midst the band of loving maidens maketh merry in the merriment of their sport. One of the maidens claspeth Hari fast to her throbbing heart, and singeth in the high Pañcama key. Yet another doth stand deeply dreaming of Madhusūdana's lotus face, whose sportive glances have caught and won her heart for its own.'

It has been claimed[1] that the work goes back to an original in Apabhrañça, and the ground adduced is the use of rime. This, however, clearly overstates the position; it is utterly improbable that the original of the poem was ever in anything but Sanskrit, and the most that can be said is that the use of rime which is regular in Apabhrañça poems may have influenced the author of the *Gītagovinda*. But in Sanskrit poetry such rime[2] as we find probably is to be derived from the fondness for Yamakas, the repetition of groups of syllables; when this repetition takes

[1] Pischel, *Die Hofdichter des Lakṣmaṇasena*, p. 22.

[2] Jacobi, *Bhavisatta Kaha*, pp. 51 f. Cf. Vāsudeva's Yamakakāvyas (chap. iv, § 7), *Ghaṭakarpara*, *Nalodaya*, Ānandatīrtha's *Yamakabhārata* (*Madras Catal.*, xx 7954); Çrīvatsāñka's *Yamakaratnākara* (*ibid.* 7797), &c.

place at the end of lines in a stanza we have an approximation to rime. Yamakas are dealt with at length by the older school of poetics, and they are frequently found in Prākrit; indeed, Hemacandra prescribes for the Galitaka metre, frequently used in Prākrit poems, the use of Yamakas at the end of the lines. In Apabhrança poetry Yamakas seem to have been allowed also. True rime, that is when the consonant preceding the corresponding vowel differs, is ignored by the earlier writers on poetics and is first defined as Antyānuprāsa, alliteration at the end, by the *Sāhityadarpaṇa*; Hemacandra, however, in his *Chando'nuçāsana* has occasion to mention it and to distinguish it as Anuprāsa from the mere Yamaka. When used in Sanskrit poetry, it is in the main more or less accidental and is not regularly employed, nor is it common in Prākrit. The frequency with which it is approached in Jayadeva may, therefore, be due in some degree to Apabhrança influence. It may be noted also that the metre of the poem is essentially based on the Gaṇa system[1] in which the determining principle is the number of feet of four *morae*, substitution of a long for two shorts and vice versa thus being permitted and freely resorted to.[2]

[1] Jacobi, ZDMG. xxxviii. 599; SIFI. VIII. ii. 87, 94, n. 1, 113, n. 4.

[2] The effective use of the refrain is doubtless borrowed from religious verse; it is found in the *Ṛgveda*, and in the classical religious lyric, in which also is found rime (e.g. the *Mohamudgara*). See the *Dakṣiṇāmūrtistotra*, *Nirvāṇadaçaka*, *Hastāmalakastotra*, and *Carpaṭapañjarikāstotra* ascribed to Çaṅkara.

IX

LYRIC POETRY AND THE ANTHOLOGIES

1. *Secular Poetry*

NONE of the other secular lyrics which have come down to us is necessarily older than Bhartṛhari, certainly none need be as old as Kālidāsa. Of the many poems which must have existed in the time of Patañjali we have the merest hints, although from the *Theragāthās* and *Therīgāthās* of the Pāli canon, which may be about the same period as Patañjali, we can conclude that poetic art was steadily developing in refinement from the earlier stage of which hints are preserved in the *Ṛgveda* itself and in the *Atharvaveda* on the one hand, and in fragments of ballads, and even of a drinking song, found incidentally in Pāli texts.[1] But these earlier efforts doubtless in many cases deservedly have passed into oblivion, though we may suspect that our taste would have found pleasure in poems whose simplicity would have seemed to us rather a commendation than a cause of censure.

To Kālidāsa are ascribed, with no adequate ground, a number of poems, of which the *Çṛñgāratilaka*[2] has some claim to be deemed worthy of the honour, though it is quite illegitimate to accord it to Kālidāsa. Its twenty-three stanzas are attractive pictures of love, but they lack special distinction. The poet neatly condemns, while praising, his hard-hearted beloved :

indīvareṇa nayanaṃ mukhaṃ ambujena : kundena dantaṃ adharaṁ navapallavena
añgāni campakadalaiḥ sa vidhāya vedhāḥ : kānte kathaṁ ghaṭitavān upalena cetaḥ ?

[1] *Dīghanikāya*, 21 (GIL. ii. 32); Jātaka 512.

[2] Ed. Gildemeister, Bonn, 1841. Cf. Pischel, *Çṛñgāratilaka*, p. 27. The last stanza occurs in Amaru, and v. 3 is cited in Dhanika's *Daçarūpāvaloka* (11th cent.), at least in some MSS. In Haeberlin, 14 ff. it has twenty-one stanzas. The *Çṛñgārarasāṣṭaka* is also ascribed to Kālidāsa ; v. 7 is, v. 4 may be, his.

'Thine eyes are blue lotuses, thy face a Nymphaea, thy teeth jasmine, thy lower lip a tender shoot, thy limbs leaves of the Campaka; tell me then, beloved, how the creator formed thy heart of stone.' Pretty, if trite, is the maiden as a hunter:

iyaṁ vyādhāyate bālā: bhrūr asyāḥ karmukāyate
kaṭākṣāç ca çarāyante mano me hariṇāyate.

'This maid is a huntress, her brows the bow, her sidelong glances the arrows, and my heart the deer.' But most effective is a note of bitterness and pain:

kiṁ me vaktram upetya cumbasi balān nirlajja lajjākṛte
vastrāntaṁ çaṭha muñca muñca çapathaiḥ kiṁ dhūrta nirvañcase?
kṣīṇāhaṁ tava rātrijāgaravaçāt tām eva yāhi priyāṁ
nirmālyojjhitapuṣpadāmanikare kā ṣaṭpadānāṁ ratiḥ?

'Why dost come and kiss my lips against my will, thou shameless one in thy pretence of shame? Let go, let go, I say, the hem of my robe. Why seek with thine oaths to deceive me? I am worn through a sleepless vigil for thee; go back to her with whom thou wert then. What care the bees for the garland of flowers that hath been cast away as outworn?' This is good poetry but it is not in the manner of Kālidāsa. On the other hand, we have from an anthology a brilliant verse that can hardly but be his:

payodharākāradharo hi kandukaḥ: kareṇa roṣād iva tāḍyate muhuḥ
itīva netrākṛtibhītam utpalaṁ: tasyāḥ prasādāya papāta pādayoḥ.

'The ball whose roundness matched her breasts she beat ever and anon in anger; hence, I ween, the lotus afraid of the anger in her eyes fell at her feet to implore her pardon.'

Much less attractive is the *Ghaṭakarpara*[1] in twenty-two stanzas, which describes how a young wife at the beginning of the rains sends a message by the cloud to her absent husband, a situation the reverse of that described in the *Megha ūta*. The poem owes its title to the fact that the author at the close offers to carry water in a broken jar for any one who can surpass him in

[1] Ed. Haeberlin, 120 f.

Yamakas, alliterations consisting of repetitions in corresponding places of groups of the same letters. Hence perhaps there has been evolved the poet Ghaṭakarpara who would thus have perpetuated his name by this word-play. That the work is earlier than Kālidāsa is deduced by Jacobi [1] from the fact of this boast, which later was not justified; if, however, the poem when first written set a model in this form of composition, then it might be preserved when it had ceased to be pre-eminent on the score of its originality. This conjecture seems wholly implausible; no example of a text being preserved as a literary curiosity is known, and Ghaṭakarpara evidently was ranked higher by Indian taste than by modern opinion, for he was made one of the nine jewels of Vikramāditya's court as contemporary of Kālidāsa. The fact that a *Nītisāra* [2] in twenty-one stanzas is ascribed to him does not strengthen the case for his identity, as there is nothing distinctive in the verses.

We come to more definite chronological grounds with the name of Mayūra,[3] who flourished at Harṣavardhana's court in the seventh century and who was reputed the father-in-law [4] of Bāṇa, while Mātañga Divākara won fame comparable to both of them. The legend tells that he described so minutely the beauties of his daughter that she cursed him in anger, and he became a leper, from which unhappy state he was rescued through the aid of the sun god whom he celebrated in his *Sūryaçataka*. It seems probable enough that the legend is due to a verse of the *Mayūrāṣṭaka* which describes the appearance of a maiden who has secretly visited her lover and is returning from his side:

eṣā kā stanapīnabhārakaṭhinā madhye daridrāvatī
vibhrāntā hariṇī vilolanayanā saṁtrastayūthodgatā
antaḥsvedagajendragaṇḍagalitā saṁlīlayā gacchati
dṛṣṭvā rūpam idaṁ priyāṁgagahanaṁ vṛddho 'pi kāmāyate.

'Who is this timid gazelle, burdened with firm swelling breasts, slender-waisted and wild-eyed, who hath left the startled herd?

[1] *Rāmāyaṇa*, p. 126.

[2] Haeberlin, 504 ff.

[3] Quackenbos, *The Sanskrit Poems of Mayūra* (1917).

[4] Or brother-in-law; the legends vary; there seems no truth in the relationship. But their rivalry is attested by Padmagupta, *Navasāhasāñkacarita*, ii. 18; Zachariae, *B. Beitr.*, xiii. 100.

She goeth in sport as if fallen from the temples of an elephant in rut. Seeing her beauty even an old man turns to thoughts of love.' The heavy and tedious style, added to the number of *double entendres* implied, marks the poetry as of second-rate order, but it confirms the view that he was a contemporary of Bāṇa, for that author's style is saved only by his real brilliance from equal demerit.

So scanty are our records that the next important lyric poet of whom we have more than the name and stanzas in the anthologies is a contemporary of Jayadeva, Govardhana, whom he extols as incomparable in effective erotic descriptions. Jayadeva, however, was neither reticent about himself nor his friends, and we cannot subscribe to his eulogy. The aim of Govardhana, as he himself insists, was to raise the Yamunā in the air in the shape of elevating the simple love songs extant in Prākrit to the level of Sanskrit. His chosen medium is the Āryā verse, and he has composed in this metre, which is unquestionably borrowed by Sanskrit from Prākrit, seven hundred erotic stanzas, without inner connexion and arranged alphabetically. The poetry, however, lacks the popular flavour which marks the *Sattasaī* of Hāla, who, of course, was the model for the *Āryāsaptaçatī*, and perhaps the most interesting thing about the poem is the fact that on it was based the *Sat'saī* (1662) in Hindī of Bihārī Lāl, who has won high rank among Hindī poets, and whose work again was copied by a late Sanskrit writer, Paramānanda, in his *Çṛṅgārasaptaçatikā*. The imitation of a Prākrit model is carried to the extent of styling the sections Vrajyās; within them there is no order observed and the effort to produce 700 verses necessarily leads to repetition and many weak lines. His brothers Udayana and Balabhadra corrected and brought out his work, but the text is difficult even when free from suspicion from corruption, for the poet is fond of suggestion in lieu of expression. A more favourable idea of him is given in a verse cited by Rūpagosvāmin:

pāntha Dvāravatīm prayāsi yadi he tad Devakīnandano
vaktavyaḥ smaramohamantravivaçā gopyo 'pi nāmojjhitāḥ
etāḥ kelikadambadhūlipaṭalair ālokaçūnyādiçaḥ
Kālindītaṭabhūmayo 'pi tava bho nāyānti cittāspadam.

'O stranger, if thou art going to Dvāravatī, pray say to Devakī's son: "Dost thou never think of the cowherdesses, whom thou hast left powerless through love's bewildering spell, or of Kālindī's glades, where the sky is covered by the masses of blossom dust of the Kadamba flowers with which thou wert wont to play?"'

The anthologies[1] are the source of our knowledge of the poet Pāṇini, whose identity with the grammarian has already been denied, despite the fact that it is in accord with Indian tradition. The verses ascribed to him are undeniably proof of no small skill as a poet of love:

tanvaṅgīnāṁ stanau dṛṣṭvā çiraḥ kampayate yuvā
tayor antarasaṁlagnāṁ dṛṣṭim utpāṭayann iva.

'The youth, having seen the breasts of the fair ladies, shakes his head, as though he were seeking to rescue his gaze fast prisoned between them.'

kṣapāḥ kṣāmīkṛtya prasabham apahṛtyāmbu saritām
pratāpyorvīṁ kṛtsnāṁ tarugahanam ucchoṣya sakalam
kva sampraty uṣṇāṅçur gata iti tadanveṣaṇaparās
taḍiddīpālokā diçi diçi carantīva jaladāḥ.

'"Where hath the sun gone, after making short the nights, stealing the water of the streams, parching all the earth, and scorching every thicket?" So saying the clouds wander hither and thither seeking his presence in every lightning flash.'

pāṇau çoṇatale tanūdari darakṣāmā kapolasthalī
vinyastāñjanadigdhalocanajalaiḥ kim mlānim ānīyate?
mugdhe cumbatu nāma cañcalatayā bhṛṅgaḥ kvacit kandalīm
unmīlannavamālatīparimalaḥ kiṁ tena vismaryate?

'Why, slender maiden, dost bedew with tears stained by eye-salve the haggard cheek, that doth rest on that reddened palm? Foolish one, though the bee may in fickleness kiss the mango blossom, yet doth he ever forget the fragrance of the blooming of the young jasmine?'

vilokya saṁgame rāgam paççimāyā vivasvatā
kṛtaṁ kṛṣṇam mukham prācyā na hi nāryo vinerṣyayā.

[1] Thomas, *Kavīndravacanasamuccaya*, pp. 51 ff. Cf. Peterson, *Subhāṣitāvali*, pp. 54 ff.; JRAS. 1891, pp. 311 ff.; Pischel, ZDMG. xxxix. 95 ff., 313 ff.; *Gramm. d. Prakrit-Sprachen*, p. 33.

'Dark groweth the face of the East as she beholdeth the glow of the sun in union with the West. What woman is free from jealousy?'

gate 'rdharātre parimandamandaṁ: garjanti yat prāvṛṣi kāla-
meghāḥ
apaçyatī vatsam ivendubimbaṁ: tac charvarī gaur iva huñ-
karoti.

'When at midnight in the rainy season the dark clouds thunder deeply, then Night, unable to see the disk of the moon, crieth aloud like a cow that seeketh her calf.'

asau gireḥ çītalakandarasthaḥ: pārāvato manmathacāṭudakṣaḥ
gharmālasāñgīm madhurāṇi kūjan: saṁvījate pakṣapuṭena kān-
tām.

'Yonder dove, which dwelleth in a cool hollow of the mountain, and is skilled in all loving dalliance, cooing sweetly doth fan with its wings the loved one, wearied by the heat.'

As among the scanty remains of this poet we have the ungrammatical *apaçyatī* and *gṛhya*, narrative aorists, and as the construction of *gireḥ* in the last-cited verse is careless, we can hardly seriously suppose that the author was the grammarian, even apart from the style of the verses.[1]

The anthologies give us invaluable testimony as to other poets now lost but of real merit. To Vākkūṭa is ascribed an elegant expression of the sad fate of the lover who, parted from his beloved, looks on all sides only to find some sign which speaks to him poignantly of lost joys:

ete cūtamahīruho py aviralair dhūmayitaiḥ ṣaṭpadair
ete prajvalitāḥ sphuṭatkisalayodbhedair açokadrumāḥ
ete kiñçukaçākhino 'pi malinair añgāritāḥ kuḍmalaiḥ
kaṣṭaṁ viçramayāmi kutra nayane sarvatra vāmo vidhiḥ.

'The mango shoots here smoke with the hordes of bees, here the Açoka glows with bursting flower buds, here the branches of the Kiñçuka are coal-coloured with their dark shoots; alas, where can I rest my weary eyes? Everywhere is fate cruel to me.' Laḍahacandra sends a pretty message from a maiden to her loved one;

[1] Bhandarkar, JBRAS. xvi. 200 ff., 343 ff.; Kielhorn, GN. 1885, pp. 185 f.

gantāsi cet pathika he mama yatra kāntas: tat tvaṁ vaco hara
çucau jagatām asahyaḥ
tāpaḥ sagarjaguruvārinipātabhītas: tyaktvā bhuvaṁ virahiṇīhṛ-
dayaṁ viveça.

'Wanderer, if thou shalt come to the place where is my beloved, then tell him from me that the flame of summer that none can endure, fearing the fall of heavy rain midst thunder, hath left the earth and entered the heart of the deserted maiden.' To the poetess Çīlābhaṭṭārikā some pretty stanzas are attributed:

yaḥ kaumāraharaḥ sa eva hi varas tā eva caitrakṣapās
te conmīlitamālatīparimalāḥ prauḍhāḥ kadambānilāḥ
sā caivāsmi tathāpi cauryasuratavyāpāralīlāvidhau
Revārodhasi vetasītarutale cetaḥ samutkaṇṭhate.

'This is the husband who stole my maidenhood, these are the same April nights, these the breezes whispering in the Kadamba, fragrant with the budding jasmines, I myself too am the same: yet my heart yearns for the dalliance and the secret love that was ours below the ratan tree on the bank of the Revā.' She is accorded [1] with Bāṇa the merit of being a type of the Pañcāla style, in which sound and sense claim equal honour, and the claim is fully justified by her verses:

dūti tvaṁ taruṇī yuvā sa capalaḥ çyāmas tamobhir diçaḥ
saṁdeças sarahasya eṣa vipine saṁketakāvāsakaḥ
bhūyo bhūya ime vasantamarutaç ceto nayanty anyathā
gaccha kṣemasamāgamāya nipuṇaṁ rakṣantu te devatāḥ.

'My messenger, thou art but a tender maid, and the youth is fickle, darkness holds the sky, my commission is secret, the place of assignation is in the wood, these winds of spring entice more and more the heart; yet go and meet him in safety; may the gods guard thy skill.'

Many poems are anonymous, while others are so variously ascribed by the anthologies that no weight can be placed on the

[1] By Rājaçekhara, who mentions also Vikaṭanitambā, Vijayāñkā of Karṇāṭa as peer of Kālidāsa in the Vaidarbha, Prabhudevī Lāṭī, and Vijjakā, as well as Subhadrā. His wife Avantisundarī figures with him as an authority on poetics. Kane (*Sāhityadarpaṇa*, p. xli) suggests equating Vijjakā with Vijayāñkā, and Vijayabhaṭṭārikā, queen of Candrāditya (*c.* 660 A.D.).

names to which they are ascribed. Very simple but very pretty is:

aṅkurite pallavite korakite vikasite sahakare
aṅkuritaḥ pallavitaḥ korakito vikasitaç ca madanaḥ.

'Swollen and sprouted and budded and bloomed hath the mango, swollen and sprouted and budded and bloomed hath love.' There is a certain humour in the consolation offered to the lover who has had to abandon a very sentimental maiden:

acchinnaṁ nayanāmbu bandhuṣu kṛtaṁ cintā gurubhyo 'rpitā
dattaṁ dainyam açeṣataḥ parijane tāpaḥ sakhīṣv āhitaḥ
adya çvaḥ parinirvṛtiṁ vrajati sā çvāsaiḥ paraṁ khidyate
viçrabdho bhava viprayogajanitaṁ duḥkhaṁ vibhaktaṁ tayā.

'Her unceasing flow of tears has been distributed among her friends, her anxiety passed on to her elders, her depression has been transferred wholesale to her attendants, her fire of love deposited in her companions; to-day or to-morrow her calm will be complete, only sighs now vex her. Take heart; she has shared out the sorrow begotten of thy departure.' A very different hand gives a picture of the moon:

udayagirisaudhaçikhare tārācayacitritāmbaravitāne
siṅhāsanam iva nihitaṁ candraḥ kandarpabhūpasya.

'On the pinnacle of the palace of the mountain of dawn, under a canopy of sky bespangled with the host of the stars, the moon hath been set as a throne for Love the king.' Circumstances alter cases, as the hapless lover finds:

prāg yāmini priyaviyogavipattikāle: tvayy eva vāsaraçatāni layaṁ gatāni
daivāt kathaṁ katham api priyasaṁgame 'dya: cāṇḍāli kiṁ tvam asi vāsara eva līnā.

'When aforetime I suffered the sorrow of severance from my beloved, o night, in thee a hundred days passed away; now when fate but hardly gave me reunion, thou, shameless one, hast departed in the day itself.' Even fanning kindles love:

viramata viramata sakhyo nalinīdalatālavṛntapavanena
hṛdayagato 'yaṁ vahnir jhaṭ iti kadācij jvalaty eva.

'Stop, stop, my friends; through the wind of the fan of lotus leaves the fire that is in my heart hath in a moment rekindled.' A sadder note but a true one is found in Halāyudha:

Bhīmenātra vijṛmbhitaṁ dhanur iha Droṇena muktaṁ çucā
Karṇasyātra hayā hṛtā rathapatir Bhīṣmo 'tra yoddhuṁ sthitaḥ
viçvaṁ rūpam ihārjunasya Hariṇā saṁdarçitaṁ kautukād
uddeçās ta ime na te sukṛtinaḥ kālo hi sarvaṁkaṣaḥ.

'Here Bhima's valour was unfolded; here Droṇa in sorrow let fly his arrows; here were stolen the steeds of Karṇa; here stood Bhīṣma, lord of the car, to fight; here at Arjuna's entreaty did Hari display his full majesty; still all the places remain, but not these great ones, for time destroyeth all.'

An author to whom many stanzas are ascribed, which are found also in the collections of Amaru and Bhartṛhari,[1] is the Buddhist Dharmakīrti, of whom we know mainly as a logician of the seventh century A. D. One verse is a neat hit at the results of reputation in dimming the chance of fair judgement of poetry:

çailair bandhayati sma vānarahṛtair Vālmīkir ambhonidhiṁ
Vyāsaḥ Pārthaçarais tathāpi na tayor atyuktir udbhāvyate
vāgarthau ca tulādhṛtāv iva tathāpy asmatprabandhān ayaṁ
loko dūṣayitum prasāritamukhas tubhyam pratiṣṭhe namaḥ.

'Vālmīki has depicted the bridging of the ocean by monkeys carrying stones, Vyāsa by Pārtha's arrows; none takes exception to their exaggeration. In my works sense and sound are, as it were, weighed in a balance, but the world eagerly aims at criticism. Ah, what a thing it is to have reputation.' There is a touching picture of the beloved in separation:

vaktrendor na haranti bāṣpapayasāṁ dhārā manojñāṁ çriyaṁ
niḥçvāsā na kadarthayanti madhurām bimbādharasya dyutim
tasyās tvadvirahe vipakvalavalīlāvaṇyasaṁvādinī
chāyā kāpi kapolayor anudinaṁ tanvyāḥ paraṁ çuṣyati.

'In separation from thee the streams of her tears rob not her moon-like face of its charming beauty, nor do her sighs diminish

[1] F. W. Thomas, *Kavīndravacanasamuccaya*, pp. 47 ff.

the sweet loveliness of her Bimba-like lip; but the slender maiden's cheeks show day by day a lessening of that bright colour which was wont to vie with the glory of the ripe Lavalī.' Too great beauty is evil:

lāvaṇyadraviṇavyayo na gaṇitaḥ kleço mahān svīkṛtaḥ
svacchandasya sukhaṁ janasya vasataç cintājvaro nirmitaḥ
eṣāpi svayam eva tulyaramaṇābhāvād varākī hatā
ko 'rthaç cetasi vedhasā vinihitas tanvyās tanuṁ tanvatā?

'He counted not the wealth of beauty which he spent nor the greatness of his effort; he made her a fever of sorrow for men that dwell in blissful ease; she herself is doomed to misery since she cannot find her peer; what, pray, was the purpose of the creator when he framed that slender maiden's body?' Kṣemendra, who gives us the verse, reprobates the jingle in *tanvyāḥ*, which seems captious.

The art of building a stanza with a limited number of letters[1] leads, as we have seen both in Bhāravi and Māgha, to tasteless extravagance, but it can be used without any lack of effect, as in the following stanza ascribed to Çāçvata:

sa me samāsamo māsaḥ sa me māsasamā samā
yo yātayā tayā yāti yā yāty āyātayā tayā.

'That month seems to me a year which passes when she is gone; that year seems as a month which goes when she returns.'

Epigrams are not rare:

vyākaraṇasiṅhabhītā apaçabdamṛgāḥ kva vicareyuḥ
guruṇaṭadaivajñabhiṣakçrotriyamukhagahvarāṇi yadi na syuḥ?

'In dread of the lions of grammar, where could the deer of barbarisms flee, were there not the caverns of the mouths of teachers, actors, astrologers, doctors, and priests?' One lady finds fault with a perfect spouse:

anekair nāyakaguṇaiḥ sahitaḥ sakhi me patiḥ
sa eva yadi jāraḥ syāt saphalaṁ jīvitam bhavet.

'My husband, o friend, has all the virtues of a stage hero; now

[1] *Varṇaniyama*; cf. *Kāvyādarça*, iii. 83 ff.; Māgha, xix. 100, 102, 104, 106, 114.

if only he were my lover, my happiness would be perfect.' The doctor fares badly:

vaidyanātha namas tubhyaṁ kṣapitāçeṣamānava
tvayi vinyastabhāro 'yaṁ kṛtāntaḥ sukham edhate.

'Best of physicians, homage be thine for thy slaying of mankind; on thee Death lays all his burden and lives in happy ease.' The note in the following is lighter:

dāhajvareṇa me māndyaṁ vada vaidya kim auṣadham
piba madyaṁ çarāveṇa mamāpy ānaya karparam.

'"I am outworn by heat and fever; tell me, doctor, what remedy is there." "Drink wine by the bowl and bring me too a glass."'

Of the art of Samasyāpūraṇa we have an excellent example in the stanza ascribed by Kṣemendra to Kumāradāsa, which embodies the line mentioned in the *Mahābhāṣya*:[1]

ayi vijahīhi dṛḍhopagūhanaṁ; tyaja navasaṁgamabhīru vallabhe
aruṇakarodgama eṣa vartate: varatanu sampravadanti kukkuṭāḥ.

'Loved one, timid in our first joy of love, relax thy clinging grasp and let me go; do not the cocks, fair one, proclaim in unison the advent of ruddy dawn?' It is characteristic that Haradatta in the *Padamañjarī*, a comment on the *Kāçika Vṛtti*, gives an entirely different three lines, while Rāyamukuṭa makes Bhāravi the author of the stanza given as Kumāradāsa's by Kṣemendra. In the curious tale of Kālidāsa's death[2] we learn that king Kumāradāsa wrote on the wall of a hetaira's house the half-verse:

kamale kamalotpattiḥ çrūyate na ca dṛçyate

offering a reward for a completion which Kālidāsa, to his undoing, provided in:

bāle tava mukhāmbhoje katham indīvaradvayam?

'It is said, but never seen, that a lotus grows on a lotus. How then, damsel, is there seen on the lotus of thy face a pair of blue

[1] Peterson, JBRAS. xvi. 170; Nandargikar, *Kumāradāsa*, pp. xx ff.

[2] Nandargikar, *op. cit.*, pp. iii ff. The verse needs amendment as above. Haradatta's date is traditionally 878 A. D.; Śeshagiri, *Report*, 1893-4, pp. 13 ff.

lotuses?' To gain the reward the graceless woman slew the poet, but the king recognized the hand of his friend and forced from her the truth, burning himself in sorrow in the pyre which consumed Kālidāsa's body.

2. *Religious Poetry*

The production of hymns of praise to the gods naturally did not cease with the Vedic poets, though the gradual change of religion evoked an alteration in the gods who received adoration; beside old gods such as Çiva, Viṣṇu, and Sūrya, whose worship was perhaps from time to time strengthened by the influx of sun-worshippers from Iran, especially after the Mahomedan conquest of Persia, there appear newer figures in the pantheon such as Kṛṣṇa, Rāma, and Durgā, who in fact is often a local deity covered by the decent robe of Çiva's dread spouse. The epic shows the existence of such hymns, the Purāṇas and Tantras afford many specimens of them, while collections of a hundred or a thousand names of a god or goddess became numerous. But naturally the higher poetry invaded this field also, and the fact that philosophers were not unwilling to take part in the composition of Stotras, songs of praise, to the gods whose reality they recognized as emphatically for empirical purposes as they denied it transcendentally, lent dignity to the art. The number of Stotras preserved is vast, but many are of no poetic worth, many of very late date, and a still larger number cannot be assigned to any definite period in the absence of external evidence, and the rarity of finding any individual note in their rather stereotyped form and style.

Of early efforts to elaborate this kind of poetry we have the *Caṇḍīçataka*[1] of Bāṇa, a collection of 102 stanzas, chiefly in Sragdharā metre, in honour of Çiva's consort and in special of her feat in slaying the demon Mahiṣa; the poem serves also as a prayer, as she is invoked to protect her worshippers. Bāṇa does not impress us with any sincerity of devotion, and the poem, though laboured and sometimes clever, has little of the attraction of his romances; his demerits appear clearly enough in

[1] See G. P. Quackenbos, *The Sanskrit Poems of Mayūra* (1917), who edited and translated Bāṇa's and Mayūra's works.

a couple of stanzas which the anthologies cite as possessing merit:

vidrāṇe rudravṛnde savitari tarale vajriṇi dhvastavajre
jātāçañke çaçāñke viramati maruti tyaktavaire kuvere
vaikuṇṭhe kuṇṭhitāstre mahiṣam akiruṣam pauruṣopaghnanighnaṁ
nirvighnaṁ nighnatī vaḥ çamayatu duritam bhūribhāvā bhavānī.

'When the Marut horde fled, Savitṛ trembled, Indra dropped his thunderbolt, the moon was smitten by fear, the wind ceased to blow, Kuvera fled the field, and Viṣṇu flung aside his blunted dart, easily she smote down that Mahiṣa who had the fierceness of a snake and prided himself on his manhood; may she, the wondrous Bhavānī, remove your misfortunes.'

namas tuñgaçiraçcumbicandracāmaracārave
trailokyanagarārambhamūlastambhāya Çambhave.

'Homage to the god that bringeth healing, who is made lovely by the moon kissing his lofty head and the yak's tail, the foundation pillar of the structure of the city of the three worlds.' Indian taste preferred to Bāṇa's *Caṇḍīçataka* the work of his alleged father-in-law or brother-in-law Mayūra, of whom we have already learned as an erotic poet. The Çataka, which was doubtless composed as a compliment to the devotion of the grandfather and father of Harṣavardhana to the worship of the sun, whose deity was also revered by Harṣa despite his Buddhist leanings, celebrates in turn the rays of the sun, the horses, the charioteer, the chariot, and the great disk itself. There is distinct cleverness in many of the thoughts and Mayūra's style is elegant. Aruṇa the charioteer is compared with the actor who speaks the prologue to the drama, the rays are the ships that carry men over the dread ocean of rebirth, the cause of human sorrow, the disk is the door to the final release, the sun himself nourishes gods and men, upholds cosmic order, and is one with Brahman, Viṣṇu, and Çiva.

Mayūra was evidently fond of religious poetry, for we have in the *Subhāṣitāvali* some verses of *double entendre* in a speech between Çiva and Pārvatī:

candragrahaṇena vinā nāsmi rame kim pravartayasy evam
devyai yadi rucitam idaṁ nandinn āhūyatāṁ Rāhuḥ.

'"Without the stake of the moon (without Rāhu) I won't play." "Why make so much trouble? If 'tis Devī's will, why, Nandin shall summon Rāhu."'

āropayasi mudhā kiṁ nāham abhijña tvadañgasya
divyaṁ varṣasahasraṁ sthitvaiva yuktam abhidhātum.

'"Why misconstrue what I say? I am not speaking of your ornaments." "That is a pretty thing for a lady to say who has been sitting on my lap for a thousand of the years of heaven."' The term *añga* permits the equivoke, and in the first stanza the use of *asmi* as a quasi-particle exhibits the grammatical knowledge of the poet. Much more attractive from the poetical point of view is a genre picture:

āhatyāhatya mūrdhnā drutam anupibataḥ prasnutam mātur ūdhaḥ
kiṁcit kuñcaikajānor anavaratacalaccārupucchasya dhenuḥ
uttīrṇaṁ tarṇakasya priyatanayatayā dattahuṁkāramudrā
visraṅsikṣīradhārālavaçabalamukhasyāñgam ātṛpti leḍhi.

'While the calf, ever butting with its head, one knee slightly bent, and its tail ever moving prettily, sucks its mother's udder whence the milk drips, the cow, lowing softly in delight at her child, licks the upturned face of the young one whose mouth is flecked by spots from her milk.' Here we have a complete picture presented to our eyes and in a form which English does not permit us to approach in beauty.

Mayūra in many ways may rank as a typical exponent of the Gauḍa style as pictured by Daṇḍin. He affects epithets more or less recondite but etymologically explicable, as in *açiçiramahas* of the warm-rayed sun or *hemādri* of Meru. He is rich in alliterations and Yamakas, and in addition to metaphors and similes in abundance is fond of paronomasias of an elaborate kind, of bombast and exaggeration, and of the production of effects by the use of a series of harsh sounds matching the sense, and the variation of sounds within a stanza in order to mark changes of feeling. Characteristic cases are:

çīrṇaghrāṇāñghripāṇīn vraṇibhir apaghanair ghargharāvyaktaghoṣān
dīrghāghrātān aghaughaiḥ punar api ghaṭayaty eka ullāghayan yaḥ

gharmāṅços tasya vo 'ntardviguṇaghanaghṛṇānighnanirvighna-vṛtter
dattārghāḥ siddhasaṅghair vidadhatu ghṛṇayaḥ çīghram aṅghovighātam.

'The sun alone doth make new and heal those whose multitude of sins hath made them noseless, handless, footless, with ulcerated limbs, gurgling and indistinct speech, and noxious to the scent from afar. May his rays, to which hosts of Siddhas offer homage, swiftly cause the destruction of your sins, for his action knows no obstacles and obeyeth only that compassion which multiplieth within his heart.'

bibhrāṇaḥ çaktim āçu praçamitabalavattārakaurjityagurvīṁ
kurvāṇo līlayādhaḥ çikhinam api lasaccandrakāntāvabhāsam
ādadhyād andhakāre ratim atiçayinīm āvahan vīkṣaṇānām
bālo lakṣmīm apārām apara iva guho 'harpater ātapo vaḥ.

'May the early light of the lord of day bring you prosperity without bounds, like another Guha, bearing with it a power that hath soon quenched the pride of many a mighty star (as he a spear that quickly overcame the power of the mighty Tāraka); scornfully eclipsing even the fire and the splendour of the lovely moon (as he rideth a peacock resplendent with the flashing tips of the eyes in its tail); and may it bring joy untold to the eyes of those in the darkness (as he to the eyes of the foe of Andhaka).' We find also good instances of the figure Vyatireka, the stating of a distinction between things seemingly alike, and Virodha, apparent contradiction, the Dīpaka, and the Tulyayogitā, combination of things with the same attributes, as in *sādridyūrvīnadīçā daça diçaḥ*, 'the ten quarters with mountains, sky, earth, and oceans'. Grammatical rarities include use of *caturarcam*, *vibhu* in the active, the Vedic *çam*, while imperatives in *tāt*, benedictives, and forms like *adhijaladhi* and *vitaratitarām* are characteristic of the Kāvya. Bāṇa in the *Caṇḍīçataka* shows many of the same features, though he does not indulge in the long similes of Mayūra, but he adds life to his composition by placing about half the stanzas in the mouths of his characters, though without dialogues; thus Caṇḍī is in ten stanzas the speaker, either taunting the gods, rebuking Mahiṣa, or addressing Çiva; Mahiṣa in nineteen stanzas derides the gods or reviles Caṇḍī; Jayā, her maid, jests, or encourages the gods; while other speakers include Çiva, Kārttikeya, the gods, sages, Caṇḍī's foot, and even her toe-nails!

Contemporary of Bāṇa and Mayūra at Harṣa's court was, according to tradition preserved by Rājaçekhara, Mātaṅga Divākara,[1] also styled a Caṇḍāla, though we can hardly suppose that this epithet really means that a man of the lowest caste was a peer at court of the greater poets. Our remains of him suggest that he was a clever courtier, for one verse seems very like a panegyric of Harṣa, though it has been censured by Abhinavagupta for inelegance; the point, however, of the stanza is probably the suggestion that Harṣa is sure to have a son who will succeed him, as was doubtless, though fruitlessly, his dearest wish:

āsīn nātha pitāmahī tava mahī mātā tato 'nantaraṁ
sampraty eva hi sāmburāçiraçanā jāyā jayodbhūtaye
pūrṇe varṣaçate bhaviṣyati punaḥ saivānavadyā snuṣā
yuktaṁ nāma samastaçāstraviduṣāṁ lokeçvarāṇām idam.

'O king, the earth, sea-girdled, was aforetime thy grandmother, then became she thy mother, and now thy spouse to bring thy glory to fullness. But when a full hundred years of thy life have flown, will she be thy daughter-in-law, for this is the just fate of those to whom every science is known.'

It has been suggested that this poet is to be identified with the Jain writer Mānatuṅga, whose *Bhaktāmarastotra*[2] in honour of the Jain saint Ṛṣabha is brought into connexion with Bāṇa and Mayūra by another tale. Mānatuṅga, it is said, wrote so fine a panegyric of the sun that he was saved from leprosy; then Bāṇa in jealousy produced the *Caṇḍīçataka*, after cutting off his hands and feet, in order that he might exhibit the power of the goddess in healing her devotee in gratitude for his eulogy. Mānatuṅga, then, to prove the might of the Jinas, had himself fastened with forty-two chains and cast into a house; he uttered his poem of praise and was released forthwith. Perhaps the origin of the legend is simply the reference in his poem to the power of the

[1] Cf. Quackenbos, *Mayūra*, pp. 10 f.

[2] Ed. and trans. H. Jacobi, IS. xiv. 359 ff. Quackenbos (p. 18) dates him far too early.

Jina to save those in fetters, doubtless metaphorically applied to the bonds holding men to carnal life. Mānatuṅga may have been a contemporary of Bāṇa, but his date may well fall from 150 to 200 years later. He is no mean poet and certainly a master of the intricacies of the Kāvya style. Ṛṣabha is extolled as Buddha, Çaṅkara, the creator, Puruṣottama; hundreds of mothers bear hundreds of sons, but none a son like him; stars there are in every region of the sky, but only the east brings forth the sun. The merits of his style are obvious when contrasted with the elaboration of the forty-four stanzas of the *Kalyāṇamandirastotra*[1] of Siddhasena Divākara, written in deliberate imitation. Other Jain Stotras are of even less poetical value.

To Harṣavardhana are ascribed certain Buddhist hymns, composed, we may presume, in the last years of his reign, including the *Aṣṭamahāçrīcaityastotra*[2] and the *Suprabhātastotra*,[3] which has also been ascribed to Çrīharṣa, of the *Naiṣadhīya*. A later writer, Sarvajñamitra, is the author of the *Sragdharāstotra*[4] to Tārā, who became a very favourite deity among the theistic school of Buddhism as the mother-goddess and saviour. The legend runs that having been rich he took to religion and thus became poor. Meeting a Brahmin who begged him for money to secure his daughter a wedding, he offered himself to a king who desired a hundred men for a human sacrifice, but moved by the sorrows of his fellow sufferers composed the poem and won through Tārā's intervention the lives of all. Other Stotras of doubtful age are numerous, but it can hardly be said that they reach any high level of poetry, though some of them certainly bear every sign of true religious feeling.

It is difficult to realize that a religious motive is also present in the *Vakroktipañcāçikā*[5] of the Kashmirian poet Ratnākara, who in fifty stanzas shows a remarkable power of illustrating the ambiguities of which the Sanskrit language is capable. The following example is moderately simple. Pārvatī addresses Çiva:

[1] Ed. and trans. IS. xiv. 376 ff.; cf. IA. xlii. 42 ff.

[2] Lévi, OC. X, ii. 189 ff.; Ettinghausen, *Harṣa-Vardhana*, pp. 176 ff.

[3] Thomas, JRAS. 1903, pp. 703–22. For anthology and inscriptional verses see Jackson, *Priyadarśikā*, pp. xliii ff, and references.

[4] See G. de Blonay, *La déesse bouddhique Tārā* (1895); Hīrānanda, *Mem. Arch. Survey India*, no. 20.

[5] KM. i. 101–14; Bernheimer, ZDMG. lxiii. 816 ff.

tvaṁ me nābhimato bhavāmi sutanu çvaçrvā avaçyam mataḥ
sādhūktam bhavatā na me rucita ity atra bruve 'ham punaḥ
mugdhe nāsmi nameruṇā nanu citaḥ prekṣasva mām pātu vo
vakroktyeti haro himācalabhuvaṁ smerānanām mūkayan.

'"I love thee no more." "'Tis true, slender one, (your connexions approve me), for my mother-in-law adores me." "Neatly said, but I repeat a second time: Thou art not pleasant in my eyes." "But, dear one, just look; I am not adorned with the Nameru flowers." So Çiva silenced the smiling mouth of the daughter of the Himālaya with his equivoke; may he be gracious to you.' The first pun here depends on the ambiguity of *nābhimato*, the second simply on the fact that Çiva interprets *na me rucitas* as *nameruṇā citas.* We must suppose that Ratnākara felt that, as men delight in these refinements, so the offering of his poem to the gods would evoke their pleasure. His epic gives no ground to doubt the sincerity of his devotion to Çiva.

A lyric poet of much fervour and no mean accomplishment must be recognized in the philosopher Çañkara,[1] if we can trust the tradition which ascribes to him many hymns, especially to Devī, the mother-goddess, whom the Çāktas adored as the expression of the highest power in the universe. Çañkara's doctrine of the two aspects of truth, the higher and the lower, permitted him to adopt to the full popular beliefs and to express his feelings in a way acceptable to other than metaphysicians, and there is no reason whatever to doubt that he composed such poems. It is, of course, a different thing to say which of those allotted to him by tradition were really his. A solemn warning of the passing of time is given in the *Çivāparādhakṣamāpaṇastotra*:

āyur naçyati paçyatāṁ pratidinaṁ yāti kṣayaṁ yauvanam
pratyāyānti gatāḥ punar na divasāḥ kālo jagadbhakṣakaḥ
lakṣmīs toyatarañgabhañgacapalā vidyuccalaṁ jīvitaṁ
yasmān māṁ çaraṇāgataṁ çaraṇada tvaṁ rakṣa rakṣādhunā.

'Life perisheth daily before our eyes, youth departeth; the days departed never return again, time consumeth the world; fortune is as transient as a ripple on the waves of the ocean; life

[1] S. Venkataramanan, *Select Works of Srisankaracharya*, and the *Bṛhatstotraratnākara.*

as unstable as the lightning; guard, guard me to-day who am come to thee for safety, o giver of peace.' More prosaic is the address to Kṛṣṇa:

vinā yasya dhyānaṁ vrajati paçutāṁ sūkaramukhāṁ
vinā yasya jñānaṁ janimṛtibhayaṁ yāti janatā
vinā yasya smṛtyā kṛmiçatajaniṁ yāti sa vibhuḥ
çaraṇyo lokeço mama bhavatu Kṛṣṇo 'kṣiviṣayaḥ.

'If man meditates not on him, he becomes a beast, boar or another; if he knows him not, birth, death, fear are his portion; if he think not of him, a hundred lives as a worm await him; let him, lord of the world, my salvation, Kṛṣṇa, show himself to his worshipper.' The utter emptiness of existence is brilliantly insisted upon in the rimed *Dvādaçapañjarikāstotra*:

mā kuru jana dhanayauvanagarvaṁ harati nimeṣāt kālaḥ sarvam
māyāmayam idam akhilaṁ hitvā brahmapadaṁ tvaṁ praviça viditvā.

'Place no pride, o man, in youth, or wealth; in the twinkling of an eye time taketh all away; deem all this world to be but an illusion, and with true knowledge attain the abode of the absolute.' Devotion and confidence reach their height of expression in the *Devyaparādhakṣamāpaṇastotra*:

vidher ajñānena draviṇavirahenālasatayā
vidheyāçakyatvāt tava caraṇayor yā cyutir abhūt
tad etat kṣāntavyaṁ janani sakalalokoddhāriṇi çive
kuputro jāyeta kvacid api kumātā na bhavati.

'If I have failed to pay due honour to thy feet through ignorance of thy commands, through lack of wealth, laziness or incapacity, forgive my transgression, o mother, o gracious one, o trust of all the world; a son may be bad, but never a mother.'

pṛthivyām putrās te janani bahavaḥ santi saralāḥ
paraṁ teṣām madhye viralataralo 'haṁ tava sutaḥ
madīyo 'yaṁ tyāgaḥ samucitam idaṁ no tava çive: kuputro

'Many good sons are thine on earth, o mother, few indeed fickle as I; yet to abandon me, o gracious one, were not meet for thee; a son may be bad, but never a mother.'

Among many others a *Bhavānyaṣṭaka* and the *Ānandalaharī* in twenty Çikhariṇī verses are ascribed to Çaṅkara, while other famous hymns to Devī include the *Ambāṣṭaka* and the *Pañcastavī*, five hymns to Durgā of unknown authorship. To Kālidāsa are ascribed, without any plausibility, various Stotras, including the *Çyāmalādaṇḍaka* mainly in prose, the *Sarasvatīstotra* and the *Maṅgalāṣṭaka*, which can be reconstructed from the Tibetan of the Tanjur. A hymn in 500 stanzas, the *Pañcaçatī*, is ascribed to a mysterious Mūka, alleged to be contemporaneous with Çaṅkara, but this is very dubious. We are on much firmer ground regarding the *Devīçataka* of Ānandavardhana the writer on poetics (*c.* 850), whose hundred very elaborate stanzas hardly conform to his own theory that the poet who pays too much attention to ornament falls into the error of neglecting the suggestion which should underlie poetry, but the deviation is excused by his own admission that in panegyrics of the gods the sentiment is of secondary importance. But it must be added that Ānandavardhana is not a great or perhaps even a good poet, confirming the adage that critics seldom are. Utpaladeva's *Stotrāvalī* was written about 925; it consists of a series of twenty short hymns in honour of Çiva, some mere innovations, some more elaborate, but none of outstanding merit. In the same century probably the Vaiṣṇava Kulaçekhara wrote in honour of Viṣṇu his *Mukundamālā*; it is interesting to find a verse cited in an inscription of a place so distant as Pagan in the thirteenth century.

In the eleventh century Līlāçuka or Bilvamaṅgala[1] produced his *Kṛṣṇakarṇāmṛta* or *Kṛṣṇalīlāmṛta*, 110 stanzas in honour of Kṛṣṇa, a poem which has been very popular in India, while the anthologies cite verses from him. One exhibits fairly the merits of his simple and not unattractive style:

Kṛṣṇa tvaṁ navayauvano 'si capalāḥ prāyeṇa gopāṅganāḥ
Kaṅso bhūpatir abjanālabhiduragrīvā vayaṁ goduhaḥ
tad yāce 'ñjalinā bhavantam adhunā vṛndāvanam mad vinā
mā yāsīr iti gopanandavacasā namro Hariḥ pātu vaḥ.

'May Hari guard you, Hari who bowed low in obedience when the cowherd Nanda thus entreated him: "O Kṛṣṇa, thou art in

[1] For legends of him, see Śeshagiri, *Report*, 1893–4, pp. 57 f.

the freshness of youth, our maidens are mostly fickle, Kaṅsa is king, and we herders have necks as frail as the lotus stalk; with folded hands I entreat thee not to go without me to the Vṛndāvana wood".'

In the twelfth century we have eulogies of Kṛṣṇa from the poets who were contemporary jewels with Jayadeva at the court of Lakṣmaṇasena. They are preserved in the *Padyāvalī* of Rūpagosvāmin, well known as an ardent devotee and follower of Caitanya. To Lakṣmaṇasena himself is ascribed an amusing verse:

āhūtādya mayotsave niçi gṛhaṁ çūnyaṁ vimucyāgatā
kṣībaḥ preṣyajanaḥ kathaṁ kulavadhūr ekākinī yāsyati
vatsa tvaṁ tad imāṁ nayālayam iti çrutvā Yaçodāgiro
Rādhāmādhavayor jayanti madhurasmerālasā dṛṣṭayaḥ.

'"She was told by me to come to the festival to-day; now she has come at night, leaving the house empty; the servants are drunk; how can a lady of family go alone? Dear child, take her safely home", so said Yaçodā, and, hearing her bidding, there passed smiling looks of joyful weariness between Rādhā and Mādhava.' Umāpatidhara,[1] whom Jayadeva records as skilled in the use of recondite language, an assertion abundantly established by the array of rare words or meanings found in a Praçasti of his which has come down to us, is credited with a quite amusing picture of a bedroom scene between Kṛṣṇa and his wife, who had a good deal to complain of in his amourettes:

nirmagnena mayāmbhasi praṇayataḥ pālī samāliṅgitā
kenālīkam idaṁ tavādya kathitaṁ Rādhe mudā tāmyasi
ity utsvapnaparamparāsu çayane çrutvā vacaḥ çārṅgiṇo
Rukmiṇyā çithilīkṛtaḥ sakapaṭaṁ kaṇṭhagrahaḥ pātu vaḥ.

'"Who has told thee this falsehood, that the moment I plunged into the water I clipped close a maiden in love? Thou troublest thyself needlessly, o Rādhā"; so Rukmiṇī heard her lord Kṛṣṇa murmur in his dream as they lay side by side, and feigned to loosen his hold on her neck; be that your protection.'

Of Çaraṇa, Jayadeva tells us that he was worthy of praise for

[1] See Pischel, *Die Hofdichter des Lakṣmaṇasena* (1893). Dhoī's *Pavanadūta*, in which a Gandharva maiden sends a message to Lakṣmaṇasena, is based on the *Meghadūta*; see M. Chakravarti, JPASB. 1905, pp. 41–71.

his skill in producing extempore poetry which was hard to understand (*durūhadruta*),[1] a term which will appear as the compliment it was meant to be, if we remember that Sanskrit poets were equally proud of their ability to compose on a given theme, taking as given a verse or part of it, and of the fact that their works were highly finished products which required for due comprehension and appreciation full knowledge of metre, poetics, lexicography, and grammar. The epithet is borne out by the verses we have, for they are frequently undeniable imitations of others, as in the following elaboration of a simple stanza ascribed to Amaru:

Murārim paçyantyāḥ sakhi sakalam aṅgaṁ na nayanaṁ
kṛtaṁ yac chṛṇvatyā Hariguṇagaṇaṁ çrotranicitam
samaṁ tenālāpaṁ sapadi racayantyā mukhamayaṁ
vidhātur naivāyaṁ ghaṭanaparipāṭīmadhurimā.

'O friend, when I saw Murāri, that my whole body did not become one eye; when I heard him, that I became not a multitude of ears; when I spoke with him, that I became not one mouth; that indeed is but a sorry work of the creator's devising.'

Dhoyī or Dhoī seems to have had the epithets Çrutadhara or Çrutidhara, perhaps 'strong in memory', and Kavirāja, and the stanzas cited under these three names appear to belong to one and the same poet. There is an amusing touch in one cited by Rūpagosvāmin from Kavirāja:

kvānanaṁ kva nayanaṁ kva nāsikā: kva çrutiḥ kva ca
çikheti deçitaḥ
tatra tatra vihitāṅgulidalo: ballavīkulam anandayat prabhuḥ.

'"Where is my face? Where my eye? Where my nose? Where my ear? Where my braid?" Thus bidden the lord touched each with his flower finger, and thus he delighted the cowherdesses.'

Of many other poems mention may be made of the *Mahimnaḥstava*[2] which is a eulogy of Çiva but which has been treated

[1] Srish Chandra Chakravarti (*Bhāṣāvṛtti*, p. 7) refers the term to Çaraṇadeva, author of the *Durghaṭavṛtti*; *durūhakāvya* occurs in an epithet of Vāmana in the *Rukmiṇīkalyāṇa* (*Madras Catal.*, xx. 7850).

[2] Often printed in India. It is cited by Rājaçekhara.

also as intended to glorify Viṣṇu, ascribed to Puṣpadanta—which may, of course, not be a true name—because the work seems to be known to the *Nyāyamañjarī* of Jayanta Bhaṭṭa, and therefore must not be later than the ninth century. As curious developments—probably late—of religious fervour may be noted the *Çaṇḍīkucapañcāçikā*,[1] fifty stanzas on the breasts of Caṇḍī, by a certain Lakṣmaṇa Ācārya, and the *Bhikṣāṭanakāvya*[2] by Çivadāsa or Utprekṣāvallabha, which describes the feelings of Apsarases when Çiva in the garb of an ascetic comes to seek alms in Indra's heaven. The author with amazing taste takes this means of displaying his intimate acquaintance with the rules of the *Kāmasūtra* as to the deportment of women in love.

Some fine religious stanzas are preserved in the anthologies:

yadi nāsmi mahāpāpī yadi nāsmi bhayākulaḥ
yadi nendriyasaṁsaktas tat ko 'rthaḥ çaraṇe mama.

'If I were not a great sinner, if I were not sore afraid, if I were not devoted to things of sense, then what need would I have of salvation?' This is ascribed to Bhaṭṭa Sunandana, else unknown to fame. Equally unknown is Gaṅgādatta who writes:

abhidhāvati māṁ mṛtyur ayam udgūrṇamudgaraḥ
kṛpaṇam puṇḍarīkākṣa rakṣa māṁ çaraṇāgatam.

'Death draweth on, with weapon upraised to smite; o lotus-eyed one, protect thy pitiful suppliant.' Anonymous is a pretty picture of the child god:

karāravindena padāravindam: mukhāravinde niveçayantam
açvatthapattrasya puṭe çayānam: bālam Mukundaṁ satataṁ smarāmi.

'With his lotus hand placing the lotus of his foot in his lotus mouth as he lies in a cradle of Açvattha leaves, our baby Mukunda is my thought for ever.' A Vikramāditya is among these poets of religion, but it is impossible to determine his identity; the various verses ascribed to him are hardly by one hand.[3]

[1] Ed. KM. ix. 80 ff. (eighty-three stanzas in all).
[2] See IOC. i. 1448 f.
[3] For an eloquent appreciation of the Stotras see Sivaprasad Bhattacharyya, IHQ. 340 ff.

3. *The Anthologies*

Of both lyric and gnomic poets whose works are lost, we derive knowledge from the anthologies, which have yielded many of the citations of fine lines already made. Themselves often of comparatively late date, they preserve the work of much earlier poets, though unhappily in many cases of the authors mentioned we have no means of determining the period of their activity. Of these anthologies the oldest apparently is that edited by Dr. F. W. Thomas as the *Kavīndravacanasamuccaya*[1] from a Nepalese MS. of the twelfth century. Sections on the Buddha and Avalokiteçvara remind us of its provenance, but otherwise it contains the same material as the other texts, verses on a wide variety of subjects, love and other passions, the conduct of life, practical wisdom, and moral and political maxims. None of the poets who composed its 525 stanzas is later than 1000 A.D. Of the next century (1205) is the *Saduktikarṇāmṛta*,[2] or *Sūktikarṇāmṛta*, of Çrīdharadāsa, son of Vaṭudāsa, both servants of Lakṣmaṇasena of Bengal, an anthology including excerpts from 446 poets, largely of course of Bengal, including Gañgādhara and five others who can be placed in the period 1050–1150. Jalhaṇa, son of Lakṣmīdeva, and, like his father, minister of Kṛṣṇa who ascended the throne in 1247, wrote the *Subhāṣitamuktāvalī*,[3] which has come down in a longer and a shorter recension. It is carefully arranged according to such subjects as riches, generosity, fate, sorrow, love, royal service, &c., and is especially valuable in its section on poets and poetry which gives us definite information on a number of authors.

One of the most famous anthologies is that of Çārñgadhara, written in 1363 by the son of Dāmodara. It is arranged in 163 sections, and contains 4689 stanzas, including some by the author himself but of no distinction. With the aid of the *Çārñgadharapaddhati*[4] Vallabhadeva perhaps in the fifteenth century put

[1] BI. 1912.

[2] BI. 1912 ff.; Aufrecht, ZDMG. xxxvi. 361 ff.

[3] Bhandarkar, *Report*, 1887-91, pp. i-liv. According to *Madras Catal.*, xx. 8114 it was written for Jalha in 1257 by Vaidya Bhānu Paṇḍita.

[4] Ed. P. Peterson, BSS. 37, 1888; cf. Aufrecht, ZDMG. xxv. 455 ff.; xxvii. 1 ff.

together the *Subhāṣitāvali*[1] in 101 sections, giving 3527 stanzas of over 350 poets; the name occurs of Vallabhadeva among the poets, but it is not clear whether he claims the verses as his own or merely cites an earlier work. Of the fifteenth century is Çrīvara's *Subhāṣitāvalī*[2]; Çrīvara was son or pupil of Jonarāja, who was a commentator and also continued Kalhaṇa's *Rājataraṅgiṇī*, and he cites from more than 380 poets. As we have seen, Rūpagosvāmin's *Padyāvalī*[3] contains verses in honour of Kṛṣṇa, some of considerable merit, from a wide range of authors. Of other anthologies, small and great, many exist in manuscript or in editions.[4]

4. *Prākrit Lyrics*

Contemporaneously with the progress of the Sanskrit lyric, there was proceeding the development of a lyric in Prākrit, which later passed into Apabhraṅça probably as a result of the achievements of the Ābhīras and the Gurjaras who, though known earlier, flooded India about the time of the Hūṇa invasions and, unlike the Hūṇas, settled down and definitely affected the culture of the country. The two streams of lyric cannot have existed without coming into contact, but there is singularly little sign of serious influence on either side in the early period of the development. Prākrit lyric as we have it in the *Sattasaī*[5] of Hāla comes before us with a definite character of its own which is not reproduced in Sanskrit, though Govardhana in his *Saptaçatī* deliberately attempts to imitate it.

Of the date of Hāla it is impossible to be certain. The mechanical method[6] of assuming that he is to be looked for in the list of Sātavāhana kings and placing him in the first or second century A.D., because he ought to come about the middle

[1] Ed. P. Peterson and Durgāprasāda, BSS. 1886; cf. IA. xv. 240 ff.; IS. xvi. 209 f.; xvii. 168 ff. Another work of 222 or so stanzas by Sumati is described in IOC. i. 1533 ff.

[2] Peterson, OC. VI, III. ii. 339.

[3] IOC. i. 1534 ff. (*c.* 387 stanzas).

[4] Sāyaṇa wrote a *Subhāṣitasudhānidhi* (*Madras Catal.*, xx. 8105 ff.); Vedāntadeçika a *Subhāṣitanīvī*, KM. viii. 151 ff.

[5] Ed. and trans. A. Weber, AKM. v (1870) and vii (1881); IS. xvi; with Gaṅgādhara's comm., KM. 21, 1889. The ascription of verses in the commentators varies greatly and is probably worthless. Cf. Winternitz, GIL. iii. 97 ff.

[6] Cf. EHI. p. 220; EI. xii. 320. We find in *horā* (435) and *aṁgāraavāra* (261) knowledge of Greek astrology.

of the list, and the dynasty extended on one view from *c.* 240 or 230 B.C. to A.D. 225, is clearly fallacious. What is much more important is that, to judge from the evidence of the Prākrits of Açvaghoṣa and the inscriptions, the weakening of consonants which is the dominant feature of Māhārāṣṭrī cannot have set in as we find it in Hāla until about A.D. 200. This make it likely that the poetry was produced in the period from A.D. 200 to 450,[1] though we have no assurance of the date. Moreover, only 430 stanzas have a place in all the recensions, so that we must admit that there has been extensive interpolation. It is possible, even probable, that in its origin the *Sattasaī* was no mere anthology, but a careful collection of verses largely his own or refashioned by himself—much as Burns refashioned some of his material—on the basis of older verses, and that in course of time by interpolation and change the collection lost much of its individuality. Even as it is, it has a spirit of closeness to life and common realities which is hardly to be seen in Sanskrit poetry. This may be a characteristic of the Māhārāṣṭra people who even to-day have a certain homeliness and rough good sense. But it must not be supposed that the *Sattasaī* is folk-poetry ; the dialect is artificial, more so in some ways than Sanskrit, but it is the work of a poet or poets who wished really to express the feelings, as well as describe the externals, of the people of the land, the cowherds and cowherdesses, the girl who tends the garden or grinds corn at the mill, the hunter, the handworker. The prevailing tone is gentle and pleasing, simple loves set among simple scenes, fostered by the seasons, for even winter brings lovers closer together, just as a rain-storm drives them to shelter with each other. The maiden begs the moon to touch her with the rays which have touched her beloved ; she begs night to stay for ever, since the morn is to see her beloved's departure. The lover in turn bids the thunder and lightning do their worst on him, if they but spare her whom he loves. The tenderness of the poet shows itself when he tells how a wife, rejoicing at her husband's return, yet hesitates to don festal array lest she embitter the grief of her poor neighbour, whose husband yet delays his home-coming. The note of pathos is not absent ; when of two who have long shared joy and sorrow

[1] Cf. Lüders, *Bruchstücke buddh. Dramen*, p. 64 ; Jacobi, *Ausg. Erzählungen in Mâhârâshṭrî*, pp. xiv ff.

together one dies, he alone is really alive, it is the other who dies; there is a distant parallel, not borrowing, in Bhavabhūti's line, 'He is not dead of whom a beloved thinks.' But absence may be a joy where the heart is false; the faithless one bemoans her unprotected state, and begs her friend to come to her home, merely to secure her safety, *bien entendu*.

The varied forms of Indian love are brilliantly portrayed: from the real devotion when each looks into the other's eyes, and the twain are made one for the moment, to the domestic joys of wedded life, as when mama laughs as the little boy crawls on his father's back, when he lies at her feet in penitence for some fault, or when she shows the delighted papa the first tooth of their darling. The biting and scratching of Indian love are frankly depicted as well as the beauties of the maidens whose swelling bosoms are compared with the moon breaking through the cloud. Much is from the life of the village, but we hear also of the demi-monde of the towns, whose presence Pischel found in the *Ṛgveda* and which certainly has marked Indian literature ever since the Vedic age.

Pictures of nature, sometimes as influenced by love, sometimes independently, are frequent and charming, echoing some of the thoughts of the *Therīgāthās* in which Buddhist nuns express their close observation of nature. Autumn, the rainy season, summer, and spring all evoke effective sketches; bees hover over flowers, the peacock and the crows enjoy the pelting rain, the female antelope seeks longingly her mate, male and female ape lend comedy. Gnomic sayings are not rare, and often very pithy; a miser's money is as useful to him as his shadow to a traveller; only the deaf and the blind have a good time in the world, for the former do not hear harsh words, the latter do not see hateful faces. Other elements in the collection are fragments, dramatic or epic, or episodes of the folk-tale, as when we hear of a lady in captivity awaiting a rescuer, or women captured by robbers, or a naughty wife who pretends to be bitten by a scorpion in order to go to the house of the doctor who loves her. How far back go these fragments we do not know; our lower date for Hāla is purely speculative, though Bāṇa knew his collection, and even then we have no security for the existence even in Bāṇa's time of any particular part.

A later Prākrit anthology is the *Vajjālagga*[1] of Jayavallabha, a Çvetāmbara Jain, of uncertain date, who deliberately collects matter to illustrate the three ends of man, conduct, practical wisdom, and love; to the latter topic falls two-thirds of the whole. The stanzas are in Āryā metre, and the Māhārāṣṭrī shows signs of influence by Apabhrañça. Apabhrañça lyric stanzas are given in some numbers by Hemacandra[2] to illustrate the type of Prākrit which he styles Apabhrañça. They are of much the same character as those of Hāla. A damsel begs that her love be brought to her; a fire may burn down the house, but still men must have a fire. Another rejoices that her lover has fallen bravely in the field; hers had been the shame, had he returned dishonoured. The respect for a mother is prettily inculcated by the words of Vyāsa and the great sages who equate falling at the mother's feet in humble devotion with the act of bathing in the sacred waters of the Ganges.

[1] J. Laber, *Über das Vajjālaggam* (1913); Jacobi, *Bhavisattakaha*, p. 61. It is being edited in BI.

[2] Pischel, AGGW. v. 4 (1902).

X

GNOMIC AND DIDACTIC POETRY

1. *Gnomic Poetry*

INDIA has always delighted in the expression in verse of pithy observations on life and morals. We find the beginnings of such poetry in the *Ṛgveda*, moral stanzas are preserved incidentally in surprising number in an episode of the *Aitareya Brāhmaṇa*, such verses appear in the Upaniṣads and the Sūtras, while the *Mahābhārata* is only too rich both in gnomai and in didactic matter; philosophy, morals, practical advice for life, and rules of polity in the widest sense of that term, including the conduct of war, are flung at the reader in undigested masses. There is evidence from Patañjali that he knew such a literature, and in the *Dhammapada* of the Pāli canon we have the finest collection of *sententiae* known in India.

These maxims were not, of course, popular in the full sense of that term; they are not to be compared to proverbs racy of the soil preserved in their primitive form; they are, as in the maxims of Phokylides in Greece, the turning of the raw material by poets into finished products, and the perfection of their finish varies greatly. Some of them, doubtless, first became current in literature through having been composed or adopted by writers of the fable literature, others merely passed current from mouth to mouth until efforts were made by compilers to collect such popular currency. We need not doubt that the collector became normally an inventor at the same time. We can, indeed, hardly imagine that it would be otherwise; that would assuredly be a more than normally stupid person who could not on the models he had devise a fresh series of maxims, or at least remould the old. We see, in fact, the process at work in the case of the collections [1] which pass under a variety of names such

[1] O. Kressler, *Stimmen indischer Lebensklugheit* (1907). There are Tibetan (SBA. 1895, p. 275) and Arabic versions (Zachariae, WZKM. xxviii. 182 ff.); for Galanos' source see Bolling, JAOS. xli. 49 ff.

as *Rājanītisamuccaya*, *Cāṇakyanīti*, *Cāṇakyarājanīti*, *Vṛddha-Cāṇakya*, *Laghu-Cāṇakya*, and so on. The number of recensions is extremely large—seventeen have been distinguished and doubtless there are more, for often each manuscript shows distinct variations from any other; the compilers were eclectic, they had many sources open, and it is now quite impossible to determine anything like the original shape of the collection. That it was composed by Cāṇakya, the minister of Candragupta, is absurd; it is perfectly clear that it was passed off under his name because he was famous. We do not even know whether the first stanza in some recensions which promises a treatise on Rājanīti, the conduct of princes, can be taken as indicating that originally the collection dealt with that subject alone. At any rate the number of verses which can be assigned to that topic in extant recensions is negligible, and it seems much more likely that the stanza is the product of the imagination of some one who wished to give the collection a closer appearance of connexion with the minister. The book in its various forms varies enormously; thus one recension has 340 stanzas in seventeen chapters of equal length; another by Bhojarāja, preserved in a manuscript in Çāradā characters, has 576 verses in eight chapters. Its contents deal with general rules for the conduct of life, for intercourse among men, general reflections on richness and poverty, on fate and human effort, on a variety of ethical and religious topics. In the main the stanzas are not connected by any bond of thought, but there are exceptions. Here and there verses are clearly meant to be antithetical. In one passage we find a continuation of the habit, seen in full development in such works as the Pāli *Añguttara Nikāya* and the Jain *Sthānāñga*, to use numerical formulae to fix matters in the memory. Here the wise man is bidden to learn one thing from the lion, one from the heron, four from the cock, five from the crow, six from the dog, and three from the ass. In another group of seven verses the different kinds of Brahmin are expounded, the holy seer, the normal Brahmin, the Vaiçya, who lives by trade or agriculture, the Çūdra who sells *inter alia* meat and drink, the cat who is treacherous, the barbarian who is destructive, and the Caṇḍāla who is a thief and adulterer. There are certain quite common mannerisms in the collection such as the insistence on the use of numbers to give the total of groups sometimes of homogeneous, but also often of quite disparate things, as when one is warned not to abide in a place where there is not a king, a rich man, a learned man, a river, and a doctor. So we have a list of six bad things:

çuṣkam māṅsaṁ striyo vṛddhā bālārkas taruṇaṁ dadhi
prabhāte maithunaṁ nidrā sadyaḥ prāṇaharāṇi ṣaṭ.

'Dry meat, old women, the young sun, milk just soured, dalliance and slumber in the morning, are the six things that take away life.' A very common device is the repetition of the main word in a series of definitions, as in:

sā bhāryā yā çucir dakṣā sā bhāryā yā pativratā
sā bhāryā yā patiprītā sā bhāryā satyavādinī.

'A true wife she who is pure and clever, a true wife she who is faithful to her spouse, a true wife she whom her husband adores, a true wife she who never tells a lie.'

satyena dhāryate pṛthvī satyena tapyate raviḥ
satyena vāti vāyuç ca sarvaṁ satye pratiṣṭhitam.

'By truth the earth is supported, by truth the sun gives heat, by truth blows the wind, on truth all is established.' Even numerical enumerations may have point:

sakṛj jalpanti rājānaḥ sakṛj jalpanti paṇḍitāḥ
sakṛt kanyā pradīyate trīṇy etāni sakṛt sakṛt.

'But once do kings give orders, but once speak the wise, but once is given a maiden in marriage; all these three things are done but once.' The force of example is extolled in one of the few political maxims:

rājñi dharmiṇi dharmiṣṭhāḥ pāpe pāpāḥ same samāḥ
rājānam anuvartante yathā rājā tathā prajāḥ.

'When the king walks righteously, most righteous are the people, if he be evil, evil they also, if mediocre, the same with them; as the king, so the people.' Another maxim emphasizes the advantages of noble character:

etadartham kulīnānāṁ nṛpāḥ kurvanti saṁgraham
ādimadhyāvasāneṣu na tyajanti ca te nṛpam.

'For this reason do kings gather to themselves men of high mind, that neither at the start, the crisis, nor the finish may they play them false.' A careful structure and a deliberate attempt at rhetorical effect may be seen in the following:

kurājarājyena kutaḥ prajāsukhaṁ: kumitramitreṇa kuto 'sti nirvṛtiḥ
kudāradāre ca kuto gṛhe ratiḥ: kuçiṣyam adhyāpayataḥ kuto yaçaḥ!

'Whence can happiness come to the people through the reign of an evil king? What relaxation is there in friendship with an evil friend? What happiness in the home where the wife is a bad wife? What fame in instructing a bad pupil?'

The pedestrian character of the topics is alleviated by the use of metaphors and similes from the life of nature:

ekenāpi suputreṇa vidyāyuktena sādhunā
āhlāditaṁ kulaṁ sarvaṁ yathā candreṇa çarvarī.

'One noble son, good and wise, illuminates the whole of his kin, as the moon the night.'

satsaṅgād bhavati hi sādhutā khalānāṁ: sādhūnāṁ na ca khalasaṁgamāt khalatvam
āmodaṁ kusumabhavam mṛd eva dhatte: mṛdgandhaṁ na ca kusumāni dhārayanti.

'From association with the good fools become noble, but from association with fools noble men remain pure; the earthen vase draws to itself the odour of the flowers therein, but the flowers absorb none of the scent of the vase.'

nātyantasaralair bhāvyaṁ gatvā paçya vanasthalīm
chidyante saralās tatra kubjās tiṣṭhanti pādapāḥ.

'Be not too upright; read the parable of the wood; the erect trees are those that are felled, the crooked are left standing.' A better moral than this is taught:

varam prāṇaparityāgo na mānaparikhaṇḍanam
prāṇatyāgaḥ kṣaṇaṁ caiva mānabhaṅgo dine dine.

'Better death than dishonour; dying lasts but a moment, dishonour endures for ever.' Fatalism is similarly matched with the exaltation of asceticism:

tādṛçī jāyate buddhir vyavasāyo 'pi tādṛçaḥ
sahāyas tādṛça eva yādṛçī bhavitavyatā.

'Man's thought, man's resolve, man's companions, all are such as fate decides.' But:

yad dūraṁ yad durārādhyaṁ yac cādūre vyavasthitam
tat sarvaṁ tapasā sādhyaṁ tapo hi duratikramam.

'What is afar, what is hard to attain, what is placed near at hand, all that can be accomplished by asceticism; asceticism is hard to overcome.' Women are unpopular:

anṛtaṁ sāhasam māyā mūrkhatvam atilobhatā
açaucatvaṁ nirdayatvaṁ strīṇāṁ doṣāḥ svabhāvajāḥ.

'Untruth, haste, cunning, folly, greed, impurity, pitilessness, these are woman's innate faults.' A parable recommends the advantages of appearances:

nirviṣeṇāpi sarpeṇa kartavyā mahatī phaṇā
viṣam astu na vāpy astu khaṭāṭopo bhayaṁkaraḥ.

'If a serpent have no poison yet should he swell out his hood; be poison there or be it not, the expansion of the hood is terrifying.'

The Çloka is the prevailing metre, but there occur stanzas in other metres, especially in Bhojarāja's recension which has many in Indravajrā, Vaṅçasthā, Vasantatilaka, and Çārdūlavikrīḍita.

Other minor collections of gnomic stanzas are attributed to Vararuci—which of the many is meant is quite unknown, to Ghaṭakarpara, and to Vetāla Bhaṭṭa, under the styles of *Nītiratna*, *Nītisāra*, and *Nītipradīpa*; they contain some excellent stanzas, but their date is quite uncertain. Of far greater importance is the *Nītiçataka* of Bhartṛhari, which has already been noticed. Under the avaricious Çaṅkaravarman (883-902) of Kashmir wrote Bhallaṭa, who suffered severely from the failure of the king to reward poets. His Çataka[1] is carefully elaborated and in varied metres, and it is clear that it is not wholly original; at least one

[1] Ed. KM. iv. 140 ff. Cf. Kalhaṇa, v. 204.

stanza of Ānandavardhana, his earlier contemporary, is included in it.[1] Bhallaṭa wrote also a good deal of other poetry, to judge from citations in the anthologies, which include many well-turned verses. His style is usually fairly simple:

antaç chidrāṇi bhūyāṅsi kaṇṭakā bahavo bahiḥ
kathaṁ kamalanāthasya mā bhūvan bhaṅgurā guṇāḥ?

'Many a thorn without, many a space within; 'twere a marvel if the merits of the lotus stem were not frail.' Another allegory is one of the dust:

ye jātyā laghavaḥ sadaiva gaṇanāṁ yātā na ye kutra cit
padbhyām eva vimarditāḥ pratidinam bhūmau nilīnāç ciram
utkṣiptāç capalāçayena marutā paçyāntarikṣe sakhe
tuṅgānām upari sthitiṁ kṣitibhṛtāṁ kurvanty amī pāṅsavaḥ.

'The dust, light by nature, is deemed nought, day by day it is trampled beneath our feet and trodden into the ground; but see, dear friend, the fickle wind has tossed it high, and it settles now on the summit of the lofty mountains.'

Less original is the work of another Kashmirian poet, a certain Çilhaṇa,[2] who may also have worked in Bengal. It is clear that he was an admirer of Bhartṛhari; he borrows from him, and when he does not reproduce he alters, partly, no doubt, in order to adapt the standpoint of an earnest Vaiṣṇava to that of a Çaiva like Bhartṛhari; one stanza is borrowed from the *Nāgānanda* of Harṣa. Çilhaṇa is essentially bent on glorifying by his compilation, to which he doubtless added original matter of his own, the merits of asceticism, and there is much in him that is common to all three great religions, Hinduism, Buddhism, and Jainism. It would be difficult to assert that he is a great poet; his matter is more interesting than his manner, which is competent but hardly more than that. His date is uncertain, but before the *Saduktikarṇāmṛta* (1205), in which he is cited. Pischel has not unnaturally seen in him a mistake for Bilhaṇa, and one of Bilhaṇa's verses is actually found, at least in some manuscripts of the Çataka. Nor can the suggestion be positively disproved; it is true that Bilhaṇa is not usually a compiler, but that is not to say

[1] ZDMG. lvi. 405.
[2] Ed. K. Schönfeld, Leipzig, 1910. See Keith, JRAS. 1911, pp. 257 ff.

that he did not become one in old age: he owned wealth, as the *Vikramāṅkadevacarita* proves, and his eroticism is established by the *Caurasuratapañcāçikā*; but we know from his epic that he grew weary of the world in old age, and that he passes over his erotic poem in silence, so that we might easily believe that he renounced wealth and love and sought the delights of solitude and devotion to God. But in the absence of any old tradition we cannot press Pischel's suggestion.

The following stanzas illustrate well the minor key of Çilhaṇa's art:

tvām udara sādhu manye çākair api yad asi labdhaparitoṣam
hatahṛdayaṁ hy adhikādhikavāñchāçatadurbharaṁ na punaḥ.

'Thee, O belly, I deem wise, since thou art satisfied with mere vegetables; but quite other is my view of the accursed heart which is ever more difficult to satiate because of its hundreds of wishes.'

dadhati tāvad amī viṣayāḥ sukhaṁ: sphuratu yāvad iyaṁ hṛdi mūḍhatā
manasi tattvavidāṁ tu vivecake: kva viṣayāḥ kva sukhaṁ kva parigrahaḥ?

'Things of sense delight us here so long only as folly reigns in our hearts; in the mind of those who know the truth objects, delight, and acquisition thereof are nothing.'

vāso valkalam āstaraṁ kisalayāny okas tarūṇāṁ talam
mūlāni kṣataye kṣudhāṁ girinadītoyaṁ tṛṣṇāçāntaye
krīḍā mugdhamṛgair vayāṅsi suhṛdo naktam pradīpaḥ çaçī
svādhīne vibhave tathāpi kṛpaṇā yācanta ity adbhutam.

'Bark for a garment, twigs for a bed, the foot of a tree for a house, roots to banish hunger, water from mountain streams to quench thirst, sport with the loving gazelles, the birds as friends, the moon as a lamp by night: with such riches at their pleasure, strange that the poor should beg.'

Other works are of less interest; Çambhu wrote under Harṣa of Kashmir (1089–1101) an *Anyoktimuktālatāçataka*[1] in 108 elaborate stanzas, of no special merit. His *Rājendrakarṇapūra*,[2]

[1] Ed. KM. ii. 61 ff.
[2] Ed. KM. i. 22 ff.

a eulogy of Harṣa, is cited by Vallabhadeva freely, not his Çataka. The *Dṛṣṭāntaçataka* [1] of Kusumadeva is probably late, though it is cited by Vallabhadeva : it illustrates each maxim by an example, whence its name, and is simple and unpretentious :

uttamaḥ kleçavikṣobhaṁ kṣamaḥ soḍhuṁ na hītaraḥ
maṇir eva mahāçāṇagharṣaṇaṁ na tu mṛtkaṇaḥ.

'Only the noble can bear the pangs of sorrow ; the jewel resists the pressure of the grindstone, not the lime.'

īçvarāḥ piçunāñ chaçvad dviṣantīti kim adbhutam
prāyo nidhaya evāhīn dvijihvān dadhatetarām.

'What wonder if the rich ever hate false men ? Treasures ever conceal two-headed snakes.' The verbal form in the comparative is a frequent feature in this poetry.

dhanam api paradattaṁ duḥkham aucityabhājām
bhavati hṛdi tad evānandakārītareṣām
Malayajarasabindur bādhate netram antar
janayati ca sa evāhlādam anyatra gātre.

'If given by another even wealth is a sorrow to the noble ; it is others whose hearts it delights ; the water drops from the Malaya wind trouble the eye, though they give pleasure to the rest of the body.'

Still later probably are the *Bhāvaçataka* [2] of Nāgarāja of the Ṭāka family, or of Bhāva, his protégé, and the *Upadeçaçataka* [3] of Gumāni, as well as many other works. In the seventeenth century the great authority on poetics, Jagannātha, wrote his *Bhāminīvilāsa*,[4] admirable in many respects both as an erotic poem, an elegy, and a store of gnomic sayings, but this poetry is well beyond the limits here set.

The anthologies, which are our sources of so many lyric stanzas, are equally rich in gnomic matter, sometimes of great beauty, and there are a number of brief poems which may best be reckoned as gnomic. The most famous is the *Cātakāṣṭaka* [5] of uncertain date ; the bird will drink only the water of the clouds, and thus is a symbol of *hauteur* :

[1] Ed. Haeberlin, 217 ff.
[2] Ed. KM. iv. 37.
[3] Ed. KM. ii. 21 ff.
[4] Ed. Bergaigne, Paris, 1872.
[5] Ed. Haeberlin, 237 ff.

eka eva khage mānī vane vasati cātakaḥ
pipāsito vā mriyate yācate vā purandaram.

'No peer is there in pride for the Cātaka among the wood-dwellers; athirst he dies or makes supplication to Indra alone.'

To an unknown Bhaṭṭa Ūrvīdhara are ascribed some verses full of rough good sense:

anāhutapraviṣṭasya dṛṣṭasya kruddhacakṣuṣā
svayam evopaviṣṭasya varaṁ mṛtyur na bhojanam.

'Better death than feeding an uninvited guest who calmly sits down, though you glare angrily at him.'

ā saptater yasya vivāhapaṅktir: vicchidyate nūnam apaṇḍito 'sau
jīvanti tāḥ kartanakuṭṭanābhyāṁ: gobhyaḥ kim ukṣā yavasaṁ dadāti?

'He is a fool who goes not on marrying until seventy; his wives can live by spinning and pounding; does the bull provide fodder for the cows?' Very different is the exquisite simile which justifies pity for the worthless:

nirguṇeṣv api sattveṣu dāyāṁ kurvanti sādhavaḥ
na hi saṁharate jyotsnāṁ candraç caṇḍālaveçmani.

'The noble show compassion even to the worthless; the moon doth not withhold her light even from the Caṇḍāla's abode.' The immutability of facts is proved in the *Nītiratna*:

maṇir luṭhati pādāgre kacaḥ çirasi dhāryate
yathaivāste tathaivāstāṁ kaco kaco maṇir maṇiḥ.

'A jewel rolls before our feet, glass is placed on the head; let them be as they are, a jewel remains a jewel, and glass glass.' Royal service is exposed:

rājasevā manuṣyāṇām asidhārāvalehanam
pañcānanapariṣvañjo vyālivadanacumbanam.

'For a man to serve a king is as wise as to lick the edge of a sword, embrace a lion, and kiss the mouth of a serpent.' The evils of overcrowding are not modern alone, as Vainateya shows in a humorous stanza:

tasminn eva gṛhodare rasavatī tatraiva sā kaṇḍanī
tatropaskaraṇāni tatra çiçavas tatraiva vāsaḥ svayam

sarvaṁ soḍhavato 'pi duḥsthagṛhiṇaḥ kiṁ brūmahe tāṁ daçām
adya çvo janayiṣyamāṇagṛhiṇī tatraiva yat kunthati.

'Within the house is the kitchen, there the mortar, there too the crockery, there the children, there his own study. He has put up with all that, but what can we say of the condition of the wretched householder when his wife who to-day or to-morrow will present him with a new addition to his family must spend there her time of labour?'

2. *Didactic Poetry*

There is, of course, no clear line of demarcation between gnomic and didactic verse; the easiest mode of distinction rests on the extent and degree of unity of conception, and that permits of indefinite variety. Of early work of the pronounced didactic type very little has come down to us; Çāntideva's *Bodhicaryāvatāra* is the most distinguished effort known to us to adapt the elegances of Sanskrit poetry to the exposition of a complex philosophical and moral theme. Some of the poems ascribed to Çaṅkara may be reckoned as sufficiently elaborate to be styled didactic tracts, for example, the *Çataçlokī* [1] which in 101 Sragdharā verses sets out with some wealth of imagery the principles of the Vedānta; the *Mohamudgara*,[2] on the other hand, by the fire of its manner and the elaborate riming it affects is more lyric than didactic; much of it features as the *Dvādaçapañjarikāstotra.* Some poetic merit attaches to the *Çṛṅgārajñānanirṇaya*,[3] which in a form not common in Sanskrit gives a contest between the claims of love and of knowledge in thirty-two stanzas, the claims of love being espoused by Rambhā, those of philosophy by Çuka. The author and date are alike unknown, but the latter is hardly early.

A more interesting and quite definitely datable work is the early treatise on Indian pornography, the *Kuṭṭanīmata*,[4] advice of a hetaira, of Dāmodaragupta, minister of Jayāpīḍa of Kashmir (779–813). The book shows a young girl how to win gold for herself by the use of all the arts of flattery and feigned love, while

[1] Ed. *Select Works of Srisankaracharya*, pp. 85 ff.
[2] Ed. Haeberlin, 265 ff.
[3] Ed. J. M. Grandjean, AMG. x. 477 ff.
[4] Ed. KM. iii. 32 ff.; J. J. Meyer, *Altind. Schelmenbücher*, ii (1903).

preserving throughout a mere desire for wealth. Kalhaṇa mentions him as a poet, and Mammaṭa and Ruyyaka cite verses from him, as do the anthologies, showing that his work won considerable fame. From the point of view of literary history, it has the interest that it depicts a representation of Harṣa's *Ratnāvalī* in an effective and realistic manner. The author's style is simple but not inelegant; it begins:

sa jayati saṁkalpabhavo Ratimukhaçatapattracumbanabhramaraḥ
yasyānuraktalalanānayanāntavilokitaṁ vasatiḥ.

'Victorious is he, the mind-born god, the bee who kisses the hundred petals of Rati's face, whose abode is the glance shot from the corner of the eye of amorous maidens.' There is both wit and humour, despite their coarseness, in some of his stanzas:

çṛṇu sakhi kautukam ekaṁ grāmyeṇa kukāminā yad adya kṛtam
suratasukhamīlitākṣī mṛteti bhītena muktāsmi.

'Let me tell you, friend, of a singular thing a boorish fellow of a lover did to me to-day; I had closed my eyes in the ecstacy of the moment, when thinking me dead he took fright and let go of me.'

avidagdhaḥ çramakaṭhino durlabhayoṣid yuvā vipraḥ
apamṛtyur apakrāntaḥ kāmivyājena me rātrau.

'Death untimely, in the shape of an uncultivated fellow, rough with his work, who can't easily get women for all his youth, a Brahmin at that, departed from me at night in the guise of a lover.'

paryaṅkaḥ svāstaraṇaḥ patir anukūlo manoharaṁ sadanam
nārhati lakṣāṅçam api tvaritakṣaṇacauryasuratasya.

'A couch with a fair coverlet, a loving spouse, a pleasant seat, all these are not worth a ten-thousandth part of the secret union which takes place in a hurried moment.' With modern examples before us, it is not surprising to find that Dāmodaragupta has lavished on this work the resources acquired by a prolonged study of the *Kāmasūtra*, the text-books on poetics, and the lexicons.

Doubtless inspired in some degree by his predecessor, Kṣemendra, the polymath of Kashmir, wrote his *Samayamātṛkā*,[1] which perhaps means 'mother by convention', alluding to the fact that the hetaira-to-be is introduced by a barber as the regular go-between to an ancient expert, Kalāvatī, to be instructed in her exacting profession. The old lady, though owl-faced, crow-necked, and cat-eyed, through the passage of time since she was an expert, proves a witty instructress, and with her skilled aid the young aspirant ends by cheating a young fool and his stupid parent. Another of Kṣemendra's numerous writings is the *Kalāvilāsa*[2] which in ten sections discourses of the various occupations and follies of mankind. The hero of the book is the famous Mūladeva,[3] the personification of all trickery, who consents to educate in his own trade the young Candragupta whom his father entrusts to his care. We learn from him of the great spirit of cheating, Dambha, which has descended to earth and reigns among ascetics, doctors, lackeys, singers, goldsmiths, merchants, actors, and indeed all others; it has spread even to the world of beasts—witness the crane who parades himself as a penitent to snare the unwary fish, and is known even in the vegetable world—the trees wear bark garments just like ascetics. There is in certain respects a curious modernity in Kṣemendra's pictures; he knew wandering singers and bards who went about, gipsy-like, with pots and carts, wearing their hair long, rich in children, winning many gifts by flattery and wasting by mid-day what they had received in the morning. More medieval is the complaint made of the goldsmith with his tricks to cheat those who put work in his hands. But we are back to modernity when we find that the doctor, who has quack medicines and who has killed many a patient, is at last voted a great success and cuts a splendid figure; that the astrologer, with all his hocus-pocus and his readiness to predict what his clients wish to hear, does not even know what his wife is doing behind his back; and that the seller of patent remedies, whose head is as bald as a copper kettle, is yet prepared to guarantee an infallible cure for baldness and finds purchasers. The *Darpadalana*,[4] in seven sections, is intended to

[1] Ed. KM. 10, 1888.

[2] Ed. KM. i. 34 ff. Cf. WZKM. xxviii. 406 ff.

[3] Bloomfield, PAPS. lii. no. 212; Pavolini, GSAI. ix. 175.

[4] Ed. KM. vi. 66 ff.; trs. ZDMG. lxix. 1 ff.

show the folly of pride whether it be based on noble birth, wealth, knowledge, beauty, courage, generosity, or asceticism. The form is not uninteresting; each section begins with some gnomic sentences, and then follows a tale in which the leading character delivers himself of a long speech which in effect is a continuation of the maxims. The Buddha appears in this role in ii, Çiva in vii, where he denounces some ascetics as not worth saving, since their passions cling to them still. The *Sevyasevakopadeça*[1] in sixty-one stanzas is a little text of advice regarding servants and their masters, the *Caturvargasaṁgraha* describes the four ends of life, morality, practical life, love, and release, characteristically with more effort in the case of love than in those of the others. The *Cārucaryāçataka*[2] is a century of verses laying down the rules of good behaviour, illustrating them by references to myths and tales. The work has a certain interest, because it was used by and doubtless influenced the writing of the *Nītimañjarī*[3] of Dyā Dviveda (1494), which illustrates some 200 verses of maxims by tales culled from Sāyaṇa's commentary on the *Ṛgveda*. Probably due to Kṣemendra's influence is also the *Mugdhopadeça*[4] of Jalhaṇa, a warning in sixty-six stanzas against the wiles of hetairai.

Kṣemendra can write a fairly simple style, which appears to the best advantage in his reflections on the world and on morals, nor must we for a moment suggest that his remarks on erotics are of the character of pornography; he unquestionably had throughout his work a moral aim, however little we may care for his mode of treating difficult issues. Some of the *Kalāvilāsa* stanzas are quite pretty:

atha pathikavadhūdahanaḥ çanakair udabhūn niçākaralokaḥ
kumudaprabodhadūto vyasanaguruç cakravākīnām.

'Then slow uprose the shimmering moon, tormenting the wives of those afar, portending the awakening of the night-lotuses, and causing the female Cakravāka birds the grief of loss of their spouses.'

anañgenābalāsañgāj jitā yena jagattrayī
sa citracaritaḥ kāmaḥ sarvakāmaprado 'stu vaḥ.

[1] Ed. KM. ii. 79 ff.
[2] Ed. KM. ii. 128 ff.
[3] Keith, JRAS. 1900, pp. 127 ff., 796 f.
[4] Ed. KM. viii. 125 ff.

'May Love who, though bodiless, with women only to aid him conquered the three worlds, bestow on you, wonder-worker, all that you love.'

artho nāma janānāṁ jīvitam akhilaḥ kriyākalāpaç ca
taṁ ca haranty atidhūrtāç chagalagalā gāyanā loke.
tamasi varākaç cauro hāhākāreṇa yāti saṁtrastaḥ
gāyanacauraḥ kapaṭī hāhā kṛtvā nayati lakṣam.

'Gold is the life and all the business of life for men, yet in this world our singers with their goat-like bleats are clever enough to steal it away; when the wretched thief in the night hears the shout "Oh, Oh," he takes to his heels in panic, but the cunning thief of a singer gets a lakh of coins when his audience shouts "Oh, Oh".' The term *hāhā* expresses joy as well as fright. The denunciation of the goldsmith is quite effective:

Meruḥ sthito 'tidūre manuṣyabhūmim parityajya
bhīto bhayena cauryāc caurāṇāṁ hemakārāṇām.
tasmān mahīpatīnām asambhave cauradasyūnām
ekaḥ suvarṇakāro nigrāhyaḥ sarvathā nityam.

'Why does mount Meru keep so far away from our earth? It is in fear of being stolen by our thieves of goldsmiths. Therefore kings, when robbers and thieves are scarce, should suppress by all means in their power the goldsmith.'

Half a century younger than Kṣemendra was Amitagati whose *Subhāṣitaratnasaṁdoha*, 'Collection of Jewels of Happy Sayings,'[1] was written in 994 and his *Dharmaparīkṣā* twenty years later.[2] The former work in thirty-two chapters, usually written in one and the same metre, touches on the various aspects of Jain ethics, with an obvious polemical attitude towards Brahmanical speculations and practice. As usual, women are assailed readily (vi), and hetairai have a whole chapter to themselves (xxiv). The Āptas, the perfect men of Jainism, are described in xxviii, and the Brahmanical gods are denied the right to rank with them because they lust after women, indulge in drink, and are devoted to the world of sense. The assault on Brahmanism is resumed with much legendary matter to support it in the later work. More

[1] Ed. KM. 82; with trans. R. Schmidt and J. Hertel, ZDMG. lix. and lxi; cf. WZKM. xvii. 105 ff.

[2] N. Mironow, *Die Dharmaparīkṣā des Amitagati* (1903).

important is Hemacandra's *Yogaçāstra*,[1] written in simple Çlokas, with his own commentary in somewhat elaborate prose. The first four chapters contain as developed in the commentary a full and clear account of Jain philosophy, the last eight deal with the various duties and ascetic practices of Jainism. There is, as in Amitagati, the constant glorification of Ahiṅsā and depreciation of women, and, though Hemacandra is capable of some moderately good poetry it would be absurd to give the work any high literary rank. From this point of view greater value attaches to the little but elaborate *Çṛṅgāravairāgyataraṅgiṇī*[2] in forty-six stanzas, denouncing the love of women, by Somaprabha (1276).

[1] Ed. BI. 1907 ff.; i–iv, ZDMG. xxviii. 185 ff.
[2] Ed. KM. v. 124 ff.

XI

THE DIDACTIC FABLE

1. *The Origin of the Fable*

WE may safely assume that from the earliest times of the life of the Vedic Indians in India tales of all sorts passed current among the people, however useless it may be to discriminate them as fairy tales, Märchen, or myths or fables in the earlier stages of their development. It was, however, a distinct and important step when the mere story became used for a definite purpose, and when the didactic fable became a definite mode of inculcating useful knowledge. We do not know at what date this took place; we could not expect to find fables in the *Ṛgveda*, but we have there something which reminds us how easy it was for Indian thought to transfer to men's neighbours the habits of men. Whatever be the purpose of a famous hymn in the *Ṛgveda*[1] in which Brahmins are compared to croaking frogs as they sing at their sacrifice, it is clear that we have a recognition of a certain kinship between men and animals, which comes out clearly in the Upaniṣads,[2] where we have the allegory or satire of the dogs who search out a leader to howl food for them, the talk of two flamingoes whose remarks call attention to Raikva, and the instruction of the young Satyakāma first by a bull, then by a flamingo, then by an aquatic bird. Granting that we have not here the didactic fable, in which the actions of beasts are made the means of advising men, still we can realize how easy it was to pass to this form of instruction, and in fact we find in the epic[3] clear recognition of fables, and that not merely in the late didactic book xii but elsewhere. Not only do we hear of the bird that provided the equivalent of the golden eggs, but of the naughty cat which deceived the little mice by an appearance of virtue so that they delivered themselves into her power, and we have a *motif* which certainly is strongly suggestive

1 vii. 103. 2 *Chāndogya Upaniṣad*, i. 12; iv. 1; 5; 7 f.
3 Holtzmann, *Das Mahābhārata*, iv. 88 ff.

of the material whence developed the *Pañcatantra*. The Pāṇḍavas, it is suggested, are to be treated as the intelligent jackal treated his allies the tiger, the mouse, the ichneumon, and the wolf, when he smartly cheated them out of any share in the booty he had won with their aid. About the same time,[1] as the monumental evidence at Bharhut proves, the Buddhists were already making another use of the common belief in the close relationship of animals and man, now accentuated by the adoption by Hindus, Buddhists, and Jains alike of the doctrine of transmigration into animal as well as human forms. They chose by relating beast stories to illustrate the deeds and greatness of the Buddha and his contemporaries in past births.

We may confidently assume from the epic and from allusions to proverbs in Patañjali[2] that the beast fable was thus current, but we cannot say with any certainty whether fables had yet come to be reduced to literary form of any kind. The answer may be in the negative, for the fable as we have it in the *Pañcatantra* is indeed an elaborate production despite its seeming lack of art. It is essentially didactic, and thus must consist in part of a tale, but in part also of a moral or maxim of practical life—which may, of course, not be moral in the higher sense of the term. The fable, indeed, is essentially connected with the two branches of science known by Indians as the *Nītiçāstra* and the *Arthaçāstra*, which have this in common as opposed to the *Dharmaçāstra* that they are not codes of morals, but deal with man's action in practical politics and conduct of the ordinary affairs of every-day life and intercourse. We must not, however, exaggerate the contrast between these Çāstras, for in the *Arthaçāstra* and the *Nītiçāstra* alike there is much common sense, and that is often in accord with practical morality; at no time can we regard the didactic fable as intended merely to extol cleverness without regard to morality; there lingers around the work a distinct influence of the *Dharmaçāstra*, as was only to be expected, seeing that the *Pañcatantra* was intended for the instruction of the young and the instructors were Brahmins. But the youthful pupils were evidently not intended to be Brahmin boys either solely or mainly; tradi-

[1] *Mem. Arch. Surv. India*, i (1919), 15. On the question of dates cf. R. C. Majumdar, JPASB. 1922, pp. 225 ff.

[2] On Pāṇini, ii. 1. 3; v. 3. 106 f.; Weber, IS. xiii. 486.

tion enshrined in the *Pañcatantra* itself asserts its composition for the instruction of the sons of a prince, and with this accords the use of Sanskrit, for at the probable time of its first production, Sanskrit was already essentially the language of the Brahmins and of the high official classes in the royal *entourage*. A work of this sort, it is evident, was a very definite creation, something vastly different from mere tales regarding beasts or even the simple fable as it may have passed current orally.

The form of the fable is essentially dictated by its origin. The story is naturally related in prose, but the moral is fixed in the memory by being put in verse form, and it is natural that other didactic verses should be strewn in the tales; such an employment of gnomic stanzas is found in the *Aitareya Brāhmaṇa*.[1] The maxim embodying the truth or point of the tale naturally stands in a different position from the more general didactic stanza; it must be capable of serving as an identification label, or Kathāsaṁgrahaçloka, a verse that sums up the tale. It must, however, have been natural on the basis of such stanzas to insert in the narrative itself stanzas which are not maxims, but, like the label, refer definitely to the tale itself, and thus we achieve the use of Ākhyāna or narrative verses, but primarily at any rate as a minor feature. It is only slowly and late that the didactic fable comes to be written wholly or largely in verse.

Yet another peculiarity marks the form of the fable. It was a distinctly artistic touch to complicate and enlarge the theme, not merely by combining a number of fables to form a book, but to interweave the fables so that the whole would become a unity. This involved making the characters in the fables support their maxims by allusions to other fables, which they necessarily are asked to tell, resulting that in a fable others are normally inserted, while the process may even be carried so far as to include in such an inserted fable another inserted fable. There is, of course, nothing simple or popular in such a form; indeed, it is highly inconvenient for merely practical purposes, as the thread of the main narrative may be so interrupted as to render return to it difficult; it must have been the invention of some definite person or persons. For models we can only refer vaguely to the love of direct speech shown in the epics where, if possible, the actor is

[1] vii. 13 ff.

made to relate his own deeds, as does Odysseus among the Phaiacians. Nor would it be reasonable to doubt that those who introduced these important changes into the form of the fable, as contrasted with the simpler form we must presume it once had, were responsible for inventing many of the fables which they tell. From the popular fable they may well have borrowed a good deal in substance, but in adapting it for very definite didactic ends they must have vitally changed it. We can support this view by the wholesale alterations evidently made in the conception of fables by the Buddhists in the Jātaka book.

In view of these facts it is clear that it is not possible to speak of a Prākrit fable literature as being the precursor of the *Pañcatantra.* We have no reason whatever to suppose that any real parallel to the structure of the *Pañcatantra* ever existed, and we cannot even say that the substance of the individual tales was current among the people until much later, when the popularity of the *Pañcatantra* led to the wholesale effort to appropriate them for the humbler ranks of society much as apparently happened in the case of Aesop's fables. We may go further and hold that the fable was far more of an independent creation in Sanskrit than the popular tale or Märchen, which is free from the didactic aim of the fable and expresses much more directly the religious feelings of the people, their myth-making capacity, their belief in magic in all aspects, and the native ingenuity of humble narrators. It is in entire harmony with this obvious distinction that Indian tradition is as positive regarding the Prākrit original of the great collections of Märchen as it is silent on the existence of any Prākrit source of the *Pañcatantra.*

Clear distinctions in literature, as in everything else, are not common in Sanskrit, and no terminology was invented by writers on poetics to discriminate between the fable and the tale, though as regards the tale itself some efforts were made to discriminate the species of Kathā or Ākhyāyikā, though without success.[1] The stories in the several books of the *Pañcatantra* are styled Kathās, while in one version the title is *Tantrākhyāyika.* The terms themselves merely denote, Ākhyāyikā, narrative, sometimes minor narrative, Kathā, conversation, story, and it was hardly possible to discriminate them seriously. Nor are in fact

[1] Cf. S. K. Dé, BSOS. iii. 507 ff.

in the *Pañcatantra* fables, tales, and narratives of actual or possible human events rigidly discriminated ; it differs from the tales in that the fable element with its didactic stanzas decidedly prevails over other elements, while the tale includes the fable merely as a lesser constituent. Both profit by this absence of rigidity, which permits either a richer content and more elaborate development. Even so late a work as the *Hitopadeça* knows how to seek variety by blending the beast fable with Märchen and spicy narratives of human life.

2. *The Reconstruction of the Pañcatantra and its Origin*

The original of the numerous works which have come down to us, usually under the style of *Pañcatantra* or something equivalent, is now lost. But we can unquestionably find our way back to the substance of the original and even to a considerable measure of its form by the examination of the chief of its representatives.[1] Of these we can certainly discern four main groups. The first is the Pahlavi version of the *Pañcatantra* made before A.D. 570, but now lost, which itself can be reconstructed in substance from an Old Syrian and an Arabic version with the later texts based on the latter. The second is a version produced in north-west India, which was interpolated in the version of Guṇāḍhya's *Bṛhatkathā* which formed the basis of the *Bṛhatkathāmañjarī* of Kṣemendra and the *Kathāsaritsāgara* of Somadeva in the eleventh century. The third is represented by two Kashmir versions styled *Tantrākhyāyika*, and by two Jain recensions which derive their matter from a text akin to, but not that of, the *Tantrākhāyika*, namely the Simplicior well known through Bühler and Kielhorn's edition *in usum tironum*, and the text of Pūrṇabhadra (1199), who used also the *Tantrākhyāyika* and some other unknown version. Fourthly, we have the common ancestor of the Southern *Pañcatantra*, the Nepalese *Pañcatantra* and the popular *Hitopadeça* ; the latter two are derived from a version sister to the Southern *Pañcatantra* now lost, and the *Hitopadeça* is in considerable measure derived from another source altogether.

This is the limit of our certainty. Hertel's[2] unrelenting and

[1] See F. Edgerton, *The Panchatantra Reconstructed* (1924).

[2] *Das Pañcatantra* (1914).

fruitful labours led him to conclude that all these sources went back to a defective original (styled by him *t*), but it is clear that this is unproved. Further, he held that these four sources ought to be reduced to two, the *Tantrākhyāyika* original and 'K', the source of the other three groups, and in part of version β of the *Tantrākhyāyika* itself. This again is implausible, and the result is important, because it follows that the occurrence of any story in any two of the four versions is a strong reason for assigning it to the original text, whereas on Hertel's view significance of this kind only applies to occurrence both in the *Tantrākhyāyika* and one of the 'K' version. Nor is there any adequate ground for Hertel's further assumption of another intermediate archetype, 'N.-W.', from which the Pahlavi, the Southern *Pañcatantra* group, and the Simplicior are descended. Further, the priority of recension of the *Tāntrākhyāyika* is implausible; its omissions, which Hertel held of great importance in re-establishing the original text, are frequently not a proof of fidelity to the ultimate source, but are secondary; the recension which makes them good is thus as valuable, if not more so, than recension *a*. Fortunately, despite these divergences of opinion, we can be assured of the possibility of reconstructing the substance of the original. Edgerton accepts all of the stories held original by Hertel as genuine, and of those which he adds Hertel merely holds five doubtful and two certainly unoriginal. His grounds in no case are convincing, and the disputed tales are, probably enough, to be ascribed to the primary *Pañcatantra*.

The name of this original was almost certainly *Pañcatantra*, but the sense of the term is uncertain; does *Tantra* merely mean book, or does it indicate trick, specimen of sharp conduct, or didactic or authoritative treatise? Similarly, does *Tantrākhyāyika* denote a Nītiçāstra in the form of tales arranged in (five) books; or an authoritative text-book (for policy) in the shape of an Ākhyāyikā; or a text-book composed of instructive or didactic tales? We do not know, but it is perhaps more likely that *Pañcatantra* meant originally five subject-matters; as a title, a treatise dealing with five subject-matters. Of the state of the original we cannot say more with certainty than that it must have existed before the Pahlavi version was made, and probably for some time. That it was written long after 200 B.C., Hertel's first suggested date, is not doubted by himself; it knows the *Mahābhārata* well, and the use of *dīnāra*, the Latin *denarius*, points definitely to a time after the Christian era, though it is not sufficient to assign it to the second century A. D. at earliest.[1] Everything, however, suggests that it fell in the period of the Brahmanical restoration and expansion under the Guptas or just before their empire, with which well accords the use of Sanskrit for the instruction of princes and the distinctly Brahmanical character of the work, even if the evidence for the author having been a Vaiṣṇava is inadequate. We may reasonably accept the author as a Brahmin, but the name Viṣṇuçarman given doubtless in the prototype cannot be relied on, though it is impossible to dismiss it as certainly feigned; the author might very well have wished thus to secure remembrance of his personality. If so, then some weight may attach to the fact that Viṣṇuçarman is described as relating the tales to the sons of king Amaraçakti of Mahilāropya or Mihilāropya in the Deccan as a sign of southern origin; with this it agrees that the *Tantrākhyāyika* with the Jain versions mentions a mount Ṛṣyamūka, apparently in the western Deccan. The frame story of Book v is placed in Gauḍa, Bengal, but this is of no importance, especially as of the later versions only the *Hitopadeça* is connected with that land. Hertel's view that the work was composed in Kashmir because neither the tiger nor the elephant plays a part in the original, while the camel is known, is inconclusive in view of the late origin of the work, which would render it possible for persons in a very wide area in India to know all about the camel. The places of pilgrimage mentioned are common-place, Puṣkara, Gaṅgādvāra, Prayāga, and Vārāṇasī, so that we must leave the place of composition open.

3. *The Subject-Matter of the Pañcatantra*

The reconstructed text is unquestionably a text-book for the instruction of kings in politics and the practical conduct of everyday life, but it is also a story-book, and the author was not inclined to cut down his stories merely to the bare minimum necessary for his task of instruction. This is true to human nature,

[1] Keith, JRAS. 1915, pp. 504 .

and it doubtless accounts for the insertion of stories which are rather Märchen than fables, as the tale[1] of the strand bird which menaced the sea and the narrative in Book ii of the experiences of the mouse, Hiraṇya. Nor was the intention of the author unmoral; he had no desire to establish the doctrine that dishonesty was the best policy; his concern was to give advice of a useful character, and it is by no means essential that such advice should be immoral. Indeed, in one important case, the story of Evil-wit and Honest-wit, we have a long account simply intended to prove that honesty is the best policy, and the point is emphasized by the fact that it is Karaṭaka, a minister of the bull, who reproves his colleague Damanaka and insists that he will live to repent successful villainy. We are in fact right in the midst of the normal Brahmanical society. The ministers of the king are normally Brahmins, Brahmins are essential for sacrifices, the Brahmanical consecrations and sacraments are observed, at the new and the full moon Brahmins are fed. It is quite a mistake to regard as signs of hostility to Brahmanism such facts as allusions to the false ascetic or the greed of the priests, a distinction which they share with women and kings. The Brahmins were not a close corporation, blind to defects of individual members; they were as ready to see the defects of one another as medieval monks. Of Buddhist tendencies there is no trace whatever; Benfey's view that the original of the *Pañcatantra* was a Buddhist book was natural at the time when he could find parallels for the tales only in Buddhist books whose age he over-rated, and when it was imperfectly realized how essentially Indian in many regards Buddhism was. We now can be certain that several of the Jātaka tales are merely derived from the original *Pañcatantra* as in the case of Nos. 349 and 361 which rest on the frame story of Book i of that text. For the large and sometimes indigestible masses of political information regarding kings, ministers, and royal government, the means to win allies and alienate confederations of enemies, and to wage war, we have a parallel in the *Arthaçāstra* handed down under Kauṭilya's name; it is quite possible that it was actually known as we have it to the original *Pañcatantra*, but that cannot be proved by internal evidence, and the utterly uncertain date of the *Arthaçāstra* renders it out of the question

[1] i. 9. Cf. St. Martin's bird, Wesselski, *Mönchslatein*, p. 172.

to assert that it is older than the *Pañcatantra.* What is clear is that the *Pañcatantra* derived its information from a similar source to the *Kauṭilīya.*

The frame story of Book i is preceded by a legend of the wickedness of the sons of king Amaraçakti, who entrusts them to Viṣṇuçarman on his promise in six months to teach them polity. Then we are introduced to the topic of the separation of friends, the frame story relating how a wicked jackal brought about the estrangement of the lion, Piñgalaka, from the bull, Saṁjīvaka, who had been rescued by the lion and then was treated as his dear friend, to the disgust of the jackals, Karaṭaka and Damanaka, the lion's trusted ministers. By cunning the lion is made to distrust the bull, and finally to slay him; he repents when he sees his blood-stained paws, but Damanaka consoles him and remains his premier. The book gives ample room for political discussions, but it contains also a set of interesting fables. The fate of the ape who pulled out a wedge and was split up by it is recounted to prove the folly of interfering with what does not concern one. The necessity of investigating in lieu of mere looking at surface appearances is shown by the tale (2) of the jackal who learned by investigation that the drum whose sound had terrified was merely skin with emptiness within. Then we learn of three cases of evils brought on oneself in the tales (3 a–c) of the foolish monk who took a thief as pupil and had his cash stolen, of the jackal who ran in between and was killed by the impact of two butting rams, and of the procuress who took the place of a weaver's wife in order to further her intrigue with a patron, and suffered in consequence the loss of her nose. Tale 4 shows the advantage of guile over force; the female crow to punish the serpent who slew her offspring put the prince's gold chain in his hole and thus had him killed. Next we hear of the error of over-greed, illustrated by the heron who deceived the fish into trusting him to remove them to another lake, and so being eaten by him, but who met his just fate from a wise crab. Tale 6 proves that folly leads to ruin, as the lion was destroyed by the clever hare who caused him to leap into a well to attack his counterfeit presentment in the water. The result of cleverness inducing combined action is next illustrated by the tale of how the retainers of a lion by offering themselves to their sick master as food and being refused in turn induced the foolish camel, who was living under the lion's protection, to do likewise, whereupon the lion devoured him. Next comes a warning against attacking an enemy without knowing his prowess, illustrated by Tale 9 of the strand birds. The male bade the hen lay her eggs at the ocean's edge, but she derided the project, defending her thesis by two tales (10 and 11) emboxed in Tale 9. The first explains how the foolish tortoise lost his life by not heeding the advice of the geese, who were carrying him on a stick held in their claws, not to open his mouth while in the air; the second explains how the fish Forethought and Ready-wit escaped the fishers but Come-what-will was caught. The husband, however, insists on her acting as he bids; the sea takes away the eggs, but the bird successfully invokes, through Garuḍa, Viṣṇu's aid, and the ocean on pain of an assault by fire gives back the eggs. The tale (12) of the bird which would not take a telling, but insisted on explaining to a foolish monkey that he could not warm himself by the light of a glowworm and so irritated the monkey that he killed him, proves the truth that some people will not learn. Tale 13 tells how Honest-wit and Evil-wit disputed over a sum of money which they had together buried but which the latter had secretly dug up. In court he declares that the tree will prove as witness of the scene that his adversary was a thief, and, when it is arranged to go to the tree, he tells his father to go into its hollow and pretend to be the tree spirit. The father remonstrates, telling Tale 14, how the foolish heron induced a mungoose to eat a snake which devoured her young only to find that mungooses are connoisseurs in young birds. None the less he does his son's bidding, declares from the tree that Honest-wit is a thief, only to be burned in the tree by that outraged youth, his crime being thus exposed. The last tale is that of the merchant's son whose balance of 1,000 pounds of iron was stolen by the friend with whom he deposited it in his absence. When he asks it back he is told that mice had eaten it; he therefore steals the son of his friend, and declares that a falcon has carried him away; brought before the judge, he easily persuades him to secure the return of the balance for the son.

Book ii of the winning of friends is perhaps more attractive. It opens with the tale of the clever king of the doves, Bright-neck, who saves his retinue from the hunter's net by making them all fly up with it and then has the bonds cut by the mouse, Goldy, being careful to have his cut last. We learn next how the crow, Lightwing, makes friends with Goldy, and is introduced to his old friend, the tortoise Sluggish. Goldy then explains why he left his first home ; his tale (1) explains that he used to eat the alms begged by a monk despite the efforts of the unfortunate to put it out of his reach ; a friend comes and tells the monk that the strength of the mouse must have some cause, just as there was a reason for mother Çāṇḍilī exchanging husked rice for husked rice. The allusion is explained in Tale 2 ; a Brahmin bade his wife prepare to feed Brahmins at the change of moon, and to override her objections on the score of economy, tells Tale 3, the story of the over-greedy jackal who, having as food a boar, deer, and hunter, nibbled the end of the bowstring which killed him by splitting his throat. The Brahmin's wife yields, but a dog snuffs and defiles the sesame prepared, so she sends the pupil of her husband to exchange it for other husked rice, evoking from the master of the house where the effort to exchange is made the adage alluded to. The monk then proceeds to search for the cause of the mouse's might and finds it in a store of gold in the mouse's home which gave him magic power. This taken away, the mouse is rendered weak, and, unable to feed his followers, is abandoned by them and gives up the delusion of desiring power and riches. A fourth friend is now added in the shape of a deer ; but, wandering one day, it is caught in a snare, and, inappropriately it may be admitted, while waiting to be freed gratifies its curious friends by telling how, when young, it had been kept in captivity by a prince, until one day urged to human utterance by desire for freedom it so startled the prince that he fell afevered and only recovered when he was told the truth of the voice he had heard and released the deer. The comrades now release the deer, but the tortoise is surprised by the hunter's advent, and has to be rescued by a clever ruse on the part of the deer who pretends to be dead.

Book iii illustrates war and peace by the tale how the stronghold of the owls was burned by the crows. The origin of the war is explained as due to an error in speech, and this elicits the tale (1) of the ass in the panther's skin, which by braying lost its life;

then a second tale is adduced, the election by the birds of a king; the crow objects to the owl as hideous[1] and not fit even for a bluff, and to illustrate the use of bluffing tells Tale 3, how the clever hare by pretending to have a commission from his patron the moon—in which the Indians saw a hare instead of a face—frightened away an elephant which was destroying with its herd all the animals round a certain lake. Further, he denounces the meanness of the owl and by Tale 4 illustrates the danger of a mean king as judge by the case of the cat, Curd-ears, who ate up the foolish hare and partridge who had come to him to settle a dispute. The birds are now induced to desert the owl who remains alone, vowing vengeance on the crows. The next tale (5) shows how by deceit the crows may win, as the Brahmin was cheated out of his sacrificial goat, as he was carrying it home, by rogues who assured him that he was carrying an unclean dog. The crow minister, therefore, contrives to present himself to the owls as a suppliant who, for his good advice to the crow king, has been cast out; his friendly reception is advised and defended by two parallels. Tale 6 explains that even a thief received a kind welcome from the old man whose young wife is terrified by his intrusion into embracing warmly her spouse; Tale 7 extols the advantage of having enemies divided; the ogre who came to carry off a Brahmin and the thief who wished to steal his cows quarrelled over priority in evil-doing, so that the Brahmin woke up, drove off the ogre by a spell and the thief by his club. Only the owl, Red-eye, warns his foolish sovereign by the tale (8) of the silly carpenter who allowed his wife to dishonour him, but was deceived by her saying that she would not have any evil happen to him for the world. Red-eye also sees through the statement of the wily crow that he wishes to burn himself and be reborn an owl, proving that no such change of nature is possible by Tale 9. An ascetic rescued a mouse and made her a maiden, when she became ripe for marriage he sought a meet husband; the sun declined the proposals as the cloud was stronger than he, the cloud admitted inferiority to the wind, the wind to the mountain, and it to the mouse, so that the sage turned the maid to a mouse again. The owl king, however, persisted in permitting his enemy within the gates and is repaid by the destruction by

[1] Cf. Jātaka 270.

fire of his home. The crow king warmly rewards his minister, and on questioning him how he could bear to associate with foes is told the tale of the serpent who pretended to the frogs that he had been cursed by a Brahmin to act as their carrier; the frog king enjoys riding on him, and finding his pace diminish owing to lack of food allows him to eat up the young frogs, which he does so energetically as to devour them all.

Book iv illustrates the loss of one's gettings by the tale of the ape and the crocodile [1] who lived in such amity that the crocodile's wife became jealous, and falling sick would be content with nothing save her rival's heart. The crocodile, though sad, seeks to entice the ape to visit him, but the ape finds out his plan and saves himself by saying that his heart is kept on a fig-tree, escaping when the crocodile seeks to obtain it from the tree. The crocodile seeks to renew the friendship, but is told instead that the ape is not like the ass who came back. This constitutes the one Tale: an ass's heart and ears are demanded by a sick lion; the jackal induces an ass to come by pretending he is taking him to a she-ass; the lion springs too soon and the ass escapes, but is deluded by the jackal into a second and fatal visit. The lion then departs to perform due ceremonial before partaking of the remedy; the jackal eats heart and ears, and, when the lion demands them, asserts as irrefutable that the ass had neither heart nor ears, or else he would never have come back. Book v warns against inconsiderate action. A Brahmin is dreaming of the son to be born; his wife warns him of day-dreams by the case of Somaçarman's father; he was a Brahmin who dreamed that he would sell for twenty rupees the groats he had to buy goats, have in five years a flock sufficient to obtain 100 cows, and so become rich until he had a son born; the child would come home, and the busy mother would neglect him, whereon the chivalrous father would beat her, an action he accomplished in his dream, destroying at one stroke all hope of the riches he coveted. In point of fact a boy is born, and the wife goes to wash, leaving the child to her husband's care as they had no maid. A summons arrives from the queen and the Brahmin goes to the palace, leaving his pet mungoose in charge of the babe. On his return he finds the mungoose rushing to meet him with bloody paws and

[1] Jātaka 208; *Mahāvastu*, ii. 246 ff.

mouth; in a rage he deems his son killed and slays the beast, only to find that the blood was that of a cobra which the faithful guardian had destroyed. His wife shares his grief, and reminds him by Tale 2 of hasty action. A young merchant is bidden in a dream to slay three monks who shall present themselves, as they are treasures stored by his father in this odd form and will become when slain *dīnāras*. He obeys, carrying out the rite with a barber's aid; the barber foolishly tries to repeat the trick, but his murdered monks do not become *dīnāras*, and he perishes at the hands of outraged justice. The tone of this book, as becomes its themes, is decidedly sombre. The brevity of the two books is remarkable, but it is just as likely to have been original as to have been the product of rehandling.

Of the many maxims cited only about a quarter can be assigned to moral, religious, or philosophical thought, the rest deal with royal policy and general rules of life. The latter are far from always unmoral; the hero of Book ii is a fine character of the heroic type, proud but ever ready to sacrifice himself for his folk and his friends; the mouse also, when he ruled his subjects, worked desperately for them, and in the sphere of private life the householder is expected to be loyal, generous, and upright. There is no suggestion of approval of a low moral standard in domestic life; violators of marriage ties are clearly not admired, and lack of sensitiveness to dishonour is disapproved and ridiculed.

4. *The Style and Language of the Pañcatantra*

There can be no doubt that the work was the production of an artist. The complex emboxment of the stories, which can be seen from the analysis above, is a very different thing from the epic simplicity, and not less characteristic is the intermingling of prose with gnomic stanzas and with title stanzas giving the moral inculcated in each tale with a hint of its characters, as when the tale of the bird who annoyed an ape regarding a glow-worm is introduced with 'You cannot bend wood that is unbendable; you cannot use a knife on a stone. Know from the fate of the bird Needlebeak that you cannot teach one who will not learn.' A model for the intermingling of prose and verse has been seen in the *Jātakamālā*; but, as we have seen, the character of that work is distinctly different; the verses there carry on the narrative, as is done but very seldom in the *Pañcatantra*, and usually where the emotion demands a finer expression than prose, or where a reported verse is essentially demanded by the narrative. Thus in the deer's tale of his former captivity the verse he cites as uttered by himself is an essential factor of the story, serving the purpose of attracting the prince's ear:

vātavṛṣṭividhūtasya mṛgayūthasya dhāvataḥ
pṛṣṭhato 'nugamiṣyāmi kadā tan me bhaviṣyati?

'Ah, when will it be that I shall follow my herd as hither and thither the wind and the rain blow it on?' Emotion, on the other hand, renders appropriate among other verses clearly gnomic the use by the hypocritical crocodile of stanzas in his address to the ape:

ekaḥ sakhā priyo bhūya upakārī guṇānvitaḥ
hantavyaḥ strīnimittena kaṣṭam āpatitam mama.

'My one true friend, who hath done me so much of good, must now be slain for the sake of a woman. Woe is me.' This may even be a quoted line from another context. In the following case that explanation is less likely, nor indeed is there any reason to suppose that the author might not add to his narrative some verses of immediate relevance to the matter in hand:

prayojanavaçāt prītiṁ lokaḥ samanuvartate
tvaṁ tu vānaraçārdūla niṣprayojanavatsalaḥ.

'The world shows affection from self-interest. But thou, noblest of apes, art loving without such cause.' But verses such as these are very few, and, apart from the title-verses, the poet's effort has been devoted to finding or writing effective maxims. How far these were original we cannot possibly say in those cases in which we have no other early authority for them; but when they do not occur outside of the *Pañcatantra* we can fairly credit him with them. Some unquestionably he derived from the epic, and he may have taken thence[1] the hint for the construction of Book iii as a reminiscence of the omen, given to the defeated Kauravas by the crows who attack and destroy the owls by

[1] *Mahābhārata* x. 1 and v. 64.

night, of the victory which they can win over the Pāṇḍavas by a night onslaught on their camp, and the idea of the doves carrying off the net of their captor. We are, however, in these matters of originality reduced to conjectures.

The fact that the author was probably carrying out an original piece of work doubtless accounts for various blemishes—of which, however, later redactors remove but a few. Even in the original there seems to have been an attempt to accumulate an undue number of maxims to the same purpose, and occasionally the tales do not fit in very well, indicating that the author desired to have the tale on record even if he could not find quite an effective mode of inserting it. This is clearly the case with the interesting tale (ii. 4) of the former captivity of the deer; it has no moral, properly speaking, but it is clearly a Märchen which the author and we would ill spare; to doubt its valid ascription to the original is clearly unnecessary; though it seems rather absurd for the deer to talk when he is anxious to be set free, we find that the mouse goes on cutting as the narrative proceeds, and in Book iii there are equally irrational delays while the owls debate; the delay is excused by the intention to give political instruction, as in modern opera the musical interest excuses delays in themselves ridiculous.

The language of the author is distinctly elegant, and especially in the verses we find plays on words, *double entendres*, and other marks of polished style combined with polished and elaborate metre. Some of the verses contain rather longer compounds than are usual in the simpler style of Kāvya; but there are few, if any, cases where real complexity of sense can be ascribed to the original. It is obvious that the author had taste, and realized that over-elaboration in style was out of place in a work destined for the use of young princes, and there is a decided humour in the decision to use a more elevated style for the story (i. 7) of the louse and the flea, which tells how by permitting a flea to assault the royal person the louse, which had long enjoyed a monopoly of that privilege, lost its life, through the over-haste of the flea to savour the extremely rich ichor of the royal person. The adoption of the same style in the story of the jackal which fell into an indigo vat and passed itself off as wearing the royal purple, an interpolation (i. 8) in the original text, shows that the nuance of style had been noted early. The prose has already, though not in exaggerated form, the signs of the nominal style noted above. The past is denoted either by participles, active or passive, or the historic present; the regular use of the aorist is one of the signs of the spuriousness of the tale of the wicked procuress found in the *Tantrākhyāyika* (iii. 5). The passive construction is clearly coming to be preferred, resulting, as it does, in nominal verbal forms in lieu of finite forms, and thus according with the growing fondness for compounds. The employment of gerunds and adjectival participles is carried to excess.

Amusing as the stories are and well as they are told, though the practice of emboxment is, to tell the truth, rather irritating than otherwise in the more complex cases, the finest thing in the work is unquestionably the many excellent stanzas. Thus the virtues of magnanimity are expounded as follows:

ājīvitāntaḥ praṇayaḥ kopaç ca kṣaṇabhañguraḥ
parityāgaç ca niḥsañgo na bhavanti mahātmanām?

'Is it not the way of the magnanimous to love as long as life lasts, to be wroth but for a moment, to make sacrifices without reserve?' The might of fate is admitted:

çaçidivākarayor grahapīḍanaṁ: gajabhujaṁgamayor api bandhanam
matimatāṁ ca nirīkṣya daridratāṁ: vidhir aho balavān iti me matiḥ.

'When I contemplate the eclipsing of sun and moon, the taking alive of elephants and snakes, and the poverty of the wise, I recognize the might of fate.' The folly of accepting bad advice is expressed in a stanza which effectively matches sound and sense:

narādhipā nīcamatānuvartino: budhopadiṣṭena pathā na yānti ye
viçanti te durgamamārganirgamaṁ: samastasambādham anarthapañjaram.

'Kings who obey the advice of the low and walk not in the path set by the wise enter a maze of misfortune, in which trouble arises upon trouble and whence no exit presents itself.' The relation of fortune to master and minister is cleverly described in verse which has found its way into the *Mudrārākṣasa*:

atyucchrite mantriṇi pārthive ca: viṣṭabhya pādāv upatiṣṭhate
çrīḥ
sā strīsvabhāvād asahā bharasya: tayor dvayor ekataraṁ jahāti.

'When a minister and a king have become too elevated, fortune, planting firm her feet, strives to support them, but unable to bear the burden as being a woman she deserts one or other of the two.' There is a fine eulogy of right:

eka eva suhṛd dharmo nidhane 'py anuyāti yaḥ
çarīreṇa samaṁ nāçaṁ sarvam anyad dhi gacchati.

'Righteousness is the one friend who accompanieth man even in death, for all the rest perisheth together with the body.' The limits of possibility are asserted:

yad açakyaṁ na tac chakyaṁ yac chakyaṁ çakyam eva tat
odake çakaṭaṁ yāti na nāvā gamyate sthale.

'What is impossible is not possible, what is possible that indeed is possible; the cart cannot go on sea, nor the ship on dry land.'

A more elaborate style is not rare, as in the description of the sufferings of the Pāṇḍavas at Virāṭa's court, including the fate of Draupadī:

rūpeṇāpratimena yauvanaguṇair vaṅçe çubhe janmanā
yuktā çrīr iva yā tayā vidhivaçāt kālakramāyātayā
sairandhrīti sagarvitaṁ yuvatibhiḥ sākṣepam ājñaptayā
Draupadyā nanu Matsyarājabhavane ghṛṣṭaṁ ciraṁ candanam.

'Draupadī, like Çrī herself, had peerless beauty, youthful grace, birth in a noble house; yet by decree of fate the passage of time brought her to such a pass that for many a day she had to pound sandal in the palace of the Matsya king at the haughty bidding of maidens who insolently called her handmaid.'

5. *The Derivative Forms of the Pañcatantra*

Of the versions derived from the *Pañcatantra* that into Pahlavi will be considered later. Of the Indian texts the *Tantrākhyāyika*[1] may be given first rank by reason of its comparative closeness to the original. It may be granted that this relation has been

[1] Ed. J. Hertel, Berlin, 1910; trans. Leipzig, 1909.

exaggerated by Hertel, but, after all allowances are made, it remains still the nearest approach to the reconstructed text. Its date is uncertain and probably indeterminable. Already it had added certain stories which may be dismissed as not original. These include probably in both recensions that of the blue jackal (i. 8), the outwitting by a jackal of a camel and a lion (i. 13), the weaver Somilaka (ii. 4), king Çibi (iii. 7), the old Haṅsa (iii. 11), and the punishment[1] of the onion thief (iv. 1). In the *α* recension we have the clearly later tale of the wicked procuress (iii. 5), in recension *β* those of the jackal and the wary fox (iii. 11) and the sham warrior (iv. 3). The relation of the recensions is disputed; Hertel's view is that recension *β* was interpolated from use of the original 'K' source, whence all but the original of recension *α* are derived. It seems impossible to accept his proofs as establishing the existence of any such 'K', and, if so, the superiority of recension is open to serious doubt. Moreover, though in substance the *Tantrākhyāyika* seems original, its language appears to have been a good deal varied; we find also some attempts in recension *α* at rhythmical prose[2] unknown to the other versions.

The *textus simplicior* was composed somewhere in western India by a Jain at an uncertain date, but doubtless before Pūrṇabhadra (1199) and after Māgha and Rudra Bhaṭṭa,[3] from whom verses are taken, perhaps, therefore, *c.* 1100. It is substantially altered from the original. The five books are made more approximately equal; several stories from iii are placed in iv, to which new matter is also added. A continuation is appended to Book v, the framework of which is altered by making the story of the barber who killed the monks the main story in which the tale of the ichneumon is inserted. The frameworks of Books iii and iv are also rehandled, and new tales added also to Books i–iii. Of the quite original matter seven tales are Märchen, one a witty anecdote, two intrigues, and one a story of a fool. The most remarkable addition is the tale (i. 5) of Viṣṇu and the weaver; the latter gains access to a princess by pretending to be Viṣṇu and mounting a wooden Garuḍa, and, when the fraud is being disclosed through the folly of the king who, proud of his divine connexion, wars unsuccessfully on his neighbours and is

[1] Zachariae, *Kl. Schriften*, pp. 170 ff.
[2] See pp. 8, 69, 118.
[3] Not Rudraṭa as Hertel, *Pañcatantra*, p. 72; see *Çṛṅgāratilaka*, i. 68.

beleaguered in his city, Viṣṇu, to save his reputation, has to come down and save the city. This story itself would hardly prove Jain origin, but there is better evidence in the mention of Jain monks in lieu of Brahmin ascetics and the occurrence of Jain terms like *kṣapaṇaka*, *digambara*, *nagnaka*, *vyantara*, a species of spirit, and *dharmadeçanā*, teaching of the law. A very large number of new stanzas is found, while perhaps of the original stanzas not more than one-third was retained. The original of the text appears to have been a text akin to the *Tantrākhyāyika*; like that text the Simplicior contains the unoriginal tales of the blue jackal, the jackal outwitting camel and lion, and the weaver Somilaka.

A second Jain revision was undertaken to please a minister Soma by a monk Pūrṇabhadra in 1199.[1] The work is marked by the appearance of twenty-one new stories, including a famous one of the gratitude of animals and the ingratitude of man (i. 9), while from the *Mahābhārata* hints are taken for the story of the pious pigeon and the hunter (iii. 8). Pūrṇabhadra's version appears to rest in part on our *Tantrākhyāyika*, in part on the prototype of the Simplicior rather than on that text, and in part on some other unknown version. In this connexion it may be noted that the Jains evidently took to study of the Nītiçāstra as they became important at courts; the Āvaçyaka legends, perhaps of the seventh century, have parallels to *Pañcatantra* tales, perhaps derived from one of the older forms of that text. Some of Pūrṇabhadra's matter may have arisen in Jain circles, though his work has no special Jain touches. Its language is marred by Gujarātī and Prākrit intrusions. But, like the author of the Simplicior, he is by no means a bad writer. In his case the title appears as *Pañcākhyānaka*, a name also applied sometimes to the Simplicior. From the two Jain versions are derived various contaminations; one of these, the *Pañcākhyānoddhāra* of Meghavijaya (1659–60), is noteworthy, as it contains many fables of special interest to the investigators of connexions with the west.

The north-western version of the *Pañcatantra*, which gave rise to the reproductions of the work in the *Bṛhatkathāmañjarī*[2] and the *Kathāsaritsāgara*, seems to have been before the authors of

[1] Ed. J. Hertel, HOS. 11–13, 1908–12; trans. R. Schmidt, Leipzig, 1901.

[2] Ed. L. von Mańkowski, Leipzig, 1892.

these works in the form of a section of the prototype on which they founded their poems. This prototype was not, as will be seen, the original *Bṛhatkathā* of Guṇāḍhya, but a version made much later in Kashmir, and in it apparently the five books of the original were separated by other matter. It omitted the introduction and Tale 3 of Book i, perhaps nothing more. Its language is uncertain. Kṣemendra, however, made use also of recension β of the *Tantrākhyāyika*, whence he derives five unoriginal tales, and perhaps also the plan of keeping the books consecutive. His brevity diminishes the value of his work, but Somadeva's treatment is clear and effective in his wonted manner. He omits our other original tales, probably for reasons of his own.

The Southern *Pañcatantra*[1] exists in at least five recensions, representing the text which won currency in southern India. It is essentially in most of these versions an abbreviated account, in which, while nothing essential has been omitted, a good deal of shortening has been done; Edgerton estimates the amount preserved as three-quarters of the prose and two-thirds of the verses. It is later than Bhāravi. One tale (i. 12) of the cowherdess and her lovers is clearly unoriginal. There is no doubt that it goes back to a common original with the Nepalese version and the *Hitopadeça*, and, as these versions save the last quote a stanza of Kālidāsa, the original cannot have been older than A. D. 500. There exists a much expanded version of this text, based in part on Tamil sources with ninety-six tales in all; from this was derived in substance the Abbé Dubois' *Le Pantcha-Tantra ou les cinq ruses* (1826).

A Nepalese manuscript of the *Pañcatantra* gives only the stanzas with one prose piece mistaken for a stanza; other manuscripts give also a prose accompaniment in Sanskrit or in Newārī. The recension in this case is clearly derived from an original which was before the compiler of the *Hitopadeça*; in both alone do we find the transposition of Books i and ii.

In addition to these sources many mixed versions of the text can be found in Sanskrit; moreover, it was rendered into old and modern Gujarātī, old and modern Marāṭhī, Braj Bhākhā, and into Tamil, and it was used freely by Çivadāsa in his *Vetāla-*

[1] Ed. J. Hertel, Leipzig, 1906.

pañcaviñçatikā, the Sanskrit texts of the *Çukasaptati*, and the *Dvātriñcatputtalikā*, while its fate in western lands has been still more brilliant.

6. *The Hitopadeça*

Of the various descendants of the *Pañcatantra* the *Hitopadeça* [1] reigns in Bengal. The author gives his name as Nārāyaṇa, whose patron was Dhavalacandra, and, as one manuscript of the work is dated 1373, must have lived before then. His mention of the term Sunday, Bhaṭṭārakavāra, as a day when work should not be done is against an early date, as not until about 900 is the use of this terminology customary; [2] otherwise it is only certain that he is later than Māgha and Kāmandaki. That he wrote in Bengal is made probable by the tale in which he describes the worship of Gaurī as involving sexual relations with the wife of another man as part of the ritual, a practice notoriously approved by the Tāntrikas of Bengal. His purpose is given frankly as instruction in conduct and in Sanskrit, and his sources are stated to be the *Pañcatantra* and another anonymous book. The political interest of the *Pañcatantra* is fully maintained, for, though Nārāyaṇa adds much, he is specially fond of bringing together large selections from the *Kāmandakīya Nītisāra*. The other book, however, is not this text, but evidently some book of stories, for Nārāyaṇa has many new tales. Of the seventeen not found in other versions seven are fables, three Märchen, five tales of intrigue, and two edifying stories. Of these, one telling of the loyal Vīravara who is willing to sacrifice himself and his family to Çivā to benefit his master, taken in conjunction with the reference to the worship of Gaurī alluded to above, and the fact that each book closes with a benediction invoking Çiva's favour, shows that the writer was a Çaiva, not, as his name would suggest, an adorer of Viṣṇu.

From this *Pañcatantra* Nārāyaṇa derived the inversion of Books i and ii, so that the work starts with the winning of friends and then advances to their loss. But in Books iii and iv he went his own way; Book iii of the original he divided into two, the

[1] Ed. A. W. von Schlegel and C. Lassen (1829–31); P. Peterson, BSS. 33, 1887.
[2] Fleet, JRAS. 1912, pp. 1039–46.

first being War, the second Peace, obviously as a pendant to the pair of opposites already contained in Books i and ii. His new Book iv was composed by inventing a new frame story, and placing in it part of the stories of the original Book iii. Further, Book v of the original was divided between Books iii and iv. Book iv of the original was wholly dropped, and several stories from Book i were placed in the new Book iv. Moreover, various tales of the original were simply omitted and new ones inserted in all four books, with the result that perhaps two-fifths of the original prose and a third of the verses are found. The sources of the new matter are obscure. The tale of the mouse which a pious hermit changed into a cat, a dog, and a tiger successively, but reduced it to its original form when it sought to destroy its benefactor, is perhaps merely a revised edition of a similar anecdote in the *Mahābhārata* regarding a dog. The tale (ii. 6) of the woman who carried on an intrigue with the son of the local headman, and who was clever enough to save them both from the lad's father and her own spouse, has its original home in the *Çukasaptati*, that of Vīravara, perhaps, in the *Vetālapañcaviṅçatikā*. It itself has been rendered into several vernaculars besides Bengālī.

Nārāyaṇa's style, as intended for instruction in Sanskrit, is simple and normally satisfactorily easy; the chief difficulties occur in the verses which he took over. A considerable number of the stanzas are probably his own work, and if so he deserves considerable credit for fluent versification. Artistically, no doubt, the massing of verses is an error, but he shares the mistake with the author of the Simplicior. His language is distinctly rendered more monotonous by the devotion to passive constructions and the avoidance of any rare or difficult verbal forms or of unusual syntactical constructions. It is, therefore, surprising to find in him one stanza of unique construction:

saṁlāpitānām madhurair vacobhir: mithyopacāraiç ca vaçīkṛtānām
āçāvatāṁ çraddadhatāṁ ca loke: kim arthināṁ vañcayitavyam asti?

'Is it right to deceive the needy, with whom one has conversed in honeyed words and whom one has reduced into one's power by false contrivances, at the very moment when their faith and hopes are set on one?' The nominal use of the gerundive is decidedly a sign of a decline in feeling for grammar. The maxims are often happily framed:

martavyaṁ iti yad duḥkham puruṣasyopajāyate
çakyas tenānumānena paro 'pi parirakṣitum.

'If one but think of the sorrow that springs up in a man at the thought of death, then one would guard even a foe from that fate.' Distrust appearances:

na dharmaçāstram paṭhatīti kāraṇaṁ: na cāpi vedādhyayanaṁ durātmanaḥ
svabhāva evātra tathātiricyate: yathā prakṛtyā madhuraṁ gavām payaḥ.

'It is no justification for trusting an evil man that he recites the text-book on duty or studies the Veda; the innate nature always triumphs, as inevitably as milk is sweet.'

XII

THE BṚHATKATHĀ AND ITS DESCENDANTS

1. *Guṇāḍhya and the Bṛhatkathā*

THERE is no doubt that one of our really serious losses in Indian literature is the disappearance of the *Bṛhatkathā* of Guṇāḍhya,[1] a work which ranked beside the *Mahābhārata* and the *Rāmāyaṇa* as one of the great storehouses of Indian literary art. Its existence is asserted first definitely by name in the seventh century when Subandhu, Bāṇa in both his romances, and Daṇḍin in his *Kāvyādarça* attest its fundamental importance. Later references are not rare; we have both the text and the comment of the *Daçarūpa* of Dhanaṁjaya as evidence of its existence, it is mentioned by Trivikrama in his *Campū*, and by Somadeva Sūri in his *Yaçastilaka*, both works of kindred type, while Govardhana celebrates it in his *Saptaçatī*. A Cambodian inscription (*c.* 875) expressly mentions Guṇāḍhya and his aversion to Prākrit, and we cannot doubt for a moment the existence before A. D. 600 of a romantic work by Guṇāḍhya.

Of his personality we have an account, reproduced with little variation in three Kashmirian sources, the *Bṛhatkathāmañjarī* of Kṣemendra, the *Kathāsaritsāgara* of Somadeva, and the *Haracaritacintāmaṇi* of Jayaratha. Çiva one day, asked by Pārvatī for a new tale, related to her the substance of the *Bṛhatkathā*, *inter alia*. A Gaṇa Puṣpadanta overhearing it told it to his wife Jayā, who repeated it to Pārvatī. She in great anger cursed Puṣpadanta to lose his rank, which he was not to regain until he had met and related to a Yakṣa Kāṇabhūti the tale he had overheard, the Yakṣa being another unfortunate under a curse. Further, Mālyavant, a comrade of Puṣpadanta who had intervened to intercede for him, was cursed to leave heaven until he should have met and heard from Kāṇabhūti the tale. In course of time Puṣpadanta was born aṣ Vararuci-Kātyāyana at Kauçāmbī; becoming the minister of Nanda, he finally retired to the

[1] F. Lacôte, *Essai sur Guṇāḍhya et la Bṛhatkathā* (1908).

Vindhya and there told to Kāṇabhūti the tale of the seven emperors of the Vidyādharas, and attained release. Guṇāḍhya meantime had been born at Pratiṣṭhita or Pratiṣṭhāna on the Godāvarī as a reincarnation of Mālyavant; he is in high favour with Sātavāhana, but the latter suffers a severe mortification when during the water play with his wives he is told by his queen not to throw any more on her (*modakaiḥ*), which he in his ignorance of the laws of verbal combination misunderstands as a request to be pelted with sweetmeats—an appalling request if the ancient Indian sweets were like the modern. Dejected, he refuses to be comforted unless he can learn Sanskrit. Guṇāḍhya offers to teach him in six years, but when Çarvavarman the author of the *Kātantra* laughs at this offer, and suggests that he can do it in six months, Guṇāḍhya vows to use neither Sanskrit, Prākrit, nor the vernacular if the deed is done. It is accomplished and Guṇāḍhya wanders disconsolate in the Vindhya, where Kāṇabhūti meets him and relates the tales learned from Vararuci. Guṇāḍhya would record them, but must write in Paiçācī, the language of the goblins, as he is debarred from use of any other speech by his vow. His disciples take the vast work to the king Sātavāhana, who rejects it. Guṇāḍhya recites it to the beasts and birds, burning the manuscript as he proceeds; the beasts, intent on the sweet poetry, become thin, and the cooks in the royal kitchen no longer serve good soup. Hence the marvel is revealed and the king saves one-seventh of the 700,000 Çlokas of the original, the tale preserved in the *Bṛhatkathā*. The Nepalese version contained in the *Nepālamāhātmya* is different. We hear nothing of Vararuci-Kātyāyana, there is but one sinner Bhṛṅgin who enters the private room of Çiva and Pārvatī in bee form; he is reborn at Mathurā as Guṇāḍhya, becomes a Paṇḍit of king Madana of Ujjain, is vanquished by Çarvavarman, and is advised to write in Paiçācī by a seer Pulastya. Nothing is said of the pledge as to language, naturally enough, for Nepal lay outside the interest on this point of India proper.

The legend seems to have been known already in some form to Bāṇa, and therefore must be moderately old; how far and in what form it goes back to Guṇāḍhya, it is idle to say. The location of Guṇāḍhya is clearly different in the two sources, for it is vain to seek to make out that there has been confusion between

Pratiṣṭhāna on the Godāvarī and a place of like name at the junction of the Ganges and the Yamunā. What is clear is that Ujjaiṇ or Kauçāmbī was the scene whence Guṇāḍhya derived much of his inspiration, which is a very different thing from the place where he was in royal honour and composed his work. The cennexion with Sātavāhana, which the Kashmirian recensions suggest, is borne out to some extent by certain facts. In the first place, the Sātavāhanas were at one time patrons of Prākrit as opposed to Sanskrit literature; the evidence of the inscriptions [1] shows that Sanskrit was used by their Kṣatrapa rivals before they adopted it, and the Māhārāṣṭrī lyric flourished under them. Secondly, the mention of the study of Sanskrit in this connexion does suggest that there was a tradition regarding the time when the Sātavāhanas determined to copy the Kṣatrapas and Sanskrit became popular in court. Further we cannot go.

Nor can we say anything definite of the date of Guṇāḍhya. The connexion with the Sātavāhanas after all means nothing definite even if real, and the most important evidence we could have would be a clear [2] allusion in literature to, or employment of, the *Bṛhatkathā* before Daṇḍin or Bāṇa. It may be [3] that Bhāsa's dramas drew some inspiration from this source, but we have no strict proof. We can fairly claim that Guṇāḍhya is not later than A. D. 500, but to place him in the first century A. D. is quite conjectural, nor in reality is any other later date more assured.

Obscure also is the question of the form of the work. The Kashmirian version suggests that what Guṇāḍhya produced was a work in Çlokas, but that may be quite misleading, and on the other hand we have the express statement of Daṇḍin that a Kathā to which type he refers the *Bṛhatkathā* was written in prose. Verses may have been interwoven as in the case of the *Jātakamālā*, but this must remain a mere hypothesis, and there is no other evidence to invalidate the impression given by Daṇḍin. A prose citation

1 Bloch, *Mélanges Lévi*, pp. 15 f.; Lévi, JA. 1902, i. 109 ff.

2 The supposed Tamil version of the 2nd cent. A. D. (S. K. Aiyangar, *Ancient India*, pp. 328, 337) is too dubious in date to be evidence. The alleged version into Sanskrit by Durvinīta (? 6th cent.) is quite dubious (R. Narasimhachar, JRAS. 1913, pp. 389 f.); see Fleet, JRAS. 1911, pp. 186–8.

3 Denied by Hertel, *Pāla und Gopāla*, pp. 153 f.; cf. P. D. Gune, *Ann. Bhand. Inst.*, ii. 1 ff.

by Hemacandra may conceivably be from the *Bṛhatkathā*, but it would be quite idle to assert that it was ; it may have come from a later recension or from some other source.

The dialect used was Paiçācī, and over this term a controversy has raged, accentuated by the fact that we really cannot be sure that we have a single relic of the *Bṛhatkathā*, still less that so late a grammarian as Mārkaṇḍeya (17th cent.) actually [1] had the text before him. A further confusion has arisen from Sir G. Grierson's decision to group a certain number of north-western dialects, spoken in Kafiristan, the Swat valley, Chitral, and Gilgit, as Piçāca languages, claiming both that they have a true relation to the ancient Paiçācī dialect, and were so called because the speakers were cannibals, and thus styled Piçācas, eaters of raw flesh, by their neighbours. The assertions of the grammarians are confused and unsatisfactory, nor is the matter improved by the existence of two schools of Prākrit grammar with divergent traditions and views, especially as these are represented by comparatively late texts. But, as we have seen, there is more probability that Paiçācī was a dialect rather of the Vindhyas than of the north-west ; the hardening of *d* to *t* or of other soft letters is not, as Grierson's theory requires to make it plausible, solely a feature of the north-west, but occurs in other dialects including Pāli, and the fact that Paiçācī has but one sibilant prejudices its claim to be akin to the north-west dialects which in Açoka's time and later preserve distinctions.[2] Lacôte, however, while accepting connexion with the north-west, agrees with the view that the phenomenon of hardening is a sign of the use of an Aryan speech among a non-Aryan people, and holds that Guṇāḍhya adapted this dialect to literary purposes, avoiding any too serious deviations from Sanskrit, and, if we substitute a Vindhyan dialect spoken in a Dravidian area, we probably approach the truth. At least for the connexion with the Vindhya we have the clear assertions of the Kashmirian recension, which had no special motive for misrepresentation of the facts, and the testimony of

[1] As Grierson asserts, AMJV. i. 121 ; JRAS. 1913, p. 391. All that is said is *Bṛhatkathāyām*, and common sense forbids us to assume that Mārkaṇḍeya used it, or that the quotation is really from Guṇāḍhya's own text and not, for instance, the Kashmirian version.

[2] Chap. i, § 4.

Rājaçekhara[1] is clear in favour of the actual use of Paiçācī in a wide region, including the Vindhya area. This view is much more plausible than Lacôte's suggestion that Guṇāḍhya picked up the idea of the dialect from some visitors from the north-west, his sphere of work lying round Kauçāmbī and Ujjain, and Grierson admits that, even if originally a north-western dialect, Paiçācī might have been carried to the Vindhya.

It is impossible to determine with precision the content of the *Bṛhatkathā*; our sources are too slight, but we can gather a general impression of the task accomplished by Guṇāḍhya. The sources on which he drew were, it is clear, three in number. The *Rāmāyaṇa* gave him the *motif* of the search of a husband for a wife cruelly stolen from him soon after a happy marriage; from Buddhist legends and other traditions of Ujjain and Kauçāmbī he was deeply familiar with the tales of Pradyota or Mahāsena and the gallant and dashing hero Udayana,[2] whose love-adventures were famed for their number and variety; he was also in touch with the many tales of sea-voyages and strange adventures in far lands which were current in the busy centres of Indian trade, and with the abundant fairy-tales and legends of magic current in India. From the latter source and from Buddhist legend he derived the conception of the emperor, Cakravartin, who is the secular counterpart of the Buddha; Naravāhanadatta, his hero, is born with the thirty-two auspicious signs which assure him Buddhahood if he enter the ascetic life, universal dominion if he remain in the affairs of the world. But the empire is not of this earth; it is essentially a fairy land, the realm of the Vidyādharas, who dwell beyond the formidable defences of the Himālayas and who by reason of their magic powers have semi-divine attributes. The Vidyādharas do not appear early in Indian religion, but we can recognize easily enough in them a contamination of the old ideas of the Gandharvas with notions derived from the mysterious powers of Hindu seers and ascetics and Buddhist saints. The hero is a son of Udayana, and in effect is Udayana revised and remodelled for his new destiny, while the *Rāmāyaṇa*

1 *Kāvyamīmāṅsā*, p. 51.

2 Cf. Przyluski, *La légende de l'empereur Açoka*, pp. 74 ff.; J. Hertel, BSGW. lxix. 4 (1917); Lacôte, JA. 1919, i. 493 ff.; P. D. Gune, *Ann. Bhand. Inst.*, ii. 1 ff.; Burlingame, HOS. xxviii. 51, 62 f., 247–93.

lends the decisive element of the plot, the rape of Madanamañcukā or Madanamañjukā by Mānasavega, and the efforts of her husband to discover her, in which he has the aid of his faithful minister Gomukha. His success is accomplished simultaneously with his winning the empire of the Vidyādharas, just as the recovery of Sītā is followed forthwith by the royal consecration of Rāma. But there must have been a vital difference in the tales, for Guṇāḍhya clearly was the poet not of kings so much as of the merchants,[1] the traders, the seafarers, and even the handicraftsmen of his day; his epic was a bourgeois epic, and in lieu of the stainless purity of Rāma we have as hero a son of Udayana, even lighter in love, despite his affection for Madanamañcukā, than his father. Hence we find that certainly even in the original there must have been much said of Naravāhanadatta's other loves and many a tale of adventurous journeying as well as Märchen and fairy lore. In Gomukha we have a picture of a minister such as is Yaugandharāyaṇa in the dramas of Bhāsa, bold, energetic, courageous, if slightly devious in modern views as regards choice of expedients. The portrait of Madanamañcukā was clearly definite; she was, like Vasantasenā in the *Cārudatta* of Bhāsa and still more clearly in the *Mṛcchakaṭikā*, a hetaira who hated her position, and whose great aim was to be recognized as a woman of family (*kulastrī*), and thus be permitted legitimate marriage in lieu of compulsory polyandry. We have here perhaps a valuable chronological hint, if we could be sure that it was from the *Bṛhatkathā* that Bhāsa really drew the picture. It is striking at least, however, that the description of the eight courts and the garden of the palace of Vasantasenā in the *Mṛcchakaṭikā*, but not in the *Cārudatta*, should correspond minutely with the description of the place of Kaliṅgasenā given in the *Bṛhatkathāçlokasaṁgraha* of Budhasvāmin.

Guṇāḍhya's influence is seen also in Daṇḍin who borrowed from him, we may fairly assume, the conception of placing his kings' sons, fallen in station by the action of misfortune among vagabonds, in positions where a series of adventures drawn from low life is allied to marvellous happenings of every kind. The arrangement indeed of the story may be due to the same cause, for it resembles the scene in which Naravāhanadatta and his

[1] Cf. Foucher, *L'Art Gréco-Bouddhique du Gandhāra*, ii. 102 ff.

friends, reunited after separation, recount their adventures to one another. The fantasy of Guṇāḍhya lives on also in the *Yaçastilaka* of Somadeva Sūri and in the *Tilakamañjarī* of Dhanapāla, both of whom recognize the importance of Guṇāḍhya.[1] Moreover, the name of his hero seems from his use of it to have won acceptance in royal usage as a suitable title for a prince as well as in literature. But his enduring memorial is furnished by the versions of the *Bṛhatkathā* which have reached us.

2. *The Bṛhatkathāçlokasaṁgraha of Budhasvāmin*

Budhasvāmin, the author of the *Çlokasaṁgraha*, abbreviation in Çlokas of the *Bṛhatkathā*, is no more than a name to us.[2] The manuscripts of his work are from Nepal, but there is no mark otherwise of his Nepalese origin, which must remain merely a conjecture. The form of name is not modern; but, as it is attested from early days down to the twelfth century, the probable date of one of the manuscripts, we reach no satisfactory result from that. If he is assigned to the eighth or ninth century, it is without any special ground save that the manuscript tradition suggests that a long time has elapsed before the extant manuscripts came into being.

The work preserved is merely a fragment, though there is no adequate reason to hold that it is defective at the beginning or that it ever contained anything as to the origin of the collection of tales comparable to the legend in the Kashmirian versions and the *Nepālamāhātmya.* It is divided into cantos (*sargas*), of which twenty-eight survive, probably a mere fraction of the original, though it extends to 4,539 verses. We are carried at once *in medias res*; Pradyota dies, and is due to be succeeded by Gopāla, but the latter, learning that he is credited with having disposed of his father, insists on his brother Pālaka reigning in lieu (i). Pālaka is a bad ruler, and is induced by what he deems divine suggestion to abandon his throne to Avantivardhana, Gopāla's son (ii). The latter falls in love with the daughter of a Mātaṅga,

[1] The degree of his originality may, of course, be questioned, and no poet is without some predecessor; but his success points to a very real creative power, which permits us justly to ascribe to him the creation of the genre.

[2] Ed. and trans. F. Lacôte, 1908 ff.

Surasamañjarī, who, like her father, is really of the race of the Vidyādharas; he marries her, only to be snatched away with his bride by Ipphaka (Ityaka) a jealous Vidyādhara; they are rescued by another of these genii, and the emperor Naravāhana pronounces judgement in favour of the marriage (iii). The seers so admire the emperor's judgement that they demand from him the account of his achievement of empire; he consents to tell of the twenty-six marriages but only when Gaurī undertakes that his revelations will be kept religiously secret. He then tells the desire of his father Udayana for a son, which ultimately is granted (v, vi). When young Naravāhana grows up, he shows the signs of a Cakravartin, and a Vidyādhara, Amitagati, recognizes them and attaches himself to him; finally he wins the hand of Madanamañjukā, daughter of Kaliṅgasenā who, however, is a hetaira, thus rendering a true union impossible (vii–xi). One day Madanamañjukā disappears, but is found under an Açoka; she relates that Kubera has demanded that she should be really married to Naravāhanadatta; this desire is conceded, but shortly after the king makes the unpleasant discovery that in lieu of his beloved he is really consorting with Vegavatī. She reveals herself to him as sister of Mānasavega, a Vidyādhara, who has taken Madanamañjukā, but who cannot do her harm, just as Rāvaṇa could not put force on Sītā in her captivity. Naravāhanadatta celebrates a new marriage with her, but immediately after he is carried off by Mānasavega; falling to earth, he finds himself in a well but is rescued (xii–xv). He is now lost, and posing as a student commences a new adventure, ending in marriage with Gandharvadattā, daughter of Sānudāsa whose history is narrated at length (xvi–xviii). Two further marriages are in wait for him, that with Ajināvatī (xix, xx), and that with Priyadarçanā, whose bosom he recognized when it was revealed for a moment when she was posing as a merchant (xxi–xxvii). The next canto gives us only the beginning of a new marriage adventure, and, as so many more were still before him, the extent of the work can be guessed.

There is much to prove that Budhasvāmin followed far more faithfully his original than the Kashmirian authors. Assuming that the *Çlokasaṁgraha* was written on the same scale throughout, it may have contained 25,000 verses, certainly an adequate number but not necessarily excessive. On the other hand, comparison of relevant portions of the work with the *Kathāsaritsāgara* shows that the latter is very greatly abridged in the vital parts of the narrative, those intimately connected with Naravāhanadatta. It is a reasonable conclusion, therefore, that the Kashmirian versions contain much added matter, especially the episodes which are merely in nominal connexion with the main story. This impression is certainly strengthened by the fact that the character of Madanamañcukā and her relations with Naravāhanadatta are much more coherently set out in the *Çlokasaṁgraha*; in the Kashmirian versions both her mother and herself are provided with royal connexions, Kaliṅgadatta and Madanavega, in order to spare us the discomfort of seeing a king marry a lady of the demi-monde. The bourgeois character of Gandharvadattā and her merchant father are similarly minimized in the Kashmirian version; they spare Ajināvatī, because she was a princess, but omit Priyadarçanā as being of middle-class origin. The *Çlokasaṁgraha* again in many details serves to explain obscurities in the Kashmirian version and to motive adequately incoherent episodes. On the other hand, it is fair to note that Budhasvāmin assumes that we know the tale of Udayana, and that we need not doubt that in the original *Bṛhatkathā* it was recognized, though Budhasvāmin preferred to confine his work to the adventures of Naravāhanadatta. From the paucity of his episodes we may fairly conclude that these were not over-numerous in the original, though it is impossible to stress this point.

Budhasvāmin is unquestionably worthy of praise for his art. Admitting his debt to Guṇāḍhya does not diminish the pleasure afforded by his lively outlook on life, the complex picture of adventure and marvels which he paints, or the romance of his well-conceived characters and the kaleidoscope of the swiftly altering scenes in which they are placed by fate or their own action. He restrains his desire for mannered description of which he doubtless felt competent by the necessity of getting on with the tale, and displays his virtuosity, partly by his large vocabulary with its not rare Sanskritizations of Prākrit terms which are doubtless sometimes derived from him by the lexicographers, and partly by the revival of obsolescent forms such as aorists. As a rule, he is simple, clear, fluent without verbosity, and if he seems on the whole rather devoid of ornament the magnitude of his undertaking may be deemed excuse enough for a very venial fault.

3. *The Kashmirian Bṛhatkathā*

The older view that the *Kathāsaritsāgara* and the *Bṛhatkathāmañjarī* were directly drawn from the *Bṛhatkathā* cannot be retained[1] in view of the discovery of the *Çlokasaṁgraha*. The Kashmirian recensions show themselves at once as vitally similar in contrast with the Nepalese and leave no option but to assume that they are derived from one source, and that not the original *Bṛhatkathā*. The date of this form of the *Bṛhatkathā* is clearly impossible to decide beyond that it must have been considerably before A.D. 1000. Nor can we say who the author was, or by what process the work assumed form. It may have been the outcome of a continued process of change if the story was regarded as specially attractive. All that can be conjectured is that the work received its final form through two main processes. In the first place, the essentials of the legend of Naravāhanadatta, including his parentage, were extracted from the original of Guṇāḍhya, and abbreviated. Then, secondly, the account was expanded and completed by inserting as satisfactorily as was possible other great legend-complexes which were popular in Kashmir, making a work essentially different from the original *Bṛhatkathā* because the original theme, the adventures of Naravāhanadatta, had fallen into a position of subordinate interest and the episodes had become of predominant importance. Which the additions were it is, of course, frankly impossible[2] to say on the strength of the present evidence; the absence of the rest of the *Çlokasaṁgraha* deprives us of the one useful control. But we may reasonably hold that the additions included both the version of the *Pañcatantra* and that of the *Vetālapañcaviṅçatika* which are found in both Kṣemendra and Somadeva, but which have plainly no real or original connexion with the legend of Naravāhanadatta.

The language and form of the new text do not permit of pre-

[1] Despite F. D. K. Bosch, *De legende van Jīmūtavāhana* (1914), pp. 85 ff.

[2] Subandhu may have known the Vikramāditya legends (cf. *Vāsavadattā*. p. 110).

cise determination. It is possible that the references to Paiçācī forms and citations in the case of Hemacandra are derived from this Kashmirian text, and if so they would show that the work was handed down in a form of Paiçācī. Nor, of course, is there anything implausible in such a proceeding. It is not rare for a dialect once established to remain in use for a certain work after the original has been changed. We have the perfectly clear statement of Somadeva that the language was altered, and this can hardly mean anything less than a translation. If the original had been in Sanskrit, it seems incredible that it would not have influenced both Kṣemendra and Somadeva sufficiently to cause frequent verbal similarities, and this is not the case. The similarities which do occur, as for instance in the stories of the *Pañcatantra*, can easily be explained by the fact that both authors were dealing with a work in a dialect which admittedly was considerably more Sanskritic than the ordinary Prākrit; indeed, on one list of the relative position of Prākrits Paiçācī is ranked after Sanskrit in honour.

4. *Kṣemendra's Bṛhatkathāmañjarī*

The work of Kṣemendra [1] was probably produced in his youth like the Mañjarīs of the *Mahābhārata* and the *Rāmāyaṇa* which he composed, perhaps in accordance with his own doctrine that the would-be poet ought to undertake exercises of this kind. The character of these abridgements is well known; they are dry and sober, reproducing faithfully, though with much omission and curtailment often to obscurity, their originals, but depriving them of all life and attraction. Kṣemendra has, moreover, in lieu of seeking to write interesting summaries, thought it enough to relieve the barrenness of his versions by interpolating elegant descriptions at intervals, a procedure not to be commended, as it merely adds to the bulk of the works without serving any useful purpose. But his accuracy, which we can test for the epics, is assured, and therefore we may *a priori* assume that his account of the contents of the *Bṛhatkathā* of Kashmir accords with reality.

It appears from the coincidence of the two recensions that the

[1] Ed. KM. 69, 1901. Cf. Bühler, IA. i. 302 ff.; Lévi, JA. 1885, ii. 397 ff.; 1886, i. 216 ff.; Speyer, *Studies about the Kathāsaritsāgara*, pp. 9 ff.

original was divided into eighteen Lambhakas as its main divisions, and it is a plausible conjecture that the term applies to the victories of the hero, each section dealing with some achievement of his. As we have it in both our sources, the work begins with the Kathāpīṭha, which gives as an introduction to the tale the legend of Guṇāḍhya already noted. In Book ii, the basis of the story is furnished in the adventures of Udayana, which are carried in iii to his winning of Padmāvatī, the book taking its style Lāvānaka from the place where the first queen, Vāsavadattā, was reported to have perished, a necessary preliminary to the second espousals. In iv we have the birth of the hero, Naravāhanadatta, who is to be the emperor of the Vidyādharas. The next book, Caturdārikā, is decidedly episodical. The Vidyādhara Çaktivega comes to visit the future sovereign, and relates how he himself has reached the wonderful city of the Vidyādharas and won the four beauteous maidens whence the title of the book is derived. From this point Kṣemendra and Somadeva diverge vitally. Kṣemendra continues with the legend of Sūryaprabha (vi), a strange and remarkable tale, of how that hero rose from royal rank to becoming emperor of the Vidyādharas after a desperate struggle against his foe Çrutaçarman, who was finally induced to content himself with a minor kingdom, thanks to the direct personal intervention of Çiva himself. The tale is remarkable in its obvious blending of mythology involving Vedic and epic beliefs, Buddhist legends, and popular story matter; but in Kṣemendra's hands it suffers greatly from excessive condensation. The two books, it will be seen, have a certain relevance to each other and to the work as a whole, despite their episodic character; they deal with the career of other aspirants to emperorship over the Vidyādharas. In vii we return to the main story a little more clearly. The essence of the book is a long account of Kaliṅgadatta, father of Kaliṅgasenā, who serves merely to give his daughter a royal ancestry; Udayana is sought in marriage by her and he would gladly wed her, but Yaugandhārayaṇa resists the match, lest the king should become too much enamoured of his wife and neglect his duties, a ludicrous excuse seeing that he had already arranged two marriages for the prince. Doubtless in a more original form it was Kaliṅgasenā's character as hetaira which motived the objections. At any rate Udayana is induced to abandon the project, but he determines to allow her daughter to wed Naravāhanadatta, and the book carries us to his consent to a formal marriage. Book viii, which is very short, is styled Velā after the name of the character of whom and her husband a legend is narrated, quite episodically, but it ends with the vital statement that Madanamañcukā has been abducted by the Vidyādhara Mānasavega. The prince is desolated, but before he is to rejoin his beloved he has to be the hero of four episodic books (ix–xii). In the first he is carried off in sleep and ends by espousing another Vidyādhara maiden, Lalitalocanā, with whom he spends time on mount Malaya, but is saddened by longing for Madanamañcukā; Lalitalocanā disappears, but a hermit, Piçañgajaṭa, comforts him by telling him the tale of Mṛgāñkadatta, a prince of Ayodhyā, who won in marriage Çaçāñkavatī, daughter of his enemy Karmasena of Ujjain, who gives the book its name (ix). The next consolation is administered by Kaṇva and consists in the narration of a vast cycle of legends of the emperor Vikramāditya, though it is inconceivable that Guṇāḍhya himself could have been guilty of so flagrant an anachronism; the title is Viṣamaçīla (x). In xi, Madirāvatī, the prince is encouraged to persevere by the tale of two Brahmins who by manly effort (*puruṣakāra*) succeeded in defying the decrees of fate (*karman*) and achieving their desire, and he also recovers the missing and apparently not much regretted, Lalitalocanā. Yet another episode follows: Gomukha tells the tale of the emperor Muktāphalaketu and his beloved Padmāvatī, who gives the book its name (xii).

After this long interlude action is resumed in Book xiii, Pañca, so called because in it the prince wins five more brides, Vidyādhara maidens who are determined to espouse him. The main business, however, of the book is the effort to attain Madanamañcukā. With the aid of Prabhāvatī, a Vidyādhara, the prince penetrates to her place of confinement, using a woman's form lent by Prabhāvatī; as she, however, has to resume it, suddenly he is discovered and Mānasavega has him tried by the court of the Vidyādharas, but will not accept their decision in his favour. Prabhāvatī takes him in safety away from the Vidyādharas; ultimately he reaches Kauçāmbī, and many Vidyādharas join him for an attack on his foes. After great efforts, he attains Çiva's favour, and in a great battle slays Gaurīmuṇḍa and Mānasavega in single combat. He prepares to attack his remaining foe Mandaradeva in the north of Kailāsa, and marries the five damsels who seek his love. The next step ought obviously to be the attack on Mandaradeva, as it is in Somadeva, but there now occurs a long series of episodes which doubtless had been inserted here in the Kashmirian *Bṛhatkathā*. In Book xiv he marries Ratnaprabhā, whose name the book bears, and pays an important visit to the land of camphor, returning in a flying machine of the kind which the Yavanas, Greeks, were experts at constructing. In Book xv we have a sort of duplication of this adventure; he marries Alaṁkāravatī, and proceeds to an expedition to a White Island or Continent[1] where he worships Nārāyaṇa with an elaborate prayer written in the most finished Kāvya style; the parallel to the famous episode of the *Mahābhārata* in which sages seek the Çvetadvīpa and take part in the worship of a wonderful deity—which has been deemed a reference to actual experience of Nestorian rites or even of Alexandrian Christianity —is complete, and suggests very strongly that the Kashmirian or the original *Bṛhatkathā* borrowed the episode from the epic as we know it. The next book (xvi) is much more banal; it gives the prince another wife, Çaktiyaças, and imparts a number of unimportant episodes. We resume now in Book xvii the lost thread. Before he can attack Mandaradeva, Naravāhanadatta must receive from the sage Vāmadeva on mount Malaya the seven jewels, emblematic of sovereignty. He then reaches the north by passing under a great tunnel, and by his offer of his own head induces the dread Kālarātri, who guards the exit, to permit his passage. Mandaradeva falls, five more maidens are wed—a repetition of the *motif* in Book xiii, and the great consecration, Mahābhiṣeka, whence the book is named, is duly celebrated, the emperor insisting on his father being present. The work is now finished, but very inconveniently a further book (xviii) is necessary; under the style Suratamañjarī it tells how, after the death of Pradyota and Udayana, Gopāla and Pālaka resigned their tenure of the kingship of Ujjain, how Avantivardhana wedded the heroine, and how the two were protected against a jealous Vidyādhara by the emperor. The only

[1] Cf. W. E. Clark, JAOS. xxxix. 209–42; Garbe, *Indien und das Christentum*, pp. 193 ff.; Grierson, IA. xxxvii. 251 ff., 373 ff.

excuse for this absurd position of the tale is the fact of the existence of Book i with its account of the telling of the tale by Guṇāḍhya. In the original, as the Nepalese version shows, the episode of Suratamañjarī led up to the telling by Naravāhanadatta himself of his adventure, which would have clashed with the version of Book i, and the old exordium was, therefore, relegated to an appendix. This view is confirmed by the fact that Somadeva in his Book vi expressly tells us that Naravāhanadatta is relating his adventures in the third person, an admission that he knew that the tale of Suratamañjarī had originally been placed at the beginning of the work. On this point Kṣemendra is silent in his corresponding Madanamañcukā book (vii), but he reveals the fact in the summary (*upasaṁhāra*) with which he ends his poem, for he tells us, for the first time, that the work is supposed to be set forth by Naravāhanadatta to the sage Kaçyapa on a visit.

Two other points at once stand out revealing the defect of the original Kashmirian recension. The break between the end of Velā (viii) and the continuation in Pañca (xiii) is lamentable; but its harshness is concealed in some measure by making the intervening books recognize the plight of the prince and the endeavour to console him during his search. Evidently it was thus that the compilers of the Kashmirian recension hoped to work in not too awkwardly their extra matter, and in a sense they succeeded. The same thing cannot be said regarding the interpolation of Books xiv–xvi between Pañca and the book of triumph and consecration. The break is ludicrous; Naravāhanadatta, who is left at the end of Pañca as accepted as lord by the great majority of the Vidyādharas, but who has Mandaradeva still to overcome, is now treated for three books as a prince in the home of his father, without any consciousness of his great adventures or his imperial dignity in the land of the Vidyādharas. Here the compiler had evidently not the skill to make even a passable transition, and Kṣemendra loyally followed his incoherence. This is conclusive evidence against the original *Bṛhatkathā* ever having contained this material; no author would permit himself such confusion, while a compiler could easily slip into it when he desired to knit together varying cycles of legend.

5. *Somadeva's Kathāsaritsāgara*

Somadeva, a Brahmin of Kashmir, son of Rāma, wrote the *Kathāsaritsāgara*[1] between 1063 and 1081 in order to divert the troubled mind of Sūryamatī, a princess of Jalandhara, wife of Ananta and mother of Kalaça, his work falling, therefore, a considerable period after that of Kṣemendra. In addition to the division into Lambhakas Somadeva has one of his own composition into Tarañgas, 124 in all, the name, 'billows', being chosen obviously in relation to the title of the work, which is most naturally analysed as 'Ocean of the Rivers of Stories', rather than with Lacôte as '(Bṛhat-) Kathā, an Ocean of Rivers (of Stories)'. These divisions are not original; Kṣemendra, indeed, has subdivisions for some of the longer books which he calls Gucchas, 'clusters', in the older manner. Kalhaṇa apparently was influenced in his choice of title for his chronicle by Somadeva.

Somadeva sets out by telling his purpose, and one stanza of his has caused trouble, evoking different renderings from Hall, Lévi, Tawney, Speyer, and Lacôte:

aucityānvayarakṣā ca yathāçakti vidhīyate
kathārasāvighātena kāvyāñçasya ca yojanā.

The sense of this stanza appears to me clear: 'Literary convention and the connexion of topics have been presented as best I could, as well as the arrangement of a part of the poem so as not to offend against the sentiment of the story (or the story and its sentiment).' We have, it seems, a recognition of the fact that there has been change of order, and that it was made in order to preserve the sentiment in the tale. This accords exactly with what we find in the arrangement. In the first five books there is no change. But for the rest Somadeva was dominated by his desire to preserve the effect of the poem, and obviously this compelled the breach of the gap between Pañca and Mahābhiṣeka; in his text the transition is perfect; the former book ends with the decision of the prince to obtain the jewels necessary for the coronation of a would-be emperor, and the next book carries on

[1] Ed. Durgāprasād, NSP. 1903; trans. C. H. Tawney, BI. 1880–4. Cf. J. S. Speyer, *Studies about the Kathāsaritsāgara* (1908).

the proposal, though in a slightly casual manner which Somadeva has not altogether obliterated. This left him, however, with three books to fit in, Ratnaprabhā, Alaṁkāravatī, and Çaktiyaças, and obviously necessitated a complete overhauling of the earlier part of the poem in order not to overburden it. The solution adopted was to fit these three books, which all deal with adventures of the prince before he became emperor, in the space before Pañca and to eliminate from the earlier matter two books, which could, as not dealing with the hero's own adventures but merely being stories told to him, be fitted in as an appendix, that is the books Padmāvatī and Viṣamaçīla. The arrangement of the material before Pañca is carried out artistically in so far as an effort is made to interpose books mainly episodic with those giving important if incidental acts of the hero. Thus after the fifth book which is episodic we have the important book Madanamañcukā (vi) ; this is followed by the Ratnaprabhā (vii) ; the Sūryaprabha (viii), which intervenes before Alaṁkāravatī (ix), is essentially merely episodic ; Çaktiyaças (x) runs naturally on from Alaṁkāravatī as containing incidental stories ; then follow Velā (xi), Çaçāñkavatī (xii), Madirāvatī (xiii), the all-important Pañca and Mahābhiṣeka (xiv and xv), and, by way of appendix, Suratamañjarī, Padmāvatī, and Viṣamaçīla (xvi–xviii). One change in the actual contents of a book was necessary. In Kṣemendra and probably in the original Velā was not merely episodic ; it contained at the close the vital element of the disappearance of Madanamañcukā, which explains the grief of the king alluded to in the following books. Nothing of this sort accorded with Somadeva's plan of working in the books Ratnaprabhā, Alaṁkāravatī, and Çaktiyaças, and therefore the allusion had to disappear, although it was not possible for Somadeva to avoid leaving occasional traces in the books before Pañca in his order that Madanamañcukā had already been lost.

We may admit at once that despite his efforts Somadeva has not succeeded in producing a unified work. But the merit of the *Kathāsaritsāgara* does not rest on construction. It stands on the solid fact that Somadeva has presented in an attractive and elegant if simple and unpretentious form a very large number of stories which have for us a very varied appeal, either as amusing or gruesome or romantic or as appealing to our love of wonders on sea and land, or as affording parallels to tales familiar from childhood. Kṣemendra's example shows how, by undue condensation and obscurity, tales can lose all point and interest; Somadeva, how by care the point can be fully expressed without fatigue to the reader. We meet with the old but still amusing tales of fools, scattered in the *Kathāsaritsāgara* among the tales of its version of the *Pañcatantra*, but collected together after it by Kṣemendra; chance proves that half at least go back to a collection made before A. D. 450, used in a work by a monk Ārya Saṅghasena, and rendered into Chinese by his pupil Guṇavṛddhi in 492.[1] We hear once more of the foolish servants who, bidden protect the leather of the new trunks, take out the clothes in them and thus protect them against the rain, of the fool who insists that his father never violated chastity and that he must have been a mind-born son, of the fellow who filled himself with seven cakes and then bitterly lamented that he had not eaten the seventh first and saved the rest, and we may, if young enough, still laugh with the stones at these japes. Rogues who prosper lend another series of tales; one is ingenious; dressed as a rich merchant, he craved an interview with the king, to whom he promised for the honour of a daily repetition of the audience a gift each time of 500 *dīnāras*; the king accedes, and the courtiers, thinking that he is all-powerful with their master, bribe him until he has fifty million gold pieces, which he has the good sense to share with the king to whom he reveals his effective ruse. Much is told also of the thief, gambler, roué, but always brilliant Mūladeva,[2] who is in Indian literature the *beau idéal* of a perfect cheat but who has a son even wilier than himself. Another rascal is so clever that we may forgive him his evil deeds; he is to suffer after death an age in hell by reason of his misdeeds, but a single gift to a pious person entitles him to one day's life as Indra. Of this he takes opportunity to gather all his friends and to traverse with them the sacred places of India, thus acquiring such merit as to remain Indra. But yet this god also is lightly treated; still more often are religious ascetics denounced; one of them who in order to get into his

[1] Hertel, *Ein altindisches Narrenbuch*, BSGW. 64, 1912. Cf. the story of the foolish monkeys (Jāt. 46 and a Bharhut scene, GIL. ii. 108).

[2] PAPS. lii (1913).

possession a pretty girl frightens her father into exposing her in a chest Danaë-like, finds the wrong chest, and has his nose and ears bitten off by an ape, while the girl is rescued by a prince.

A book of tales about women seems to have been used by the compilers of the Kashmir recension, to judge from the mass of stories, unhappily often to their disadvantage; we hear of murderous women, of one who mutilates her husband in revenge for a beating, of one who regularly betrays him but insists on burning herself on his pyre, of the woman who got rid of ten husbands, and apparently met her match in the man who had disposed of ten wives, but defeated him also and became so unpleasantly notorious that she turned into an ascetic. Full of reminiscences of various Märchen *motifs* is the tale of the king whose white elephant can be healed only by the touch of a chaste woman; none of 80,000 in the kingdom can help it, until a poor young wife succeeds; the king marries her sister, immures her in a palace, and is after all betrayed. But Somadeva gives us also tales of faith and truth among women. Devasmitā revenges herself on her would-be lovers by giving them assignations, but merely in order to brand them; charming is the picture of an Indian Philemon and Baukis.[1] It is death to tell another what one has remembered of existence in a former birth; nevertheless the queen of Dharmadatta and her husband are alike seized with the feeling that they must tell each other of their suddenly aroused memories. The story is pretty; the lady was a faithful servant in the house of a Brahmin, while her husband was the loyal retainer of a merchant; they lived together in poverty, eating the little they had over when gods, ancestors, and guests had taken their share. In time of famine a Brahmin comes, the husband gives him the little they had, and then his life leaves him, indignant that he had preferred the Brahmin to himself. His wife follows him in death, and the same fate again meets them when they have exchanged these memories of a faithful love.

The religious world of Somadeva reminds us of the superstitious nature of the people of Kashmir; we can hardly doubt that the Kashmir recension added readily anything that seemed interesting in this regard, even if Somadeva himself is rather

[1] J. S. Speyer, *Die indische Theosophie*, pp. 97 .

inclined to rationalizing Märchen. Çiva and Pārvatī in her dread forms are the great deities, though Viṣṇu inevitably appears in the episode of Naravāhana's visit to the Çvetadvīpa. Human offerings are specially frequent, the Pulindas, the Bhillas, are regarded as ever on the outlook for victims for the goddess to whom Jīmūtavāhana is prepared to offer homage before his act of self-sacrifice. Witchcraft is taken as a matter of course, and many details are given of the dreadful deeds of the witches and of the horrible scenes enacted nightly at the places where the dead are burned or flung out as prey for beasts, birds, and the ghouls who haunt these cemeteries; in his eeriness of description Somadeva is a match for the author of the *Mālatīmādhava*. Buddhistic traits are not rare, though only sporadic; it must be remembered that, as we know from Kalhaṇa, Buddhism had in a degraded form a strong hold in Kashmir. A number of tales are told to relate the action of Karman in determining man's life; we have a legend of a prince who tears out an eye because women loved so deeply his beauty, a parallel to the *Mittavindaka Jātaka*, and the legend of Jīmūtavāhana, though the Buddhist origin of that has been questioned.[1] The *Vetālapañcaviñçatikā* legends show distinct Buddhist traits. On the other hand, we have frequent mention of the worship of the Liñga, Çiva's phallic symbol, and of the Mothers, and popular superstition is everywhere abundant. The gods and minor spirits mingle freely in ordinary life, innumerable apparent mortals are merely beings driven from heaven by curses who can be restored to their former estate by some act of cruelty or kindness. The love of the marvellous is fully satisfied by tales of adventures at sea, with shipwrecks and subterranean palaces, or not less marvellous wanderings on land to strange places like camphor-land where princesses can easily be won. The loves of Naravāhanadatta are too numerous and too inevitable—for they are all fore-ordained even if we are only told so at the end—to be exciting, but there are many others recounted in episodes, and a picture or a dream often proves the starting-point for a deep if transient affection. Nor can we ignore the interest lent by the inclusion of effective versions of the Vetāla cycle, of the *Pañcatantra*, of anecdotes of

[1] Bosch, *De legende van Jīmūtavāhana*, pp. viii, 143 ff.

Vikramāditya, as well as those in the less satisfactory book Padmāvatī.

Somadeva's taste is shown by the fact that, though he likes to conclude a tale with a different metre, only 761 of his 21,388 verses are in more elaborate metres, and he resists the temptation to indulge himself in word-plays, contenting himself with the swift easy flow of the simple narrative. He permits himself in his metre a certain lightness of touch exhibited in minor negligences, which in no way make it inaccurate, but save it from the pedantry of following in absolute strictness the rules regarding caesuras and Sandhi rigorously adopted by the great Kāvya writers. His abnegation is the more remarkable because he obviously could have won repute as a poet in the elaborate style. As it is, we owe him many happy passages in which simplicity is not inconsistent with ornament. Thus we have the description, brief but effective, of a storm at sea:

aho vāyur apūrvo 'yam ity āçcaryavaçād iva
vyāghūrṇante sma jaladhes taṭeṣu vanarājayaḥ.
vyatyastāç ca muhur vātād adharottaratāṁ yayuḥ
vāridher vārinicayā bhāvāḥ kālakramād iva.

'The forests on the banks of the sea shook to and fro as though amazed at the wondrous force of the gale, and inverted by the wind the waves went up and down as do men's hopes through the force of fate.' The good deed of the Gandharva, who saves the prince from the well into which he had fallen, is summed up in an admirable line:

parārthaphalajanmāno na syur mārgadrumā iva
tapacchido mahāntaç cej jīrṇāraṇyaṁ jagad bhavet.

'Were there not high-souled men born to do good to others, like wayside trees which dispel the heat, this world were nothing but a worn-out forest.' There is a very pathetic picture of the death of Çūrasena; he was a Rājput and had to obey his king's summons, despite his love for his wife Suṣeṇā; she awaits his promised return and, when he comes not, her breath leaves her body as if consumed by the forest fire of love. Her husband meantime, scarce able to leave his lord, is hastening to her on a swift camel:

tatrāpaçyad gataprāṇām priyāṁ tāṁ kṛtamaṇḍanām
latām utphullakusumāṁ vātenonmūlitām iva.
dṛṣṭvaiva vihvalasyaitāṁ kurvato 'ṅge viniryayuḥ
pralāpaiḥ saha tasyāpi prāṇā virahiṇaḥ kṣaṇāt.

'There saw he his wife lying dead in all her finery like a creeper in full bloom that the wind hath uprooted; seeing her he grasped her in his arms, beside himself with grief of separation, and his breath straightway departed with his lamentations.' There is a brilliant description of summer:

bhrāmyataç ca jagāmāsya bhīmo grīṣmartukesarī
pracaṇḍādityavadano dīptatadraçmikesaraḥ.
priyāvirahasaṁtaptapānthaniḥçvāsamārutaiḥ
nyastoṣmāṇa ivātyuṣṇā vānti sma ca sakīraṇāḥ.
çuṣyadvidīrṇapañkāç ca hṛdayaiḥ sphuṭitair iva
jalāçayā dadṛçire gharmaluptāmbusampadaḥ.
cīrīcītkāramukharās tāpamlānadaladharāḥ
madhuçrīvirahān mārgeṣv arudann iva pādapāḥ.

'And as he wandered there came on him the dread hot season in lion shape with the blazing sun for mouth and his fiery rays for mane. The winds blew with cruel heat as though warmed by the dolorous sighs of travellers parted from their loved ones. The tanks, their waters wasted by the heat, with their drying white mud seemed to show their broken hearts. The trees bewailed the departure of the glory of spring with the shrill moaning of their bark, their lips of leaves being parched by the heat.'

XIII

THE ROMANTIC AND THE DIDACTIC TALE

1. *The Romantic Tale*

THE fame of the *Bṛhatkathā* has resulted in comparatively few other tales being preserved in works of early date. The *Vetālapañcaviṅçatikā* was doubtless originally part of a distinct cycle, but it is preserved for us in its oldest form in Kṣemendra's *Bṛhatkathāmañjarī*[1] and Somadeva's *Kathāsaritsāgara*.[2] We have several other recensions, of which that of Çivadāsa[3] is in prose and verse, which may represent the original form of the tales, though that is mere speculation, and a verse original has been claimed.[4] One recension of an anonymous author[5] is no more than a prose version based on Kṣemendra, and Kṣemendra's verses have here and there found their way into the codices of Çivadāsa. The late recension of Jambhaladatta[6] has no verse maxims, and it has been suggested that its form of the tales is in some respects older than that shown by the other recensions, but this is by no means clear. An abbreviated version by Vallabhadāsa[7] is also known, and the text has been freely rendered into modern Indian vernaculars and also exists in the Mongolian Ssiddi-Kür.

Trivikramasena, or as the later accounts have it Vikramāditya, is in receipt annually of a fruit from an ascetic, which he hands over to his treasurer, until accidentally he finds that each contains a jewel. In gratitude he offers aid to the ascetic who asks him to go to a cemetery and bring down from a tree a corpse which is on it. The king agrees to act, but is startled to find that a ghoul, Vetāla, has taken up its abode in the corpse, yet persists in his purpose. The corpse denizen, however, lightens

[1] ix. 2. 19 ff.
[2] lxxv–xcix.
[3] Ed. H. Uhle, AKM. viii. 1, 1914.
[4] Bosch, *De legende van Jīmūtavāhana*, pp. 22 ff.
[5] Ed. AKM. viii. 1; another version (MS. 1487 A. D.), BSGW. 66, 1914.
[6] Ed. Calcutta, 1873.
[7] Eggeling, IOC. i. 1564 f.

the way by telling a story ending in a question as to the answer to a riddle, and on the king solving it the corpse falls off and returns to its original place. The king, however, finally is defeated, and is silent. The demon then reveals to him that the evil ascetic is seeking in reality to slay him, and at his bidding the king asks the ascetic to show him how to perform the prostration required in the rite which is to be performed with the corpse, and hews off the evil-doer's head. The stories have often much spirit and point; the king is silenced by the question of the relationship *inter se* of the children of a father who marries the daughter of a lady whom his son espouses. This weird tangle arose from rash vows and honour combined; the king and his son had seen the footprints of two ladies and the son induces his sire to marry the one with large, he the one with small feet, and it turned out that the mother was the *petite* beauty. Difficult again is the question how the hand of a girl should be disposed of, when she has been rescued from a demon by the united work of three lovers, one of whom finds by his skill the place where she is hidden, the other by magic provides an aerial car to seek for her, and the third by valour slays the demon; the king gives the palm to valour. Which again is the nobler, the husband-to-be who permits his beloved one a last assignation, the robber who lets her pass him unscathed when he knows her mission, or the lover who returns her unharmed when he learns of the husband's noble deed? A youth vows his head to Bhaṭṭārikā if he win a fair maid as wife; he pays his debt, his friend finds his corpse and imitates his deed, fearful of suspicion of murder; the wife finds the headless bodies, the goddess pities, and bids her restore the heads, but she errs. Which is her husband? The body with the true head, replies the king, for the head is the noblest member. Or we have the strange case of the son of a thief brought up by a Brahmin, adopted by a king, at whose offering to the spirits of the dead three hands appear to demand the sacrifice. Among these Märchen or novelettes there is one distinctly Buddhist tale, though Durgā is the chief figure in the book taken as a whole, which is distinctly a product of the spirit of the Tantras. A king desires a human sacrifice for his own benefit, parents and the Brahmin priest seek to carry it out, the demon is ready, but the little child to be offered laughs at their shameless folly in ignoring the transient nature of all earthly things, and his life is spared.

Çivadāsa's recension cannot well date before the twelfth century and may be later. It contains not merely maxims in verse—often collected from well-known sources, including a verse of Rudra Bhaṭṭa—but also some narrative verse, and in so far approaches the style of the Campū. One fine stanza probably quoted[1] is worthy of citation:

no manye dṛḍhabandhanāt kṣatam idaṁ naivāñkuçodghaṭṭanaṁ
  skandhārohaṇatāḍanāt paribhavo naivānyadeçāgamaḥ
cintāṁ me janayanti cetasi yathā smṛtvā svayūthaṁ vane
  siṅhatrāsitabhītabhītakalabhā yāsyanti kasyāçrayam.

'Not the wounds, I ween, that my body suffers from my tight bonds, nor the blows of my master's hook, nor the shame of bearing him on my shoulders and enduring his strokes, nor the loss of my home, bring such sorrow to my heart as the thought, "To whom can the young calves, terrified to death by the lion's onslaught, now have resort for aid?"' An ingenious alliteration is also pretty:

sa dhūrjaṭijaṭājūṭo jāyatāṁ vijayāya vaḥ
yatraikapalitabhrāntiṁ karoty adyāpi Jāhnavī.

'May Çiva's matted locks further your success, locks among which the Ganges' presence seems to place one white hair.'

Interesting is the *Çukasaptati*,[2] seventy tales of a parrot, of which we have two recensions, both of uncertain date, but which was certainly known in some form to the Jain Hemacandra[3] and doubtless existed long before it was finally reduced to the form in which we have it. The two recensions best known are the *ornatior* and *simplicior* of Schmidt. The latter is not the earlier; it is clearly an abbreviated version of a text something like the Ornatior, as is shown by the fact that it not rarely leaves us in the

[1] Ascribed to Pāmpaka by Çrīdharadāsa, iv. 214.

[2] Simplicior, ed. AKM. x. 1, 1897; trans. Kiel, 1894; shorter version, ZDMG. liv. 515 ff.; lv. 1 ff. Ornatior ed. A. Bay. A. xxi. 2, 1901; trans. Stuttgart, 1899. Four tales ed. and trans. Kiel, 1890; notes on Simplicior, ZDMG. xlviii. 580 ff. all by R. Schmidt, who has edited a Marāṭhī version, AKM. x. 4. In some MSS. all sorts of bad Sanskrit appear.

[3] Hertel, *Pañcatantra*, pp. 240 ff.

dark as to the precise point of the stories. The form of the original must probably have been simple prose, interspersed with gnomic verses and with some narrative verses at the beginning and end of each of the tales. The framework is amusing. Haradatta, a merchant, has a foolish son Madanasena who spends his whole time in love-passages with his young wife. His father is induced to give him the present of a parrot and a crow, wise birds, embodiments of Gandharvas, whose wise talk converts the son to virtue's ways, so that when going on a journey he entrusts his young wife to them. She regrets his loss but is ready to find another to console her, and the advice of the crow merely meets with a threat to wring his neck. The wiser parrot approves her deed, provided she is smart enough if she finds herself in a hole to get out of it as cleverly as Guṇaçālinī did. The curiosity of the lady is aroused, and by telling her tales and asking her how one should act at the critical moment the bird maintains her virtue until her husband returns. The tales are hardly edifying; about half of them deal with breaches of the marriage bond, while the rest exhibit other instances of the cunning usually of hetairai or clever decisions of arbitrators, as when Mūladeva appears as asked to decide which of two hideous wives of demons is the better-looking. Two famous incidents contained in the collection are the judgement of Solomon and the parallel to the fabricated ordeal in Tristan and Isolde. As usual, religion plays its part in helping immorality; religious processions, temples, pilgrimages, marriages, sacrifices, all are convenient occasions for assignations, the fleeing lover is declared by the ingenious wife to be the ghost of the paternal ancestor, and so forth.

The Ornatior seems to be by a Brahmin Cintāmaṇi Bhaṭṭa, who used the Jain *Pañcatantra* recension of Pūrṇabhadra (1199), though it is quite probable that an older form of the *Çukasaptati* was the source whence some at least of the tales of unfaithful wives were taken by the *Pañcatantra*. The Simplicior seems to be the work of a Çvetāmbara Jain, and it has been suggested that it is ultimately derived from a metrical form, while the occurrence of Prākrit verses has further given rise to the view that the collection may have been originally in Prākrit. The question does not admit of definite solution, nor is the work of great interest save in connexion with its western offshoots and its effect on vernacular literature. The eastern Rājasthānī version[1] is made from a Sanskrit original by Devadatta, son of Puruṣottamadeva, of unknown date; in it the judgement of Solomon is pronounced by a damsel.

Still less attractive is the *Siṅhāsanadvātriṅçikā*,[2] thirty-two tales told by the statues of maidens on a throne which is alleged to have been discovered by Bhoja of Dhārā in the eleventh century, when that king desired to seat himself on it. The throne, it turns out, had been won by Vikramāditya as a gift from Indra, and after his death in battle against Çālivāhana had been buried in the earth, and the thirty-two spirits bound there in statue form tell tales of the great monarch and receive release. The tales are far from exciting, and in the Jain recension of Kṣemaṁkara are ruined by being framed so as to make out the king to be a model of generosity who spent his substance in gifts to the priests of what he won by his great deeds of valour. The form of the work in this recension is marked by the presence of narrative verses at the beginning and end of each prose tale. More like the original form is perhaps the south-Indian version with gnomic verses and occasional narrative verses mingled in its prose. Another version consists of verse, while in a north-Indian recension the stories are lost in the morals. The Bengal version ascribed to Vararuci is merely based on the Jain recension, itself alleged to have used one in Māhārāṣṭrī. The work is clearly later than the *Vetālapañcaviṅçatikā*, but that gives no definite date, and it is not at all likely that it really was written for or under Bhoja of Dhārā. It contains the well-known tale of the king who gives to his dearly beloved wife the fruit which drives away age, only to find that it has passed from her to the master of horse and from him to a hetaira; in disgust the king abandons his throne. Vikramāditya's adventures are also the subject of an alleged epic in thirty chapters, the *Vīracaritra*[3] of Ananta, whose real hero is rather Çūdraka, once co-regent of Çālivāhana, but later a supporter of the descendants of Vikramāditya; of the *Çālivāhanakathā*[4] in eighteen cantos, partly in prose, by Çivadāsa; of the

[1] *Suvābahuttarīkathā*; Hertel, *Festschrift Windisch*, pp. 138 ff.
[2] Weber, IS. xv. 185 ff.; F. Edgerton, AJP. xxxiii. 249 ff., and ed. HOS. 1926.
[3] H. Jacobi, IS. xiv. 97 ff.
[4] Eggeling, IOC. i. 1567 ff.

Mādhavānalakathā[1] in simple prose with Sanskrit and Prākrit stanzas by Ānanda, pupil of Bhaṭṭa Vidyādhara; the anonymous *Vikramodaya*[2] in verse; the Jain compilation of the fifteenth-century *Pañcadaṇḍacchatraprabandha*,[3] &c. In this work he appears as a magician and master of black magic, while in the *Vikramodaya* he is a learned parrot who issues another version of Solomon's judgement.[4]

The close contact of the literature of tales with the people is shown by the fact that later we find apparent Sanskrit versions of vernacular works as in the *Bharaṭakadvātriṅçikā*,[5] tales intended to deride Brahmins, and obviously of Jain inspiration. Çivadāsa's *Kathārṇava*,[6] thirty-five tales including stories of fools and thieves, is also late, and in Vidyāpati's *Puruṣaparīkṣā*,[7] a collection of forty-four stories, we have the work of an author who won in the latter part of the fourteenth century fame as a Maithilī poet. To the same century belong also the unhistorical but interesting legends of authors and other important persons contained in the *Prabandhacintāmaṇi*[8] and the *Prabandhakoça*[9] of the Jain writers Merutuṅga and Rājaçekhara, while that collection of witty but quite untrustworthy legends of the court of Bhoja, the *Bhojaprabandha*[10] of Ballālasena, is of the sixteenth century.

2. *The Didactic Tale*

The tale which is aimed directly at edification rather than amusement is specially richly presented in Jain literature; the Jains were very fond of stories, but they demanded a moral, and hence their writers were often led to spoil good stories such as the legends of Vikramāditya by seeking to make the participants

[1] Ed. Pavolini, OC. IX, i. 430 ff.; GSAI. xxii. 313 ff.; H. Schöhl, *Die Strophen der M.* (1914).

[2] Zachariae, *Kl. Schriften*, pp. 152 ff., 166 ff.; IOC. i. no. 3960. Ch. 7 has a parallel in *Mahāvastu*, iii. 33 ff. (imaginary debts and like repayment).

[3] Ed. and trans. ABA. 1877.

[4] Zachariae, p. 154, n. 1 refers to the literature.

[5] Ed. J. Hertel, Leipzig, 1921; trans. *Ind. Erzähler*, 1922; *c.* A.D. 1400.

[6] Weber, *Ind. Streifen*, i. 251 f.; Pavolini, GSAI. ix. 189 f.

[7] Ed. Bombay, 1882.

[8] Trans. C. H. Tawney, BI. 1901 (date 1306).

[9] Hultzsch, *Reports*, iii. p. vi (1349).

[10] Ed. NSP. 1913; L. Oster, *Die Rezensionen des Bh.* (1911).

in high adventure rather tedious exponents of Jainism. First place among these works must be assigned to the *Pariçiṣṭaparvan*,[1] a supplement to his epic *Triṣaṣṭiçalākāpuruṣacarita* by Hemacandra. In it he deals with the oldest teachers of the Jain faith, and the tales he relates are no longer mythic and epic, but distinctly of the ordinary variety of folk-tale. We hear, for instance, of the incest of brother and sister, children of a hetaira; it is characteristic that the situation is less appreciated on its tragic side than from the point of view of the relationships resulting, a point raised in more innocent circumstances in the last of the tales of the Vampire. The historical figure of Candragupta is made the subject of strange legends, one of the most curious making out that he died a pious Jain.[2] We are told[3] of the monk who showed the constancy required for living with a hetaira during the whole rainy season without breaking his vow of chastity; another, who had shown courage enough to spend the same period in the company of a lion, essays the task but fails; piety however requires that the hetaira should convert him once more to the ways of virtue and herself become a nun.[4]

The Jain Caritras and Purāṇas which contain many legends do not normally attain the level of literature, but more importance attaches to the elaborate allegory of human life in the form of a tale written in 906 by the renowned author Siddha or Siddharṣi. A late and doubtless unreliable authority[5] tells that he was induced to adopt Jainism because his young wife and his mother, annoyed at his late hours, one night insisted on shutting the door on him, so that he went to the always open door of some Jains and refused to give up his intention of becoming a Jain monk. The same authority puts him down as a cousin of the famous poet Māgha. In point of fact the *Upamitibhavaprapañcākathā*,[6] which is in prose with considerable numbers of stanzas interposed

[1] Ed. H. Jacobi, BI. 1891; sel. trans. J. Hertel, Leipzig, 1908; Keith, JRAS. 1908, pp. 1191 f.

[2] Smith (EHI. pp. 154, 458) strangely believes this legend.

[3] viii. 110 ff.

[4] i. 90 ff. (Valkalacīrin) is a variant of Ṛṣyaçṛṅga; ii. 446 ff., the ordeal of an adulteress, is trans. J. J. Meyer, *Isoldes Gottesurteil* (1914), pp. 130 ff.

[5] The *Prabhāvakacaritra* of Prabhācandra and Pradyumna Sūri (1250 A. D.), a continuation of Hemacandra's *Pariçiṣṭaparvan*.

[6] Ed. BI. 1899 ff. Trans. A. Ballini, GSAI. xvii–xix, xxi–xxiv.

from time to time, is by no means badly written, and the author has kindly supplied a key at the end of the introduction to the allegory, so that it is not difficult to follow. His Sanskrit, which he deliberately chose because it was a sign of culture, is not difficult—indeed, he promises that it will be as easy to follow as Prākrit, but the impression of the work as a whole is, as in the case of most allegories, one of unrelieved dreariness, no doubt partly due to the extreme difficulty in making anything picturesque out of the dry and scholastic Jain tenets and the somewhat narrow views of life prevalent in Jain circles.

Of simpler type are the many Kathās or Kathānakas in which well-known *motifs* are adapted to illustrate Jain tenets. These are numerous in the Prākrit literature, being preserved both in commentaries on the canon and separately, and in Sanskrit form they tend to be late. Two interesting tales are the *Campakaçreṣṭhikathānaka*[1] and the *Pālagopālakathānaka*[2] of Jinakīrti, who wrote in the first half of the fifteenth century. The former takes the form of a frame story enclosing three tales, one of Rāvaṇa's vain effort to avoid fate, while in the latter we have with other matter a version of the tale of a woman who accused of attempts on her honour the youth who has refused to yield to her seductions. The *Samyaktvakaumudī*[3] illustrates the plan of inserting tales within a narrative; the pious Arhaddāsa relates to his eight wives and they to him how they obtained true religion (*samyaktva*), their tales being overheard both by a king who wanders about his capital and a thief. On the other hand the *Kathākoça*,[4] also of unknown date, is a series of tales without connexion, in bad Sanskrit with verses in Prākrit, which gives a very poor Jain version of the *Nala*.[5]

[1] A. Weber, SBA. 1883, pp. 567 ff., 885 ff.; J. Hertel, ZDMG. lxv. 1–51, 425–70.

[2] J. Hertel, BSGW. lxix. 4; *Indische Erzähler*, vii (1922); Bloomfield, TAPA. liv. 164 ff.

[3] A. Weber, SBA. 1889, pp. 731 ff.

[4] Trans. C. H. Tawney, London, 1895.

[5] Hemavijaya's *Kathāratnākara* is trans. Hertel. Rājaçekhara (14th cent.) in his *Antarakathāsaṁgraha* (cf. Pullé, SIFI. i. 1 ff.; ii. 1 ff.) has a version of the judgement of Solomon (Tessitori, IA. xlii. 148 ff.; Hertel, *Geist des Ostens*, i. 189 ff.).

XIV

THE GREAT ROMANCES

1. *The Age and Works of Daṇḍin*

OF Daṇḍin we know really nothing save what can be gathered from his works and late tradition. The latter asserts his authorship of three books, and it is generally conceded that of these we have two, the *Daçakumāracarita* and the *Kāvyādarça*. The third has been variously identified; the view of Pischel that it was the *Mṛcchakaṭikā* was based in effect merely on the general resemblance of social relations described in the drama and in the *Daçakumāracarita* and the anonymous citation of a line found in the drama by the *Kāvyādarça*. Now that we know that the line is found also in Bhāsa, the argument is less strong than ever. But it is very dubious if the *Chandoviciti* referred to in the *Kāvyādarça* is intended by Daṇḍin to be his own work, and even if it were it is possible that it and the *Kālaparicchheda* also alluded to were mere chapters to be appended to the *Kāvyādarça*. Even the identity of authorship of the *Kāvyādarça* and the *Daçakumāracarita* has been doubted on various grounds. It has been pointed out [1] that the vulgarity and occasional obscenity of language in the romance accord ill with the insistence in the *Kāvyādarça* on freedom from coarseness, and certain real or alleged inelegancies of diction have been asserted to be impossible in an author who wrote on poetics. But neither contention is of serious value. Apart from the notorious difference between precept and practice, it is perfectly possible and even probable that the romance came from the youth of Daṇḍin and the *Kāvyādarça* from his more mature judgement, while most of the alleged errors in grammar may safely be denied or at least are of the type which other poets permit themselves.[2]

The date of Daṇḍin is still open to dispute, and if the *Kāvyādarça* were not to be taken into account would be even more difficult to determine than it actually is. If, for reasons which will be given later, we place the *Kāvyādarça* definitely before

[1] Agashe, ed. pp. xxv ff.

[2] The ascription to him of the *Avantisundarīkathā*, of which we have a fragment, is quite implausible; S. K. Dé, IHQ. i. 31 ff.; iii. 394 ff.

Bhāmaha (*c.* A. D. 700), there is no reason to assert that he wrote much earlier, and the chief impression conveyed by the *Daçakumāracarita* is that its geography [1] contemplates a state of things anterior to the empire of Harṣavardhana, and that its comparative simplicity suggests a date anterior to the work of Subandhu and Bāṇa. Nor is there anything to suggest a later date. The corruption of manners adduced by Wilson in favour of the legend which makes him an ornament of the court of Bhoja of Dhārā, so far as it was real, merely represents a regular feature of one aspect of Indian life.

2. *The Daçakumāracarita*

It is very probable that it was from Guṇāḍhya that Daṇḍin derived the conception of the plot of the romance.[2] The device by which Naravāhanadatta and his companions, reunited after strange adventures, repeat the account of what has befallen each of them is strongly suggestive of the device by which the ten princes of Daṇḍin's tale expound their fortunes when reunited after their original separation. The idea is ingenious, for it provides a certain measure of unity in what else would be merely a series of unconnected stories. If Hertel is right, however, Daṇḍin's plan would have extended far beyond what he has accomplished ; he finds allusions to a scheme which would have told of the history of king Kāmapāla and his five wives in three different births on earth, so that what we have is a mere fragment. It may be true that Daṇḍin contemplated some such work, but there is really no proof of it, and still less that he ever actually wrote it. Indeed, Hertel himself holds that he left even the *Daçakumāracarita* itself as we have it, with an abrupt beginning and incomplete, his purpose of carrying out his undertaking having been frustrated for some cause or other. This is of course conjectural, nor can any conclusion be drawn from the fact that so many efforts [3] were later made to supply a beginning and to end the

[1] Collins, *The Geographical Data of the Raghuvaṃśa and Daśakumāracarita* (1907), p. 46.

[2] Ed. G. Bühler and P. Peterson, BSS. 1887–91 (2nd ed. by Agashe); A. B. Gajendragadkar, Dharwar. Trans. J. J. Meyer, Leipzig, 1902; J. Hertel, Leipzig, 1922; Weber, *Ind. Streifen*, i. 308 ff.

[3] For one by Bhaṭṭa Nārāyaṇa see Appendix in Agashe's ed.; there is one in verse by Vināyaka ; a continuation by Cakrapāṇi and a revision by Gopīnātha (IOC. i. 1551 f.) exist.

text to prove that, if these parts of Daṇḍin's work had ever existed, they would not have been lost. The fates of books are far too uncertain to admit of such reasoning being decisive.

What is certain is that we have in our manuscript quite frequently beside the text of the work proper an introduction, Pūrvapīṭhikā, and in one manuscript and its derivatives a conclusion, Uttarapīṭhikā. That these are no part of Daṇḍin's work seems suggested at once by the names, and this conclusion is confirmed by overwhelming evidence. The Pūrvapīṭhikā ought to lead up merely to the first tale in the text of the romance, but in point of fact it gives tales of two princes in order to make up the number of ten, Daṇḍin's own work extending only to eight, the last imperfect. Moreover, the contents of the introduction by no means correspond precisely with the facts made clear in the romance itself. Thus, while in the ancestry of the princes Rājavāhana, Puṣpodbhava, Apahāravarman, and Upahāravarman there is no discrepancy of moment, the accounts of Arthapāla, Pramati, and Viçruta cannot be reconciled. In Daṇḍin Arthapāla and Pramati are Kāmapāla's sons by Kāntimatī and Tārāvalī, in the introduction Arthapāla is Tārāvalī's son and Pramati is not his half-brother but merely a son of the minister Sumati, a misunderstanding of a passage in Daṇḍin. Viçruta, again, to Daṇḍin is descended from the merchant Vaiçravaṇa and grandson of Sindhudatta, in the introduction it is the minister Padmodbhava who is his grandfather. It is probable that the ancestries of the princes Somadatta, Mitragupta, and Mantragupta given in the introduction are mere figments, that of Mantragupta being given as Sumantra from a mere misreading in Daṇḍin, while in reality the princes in Daṇḍin's own view were sons of the three remaining wives of Kāmapāla himself, and therefore half-brothers of the hero Rājavāhana. Moreover, when in Daṇḍin Caṇḍavarman finds Rājavāhana with the princess, he denounces him as an impostor who has under the cloak of religion corrupted the people and made them believe in false gods, but the introduction has nothing of this, and in lieu of making the prince a clever trickster has to provide him with an accomplice in the shape of a magician in order to accomplish his ends. So, again, in Daṇḍin we hear of a younger brother as guilty of aiding the prince to obtain access to the princess's harem, while the introduction has provided him with the magician for this very end. Upahāravarman's own tale is that he was brought up by a monk, the introduction gives the duty to the king. It is clear, too, that the scene at the end of the introduction does not accord with the beginning of the text. Daṇḍin conceives Rājavāhana and his princess as already having enjoyed the sweets of love, and depicts the prince seeking to win a revival of her passion by tales of the ancient loves of gods and saints,[1] to which she responds. The introduction with incredible bad taste treats the occasion as the first scene between the two, and represents the prince as seeking to make his love repeat what he has been telling her, for the pleasure of listening to her doing so. Moreover, the matter imparted to the loving maiden was not in his view erotic, but an account of the fourteen worlds as a lesson on Brahmanical cosmography. We may safely say that the author of this stupidity was not Daṇḍin, whose own purpose doubtless was, as in chapter vi, to insert just before our present text some anecdotes of ancient love stories. The case against the Uttarapīṭhikā is even more convincing, for it is obvious from the end of the text that Daṇḍin was about to paint the model of a wise ruler, a task which the present conclusion does not even attempt. The fact that other efforts to supply an introduction are known is additional proof that the existing Pūrvapīṭhikā was not accorded general acceptance as Daṇḍin's work. It is possible that two hands are to be distinguished even in the Pūrvapīṭhikā itself.

3. *The Content and Style of the Daçakumāracarita*

It has been suggested[2] that the romance is really to be regarded as a didactic work, an attempt to teach the doctrines of the Nītiçāstra in narratives of attractive character. This we may fairly pronounce to be an exaggeration and an injustice to the author, whose real aim we may be sure was to give pleasure, however ready he might be to show himself an expert in the rules of polity as well as those of the Kāmaçāstra. His distinctive quality is the application to the simple tale of the grand manner of the Kāvya, though in a moderation which is utterly lost in the case of Subandhu and Bāṇa. Doubtless he had predecessors in

[1] Cf. the *Kāmasūtra's* insistence on the love of women for tellers of tales (p. 260).

[2] Hertel, trans. iii. 8 ff.

the attempt, though they are lost to us and we cannot even say whether the Bhaṭṭāra Haricandra to whom Bāṇa refers in the introduction to his *Harṣacarita* as a fine author of prose was a predecessor of Daṇḍin. It may be conjectured that the application of the Kāvya style to prose had its origin in panegyrics such as are seen in the inscriptions of Rudradāman and Hariṣeṇa which we have already considered, and that it was only later that it was thought suitable to apply similar methods to tales. The application, of course, made the tale vitally different from its effect in its more simple form. The work of Guṇāḍhya, even through its changed forms, as it has come down to us gives the definite impression of swift and easy narrative, the poets not pausing to exercise their descriptive talents; Daṇḍin leads the way to the result that the narrative is a mere skeleton, the descriptions the essence.

In Daṇḍin, however, we are far from the period when an exercise in style is aimed at. The main interest of the romance lies in the substance,[1] with its vivid and picturesque account of low life and adventure, of magicians and fraudulent holy men, of princesses and ruined kings, of hetairai, of expert thieves, of fervent lovers, who in a dream or by a prophecy are urged on to seek the beloved. The world of the gods is regarded with singularly little respect, and the ministers to holiness are equally far from finding favour. Not that there is a total disregard of moral considerations; one prince consoles himself for his action in seeking to secure the wife of another, and slaying to fulfil the end, by moral principles. It is legitimate according to the text-books to abandon one of the three ends of man, duty, profit, and love, if it tends to the attainment of the other two, and if he has violated duty he has enabled his parents to escape from captivity, has secured himself the delights of love and the possession of a realm. Apahāravarman again is a prince of thieves; he plans on the model laid down by Karṇīsuta, author of an unhappily lost text-book on the art, to rob a city in order, it is true, to reimburse an unfortunate who has been robbed by a hetaira;

[1] How far original is unknown. In vi the insertion of stories has a parallel in the *Kathāsaritsāgara* where the Vetāla stories come in the report of the sixth minister, and there is a parallel for Nitambavatī. The figures of the ungrateful and the ideal wives here have parallels in Jātakas 193 and 546; Winternitz, GIL. iii. 357.

moreover, he understands that there are too many misers in residence. Mantragupta in disguise worms himself into the confidence of a foolish king, persuades him to bathe in the sea in order to acquire greater beauty, murders him, and parades himself before the people as the new form of the king, extolling the wonderful deed that has been accomplished, which has put to shame all mockers as to the powers of the gods to work miracles. Viçruta in order to secure his protégé's restoration to power makes use both of the temple and the name of Durgā to perpetrate a successful fraud. The gods appear as justifying the most disgraceful deeds; the moon god is cited as justifying adultery, the hetaira in her successful effort to pervert the pious ascetic can find authority in the scandals regarding heaven. The ascetic is far from being adamant, and it is not Brahmins alone who are subject to satire; the merchant whom she plunders down to his loin-cloth abandons that also and becomes a Digambara Jain monk, but confesses that the sublime teachings of the Jina are but a swindle. The Brahmins again with their reports of evil, requiring a special sacrifice with vessels of pure gold, are derided, while nuns are all go-betweens and one Buddhist lady is the head procuress in the service of a hetaira. The might of fate does not rule the affairs of these active princes; true, Apahāravarman when caught stealing, Pūrṇabhadra captured by robbers, ascribe to this cause their mishaps, but they both are ready and able by human exertion to defeat effectively the decrees of that unstable deity.

The realism of Daṇḍin's outlook is entirely in accord with one strain of Indian tradition, that which from the *Ṛgveda* onwards notes and describes the sins of the gods, without any moral protest. It stands out the more prominently when it is compared with the pious attitude of the author of the Pūrvapīṭhikā. To him the sacrifice is the power that brings the gods; Rājahaṅsa is praised because of his devotion to the priests, the gods on earth, while Daṇḍin denies them that appellation save in one passage where his use for them of *dharaṇitala-taitila* is sneering, the term meaning also 'rhinoceroses'. The king's domestic priest possesses the full holiness of Brahman himself, and despite his appalling deeds the Brahmin Mātaṅga, because he died in saving another Brahmin, after an interesting tour of inspection of Yama's hells is restored to life, and by his devotion to Çiva is rewarded with the aid of Rājavāhana to enable him to win an Asura princess and lordship of the nether regions. Not valour but Çiva's club gives the king of Mālava victory over Rājahaṅsa. Daṇḍin makes a joke out of Mārkaṇḍeya's curse which condemns Suratamañjarī, whose pearl necklace fell on the ascetic when bathing, to become a silver chain. The Pūrvapīṭhikā parts Çāmba from his wife for two months because of the curse of a water-fowl. The princes no longer are free agents; the great Vāmadeva and his acolytes protect and guard the father and the princess; Rājavāhana can win his princess only by a Brahmin's aid.

Characteristic of Daṇḍin is his power of characterization which is not content with making alive the more important figures on his stage, but invests with life and reality the minor personages. The ascetic Marīci, the merchant Vasupālita, and their seducer Kāmamañjarī, the old Brahmin who meets Pramati at the cock-fight and seconds him *con amore* in the trick to win his bride, improving on his instructions, the police commandant Kāntaka, who is deluded into believing that the king's daughter is in love with him and treasures the nurse's soiled garment as a pledge of affection, and the nurse herself, Çṛgālikā, who seconds Apahāravarman's efforts to win the princess, are all depicted with liveliness, force, and insight. Nor is Daṇḍin limited in range; in chapter viii we have a deeper note in the characterization of the young king Anantavarman, his loyal minister Vasurakṣita, whom he casts aside because his advice is too wise for his taste, and the shallow but witty courtier Vihārabhadra whose advice leads to the utter ruin of realm and king.

The humour and wit of the author are remarkable and far more attractive to modern taste than are usually these qualities in Indian works. The whole work is pervaded by the humour of the wild deeds of the princes, their determination to secure what they wish, and their light-hearted indifference to the morality of the means which they employ. The deception of Marīci [1] by the hetaira is perfectly drawn; the damsel pretends to be enamoured of the holy life, the ascetic warns her of the trials and advises her mother, who is shocked at her daughter's indifference to duty, to let her stay a short time to experience what her purpose means;

[1] Lüders' comparison of the Ṛṣyaçṛṅga legend (GN. 1897, p. 109) is needless. For Christian parallels see Günter, *Buddha*, pp. 233 ff.

alas, it is the ascetic who learns many things not suitable for ascetics. The silver chain which binds the captive turns itself into a beautiful maiden in an unexpected but delightful way. Queen Vasundharā finds a brilliant way of spreading a false rumour ; she invites the oldest of the citizens and the highest of the ministers to a secret conclave at which under the most solemn pledge of secrecy she reveals the *canard*. There is admirable wit in Apahāravarman's pious resolve to bring into a better frame of mind the misers of Campā by revealing to their eyes the perishable nature of all that is earthly, in vulgar parlance by stealing their money. Mitragupta offers Candrasenā a magic ointment to make her appear like a female ape to the prince, but she replies that she does not wish in this life to be parted from her mortal body. Arthapāla finds in the earth a lovely damsel whom he likens to the goddess of royal sovereignty who has taken refuge in the earth to avoid the sight of so many bad kings. Upahāravarman makes a very bitter jest at the expense of king Vikaṭavarman who is under the impression that he is his beloved queen ; to confirm him in this view he asks him to swear to confine his love in future with his new form to the queen alone : the fool is prepared to take the oath but Upahāravarman continues: *kiṁ vā çapathena ? kaiva hi mānuṣī mām paribhaviṣyati ? yady apsarobhiḥ saṁgacchase saṁgacchasva kāmam. kathaya kāni te rahasyāni. tatkathanānte tvatsvarūpabhrañçaḥ.* 'Nay, what need of an oath ? What woman can vie with me ? But if thou wouldst mate with the Apsarases, thou mayst do so at pleasure. Tell me thy secrets ; when thou hast told, thy change of shape will come to pass.' The foolish king little knows the meaning of the words which portend his wedlock with a denizen of the next world, and a change not to a fairer form but the passing of this mortal life.

In the arrangement of his work Daṇḍin shows distinct judgement. He varies his tone ; from the light-hearted or grim humour of chapters ii and v we pass to the earnest tragedy of chapter viii. He alters his form ; while most of the books are without break of subject, in chapter vi we have four clever tales, those of Dhūminī, Gominī, Nimbavatī, and Nitambavatī, told in succession to illustrate the maxim that cunning alone is able to accomplish the most difficult ends. If the work had been completed, as we have seen, before the present opening, we should doubtless have had some pictures of ancient love scenes.

Daṇḍin is unquestionably masterly in his use of language. He is perfectly capable of simple easy narrative, and in the speeches which he gives to his characters he avoids carefully the error of elaboration of language. But he is prepared to exhibit his talent and command of the language in descriptions and in these he is markedly an adherent of the Vaidarbha style, and excels, as a traditional estimate holds, in pleasing sound effects. He aims both at exactness of expression and clearness of sense, at the avoidence of harsh sounds and exaggeration or bombast; he attains beauty, harmony of sound, and effective expression of sentiment. He makes free use, but with reasonable moderation, of the right in prose to construct long compounds, but they in the main are not difficult of comprehension. His desire to vary his forms of description is marked and receives effective illustration. Twice he has to describe the beauty of a slumbering maiden; in the first case [1] he resorts to a complete catalogue of all her perfections as the hero gazes on her and notes them in minutest detail through her thin garments; in the second case there is no realistic description, but four similes from mythology and nature serve to express her loveliness.[2] Yet again a picture is given of beauty unveiled, but the occasion is different; the hero sets up as an astrologer, and in this capacity has the privilege of inspecting youthful beauty presented to him to ascertain if it possesses the auspicious signs of suitability for marriage.[3] Reference has already been made to the witty close of the description of the beautiful maiden of the underground dwelling, where the jest is given special point by following on several more stereotyped complimentary epithets.[4] Another description is decidedly ingenious and is addressed to the lovely one herself: *bhāmini nanu bahv aparāddhaṁ bhavatyā cittajanmano yad amuṣya jīvitabhūtāṁ Ratim ākṛtyā kadarthitavatī dhanuryaṣṭim bhrūlatābhyāṁ bhramaramālāmayīṁ jyāṁ nīlālakadyutibhir astrāṇy apāṅgavīkṣitavṛṣṭibhir mahārajanadhvajapaṭāṅçukaṁ daçanacchadamayūkhajālaiḥ prathamasuhṛdam malayamārutam parimalapaṭīyasā niḥçvāsapavanena parabhṛtarutam atimañjulaiḥ pralāpaiḥ puṣpamayīm patākām bhujayaṣṭibhyāṁ digvijayārambhapūrṇa-*

[1] ii. p. 62. [2] v. p. 13. [3] vi. p. 31. [4] iv. p. 10.

kumbhamithunam urojayugalena krīḍāsaro nābhimaṇḍalena samnāhyarathamaṇḍalaṁ çroṇimaṇḍalena bhavanaratnatoraṇa-stambhayugalam ūruyugalena līlākarṇakisalayaṁ caraṇatalapra-bhābhiḥ. 'Hast thou, gracious lady, not wrought much wrong on our lord Love? Hast thou not utterly eclipsed with thy form Rati, who is all his life to him; with thy creeper-like brows the staff of his bow; his bowstring formed of a row of bees with the flashings of thy dark locks; his arrows with the showers of thy sidelong glances; the silk of his saffron-dyed banner with the ruddy rays darting from thy lips; his dearest friend, the wind from Malaya, with the sweet fragrance of thy breath; the Kokila with thy charming utterance; his flower ensign with the flagstaffs of thy arms; the two bowls which were filled when he started to conquer the world with thy two rounded breasts, the lake in which he plays with the circle of thy navel; the rounded frame of his battle-chariot with thy round hips; the twin pillars of the jewelled arch of his palace with thy twin thighs; the lotus behind his ear with which he plays with the gleaming red of the soles of thy feet?' The same variety is seen in his many changes of expression in describing the dawn and the sunset, which he delights to do. So Upahāravarman sees the dawn thus: *cintayaty eva mayi mahārṇavonmagnamār-taṇḍaturañgamaçvāsarayāvadhūteva vyavartata triyāmā samu-dragarbhavāsajaḍīkṛta iva mandapratāpo divasakaraḥ prādur āsīt.* 'While yet I pondered, night passed away, as though wafted away by the hot breath of the steeds of the sun as he emerged from the mighty ocean, and the sun stood revealed, but yet feeble his might as though he had been paralysed by his dwelling within the bosom of the sea.' There is a very effective example of the simplicity and vividness of his style in his account in the legend of Dhūminī of the appalling famine which led to the tragic events of that tale: *kṣīṇasāraṁ sasyam oṣadhayo bandhyā na phalavanto vanaspatayaḥ klībā meghā bhinnasrotasaḥ sravantyaḥ pañkaçeṣāṇi palvalāni niḥsyandāny utsamaṇḍalāni viralībhūtaṁ kandamūlaphalam avahīnāḥ kathā galitāḥ kalyāṇot-savakriyā bahulībhūtāni taskarakulāny anyonyam abhakṣayan pra-jāḥ paryaluṇṭhann itas tato balākāpāṇḍurāṇi naraçiraḥkapālāni paryahiṇḍanta çuṣkāḥ kākamaṇḍalyaḥ çūnyībhūtāni nagaragrā-makharvaṭapuṭabhedanādīni.* 'The corn lost all its strength, the herbs became barren, the trees bore no fruit, the clouds rained not, the beds of the streams became dry, the tanks were reduced to mud, the springs ceased to flow, bulbs, roots, and fruits were hard to find, all ceased to converse or celebrate auspicious events, hordes of robbers became more common, people ate one another in their hunger, men's skulls, bleached white as cranes, rolled about, great flocks of starving crows flew around, while cities great and small, market-places, villages, and other resorts of men were abandoned.' It is significant that the author of the Pūrvapīṭhikā is quite unable to vie in description with his model, though he exaggerates the length of his compounds and in the introduction commits himself to a stanza playing on Daṇḍin's name. He commits also the grave fault of excessive use of alliterations, perpetrating the continuous riming effect of: *kumārā mārābhirāmā rāmādyapauruṣā ruṣā bhasmīkṛtārayo rayopahasitasamīraṇā raṇābhiyānena yānenābhyudayaçaṅsaṁ rājānam akārṣuḥ.* 'The princes, beautiful as Māra himself, with the heroism of Rāma and other heroes, reducing their enemies to ashes in their rage, in their swiftness defeating even the wind, advancing in their chariots to battle assured the king of victory.' It may be doubted whether it is not to his carelessness rather than to clerical errors or to learned pedantry that we should ascribe the incorrect forms *mahadāyudha*, *mahadabhikhyā*, *mahadāçā*, *āvoci*, *çāsan*, *adaṅçi*, presented by manuscript tradition.[1] These are very different from the forms which have been censured in Daṇḍin, such as *āliṅgayitum*, *brāhmaṇabrūvaḥ*, *enaṁ anuraktā*, which are clearly defensible as they stand.

It must not, however, be denied that we see traces here and there of the desire even in Daṇḍin to strain language. The *tour de force* by which chapter vii is spoken by Mantragupta without any labial letters[2] because his loved one had bitten him so deeply on the lower lip that he could not form labials is noteworthy but hardly admirable, and in chapter ii we find a piece[3] of complex argument elliptically expressed which might do credit

[1] For differences in language between the Pūrvapīṭhikā and the text of Daṇḍin, see Gawroński, *Sprachl. Untersuchungen über das Mṛcchakaṭika und das Daśakumâracarita* (1907), pp. 47 ff.

[2] In *Kāvyādarça*, iii. 83, the difficulty of the feat is recognized. Cf. Jacobi, ZDMG, xl. 99. Pindar is credited with writing a poem without *s*; cf. Ohlert, *Rätsel und Rätselsprüche*, pp. 3 ff.

[3] p. 50, ll. 7 ff. (ed. Bühler).

for difficulty of comprehension to Subandhu or Bāṇa. But in him these deviations are exceptions, and though Indian taste would never have ranked his style with that of the other great romancers it is greatly to be preferred on modern standards. In one point, however, Daṇḍin surpasses Subandhu. He obeys the rule that the perfect shall only be used in describing what is not part of one's personal experience.[1] Hence in the narratives of the princes the perfect is excluded, although it is permitted in the four short tales inserted in chapter vi; in the princes' narrative he uses only imperfects, aorists, the historical present, and participles, active and passive. His frequent use of aorists is doubtless a sign of his familiarity with grammar and his anxiety to exhibit the fact.

4. *Subandhu*

Of Subandhu we know as little as of Daṇḍin. He appears first in Bāṇa who mentions in the introduction to the *Harṣacarita* the *Vāsavadattā* as quelling the pride of poets, and in the *Kādambarī* in celebrating his own work he uses the epithet *atidvayī*, 'surpassing two,' which is believed to refer to the *Vāsavadattā*[2] and the *Bṛhatkathā* of Guṇāḍhya. That Subandhu's work is meant is not now very seriously questioned, Peterson himself having long since withdrawn his suggestion to that effect. Subandhu's name appears with those of Bhāsa, Kālidāsa, and Haricandra in Vākpatirāja's *Gaüḍavaha*; he is classed with Meṇṭha, Bhāravi, and Bāṇa by Mankha in his *Çrīkaṇṭhacarita*; and Kavirāja in the *Rāghavapāṇḍavīya* boasts that Subandhu, he, and Bāṇa are masters of ambiguous diction; while a Kanarese inscription of A.D. 1168 ascribes to him mastery in Kāvya. Quite late tradition makes him a contemporary of the legendary Vikramāditya and a nephew of Vararuci. But the only reference to that monarch shows him to have been in the remote past, and the date of Subandhu must depend on his priority to Bāṇa, which is borne out by a mass of obvious coincidences in diction, and on the other hand by his own literary allusions. Of the many works known to the poet most are decidedly older, such as the epics, the *Kāmasūtra*, the *Chandoviciti* section of the

[1] Speyer, *Sansk. Synt.*, p. 248.

[2] Ed. F. Hall, BI. 1859; South Indian text, ed. L. H. Gray, CUIS. 8, 1913, with translation. Cf. Peterson, *Subhāṣitāvali*, p. 133.

Nāṭyaçāstra, and the *Bṛhatkathā*; but he knew well not only the Upaniṣads but also the Nyāya and Mīmāṅsā schools of philosophy and Buddhism. One passage enables us to fix an upper date with some certainty; he describes a maiden as *nyāyasthitim iva Uddyotakarasvarūpām Bauddhasaṁgatim iva Alaṁkārabhūṣitām.* It is impossible to doubt that Uddyotakara is referred to; perhaps the reference following is to Dharmakīrti, the Buddhist logician, as Çivarāma asserts, because we know now that Uddyotakara possibly used and was used by Dharmakīrti, and nothing can be more natural than to find the two together. This means,[1] however, in view of the evidence available as to Dharmakīrti's date, that Subandhu must be placed in the second quarter of the seventh century and that he was only a contemporary of Bāṇa whose work came to fruition before Bāṇa's. Unlike that author, he cannot have enjoyed the patronage of Harṣavardhana, and we may presume that his activity was carried on at some other capital.

5. *The Vāsavadattā*

Though the name Vāsavadattā is famous in Indian literature, we do not find in it any parallel for the tale of Subandhu, unless we infer from the mere name recorded as the subject of an Ākhyāyikā by Patañjali on Kātyāyana[2] that he knew of this story, a most implausible theory. Nor is it of much consequence whether we regard the work as falling technically into the category of Ākhyāyikā or Kathā. Bāṇa[3] indeed, seems to suggest the former appellation as appropriate, but while Daṇḍin[4] is no doubt right in dismissing controversy on this point as foolish, it is clear that, if distinctions are made, the *Vāsavadattā* accords with the nature of a Kathā. Thus, if we take the essential feature of an Ākhyāyikā to be that it is told by the hero, is divided into Ucchvāsas, has passages in Vaktra[5] and Aparavaktra metres, these characteristics do not suit the text; if, on the other hand, we adopt Amarasiṅha's[6] distinction and make the subject-matter

[1] Keith, JRAS. 1914, pp. 1102 ff. The *Alaṁkāra* is not to be regarded as a work on poetics.

[2] On Pāṇini, iv. 3. 87; cf. on iv. 2. 60.

[3] *Harṣacarita*, v. 10.

[4] *Kāvyādarça*, i. 23 ff.

[5] Cf. Subandhu (ed. Hall), p. 184.

[6] i. 6. 5.

of the Ākhyāyikā traditional as opposed to invented by the poet, the *Vāsavadattā* seems to disagree with the description of the Ākhyāyikā. The similarity of the tale to the manner of the *Kādambarī*, which is clearly a Kathā, is practically decisive in favour of that genre.[1] But, accepting as we may the originality in some degree of the poet, we may admit that he makes use of the whole stock-in-trade of Indian narratives, the seeing in a dream of one's future mate, the overhearing of the chatter of birds, magic steeds, the fatal effect of ascetics' curses, transformations of shape, and recovery of one's true form by a lover's embrace. It is essentially the aim of the poet not to trouble himself with the plot or the characters but to display his virtuosity in language.

King Cintāmaṇi has a beautiful son, Kandarpaketu, who in a dream beheld a girl of beauty exceeding his own ; sleep leaves him and with his friend Makaranda he sallies forth to seek the unknown. In the Vindhya as the prince lies sleepless he overhears the curtain-lecture of an indignant Maina bird to her husband, who defends himself for late hours by telling how the monarch Çṛñgāraçekhara has a peerless daughter, Vāsavadattā, who in a dream has seen the lovely vision of a youth, of whom she is deeply enamoured. She has sent her confidante Tamālikā to bear to the youth an assurance of her deep love. There is no difficulty in securing the meeting of the two at Pāṭaliputra, but the prince learns to his horror that the king, wearied of her unwedded state, means forthwith to marry her to the Vidyādhara chief Puṣpaketu. The lovers therefore flee by means of a magic steed to the Vindhya where they fall asleep. Awakened, the prince finds to his sorrow that the maiden has departed, and in his despair he is only kept from self-destruction by a voice from the sky promising him reunion. After long wandering he finds a statue which at his touch awakens to life as his beloved, and in rêunion they live in great happiness in Kandarpaketu's capital. The plot it will be seen is negligible, not even worth serious criticism, but it would be quite unjust to accuse Subandhu of indecency or savagery as one distinguished editor did. To apply

[1] The story contains the taking of a maiden, a battle (pp. 290 ff.; Nobel's denial (*Indian Poetry*, p. 185) is an oversight), separation, and success, as required by Bhāmaha (i. 27), and seems original.

mid-Victorian conceptions of propriety to India is obviously absurd and wholly misleading. Indian writers, not excluding Kālidāsa, indulge habitually *con amore* in minute descriptions of the beauty of women and the delights of love which are not in accord with western conventions of taste. But the same condemnation was applied by contemporaries to Swinburne, and Shakespeare's frankness is more resented by English than by German taste. What is essential is to repel the connexion of such descriptions with immorality, and to assert that they must be approved or condemned on artistic grounds alone. There is all the world of difference between what we find in the great poets of India and the frank delight of Martial and Petronius in descriptions of immoral scenes.

What we have in Subandhu is an exercise in style applied in descriptions of mountain, river, stream, the valour of the prince, the beauty of the heroine, and the strife of the contending armies, whose struggle led to the loss of the princess, who unwittingly trespassed into the garden of an ascetic and was cursed by him with the customary injustice of his kind to become a stone. Of serious characterization there is nothing whatever; Subandhu's own claim is that he is a storehouse of cleverness in the composition of works in which there is a pun in every syllable (*pratyakṣaraçleṣamayavinyāsavaidagdhyanidhi*), and this is carried out in prose with occasional verses interspersed and with an introduction in verse. Subandhu's translator has generously—and not without justice—claimed for him a true melody in the long rolling compounds, a sesquipedalian majesty which can never be equalled except in Sanskrit, a lulling music in the alliterations, and a compact brevity in the paronomasias which are in most cases veritable gems of terseness and twofold appropriateness. In fact Subandhu's ideal was clearly the Gauḍa style with its enormous compounds, its love of etymologizing, its deliberate exaggeration, its love of harsh sounds, its fondness for alliteration, its attempt to match sense closely with sound, its research for recondite results in the use of figures and above all in paronomasias and cases of apparent incongruity. How far Subandhu's accomplishment was original we cannot say in the absence of so much literature now lost, but Daṇḍin certainly is very different in style, and it is of interest that in the period after Subandhu we begin to find in inscriptions [1] a rather free use of paronomasias and the figure incongruity (*virodha*). Thus, as a parallel to Subandhu's *dhanadenāpi pracetasā*, 'who is Kubera, yet also Varuṇa, for he is generous, yet wise,' we have *dhanado 'pi na pramattaḥ*, 'he was Kubera, not Varuṇa, for he was generous, not inattentive.' It must, however, be said that alliteration, pretty when used with a point, becomes tedious when practised too often, and it is impossible not to be wearied by a string of puns even if they cannot be styled obscene and are at the worst only dull. Granted that the poet's fancy [2] is able, with the resources of the Sanskrit language, to find a vast variety of clever *double entendres*, moderation and judgement are conspicuously lacking throughout in Subandhu. Moreover, he has to perfection the capacity of constructing a vast sentence which rests on a single verb, while in its enormous compass by means of a series of epithets, each composed of a long compound, it contains infinitely more matter than the mind can conveniently assimilate at one time. The disadvantage of the prose form is here abundantly apparent; the stanza compels compression and a certain moderation, and Subandhu has verses [3] which show that, when placed under restraint, he was capable of really effective writing. The picture of the lion's attack lacks puns and is admirable.

paçyodañcadavāñcadañcitavapuḥpaçcārdhapūrvārdhabhāk
stabdhottānitapṛṣṭhaniṣṭhitamanāgbhugnāgralāṅgūlabhṛt
daṅṣṭrākoṭiviçaṅkaṭāsyakuharaḥ kurvan saṭām utkaṭām
utkarṇaḥ kurute kramaṁ karipatau krūrākṛtiḥ kesarī.

'See, the lion, raising the hind quarters of his fair body, with the fore quarters depressed, his tail, slightly bent, remaining poised over his firm arched back, his cavernous mouth terrible with the tips of his fangs, tossing aloft his mane, with ears erect, doth make, with aspect dread, his assault on the lord of elephants.' The picture of the lion is perfect in every detail, and the alliterations rather heighten the effect, while the frequent use of *ṭ* and

[1] Gwalior inscr. (874–5) EI. i. 157; cf. inscr. of Govinda III (807–8), EI. vi. 246 ff. and others (Gray, p. 31).

[2] Here and there he reduced to prose older verses; Zachariae, *Gurupūjākaumudī*, pp. 38 ff.

[3] After the twelve Āryās of the introduction there are only three cases of verses, Āryā, Çārdūlavikrīḍita (2); Çikhariṇī, Sragdharā; Āryā.

harsh sound-combinations makes the effect all the more impressive, illustrating what in poetics ranks as Svabhāvokti, which is in essentials a vivid description. An instance of the figure Sahokti, unified description, which is found already in the *Rāmāyaṇa*, is found in: *samaṁ dviṣāṁ dhanuṣāṁ ca jīvākṛṣṭiṁ yodhāç cakruḥ.* 'The warriors drew at once their bow-strings and took their enemies' lives.' The figure Utprekṣā, lively fancy, is seen in many imaginative flights, such as the description of the moon as: *dadhidhavale kālakṣapaṇakagrāsapiṇḍa iva niçāyamunāphenapuñja iva menakānakhamārjanaçilāçakala iva*, 'white as curd, shaped like a ball of food for an ascetic's meal, as it were a mass of the foam of the Yamunā, night, a sliver of stone for the polishing of Menakā's nails.' Akin to this is the mental picture involved in supposition, Sambhāvana: *tvatkṛte yānayā vedanānubhūtā sa yadi nabhaḥ patrāyate sāgaro melānandāyate brahmāyate lipikaro bhujagarājāyate kathakas tadā kim api katham apy anekayugasahasrair abhilikhyate kathyate vā.* 'The sorrow that this maiden hath endured because of thee might be written or told only in some way or another in thousands of æons, if the sky became the paper, the sea the inkwell, Brahman himself the scribe, and the Lord of Serpents the narrator.'[1] Within limits puns are attractive, as in the verse:

sa rasavattā vihatā na vakā vilasanti carati no kaṅkaḥ
sarasīva kīrtiçeṣaṁ gatavati bhuvi Vikramāditye.

'Moisture is gone (eloquence is destroyed), the cranes sport not (new men plume themselves), the heron is gone (who devours not whom?), like a lake Vikramāditya hath left the earth, save indeed in fame.' Even on a larger scale it may be effective:

jīvākṛṣṭiṁ sa cakre mṛdhabhuvi dhanuṣaḥ çatrur āsīd gatāsur
lakṣāptir mārgaṇānām abhavad aribale tadyaças tena labdham
muktā tena kṣameti tvaritam aribalair uttamāṅgaiḥ praviṣṭā
pañcatvaṁ dveṣisainye gatam avanipatir nāpa saṁkhyāntaram.

'The king on the battlefield drew to himself the life (string) of his bow; yet the enemy perished. In the host of the foe suppliants received a lakh of gold (the king's arrows found their mark), yet the glory (due to them for generosity) was won by him. Thinking he had abandoned the earth, the foe swiftly

[1] For parallels cf. R. Köhler, *Kl. Schriften*, iii. 293 ff.; Zachariae, *Kl. Schriften*, pp. 205 f.

occupied it with their heads (the king losing patience, the foe was swiftly laid low with head on earth in death). The hostile host five times sought battle (met with death); the king needed no higher number (as all were disposed of).' Still, while this commingling of the pun, Çleṣa, and apparent incongruity, Virodha or Virodhābhāsa, is ingenious, it is clearly fatiguing when kept up. Still more irritating is the further development in the figure of exhaustive statement, Parisaṁkhyā, when it is intended to express by words not only their literal sense but a denial of what might be the sense if a pun were intended; thus in *netrotpāṭanam munīnām* we are to see the sense 'there was plucking out of roots in the case of wormwood trees only (for ascetics do not pluck out their eyes).' Sound effects are sometimes ingenious, as in the following Yamaka describing the wind: *āndolitakusumakesare keçareṇumuṣi raṇitamadhuramaṇīnāṁ ramaṇīnāṁ vikacakumudākare mudākare*, 'rocking the filaments of the flowers, stealing the pollen from the hair of fair damsels with sweet chiming jewels, expanding many a lotus, and causing delight.' But alliteration, Anuprāsa, can be merely tedious, as in the description of the Revā as: *madakalakalahaṅsasārasarasitodbhrāntabhāḥkūṭavikaṭapucchacchaṭāvyādhūtavikacakamalakhaṇḍavigalitamakarandabindusandohasurabhitasalilayā*, 'whose waters were fragrant by the many drops of juice fallen from the fragments of full-blown lotuses shaken by many a monstrous tail of fish scared by the notes, indistinct through passion, of the geese and herons.' It is clear that this is an utter abuse of language.[1] The work would indeed be unreadable, were it not for the care taken by the author to vary his long compounds by occasional short words in order to permit the reader to breathe and gain some comprehension of what has gone before, and notably in occasional short dialogue passages, as when he describes the talk of lovers at night, he realizes the necessity of the use of short sentences. But if his tale is of the genus Kathā, he does his best by length of compounds to establish the falsity of the suggestion of Ānandavardhana[2] that the compounds of Ākhyāyikās can be longer than those of the Kathā.

[1] Cf. Peterson's denunciation of the 'graceless string of extravagant and indecent puns'. Martial has equally been too freely censured for indecency, e.g. Teuffel-Schwabe, *Hist. Rom. Lit.*, § 322. 5.

[2] *Dhvanyāloka*, pp. 143 ff., cf. 134 ff.

6. *Bāṇa's Life and Works*

Bāṇa has most fortunately preserved for us some account of his fame by giving up the first two and a half chapters of his *Harṣacarita* to an account of himself and his family. He was a Brahmin of the Vātsyāyanas, whose mythical origin he depicts in detail; his great-grandfather Pāçupata had a son Arthapati who had eleven sons, of whom Citrabhānu married the Brahmin lady Rājyadēvi and had as son Bāṇa. His mother died young, and his father brought him up with tender care until, after his initiation at the age of fourteen, he died untimely; the history of this part of his life is hinted at in the touching picture at the beginning of the *Kādambarī* of the fate of the young parrot. After his father's death Bāṇa mixed, it is clear, in dubious company, though in part it was literary, including a poet in the vernacular (*bhāṣākavi*), Īçāna, the Prākrit poet Vāyuvikāra, two panegyrists, a painter, two singers, a music teacher, an actor, a Çaiva devotee, a Jain monk, a Brahmin mendicant, and many others. A fit of wandering seized him and he went far, acquiring evil repute in abundance. But by consorting with the wise and the good he claims to have redeemed a misspent youth, and finally returned to his home at Prītikūṭa. When there he received a royal summons through Kṛṣṇa, brother of Harṣavardhana, who as a friend warned him to make his peace with the king—which suggests that Bāṇa had been engaged in something worse than sowing wild oats. At any rate he went to the royal camp, and was received with marked coldness even according to his own account by the king, but shortly afterwards received the royal favour. That is all we know definitely of his fate in life. He proceeds to tell us that he recited the *Harṣacarita* because on a visit home he was asked to speak of the great king, but the story is unfinished, and what is more striking, the *Kādambarī* also is incomplete, though an end was made for it by his son Bhūṣaṇa Bhaṭṭa or Bhaṭṭa Pulina, who states that he did so because regret was felt at the incomplete condition of the work. It is by no means clear which of the two works really was written first, though there is a good deal to be said for the priority of the *Harṣacarita*. We may, however, believe that there was much touching-up of either tale during Bāṇa's lifetime.

Of Bāṇa's date we are approximately certain; he must have been fairly young when Harṣavardhana in his greatness patronized him, and we have no reason to suppose that he first became acquainted with the king early in his reign.[1] It is assumed in the *Harṣacarita* that the king disposed of his enemy, the Gauḍa king, and as reference is made to the king's vow to assume the garb of a Buddhist mendicant when he has punished his brother's murder, we may assume that Bāṇa was well aware of the Buddhist sentiments which Hiuen Tsang so fully records. We may hold, therefore, that Bāṇa wrote late in his reign, which ended in 647, and this is borne out by his mention of the *Vāsavadattā*, which he clearly imitated. Of the legend which makes him a son-in-law of the poet Mayūra we can find no confirmation in his narrative, for among his associates he merely mentions a snake-doctor Mayūraka, and it would be amazing if he really passed over without allusion his being his father-in-law. He was, it will be seen, a Brahmin of pure race, of means, and royal favour, but he was clearly far from bigoted; he presents to us abundant and detailed proof of the amity in which Buddhists and very many kinds of Hindu sectaries lived together, discussing and disputing, but without the rancour which the Chinese pilgrim's reports suggest sometimes showed itself against the Buddhists.

Besides his two romances, Bāṇa is credited with the *Caṇḍīçataka* and with the play *Pārvatīpariṇaya*. The feebleness of that work both in construction and style might have deterred critics from accepting the attribution, and in point of fact it is clear that it was the production of Vāmana Bhaṭṭa Bāṇa in the fifteenth century.[2] The ascription of the *Ratnāvalī* to him is also merely an idle surmise, for the limited imagination and restrained diction of the author of that piece are wholly unlike the over-fertile conception of Bāṇa and his amazing command of words. Later tradition recognized in him the poet who received, indeed, rich rewards from his royal patron, but whose picture of the king

[1] This is assumed by all who ascribe Bāṇa to *c.* A.D. 620. We cannot even say that he did not know of Pulakeçin's interruption of Harṣa's joy, recorded in an inscription of some poetic merit; EHI. p. 353.

[2] R. Schmidt, AKM. xiii. 4 (1917). He wrote a *Nalābhyudaya* (TSS. 3, 1913) and the romance, imitating Bāṇa, *Vemabhūpālacarita*.

lived on for ever, long after the elephants and the jewels given to the singer had passed into nothingness.[1]

7. *The Harṣacarita*

Bāṇa opens the *Harṣacarita*[2] by a brief summary in verse of the models in poetry whom he admired, the author of the *Bhārata*, the writer of *Vāsavadattā*, the prose of Haricandra—to us merely a name, Sātavāhana's treasure of song, the poem of Pravarasena, doubtless the *Setubandha* in Prākrit, Bhāsa's plays, Kālidāsa's flowers of speech, honey-sweet, and the *Bṛhatkathā*. He records the love of the north for plays on words, of the west for sense, of the south for poetical fancy, Utprekṣā, and of Gauḍa for pomp of syllables, and admits that it is hard to combine, what he evidently holds as ideal, a fresh subject-matter, a diction not common, double meanings obtained without forcing, a dominant sentiment clearly expressed, richness in sonorous words. Then he pronounces his purpose in a stanza often misunderstood:[3]

Āḍhyarājakṛtotsāhair hṛdayasthaiḥ smṛtair api
jihvāntaḥ kṛṣyamāṇeva na kavitve pravartate.

'The mighty deeds of my great king, which fill my heart though remembered only, restrain my tongue and forbid it to proceed to the poet's task.' This seems a clear intimation that he is to celebrate deeds of Harṣa which he heard of from others, but which none the less filled so fully his heart as almost to prevent utterance.

Bāṇa then proceeds in chapter i to relate the descent of his family and his own life to the end of his rash youth. Chapter ii carries us no further than the reception of the message and his journey to the royal camp, where he sees and admires so fully the points of the king's great steed that he can hardly exceed his accomplishment of hyperbole in his description of Harṣa himself. Chapter iii relates how Bāṇa, on a visit home, received

[1] Soḍḍhala, *Udayasundarīkathā*, p. 2; *Kāvyaprakāça*, i. 2; *Subhāṣitāvali*, 150.

[2] Ed. NSP. 1918; trans. E. B. Cowell and F. W. Thomas, London, 1897; ed. A. Führer, BSS. 1909; P. V. Kane, Bombay, 1918; S. D. and A. B. Gajendragadkar, Poona, 1919.

[3] Nobel (*Indian Poetry*, p. 179) still talks of Āḍhyarāja's *Utsāha*. Pischel (GN. 1901, pp. 485–7) first recognized him as Harṣa.

entreaties to tell of the king and how he complied. A long description of Sthāṇvīçvara, the capital of the race whence the king sprang, leads up to a eulogy of a mythical king Puṣpabhūti and an elaborate description of his friend and associate in adventure, Bhairavācārya. In chapter iv, after a vague allusion to the glorious kings sprung from Puṣpabhūti, we are abruptly carried to Prabhākaravardhana, whose great deeds are lightly alluded to, while the stress of the tale deals first with the queen's behaviour during the time when her first child was yet unborn, the mirth and wild revelry in the city when Rājyavardhana was born, the births of Harṣa and his sister Rājyaçrī, and the wedding of the latter to the Maukhari Grahavarman, evidently an event of great political importance to the family. With great skill, on this picture of happy wedlock and joyful celebration of a glad event follows a chapter of unrelieved tragedy. Rājyavardhana is bidden attack the Hūṇas and departs with his great host; Harṣa accompanies him, but is attracted to go hunting, whence he is rudely recalled by learning of the grave illness of his father. He comes back to find the whole capital convulsed with anxiety, and in a series of brilliant pictures we are shown the illness of the fevered king whose anguish nothing can relieve, the certainty of a fatal issue, the suicide of Harṣa's mother whence her son vainly would have stayed her, the final passing away of the great king after an oration to his son whose sincerity can be felt under the embroidery of Bāṇa's imagination, his obsequies, and the deep mourning of the prince. From this stupor he is aroused by the return of Rājyavardhana, who is eager to throw on Harṣa the duties of sovereignty and to abandon himself to grief; Harṣa urges constancy and resolve, and at the moment of indecision the dread news is brought; the Mālava king has slain Grahavarman and imprisoned Rājyaçrī. Rājyavardhana determines to proceed at once to punish the miscreant, commanding Bhaṇḍi to follow with 10,000 horse, and declining Harṣa's aid, lest it be doing too much honour thus to accumulate forces against so worthless a prince. Harṣa remains at home in gloom, swiftly to be deepened by the report of Rājyavardhana's success over the Mālava king but of his treacherous murder by a Gauḍa king; Harṣa would wage immediate war, but Skandagupta gives sage advice, reinforced as usual by many a parallel from legend; Harṣa obeys and prepares for war, while omens of evil menace the fate of his enemies. Chapter vii pictures in extraordinary vividness of detail the movements of an Indian army with its utter confusion, its vast masses of impedimenta, its countless camp-followers from the ladies of the court to the meanest hangers-on, the destruction wrought on the countryside, the vain claims of the landholders for exemption from pillage. We hear too of an ambassador from the king of Assam who tenders to the king a present of an umbrella of great beauty, and in due course the king reaches the Vindhya, again described in picturesque and minute detail. Chapter viii presents to us the figure of Nirghāta, a young mountaineer, who is to aid Harṣa in seeking in the Vindhya region for Rājyaçrī, who has escaped from her confinement and is believed to be wandering in that forest region. By his advice the king seeks the holy ascetic Divākaramitra, whose hermitage, with its pious animals who have imbibed the Buddhist faith, is brilliantly portrayed. The king asks his aid, and as the holy man is regretfully admitting that he has not heard of the princess an ascetic enters with the news that a lady is about to burn herself in despair, and asks the holy man to comfort her and stay her deed. The king rushes to find his sister on the point of perishing with her maidens; he restrains her and takes her to the sage. The princess begs to be allowed to end a life that now is worthless to her; the sage, however, with wise words restrains her action and bids her live as her brother begs. Harṣa then asks him to come with him and comfort and guide his sister while he carries out his vow of vengeance; this accomplished both will adopt the red garments of the faith. The sage gladly agrees; the party returns to the camp, and the book breaks off in a description of the advent of night while the tale of the recovery of Rājyaçrī is being told.

Historically we may say that the work is of minimal value, though in our paucity of actual records it is something even to have this. But chronology is weak and confused, it is extremely difficult to make out the identity of the king of Mālava,[1] and even the Gauḍa king is only indirectly indicated as Çaçāñka,

[1] Cf. Smith, EHI. pp. 350 ff.; R. Mookerji, *Harsha*, pp. 50 ff.

whose name is given by Hiuen Tsang.[1] Bāṇa has not attempted to make intelligible the course of events which rendered it possible for the Gauḍa king to come into hostile contact with Rājyavardhana in or near Mālava, and it is difficult not to suppose that he desired, writing at a considerable distance of time, to leave what was long past in a vague position. What he does supply to history is the vivid pictures of the army, of the life of the court, of the sectaries and their relations to the Buddhists, and the avocations of a Brahmin and his friends.

8. *The Kādambarī*

The *Harṣacarita* ranks as an Ākhyāyikā, and in fact it has been adopted as the model of that form by later writers on poetics such as Rājaçekhara. It is divided into Ucchvāsas, contains occasional verses, and if not narrated by the hero, Harṣa, is at least narrated by the sub-hero, Bāṇa himself, whose history takes up the first two and a half chapters. The *Kādambarī*, on the other hand, is a Kathā, and it lacks the distinctive marks of the Ākhyāyikā. In point of fact it has a complex structure of its own, for it consists of a long narrative in which are interwoven other narratives given by characters of the work. In a sense, therefore, if it were worth while seeking to fix terminology in a manner which was unknown to Indian writers, a Kathā might be deemed [2] a complex Ākhyāyikā, one in which a main narrative was the mode in which sub-narratives came to be set forth in due place. The essence of the form of the *Kādambarī* is the use of these sub-narratives to explain matters which the main narrator could not himself know; he does not gather all his information into a whole and set it out in an ordered fashion, but he allows us to have it as the matters came to the knowledge of his hero during the course of his actual experience. This is a definite and marked plan which makes the *Kādambarī* in point of structure very different from the *Daçakumāracarita* or a text like the *Pañcatantra*, in which sub-narratives are included. It may originally have been the plan of the *Bṛhatkathā* as Guṇāḍhya

[1] For a defence of him see Majumdar, *Early Hist. of Bengal*, pp. 16 ff.

[2] F. Lacôte, *Mélanges Lévi*, pp. 250 ff. For comments on the valueless distinctions in Indian writers, see Nobel, *Indian Poetry*, pp. 156 ff.; S. K. Dé, BSOS. iii. 507 ff., who themselves differ on one vital point, the content of the Kathā.

conceived it, though that characteristic is lost in the versions which have come down to us, and in any case it is very dubious if the same plan were ever systematically carried out in that work. But it is interesting to note how, in the *Kādambarī* and probably in the *Bṛhatkathā* tale whence the story is largely derived, we find the highest perfection of a manner beloved in India, the inclusion of one tale within another. In the logically simplest form we have it in the Jātaka style where a tale of old is led up to by a tale of to-day, and the story ends with the application to to-day of the legend of the past. In such works as the *Vetālapañcaviṅçatikā* there is a closer approach to the *Kādambarī* inasmuch as the tales of the Vampire are all connected with the main purpose of the king, and thus, though distinct in themselves, serve to help on one main purpose. In the *Pañcatantra* we reach a further improvement, for the stories, in themselves unconnected and many told to illustrate principles, are put in the mouths of the characters of the frame story, or in the case of narratives included in subordinate stories in the mouths of the persons of the latter. Yet a closer approach is achieved in the *Daçakumāracarita* in so far as the princes each narrate their own experiences, thus introducing a degree of life which is wanting in the other forms, for in the Jātakas, though the Bodhisattva tells a tale of what was really his past experience, it is not narrated in the first person. As the idea of the *Daçakumāracarita* is doubtless borrowed from the *Bṛhatkathā*, we have an additional proof of the free use there of this device of first-hand narrative which is still further developed in the *Kādambarī*,[1] because the whole of the tales told are essentially part of one complex action, unlike those of the princes of the romance of Daṇḍin. But in one respect there is more semblance of realism in the *Daçakumāracarita*; the *Kādambarī* places its main narrative in effect in the mouth of the sage Jābāli, who knows by his great insight the tale he relates; he places himself largely at the point of view of the hero Candrāpīḍa, but that prince is not actually the narrator. The adoption of this device had already taken place in the *Bṛhatkathā*, where we find a close

[1] Ed. P. Peterson, BSS. 1883; P. V. Kane, Bombay, 1920; trans. C. M. Ridding, 1906. V. 2 of the introduction is copied in a Pallava inscr. of Amarāvatī, *South Ind. Inscr.*, i. 26; Kielhorn, GN. 1903, pp. 310 f.

parallel in substance and form to the *Kādambarī* in the tale of king Sumanas. Doubtless both Somadeva and Kṣemendra may have been influenced by Bāṇa's work, and the latter certainly was, but there is no ground whatever to suspect that the Kashmirian compilers borrowed the tale from Bāṇa. In every respect the relation between what we can reconstruct as the original and Bāṇa is that of development and elaboration in the romance.

The poet opens his work with some stanzas in which he suggests that his Kathā is seeking favour by its novel subject and phraseology, its brilliant vivid descriptions, its resplendent similes and Dīpakas, figures where one word serves as predicate to series of clauses. We learn then of Çūdraka of Vidiçā on the Vetravatī river; to him a Caṇḍāla maiden of wondrous beauty brings a parrot, and after persuasion it tells the following narrative. In its youth it lost its mother and was tenderly reared, like Bāṇa, by its father, who was killed by a Çabara; the young parrot was taken by Hārīta to the hermitage of his father, Jābāli, who looks kindly at the bird and says that it is reaping the fruit of past misconduct. On entreaty Jābāli tells the tale which the parrot repeats. We hear of Tārāpīḍa of Ujjain and his minister Çukanāsa; the moon seems in a vision to enter the queen who bears a glorious son, Candrāpīḍa, while Çukanāsa is blessed with Vaiçampāyana, born of a lotus placed in his wife's bosom. The two grow up in loving amity; at sixteen, when both have been fully trained, they are brought home from the place in which they have spent their time, and Candrāpīḍa receives the gift of a wondrous horse, Indrāyudha, and from the queen a maiden Pattralekhā, a captive daughter of the king of Kulūta. With his steed to aid him and the sage counsel of Çukanāsa to guide him, he enters on a campaign of world conquest lasting three years. But one day, seeing a pair of Kinnaras[1], quaint semihuman animals, he pursues them so far that he is lost and arrives at a lovely lake graced by the presence of a lovelorn maiden, Mahāçvetā. On his persuasion she tells her tale in the first person. She is daughter of a Gandharva and an Apsaras; she had seen a beautiful ascetic boy, Puṇḍarīka, and his friend, Kapiñjala, learned that the former was the mind-born son of

[1] Cf. Foucher, *L'Art Gréco-Bouddhique du Gandhāra*, ii. 21 f.

Lakṣmī, goddess of beauty, and the ascetic Çvetaketu, had loved him, but too late to prevent his death from unfulfilled longing. At this point she faints but, revived by Candrāpīḍa, proceeds to the end. She had decided to die, but, as she was about to ascend the pyre a majestic figure descended from the sky, took up Puṇḍarīka's body and promised her reunion if she lived; hence her decision to live at lake Acchoda awaiting her beloved. We are then told how Candrāpīḍa learns of her friend Kādambarī of like descent, who will not wed because her friend remains a maiden; Mahāçvetā takes the prince with her to visit her friend, of whom Candrāpīḍa becomes deeply enamoured while she shares his love. But, before the two have plighted troth, Candrāpīḍa is compelled by a summons from his father to return, and, leaving Pattralekhā with Kādambarī for a few days, he hurries on, bidding Vaiçampāyana bring back his forces. He is received with joy at Ujjain, but is tormented by love, and gladly hears of his dear one from Pattralekhā; at this point Bāṇa's work ends and his son's continuation begins. Further news comes from Keyūraka, increasing Candrāpīḍa's desire to return to Kādambarī, but he must await Vaiçampāyana and the host. The latter comes, but the officers tell the sad tale of the fact that Vaiçampāyana had insisted on staying at the lake as one distraught; the king suggests that Candrāpīḍa has done him some wrong, but Çukanāsa hotly defends the prince and blames his son, while Candrāpīḍa is convinced that Vaiçampāyana is blameless. Permitted to seek him, he proceeds to the lake, and finds Mahāçvetā in even more profound grief than before. She narrates her tale: Vaiçampāyana had fallen in love with her, she, true to Puṇḍarīka, had repulsed him, and, wearied with his parrot repetitions of love, had cursed him to become a parrot, whereupon he had forthwith died. This is too much for Candrāpīḍa who dies straightway. Mahāçvetā mourns him, when Kādambarī with Pattralekhā enters, resolves on death, prepares the pyre, when a light breaks forth from the bed and a voice from heaven tells Mahāçvetā that Puṇḍarīka's body is incorruptible in heaven, while Kādambarī is to guard Candrāpīḍa's body until the curse which slew him is over. Pattralekhā, who had fainted, awakes, springs on Indrāyudha who is among the mourners, dashes into the lake whence emerges Kapiñjala. He now takes up the tale;

when Puṇḍarīka's body was carried away, he had followed and the Moon had deigned to explain the happening; dying, Puṇḍarīka had cursed him, though blameless, to suffer himself on earth the pangs of that love which was destroying him. He in turn has vowed that Puṇḍarīka should share his misfortunes and had taken the body away to keep until the appointed time of his own descent to earth. Kapiñjala was returning with this news, when he was cursed by a semidivine being, over whom he ran, to become a horse; on entreaty the curse was modified to end this condition on his master's death, and he learned that the Moon and Puṇḍarīka were about to be incarnated as Candrāpīḍa and Vaiçampāyana, and he as the horse Indrāyudha. So saying, Kapiñjala goes out to seek Çvetaketu's advice to end the curse; of Pattralekhā he knows nothing. Mahāçvetā and Kādambarī decided to spend the time together beside the body of the prince which became lovelier every day, and Tārāpīḍa and Çukanāsa with their wives joined in the vigil. Here ended Jābāli's tale, and the parrot knew the truth, that it was Vaiçampāyana dreeing the weird appointed for him. The impatient parrot desires to know its future fate, but is rebuked for its haste, and told that it would have as brief a life in its new condition as when Puṇḍarīka. It is consoled by the advent of Kapiñjala, sent to it by Çvetaketu with the news that he and Lakṣmī, ashamed of past neglect, are now engaged in sacrifice to end the curse, and that it must stay peacefully in the hermitage until the due season. Impatient, however, it flies off, is caught by a Caṇḍāla for his princess, who has brought it to the king; this is all it knows and here ends its tale, which the poet resumes. The Caṇḍāla maiden reveals herself as Lakṣmī, mother of the parrot, who had captured it to save it from the consequences of filial disobedience; she bids the king now quit this life and both he and the parrot at once perish, thus completing the human lives in which they had to suffer. At this moment Candrāpīḍa comes to life in Kādambarī's eyes, Puṇḍarīka descends from the sky, all are reunited, Candrāpīḍa places Puṇḍarīka on the throne, and in devotion to his parents spends his time partly at Ujjain, partly at Hemakūṭa, Kādambarī's parental home, and partly in the moon, his own abode, while Pattralekhā is revealed as Rohiṇī, best beloved of the queens of the Moon.

We can see from the *Kathāsaritsāgara*[1] that Bāṇa has followed in his part very faithfully the main outlines of the story, though the names in the two versions are quite different, and the Kashmirian version has the Himālaya and Vidyādharas for the more southern regions and Gandharvas and Apsarases of Bāṇa. Bāṇa, moreover, expands and duplicates; he creates the attractive character of Çukanāsa, wise and loyal, and brings Vaiçampāyana in as comrade of Candrāpīḍa; he has even two Kinnaras for the one of the tale, and develops the theme of his hero's birth as he does that of the children in the *Harṣacarita.* All his own are his brilliant descriptions and his elaborations of the signs of love in his hero and heroine. In the tale, however, after the prince's departure the princess, Makarandikā, annoys by her grief her parents so deeply that she is cursed to become a Niṣāda maiden, while her father it is who, ashamed of his action, dies and becomes the parrot, who repeats the tale of its own experiences and what it heard Pulastya recite to king Sumanas. At the court of that prince Somaprabha is reunited to the Niṣāda maiden, who resumes her true shape, and it is the king who is revealed as Raçmimant, mind-son of the sage Dīdhiti, and is united to Manorathaprabhā, while the parrot is released and reaps the fruit of its asceticism.

This is indeed a strange tale, and to those who have no belief in rebirth, or even in a reunion after this mortal life, its appeal must be gravely diminished, and the whole must seem rather a fantastic if not idle romance with uninteresting characters living in an unreal atmosphere. But from the point of view of Indian belief the case is far other, and the story may justly be deemed replete with the tenderness of human love, the beneficence of divine consolation, the pathos and sorrow of death, and the abiding hope of reunion after death as a result of unswerving fidelity to love. To Indian minds also there is a strong appeal in the element of the miraculous, nor to them is there anything save attraction in the wonderful history of the Moon and Puṇḍarīka, even the appearance of the latter in parrot form has nothing ludicrous when it is believed that human beings do pass from one body to another. Bāṇa's treatment of love is refined and graceful, and shows itself at its best in the scenes between

[1] lix. 22 ff.; *Bṛhatkathāmañjarī*, xvi. 183 ff.; Mańkowski, WZKM. xv. 213 ff.

Kādambarī and the prince; in his account of the feelings of Kādambarī from the time when she mounted the terrace of her palace to gaze on the prince, Bāṇa achieves a wonderful insight into the currents of youthful passion and virgin modesty which sway a girl's mind when first she is moved to love.[1] All credit is also due to him for his effective characterization of so many minor characters; to Tārāpīḍa, Vilāsavatī his queen, and, above all, to Çukanāsa he has imparted both life and colour, while the devotion of Pattralekhā is touchingly portrayed.

There is also no lack of movement, and Bāṇa is perfectly well aware of the advantage of contrast, as when he brings vividly before us the innocent life of the parrots under their Çalmalī tree or the peaceful quiet of Jābāli's hermitage, on the one hand, and the pomp and display of the courts of Çūdraka and Tārāpīḍa on the other. His sense of drama is revealed by the introduction with its brilliant portraits of Çūdraka and the Caṇḍāla maiden, while his love for nature and his close observation reveal themselves in his descriptions of the Himālaya, of lake Acchoda, of Mahāçvetā's abode, and in minor touches throughout. As in the *Harṣacarita* he blends description of nature's own beauties with those of the cities and works of men's hands, so we can set his pictures of palaces and towns against those of hermitage and country. The political insight which reveals itself in the discourses of the *Harṣacarita* is again exhibited in Çukanāsa's admonitions to the young prince, and the advice of Kapiñjala to Puṇḍarīka. We seem, however, to find a more mature view and a deeper insight into the springs of human action in the *Kādambarī* than in the *Harṣacarita*, supporting the conclusion as to the later date of the *Kādambarī*.

It would, however, be unfair to ignore the grave defects of Bāṇa, not merely in respect of style, but also of structure, for nothing will make the *Kādambarī* other than difficult to follow in its complex of past and present lives, and its lack of proportion; the descriptions are always overdone, especially in the case of Mahāçvetā and of the temple of Caṇḍikā; Bāṇa does not let his reader see the wood for the trees; in his devotion to the beauties of the evening or morning, or the rising of the moon, or the limbs of his heroine, he often loses sight of the plot itself.

[1] Cf. Apollonius Rhodius' view of Medea.

Of his son little need be said. He unquestionably is inferior to his father, even if we may excuse his hurried treatment of the remainder of the plot on the score of its inherent difficulties. He prolongs the description of Kādambarī's lovelorn condition out of reason, while he is deficient in his father's fertile imagination, and cannot draw on his wealth of mythological knowledge and observation of Indian flora and fauna. Moreover, he attempts no parallel to Çukanāsa's display of knowledge of life.

9. *Bāṇa's Style*

Weber,[1] who was rarely moved to wrath, made once a most effective protest against Bāṇa's defects of style; he condemned him, as compared with Daṇḍin, for a subtlety and tautology which were repugnant, the outrageous overloading of single words with epithets, the construction of sentences in which the solitary verb is held over for pages, the interval being filled by epithets and epithets upon these epithets, these epithets moreover frequently extending over more than a line in the form of compounds, so that Bāṇa's prose is an Indian wood where progress is impossible through the undergrowth until the traveller cuts out a path for himself, and where even then he is confronted by malicious wild beasts in the shape of unknown words to terrify him. The censure is just; Bāṇa revels in the construction of sentences consisting of heaped up epithets in compound form, throwing away all the advantages of an inflected language; moreover he loves to pile up in these compounds double meanings, and these he brings about repeatedly by the use of rare senses of ordinary words or the use of utterly abnormal phraseology. He shows his exact knowledge of grammar in many points, and adheres to the due use of the perfect, as against Subandhu who employs it as a narrative tense without the restriction of reference to matters not within the experience of him who uses it. His employment of the figures of speech is unwearying, and he is largely dominated by the desire to produce prose which shall be rhythmical. His long compounds are often clearly built up and interspersed with

[1] Accepted by M. R. Kāle, *Kādambarī*, p. 25. Weber's treatise on the romances is in *Ind. Streifen*, i. 308–86.

shorter words simply in order to achieve this effect which Daṇḍin and other writers of poetics extol under the style of Ojas, strength. Like other Indian authors he clearly attaches to this end an importance foreign to our conceptions, but part at least of his influence on later writers such as Dharmadāsa, Govardhana, and Jayadeva must be assigned to his sound effects as well as to his brilliance in figures of speech, to which they no doubt, from a modern point of view, attached undue merit. But it is fair to remember that Bāṇa is by no means without sense of propriety; he can resort to brief interchange of speeches when he deems it fit, Kapiñjala's advice to Puṇḍarīka is direct and forcible, and the ejaculations of the maidens of the queen Rājyaçrī when on the point of lighting the pyre, or of the dying king Prabhākaravardhana, are perfectly phrased. In its own way there is a model of force in the picture of the exclamations of the motley host of the royal army and the cries of the despairing villagers who are being plundered right and left. Nor is Bāṇa at all incapable of epigrammatic brevity, though unhappily he too rarely practises it.

The description of the doorkeeper,[1] a maiden, in the *Kādambarī* exhibits his normal style: *ekadā tu nātidūrodite navanalinadalasampuṭabhidi kiṁcidunmuktapāṭalimni bhagavati sahasramarīcimālini rājānam āsthānamaṇḍapagatam aṅganājanaviruddhena vāmapārçvāvalambinā kaukṣeyakeṇa saṁnihitaviṣadhareva candanalatā bhīṣaṇaramaṇīyākṛtir aviralacandanānulepanadhavalitastanataṭonmajjadairāvatakumbhamaṇḍaleva mandākinī cūḍāmaṇipratibimbacchalena rājājñeva mūrtimatī rājabhiḥ çirobhir uhyamānā çarad iva kalahaṅsadhavalāmbarā jāmadagnyaparaçudhāreva vaçīkṛtasakalarājamaṇḍalā vindhyavanabhūmir iva vetralatāvatī rājyādhidevateva vigrahiṇī pratīhārī samupasṛtya kṣititalanihitajānukarakamalā savinayam abravīt.* 'Once, when the sun, garlanded with a thousand rays, bursting open the fresh lotus buds, relaxing something of his ruddy hue, had risen no great space in the sky, to the king seated in the presence chamber, came the keeper of the door, and with bent knee and lotus-like hand touching the ground addressed his majesty. Her form was lovely, yet dread, even as a sandal plant wherein lurks

[1] For the representation of such a Yavanī in art see Foucher, *L'Art Gréco-Bouddhique du Gandhāra*, ii. 70 ff.

a snake, by reason of the sword which she wore at her left side, belying her womanhood; she was as it were the Ganges, her bosom whitened by sandal showing like the temples of Airāvata as he emerges from his bath; through her reflection in their crest jewels she was as it were an embodiment of the king's order, borne on the heads of obedient princes; by the whiteness of her robe which vied with the swans, she resembled the autumn when they return home; she conquered all the assembled kings as did the edge of Paraçurāma's axe; with the cane wand which she bore she resembled the Vindhya forest land, and she seemed none other than the guardian deity of the realm in human shape.' We would no doubt be unjust to Bāṇa if we held that he did not realize the humorous side of these exaggerations, just as he no doubt saw the comic aspect of the putting of his tale into the mouth of a parrot, and enjoyed as much as we should his remark on Skandagupta: *nṛpavaṅçadīrghaṁ nāsavaṅçaṁ dadhānaḥ*, 'with a nose as long as his sovereign's pedigree,' which has been solemnly censured by unimaginative stolidity. Against this peaceful picture we may set the striking picture of the return of Bhaṇḍi with the news of Rājyavardhana's death: *malinavāsā ripuçaraçalyapūritena nikhātabahulohakīlakaparikararakṣitasphuṭaneneva hṛdayena hṛdayalagnaiḥ svāmisatkṛtair iva çmaçrubhiḥ çucaṁ samupadarçayan dūrīkṛtavyāyāmaçithilabhujadaṇḍadolāyamānamaṅgalavalayaikaçeṣālaṁkṛtir anādaropayuktatāmbūlaviralarāgeṇa çokadahanadahyamānasya hṛdayasyāṅgāreṇeva dīrghaniçvāsaveganirgatenādhareṇa çuṣyatā svāmivirahavidhṛtajīvitāparādhavailakṣyād iva bāṣpavāripaṭalena paṭeneva prāvṛtavadanaḥ viçann iva*, 'His raiment was besmirched and he manifested his grief by his heart which was filled with the foe's darts and arrows, as though they were clamps of iron to restrain it from breaking, and his beard which lay over the heart on which his master's good deeds were engraved. On his long arm, relaxed from lack of exercise, was as sole ornament his lucky bracelet. His parched lip, faintly coloured through neglect of use of betel, protruded under the stress of his long sighs like a coal from a heart afire with sorrow, and he covered his face with a mantle of tears as though in shame for the sin of living when his master had fallen.' Yet Bāṇa can be brief, though he must be pointed, as in Harṣa's oath; *çapāmy āryasyaiva pādapāṅ-*

susparçena yadi pariganitair eva vāsaraiḥ sakalacāpacāpaladur-lalitanarapaticaraṇaraṇaraṇāyamānanigaḍāṁ nirgauḍāṁ na karomi medinīṁ tatas tanūnapāti pītasarpiṣi pataṅga iva pātakī pātayāmy ātmānam, 'By the dust of my noble one's feet I swear that, if I do not within a measured tale of days make the earth without a Gauḍa and cause it to resound with the fetters on the feet of kings made haughty by the elasticity of their bows, I will hurl myself, worthless as I shall be, like a moth on to a flame fed of oil.' Even in the death scenes of Harṣa's mother and father epigram must prevail: Prabhākaravardhana thus addresses his darling boy: *mahāsattvatā hi prathamam avalambanaṁ lokasya paçcād rājajīvitā. sattvavatāṁ cāgraṇīḥ sarvātiçayaçritaḥ kva bhavān kva vaiklavyam? kulapradīpo' sīti divasakarasadṛçatejasas te laghukaraṇam iva. puruṣasiṅho' sīti cauryapaṭuprajñopabṛṅhita-parākramasya nindeva. kṣitir iyaṁ taveti lakṣaṇākhyātacakra-vartipadasya punaruktam iva. gṛhyatāṁ çrīr iti svayam eva çriyā gṛhītasya viparītam iva*, 'Magnanimity is the mainstay of this world, next royal blood. How incompatible is weakness with thee who art the first of the magnanimous, endowed with every perfection? Shall I call thee lamp of our line? That were almost a making light of thee whose brilliance matcheth the sun. To call thee lion of men is as it were a censure to one whose prowess is manifested not alone in heroism but in keen intelligence. 'Twere tautology to say, "The earth is thine", when thou bearest the clear signs of imperial splendour to come. 'Twere contradiction to bid thee grasp the goddess fortune when she already hath thee in her embrace,' and so on until the poet grows weary, for there is no logical end to these elegancies. Rhythmical effects and alliterations abound and often are happy: *apratihataratharaṅhasā Raghuṇā laghunaiva kālenākāri kaku-bhāṁ prasādanam*, 'In a brief space with the irresistible onset of his chariot Raghu brought peace to the world.'

Bāṇa's fondness of figures is obvious, and metaphors, similes, seeming incongruity, exemplification, Sahoktis, as in the description of Rājyaçrī as *akulāṁ keçakalāpena maraṇopāyena ca*, 'bewildered with dishevelled locks and as to the means of death,' *dagdhāṁ caṇḍātapena vaidhavyena ca*, 'burnt with the fierce heat and the pains of widowhood', and others abound. Among his few verses is a fairly good example of lively fancy, Utprekṣā:

jayaty Upendraḥ sa cakāra dūrato: bibhitsayā yaḥ kṣaṇalabdhalakṣyayā
dṛçaiva kopāruṇayā ripor uraḥ: svayam bhayād bhinnam ivāsrapāṭalam.

'Supreme is that Upendra, who by his mere glance from afar which struck at once its mark with angry red, made the breast of his foe ruddy with gore as though in fear it had burst open of its own accord.' A good instance of hyperbole, Atiçayokti, is presented in his eulogy of his preceptor:

namāmi Bharvoç caraṇāmbujadvayaṁ: saçekharair Maukharibhiḥ kṛtārcanam
samastasāmantakirīṭavedikā-: viṭaṅkapīṭholluṭhitāruṇāṅguli.

'I revere the lotus feet of Bharvu, worshipped by the Maukhari princes with diadems on their heads, whose toes gleamed red as they moved on the lofty footstool formed by the crowns of all the feudatories of the realm.'

The number of verses used by Bāṇa is small, though less limited than in the case of Subandhu. Bāṇa does not observe the rule laid down by Bhāmaha[1] that the Ākhyāyikā should contain at the beginning of each Ucchvāsa Vaktra and Aparavaktra verses announcing the subject of the chapter. The first Ucchvāsa of the *Harṣacarita* has an introduction on poetry; the others have two verses, but the form is either two Āryās or a Çloka and an Āryā. In the body of the chapters we have an Aparavaktra in i; three stanzas Vasantatilaka, Çārdūlavikrīḍita and Aparavaktra in ii; two pairs, Āryā and Sragdharā in iii; a pair of verses, Vaktra and Aparavaktra, and a detached Āryā in iv; a Çloka and an Aparavaktra in v; and an Āryā in vi; the last two have no inserted verses. The Vaktra of Bāṇa is not the Çloka as in the metrical textbooks, but a sort of Çloka with a spondee at the close of the even lines. The *Kādambarī* after its verse prelude is essentially in prose.

[1] i. 26. Nobel (*Indian Poetry*, pp. 178, 187) argues that both Daṇḍin and Bhāmaha cannot have known Bāṇa's work; as regards Bhāmaha this can hardly be true in respect of time, but he may have lived far away. In Rudraṭa we have accounts of the Kathā (xvi. 20–3) and Ākhyāyikā (xvi. 24–30) which obviously are based on Bāṇa; cf. S. K. Dé, BSOS. iii. 514 f.

XV

THE LATER ROMANCES AND THE CAMPŪS

1. *The Romances*

BĀṆA has set a model which it was easy to admire, but infinitely hard to follow with any success, and in fact we have nothing later which can be set for a moment beside him. Criticism[1] of him was not specially intelligent; he was classed with Çīlābhaṭṭārikā, one of the few poetesses of India who used Sanskrit, as a model of the Pāñcāla style, in which sense and sound were of equal importance, an assertion in no sense true. He found an imitator in Dhanapāla, son of Sarvadeva, and brother of Çobhana; he lived under the patronage of Sīyaka and Vākpati of Dhārā, though Merutuñga[2] places him also at Bhoja's court and tells us a tale of his dispute with his family and final reconciliation to his brother. He wrote in A.D. 972-3 the Prākrit lexicon, *Pāiyalacchī*, and, after becoming a Jain, the *Ṛṣabhapañcāçikā* in fifty Prākrit stanzas. His romance is styled *Tilakamañjarī*[3] after the heroine, and it has clearly been his aim to seek to draw as many parallel pictures to those of the *Kādambarī* in describing this lady's love of Samaraketu. He recognizes his debt, and perhaps that is the best that can be said of him.

Another Jain effort to rival the *Kādambarī* is seen in the *Gadyacintāmaṇi*[4] of Oḍayadeva, alias Vādībhasiṅha, a lion to the elephants of counter disputants. He was a Digambara Jain, pupil of Puṣpasena, whom he lauds in the usual exaggerated style, and his work deals with the legend of Jīvaka or Jīvandhara, which is also the topic of the *Jīvandharacampū*. His imitation of Bāṇa is flagrant, including an effort to improve on the advice given by the sage Çukanāsa to the young Candrāpīḍa. Other Jain

[1] Kane, *Kādambarī*, p. xxv.

[2] *Prabandhacintāmaṇi*, pp. 60 ff. (trans. Tawney).

[3] Ed. KM. 85, 1903. Cf. Jacobi, GGA. 1905, p. 379.

[4] Ed. Madras, 1902. Cf. Hultzsch, IA. xxxii. 240; ZDMG. lxviii. 697 f.

Kathās hardly attempt, and certainly do not reach, the stage of comparison with the true romances.[1]

2. *The Campūs*

The romances contain here and there a few stanzas but they are normally and effectively in prose, and the literary compositions styled Campūs, a name of unknown sense, differ vitally from them in that they use prose or verse indifferently for the same purpose. In this Campūs differ from other forms of literature in which verse is mingled with prose; the verses in these cases are either gnomic, or they serve to summarize the context of the story, as do the title verses of the *Pañcatantra*, or occasionally they appear to lend greater effect to some point in the narrative as when a short speech is made in pointed form, or a specially important idea is thus underlined. But it was not surprising that the use of verse freely side by side with prose should occur, especially when works could be written in either indifferently, and we have in the *Jātakamālā*, on the one hand, and in the inscription of Hariṣeṇa on the other, clear cases of something which may be deemed fairly like the Campū, and Oldenberg[2] has adduced analogous cases in the Jātaka book. But it is only from a late period that we have works written in the full Kāvya style in which the poet shows now his ability in prose and now in verses, without seeking to reserve verses for any special end.

The oldest extant is probably the *Damayantīkathā*[3] or *Nalacampū* of Trivikrama Bhaṭṭa, whom we know as the author of the Nausari inscription of the Rāṣṭrakūṭa king Indra III in A.D. 915, and who is also mentioned as author of the *Madālasācampū*. The tale runs that his father Devāditya, a court Paṇḍit, was absent from his post when a rival came forward to challenge him, with the result that the son aided by Sarasvatī composed the *Nalacampū*, which was left unfinished because his father returned and rendered his son's action needless. The story is

[1] On the fragmentary *Avantisundarī* ascribed to Daṇḍin—wrongly—see S. K. Dé, IHQ. i. 31 ff.; iii. 395 ff.

[2] GN. 1918, pp. 429 ff.; 1919, pp. 61 ff.

[3] Ed. NSP. 1885. He was of the Çāṇḍilya family and son of Nemāditya (EI. ix. 28).

elaborated with the usual defects of long sentences, consisting of epithets heaped on epithets in long compounds, with double meanings, alliterations and jingles complete. The author mentions Bāṇa, and himself is referred to in the *Sarasvatīkaṇṭhābharaṇa.* His verses are no more than mediocre; there is the usual combination of simile with a double meaning in his critique of poets given in anthologies:

apragalbhapadanyāsā jananīrāgahetavaḥ
santy eke bahulālāpāḥ kavayo bālakā iva.

'Some poets are like children; their diction is as tottering as their feet, they disgust people (they cause delight to their mothers), they chatter much (they have many endearments).' This is clearly frigid, and his elaborate stanzas are still less attractive.

To a Jain of the same century, a contemporary of the Rāṣṭrakūṭa Kṛṣṇa and protégé of his feudatory, a son of the Cālukya Arikesarin II, we owe the much more important work, *Yaçastilaka*,[1] written in 959. Somadeva was a Digambara Jain and he wrote, as did all Jains, with an eye to the salvation of mankind by means of the Jain faith, and in fact the last three sections of his book serve as a manual of lessons for laymen. The tale itself, however, is not at all dull. In the rich Yodheya country there was a city Rājapura ruled by Māridatta, a sensualist, who has decided on the advice of his family priest to offer to the goddess of the family, Caṇḍamāri-devatā, a pair of all living things, including human beings. He is ready to sacrifice when there come before him an ascetic pair, boy and girl, who have been induced to come to the place of sacrifice; at the sight of them the darkness passes away from his mind. At this point the author, with an awkward transition, explains their presence; an ascetic, Sudatta, has just arrived at the outskirts of the town, and rejecting a garden for its encitements to love, and a burning place as needlessly repulsive, has taken up his abode on a small hill. In his train are two young people, the children of Māridatta's own sister by Yaçomati, son of king Yaçodhara, and the sage, knowing the future, sends them where he knows the royal guards will accost them and take them to the king for sacrifice.

[1] Ed. KM. 70, 1901–3. Cf. Peterson, *Report*, ii. pp. 33 ff.

The king, however, treats them with honour, having bethought him that his niece and nephew were reported to have adopted the ascetic life, and questions them as to their history. In Āçvāsa ii the youth, who enjoys like his sister the rare gift of knowledge of past births, tells a curious tale. There was a king of Ujjain, Yaco'rtha,[1] and his wife Candramatī bore him a son, Yaçodhara, whom on the sight of his whitening hair the father placed on the throne, retiring to contemplation. The life of Yaçodhara is described, and the poet displays his knowledge of policy in conversation between the king and a minister, in which are set out with legendary examples the fate of kings who choose bad ministers, and of kings who cast aside their faithful servants. Yaçodhara seems ideally happy, he delights in the Veda of the bow, but one night he finds that his wife leaves his side for a guilty intrigue. He meditates slaying her, but is deterred by the scandal, and his mother, who suspects the truth, seeing his sudden aversion to life, counsels him to perform a sacrifice including the slaughter of all kinds of animals. The king, however, will have nothing to do with sacrifices destructive of life, and there ensues a polemic between him and his mother on the Jain faith, to which she realizes that he is tending. He argues, however, that offerings to the dead are absurd, and that crows are the real recipients of the bounty tendered, while the idea of water as purifying is ridiculed. A vast array of poetical authority is adduced by the king, who quotes almost all the great poets down to Rājaçekhara, and the queen, perhaps wearied by his eloquence, compromises on a cock of flour. The wicked wife, however, sees her chance, insists on cooking the mixture, inserts poison and ends the mother and son alike (iii). In Āçvāsa iv we have the account of the fate of the mother, son, and wife in later births as the result of their crimes, the slaying even of an effigy of a cock being a sin. The wicked wife repeats in these rebirths her evil deed. At last, however, the cycle is complete, and the mother and son are reborn, with knowledge of the past as the twin children of Yaçomati and the sister of Māridatta. Needless to say, the king is now induced (v) to take instruction from Sudatta, and in the end is converted along with the goddess and his people.

[1] Hertel (*Pāla und Gopāla*, pp. 81 ff.) summarizes the parallel works of Māṇikya Sūri and Vādirāja Sūri. His Yaçogha (p. 92) may be an error.

While it can hardly be said that Somadeva complies with the principle laid down in such late works as the *Sāhityadarpaṇa*,[1] that verse should be used for passages where sentiment is to be prominently expressed (*sarasaṁ vastu*), since he often employs it without much impressment, it is certain that he is a poet of taste and good sense. His defence of critics against ignorance of poetry because they are not composers is:

avaktāpi svayaṁ lokaḥ kāmaṁ kāvyaparīkṣakaḥ
rasapākānabhijño 'pi bhoktā vetti na kiṁ rasam?

'Though people in general cannot express themselves, still they are good judges of poems. Though one has no skill in the art of producing sweet flavours, does not he who partakes of food know them perfectly well?' The king's commonsense is clear:

saritsarovāridhivāpikāsu: nimajjanonmajjanamātram eva
puṇyāya cet tarhi jalecarāṇāṁ: svargaḥ purā syād itareṣu paçcāt.

'If descent into and emerging from river, lake, sea, or tank, were enough for salvation, then heaven would belong preeminently to those that dwell in the water, and secondarily only to other creatures.' The king's joy in the bow is well expressed:

yāvanti bhuvi çastrāṇi teṣāṁ çreṣṭhataraṁ dhanuḥ
dhanuṣāṁ gocare tāni na teṣāṁ gocare dhanuḥ.

'Of all the weapons on earth the bow hath preeminence; it reacheth all, but none can attain it.' The folly of human desire is repeatedly derided as in:

tvam mandiradraviṇadāratanūdvahādyais: tṛṣṇātamobhir anubandhibhir astabuddhiḥ
kliçnāsy aharniçam imaṁ na tu citta vetsi: daṇḍaṁ Yamasya nipatantam akāṇḍa eva.

'O heart, thou dost torment thyself night and day, fettered by the darkness of desire for home, wealth, wife, and child, and dost

[1] vi. 336 (332) reading *padyair* with Peterson, *Report*, ii, p. 34. There is a *v. l. gadyair* (Nobel, *Indian Poetry*, p. 168, who has overlooked Peterson's view). The sense is dubious; Peterson's view is that the definition of Kathā has this work or type in view.

heed not that the rod of Death is falling even now all unexpected upon thy head.'

Another Jain Campū known to us is the *Jīvandharacampū*[1] of Haricandra, which is based on the *Uttarapurāṇa* of Guṇabhadra, and cannot be before A.D. 900. Whether this writer is the same as the Haricandra, the Digambara, who wrote the *Dharmaçarmābhyudaya* in twenty-one cantos, must remain uncertain, but that author copied both Māgha and Vākpati, and thus there is no chronological difficulty in the suggestion. Both works are of the type of respectable dullness.

Of Brahmanical Campūs one, the *Rāmāyaṇacampū*,[2] is ascribed to Bhoja and Lakṣmaṇa Bhaṭṭa; there is a *Bhāratacampū*[3] by Ananta, in twelve Stabakas, of uncertain date. More definitely dated is the *Udayasundarīkathā*[4] of Soḍḍhala, a Vālabha Kāyastha of Lāṭa, who wrote *c.* A.D. 1000 under the patronage of king Mummuṇirāja of the Konkan. The model of the writer was the *Harṣacarita* of Bāṇa, and in imitation of him he gives not merely facts regarding his own lineage, but also some twenty-five stanzas on earlier poets. Of Bāṇa he says:

Bāṇasya Harṣacarite niçitām udīkṣya: çaktiṁ na ke 'tra kavitāstramadaṁ tyajanti?

'Who, seeing the sharp spear of Bāṇa in his *Harṣacarita*, would not lose all delight in the arms of poetry?' There is, however, little sign of keen insight in his verse, and he merely utters, as a rule, some vague generality as in:

babhūvur anye 'pi Kumāradāsa-: Bhāsādayo hanta kavīndavas te yadīyagobhiḥ kṛtināṁ dravanti cetāṅsi candropalanirmalāni.

'Others, too, there were, Kumāradāsa, Bhāsa among them, moons of poetry through whose words the hearts of the makers, pure as the moon stone, are made to melt.'

Late, but of special interest are the *Svāhās[udh]ākaracampū*[5] of Nārāyaṇa written in the seventeenth century, which describes

[1] Ed. Tanjore, 1905. Cf. Hultzsch, IA. xxxv. 268.

[2] Ed. NSP. 1907. The *Navasāhasāṅkacarita* of Çrīharṣa was a Campū (*Naiṣ.* xxii. 51).

[3] Ed. Madras and Bombay, 1903.

[4] Cf. *Kāvyamīmāṅsā* (GOS.), pp. xii f.; ed. *Gaekwad's Or. Series*, 1920.

[5] Ed. KM. iv. 52 ff.; Pischel, *Die Hofdichter des Lakṣmaṇasena*, p. 29.

the loves of Agni's wife Svāhā and the Moon in an idyllic manner which has been compared by Pischel with Homer's picture[1] of the loves of Ares and Aphrodite, and the *Çañkaracetovilāsacampū*,[2] written by a poet Çañkara in honour of Cetasiṅha, whose name figures prominently in the transactions of Warren Hastings. Of these poems the former is admittedly a product of the art of extempore composition (*āçukavitā*), of which poets were inordinately and most foolishly proud.

[1] *Od.* viii. 266 ff.

[2] Aufrecht, *Bodl. Catal.*, i. 121. For other texts cf. *Madras Catal.*, xxi. 8180 ff.

XVI

THE AIMS AND ACHIEVEMENT OF SANSKRIT POETRY

1. *The Aims and Training of the Poet*

INDIAN poets and authors of works on poetics are in substantial agreement in their views of the poet's purpose.[1] The two great ends which appeal to them are the winning of fame and the giving of pleasure; even after the poet has gone to heaven, Bhāmaha says, his body remains on the earth, pure and pleasant in the shape of his poem. No doubt other ends may be added; Bhāmaha himself mentions skill in regard to duty, practical life, love, and final release, and in the arts, but these are merely subsidiary matters, which can be gained by other means and are not therefore worthy of mention. Nor is instruction a necessary part of the aim of the poet, though it may be designed by him; if this is his purpose he serves the purpose of the persuasion of a lovely lady as opposed to the religious teachers who can command or the authors of scientific treatises who advise as friends. The pleasure of poetry accrues to the reader or auditor; when pressed, Indian theory does not admit that the pleasure lies in the creation; it is appreciated by the poet when, his work accomplished, he becomes the critic and in this capacity partakes of the sentiment which, relished, is the purest form of delight. We have here a parallel to the doctrine that it is the spectator, not the actor, who enjoys the sentiment of a drama.

If, however, the poets desired their own fame, they were conscious that they could not achieve it without patronage, and this was naturally to be sought primarily from the king, or failing him from some rich patron. The motives which should influence kings are expressed repeatedly and most effectively. The glory of ancient kings, Daṇḍin assures us, mirrored in speech, endures after they have passed away; the fruits of men's deeds, heaven

[1] F. W. Thomas, *Bhandarkar Comm. Vol.*, pp. 397 ff. Cf. above, chap. ii, § 5.

&c., may pass away, says Rudraṭa, but the poet can preserve their names for ever, and Kalhaṇa, as we have seen, is most emphatic on this score.[1] In Rājaçekhara we have the utmost insistence on the duty of the king, both in regard to poetry and the sciences; he is to hold a formal durbar at which a vast array of poets and others are to be present and to examine the merit of the work presented for consideration, and he should reward poets according to their merits, following the example of Vāsudeva, Sātavāhana, Çūdraka, and Sāhasāñka. He is also to set up assemblies of Brahmins, Brahmasabhās, in the great cities of the realm in order to have tests applied to works presented there for approval, and we have given to us lists of the great poets Kālidāsa, Meṇṭha, Amara, Rūpa, Sūra,[2] Bhāravi, Haricandra, Candragupta, acclaimed at Ujjain, while the writers of Çāstras, Upavarṣa, Varṣa, Pāṇini, Piñgala, Vyāḍi, Vararuci, and Patañjali, were approved at Pāṭaliputra. The *Bhojaprabandha*, though late and unhistorical, presents us with amusing pictures of such contests at court, and similar pictures are drawn in the *Prabandhacintāmaṇi*, showing that Rājaçekhara's ideal was not seldom realized, while a more formal picture of a Sabhā is given by Mañkha. Nor need we doubt that the relation between poet and king was happy for both; if Bāṇa's wealth through the generosity of Harṣa was famous, there is much truth in the anonymous poet who asks where are departed the loads of gold, the rutting elephants bestowed by the great king on Bāṇa's merits, whereas his glory limned in the poet's flowing verses will not pass away even at the aeon's waning.

Poets, of course, hoped that kings would be men of taste, but they remembered also that they sought a wider audience than kings, and that to be permanent in renown they must capture the fancy of the man of taste (*rasika*) whose expert judgement would test their works. Such a man is one who has deeply studied poetry so that there is no flaw in the mirror of his mind, and who can thus by reason of sympathy identify himself with the writer's aim. Such a man will feel his heart stirred as by the drinking of much wine when he hears a true poem; his hair will thrill, his head tremble, his cheeks redden, his eyes fill with tears, his voice falter

[1] Cf. *Subhāṣitāvali*, 150, 160, 167, 186.

[2] Perhaps Ārya Çūra.

when he seeks to repeat the poet's words.[1] And, as we have seen, these effects the true poet will experience in himself when he places himself in the position of a reader, and thus enjoys objectively and dispassionately the aesthetic pleasure of his own creations.

But to produce such fine poetry is the result of many factors. There must be genius (*pratibhā*), there must be culture (*vyutpatti*), there must be practice (*abhyāsa*); Daṇḍin, indeed, disagreeing with others like Bhāmaha, insists that even in the absence of genius or fancy, much may be accomplished by dint of the other two, and all are agreed in demanding the combination of all three for the highest poetry. The idea that from a simple uncultured soul there might well up a stream of poetry limpid and undefiled would certainly not have appealed to Sanskrit poets, and the writers on poetics demand from them, and they take pains to show that they possess, a vast fund of useful information. Vāmana gives us a quite clear list of what a poet requires to know. He must have worldly knowledge, understand what is possible or not; he must be a master of grammar, must know the correct meanings of words as shown in dictionaries; must study metrics; must be expert in the arts, including singing, dancing, and painting; and study the Kāmaçāstra, so as to be aware of the usages of love. Again, he must study politics, so as to know what is policy and the reverse, and to gather propriety of incident. These, however, are by no means all the duties of the poet. He has certain miscellaneous matters still to attend to: he must make himself acquainted with existing poetry, practise the writing of poems or at least parts of poems, show reverent obedience to masters who instruct him in the art of poetry, practise the choosing of the right word which when found could not possibly be changed without injury to the poem. His talent must be concentrated by attention to his aim, and for this purpose the early morning is the best, a doctrine which may be supported by the testimony of Kālidāsa and Māgha.

Refinements on the doctrine of the sources of poetry yield little of value. Rājaçekhara[2] discusses the function of imagination (*pratibhā*) as creative or discriminative, a distinction which

[1] *Subhāṣitāvali*, 158, 163, 165. The importance of inspiration is recognized in Buddhist tradition, *Aṅguttara Nikāya*, ii. 230, where poets are classed on the basis of reflection, study, subject-matter, or inspiration.

[2] *Kāvyamīmāṅsā*, iv.

really deals with the distinction between the power to create and the power of appreciation. Kālidāsa is cited as discriminating between the two capacities. Rājaçekhara is also interesting for his picture of the poet, who is essentially to be a man of fashion and wealth. His house is to be well garnished, with rooms meet for each season, a shady garden with lakes, ponds, a pavilion, a bathing-place, a palanquin, swans, and Cakora birds. The poet must be pure in speech, mind, and body; he is to have short-clipped nails, be anointed, wear a splendid but not gaudy garment, chew betel after meals. His retinue must match his elegance; the menials shall speak Apabhrança, the maids Māgadhī, the ladies of the harem Sanskrit and Prākrit, his friends all languages; his writer should have the same capacity and be himself a poet. Some even might go so far as to insist on special rules of speech in the household, like the Magadhan Çiçunāga who prohibited the use of cerebrals save *ṇ*, sibilants and *kṣ* in his hearing, while Kuvinda of Çūrasena would not have harsh consonants used, Sātavāhana of Kuntala insisted on Prākrit only, Sāhasāñka of Ujjain demanded Sanskrit from his court. The poet's day is neatly divided; he is to rise early, pay devotion to Sarasvatī, goddess of learning, study sciences and their accessories, then give a period to composition, take his midday meal, thereafter engage in a discussion on his poem or poetry in general (*kāvyagoṣṭhī*), later examine his poem with some intelligent friends, in the evening repeat his worship of the goddess, and in the early part of the night write out his final version. All this, of course, is somewhat tainted with artificiality, but everywhere in Rājaçekhara, as in his distinction of poets according to the part played by science in their works, we are faced with the fact that poetry was essentially a learned pursuit, the product of much cultivation.

Rājaçekhara devotes much attention to an issue which his predecessors less completely discuss, the issue of the borrowing of phrases and ideas by one poet from another. Ānandavardhana [1] is not anxious for overmuch borrowing; the province of poetry is unlimited, though for centuries hundreds of poets have been writing. There may be resemblances between the works of two inspired poets; of such similarities we must disapprove those in

[1] iii. 12 f.

which we have such a relation as that of a thing and its image, or an object and a picture thereof, but similarity such as exists between two men is not to be condemned. Rājaçekhara[1] gives us divergent views on the issue of borrowing phrases or part or even the whole of a stanza, and though he discriminates between mere stealing and appropriation his views turn out to be lax. He cites indeed the excellent maxim that while other thefts pass away by lapse of time the theft of words endures even to sons and grandsons, but only to cite his wife Avantisundarī's excuses for appropriation, whether in words or matter. Thus he may say, 'I have a reputation, he has none; I enjoy a secure position, he is a climber; this is inappropriate in him, appropriate in me, his words are like a tonic, mine like wine, that is, our styles are different; he ignores specialities of dialect, I attend to them; no one knows that he is the author; the author lives a long way off; the book he wrote is obsolete; this is the work of a mere barbarian.' These excuses were evidently duly availed of by later writers in Sanskrit, and they are too well known in modern practice to render serious condemnation in point. Rājaçekhara's own view is stated in the doctrine that 'there is no poet that is not a thief, no merchant that does not cheat, but he flourishes without reproach who knows how to hide his theft. One poet is a creator, another an adapter, another a coverer up, another a collector. He who here sees something new in word, sense, phrase, and writes up something old, may be accounted a great poet.' As regards theft of matter Rājaçekhara propounds a doctrine which attained acceptance, and is summed up by Hemacandra.[2] The relation of imaging is condemned, being defined as 'the case where the sense is entirely the same but there is a setting in other expressions. In the case of the copy the subject is made to appear different by a moderate elaboration of particulars, and this is a superior form to the previous. Corporeal resemblance is the case where, with difference of subject, there is apprehension of identity because of great similarity; even clever poets produce such works. In the form named 'foreign city entrance', there is identity in substance, but the garnishing is widely different and even excellent poets adopt this mode. There

[1] *Kāvyamīmāṅsā*, xi ff.; cf. Kṣemendra, *Kavikaṇṭhābharaṇa*, ii. 1.

[2] *Kāvyānuçāsana*, pp. 8 ff.

is, of course, another side to this process; Bāṇa distinctly condemns in the preface to his *Harṣacarita* the poet who modifies phrases and hides the signs of authorship, as a thief, worthy of condemnation.[1]

The process of copying, of composing verses for practice in metre without much regard to sense, and the working up of commonplaces, resulted in a large number of poetical conventions being established, which the Kāvyas repeat almost mechanically; the Cakravāka bird is parted at night from its mate and affords a constant reminder of human suffering; the Cakora is fabled to subsist on the moonbeams, and its eyes redden at the sight of poisoned food; the Cātaka drinks the waters of the clouds alone; the Haṅsa discriminates milk in water; fame and laughter alike are white; affection is redness; darkness can be handled; the mouth of envy is two-tongued and filled with poison, the toe-nails of the king are burnished by the crest jewels of the vassals who lie prostrate at his feet; the day lotuses close their calyx eyes in the evening; the Açoka blooms beneath the touch of the beloved's foot, and a large number of *motifs* are rehandled by poet after poet. Rājaçekhara[2] deals fully with these poetic conventions, which he prosaically explains as really due to observations made at different places and times from ours. Thus we find the rule that lotuses always exist in rivers, swans only in water, every mountain has gold and jewels; or, again, facts are ignored, as when the jasmine is denied the right to exist in spring, sandal trees are said to have neither flowers nor fruit, and Açokas denied fruit. Or, again, there are artificial restrictions on the existence of things; dolphins exist only in the ocean, pearls only in Tāmraparṇī. He illustrates the same style of conventions for substances, actions, qualities, and gives us the characteristics of the seasons as they are established by the poets. There is also much repetition of wider ideas, and interesting collections have already been made of variant treatments of ideas in Hindu fiction: such *motifs* are the art of entering another's body, the laugh and cry *motif*, talking birds, the act of truth, the Dohada or craving of pregnant women, false ascetics and spurious nuns, the Joseph and Potiphar *motif*, the idea of avoiding fate, the

[1] Cf. Someçvara, *Surathotsava*, i. 37, 39.

[2] *Kāvyamīmāṅsā*, xiv ff.

fable of the crow and the palm tree, change of sex, and many others important or trivial.[1]

Another fact of importance in the development of Sanskrit literary taste was the fondness for the composition of poetry *ex tempore* or at least on a given theme with the least possible delay. This device might easily lead to undue regard for a complete and ready command of conventions enabling the poet to turn out verses with the greatest possible speed. The praise bestowed on the quick-writing poet Çīghrakavi [2] to us must seem exaggerated, but the existence of the feeling is clearly attested. Less reprehensible as an essay in poetic skill was the practice of Samasyāpūraṇa,[3] when a poet constructed a stanza usually on a single line given to him. Tradition ascribes proficiency in this amusement even to Kālidāsa.

2. *The Achievement*

It is easy to see the defects in Sanskrit poetry and still easier to exaggerate them. The difficulty of the language is added to by the elaboration given to it by poets who were writing always for highly cultured audiences and who had no chance of winning reputation and wealth by anything that was commonplace or simple. The long compounds which are affected by some poets even in verse and which are *de règle* in poetic prose are sometimes obscure; they are always a barrier to quick comprehension by all who are not deeply imbued with the spirit of the Kāvya literature. The elaborate alliterations and assonances which had to the Indian ear a definite aesthetic relation to the sense conveyed are less easy for us to appreciate, especially as the blending of sound and sense has been less eagerly pursued and much less successfully attained by western poets, so that we are apt to dismiss as pedantic the careful rules of the writers on poetics who came to divide styles largely on the basis of sound effects.

[1] Bloomfield, JAOS. xxxvi. 54–89; PAPS. lvi. 1–43; *Festschrift Windisch*, pp. 349–61; Burlingame, JRAS. 1917, pp. 429–67; Bloomfield, JAOS. xl. 1–24; xlii. 202–42; TAPA. liv. 141–68; Brown, JAOS. xlvii. 3–24; AJP. xlvii. 205 n.

[2] Cf. *Nalacampū*, p. 16; Someçvaradeva's Praçasti, 114 (EI. i. 21); *Gītagovinda*, i. 4.

[3] *Kāmasūtra*, p. 33; *Çārṅgadhara Paddhati* xxxii; Merutuṅga and Ballālasena give many examples; Aufrecht, ZDMG. xxvii. 51.

Moreover, the love of double meanings, which is essential in Subandhu and Bāṇa and much loved by many other poets, is perplexing, and demands from us an intellectual strain which was doubtless not exacted from the select coteries who admired the poems when they were first produced. Nor is it easy for us to appreciate the constant effort slightly to improve on phrases and ideas which have been given currency by an earlier poet, an attempt which is unquestionably apt to lead to forced uses of language and lack of simplicity. Still less of course can we appreciate those tricks in poetic form and grotesque experiments in the use of but one or two letters to make up the consonants in a line which Bhāravi and Māgha, not to mention minor poets, were willing to carry out. Nor does the elaboration of the poetic vocabulary, based largely on the free use of poetical dictionaries, appeal to us, and the rich variety of conventional ornaments unquestionably soon palls.

Apart from defects of style we miss in Sanskrit literature the revelation of personal character by the poets in their poems; Sappho, Catullus, Lucretius, distant as they are from us, produce an impression infinitely more vivid than does any Sanskrit poet. Those that have come down to us preserve far more of the calm of Vergil; the writers on poetics appreciated to the full the generalizing power of poetry, its impersonal character, its duty of suggestion in lieu of expression, and their appreciation was due to the practice of the great poets. They live moreover in a world of tranquil calm, not in the sense that sorrow and suffering are unknown, but in the sense that there prevails a rational order in the world which is the outcome not of blind chance but of the actions of man in previous births. Discontent with the constitution of the universe, rebellion against its decrees, are incompatible with the serenity engendered by this recognition by all the Brahmanical poets of the rationality of the world order. Hence we can trace no echo of social discontent; the poets were courtiers who saw nothing whatever unsatisfactory in the life around them. Nor in the classical period do we find them much moved by patriotism; they wrote, so far as we have them, in times when national feeling was not excited by any foreign attack, and the clashes between neighbouring kings appeared to them in the light of the normal occupation of the warrior class. Political liberty within the state was undreamed of; the fiery passion which ennobles Lucan is impossible for an Indian poet. The Buddhist writers glorified their teacher and magnified his doctrine, but in the main they are too deeply affected by the Brahmanical spirit to move beyond the confines of emotion allowable. It is in Çāntideva above all that we find a deep seriousness, which blends in the most curious and inconsistent manner with a denial of the reality of the universe.

The conventionality of the themes of the poets may be admitted, and due regard had to the limit of their range and outlook, but the fact of the great merit of Sanskrit poetry remains unquestioned. At their best the poets had complete command of the ordinary emotions which appeal most deeply to the human heart; they know to the full the nature of love, in youth and in wedlock, of sorrow, of the joy of union and the pangs of separation, of the utter hopelessness induced by the loss in death of the beloved, or its mitigation by the assurance of reunion in a life to come. Moreover, their love of nature is intimate and real; whether because of their belief in transmigration or simply through natural sympathy, they look on life of all kinds with a kindly eye, and they share in the feelings of nature, as they assume it to share in the vicissitudes of man. Nor do they ignore the more manly virtues; heroism, constancy, uprightness, self-sacrifice, all receive their meed of recognition in energetic portrayal. Humour comes naturally to many of them, and the wit of their paronomasias is often unquestionable and strikingly effective. Their descriptive power is undeniable and applies equally to scenes from life and to cameos of nature. Their miniature-painting, illuminated by the brilliant condensation of style and set off by the effective and melodious metre, while the sounds are skilfully chosen to match the sense, often achieves perfection in its kind. But the ability of the authors is not limited to description; they are capable of rapid and luminous narrative, and even if they smack sometimes of the Arthaçāstra the speeches of their characters are lacking neither in force, vigour, nor logical power.

It is not, of course, given to many poets to excel in epic, and we have many fine lyric stanzas from poets who failed to produce anything distinguished on a larger scale. The highest merit belongs also to the expression in verse of maxims on life; deeply original they seldom are, but the power of giving impressive utterance to the essential facts of human life belonged to men like Bhartṛhari in the highest degree, and many others have recorded impressions with complete adequacy of language. It is in the romances of Subandhu and Bāṇa that we feel most the serious defects of Sanskrit prose style, and even with these drawbacks Bāṇa deserves his reputation both for the depth of his feeling of the nature of love and for the vigour and fire of his pictures of the court of Harṣa, of the death of Prabhākaravardhana, and the martial preparations of the king.

The merits of India in the fable and the fairy tale have never been ignored, and in addition to the interesting character of the imaginative production of India in these genres there must be set to her credit the easy and elegant style of the original *Pañcatantra* and Somadeva's skill in rapid yet pleasing and pointed narrative. History never succeeded in winning a real place in Indian literature, though panegyrics are often clever and valuable as sources of historical information, but Kalhaṇa was not merely an interesting chronicler; often he achieves true poetry, and for the period with which he was almost contemporary his work has all the interest possessed by Lucan's *Pharsalia.* Widely different as were the two men by temperament, the studied elaboration of their style and the fine effects of which they are capable attest a real similarity of genius.

It is natural to compare Sanskrit writers with the Greeks of the Alexandrian age or the post-Augustan Latin poets, and there is no doubt some justice in the parallels drawn between the literatures. They are essentially the outcome of study and of the deliberate and conscious use of older models.[1] But it would be unjust to suggest for a moment that the Sanskrit poets were in general only on the level of the Alexandrians or of Statius. If we allow this to be true of Māgha, it could hardly be asserted of Bhāravi, and Kālidāsa merits comparison with all but the greatest of poets, superior by far to men as able as Ovid and

[1] For the Roman practice of recitation and its effect on literature and French and other parallels see Mayor, *Juvenal*, i. 173 ff.; Friedländer, *Sittengesch.*, iii. 601; Rohde, *Der griech. Roman*, pp. 303 ff.; Heitland in Haskins's *Lucan*, pp. xxxiv f., lxiii ff. H. E. Butler (*Post-Augustan Poetry*), and U. von Wilamowitz-Moellendorff (*Hellenistische Dichtung in der Zeit des Kallimachos*) deal adequately with these periods. Cf. Butcher, *Greek Genius*, pp. 245 ff.

Propertius.[1] Of English writers Tennyson has much in common with him in calmness of outlook and in delicacy of beauty of phrase, coupled with restraint and balance, but Tennyson lacked entirely the dramatic talent which is evinced so remarkably in the *Çakuntalā*.[2]

The similarities, however, between the Alexandrians, the Flavians, and the lesser masters of the Kāvya are as interesting as they are natural. Encyclopaedic learning is common to all three; Apollonios does his best to weary us of the *Argonautika* by his intempestive geographical dissertations, and Lucan, despite his youth, loses no opportunity of showing his mastery[3] of the Roman counterpart of the Indian Kalās. The subject-matter is, on the whole, sacrificed to the form; threadbare legends, descriptions of scenery, and commonplace reflections are crowded in without regard to appropriateness; Māgha is no greater a sinner than Apollonios or Lucan, and Valerius Flaccus and Statius are infinitely worse than he. Point, antithesis, and metaphor became essential; it was demanded of the Roman poets that they should like the prose authors adorn their writings with *sententiae*, *lumina orationis*; success was often achieved in this genre. There is a remarkable similarity between the average stanza of a Kāvya and the style of post-Augustan poetry. 'Almost every group', writes Merivale,[4] 'of three or four lines in Statius constitutes in itself an idea, perhaps a conceit, a play of thought or of words; it fastens itself like a burr upon the memory: such is the distinctness of his vision, such the elaborate accuracy of his touch. The epigram is the crowning result of this elaborate terseness of diction, and this lucid perception of the end in view. The verses of Martial are the quintessence of the Flavian poetry.' This holds good no less of Kallimachos and the Greek epigrammatists, who come nearest to achieving similar effects to Sanskrit poets. Latin prose felt the effects of poetry; it became poetical in construction, vocabulary, and ornaments. Old and obsolete words were revived, new words invented or existing terms given new

[1] For an eloquent defence of Propertius, see Postgate's ed. pp. lvii ff. He approaches more closely to the complexity of Indian poetry than does Ovid's pellucid simplicity. Cf. also Sellar, *Horace and the Elegiac Poets* (1892).

[2] Matthew Arnold's polish is no compensation for his lack of force.

[3] Heitland in Haskins's *Lucan*, pp. li ff.

[4] *Romans under the Empire*, chap. lxiv.

senses, and bold metaphorical transfers of meaning were affected,[1] all phenomena which occur freely in the ornate prose of the Sanskrit romances. As we have seen, Subandhu shows traces of the appropriation of verses for his work, and Tacitus himself is full of reminiscences of Vergil; Kalhaṇa in his turn freely adapts to poetry the happier turns of Bāṇa's prose.[2] In prose and poetry alike we find in the silver age of Latin literature the love of strained expression and involved constructions and a search after metaphorical expression which is often artificial; Lucan, Statius, and Valerius Flaccus offer abundant examples of unsuccessful similes which make the Sanskrit poetaster's[3] comparison of an orange with the freshly shaved chin of a drunken Hun quite pardonable.

But Sanskrit poets had advantages denied to some of the Alexandrians and post-Augustans. Their outlook on religion was one which it is perhaps difficult for us to appreciate, but it accepted a reality in the tales of the gods such as Viṣṇu or Çiva which was obviously not felt by Kallimachos in his playful treatment of the loves of the deities, or by Apollonios in his revival of the Homeric outlook long after it had ceased to have any reality, still less by Lucan, Statius, or Valerius Flaccus, to whom the gods were no more than machinery sanctioned by Vergilian usage. The Sanskrit poet might regard the gods as ultimately real only in a secondary sense, but he had no difficulty in treating them as something more than idle abstractions. Again, these poets had a deep appreciation of nature and feeling for its beauties which is rare in classical poets of Greece or Rome; it is more akin to the spirit of Theokritos, but, unlike that author, Indian poets expressed not a somewhat artificial appreciation of country scenes as they attracted a poet used to town life, but a natural affection which is not really disguised by their placid acceptance of a large number of purely poetic conventions in their descriptions. It may become tedious to find the themes of the seasons, the dawn, the rising and setting of the moon, and kindred topics so often dealt with in the Kāvya, but taken each by itself

[1] Seneca, *Ep.*, cxiv, § 10.

[2] Stein, *Rājataraṅgiṇī*, i. 133; Thomas, WZKM. xii. 33; JRAS. 1899, p. 485.

[3] *Sāhityadarpaṇa*, 622. Pindar's elaborate similes, bold metaphors, and effective compounds (cf. Gildersleeve, *Pindar*, pp. xl ff.) offer an interesting parallel to the best Indian Kāvya.

these pictures are often accomplished works of art with which Greek and Roman poets have nothing strictly comparable in finish or merit. Nor in their appreciation of love in all its phases have the Sanskrit poets any equal among the Alexandrians save Apollonios in his splendid picture of Medea, while the post-Augustans cannot vie with him despite the real ability of Statius. There is, moreover, a deep gulf between the reticence of Greek and Roman alike in the treatment of love and the frankness of the poet of India; the *Ars Amatoria* of Ovid aided to secure his permanent exile,[1] and the Flavians show no signs of its influence, while Sanskrit poets would have been discredited if they had not been skilled in the topics of the Kāmaçāstra, and been able to depict beauty of form and the delights of dalliance. In this sense they are far more akin to the spirit of romance than are the Greeks or their Roman followers. Indian poets also have a happier outlook on life than the disillusioned Alexandrians or the somewhat depressed post-Augustans;[2] they lived in a simpler world, were not vexed by political problems or memories of lost liberty, and were parts of a social system and believers in a scheme of life which, if incapable of producing the magnificence of Vergil's vision of the world to come, at least offered something more exhilarating than the systems of Epicureanism or Stoicism.

Moreover, the Sanskrit poets had command of a language capable of finer sound effects than even Greek at its best; they could successfully manage metres of great complexity but remarkable beauty, and they were conscious experts in the task of matching sound to sense, an art practised indeed by Greek and Roman poets alike, but with far less adequate means and with much less subtlety. Their use of alliteration is often overdone, but they resemble Vergil in their power to make it yield effective results, an art in which his followers and notably Lucan were markedly deficient. Their love of metaphor and simile doubtless led them at times to commit faults of taste and to a display of erudition rather than of judgement; but often they show a richness of fancy and power of happy phraseology which is not

[1] Teuffel-Schwabe, *Rom. Lit.*, § 247. The deplorable taste of i. 289 ff. cannot be excelled in India. Characteristically Indian are e.g. *Amores*, i. 5; ii. 15.

[2] All the greater classical poets have a vein of sadness; cf. Tyrrell, *Latin Poetry*, pp. 159 ff.; Butcher, *Greek Genius*, pp. 133 ff.

paralleled either in Greek or Latin poetry. Moreover, though we may easily find their paronomasias [1] tedious, there is no doubt that they are frequently rightly called models of twofold appropriateness, and the free employment of figures of speech is often superior to the somewhat rhetorical manner which was introduced into Latin poetry by the practice of declamation in the oratorical schools, which Juvenal so forcibly derides.

[1] English lends itself only to comic effects, but Greek and Latin authors alike use this device with serious efforts at beauty; cf. Cope, *Aristotle's Rhetoric*, p. 320, n. 1.

XVII

THE WEST AND INDIAN LITERATURE

1. *The Fables and Märchen of Greece and India*

THE obvious parallelisms between Indian and Greek fairy tales and fables have never been ignored, and have evoked lively controversies. Wagener[1] held that Greece was the recipient, but both Weber[2] and Benfey[3] came to the conclusion that the Indian fables were borrowed from Greece, and for this view there could be adduced the question of chronology; the Greek fable is clearly in existence in the time of Hesiod, is hinted at in Homer, appears definitely in Archilochos and Simonides, and is developed into an important branch of literature, though the actual date of our collections is less certain. Herodotos, however, knew of Aisopos as a fable-teller, and Babrios (*c.* A.D. 200) and Phaedrus (*c.* A.D. 20), if themselves late. drew from earlier sources. Benfey complicated the position by holding that fairy tales were normally Indian in origin, thus establishing a dualism which was difficult to defend. Keller[4] contended for the priority of India, and this view has recently been revived and insisted upon.[5] As a chronological consideration stress has been laid on the monumental evidence in India, especially at Bharhut of the third or second century B.C., for the existence of beast fables, and some would accept the Jātaka stories as already existing in the fourth or fifth centuries B.C., although this is manifestly dubious. Various criteria have been imagined by which to decide priority; Weber preferred the test of simplicity, naturalness, or naïveté, Benfey thought that incompleteness was often a sign of greater age, while Keller laid stress on the doctrine of logical sequence and conformity to the habits

[1] *Les Apologues de l'Inde et les Apologues de la Grèce* (1854).

[2] IS. iii. 327–73; SBA. 1890, p. 916.

[3] Trans. of *Pañcatantra*, I. x ff.

[4] *Jahrbücher f. klass. Phil.*, iv. 309–418.

[5] e.g. by Hertel, Cosquin, H. Lüders (*Buddh. Märchen*, p. xiii). Cf. G. d'Alviella, *Ce que l'Inde doit à la Grèce* (1897), pp. 138 ff.

of animals as revealed in nature. Thus he developed the argument that the fact of the jackal following the lion to partake of the remains of his kill is true to nature, and easily suggests to the early fabulist the conception of making him minister to the lion as king of beasts, whence, as the minister must according to Indian tradition be a miracle of cunning, the jackal is thus reputed; in Greece where the fox appears in the role of the jackal, his position is unexplained, for he is not in reality a very cunning animal. Unhappily this ignores, apart from the fact that it is fancy, not fact, that creates a world of intelligent beasts, the possibility that the fable had its origin neither in India nor in Greece, but was a product of lands intermediate between these countries. Weber justly contended that, if the relation of lion and jackal came thence to Greece, it would have to be changed to suit Greek conditions, while, if it later reached India from Greece, it would have been necessary there to reinstate the jackal. Or, more naturally, it may be held that the fable reached both west and east from the common source in the early fables connected with the name of Aisopos. We cannot ignore the possibility of Egypt having played a part in the genesis and transmission of fables, and Diels[1] has with special reference to Kallimachos claimed for Lydia a substantial share in the work of diffusion. Hertel,[2] again, has insisted that the idea of making use of fables to given instruction in politics is essentially Indian, and on the strength of it has claimed for India originality in respect of the best Greek fables; but the assertion is as little capable of proof as the claim that Greece excels in witty and pointed fables which in India have often suffered watering down at the hands of Buddhist and other preachers.

Nor in any account can we omit to recognize the fact that in Märchen at least we may have old myths and that something must be allowed, as Grimm demanded, for the old common possession of the Indo-European people. In the tales of Herakles, Thorr, and Indra we have certainly some of this old mythology. More speculative is Kern's[3] ingenious comparison of the ape king, who in a Jātaka makes himself a bridge for his following over the Ganges, and a similar exploit of the Irish king

[1] *Int. Wochenschrift*, iv. 995.
[2] ZDMG. lxii. 113.
[3] *Gurupūjākaumudī*, pp. 93 f.

Bran, with which he suggests that the function of the Roman pontifex may be connected. We have accordingly a great field of possibilities; borrowing of India from Greece, of Greece from India, of both from a common source in Egypt or Asia Minor and Syria; common inheritance from Indo-European times, or from even further back if it is deemed worth while seeking to penetrate further into the past; and independent development due to the similar constitution of the human mind. In the face of these possibilities it will be found increasingly difficult to reach any clear decision in any particular case, while any general conclusion is absolutely out of the question. It must further be remembered that there must be admitted movements to and fro; a good story may be invented in Greece, pass to India, and return to Greece; Pausanias[1] already tells us before 180 A.D. of the snake who protected a child but was taken for its murderer and killed; it is difficult not to see in this the origin of the touching tale of the Brahmin who slays the ichneumon which had killed the snake attacking its master's child, a legend which is famous in the form of Llewelyn and Gelert, a dog replacing the mongoose, and which can be traced widely over Europe.

In many cases chronology is decisive against Indian influence on Greece being plausible. Thus a Corinthian vase[2] shows us the existence of the fable of the fox and the raven in the sixth century B.C., while in India we have the story of the fox and the crow only in the Jātaka and, therefore, of uncertain date. A painting by Polygnotos in the Lesche at Delphi of Oknos and his ass affords better evidence than the Jātaka tale of the rope-maker and the female jackal who undoes his work unperceived, both accusations of man's industry and woman's waste.[3] Demokritos knew the story of the eagle who dropped the tortoise, which in India appears as the swans who let the same animal fall. The goat which swallowed a razor was the subject of a Greek proverb,[4] and occurs in a Jātaka. The mice which eat iron in the *Pañcatantra* and a Jātaka are known already to Seneca and Herondas. The fable related of Daidalos in Sophokles' *Kami-*

[1] x. 33. 9. Cf. Bloomfield, JAOS. xxxvi. 63 ff.

[2] *Philologus*, lxxiv. 470. On classical fables, cf. Hausrath, Pauly-Wissowa, *Realencycl.*, vi. 1724 ff.; *Achiqar und Äsop* (1918); G. Thiele, *Neue Jahrbücher f. d. klass. Altertum*, xxi. 377 ff.

[3] Pausanias, x. 29.

[4] ZDMG. xlvii. 89 ff.; lxvi. 338.

kioi[1] is far better attested for Greece than for India in a late Jātaka. The claim that the account in Herodotos and Sophokles alike of a sister's preference for a brother's life to that of a husband, since she cannot have another brother, need certainly not be traced to a Jātaka, and the attempt to derive the delightful story of how Hippokleides lost his marriage by reason of his dance from the similar tale of the peacock in the Jātaka is curiously absurd. In these cases we have to do with ideas which would naturally enough develop themselves in men's minds independently. Nor does there seem any conclusive ground for holding that the tale of the ass in the lion's skin is older in either country. In the version in Greece the ass itself assumes a lion's skin and is betrayed by the wind blowing it away; the Indian versions are more prosaic; the ass is given a skin by its owner to allow it to steal corn, and betrays itself by its cry.

The same doubt as to priority constantly occurs;[2] the story of the jackal which revealed its nature by its cry has a parallel in Phaedrus; so has the story of the ungrateful snake which bit its rescuer; the panther treats the goat as does the wolf the lamb in Phaedrus; the gods of Phaedrus who wish to drink up the stream have their parallel in the crows which would drain dry the sea; the *motif* of the bald-headed man and the fly, used with comic effect in Phaedrus, is turned to tragedy in the Jātaka; we find in Phaedrus the old tale of the eagle and the tortoise, and in India the swans in place of the eagle. The fable of the fox which compels the eagle to restore its young, which Archilochos knew, has been paralleled with a tale in the *Pañcatantra* of a crow and a snake, but the discrepancies are too great; nor is the parallel of the wolf, which a crane helps, in Phaedrus to the tale of the lion and the woodpecker sufficiently close to prove priority on either side.

Much that has been adduced definitely[3] in favour of Greek priority is extremely dubious. The Trojan horse, however, is much older than the capture by an elephant of wood filled with soldiers of Udayana, but the *motif* is traced also in Egypt,[4] and

[1] Zachariae, *Kl. Schriften*, pp. 108 ff.

[2] Günter, *Buddha*, pp. 52 ff.

[3] e.g. Polykrates' ring and the ring in the *Çakuntalā*; Surendranath Majumdar Sastri, JBORS. 1921, pp. 96 ff.; Jāt. 288.

[4] v. d. Leyen, *Archiv f. d. Stud. d. neueren Sprachen*, cxv. 6.

cannot be deemed too recondite to be original in India. The love of Phaidra for Hippolytos is striking, but the *motif* is found in the Jātaka [1] and belongs to human nature. The device of consoling the living for the dead by striking means is ascribed to Demokritos, is found in Lukianos, in Julian's letters, and in pseudo-Kallisthenes, but it also is attested by the Chinese version of the Tripiṭaka, which bids the mourner bring fire from a house where none has died. Androclus' grateful lion has an Indian parallel in the grateful elephant; Milo's death reminds us of the foolish ape in the *Pañcatantra*; India knows of paintings which deceive by likeness to life, as Parrhasios deceived even Zeuxis by his painted curtain. The tale of how an adulteress clears herself by a cunningly devised oath is early enough in India to have been deemed the source of Isolde's falsehood,[2] but we have the same idea in the oath of Ovid's Mestra.[3] The effort to find in the tract *Physiologos* the proof of Indian influence on the western legend of the unicorn or the source of Caesar's tale of the elks of the Black Forest, which cannot rise if once they fall to the ground, is clearly a failure. From India may be borrowed the tale of the Charadrios, a bird which bears jaundice to the sun, but, as this idea is extremely early in India, it may be an ancient Indo-European belief.

In some cases more certainty of borrowing exists. The complex legend of Rhampsinitos in Herodotos, which he learned in Egypt, appears before A.D. 300 in India and can hardly be other than a borrowing there.[4] But instances of this sort are rare and the issue of priority between India and Greece normally remains open. Little can be gained from general considerations such as the fact of belief in transmigration in India, the fondness of the Indian mind for romance, or the number of idle wanderers, religious men of various kinds, who went about India and perhaps beyond, telling and hearing tales. There seems to be no necessary connexion between beast fables and the belief in transmigration, for such fables exist among many peoples and represent a period when beast and human lives were not regarded as

[1] Bloomfield, TAPA. liv. 145 ff.

[2] J. J. Meyer, *Isoldes Gottesurteil*, pp. 218 ff.

[3] Rohde, *Griech. Roman*, p. 515.

[4] Frazer, *Pausanias*, v. 176 ff.; G. Paris, RHR. lv. 151 ff., 267 ff.; Huber, BEFEO. iv. 701 f.; Niebuhr, OLZ. 1914, p. 106.

so distinct as they are in modern times; love of tales is recorded of others as of the people of Miletos, and wanderers of all kinds were evidently as common in the ancient as in the modern world. What presents much greater certainty is the actual translation of important Indian books and the transmission thus of much of fable and fairy tale to western lands, but that cannot be proved for an early date. It is difficult to believe we must[1] go to India for the idea of the gratitude of animals when we know that Agatharchos, a contemporary of Alexander the Great, told the tale of the dolphin, which rewarded kindness by saving during a shipwreck the life of the youth who bought him from some fishermen. On the other hand, it is not necessary to find in the Aisopian fable of the fox which ate the heart of the deer killed by the sick lion and then denied that the beast had had a heart, the prototype of the jackal who ate the heart and ears of the ass and declared it never had them or it would not have been killed.

2. *The Translations of the Pañcatantra*

The enterprise of the physician Burzōe, who under Chosrau Anōsharwān (531–79) translated a version of the *Pañcatantra* into Pahlavi, was a work of the utmost importance for the Indian fable literature.[2] It is lost, but by A.D. 570 it was rendered by one Būd into Syriac, and about 750 an Arabic version was made by Abdallah ibn al-Moqaffaʿ from which the western versions are derived. The Syriac version is preserved in one manuscript and is imperfect, the Arabic is clearly expanded from the original, which seems to have consisted of five books corresponding to the *Pañcatantra*, five or eight other books taken from a different source[3]—whether or not the fusion was accomplished in India before Burzōe—and two books regarding his mission and his introduction. Of these fifteen chapters the Syriac has only ten,

[1] Cosquin, *Études folkloriques*, p. 21.

[2] Hertel, *Das Pañcatantra* (1914); ZDMG. lxxii. 65 ff.; lxxiv. 95 ff.; lxxv. 129 ff.

[3] From the *Mahābhārata*, xii. 138. 13 ff.; 139. 47 ff.; 111. 3 ff., three are taken; one is Buddhist (cf. A. Schiefner, *Bharatae Responsa* (1875) in Tibetan; Zachariae, *Kl. Schriften*, pp. 49 ff.); one the tale of the man in the well (see Nöldeke, *Burzōes Einleitung zu dem Buche Kalīla wa Dimna*, 1912); one of the lion and jackal also probably Buddhist; one of grateful beasts and ungrateful men; one of four friends, perhaps Buddhist; one of the mouse king and his minister is Indian in spirit.

while the Arabic has twenty-two in all. The title of the work was clearly derived from Karaṭaka and Damanaka, the two jackals who figure in the first book of the *Pañcatantra*, variants of whose names occur regularly as the title of the translations, while the character of the work was somewhat altered by the inclusion of tales which were distinctly of a moral character.

From the Arabic version came in the tenth or eleventh century a fresh Syriac translation, and at the close of the eleventh century the Greek version of Simeon, son of Seth, which in its turn produced an Italian version of 1583 by Giulio Nuti, two Latin and one German versions, and various Slav reproductions. But more importance attaches to the Hebrew version of the Rabbi Joel (*c.* 1100), whence was made by John of Capua between 1263 and 1278 the *Liber Kelilae et Dimnae, Directorium vitae humanae*, of which two printed editions appeared in 1480. From a manuscript was made by Anthonius von Pforr the German translation, *Das buch der byspel der alten wysen*, which was repeatedly printed from 1483 onwards, and in addition to influencing deeply German literature was rendered into Danish, Icelandic, and Dutch. A Spanish version appeared in 1493, based on it, an Italian by Agnolo Firenzuola in 1546 which was translated into French in 1556, while a direct Italian version, that of A. Doni, came out in two parts in 1552, and the first part was translated into English by Sir Thomas North as *The Morall Philosophie of Doni* in 1570.

Another important translation was that made from the Arabic in 1142 or 1121 by Abu 'l-Maālī Naṣrallāh ibn Muhammed ibn ʿAbd al-Hamīd, for it produced the Persian *Anwāri Suhailī* by Ḥusain ibn ʿAlī al-Wāʿiẓ between 1470 and 1505, whence came numerous translations into eastern languages, and which became known in France in 1644 by the translation by David Sahid and Gaulmin; this, again, was soon rendered into English, German, and Swedish. Moreover, the Persian original was rendered into Turkish by ʿAlī bin Ṣāliḥ between 1512 and 1520, and it was rendered into French by Galland and Cardonne, the French then being translated into German, Dutch, Hungarian, and even Malay.

Other renderings from the Arabic were less fertile; the Hebrew version of Jacob ben Eleazer in the thirteenth century is only in part preserved, the old Spanish version (*c.* 1251) and John of

Capua's work afforded material to Raimundus de Biterris who prepared his *Liber de Dina et Kalila* for Johanna of Navarre. The Italian Baldo in the early twelfth century used some version for his *Novus Esopus*. La Fontaine in the second edition of his *Fables* in 1678 expressly states that the greater part of his new matter is derived from the Indian sage Pilpay, in whose name we may recognize the Sanskrit Vidyāpati, lord of learning.

3. *The Çukasaptati*

Another case of translation which is certain is that of the *Çukasaptati*, whose existence, as we have seen, is attested by Hemacandra in the twelfth century when he cites an episode, not in our texts, in which the parrot is caught by a cat, proving probably that variant recensions were already in existence. By the beginning of the fourteenth century there already was extant a rude Persian version which displeased the refined taste of Nachshabī, a contemporary of Hāfiz and Saʿdī, who in 1329–30 produced the *Tūtīnāmeh*,[1] which a hundred years later was rendered into Turkish and in the eighteenth century evoked a fresh version by Kadiri. The *Tūtīnāmeh* rejected part of its original as unsuitable, substituting other tales partly from the *Vetālapañcaviṅçatikā*. From the Persian version many tales passed to western Europe *via* Asia, and one of the tales was made famous by Gottfried's *Tristan und Isolde*, in which occurs the account of the ordeal which was used to deceive by proving Isolde's innocence. In India the episode is old, for it occurs in a Chinese fifth-century version of an Indian tale and in a confused form is extant in the Jātaka book.[2]

4. *Other Cases of Contact between East and West*

Tales which cannot be traced thus definitely to Indian sources may yet readily be assumed to have reached the west from India in view of these proved facts. Nor is it difficult to imagine modes of transmission[3]; apart from literature, tales pass easily enough

[1] Pertsch, ZDMG. xxi. 505–21. The Persian of Kadiri was translated by C. J. L. Iken (1822), the Turkish by G. Rosen (1858).

[2] Chavannes, *Cinq cents contes*, i. no. 116; Jātaka, 62; Zachariae, *Kleine Schriften*, pp. 282 f.; J. J. Meyer, *Isoldes Gottesurteil*, pp. 74 ff.

[3] For the period to A. D. 600 see Kennedy, JRAS. 1917, pp. 226 ff.

from mouth to mouth, and the Crusades resulted in prolonged intercourse between Christians and Mahomedans. Then the Arab rule in Spain served to mediate between the civilizations of west and east, and the Jews in their turn played an important part as intermediaries. The influence on the Mongols in this regard has been exaggerated by Benfey, but doubtless under-estimated by Cosquin.[1] There is no reason to doubt that the Gipsies[2] helped to spread tales, as their Indian origin is well established. Byzantine literature,[3] again, must have been a factor in the literary diffusion of stories. But it would be absurd to assume that the borrowing was all from one side, as Benfey was inclined to do as regards fairy tales. Cosquin has, indeed, done much to defend this thesis by his efforts to prove that the better-motived tales are often Indian; Lang, with various qualifications, and Bédier have insisted instead on the independent generation of tales in different places, while Antti Aarne has endeavoured to work on the basis that every country may produce tales, but these tales wander far and wide, so that the end of research is to establish *motifs* which belong to one country or another; thus a group of ideas centring in a magic ring is Indian in origin, another dealing with three magic substances is British and French, another centring in a magic bird is Persian. In most cases it may be frankly admitted that it is extremely difficult to achieve any satisfactory result.

A certain degree of assurance may be felt regarding the familiar tale of Sinbad. The Arabian historian Masūdi, who died in 956, expressly ascribes to the *Kitāb el Sindbād* an Indian origin; this work corresponds to the Persian *Sindibādnāmeh*, the Syriac *Sindban*, the Arabic 'Seven Viziers' which is found in manuscripts of the *Arabian Nights*, the Hebrew *Sandabar*, the Greek *Syntipas*,[4] and a mass of European tales. The plan of the work is taken from the *Pañcatantra*; a king entrusts his son to a wise man who undertakes to teach him wisdom in six months; the Indian *motif* of telling tales to save the life of some one, here a prince condemned to death, is found, and the stories

[1] Cosquin, *Études folkloriques*, pp. 497 ff.

[2] Wlislocki, ZDMG. xli. 448 ff.; xlii. 113 ff.

[3] E. Kuhn, *Byzant. Zeitschrift*, iv. 241.

[4] H. Warren, *Het indische origineel van den Griekschen Syntipas*; Hertel, ZDMG. lxxiv. 458 ff.

have usually Indian parallels; that of the ichneumon is taken from the *Pañcatantra*, and the others are often specimens of women's tricks to cover their infidelities, which are common in India, forming as it were a supplement of the *Pañcatantra*. The Greek *Syntipas* contains various passages which can only be read successfully by recognizing that they are merely corruptions of a Sanskrit original, and everything supports the conclusion that we have here another case of an Arabic original rendered from a Pahlavi translation of a Sanskrit text.

It is natural to extend the doctrine and to find the original of the Arabian *Thousand and One Nights* in India,[1] and something substantial has been done in this direction by proving that the prologue and setting of the tales are a contamination of *motifs* which are quite well known in India. Thus we have the Jain legend of Kanakamañjarī, who retains for six months the undivided love of the king by the device of beginning a tale each night but not finishing it. Again, we have in a Chinese rendering of a Buddhist tale (A.D. 251), in the *Kathāsaritsāgara*, and in Hemacandra, variations of the theme of the man who is utterly depressed by finding out that his wife is unfaithful, but recovers happiness because he discovers that the king himself is equally being made a mock of. The further adventure of Shahriar and Shahzeman has a parallel in the *Kathāsaritsāgara*. There are other traces of Indian influence in the tales, and it is clear that it is impossible to ascribe them to borrowing from Persia; translations from Persian into Sanskrit are normally late, as in Çrīvara's *Kathākautuka*[2] written on the theme of Yusuf and Zuleikha under Zainu-l-'Abidīn in the fifteenth century. The only matter that can be in doubt is the extent of the influence; certainly there is nothing in this case to prove the taking over of a whole cycle of stories from an Indian work, now lost.

In Europe, apart from the translations enumerated, traces of real Indian origin are hard to prove.[3] A Carolingian poem of the

[1] Cosquin, *op. cit.*, pp. 265 ff.; Przyluski, JA. ccv. 101 ff., who finds in the Svayaṁvara of India a relic of the Austroasiatic festival dance at which young people were mated. Cf. Macdonald, JRAS. 1924, pp. 353 ff.

[2] Ed. and trans. R. Schmidt (Kiel, 1898).

[3] Günter, *Buddha*, pp. 99 ff. The famous tale of the poison maiden in Indian literature and in the west—told of Aristotle and Alexander in the *Secretum Secretorum* (cf. Hawthorne, *Rappaccini's Daughter*), is discussed by Penzer, *Ocean of Story*, ii. 311 ff.

ninth century tells how a hunter slew a boar, was himself killed by and caused the death of a snake, which is a feeble tale in comparison with the Indian story of the greedy jackal who was lucky enough to find a hunter who had killed a deer, and had also slain a boar which killed him, but meets death through eating first out of the spirit of thrift the bowstring. Peter Alfonsi (twelfth century) knows a tale which occurred in Barzōe's introduction to his version of the *Pañcatantra* and some other Indian narratives, but merely as handed down in Arabic. Walter Mapes' knowledge is doubtful, but Marie of France has clear parallels, and the bird of St. Martin recounted by Odo of Sheriton (*c.* 1215), which held up its limbs to keep up the sky but appealed in terror to the saint when a leaf fell on it, can be traced to the *Mahābhārata* and the *Pañcatantra.* Nigel of Canterbury's knowledge (*c.* 1180) of the tale of the ingratitude of man as contrasted with that of animals is not necessarily borrowed, nor is the *motif* of the fatal letter and its bearer in Saxo Grammaticus probably Indian, seeing that we have already the conception in Homer. James of Vitry, bishop of Ptolemais, a Crusader, in his *Exempla* tells from hearsay the stories of the Brahmin who was cheated by rogues, of the Brahmin who built castles in the air, and of the son who was going to bury his too long-lived grandfather, while his own son prepared a grave for him. In the *de diversis rebus praedicabilibus* of the Dominican Étienne of Bourbon, who died *c.* 1260, we find a version of the story of the blind and the lame, well known in Jain texts,[1] and a variant of the judgement of Solomon [2] in which two women dispute over a ball of wool and the issue is decided by asking what was the kernel used on which to wind the material [3]; the Indian tale, found in a Chinese version, in Buddhaghosa, and the *Çukasaptati*,[4] of his stepfather's device of ridding himself of the Bodhisattva appears in Étienne as the tale of the page whose prince, suspecting him of an intrigue, sends him to the workers at his oven who have instructions to

[1] Hertel, *Geist des Ostens*, i. 248 ff.

[2] Cf. Hertel, *loc. cit.*, 189 ff. on the issue of the ultimate original of the Indian versions of 1 Kings, iii. 16; Jātaka, 546.

[3] Zachariae, *Kl. Schriften*, pp. 84 ff.

[4] Cf. the legend of St. Elizabeth of Portugal, Cosquin, *Études folkloriques*, pp. 73 ff., who (p. 160) insists on the exchange of persons or messages as distinguishing these tales from such cases as Bellerophon.

fling into it the first who comes with a royal message. Étienne also tells us of the innocent hound, transmuted into St. Guinefort and an object of worship, whose tomb he insisted on destroying. The *Gesta Romanorum* contains various stories which may be of Indian origin; one in a manuscript of 1469 [1] is so elaborate as to leave no doubt of its origin, for it tells of how a knight who was taught in gratitude the language of the beasts managed to escape revealing it to his wife, a famous Jātaka tale. On the other hand it is impossible to ignore independent development; if Heinrich Seuse (*c.* 1330) illustrates the idea of eternity by telling of a bird which once in 100,000 years picks up a grain of corn from a millstone of the size of the earth (the period until the stone shall be made bare is but a moment in comparison with eternity), it is far-fetched to claim derivation from the Indian conception of a world age as longer than the period taken by a man who once in a hundred years rubs a mountain with a silk cloth to level it with the ground.

From the late middle ages comes evidence of the borrowing of several stories of cleverness, as in the story of the man who finds out guilty servants by more or less accidental observations made at table.[2] The seven-league boots of fairy tale are found in the *Kathāsaritsāgara* and may be Indian, but many other *motifs* are hardly to be assigned to one nation; thus we have the hero who is vulnerable in one spot only much earlier in Greece than in India and independently probably in Germany; the tree which yields what it is asked for depends on the widespread belief in tree spirits; the man or animal which yields gold attests, though early in India, to community of ideas rather than borrowing; the burning of a skin which frees the enchanted prince seems ethnic. Various peoples know of flying birds which carry heroes on long journeys. Circe in the *Odyssey* need not be the source of the Yakṣiṇī of the tale of Niçcayadatta in the *Kathāsaritsāgara*.[3]

Of interesting *motifs* due to India Cosquin [4] offers a good example in the *Mahosadha Jātaka* tale of how a faithful wife served gallants who sought to seduce her in her husband's

[1] Günter, *Buddha*, pp. 122 ff.

[2] Cf. Forke, *Die indischen Märchen*, pp. 36 f.; Zachariae, *op. cit.*, pp. 138 ff.

[3] See Tawney's trans., i. 337 ff.; cf. the Sirenes of *Od.*, xii. 39 ff. and Jātakas 41, 96, 196, 439; *Mahāvaṅsa* (Geiger, p. 25).

[4] *Études folkloriques*, pp. 457 ff.

absence, ending up with conveying them in jars before the king, an episode which is proved ancient by a relief at Bharhut on which is depicted the opening of three coffers in each of which is a prisoner. The story is preserved in perhaps a more original fashion in the Kashmirian *Bṛhatkathā* legend of Upakoçā, who induces the gallants to take a bath and has them blackened by a sticky preparation, in which condition they are revealed to the king. It seems difficult to doubt that this is the source of the inferior version in the fable of Constant du Hamel and Isabeau in the thirteenth century. A variant of the same idea appears in the story of Devasmitā in the Kashmirian *Bṛhatkathā*, and it is probable enough that we must seek an Indian original for the form of the legend as it appears in the *Gesta Romanorum* (*c.* 1300), in the romance of Perceforest, and in the fifteenth-century English poem, *The Wright's Chaste Wife.* It is tempting no doubt to find [1] in the common idea of the ogre and the fascinating daughter who helped the lover to deceive her father, who despite his wickedness is stupid, the result of the Indian idea preserved in the Kashmirian *Bṛhatkathā* of the youth who is aided by the daughter of a Rākṣasa whose stupidness she asserts is due to his origin, to win her hand by accomplishing all the impossible feats set to him. But proof is wanting. Another tale,[2] which has a fair chance of being Indian in origin, is the type of the boiling cauldron and the pretended lack of skill as in the case of Vikramāditya, who is saved by the warning given by a skull from the ruse of a Yogin who bids him turn round a cauldron into which he means to fling him; the king asks to be shown how to act and slays the miscreant by his own device. The tale [3] of the cat who held a candle for the king but at last lets it go at the sight of a third mouse, though he has permitted two to pass unnoticed, may be of Indian origin, but that is clearly not proved; it is, however, probable that the idea of the vigil of Solomon and Marcolphus, well known in the fourteenth century, is due to India, where the tale of Rohaka [4] and the king of Ujjain is known in the twelfth century and that of Pradyota and a Gandhāran is

[1] Cosquin, *op. cit.*, p. 25.

[2] *Op. cit.*, pp. 349 ff.

[3] *Op. cit.*, pp. 401 ff.

[4] On him cf. Zachariae, *op. cit.*, pp. 66, 94 f., 190; Pullé, *Uno progenitore Indiano del Bertoldo* (1888).

found in the Kanjur, in the ninth century. Nor is the idea of the magician and his apprentice [1] who assumes all sorts of forms to emerge from different impasses unique; the legend of Mestra in Ovid [2] shows that tales of this sort could easily arise in independence of India, where indeed the *motif* is not specially important.

5. *The Romance in Greece and India*

It is natural that efforts should have been made to prove the derivation from Greece of the Indian romance, as it appears seemingly full-fledged in the works of Subandhu, Bāṇa, and even in some degree Daṇḍin. Peterson's [3] argument for Greek influence, strictly limited in scope, was based in part on the indubitable fact of Greek influence on astronomy and astrology, and in part on the new spirit which he discerned in the romances, which clothed with flesh and blood the dry bones of the simple tale with its rapid but monotonous stream of adventures. He quoted, however, in support of his view merely passages illustrating the affection of Achilles Tatius in his tale of Kleitophon and Leukippe for minute descriptions of the beauty of the beloved, the effect of love upon man, and the love which other things have for each other, citing the story of the affection of the male palm for the female palm, which is given fruition by the grafting of a shoot into the heart of the male. To this Reich [4] has added merely a list of similarities; thus we find both in Indian and in Greek romance the conception of love at first sight, of lovers revealed to each other in a dream, the swift change of fortune from good to evil and then back to prosperity, adventure and shipwreck at sea, heroes as well as heroines of wonderful beauty, free use of detailed description both of love and of nature. All these things may be admitted, but clearly they do not prove borrowing, though they render it possible. The tale of the loves of the palms, it is clear, suggests Syria rather than either Greece or India; it is decidedly different from the Indian wedlock of the mango and the jasmine recorded in the Kāvyas.

[1] Cosquin, *op. cit.*, pp. 497 ff. For other suggestions see *Les contes indiens et l'occident* (1922), where *inter alia* he deals with the slipper *motif* in India.

[2] *Met.*, viii. 847 ff.

[3] *Kādambarī*, pp. 98 ff.

[4] DLZ. 1915, pp. 553 ff., 594 ff.

More definite evidence is adduced by Rohde [1], and by Weber [2] who holds that we find the *motif* of the *Vāsavadattā*—which, it must be remembered, has no known antecedent in India—in a tale recounted by Athenaios on the authority of Chares of Mytilene, an official of Alexander the Great. This tale of Zariadres and Odatis contains the *motifs* of lovers who see each other in a dream, and are finally united through the intervention of the maiden's marriage ceremonial in which she enjoys the right of choice. But even if we compare the awakening of Vāsavadattā at her lover's embrace to the story of Pygmalion and Galatea, and find parallels in the Greek romance for armies which war for the possession of a maiden, we have the fact that the tale admittedly in the Greek version is not Greek, and in point of fact in Firdausī we learn that the daughter of the emperor of Rome sees her lover Gushtasp in a dream and herself claims him as husband. The choice of a husband in this way by a princess is an early Indian practice, and the Persian tale may easily have come from India in the first place.

A different aspect was given to the hypothesis by F. Lacôte,[3] when he claimed that Guṇāḍhya himself was under Greek influence, thus departing from Peterson's contrast between the predecessors of the romances and these works. But his opinion later [4] changed, and he adduced evidence in favour of the borrowing of the Greek romance from India. Of his evidence, part may be at once dismissed as being irrelevant to the question of origin, as it concerns merely incidents and might therefore be borrowed without the romance as a whole being adopted by Greece from India. In any case, however, these details seem inadequate to prove their case; the plant which cures wounds in three days has been compared to the *vraṇasaṁrohaṇī* plant of India, but it belongs to the most primitive period of Greek as well as Indian medicine. The unwinking eyes and feet that touch not the ground which mark out the gods from men is Indian, but the latter detail at least is recognized by the artists of the Roman Empire, and Kalasiris shows that the *Iliad* [5] was believed to be the authority for both the assertions.

[1] *Griech. Roman*², pp. 47 ff. [2] IS. xviii. 456 ff.

[3] *Essai sur Guṇāḍhya*, pp. 284–6.

[4] *Mélanges Lévi*, pp. 272 ff. See Keith, JRAS. 1915, pp. 784 ff.

[5] N. 71 f.; A. 200, which prove that in gait (cf. Vergil: et vera incessu patuit dea) and eyes gods revealed their divinity.

When Theagenes and Chariklea see each other for the first time, they seem to recognize each other as if they had known each other before; this is not merely a common feeling among modern people, but Plato had a doctrine of recollection which was far more likely to be present to a Greek author than an Indian romance *motif.* In the general purpose of the romances there is absolutely nothing un-Greek. On the contrary, the *Aithiopika* justifies the trials of its hero by the doctrine that he and his beloved had to be brought almost to death in order that the Aithiopians might cease to practice human sacrifice. The fate that elsewhere governs the progress of events is essentially Greek, more Greek than Indian, and it is most significant that nothing is said of the misfortunes which fall on the heroes being due to evil deeds done in past lives. Moreover, it is striking that in all the complex adventures recounted in the Greek romances we do not have Indian scenes or episodes, though there was abundant room for them, and the authors of the romances were largely themselves Orientals, not natives of Greece proper.

There remains, therefore, the argument from form. Lacôte contends that the Kathā form was original in India, that there alone did it develop, and that it was borrowed by the Greek romances from India. Every part of the proof is defective. The Kathā manner in its simpler forms is the most natural [1] of all, and Lacôte admits that we have it in the *Odyssey*, but he holds that it was not developed in Greece. Of this there is no proof whatever; the dialogues of Plato, which are reported conversations, he admits to be exceptions to his rule, but holds that the manner was confined to philosophy, which borrowed it from the Mimes of Sophron. This is a very implausible assumption, and is further contradicted by the evidence. We know of the love of Greece for tales, the story-tellers of Sybaris and Ephesos were famous, there is the evidence of Apuleius, who refers to his *Metamorphoses* in the words *ut ego tibi sermone isto Milesio varias fabulas conseram.*[2] It is a perfectly fair deduction to make from this definite statement that the Ephesian tales known to Apuleius —including doubtless Aristeides' *Ephesiaka* which were rendered

[1] It is found early in Egypt, and the emboxing of stories there is very early; Maspero, *Contes populaires de l'Égypte ancienne* (1906), pp. 23 ff.

[2] Teuffel-Schwabe, *Rom. Lit.*, § 367; H. Lucas, *Philologus*, 1907, pp. 29 ff.

by Sisenna,[1] already exhibited the form of a framework story with reports of experiences of the actors inserted. In Ovid's *Metamorphoses* (v) Pallas's adventures include meeting and hearing tales from the Muses, in whose account of Demeter and Proserpina are inserted two narratives by Arethusa; in xiv in Aeneas' adventures we have Macareus' narrative to Achaemenides, in which is inserted a tale by a maiden of Circe's. We have, therefore, no conceivable need to seek in India for the prototype, especially as chronology is all against the suggestion. We know nothing that we can prove of the actual manner of the *Bṛhatkathā* and its date is utterly uncertain, assuredly not early enough to make dependence even possible,[2] while as regards the *Vāsavadattā* we know that it is later than any extant Greek romance of the period dealt with by Lacôte. A further insuperable difficulty would be the fact that Lacôte thinks of popular transmission, recognizing that no Greek could understand a real Indian romance in Sanskrit, while such transmission would certainly give only tales, not the elaborate construction which is the one point which could be used to prove derivation.

In point of fact there is no general agreement in the Greek romances as regards form; it would have been strange if there had been, for Greek writers are usually successful in achieving originality. Heliodoros sometimes relates himself the tale, sometimes brings the actors before us in conversation to tell of their doings, just as does Homer; Xenophon is a simple narrator; Achilles Tatius puts his tale into the mouth of Kleitophon, but the latter relates it as if he were an outsider, recording what happened to himself and to the heroine impartially. It is only in Antonius Diogenes that we find anything more complex. There the story opened with a letter from the author to his sister, sending her a copy of a letter from Balagros to Phila, enclosing a note drawn up by one Erasinides of a conversation between Deinias and Kymbas. Deinias's narrative consists largely of a story told to him by Derkyllis, in which are inserted reports to Derkyllis by Astraios and Mantinias, and again by Astraios

[1] Teuffel-Schwabe, § 156.

[2] There is Apuleius' own work (*c.* A. D. 160) and Lukianos' Λούκιος ἢ ὄνος, as well as Petronius' *Satirae* (Teuffel-Schwabe, § 305), and above all Ovid's work. The *Arabian Nights* manner, as Tyrrell (*Latin Poetry*, p. 123) says, is not a great success there.

to Derkyllis and Mantinias; at the close of Derkyllis' narrative Deinias reports what he heard from Azulis, and the close of Deinias's conversation with Kymbas is followed by the final note of Erasinides. This is complex, no doubt, but a perfectly natural development, just as the Indian Kathā in *Vāsavadattā* is a natural development from simpler forms. The further parallels drawn by Lacôte are invalid; the letter from the author to Faustinus, which seems clearly to have been in an appendix, is only remotely similar to the introductions to the *Vāsavadattā* and Bāṇa's works, while the statements at the head of each book of the work as to stories parallel to the marvels he relates have no real resemblance to the introductory verses prefixed to each chapter of the *Harṣacarita* only, which, it may be added, is not in the slightest degree in form like the work of Antonius. Nor, it must be admitted, is it altogether reasonable to ignore the fact that, while the Greek romances are silent as to India, the existence of Yavanas and their cunning, especially in the fabrication of aerial ships, is referred to in the Kashmirian *Bṛhatkathā*, which knows their skill in architecture, and Budhasvāmin attests the use of Greek beds, suggesting that even the original *Bṛhatkathā* may have known of the Greeks as cunning and skilled craftsmen.[1]

Denial of any relation of interdependence is also asserted by L. H. Gray,[2] who calls attention to many parallels, letters between lovers, long-winded lamentations, threats of suicide, the stories within stories, descriptions of nature, detailed personal descriptions, learned allusions and citations of precedents, even strained compounds, and alliterations, parisoi,[3] homoioteleuta, and other figures of rhetoric which recall the Sanskrit Anuprāsa and Yamaka. But he insists that the least part of the Sanskrit romance is the thread of the story or the adventures of its characters; all the stress is laid on rhetorical embellishment, minute description of nature, detailed characterization of exploits, and of mental, moral, and physical qualities. In the Greek romance, on the other hand, the essence is the narrative of one

[1] Cf. Lacôte, *op. cit.*, p. 286. The existence of a Greek and Eurasian population in Gandhāra for a couple of centuries at least (Foucher, *L'Art Gréco-Bouddhique du Gandhāra*, ii. 448 ff.) cannot be ignored.

[2] *Vāsavadattā*, pp. 35 ff. Cf. G. N. Banerjee, *Hellenism in Ancient India*, pp. 258 ff.

[3] Cf. Aristotle, *Rhet.* iii. 10 ff.

improbable adventure after another, fine writing is practically discarded, description and appreciation of nature are essentially neglected. To the latter assertion there is of course admitted an exception in the case of the *Poimenika* of Longus, but that author derives directly from Theokritos, Bion, and Moschos, while the Sanskrit romance owes its love for nature to Indian feeling. The *Daçakumāracarita* with its affinities to the picaresque romance is without real parallel in the Greek romances, though it has affinities to the *Satirae* of Petronius.

An interesting parallel is drawn by Gray between the manner of Lyly in his *Euphues* and that of Subandhu. They agree in laying all stress on form rather than subject-matter, though Lyly has a didactic end foreign to Subandhu. Lyly employs the device familiar in India of emboxing a story within a story, as in the case of the tale of Callimachus, which itself includes the story of the hermit Cassander. Moreover, his paronomasias, his alliterations, his antitheses, and his learned allusions are in close harmony with the Indian practice. The instance is valuable as a reminder that parallels may arise without borrowing on either side.

6. *The Hexameter and Indian Metre*

An interesting suggestion has been made by Jacobi[1] that the Dohā metre of Apabhrança, with which may be compared the Dodhaka metre of Classical Sanskrit poetry, in so far as both are essentially originally dactylic in structure, is to be traced back to the Greek hexameter, the Dohā being the result of combining two hexameters into a stanza and then dividing it in the usual Indian manner into four lines. The Ābhīras, he contends, were situated in Gandhāra and the neighbourhood during the period of the influcnce of the Greco-Bactrian kings, and they must have eventually felt the need for a rendering into an Indian speech of the Homeric poems which, as Dio[2] tells us, the Greeks loved so dearly, and clung to even when they had lost much else of Hellenic character. The version of Homer thus made for the educated classes would probably be in the metre of the original,

1 *Festschrift Wackernagel*, pp. 127 ff.

2 *Or.* liii. 6. On the amount of Greek known in India cf. Kennedy, JRAS. 1912, pp. 1012 ff; 1913, pp. 122 ff.; 1917, pp. 228 ff.; Thomas, 1913, pp. 1014 f.

and thus the Dohā would grow up as the peculiar metre of the Ābhīras and would cling to Apabhrança poetry. A parallel may be seen in the great influence exerted on Bengal prose literature by the missionaries of Serampore.

Jacobi's theory rests naturally on the validity of the assertion of Dio that the Indians had a translation of Homer, which is repeated by Aelian, who asserts the same of the Persian kings, and who may have used the same source as Dio, although it is possible that he merely copies the latter. The general view[1] that Dio's reference is really to the *Mahābhārata* as the Indian equivalent of Homer is possible, but there is no doubt that it is not proved. Jacobi strengthens his case by pointing out that from the later sculpture of India we should never be able to demonstrate Hellenistic influence, were it not for the Gandhāran art, which being permanent has survived to testify to the strength of Greek art, and it might be added that the proof of the influence of Greek painting has probably been lost through the disappearance of the frescoes which once existed in abundance in Gandhāra.[2] But, granting that the tale of Dio may have foundation, it must be admitted that it does not seem possible to accept as even probable the origin suggested for the Dohā; the dactylic form is easy to explain independently. It must, however, be said that the effort of Leumann[3] to reconstruct an Indo-European metre with a quantitative basis, of which the Dohā would be a descendant, is clearly a mere *tour de force*, resting on utterly inconclusive evidence.

[1] Weber, IS. ii. 161 ff.

[2] Cf. Foucher, *L'Art Gréco-Bouddhique du Gandhāra*, ii. 402 f.

[3] *Festschrift Wackernagel*, pp. 78 ff. and elsewhere. His work is vitiated by a complete failure to weigh evidence and inability to meet criticism. By his methods anything could be proved. Meillet and Weller (ZII. i. 115 ff.), whom he attacks, are far sounder.

XVIII

THEORIES OF POETRY

1. *The Beginnings of Theory on Poetry*

IT is very possible to exaggerate the effect of theories of poetics [1] on Indian poetry and to ignore the fact that in India as elsewhere the poets set the models on which theory was built, and that it was only gradually that the effect of the text-books on poetics came to be of ever-increasing importance. It is little short of absurd to imagine Kālidāsa as laboriously striving to conform to rules which in his time were, to the best of our knowledge, only in process of formulation, and which in any case were, as we can see from our extant sources, always being laid down with distinct divergences of emphasis and detail. Of the age of the study of poetics we can say little, but the fact that Pāṇini does not mention Alaṁkārasūtras, while he does recognize Naṭasūtras, certainly suggests that dramaturgy came before a general survey of poetics, even if we do not believe that Pāṇini knew a fully developed drama. With this accords the fact that, beyond vague references to Kāçyapa and a Vararuci, and Yāska's knowledge of discussions of similes, Upamās,[2] we have no certain information on poetics until it occurs as a subordinate element in chapter xvi of the *Bhāratīya Nāṭyaçāstra*, which is essentially a treatise of dramaturgy and which may be placed conjecturally somewhat earlier than Bhāsa and Kālidāsa, though there is no strict proof of date. The great merit of this treatise, a compilation unquestionably from previous works, is that it develops the doctrine of sentiment, Rasa, with its eight subdivisions as erotic, comic, pathetic, and those of horror, heroism, fear, disgust, and wonder. Sentiment is a condition in the mind of the spectator of a drama, or, we may add, the hearer or reader of a poem,

[1] See S. K. Dé, *Sanskrit Poetics* (1923–5); P. V. Kane, *Sāhityadarpaṇa* (1923); Hari Chand, *Kālidāsa et l'art poétique de l'Inde* (1917); V. V. Sovani, *Bhandarkar Comm. Vol.*, pp. 387 ff.; Trivedī, pp. 401 ff.

[2] *Nirukta*, iii. 13; cf. Pāṇini, ii. 1. 55 f., 3. 72.

produced by the emotions of the characters, and the emotions, Bhāvas, are excited by factors which may either be the object of the emotion, as the loved one is in the case of love, or serve to heighten it, as does the spring season. The emotions manifest themselves in effects of various kinds, and they are essentially distinct in psychological character among themselves, while the sentiments, though subdivided according to the emotions which excite them, are nevertheless essentially one in feeling, and this feeling, which later authorities seek more clearly to define, is a special purely aesthetic emotion comparable to the bliss obtained in contemplation of the absolute by the intellect which can comprehend it.[1]

This, however, is not the side of the *Nāṭyaçāstra* which was fated to elicit the chief attention of writers on poetics as opposed to dramaturgy. Poetics developed, if it did not originate, in distinction from dramaturgy, and writers on it were long content to refer merely to that science. The topics which were to engage writers on poetics, however, appear in elementary, though not undeveloped, form in the *Nāṭyaçāstra*. It recognizes four figures of speech, the simile, Upamā, the metaphor, Rūpaka, the Dīpaka, in essence the use of one predicate to many subjects or one subject to many predicates, and the Yamaka, repetition of syllables or alliteration. There is no distinction of figures as those of sound, Çabdālaṁkāra, and of sense, Arthālaṁkāra, and it is significant of early poetry that there are given ten kinds of Yamakas, but only five of Upamās. The Yamakas remain prominent in the older school of poetics, including Bhaṭṭi, Daṇḍin, Vāmana, Rudraṭa, and the *Agni Purāṇa* section on poetics, but Bhāmaha already admits but five kinds and Ānandavardhana and Mammaṭa make it clear that the figure has no real aesthetic importance, though in later as well as older poetry, for instance, the *Ghaṭakarpara*, it is freely used, serving in lieu of rhyme. Further, serving like the figures to bring out the sentiment, are given the ten qualities and the ten defects; it is characteristic of the beginnings of the science that the defects are given positively and the qualities given as the negation of the defects, while in fact it is impossible thus to connect the two lists. Moreover, the details of the lists are obscure, and differently interpreted

[1] See Keith, *Sanskrit Drama* (1924), pp. 314 ff.

both by the later writers on poetics and by the commentators on the Çāstra. On one view [1] the defects are: absence of a complete meaning; incongruity with the context; tautology; ambiguity; violation of syntactical regularity; grammatical errors; break of metrical rules as to pause; misuse of long or short syllables in metre; breach of euphonic rules; and inconsistency as to place, time, artistic usage, popular belief, logic, or science. The qualities are: Çleṣa, possibly in the sense of suggested sense; Prasāda, clearness; Samatā, evenness implying ease of comprehension; Samādhi, superimposition of something special in the sense; Mādhurya, sweetness; Ojas, strength arising from the use of compounds with respect to suitable concatenations of letters; Saukumārya, smoothness arising from happy metres and conjunctions; Arthavyakti, explicitness of sense; Udāra, elevation of subject and sentiment; and Kānti, loveliness, delighting the mind.

Of developments after the Çāstra we know nothing definite, and we can only guess at the stages by which new figures were found out. If we can take Bhāmaha's account as helping us historically—which is a pure assumption not suggested in any way by that author—we may hold [2] that the first step was to distinguish Anuprāsa, alliteration, from Yamaka, the former affecting only single letters, the latter involving the repetition of syllables. But it is much more dubious if the fact that Bhāmaha mentions after this set of five a set of six has any chronological conclusion, and the figures themselves are rather more complex than can be supposed to have been early. They are: Ākṣepa, paraleipsis, the denial of one thing to imply another; Arthāntaranyāsa, corroboration, the adduction of some instance or principle to prove an assertion; Vyatireka, contrast by dissimilitude; Vibhāvanā, abnormal causation, when something comes about by some unusual reason; Samāsokti, brevity, suggestion by metaphorical expressions; and Atiçayokti, hyperbole. Possibly to this period has been referred the figure Vārttā, which, however, was not generally accepted, though Daṇḍin perhaps,[3] treats it as a sort of Hetu, cause. Our trust in the whole theory is seriously undermined when we find that to a third period of development

[1] Bhāmaha, iv; logical faults are given in v. For Bharata's list see xvi. 84 ff.

[2] Jacobi, SBA. 1922, pp. 220 ff.

[3] If Jacobi rightly refers ii. 244 to it.

are assigned three new figures: Yathāsaṁkhya, relative order; Utprekṣā, poetical fancy; and Svabhāvokti, description of the nature of a thing in its reality as appreciated by the poetic imagination; and that the fourth period is made to recognize the large number of figures, twenty-four more, in Bhāmaha. What is really clear is that the *Bhaṭṭikāvya*,[1] Daṇḍin, and Bhāmaha all had before them a large number of figures which they treat in slightly different ways, Bhāmaha for instance rejecting the forces of cause, Hetu, Sūkṣma, and Leça, accepted by Daṇḍin. To assert even a common source for Daṇḍin and Bhāmaha as opposed to Bhaṭṭi is beyond our means of proof, and to ascribe to Medhāvin the invention of Utprekṣā is quite invalid.

2. *The Early Schools of Poetics*

In Daṇḍin we come, as usual in Indian scientific literature, to an authority who used freely many predecessors whose works are lost, and who, therefore, presents us with a fully developed and elaborate doctrine. Daṇḍin was doubtless the author of the *Daçakumāracarita* and his relation to Bhāmaha has been keenly discussed.[2] The difficulty of decision rests on the fact that both authors can be made out to be attacking each other's views, but that there is nothing whatever strictly to prove that they are not dealing with views expressed by some predecessor of the other, as we know for certain in the case of Bhāmaha that he used[3] Medhāvin, who must have expressed opinions similar to those assailed by Daṇḍin. It is, however, on the whole, probable that Bhāmaha knew Daṇḍin, while Daṇḍin did not use him, and with this agrees the generally less refined views of Daṇḍin as in his enumeration of thirty-two kinds of simile, which Bhāmaha reduces to four. Daṇḍin's rejection of the difference between Kathā and Ākhyāyikā seems thoroughly sound, while Bhāmaha's defence seems specially directed against Daṇḍin. It is striking also that Daṇḍin never notices one of the

[1] Cf. on Canto x Nobel, in *Muséon*, xxxvii.

[2] Kane, *Sāhityadarpaṇa* (1923), pp. xxv ff.; M. T. Narasimhiengar, JRAS. 1905, pp. 535 ff.; Pathak, JBRAS. xxiii. 19; IA. xli. 236 ff., support Bhāmaha's posteriority against Trivedī, IA. xlii. 258 ff. R.; Narasimhachar, IA. xli. 90 ff.; xlii. 205; Nobel, ZDMG. lxxiii. 190 ff.; Hari Chand, *Kālidāsa*, pp. 70 ff.; Jacobi, *loc. cit.*

[3] ii. 40, 88; Medhāvirudra, Nami on Rudraṭa, xi. 24. Cf. *Kāvyamīmāṅsā*, p. 12.

many verses adduced by Bhāmaha to expound his views. The matter is not, indeed, of the highest importance, for it is not supposed in any case that Daṇḍin lived long after Bhāmaha, who certainly used the works of Uddyotakara (*c.* 650) and probably knew the *Nyāsa* of Jinendrabuddhi (*c.* 700). On the whole, having regard to the facts regarding the *Daçakumāra-carita*, which suggests that it precedes Subandhu and Bāṇa, we may place Daṇḍin some generations before Bhāmaha.

To Daṇḍin poetry appears under the metaphor of a body of words determined by the sense which it is desired to set out, and that body is ornamented, the term Alaṁkāra here being used in the most general sense to cover anything which lends beauty to the poem as ornaments do to the human body. A poem may consist of verse, prose, or both, as in the drama and the Campū; no Indian writer on poetics allows himself to be led astray into demanding verse form as a condition of poetry. This, of course, was a natural conclusion from the fact that law, medicine, astronomy and astrology, grammar, and philosophy had all been composed in verse, so that outer form was obviously no criterion between the literature of knowledge and that of power. Of verse forms Daṇḍin enumerates the Sargabandha or Mahākāvya, the characteristics of which we have already noted; Muktaka, single verses; Kulaka, groups of up to five verses; Koça, unconnected verses by different authors; Saṁghāta, similar verses by one author. Of prose he mentions Kathā, Ākhyāyikā, and Campū, recognizing as current the difference between the first two, but rejecting it as quite artificial and not even in accordance with practice. The use of different languages is admitted, Sanskrit, Prākrit, Apabhrança, and mixtures of these being allowed, seen in the Mahākāvya in Sanskrit, in poems in the Skandhaka metre in Prākrit, in the Āsāra in Apabhrança, and the Nāṭaka, drama, in a mixed form.[1] Daṇḍin also recognizes the distinction between a poem to be heard and one to be seen, but refers to works on dramatic art for consideration of the latter.

Of special interest is the new presentation of the doctrine of qualities. It is clear that before Daṇḍin there had developed the doctrine of schools or paths, Mārga, of poetry, and Bāṇa refers

[1] The sense of the terms is not given by Daṇḍin, and is dubious; the last may be poems in one metre. Osara is a *v.l.*

to four of them, as we have seen. Daṇḍin declares for the existence of two types, holding that subvarieties are incalculable, and he sets them against each other as the Vaidarbha and Gauḍa, the former the southern, the latter the eastern, the distinguishing marks being the presence in the former of ten qualities which the other does not usually accept. Daṇḍin shows clearly that these distinctions are not his own, and his descriptions are here and there suggestive of doubt on his own part as to what is meant, a doubt increased by divergences of view among the commentators. One quality, indeed, is admitted to be liked even by the Gauḍas, perspicuity of sense; if the ocean is referred to as red, that requires the addition of the words 'through the blood of the serpents.' But the merit of clearness, Prasāda, applicable to the use of words in a natural way, is not attractive to the Gauḍas; they like a phrase such as *anatyarjunābjanmasadṛkṣāñko balakṣaguḥ*, 'the white-beamed (moon) has a spot similar to the not-very-white water-born (lotuses)', where the rare expressions are excused in the Gauḍa view by their being etymologically derivable. Udāratva signifies the presence in a sentence of a distinguished quality, thus giving elevation of style, as in:

arthināṁ kṛpaṇā dṛṣṭis tvanmukhe patitā sakṛt
tadavasthā punar deva nānyasya mukham īkṣate.

'Once the sad eye of suppliants hath fallen on thy face, o king, it taketh there its abode, and gazeth not at the face of any other.' Another explanation given by Daṇḍin himself makes elevation the result of the use of ornamental epithets such as *līlāmbuja*, toy-lotus, *krīḍāsaras*, play-lake, *hemāñgada*, gold bracelet. Kānti is the grace of beauty, which is in harmony with nature, as opposed to the exaggeration, Atyukti, of the Gauḍa style; the two are neatly contrasted: the Vaidarbha has:

anayor anavadyāñgi stanayor jṛmbhamāṇayoḥ
avakāço na paryāptas tava bāhulatāntare.

'O maiden with faultless limbs, there is not space enough between thy creeper-like arms for the expansion of those swelling breasts.' The Gauḍa exaggerates:

alpaṁ nirmitam ākāçam anālocyaiva vedhasā
idam evaṁvidham bhāvi bhavatyāḥ stanajṛmbhaṇam.

'Surely the creator hath made this world too narrow, foreseeing not so great an extension of thy breasts.' Samādhi denotes metaphorical expression, and Daṇḍin shows how words normally vulgar can be used if the sense be no longer literal, as in the case of *vam*, vomit, *niṣṭhīv*, and *udgṛ*, spit out.

These five qualities are clearly essentially connected with sense, a sixth, Mādhurya, sweetness, is defined as possessing Rasa, which here denotes rather tastefulness than sentiment as taken by Bühler among others, and this is a quality of sense as well as of sound, for it applies to the extent of forbidding the use of expressions suggesting vulgar ideas, requiring that love should be alluded to in decently veiled phrases. It, however, also has to do with tasteful arrangement of sounds, and in this there is a divergence between the styles, for the Vaidarbha likes the combination of harmonious sounds, while the Gauḍa prefers the more obvious and blatant device of alliteration outright. The Vaidarbha also demands Sukumāratā, gentleness, which means the use of syllables which are not rough sounding, while the Gauḍas like harsh sounds when they serve to accord with the sentiment expressed. Thus we have for the Vaidarbha the pleasing if in sense negligible:

maṇḍalīkṛtya barhāṇi kaṇṭhair madhuragītibhiḥ
kalāpinaḥ pranṛtyanti kāle jīmūtamālini.

'Making circles of their tails the peacocks dance in the season of the clouds, uttering sweet cries.' Contrast the Gauḍa fiery utterance:

nyakṣeṇa kṣapitaḥ pakṣaḥ kṣatriyāṇāṁ kṣaṇād iti.

'In a moment the host of the warriors was destroyed by Paraçurāma.' There is again a distinction as to Samatā, evenness: the Vaidarbha style likes the letters to be soft, harsh, or well mixed, but the Gauḍas do not object to unevenness, and the poetry aiming at brilliance or bombast of both sense and ornament (*arthālaṁkāraḍambara*) is recognized as having won fame. The Vaidarbhas also like Çliṣṭa, stability,[1] diction which is not loose, i.e. composed of easily pronounced syllables—while the Gauḍas do not mind the latter defect, provided it be alliterative;

[1] In i. 43 this seems the best sense; Lüders in Nobel's *Indian Poetry*, p. 107, n. 12.

thus to express the common idea of a jasmine wreath and its attendant bees the Vaidarbhas say: *mālatīdāma laṅghitaṁ bhramaraiḥ*, the Gauḍas *mālatīmālā lolālikalilā*. Finally both styles like force, Ojas, consisting of lengthy compounds, or rather of a large number of compounds, both in prose and poetry in the Gauḍa view, in prose only in that of Vaidarbhan usage, though the latter would evidently sanction it if it was set off by short words as in:

payodharataṭotsaṅgalagnasandhyātapāñçukā
kasya kāmāturaṁ ceto vāruṇī na kariṣyati?

'Whose heart is not made lovesick by the sight of the western sky, whose garment, the evening sun, hangs on the slopes of the clouds that are her breasts?' The poet recognizes that varieties of compounds are made by the mingling of syllables long and short.

Daṇḍin insists that to produce the effective poetry he has praised are necessary natural genius, which arises from impressions formed in earlier births, much study, and great application, and, recognizing that the first requisite may be unattainable, allows concentration on the second two. He then proceeds, in Book ii of the *Kāvyādarça*, to define Alaṁkāras as those qualities which produce charm in poetry, some of which have been already mentioned in dealing with the difference of styles, while those common to both styles are enumerated in ii and iii, the figures of sense coming first, than those of sound, treated from our point of view at absurd length. The early state of Daṇḍin's views is shown in his failure to distinguish quality and figure, and in his making no effort to explain the poetic effect of figures save by mere generalities. Nor has he any scheme of division of figures, and in a manner somewhat startling we find that he ranks as a figure, the first of all, Svabhāvokti, natural description as a thing appears to a poet. This figure—or rather ornament—is of a quite special kind, for it is classed as opposed to all the rest of the figures of sense, which are classed under Vakrokti, crooked, non-natural, figurative, speech. The meaning of the distinction must be that in the former case the poet, by his discernment, sees the essence of a thing—using that term in the widest sense, be it an individual thing, or a species, or a quality or action—and sets it out in plain speech: in the latter he describes not necessarily with special intuition, but with figurative language. He has already insisted, in his account of the qualities, on the supreme importance to the poet of the use of metaphor.

The actual list of figures[1] is a curious mixture including much that we should not reckon figures of a distinct kind, as well as figures more naturally so styled. We have in his order the simile in thirty-two varieties, the metaphor, the Dīpaka, Āvṛtti, repetition in the sense of the use, e.g., of four different verbs with one meaning as a quasi contrast to the Dīpaka, Ākṣepa, Arthāntaranyāsa, Vyatireka, Vibhāvanā, Samāsokti, hyperbole, poetic fancy, and then three figures rejected by Bhāmaha, Hetu, Sūkṣma, and Leça. These express cause, convey a meaning by adroit hint or gesture, or conceal something which has almost come to light; but Daṇḍin gives us an alternative view of Leça, a rebuke or eulogy. Then come order; Preyas, the expression of pleasure; Rasavat, the expression of one or other of the sentiments; Ūrjasvin, that of vigour; Paryāyokta, the expression indirectly of something which cannot openly be avowed; Samāhita, mentioning some fact which has come to afford aid to one's end; Udātta, description of something noble or elevated; Apahnuti, seeming denial to affirm more strongly; Çleṣa, double meaning; Viçeṣokti, description of a special distinction; Tulyayogitā, putting like things together; Virodha, seeming incongruity; Aprastutastotra, indirect praise; Vyājastuti, praise concealed as censure; Nidarçana, reference to a like result; Sahokti, mention of two things as happening together; Parivṛtti, exchange of objects; Āçis, benediction; Saṁkīrṇa, mixing of figures; and Bhāvika. The latter is a quality applicable to the whole of a composition and expresses the purpose and mind of the poet; it reveals itself in the making of all the different elements of the plot aid one another to their end, the avoidance of needless qualifications, the description of things in their place, and the exposition of even a difficult matter by due regard to orderly exposition. This quality, we can see, would, if Daṇḍin had had

[1] Cf. Kane, *Sāhityadarpaṇa*, pp. I ff. Nobel (*Beitr. z. ält. Gesch. d. Alaṁkāraçāstra* (1911); ZDMG, lxvi. 283 ff.; lxvii. 1 ff.; lxxiii. 189 ff.) deals with some of the figures, but not always satisfactorily; his desire to place Bhāmaha before Kālidāsa leads him to deny the former's obvious reference to the *Meghadūta* (*Indian Poetry*, p. 15), even though he realizes that Kālidāsa was really the older.

any idea of order, have been conjoined with Svabhāvokti; we may compare Aristotle's [1] ἐνέργεια. It is important to note that Daṇḍin expressly mentions the view of some authors which made a hyperbole implicit in every figure whatever, and he himself lays it down that in every form of Vakrokti the use of the Çleṣa enhances the beauty, thus according approval to the practice of Subandhu and Bāṇa and of himself in his less immoderate action in the *Daçakumāracarita.*

Book iii of the *Kāvyādarça* develops at great length the doctrine of Yamakas, leading us to the stanza with one consonant, *n*, only; then follow riddles and finally the ten defects of poetry much as in the *Nāṭyaçāstra.* But nothing of real value is here found.

The doctrines of Daṇḍin found an echo and completion in those of Vāmana,[2] who is doubtless to be placed at the end of the eighth century.[3] We have in him the emergence, however, of a new idea, that of the soul of poetry as opposed merely to the body. As later than both Daṇḍin and Bhāmaha he has a more developed idea of the nature of Kāvya; it is not merely words and meaning or sense, but there must be qualities and figures as well. But he also seeks to fit all the elements in Daṇḍin into a scheme, based on the doctrine of Rīti, a new word for style. The soul of poetry is style which is a specified arrangement of words, the term specified referring to distinction according to the qualities possessed which are the cause of charm in poetry, while the figures are ranged as things which add to the charm. He admits three kinds of Rīti, Vaidarbhī, Gauḍī, Pāñcālī, so styled because found among the local poets, but not due to local causes. The Vaidarbhī is perfect and has all the qualities. The Gauḍī is accorded the qualities of Kānti and Ojas, understood here in the sense of many compounds which are of great length, and high-sounding words, a statement illustrated by a famous stanza of Bhavabhūti. The Pāñcālī has sweetness and gentleness, Mādhurya and Saukumārya, like the style of Purāṇas. The Vaidarbhī is strongly insisted on, the other two disparaged, and

[1] *Rhet.* iii. 10, 16. On metaphor, cf. c. 2.

[2] *Kāvyālaṁkāra* with *Vṛtti*, ed. KM. 15, 1895; Vāṇīvilāsa Press, 1909; trans. G. Jhā, IT. iii and iv.

[3] Minister of Jayāpīḍa of Kashmir (779–813); Jacobi, ZDMG. lxiv. 138 f.

a pure form of Vaidarbhī is expressly commended which uses no compounds, thus allowing full play to the qualities of sense. The qualities in Vāmana are now rearranged as qualities of sound and of sense, each having two aspects, with results far from satisfactory as regards clearness, and disadvantageous as departing from the normal use of the terms established in Daṇḍin. Under the quality beauty Vāmana includes the feature of implying sentiment, which Daṇḍin places in the figures Preyas, Rasavat, and Ūrjasvin, and perhaps in the quality Mādhurya, while the quality of perspicuity covers the Svabhāvokti of Daṇḍin. Under the qualities also room is found for the odd figure Bhāvika, whose awkward position in Daṇḍin's view has been noted.

Vāmana's treatment of figures is important for his reduction of their importance as elements in poetry; the qualities are vital, the figures not: they are related rather to the body, word and meaning, of poetry than to the style which is the soul. Further, he insists that the simile lies at the bottom of all figures and to achieve this result has to omit various figures, in addition to those above mentioned, such as Udātta, Paryāyokta, and Sūkṣma, while others he defines differently. Vakrokti to him is a special mode of metaphorical expression, not the generic term for all figurative speech as in Daṇḍin.

As opposed to Daṇḍin we find in Bhāmaha's *Kāvyālaṁkāra* [1] a decided preference for a system which insists on the figures as the essential feature of the poetry whose body is word and sense. Bhāmaha definitely rejects outright the distinction of two styles, and the qualities which he does recognize are connected generally with poetry, not with any special style. Moreover, he shows the reduction of qualities to three, which is characteristic of later thought, though he does not specifically deal with the matter as do the later writers, who reduce Daṇḍin's ten to their categories. He mentions, however, as sweet, a poem which is agreeable to hear and has not too many compounds, and a clear poem is one which can be understood by even women and children; strength he understands as usual as connected with long compounds, and he implies that this is incompatible with clearness as well as sweetness. He has, however, no clear marking line between qualities and figures; he mentions clearness and sweetness in

[1] Ed. as App. viii to K. P. Trivedī's ed. of *Pratāparājayaçobhūṣaṇa*, BSS. 1909.

close proximity to his account of figures, and he describes Bhāvikatva as a figure or quality indifferently. He definitely insists on the distinction of figures into those of sound and sense, and he more or less vaguely is conscious of the doctrine which regards the essential feature of poetry to be figurative expression, Vakrokti. For the two-fold division of subject-matter of poetry favoured by Daṇḍin, which recognizes traditional matter and invention, he substitutes one admitting also foundation on the arts or sciences. His division of classes of poetry is five-fold, the Sargabandha, drama, Akhyāyikā, Kathā, and detached verses, and he defends the distinction between Kathā and Ākhyāyikā on quite worthless grounds. But he insists that there is a common element in all poetry, Vakrokti, while he denies, accordingly, to Svabhāvokti the right to be styled a figure at all. This figurative expression he identifies with hyperbole, which is explained as an expression surpassing ordinary usage, meaning no doubt a poetical conception as opposed to the prosaic everyday conception of facts. Bhāmaha examines the various figures from this point of view, and his work in this regard was carried on by Udbhaṭa, the contemporary of Vāmana, whose *Alaṁkārasaṁgraha*[1] deals with forty-one figures, including three varieties of alliteration. His *Bhāmahavivaraṇa* is lost, and from Pratīhārendurarāja, pupil of Mukula, who wrote *c.* 950, and commented on Udbhaṭa, we learn little of importance. Of no historical importance is Bhāmaha's treatment of defects, in which he gives a new list of ten additional to the tradition alone (Book iv), while in Books v and vi he describes logical and grammatical errors in poetry.

There are in Udbhaṭa hints of new views which later had some effect. The ascription to him of the doctrine that sentiment is the soul of poetry is due to an error, a verse cited by Pratīhārendurāja being wrongly ascribed to him. But he did lay some stress on the element of sentiment in poetry and he added to the list of eight of the *Nāṭyaçāstra* a ninth, the calm. Further, while he ignored, like Bhāmaha, the styles of Daṇḍin, he introduced a new classification based entirely on sound effects, primarily alliteration, in the shape of the theory of three Vṛttis, manners, classed as elegant (*upanāgarikā*), ordinary (*grāmyā*), and harsh (*paruṣā*). In treating figures he adds Dṛṣṭānta, exemplification,

[1] Ed. Jacobi, JRAS. 1897, pp. 829–53; BSS. 1925.

and Kāvyaliñga, poetical causation, divides simile according to the grammatical form of expression, as by suffixes like *vat*, and starts the investigation of the relations of double meaning to other figures, which is later developed, as well as the complex issue of the different kinds of blending of figures, Saṁsṛṣṭi and Saṁkara.

Rudraṭa, who wrote before 900 and probably in the earlier part of the ninth century, the *Kāvyālaṁkāra*,[1] in sixteen chapters of Āryā verses, makes no innovation in theory, but belongs essentially to the school which, without scientific investigation, accepted as its duty the enumeration of figures. He seeks to divide figures on the base of sound and sense, and then to subdivide on principles of his own; under those of sound he classes figures on the basis of equivocation (*vakrokti*), paronomasia (*çleṣa*), pictorial effects (*citra*), alliteration and Yamakas; those of sense are based on reality, similitude, hyperbole, and coalescence. This results in a repetition of some figures under different heads, and his plan of division received no general acceptance, though Mammaṭa adopted some of his figures, and his new interpretation of Vakrokti as an equivoke based on paronomasia or intonation (*kāku*), though rejected by Hemacandra, prevails from Mammaṭa onwards over the wider sense of Daṇḍin or the narrower interpretation as a figure based on similitude of Vāmana. He generalizes and extends the manners of Udbhaṭa, in whom they seemed to be restricted to alliterative effects, by laying down five manners of letters (*varṇa*), sweet, harsh, pompous, dainty (*lalitā*), and excellent (*bhadrā*). But he accepts also the styles, Rītis, of Vāmana, though under the influence of Bhāmaha we find them looked at in a new light. They now number four, and the distinction is based on the use of compounds. The Vaidarbhī has none, verbal prefixes not ranking as compounding elements. Pāñcālī compounds up to three words, Lāṭīyā five to seven, and Gauḍīyā any number. His debt to Daṇḍin is seen in his dealing at great length with Yamakas and developing the idea of Citra, tricks in poetic form, such as Māgha declares to distinguish poetry

[1] Ed., with the comm. of Namisādhu, a Jain (1068), KM. 2, 1909. Rudraṭa is son of Vāmuka and is also called Çatānanda. His difference from Rudra Bhaṭṭa was proved by Jacobi, WZKM. ii. 151 ff.; ZDMG. xlii. 425. Rudra Bhaṭṭa is known to Hemacandra (p. 110); his *Çṛṅgāratilaka* is ed. Pischel, Kiel, 1886.

in his day, but which Bhāmaha and Udbhaṭa ignore, while Udbhaṭa also passes over Yamakas. A novel feature is the introduction in four chapters of the theory of sentiment which, however, is in no wise brought into vital connexion with his subject, but stands in a merely formal collocation. He recognizes ten sentiments, adding the feelings of calm and friendship to the traditional list.

Still less important from the point of view of theory is the *Kāvyamīmāṅsā* of the dramatist Rājaçekhara (*c.* 900) which is a work in other regards of no small interest and originality. He conceives of the Kāvyapuruṣa, the spirit of poetry, son of Sarasvatī, and the Sāhityavidyā, science of poetics, who becomes his bride, the term Sāhitya being derived, we may believe, from the old doctrine of the union of word or sound and sense to make a poem, as laid down by Bhāmaha, Māgha, and others. He distinguishes carefully science, Çāstra, and poetry, and analyses the divisions of the former; he discusses at length the relation of genius, poetic imagination, culture, and practice in making a poet and classifies poets on this score. A further classification is based on the fact that a poet may produce a Çāstra, or a poem, or combine both in varying proportions, and of poets in the narrower sense he makes eight illogical groups. His own conception of poetry appears traditional; he defines it as a sentence possessing qualities and figures, and he accepts Vāmana's doctrine of styles which are the outcome of Sāhityavidyā's wanderings in diverse lands. The sources of poetry are touched on, and the subject-matter as concerned with men, divine beings, or denizens of hell is investigated. Very interesting is the discussion of borrowing from earlier works; it is recognized as justified by freshness of idea and expression, and elaborate illustration is given of thirty-two different ways of evading improper plagiarism. Important also is the consideration of poetical conventions, and we are given a geography of India and many remarks on the seasons with their appropriate winds, birds, flowers, and action. Rājaçekhara also gives curious details of the likings of different parts of India for certain languages and their mode of mispronouncing Sanskrit. The Magadhas and others east of Benares are blunt in Prākrit, good at Sanskrit, but the Gauḍas are thoroughly bad in Prākrit, the Lāṭas dislike Sanskrit but use

Prākrit beautifully, the Surāṣṭras and Travaṇas mix Apabhrança with Sanskrit, the Draviḍas recite musically, Kashmirian pronunciation is as bad as their poetry is good, Karṇāṭas end up sentences with a twang, northerners are nasal, the people of Pañcāla sweet and honey-like. Women poets are recognized, and sex barriers despised, while of the ten grades of poets the rank of Kavirāja, held by Rājaçekhara, comes seventh even above the Mahākavi himself. Great stress is laid on the assemblies at which poets were judged and where the prize given by the king included crowning with a fillet and riding in a special chariot. The poet's paraphernalia is given, chalk, a board, palm leaves, birch bark, pen and ink.[1] More important is the insistence on the equal rights of all four forms of speech : Sanskrit ; Prākrit, elegant, sweet, and smooth ; Apabhrança also elegant, as lọved in Marwar, Ṭakka, and Bhādānaka ; and Bhūtabhāṣā current in Avantī, Pāriyātra, and Daçapura, while the people of the Madhyadeça used all equally well. The people of that land show also their admixture by their colours, brown like the easterners, dark like the southerners, white like the westerners, while the northerners are fair. When we add that he quotes extensively including the *Mahimnaḥstotra*, gives many fine verses and some anecdotes, and is usually lively if pedantic, the merits of his work can be appreciated.[2]

3. *The Doctrine of Dhvani*

Rājaçekhara lived at a time when a new doctrine, that of Dhvani, tone, had been steadily winning its way to power. It is represented for us by the metrical Kārikās preserved in the *Dhvanyāloka*[3] of Ānandavardhana of Kashmir (*c.* 850) with its

[1] On these matters see Bühler, *Indische Palaeographie* ; Hoernle, JASB. lix. pt. i. no. 2 ; on the use of paper, Waddell, JRAS. 1914, pp. 136 f. ; Haraprasād, *Report*, i. p. 7 ; on the claim of Indian writing as indigenous, not of Semitic origin, see Bhandarkar, POCP. 1919, ii. 305 ff.

[2] Ed. *Gaekwad's Oriental Series*, 1916. Many stanzas on poets by Rājaçekhara probably came from some lost work, perhaps the *Haravilāsa* ; cf. Bhandarkar, *Report*, 1887–91, pp. ix ff ; Peterson, JBRAS. xvii. 57–71 ; for an exposure of forged verses adduced to support an attack on Bhāsa's authorship see G. Harihar Sastri, IHQ. i. 370 ff. ; K. G. Sesha Aiyar, 361 ; a bad case invites worse arguments ; cf. Keith, BSOS. iii. 623 ff. ; T. Gaṇapati Śāstrī, 627 ff.

[3] Ed. KM. 25, 1911 ; trans. H. Jacobi, ZDMG. lvi and lvii.

super-commentary by Abhinavagupta, *Locana*.[1] The Kārikās assert that the doctrine is old, but if so we must assume that it had not won much success, and it may be that the author referred really to some not distant predecessor, justifying himself by the view that the doctrine was implicit in the older writers. His name was possibly but not certainly Sahṛdaya, which at best is merely an epithet, and he must have written early in the ninth century. At any rate by the ability of his commentators and by the adoption by Mammaṭa of the doctrine the new view won on the whole a dominant position in Indian poetics.

The theory finds its origin in the analysis of language and meaning. The phrase, a herdsmen's station on the Ganges, is obviously as it stands absurd; the denotation (*abhidhā*) gives no sense, and we are obliged to find a transferred sense (*lakṣaṇā*) which gives us the sense of a station on the bank of the Ganges. This shows the incompatibility of the literal sense as one factor, and the possibility of giving an allied meaning as another. But this is not all; there is brought to us by such a phrase deliberately used in poetry a sense of the holy calm of such a station situated on the sacred stream with all its associations of piety. This, it is contended, is not given by implication, but by the power of suggestion which is derived from the poet's purpose (*prayojana*) in applying the phrase. This doctrine of suggestion which the grammarians did not accept could be based on a philosophical opinion of the grammarians themselves. They recognized the Sphoṭa,[2] a mysterious entity, a sort of hypostatization of sound, of which action sounds were manifestations, and the same idea of the revelation of something inherent (*vyañjanā*) is found in the Vedānta, where all is a manifestation of the underlying reality, the Brahman or absolute. There were common-sense people [3] who held that all could be put down to denotation; a word might be regarded like an arrow which could pierce armour and slay the foe in a single movement, without inventing new phases of operation, while yet others [4] claimed that the signification, Tātparya, resulting from the taking of words together in a sentence explained all that was

[1] Ed. KM. 25 (i–iii); Dé, Calcutta, 1923 (iv).

[2] E. Abegg, *Festschrift Windisch*, pp. 188 ff.; ZDMG. lxxvii. 207ff.

[3] Dīrghavyāpāravādin school, dubiously ascribed to Lollaṭa (Dé, *Sanskrit Poetics*, ii. 192, n. 16).

[4] Abhihitānvayavādin school of Mīmāṅsā.

required, and others[1] again held that even this idea of Tātparya was needless, because the words had the power *per se* of conveying their relations with other words to make up a whole. A further school, which became more insistent later, declared that suggestion was not real, and that what was explained by suggestion ought to be accounted for by inference. From the mention of the station on the Ganges one at once inferred the intention of the speaker to convey the ideas of purity, &c.

But the holders of the doctrine of Dhvani remained unconvinced, and on the basis of their theory they declared that the soul of poetry was not style nor sentiment, but tone, Dhvani, by which they meant that an implied sense was the essence of poetry. What was suggested might be threefold, either a subject, or a figure, or a sentiment and, while these three possibilities are admitted by the more orthodox members of the school, including Ānandavardhana and Mammaṭa, Abhinavagupta went much further and declared that in reality all suggestion must be of sentiment, holding that in the long run suggestion of subject and figure reduced themselves to this. Viçvanātha, author of the *Sāhityadarpaṇa*, followed his lead, but this never became the accepted doctrine, for the writers realized that, by attempting thus to limit suggestion, they would cut out a good deal of admitted poetry. Suggestion, however, can be expressed in two ways, for it may rest on the metaphorical sense of words, in which case we have the species of Dhvanikāvya where the literal meaning is not intended at all (*avivakṣita-vācya*), thus making provision for the ordinary view which attached great importance to metaphor or simile as the base of poetry. Or, again, the literal sense may be intended, but a deeper suggestion implied, in which case we have the type where the literal sense is meant but ultimately comes to something deeper (*vivakṣitānyapara-vācya*). Here, again, we have two different cases, for the process of apprehension may be instantaneous (*asaṁlakṣya-krama*), which is the rule in respect of suggestion of sentiment, or due to a perceptible process (*saṁlakṣya-krama*), as in the suggestion of subject and figure. The process of apprehension of sentiment is comparable to the piercing of a hundred lotus leaves with one needle; there is a process by which the factors induce the senti-

[1] Anvitābhidhānavādin school.

ment, but it is so rapid as to seem instantaneous. It is clear also that the rising up of sentiment is not the result of inference; it can come into being only in a person who has had in previous lives experience which gives him aesthetic susceptibilities, makes him a feeling heart or connoisseur (*sahṛdaya*), and in him it arises as a perfectly unique emotional experience, comparable only to the bliss of cognition of the absolute,[1] a transcendental (*alaukika*) joy. He who sees on the stage, or reads in poetry, the factors which are connected with sentiment presented, does not regard them as external to himself, whether as the property of the actor or of the hero of the play or poem, nor does he appropriate them to himself; he sees them under the aspect of universality, and this causes the sentiment to be unique and pleasurable, whatever the corresponding emotion, as a personal possession, would be. What in real life would be horror, thus as a sentiment is exquisite joy. We have, it is clear, a real effect to explain the nature of disinterested aesthetic pleasure arising from literature.

But the system does not deny the right to rank as poetry of poetry which contains only in a secondary degree suggestion (*guṇībhūta-vyaṅgya*). This head helped them to find a place for the doctrines of the older writers who accepted in certain figures the expression of sentiment, as in the Preyas, Rasavat, and Ūrjasvin of Daṇḍin. Moreover, it served to include cases in which these writers found that one figure lay at the base of others, as when Vāmana found simile in all, and Bhāmaha held that in all figures there lay hyperbole, a view mentioned by Daṇḍin also. Finally the system, though not its sterner advocates, confessed that they must permit the kind of poetry called Citra, picture, in which there was mere beauty without any suggested sense at all. The beauty may be of sense or sound.

It remained to seek some way of dealing with the qualities and figures and the styles or manners of the earlier writers, so as to find them a just place. One great simplification was effected by reducing the number of qualities, restricting their extension to sound effects, and by merging in them both the Rītis of Vāmana and the Vṛttis of Udbhaṭa, which were at the same time practically identified. This became possible through the adop-

[1] This is, we must remember, identic with the bliss which is part of the absolute as one, being, thought, and joy.

tion of a new doctrine as to the relation of qualities to the poem; the sentiment being regarded as the vital element, the qualities are related to it as the soul of the poem, in the same way as heroism is an attribute of the soul of man. This fact, however, precludes us from regarding qualities as stereotyped in the old fashion; everything depends on the sentiment, and what relatively to sentiment would be a quality might in the abstract be a defect. If, then, we admit qualities, they must be such as are never defects, and they must be positive in nature, not mere lack of defects, and distinct in character. On this score we can dismiss Vāmana's Çleṣa, Samādhi, and Udāratā as merely forms of Ojas, strength; Saukumārya and Kānti are no more than the absence of the faults of harshness and vulgarity; and Samatā, evenness, is in some cases positively a blemish. We have thus left just three qualities, and these of sound only, there being no need in the views of the school, which Mammaṭa in special develops very clearly, to allow of qualities of sense. These are strength, which is regarded as causing, or as Viçvanātha insists, coincident with an expansion (*vistara*) of the mind, and which has its proper place in the sentiments of heroism, horror, and disgust; sweetness, which stands in a like relation to a melting (*druti*) of the mind, and is normally present in the sentiment of love-in-union, but appears also, rising in degree in order, in pathos, love-in-separation, and calm; and clearness, including the older Arthavyakti, which corresponds to an extension or pervasion (*vikāsa*) of the mind. The idea of these psychological equations was probably borrowed from Bhaṭṭa Nāyaka who in his theory of the enjoyment (*bhoga*) of sentiment spoke of these three conditions of the mind. In concrete terms the characteristics of the three qualities of sound are given by Mammaṭa as depending on arrangement of letters, compounds, and style of composition; thus sweetness depends on the use of all the mutes (save linguals) with the corresponding nasals; *r* and *ṇ* with short vowels; and no compounds or short compounds; strength arises from the use of double consonants, or consonants followed by the corresponding aspirate; conjuncts of which *r* forms part; lingual letters save *ṇ*; the palatal and lingual sibilants; long compounds; and a formidable, loaded, composition; no special rules are given for clearness. It is obvious that Mammaṭa is here incorporating much of what Udbhaṭa taught regarding his Vṛttis, the characteristics of the Upanāgarikā and Paruṣā forms being closely similar, and thus it is possible for Mammaṭa to bring the Vṛttis under qualities. Nor, as he includes the use of compounds in his treatment, does he find it difficult to include the styles of Vāmana, as brought into close relation to compounds by Rudraṭa. It is, of course, all rather artificial, and very much of an effort to harmonize without real care for the facts, but it is normal and plausible enough.

In the case of the figures a definite line is drawn between them and the qualities. The figures are only of importance in so far as they seek to enhance the sentiment; they do not, however, act directly on the sentiment, but they aid it by decorating the body, sound and sense, just as the soul of a man has as attributes the qualities, while ornaments such as a necklace affect his body directly. If figures do not aid the sentiment, then they are merely forms of speech, and their place is in poetry of the third type, Citra, pictorial poetry which Viçvanātha denies outright the name of poetry.

Ānandavardhana give much else of great interest, and his remarks on compounds are sensible and just; he allows them freely in Ākhyāyikās, but he points out that even there where pathetic, or love-sorrow effects are aimed at such compounds are not suitable, and in the Kathā they should be employed in moderation. The doctrine of Doṣas, defects, is treated from the same point of view as that of qualities; tautology, for instance, may become an excellence if the suggested sense is made more effectively felt by means of it. But as with qualities, there may be real faults which are always such; the Dhvanikāra insists that in love there is always a defect in using unmelodious (*çrutiduṣṭa*) expressions, though such are in good taste in the heroic or the horrible sentiments.

4. *The Critics and Supporters of the Doctrine of Dhvani*

The idea of suggestion did not pass unchallenged. Bhaṭṭa Nāyaka in the *Hṛdayadarpaṇa*,[1] perhaps an independent work

[1] Cf. M. Hiriyanna, POPC. 1919, ii. 246 ff., who regards him as expressing the Sāṁkhya view of aesthetic joy as arising beyond nature to something finer if not real, while the Vedānta view rests on the revelation of the absolutely real which is joy.

though there is some evidence of it having been a commentary on the *Nāṭyaçāstra*, who wrote before Abhinavagupta, insisted on his own theory of the effect of words. In addition to denotation, he ascribed to them the faculty of generalization, Bhāvakatva, which consists in making the meaning intelligible as universal to the audience, while a third power, Bhojakatva, results in the audience relishing the enjoyment of the poem. This condition is one of an enjoyment which cannot be described, but which is marked, as we have seen, by the melting, expansion, and extension of the mind. The loss of his work makes it very difficult to appreciate what Nāyaka exactly intended to convey.

More fortunate is Kuntala, probably a contemporary of Abhinavagupta, whose *Vakroktijīvita*[1] is an effort to present in a new and improved form the idea vaguely present to Bhāmaha and those who laid stress on figures as the essential feature of poetry. He insists that Vakrokti, crooked or figurative speech, is the life of poetry, distinguishing it from science and any merely ordinary or natural mode of expressing facts of any sort. It is, therefore, a deviation from the ordinary language of life in order to produce a certain striking effect (*vicchitti*), or an imaginative turn of speech (*bhañgī-bhaṇiti*). Poetry, therefore, is to be defined as embellished sound and sense, the embellishment being figurative speech, and as this is the only Alaṁkāra possible, and as it is essential to poetry, it is absurd to have any definition which omits figures or makes them subordinate. He goes in great detail through all the forms of poetry in order to show that the principle of Vakrokti covers adequately all developments, citing copious examples from the poets, especially Kālidāsa. It is to the imagination or skill of the poet, his work (*kavikarman*), that we owe the presence of Vakrokti in any poem, and this work can be classed according as he exhibits it in regard to the letters, to the base or termination of words, to a sentence, a particular topic, or a treatise as a whole. It is clear that we have here in part a reminiscence of the doctrine of an element of hyperbole in all poetry asserted by Bhāmaha ; a poem attains at best a transcendental charm (*lokottara vaicitrya*), which can be judged in the long run only by the man of taste, a result

[1] Ed. S. K. Dé, Calcutta, 1923.

in which Kuntala agrees largely with the theory which he attacks.

The strength of this position is clearly the room it finds to allow of accepting figures on their own merits, and not as ancillary to a sentiment as essential features of poetry; we have their cause in the poet's imagination (*kavipratibhā*), and their effect is a definite fact, a species of charm. Mammaṭa gladly accepts this fact and, when figures do not affect sentiment, still declares that they have charm (*vaicitrya*), and Ruyyaka built up his treatment of figures on this basis. To complete his theory Kuntala naturally endeavours to bring both sentiment and suggestion under the scope of his principle, with just as much success as the opposite effort achieved.

Mahiman Bhaṭṭa,[1] who was later than Abhinavagupta, developed in lieu a doctrine which declined to accept the views of Kuntala, but claimed that Dhvani could always be reduced to inference (*anumāna*), and that there was no such thing as immediate apprehension of sentiment, but that between the factors and the result there intervened some space, however short, during which the function of inherence was active. He criticized severely the failure of Dhvanikāra to give a definition of poetry which would be comprehensive, and in his second chapter he deals at some length, incidental to his main object, with propriety (*aucitya*) dealing with defects of sense, such as the wrong use of the factors, &c., and of form, such as the failure to co-ordinate the parts of a proposition, break in regular order, violation of syntax, tautology, and pleonasm. The work, however, is hardly of much consequence, for it deals merely with the question of the form of apprehension which is artistically of negligible importance.

Other authors remained outside the sphere of the influence of the new doctrine. Thus the section on poetics of the *Agni Purāṇa*,[2] which is of uncertain date, and Bhoja's large *Sarasvatīkaṇṭhābharaṇa*[3] show that other theories were prevalent, though their scope extended to minor issues. The Purāṇa adopts the

[1] *Vyaktiviveka*, with comm. (poss. by Ruyyaka), TSS. 5, 1909.

[2] cc. 336–46. Kane (*Sāhityadarpaṇa*, pp. iii–v) puts it after Ānandavardhana, contrary to Dé's view (*Sanskrit Poetics*, i. 103).

[3] Ed. A. Borooah, Calcutta, 1883–4.

ordinary definition of poetry as possessing qualities and figures and being free from defects, while Bhoja requires it to possess sentiment, but neither has any effective discussion of the vital character of poetry. The Purāṇa, however, recognizes the doctrine of styles, making four as in Rudraṭa, and combining their marks of distinction so as to include the kinds of letters used, the length of compounds, and the use of metaphor. Bhoja adds two more styles, Āvantikā, intermediate between Vaidarbhī and Pāñcālī, and Māgadhī, which is a defective style (*khaṇḍarīti*). The Purāṇa introduces a new complication in the shape of distinguishing particular and general qualities; the latter are given as seven of sound, six of sense, and six of both, while figures are classed as of sound, of sense, and of both. Bhoja accepts this and gives absurdly twenty-four of each. His extensive citations and authority lent him some popularity without affecting substantially poetic theory. His treatment of sentiment in the *Sarasvatīkaṇṭhābharaṇa* is supplemented by the *Çṛṅgāraprakāça* where, as in Rudra Bhaṭṭa's *Çṛṅgāratilaka*, the erotic sentiment is made the chief feature.

The doctrine of Dhvani was adopted by Mammaṭa, as we have seen, who with Alaṭa (Alaka, Allaṭa) set out the theory in the *Kāvyaprakāça*[1] about 1100 in a complete and careful form in the shape of Sūtras with a commentary; the theory of a different origin of these two is unfounded, and his coadjutor aided him or wrote parts of Ullāsas vii and x at least. Mammaṭa attempted to supply the lacuna criticized by the *Vyaktiviveka* and defined a poem as sound and sense, free from defects, possessing qualities and sometimes figures, ignoring as essential sentiment, although he makes the qualities essentially attributes of the sentiment, a defect which Viçvanātha sought to remedy by defining poetry as having sentiment as its soul, rejecting thus either subject or figure as a real object of suggestion. Mammaṭa has three qualities, reducing others to them and including under them the styles and manners of earlier writers, while defects he classes as those of sentiment, of word, proposition, and sense, a division later often followed. Figures he treated as of sound,

[1] Ed. with various commentaries, Calcutta, 1866; Benares, 1866; BSS. 1917; ĀnSS. 1911; KM. 63, 1897. Cf. Sukthankar, ZDMG. lxvi. 477 ff., 533 ff. Trans. G. Jhā, Benares, 1918. Māṇikyacandra's comm. (1160 A. D.) is ed., Mysore, 1922.

of sense, and, a small number, of both. Viçvanātha's *Sāhitya-darpaṇa*[1] (*c.* 1350) largely follows Mammaṭa, but it uses also the treatises on drama which it includes. He, however, accepts the doctrine of styles, regarded as an arrangement of words (*pada-saṁghaṭanā*) in a special way and admits four: Vaidarbhī or dainty, with letters indicating sweetness and no or short compounds; Gauḍī, with letters indicating strength and long compounds; Pāñcālī, containing other letters than those mentioned and compounds of five or six words; and Lāṭī, intermediate between Pāñcālī and Vaidarbhī. On figures he shows often the influence of Ruyyaka. His work takes the now usual form of Sūtra and commentary. Similar in spirit and manner are the *Ekāvalī*[2] of Vidyādhara and the *Pratāparudrayaçobhūṣaṇa*[3] of Vidyānātha, both written *c.* 1300, the one for Narasiṅha of Orissa, the other for Pratāparudra of Warangal, whose glory is celebrated in a drama included in it to illustrate the rules of dramaturgy. Both are more orthodox than Viçvanātha in accepting subject and figure as objects of suggestion as well as sentiment. Vidyādhara, however, follows Bhoja in enumerating twenty-four qualities in defiance of the reduction of this head to three of sound only by the school.

In the contemporary of Mammaṭa, Hemacandra, we find a placid borrowing from Mammaṭa, Abhinavagupta, Rājaçekhara, the *Vakroktijīvita*, and so on. His *Kāvyānuçāsana*,[4] with the *Viveka* by himself, is destitute of originality, but contains a section on dramaturgy. Even less valuable are the works of the two Vāgbhaṭas, of the twelfth and thirteenth centuries respectively, who wrote the *Vāgbhaṭālaṁkāra*[5] in verse and the *Kāvyānuçāsana*[6] in the normal form. The older tries a new definition of poetry to include quality, figure, sentiment, and style, but makes no effort to weld these into a whole, while he adopts the old set of ten qualities; the younger accepts Hemacandra's definition, which is merely a rehash of Mammaṭa's in a worse form, and allows only three qualities. Neither seems to

[1] Ed. and trans. BI. 1851–75; Kane, Bombay, 1923. Cf. Keith, JRAS. 1911, pp. 848 f.

[2] Ed. BSS. 63, 1903.

[3] Ed. BSS. 65, 1909.

[4] Ed. KM. 71, 1901.

[5] Ed. KM. 48, 1915.

[6] Ed. KM. 43, 1894.

accept Dhvani as essential; the younger mentions it under the figure Paryāyokta and refers readers to Ānandavardhana.

Of very different importance is the work of Ruyyaka, the teacher of Mañkha, who wrote (*c.* 1100) the *Alaṁkārasarvasva*,[1] text and commentary, though the commentator Samudrabandhu[2] (*c.* 1300) ascribes the comment to Mañkha, who may have helped in his teacher's work. Ruyyaka summarizes cleverly all earlier systems and asserts the validity of the Dhvanikāra's view. His own aim is to deal with the pictorial poem which does not suggest anything, and therefore with figures which are its essence. In doing so he clearly accepts the principle of the *Vakroktijīvita* that it is a certain charm which gives a figure its being and value. Such charm does not permit of exact description, as it is as infinite as the poet's imagination which produces it, but it is this which forms the basis of any figure, and justifies our asserting that it is a figure and differentiating it from others. In detail he often follows with improvements Udbhaṭa whom he much admired. He disagrees with Mammaṭa on the vexed issue of Çleṣa; the latter admitted figures both of sound and sense in this case, basing the distinction on the fact that in Çabda-çleṣa the substitution of a synonym would ruin the effect, in Artha-çleṣa it would make no difference. Ruyyaka's view is that the real thing to consider is whether the word in question yields the double meaning without change of form, that is by having another sense, when it is Artha-çleṣa, or whether the word must be differently divided and read when it is Çabda-çleṣa. He rejects, on the other hand, Udbhaṭa's dogma that a Çleṣa destroys the operation of any other figure with which it is joined. Though comparatively early in date, Jayadeva's *Candrāloka*[3] is no more than a convenient manual of figures with happy illustrations, on which (*c.* 1600) Appayya Dīkṣita the polymath based his *Kuvalayānanda*.[4] Very different is the *Rasagañgādhara*[5] of Jagannātha (*c.* 1650), where we find the revised definition of poetry as sound expressive of a charming idea (*ramaṇīyārthapratipādakaḥ çabdaḥ*), and charmingness is ascribed to knowledge begetting

[1] KM. 35, 1893; trans. H. Jacobi, ZDMG. lxii.

[2] TSS. 40, 1915.

[3] Ed. Calcutta, 1917.

[4] Ed. and trans. Calcutta, 1903. Cf. IOC. ii. 340 ff.

[5] Ed. KM. 12, 1913. Cf. Jacobi, GN. 1908, pp. 1 ff.

transcendental pleasure (*lokottarāhlāda*); this characteristic of pleasure is a distinct entity which one realizes by experience, and it is also denoted by Camatkāratva. The cause of this form of pleasure is a form of meditation (*bhāvanā*), consisting of continued application to the object characterized by the pleasure. It is quite different from the joy produced by the thought of the meaning of what is said to one, e. g. 'A son is born to you.' Poetry, therefore, can be redefined as sound expressing a sense which is the object of a contemplation producing transcendental pleasure. This is, it will be seen, a development to a logical conclusion of the doctrine of the enjoyment of sentiment; that was essentially universal and impersonal, therefore purely pleasurable, and this test Jagannātha now applies to the whole field of poetry. In his treatment of figures in like manner he applies, but more ably even than Ruyyaka, and very critically as regards earlier writers, the test whether any alleged figure produces charm of a different kind from some other accepted figure.

Of other treatises it is necessary to mention the works of the polymath Kṣemendra, *Aucityavicāra*[1] and *Kavikaṇṭhābharaṇa*,[2] as they stand rather apart from the ordinary line. In the former Kṣemendra develops the conception of Aucitya, propriety as essential to sentiment, indeed the life of sentiment, and as founded in the charm underlying the relish of sentiment. He finds twenty-seven cases in which propriety can be exhibited or violated, and the value of his work lies in his rich illustration and his criticisms of what he deems defects. Such critiques on an extended scale are rare, and Kṣemendra is a better critic than a poet. The *Kavikaṇṭhābharaṇa* discusses the possibility of becoming a poet, the issue of borrowing on a small or large scale, and the legitimacy of doing so in the case of the epic and similar works, the charm of poetry with illustration of its ten aspects, the defects and excellencies with regard to sense, sound, or sentiment, and the various arts which a poet ought to be familiar with. The *Kāvyakalpalatā*,[3] with a commentary, by Arisiṅha and Amaracandra (13th cent.) is still more of a practical book of

[1] Ed. KM. i. 115 ff.; Peterson, JBRAS. xvi. 167 ff.
[2] Ed. KM. iv. 122 ff.; I. Schönberg, SWA. 1884.
[3] Ed. Benares, 1886. Cf. IOC. i. 339 ff.; ii. 337 f.

advice to poets, while Bhānudatta in the fourteenth century wrote on sentiment in his *Rasamañjarī*[1] and *Rasataraṅgiṇī*.[2]

In the *Sarasvatīkaṇṭhābharaṇa*[3] we find an elaborate discussion of a theme dealt with in some detail by Rudraṭa alone of the earlier writers, the mingling of languages. Thus, while we may and normally do have a single language used throughout, we may have cases in which the same words can be read, for instance, both as Sanskrit and Prākrit with one and the same meaning; or, again, a verse may be made up of distinct parts in different languages, or different languages may simply be mixed together, giving a consecutive sense, or they may be written consecutively without such a sense, or degraded forms of Prākrit or Apabhrança may be used in parody or in imitation. Rudraṭa[4] mentions the two simple forms in which the same words can be read in another language in the same sense or in a different sense. Of this we have an early example in Canto xiii of the Kāvya of Bhaṭṭi, where the text can be read as Prākrit as well as Sanskrit without alteration of sense. There is little to be said for these absurdities, though occasional instances of happy adoption of these devices can be cited.

On the classification of figures of speech no serious thought appears to have been expended. Mammaṭa, whose actual treatment of individual figures dominates Ruyyaka, gives no guidance, while Ruyyaka[5] offers a division of figures of sense based on the principles of comparison (*aupamya*), incongruity (*virodha*), linked succession (*çṛṅkhalā*), logical reasoning (*nyāya*), sentence economy (*vākyanyāya*), popular maxims (*lokanyāya*), apprehension of a secret sense (*gūḍhārthapratīti*), and combination of figures (*saṁsṛṣṭi* or *saṁkara*). Nothing substantial is added to this in the later texts by Vidyādhara and Viçvanātha. It is not worth while investigating the precise meaning attached to this division, especially as some of the figures included in these divisions, such as Yathāsaṁkhya in which, for instance, epithets are asserted in

[1] Ed. BenSS. 83, 1904.

[2] Ed. Benares, 1885; Regnaud, *Rhétorique Sanscrite* (1884).

[3] ii. 17 with Ratneçvara's comm. Cf. Rāma Tarkavāgīça, iii. 15. 4 ff. (AMJV. III. i. 138 ff.); Schubring, *Festgabe Jacobi*, pp. 89 ff.

[4] iv. 10–23. Cf. *Sāhityadarpaṇa*, x. 10 (642).

[5] Cf. Kane, *Sāhityadarpaṇa*, pp. 336 f.; Trivedī, *Ekāvalī*, pp. 526 f.; Ruyyaka, pp. 143, 148, 164.

the same order as the subjects are set out, are denied any true quality of charm by Jayaratha and Jagannātha. The division even in Ruyyaka is not logical, manifesting a characteristic defect of Sanskrit investigation, and in a number of cases the justification for the existence of distinct figures is quite wanting. The validity in other cases of the distinctions does exist, and the real criticism is that it is hardly worth while inventing special terms for the variant forms. Thus the idea that the face of the beloved is like the moon can be utilized to illustrate a long series of figures, based on similarity. 'Thy face is like the moon' is simile, Upamā; 'The moon is like thy face' is the converse, Pratīpa; but in 'Thy face shineth ever, the moon by night alone' we have contrast, Vyatireka. 'The moon doth reign in heaven, thy face on earth' illustrates typical comparison, Prativastūpamā, while 'In the heaven the moon, on earth thy face,' is an instance of exemplification, Dṛṣṭānta; illustration, Nidarçanā, is seen in 'Thy face doth bear the beauty of the moon,' and indirect eulogy, Aprastutapraçaṅsā, in 'The moon doth pale before thy face.' Or the simile may be repeated, Upameyopamā, 'The moon is like thy face, thy face is like the moon,' or we have remembrance, Smaraṇa, 'The sight of the moon doth bring thy face before me.' Or we have metaphor, Rūpaka, in 'Thy moon-face,' which develops into commutation, Pariṇāma, in 'By thy moon-face, the heat of passion doth wane.' In 'Is this thy face or the moon?' we have doubt, Saṁdeha; in 'The Cakora, thinking it to be the moon, flieth toward thy face' confusion, Bhrāntimat; while different representations, Ullekha, may be seen in 'This the moon, this the lotus; so the Cakora and the bee fly to thy face.' Or we may have negation, Apahnuti, 'This is the moon, not thy face,' or self-comparison, Ananvaya, 'Thy face is like thy face alone,' with which may be compared the famous verse of the *Rāmāyaṇa*[1] cited above. Or we may have lively fancy, Utprekṣā, as in 'This is indeed the moon,' or hyperbole, Atiçayokti, in 'This is a second moon.' Or we may have equal pairing, Tulyayogitā, 'The moon and the lotus are vanquished by thy face,' or illumination, Dīpaka, as in 'Thy face and the moon rejoice in the night.'[2] Or, to conclude, we have the typical comparison,

[1] Above, chap. ii, § 3.

[2] Dé, *Sanskrit Poetics*, ii. 87 f.

Prativastūpamā, in another form illustrated by a beautiful verse from the *Çakuntalā*, as a welcome change from these aridities:

mānuṣīṣu kathaṁ vā syād asya rūpasya sambhavaḥ?
na prabhātaralaṁ jyotir udeti vasudhātalāt.

'Nay, how could such beauty be born among men? Not from the earth doth the tremulous loveliness of the lightning arise.'

PART III

SCIENTIFIC LITERATURE

XIX

THE ORIGIN AND CHARACTERISTICS OF THE SCIENTIFIC LITERATURE

1. *The Origin of the Çastras*

IN India, at any rate, science, Çāstra or Vidyā, arises in very close connexion with religion. The Vedic period saw the development of definite sacrificial schools, which preserved the tradition of one or other of the four Vedas, sometimes developing a special recension of that Veda, sometimes showing their individuality by producing a Brāhmaṇa, or, much more often, a Sūtra of their own. These Vedic schools, however, gradually passed away, though we have evidence that in an attenuated form they persisted for many centuries after their importance had greatly diminished. What happened was the inevitable rise of specialization. As life went on, more and more topics arose which the schools could not adequately master, and special schools arose which cut across the old divisions, though we may conjecture that in their origin they were formed within the Vedic schools as specialists in one branch of the work of the school itself. If so, it was inevitable that they should tend to expand and to take into consideration the similar issues arising in regard to the work of other schools. If, for instance, in a Ṛgvedic school the need for grammatical study produced a special school of Vaiyākaraṇas, grammarians, they would tend to amalgamate with any grammarians who studied the *Yajurveda* and to extend their interest to the Vedas in general. At any rate Yāska, perhaps *c.* 500 B.C., knows of schools of Vaiyākaraṇas, of Nairuktas, etymologists, and of Yājñikas, persons who concerned themselves with the sacrifice, and the grammar of Pāṇini is sufficient proof that there existed a grammatical school which was willing to include in its work usages of different Vedas and different schools of the same Veda. The Vaiyākaraṇas are, of course, the direct ancestors of the science of Grammar in classical times; the Nairuktas, though they give an impulse to lexicographical studies, can hardly be said to be the direct cause of the existence of the Koças, which were largely influenced by the necessity of the writers of Kāvya, who required to have collections of words for aid in composing their poetry.

Yet another early development within the Vedic period was the building up of schools of Law in the wide sense of that term which includes religious and civil and criminal law. This must have been done together with the development of society and the necessity for having some standards to guide the Brahmins who acted as advisers and judges to the ruling class. The Smṛti of Manu presupposes a considerable period of development during which there arose professional schools, to one of which is due the production of a work such as that Smṛti which claims not to guide the life of any single community, but to be a general guide for all the classes of the state. Only slowly and imperfectly within these schools was there developed a separation, never complete, of religious and secular law.

In another field of learning we can clearly see the development of expertise. The Vedic sacrifice demanded a rudimentary knowledge of the calendar and elementary conceptions of mensuration. Definite ideas of these subjects were slow of development, and were at first handed down merely in close connexion with each Veda; we still have different recensions of the Jyotiṣa on astronomy and the Çulbasūtras on the making of altars and kindred matters. But inevitably from these beginnings developed a wider geometrical, astronomical, and astrological science, which we find under the comprehensive title of Jyotiṣa and which is studied in distinct schools. Medicine, again, appears first in the spells of the *Atharvaveda*, and was fostered by the schools of magic practices which produced such a work as the *Kauçika Sūtra* of that Veda; but its Vedic connexion is less close than in the case of most of the sciences we have mentioned, and it is dubious conjecture that what surgery and anatomical knowledge it possessed was furthered by the practice of dissecting animals for the sacrifice and less often even man in the human sacrifice.

The Vedic schools developed also a tendency to mysticism which is seen in the Āraṇyakas and the Upaniṣads, which are attached more or less closely to the great Brāhmaṇas. We may see in these works a tendency to fissure within the Vedic schools themselves: some preferred the sacrifice and the ritual, others sought to go behind it to the significance of the sacrifice, of the gods to whom it was offered, of life and man, and of the universe. The Upaniṣads are clearly in origin closely connected with Vedic schools, but their ideas inevitably transcend the school limit and prepare the way for that period of intellectual exchange which issues in the systems of philosophy, which, we may be sure, were not the outcome of any Vedic school as such. Theology and theosophy naturally, with the gradual transformation of the Vedic system, passed beyond the sphere of the old schools and were handed down in new forms of organization.

Nor is it certain that we can divorce the Kāmaçāstra, the science of love, from Vedic beginnings. We may, indeed, conclude from hints [1] in the Vedic texts that genetics occupied the attention of sages of these schools, though little of their wisdom has been preserved for us. Naturally the subject would tend to spread beyond any individual school, and become, as it remained, the object of special study, treated with precisely the same care and detail as any other scientific subject.

The study of metre was doubtless encouraged by the mystic importance attached in Vedic times to the metre of the sacred texts, and Chandas, metrics, is reckoned one of the six Vedāñgas, but its importance and character were early affected by the need of affording guidance to writers of Kāvya and other forms of literature, so that even the Vedāñga presents itself as largely connected with secular metres. Poetics, on the other hand, was hardly in any sense Vedic, and represents an independent secular science. Largely the same remark may be applied to the Arthaçāstra or Nītiçāstra, but there is some connexion between it and the Dharmaçāstra, even when both were distinctly developed, and we may quite legitimately suppose that the original schools of Dharmaçāstra included in their scope the matters which later became specifically the objects of Arthaçāstra, politics, practical knowledge, technique in matters not primarily sacrificial. It is less certain that the Kāmaçāstra was taught in the same schools along with the primitive Arthaçāstra under the aegis of the Dharmaçāstra, though this may well have been the case. But at

[1] *Bṛhadāraṇyaka Upaniṣad*, vi. 4.

least there is no doubt of the dominant influence of religion on the growth of Sanskrit scientific literature.

2. *The Characteristics of the Scientific Literature*

Owing to its inheritance of Vedic tradition, Sanskrit science greatly affected the Sūtra form of composition. The exact causes of this development in the Vedic literature must remain obscure; paucity of writing material, expense in procuring it, or similar causes can hardly be seriously adduced. Rather it may be ascribed to the character of the teaching of the schools, which was oral and always in a sense esoteric. The teacher expounded his subject orally, and it was convenient but also sufficient to sum up the pith of his discourse in short sentences, which would be significant to those who knew the key to their meaning but of little import to those who did not. The plan remained in use [1] beyond all in the philosophical schools, where doctrines were as in the Upaniṣads something sacred and secret, and it is precisely this character which renders the Sūtras of the philosophical schools so enigmatic, and allows, for instance, the *Brahma Sūtra* to become the source of quite distinct and even incompatible doctrines. But a decisive step was taken when the Sūtras were supplemented by the composition of Bhāṣyas written in a new and interesting style. It is based on the principle of reproducing the dialogue between teacher and student, and, moreover, is often cast in the form of adducing a topic, then bringing forward a partial solution, or prima facie view (*pūrvapakṣa*), which is dealt with, corrected, and revised in the final opinion (*siddhānta*). We need not suppose that the objections discussed were always really views held; the style once adopted naturally would lead to the positing of possible objections, and indeed this form of putting the matter is not at all rare, the abbreviated form of words *iti cen na*, being used to denote, 'if so and so is put forward, then we reply that this is not the case,' for the reason which is then introduced.

The style of the Bhāṣyas undergoes a clear development; Çaṅkara, for instance, is more advanced than the *Mahābhāṣya* on

[1] See, e. g., the late *Āyurvedasūtra* (Madras, 1922), which is based on old and 15th-century work.

the grammar of Pāṇini or the Bhāṣya of Vātsyāyana on the *Nyāya Sūtra*. We pass from a reproduction of a discussion to an essay or lecture, and later still is developed the very stiff, if scientific, philosophical style which appears equally in the handbooks of poetics and in such sciences as philosophy and law. The essence[1] of it lies in the insistence on the use of nouns only, verbs being practically eliminated, and in the pregnant employment of particles and of case relations, together with the use of compounds, sometimes of great length. It may be admitted that it is possible to attain great precision in this manner, for in a technical subject-matter compounds can be used so rigidly as to be clear in sense, even when long and complex, but on the other hand it is impossible to regard such products as literature. The Sūtras also have a serious effect on all future work, for they are normally regarded as definitive, and therefore not to be altered, checking development in the substance of the science. A partial way out was found in the case of grammar, where Vārttikas grew up to correct or modify the Sūtras of Pāṇini, but the term Vārttika is not applied in the case of other sciences, though we have in Vātsyāyana occasional sentences which might be deemed Vārttikas to the *Nyāya Sūtra*.[2] On the other hand we come here and there in philosophic works upon Sūtras which are not preserved in our Sūtra texts.

The formal Sūtra style never grew obsolete,[3] and it is predominant in Grammar, appears in the leading work on Metrics, was often adopted in Poetics, was normal in the great schools of Philosophy, and is claimed for the *Arthaçāstra*, in which, however, in the leading text we have a complex of Sūtra and Bhāṣya in one by the same hand which deviates distinctly from the orthodox style, and the same remark applies to the *Kāmasūtra*. The *Bhāratīya Nāṭyaçāstra* contains here and there reminiscences of the Sūtra style, but it has passed over on the whole to a different form of composition, that of Çlokas.

[1] Jacobi, IF. xiv. 236 ff.; V. G. Paranjpe, *Le Vârtika de Kâtyâyana*, pp. 50 ff., who compares the *Mīmāṅsā Sūtra* and the *Mahābhāṣya*.

[2] Cf. Windisch, *Über das Nyâyabhâshya* (1888).

[3] Thus the *Āyurvedasūtra* (*Bibl. Sansk.*, 61) is quite a modern composition, as proved by the learned editor, Dr. R. Shamasastry. In scientific works, medicine, architecture, astrology, incorrect and barbarous Sanskrit is common; cf. *Vidyāmādhavīya*, intr.

The discussions at the Sabhās held by kings and rich patrons were undoubtedly in some measure responsible for the form of exposition. Any new doctrine which desired to establish itself was only able to do so, if its supporter could come forward on such an occasion and by his advocacy secure the verdict of those assembled and the favour of the king or patron of the assembly. Doubtless this accounts in large measure for the scholastic and dialectic type of Indian scientific literature, including many of its worst features. In philosophy, for instance, it is extremely irritating to find really profound thoughts interrupted by what are merely scholastic and pedantic arguments, where a clear exposition would be far more attractive to western taste. To the readers of the works of the philosophers, however, such a form of literature would have appeared dry and over-simple, though the appalling results of scholastic subtlety can be seen in the fact that the whole of logical literature after Gañgeça, and all the commentaries on the Vaiçeṣika philosophy after Udayana could be spared without any real loss to Sanskrit literature.

In the great period of Sanskrit literature at any rate experimental science was at a low ebb, and little of importance was accomplished in those fields in which experiment is essential.[1] Medicine developed a considerable knowledge of symptoms and treatment of diseases, but surgery was banned by reason of the Brahmanical and general Indian fear of impurity through contact with the dead, and the acceptance of demoniac sources of disease hampered serious research. The mathematical achievements of India lay in the field of algebra and in the invention of a valuable system of notation. Far more was accomplished in fields of human action ; if political theory never reached any high development, legal studies were conducted with much acumen. The form of the Dharmaçāstras corresponds in an interesting manner with the more humane character of their contents. They are handed down in Çlokas, for which we have in the Dharmasūtras, of which they are ultimately descendants, occasional memorial verses summing up or illustrating doctrines. In verse form

[1] B. Seal (*The Positive Sciences of the Ancient Hindus*) holds a much more favourable view, but he reads new ideas into old texts. The influence of western science has now evoked brilliant reactions in India, including a revolution in our ideas of plant life.

maxims on human life naturally won far greater circulation than prose Sūtras, and this form of composition, which was unquestionably aided by the example of the epic, was often adopted for scientific works, even in non-humanistic branches of learning. The Çloka was easy to write and easy to remember, but not unnaturally it did not content all authors, some of whom, like Varāhamihira and Bhāskara in the field of astrology and mathematics, proceeded to develop their scientific doctrines in elegant and complex metres. In other cases the Āryā, which, like the Çloka, is a comparatively simple metre, won acceptance, as in the *Sāṁkhyakārikā*, in which the doctrines of the Sāṁkhya philosophy were succinctly set forth. Technical science was often reduced to roughly fashioned Çlokas which were popular for medical recipes, though even for those we find cases of more complex metres being employed. But there remained instead the alternative of a prose exposition with verses interspersed here and there to corroborate or sum up or illustrate doctrines laid down, as is the case with the medical Saṁhitās.

A phenomenon of interest, common to prose and verse alike, is the tendency to use homely metaphors or similes and to illustrate doctrines by the facts of ordinary life. The danger of such illustrations was, of course, not avoided; similitudes were held to explain difficulties, without realization that they did not cover adequately the ground; the lamp which illumines itself is given us to explain self-consciousness, without recognition that the parallel is really misleading. But a number of popular illustrations became hardened into regular use, and figure as Nyāyas.[1] Thus the grammatical principle that the more important element in a compound coupling two things should come first is popularized and generally used as a scientific principle, *abhyarhitam pūrvam*. The amusing proverb *avatapte nakulasthitam*, 'a mongoose's standing on hot ground,' serves to describe the man who does not stick to his undertaking. The expert who forgets his rules is hit by the proverb, *açvārūḍhāḥ kathaṁ cāçvān vismareyuḥ sacetanāḥ*, 'How could intelligent people, when sitting on horses, forget their mounts?' A painful dilemma is well expressed by *ito vyāghra itas taṭī*, 'A tiger on the one side, a precipice on the other.' An embarrassing position is not badly

[1] See Jacob, *Laukikanyāyāñjali*, 3 pts., 1908 ff.

described as *ubhayataḥpāçā rajjuḥ*, 'a rope which binds at both ends.' The *tṛṇabhakṣaṇanyāya* illustrates submission, for the ancient Indian usage spared the man who took grass in his mouth to signify that he yielded himself to the mercy of the conqueror. Wasted effort is expressed by the maxim of *çvapucchonnamana*, 'trying to straighten a dog's tail.' The united effect of words in conveying meaning is likened to the joint action of men in lifting a palanquin, *çibikodyacchannaravat*. Quaint and interesting is a very old Nyāya: *mahārṇavayugacchidrakūrmagrīvārpaṇanyāya*, 'the chance of a tortoise putting its neck into the hole of a yoke which is floating about on the mighty ocean.' The allusion is to a thing of great difficulty, illustrated by the mere chance which would cause a tortoise, which comes to the surface once only in a hundred years, accomplishing the difficult feat referred to.

A characteristic which in greater or less degree pervades the whole of the scientific literature is the love of subdivision and of inventing distinctions. Everything has to be schematized without regard to the nature of the subject-matter. Thus in the *Kāmasūtra* even the meticulous specification of detail of this kind is carried out with perfect solemnity, and in the sphere of international relations as treated in the *Arthaçāstra*, in lieu of concrete investigation of actual relations between historical tribes, we have a complete scheme of theoretical connexions based on the possibility of relations with adjacent and more distant kingdoms.[1] The historical method in fact is normally lacking, yielding to the more attractive habit of analysis of a somewhat superficial character and deduction from bases which have not been sufficiently established. In the subdivisions of which India is so fond there is often much ingenuity in finding legitimate grounds of distinction, but there is always present the tendency to lose sight of the broad and important lines of demarcation while concentrating on minutiae. Moreover the practice of accepting as given what has been traditionally handed down has a serious effect. It often results in ingenious efforts to reinterpret the old, in lieu of frankly abandoning it, thus causing waste of energy in subtleties, as when the traditional account of inference is rendered quite

[1] Narendranath Law, *Inter-State Relations in Ancient India* (1920).

differently with equal assurance by each commentator.[1] In other cases it brings about the acceptance and defence by sophistic grounds of what is plainly untenable. There was, of course, constant progress, for instance in the sphere of law, but it was hampered by the necessity of making out that change was not really taking place, and that new customs were really allowed by Manu or some other Smṛti. In astronomy we see even a competent author like Brahmagupta attacking sensible innovations of Āryabhaṭa on the score that they depart from traditional knowledge.

Poetical form moreover was often injurious. It led to the use of redundant expressions merely to fill up the verses, or on the other hand to undue condensation and ellipsis, with resulting obscurity. Clearness was much furthered by the adoption of the later scientific style which is seen at its best probably in the expositions of law and in the works on poetics; Vijñāneçvara, Ānandavardhana, and Ruyyaka in their prose expositions prove decisively the superiority of this form to the obscurity left by the use of verse. The controversy which exists as to the exact meaning of Bhāmaha's description of the Ākhyāyikā and Kathā would have been avoided had he written in prose.[2]

[1] Cf. A. B. Dhruva, POCP. 1919, ii. 251 ff.

[2] i. 27, giving the characteristics of a mark of the poet's imagination and of containing the seizure of a maiden, a struggle, separation, and the hero's triumph, is held by Dé (BSOS. iii. 507) to apply to the Ākhyāyikā, by Nobel (*Indian Poetry*, p. 157) to refer to the Kathā. Both agree in censuring Daṇḍin for misunderstanding Bhāmaha, which in the circumstances is amusing.

XX

LEXICOGRAPHY AND METRICS

1. *The Origin and Characteristics of Sanskrit Lexicography*

THE oldest lexicographic work[1] carried out in India is recorded in the *Nighaṇṭavas*, collections of Vedic terms, of which the most important are the lists handed down to us with the *Nirukta* of Yāska.[2] These, however, differ in many respects from the Koças of classical literature. They were drawn up for practical purposes like the latter, but in the case of the Nighaṇṭu literature the purpose was essentially interpretation of sacred texts which were becoming more and more obscure, while the Koças were prepared to help poets to a supply of words. In accord with this we find dictionaries attributed to such poets as Bāṇa, Mayūra, Murāri, and Çrīharṣa, who composed one of terms for use in double meanings, *Çleṣārthapadasaṁgraha.*[3] The Nighaṇṭus further contained not merely nominal but also verbal forms, the Koças only nouns and indeclinables, and while the former dealt with one special text, the latter are not based on any special text. In keeping with the new spirit the Koças are in verse, usually Çlokas but also Āryās, and, by incorporating expressions from many of the arts which a poet was expected to have mastered, they saved him labour. The composition of such works may have been fostered by the existence of the Dhātupāṭhas and other lists of the grammarians, but this is conjectural.

Of lexica two main classes exist—synonymous, in which words are grouped by subject-matter, and homonymous (*anekārtha, nānārtha*), but the important synonymous dictionaries usually include a homonymous section. As the books were intended,

[1] On the subject see Th. Zachariae, *Die indischen Wörterbücher* (1897). Koça and Koṣa both occur.

[2] See S. Varma, POCP. 1919, ii. 68 ff. Cf. R. D. Karmarkar, *ibid.*, 62 ff.

[3] Burnell, *Tanjore Catal.*, pp. 48 ff. Similarly Amara appears as a poet, Thomas, *Kav.*, p. 22; cf. above, p. 339.

not for reference, but for learning off by heart, the principle of alphabetic order was not considered essential; they are, accordingly, divided on various principles, often on more than one; thus the longer articles may come first, or the arrangement may be by the final consonants or the initial letters or the two combined, or the number of letters; in some cases information is given as to gender, sometimes with an appendix on it, and gender occasionally is taken into account in fixing the order. Synonyms, of course, appear in the nominative, compounded or otherwise as metre and convenience dictate; homonyms may be treated in the same way, or the different senses may be put in the locative. The older writers, of whom we have but fragments, were indifferent to order and willing to give long definitions; the later are extremely unwilling to waste space and are proportionately obscure. Moreover, the text of the lexica is seldom in a satisfactory condition.

2. *The Extant Lexica*

As usual in India the older works were obscured by the later, and we have only names and odd citations of important writers, such as Kātyāyana, to whom a *Nāmamālā* is ascribed, Vācaspati and Vikramāditya, authors of a *Çabdārṇava* and a *Saṁsārāvarta*, and Vyāḍi, whose *Utpalinī* is often cited, and included Buddhist terms. The fragments of a dictionary exist in the Weber manuscript found in Kashgar.[1] But one of the earliest texts preserved for us is the *Nāmaliñgānuçāsana*[2] of Amarasiṅha, called usually the *Amarakoça*. Its author is also known as a poet, and was certainly a Buddhist who knew the Mahāyāna and used Kālidāsa. His lower limit of date is dubious, he is not certainly known to the *Nyāsa* of Jinendrabuddhi (A.D. 700), but the decline of Buddhism in India renders it improbable that he lived after the eighth century; his ascription to the sixth, however, rests on nothing better than the assertion that he was a jewel of Vikramāditya's court.[3] The work is synonymous, arranged in three books by subjects, with an appendix in the last on homonyms, indeclinables, and genders. Of its many commentators, special

[1] Hoernle, JASB. lxii. 1. 26 ff. [2] Ed. TSS. 1914–17.
[3] Cf. Bhandarkar, *Vaiṣṇavism*, p. 45; Keith, IOC. ii. 303.

merit attaches to the works of Kṣīrasvāmin (11th cent.), Vandyaghaṭīya Sarvānanda (1159), and Rāyamukuṭamaṇi (1431) who used sixteen earlier writers. An important supplement of rare words is afforded by the *Trikāṇḍaçeṣa* of Puruṣottamadeva, who wrote also, after twelve years' work, the shorter *Hārāvalī*, including synonyms and homonyms; these give a rich store of very rare terms, many from Buddhist texts.[1] Perhaps as old as Amara is Çāçvata, whose *Anekārthasamuccaya*[2] betrays age by its arrangement of its homonyms according as the explanation takes a whole verse, a half verse, a quarter verse; indeclinables conclude the work.

Other dictionaries are decidedly later. From *c.* 950 we have the short *Abhidhānaratnamālā*[3] of the poet-grammarian Halāyudha, and a century later Yādavaprakāça's *Vaijayantī*,[4] which is of great bulk and arranges its words by syllables, genders, and initial letters. The twefth century gives a rich variety. Preeminent are Hemacandra's works; the *Abhidhānacintāmaṇi*[5] deals with synonyms in six sections, beginning with Jain gods and ending with abstracts, adjectives, and particles, and is supplemented by the botanic dictionary *Nighaṇṭuçeṣa*; the *Anekārthasaṁgraha*[6] deals with homonyms in six sections, beginning with one-syllable and ending with six-syllable words arranged by initial letters and end consonants. The Jain Dhanaṁjaya wrote between 1123 and 1140 his *Nāmamālā*; Maheçvara's *Viçvaprakāça*[7] falls in 1111, while Mañkha's *Anekārthakoça*[8] with his own comment, which uses Amara, Çāçvata, Halāyudha, and Dhanvantari, is rather later, and Keçavasvāmin's *Nānārthārṇavasaṁkṣepa*[9] falls about 1200. To the fourteenth century belongs the *Anekārthaçabdakoça*[10] of Medinīkara, which is often cited by commentators, as well as the *Nānārtharatnamālā*, written by, or for, Irugapa, general of Harihara.[11]

Of uncertain date are minor works dealing with words of one syllable, *Ekākṣarakoça*, or with words of different forms, *Dvirūpa-* or *Trirūpa- koça*, medical or astronomical or astrological glos-

[1] Cf. Zachariae, *Bezz. Beitr.* x. 122 ff. (before 1150).
[2] Ed. Zachariae, Berlin, 1882.
[3] Ed. Th. Aufrecht, London, 1861.
[4] Ed. G. Oppert, Madras, 1893.
[5] Ed. St. Petersburg, 1847.
[6] Ed. Vienna, 1893.
[7] Ed. ChSS. 1911.
[8] Ed. Vienna, 1897; cf. SWA. cxli. 16 ff.
[9] Ed. TSS. 1913.
[10] Ed. Calcutta, 1884.
[11] Śeshagiri, *Report*, 1893-4, pp. 41 f.

saries. Buddhist texts revived the Vedic Nighaṇṭus, as they produced works specially written for their interpretation and in prose form; thus the best known, the *Mahāvyutpatti*,[1] gives elaborate information on many Buddhist topics, and includes verbal forms, phrases, and sentences. It is characteristic of the bitter relations between Hindus and Mahomedans that it is not until the time of Akbar that we find the Persian-Sanskrit dictionary *Pārasīprakāça*,[2] and in 1643 the work of the same title by Vedāñgarāya on astronomical and astrological terms.

In 972 Dhanapāla wrote for his sister Sundarī the *Pāiyalacchī* (*Prākṛtalakṣmī*) *Nāmamālā*,[3] a Prākrit dictionary which was used by Hemacandra in producing his *Deçīnāmamālā*[4] with commentary, in which he seeks to give Deçī words, that is, terms neither identic with Sanskrit (*tatsama*) nor derived thence by ordinary processes (*tadbhava*). Some of these words are referable to Sanskrit, but most are not, and their provenance is still extremely uncertain.[5]

The scientific value of this lexicographical work cannot be said to be high, nor could this be expected from writers who merely aimed at a practical result. Especially in the later lexica there are cases of words being inserted which merely rest on misreadings of texts or on misinterpretations, and frequently poets have been misled to use words in incorrect senses because they were given as synonyms of some other word in one of its senses, and the synonymity has been generalized. But we are rarely in a position to decide definitely on these points.

3. *Treatises on Metre*

The Brāhmaṇas already show interest in matters metrical,[6] and sections of the *Çāñkhāyana Çrautasūtra*, the *Nidāna Sūtra*, the *Ṛk-Prātiçākhya*, and Kātyāyana's *Anukramaṇīs* to the *Ṛgveda* and the *Yajurveda* deal with metre. The topic ranks as

[1] Ed. J. P. Minayeff, BB. 13, 1911.

[2] A. Weber, *Über den Pârasîprakâça* (ABA. 1887).

[3] Ed. G. Bühler, *Bezz. Beitr.*, iv. 70 ff.

[4] Ed. R. Pischel, BSS. 17, 1880.

[5] Jacobi, *Bhavisattakaha*, pp. 62 f., 65 f., 69; Grierson, MASB. viii. 2 (*The Prakrit Dhātvādeśas*). His theory of semi-Tatsamas (JRAS. 1925, pp. 221 f.) is certainly too widely stated.

[6] Cf. Weber, IS. viii; SIFI. viii; H. Jacobi, ZDMG. xxxviii. 590 ff.; xl. 336 ff.

the Vedāñga Chandas, and a Sūtra of this name is ascribed to Piñgala,[1] the importance of which for the classical literature has already been mentioned, for the work is far more concerned with classical than Vedic texts. The text ascribed to Piñgala[2] on Prākrit[3] metres is much later. Piñgala adopts the system of algebraic symbols, using *l* for a short (*laghu*), *g* for a long (*guru*) syllable, *m* for a molossus, and so on. He is clearly earlier than chapters xiv and xv of the *Nāṭyaçāstra* which deal with metre, and the section of the *Agni Purāṇa*[4] on this topic is derived from Piñgala. Yet it must be said that neither he nor either of these texts describes fully or accurately the Çloka metre as we know it from the texts. We must, therefore, be uncertain whether his work was the guide by which the poets steered their course. What is clear is that we have no certainly early text other than his. The *Çrutabodha*[5] is attributed to Kālidāsa, but there is no ground for the ascription. It illustrates, while describing, the verses. Vararuci is also sometimes credited with this text. More definite is the fact that a chapter (civ) in the *Bṛhatsaṁhitā* of Varāhamihira describes metres simultaneously with planetary movements, and that Bhaṭṭotpala in his comment cites a textbook by an Ācārya. The view[6] that Daṇḍin wrote on metre is uncertain, though Bhāmaha may have done so, and from Kṣemendra we have the *Suvṛttatilaka*.[7] In book i he describes, with verses from his own works as illustrations, the metres; in ii he deals with defects in metre with many useful citations; and in iii he discusses the use of metre according to the nature of the work, poetry, science, or a combination in which one or the other predominates. He ends by demanding variety of metres from poets, but admits that great writers have often preferred some special metre, as did Pāṇini the Upajāti, Kālidāsa the Mandākrāntā, Bhāravi the Vañçasthā, Bhavabhūti the Çikhariṇī, &c.

Hemacandra as usual has written a compilation, the *Chando'*-

[1] Ed. with Halāyudha's comm. (*c.* 950), KM. 81, 1908.

[2] Ed. KM. 41, 1894. It is dated not before the fourteenth century by Jacobi, *Bhavisattakaha*, p. 5.

[3] Cf. Ratnaçekhara's *Chandaḥkoça*; Schubring, ZDMG. lxxv. 97 ff.

[4] cc. 328–34. For Bharata see Regnaud, AMG. ii.

[5] Ed. Haeberlin, 9–14.

[6] Jacobi, IS. xvii. 442 ff.

[7] Ed. KM. ii. 29 ff.

nuçāsana,[1] while Kedāra Bhaṭṭa's *Vṛttaratnākara*,[2] which describes 136 metres and was written before the fifteenth century, has been widely used, and the *Chandomañjarī*[3] of Gaṅgādāsa is also well known.[4]

4. *The Metres of Classical Poetry*

Our authorities leave us wholly in the dark regarding the development of metre between the Vedic and the classical periods of Sanskrit, and it is hardly very profitable speculating exactly why there grew up in Sanskrit poetry the use of metres with a determined length of quarter-stanzas or lines, each line being built exactly on the same model, while the first two and the last two lines were more closely combined than the second and the third, between which a complete caesura was essential. We can, it is true, in the case of both the Çloka[5] and the Triṣṭubh and Jagatī styles[6] see the process of hardening going on slowly in the Vedic and epic literature, doubtless under the growing desire for symmetry which was offended by the freedom of the Vedic and epic verses. The definite rules regarding the close of the line came to be applied throughout, and, when this was complete, longer lines were essayed on the same principle. In these longer lines we find operative a principle which is dropped in the Triṣṭubh and Jagatī styles, that of caesuras in definite places, which were doubtless felt to be made necessary if the verses were to retain elegance of form; the definitions of the metres are careful to make it clear where these caesuras are to be, and normally good poets insist on having full caesuras at these points, that is the end of an inflected word, though weak caesuras, at the end of some member of a compound or of a prefix, may legitimately occur,[7] and caesuras may be obscured by Sandhi.

[1] Bühler, *Hemachandra*, pp. 33, 82.

[2] Ed. Bombay, 1908. Mallinātha (cf. p. 435) uses it.

[3] BSGW. vi (1854), 209.

[4] Nārāyaṇa wrote in 1545 the *Vṛttaratnākara*; Dāmodara a *Vāṇībhūṣaṇa* (IOC. i. 305).

[5] GN. 1909, pp. 219 ff.; cf. Hopkins, *Great Epic*, pp. 219 ff.

[6] GN. 1915, pp. 490 ff.; cf. Hopkins, *op. cit.*, pp. 273 ff.; GN. 1919, pp. 170 ff.

[7] Halāyudha, IS. viii. 462–6. He allows even, e. g., *Kamalen|ālokyate*; Jackson, *Priyadarśikā*, pp. xcvi f.

Metres measured by number of syllables and, except in the case of the Çloka, strictly regulated as to the quantity of the syllables, are thus predominant in classical poetry. But, probably from popular poetry, there came to be used metres in which only the sum total of the morae was absolutely fixed, there being indeed certain restrictions as to the mode in which these morae could be made up, but such restrictions allowing a variation in the number of syllables, the Mātrāchandas. The most common form of this type is the very simple Vaitālīya consisting of two half-verses of 30 morae each, 14 plus 16 in the two lines of each half-verse, made up as follows: ⏑⏑ ⏑⏑ ⏑ ⏑ – ⏑ – ⏑ ⏓ ‖ ⏑⏑ ⏑⏑ – ⏑ ⏑ – ⏑ – ⏑ ⏓. If each line is lengthened by a long syllable we have the Aupacchandasika metre. More complex is the case of the Āryā,[1] which is recognized by metrical treatises as a Gaṇacchandas, the number of morae and the number of feet (*gaṇa*) being fixed. Thus the ordinary form of the Āryā has $7\frac{1}{2}$ feet to the half-verse with 4 morae in each, 30 in all; the 4 morae can take the forms ⏑ ⏑ ⏑ ⏑, – –, – ⏑ ⏑, ⏑ ⏑ –; in the second and fourth feet ⏑ – ⏑ is also permitted; in the sixth only ⏑ ¦ ⏑ ⏑ ⏑ or ⏑ – ⏑, while the last is monosyllabic. The second half-verse in the most usual form has in the sixth foot one short syllable, giving 27 morae, but we can have the position reversed, 27 plus 30 morae, Udgīti; or 30 plus 30, Gīti; or 27 plus 27, Upagīti; or 32 plus 32, Āryāgīti. If there is no caesura after the third foot the verse ranks as Vipulā; if in the second, fourth, and sixth feet the amphibrach is essential, as Capalā.

Of the metres measured by syllables, Akṣaracchandas, the following have been mentioned as found in classical poetry, and their schemes are given below, each consisting normally of four lines of the type given, with caesuras indicated by perpendicular lines:

Acaladhṛti: ⏑ ⏑ ⏑ ⏑ ⏑ ⏑ ⏑ ⏑ ⏑ ⏑ ⏑ ⏑ ⏑ ⏑ ⏑ ⏑ (16)
Anavasitā: ⏑ ⏑ ⏑ ⏑ – – – ⏑ ⏑ – – (11)
Aparavaktra[2]: ⏑ ⏑ ⏑ ⏑ ⏑ ⏑ – ⏑ – ⏑ – (11) ‖ ⏑ ⏑ ⏑ ⏑ – ⏑ ⏑ – ⏑ – ⏑ – (12)
bis
Açvalalita: ⏑ ⏑ ⏑ ⏑ – ⏑ – ⏑ ⏑ ⏑ – | – ⏑ ⏑ ⏑ ⏑ – ⏑ – ⏑ ⏑ ⏑ – (23)

[1] Apparently originally sung; cf. Jacobi, ZDMG. xxxviii. 599 ff.; cf. xl. 336 ff.; SIFI. VIII. ii. 84 ff.

[2] On the origin of this metre from the Puṣpitāgrā, cf. Hopkins, *Great Epic of India*, p. 340.

Indravajrā : – – ⏑ – – ⏑ ⏑ – ⏑ – ⏓ (11)
Upendravajrā : ⏑ – ⏑ – – ⏑ ⏑ – ⏑ – ⏓ (11)
Upajāti, a combination of stanzas of lines of Indravajrā and Upendravajrā
Utsara : – ⏑ – ⏑ ⏑ ⏑ – ⏑ ⏑ – ⏑ ⏑ – ⏑ – (15)
Udgatā[1] : ⏑ ⏑ – ⏑ – ⏑ ⏑ ⏑ – ⏑ | ⏑ ⏑ ⏑ ⏑ ⏑ – ⏑ – ⏑ – (10+10) = *a*+*b*
– ⏑ ⏑ ⏑ ⏑ ⏑ ⏑ – ⏑ ⏑ – | ⏑ ⏑ – ⏑ – ⏑ ⏑ ⏑ – ⏑ – ⏑ – (11+13) = *c*+*d*
Upajāti, mixture of Indravajrā and Vaṅçasthā lines
Kalahaṅsa : ⏑ ⏑ – ⏑ – ⏑ ⏑ ⏑ – ⏑ ⏑ – – (13)
Kusumavicitrā : ⏑ ⏑ ⏑ ⏑ – – | ⏑ ⏑ ⏑ ⏑ – – (12)
Kokilaka (Narkuṭaka, Avitatha) : ⏑ ⏑ ⏑ ⏑ – ⏑ – ⏑ | ⏑ ⏑ – ⏑ ⏑ | – ⏑ ⏑ – (17)
⏑ ⏑ ⏑ ⏑ – ⏑ – | ⏑ ⏑ ⏑ – ⏑ ⏑ – ⏑ ⏑ –
⏑ ⏑ ⏑ ⏑ – ⏑ – ⏑ ⏑ ⏑ – ⏑ ⏑ – ⏑ ⏑ –
Kṣamā : ⏑ ⏑ ⏑ ⏑ ⏑ ⏑ – | – ⏑ – – ⏑ – (13)
Citralekhā : ⏑ ⏑ – ⏑ ⏑ – ⏑ – ⏑ – | ⏑ ⏑ ⏑ – ⏑ – ⏑ (17)
Jalaḍharamālā : – – – – | ⏑ ⏑ ⏑ ⏑ – – – – (12)
Jaloddhatagati : ⏑ – ⏑ ⏑ ⏑ – | ⏑ – ⏑ ⏑ ⏑ – (12)
Tanumadhyā : – – ⏑ ⏑ – – (6)
Tāmarasa (Lalitapada) : ⏑ ⏑ ⏑ ⏑ – ⏑ ⏑ – ⏑ ⏑ – – (12)
Tūṇaka : – ⏑ – ⏑ – ⏑ – (7) || ⏑ – ⏑ – ⏑ – ⏑ – (8) *bis*
Toṭaka : ⏑ ⏑ – ⏑ ⏑ – ⏑ ⏑ – ⏑ ⏑ – (12)
Triṣṭubh, mixtures of Vātormī, Çālinī, Indravajrā, Vaṅçasthā lines
Daṇḍaka : ⏑ ⏑ ⏑ ⏑ ⏑ ⏑ + 17 (– ⏑ –) and variants
Dodhaka : – ⏑ ⏑ – ⏑ ⏑ – ⏑ ⏑ – – (11)
Drutapada : ⏑ ⏑ ⏑ – ⏑ ⏑ ⏑ – ⏑ ⏑ – – (12)
Drutavilambita : ⏑ ⏑ ⏑ – ⏑ ⏑ – ⏑ ⏑ – ⏑ – (12)
Dhīralalitā : – ⏑ ⏑ – ⏑ – ⏑ ⏑ ⏑ – ⏑ – ⏑ ⏑ ⏑ – (16)
Dhṛtaçrī : ⏑ ⏑ ⏑ ⏑ – ⏑ – ⏑ ⏑ ⏑ – ⏑ ⏑ – ⏑ ⏑ – ⏑ – ⏑ – (21)
Nandana : ⏑ ⏑ ⏑ ⏑ – ⏑ – ⏑ ⏑ ⏑ – | ⏑ – ⏑ – – ⏑ – (18)
Puṣpitāgrā : ⏑ ⏑ ⏑ ⏑ ⏑ ⏑ – ⏑ – ⏑ – – (12) || ⏑ ⏑ ⏑ ⏑ – ⏑ ⏑ – ⏑ – ⏑ – – (13) *bis*
Pṛthvī : ⏑ – ⏑ ⏑ ⏑ – ⏑ – | ⏑ ⏑ ⏑ – ⏑ – – ⏑ – (17)
Prabhā : ⏑ ⏑ ⏑ ⏑ ⏑ ⏑ – ⏑ – – ⏑ – (12)
Prabhāvatī : – – ⏑ – | ⏑ ⏑ ⏑ ⏑ – ⏑ – ⏑ – (13)
Pramadā : ⏑ ⏑ ⏑ ⏑ – ⏑ – ⏑ ⏑ ⏑ – ⏑ ⏑ – (14)
Pramāṇikā : ⏑ – ⏑ – ⏑ – ⏑ – (8)
Pramitākṣarā : ⏑ ⏑ – ⏑ – ⏑ ⏑ ⏑ – ⏑ ⏑ – (12)
Praharaṇakalitā : ⏑ ⏑ ⏑ ⏑ ⏑ ⏑ – | ⏑ ⏑ ⏑ ⏑ ⏑ ⏑ – (14)
Praharṣiṇī : – – – | ⏑ ⏑ ⏑ ⏑ – ⏑ – ⏑ – – (13)
Bhadrikā : ⏑ ⏑ ⏑ ⏑ ⏑ ⏑ – ⏑ – ⏑ – (11)
Bhujaṅgaprayāta : ⏑ – – ⏑ – – ⏑ – – ⏑ – – (12)
Bhujaṅgavijṛmbhita : – – – – – – – – | ⏑ ⏑ ⏑ ⏑ ⏑ ⏑ ⏑ ⏑ ⏑ ⏑ – | ⏑ – ⏑ ⏑ – ⏑ – (26)

[1] Cf. Jacobi, ZDMG. xliii. 464 ff. ; SIFI. VIII. ii. 108 ff.

Bhramaravilasita : – – – – | ∪ ∪ ∪ ∪ ∪ ∪ – (11)
Mañjarī : ∪ ∪ – ∪ – | ∪ ∪ ∪ – ∪ – – ∪ – (14)
Mañjubhāṣiṇī : ∪ ∪ – ∪ – | ∪ ∪ ∪ – ∪ – ∪ – (13)
Maṇiguṇanikara : ∪ ∪ ∪ ∪ ∪ ∪ ∪ ∪ | ∪ ∪ ∪ ∪ ∪ ∪ – (15)
Mattamayūrā : – – – – | – ∪ ∪ – – ∪ ∪ – – (13)
Mattā : – – – – | ∪ ∪ ∪ ∪ – – (10)
Madhyakṣamā : – – – – | ∪ ∪ ∪ ∪ ∪ ∪ | – – – – (14)
Mandākrāntā : – – – – | ∪ ∪ ∪ ∪ ∪ – | – ∪ – – ∪ – – (17)
Mahāmālikā (Vanamālā) : ∪ ∪ ∪ ∪ ∪ ∪ – ∪ – – | ∪ – – ∪ – – ∪ – (18)
Mālatī : ∪ ∪ ∪ ∪ – ∪ ∪ – ∪ – ∪ – (12)
Mālinī : ∪ ∪ ∪ ∪ ∪ ∪ – – | – ∪ – – ∪ – – (15)
Meghavitāna : ∪ ∪ – ∪ ∪ – ∪ ∪ – – (10).
Meghavisphūrjita : ∪ – – – – – | ∪ ∪ ∪ ∪ ∪ – | – ∪ – – ∪ – – (19)
Rathoddhatā : – ∪ – ∪ ∪ ∪ – ∪ – ∪ – (11)
Rukmavatī : – ∪ ∪ – – | – ∪ ∪ – – (10)
Rucirā : ∪ – ∪ – | ∪ ∪ ∪ ∪ – ∪ – ∪ – (13)
Lalitā : – – ∪ – ∪ ∪ ∪ – ∪ – ∪ – (12)
Vaṅçapattrapatita : – ∪ ∪ – ∪ – ∪ ∪ ∪ – | ∪ ∪ ∪ ∪ ∪ ∪ – (17)
Vaṅçasthā : ∪ – ∪ – – ∪ ∪ – ∪ – ∪ ∪ (12)
Upajāti, stanzas of Indravaṅçā and Vaṅçasthā lines
Vasantatilaka : – – ∪ – ∪ ∪ ∪ – ∪ ∪ – ∪ – – (14)
Vātormī : – – – – | ∪ ∪ – – ∪ – – (11)
Vidyunmālā : – – – – | – – – – (8)
Vilāsinī : ∪ ∪ ∪ ∪ – ∪ – ∪ ∪ ∪ – ∪ – ∪ ∪ ∪ – (17)
Vaiçvadevī : – – – – – | – ∪ – – ∪ – – (12)
Çārdūlavikrīḍita : – – – ∪ ∪ – ∪ – ∪ ∪ ∪ – | – – ∪ – – ∪ – (19)
Çālinī : – – – – | – ∪ – – ∪ – – (11)
Çikhariṇī : ∪ – – – – – | ∪ ∪ ∪ ∪ ∪ – – ∪ ∪ ∪ – (17)
Çuddhavirāj : – – – ∪ ∪ – ∪ – ∪ – (10)
Çrīpuṭa : ∪ ∪ ∪ ∪ ∪ ∪ – – | – ∪ – – (12)
Sumānikā : – ∪ – ∪ – ∪ – (7)
Suvadanā : – – – – ∪ – – | ∪ ∪ ∪ ∪ ∪ ∪ – | – – ∪ ∪ ∪ – (20)
Sragdharā : – – – – ∪ – – | ∪ ∪ ∪ ∪ ∪ ∪ – | – ∪ – – ∪ – – (21)
Sragviṇī : – ∪ – – ∪ – – ∪ – – ∪ – (12)
Svāgatā : – ∪ – ∪ ∪ ∪ – ∪ ∪ – – (11)
Hariṇapluta : ∪ ∪ – ∪ ∪ – ∪ ∪ – ∪ – ‖ ∪ ∪ ∪ – ∪ ∪ – ∪ ∪ – ∪ – (*a* = 11 ; *b* = 12) *bis*
Hariṇī : ∪ ∪ ∪ ∪ ∪ – | – – – – | ∪ – ∪ ∪ – ∪ – (17)

The rules observed in the Çloka are strict. Each half-verse is composed of two lines of eight syllables, and the whole falls naturally into four feet of four syllables each. The fourth must be a diiambus ; if the second is ∪ – – ⏓, then all possible forms of the third are permissible save ⏓ ⏓ ∪ ⏓, while in the first in this case the only restriction is that it must not be – ∪ ∪ ⏓ or ∪ ∪ ∪ ⏓.

If, however, the second foot assumes any other shape, there are definite restrictions affecting the first foot, born of the desire to prevent undue monotony of metre. In these cases the same restrictions apply to the third foot as in the normal form. This gives us for the first two feet of the irregular forms, Vipulās:

Vipulā I ⏓ – ⏑ – / ⏓ ⏓ – – ⏑ ⏑ ⏑ ⏓
" II ⏓ – ⏑ – – ⏑ ⏑ ⏓
" III ⏓ – ⏑ – – | – – ⏓
" IV ⏓ ⏓ ⏓ – ¦ – ⏑ – ⏓

The use of Vipulās seems to be mainly a question of individual taste and style, and, as has been mentioned, the writers on metre show no real comprehension of the rules of the metre.[1]

[1] On the specific characters of the metres see A. S. Bhandarkar, POCP. 1919, i. pp. clvi f. In Vipulas I and II a long final is normal.

XXI

GRAMMAR

1. *The Beginnings of Grammatical Study.*

IN the Brāhmaṇas of the Vedic period we find sufficient proof[1] that, as in Greece, grammatical study in India began with consideration of such points as pronunciation and euphonic combination, and the discrimination of parts of speech which gives us terms such as *vibhakti*, case termination, *vacana*, number, *kurvant*, present tense. Possibly hence it derived its name Vyākaraṇa, though that is often deduced from the later practice of analysis of forms. We find already in Yāska the terms *nāman*, noun, *sarvanāmam*, pronoun, *ākhyāta*, verb, *upasarga*, preposition, *nipāta*, particle.[2] The next stage is not represented in the Brāhmaṇas, but is fully in being in Yāska's time; it consists of the analysis of forms, as opposed to the reckless etymologies of the Brāhmaṇas and Plato; we do not know how this came to be arrived at, though it is a plausible conjecture which finds the motive in the fact that in compounds in Sanskrit the first word appears in its stem form without terminations. From this it was fairly easy to distinguish stem and termination in nouns, and then to advance to distinguish in verbs root, terminations and tense and other affixes, and to arrive at the doctrine of the derivation of nouns from nouns by Taddhita suffixes, of nouns from verbs by Kṛt suffixes. A further step was to declare as did Çākaṭāyana that all nouns are derived from verbs, to which Gārgya objected that if this was so, it followed that every thing should have as many names as it had activities, and every name should apply to everything which had the activity it connoted. But the supporters of Çākaṭāyana carried out their principle, and to this period goes back in substance, not in its present form, the *Uṇādisūtra*, con-

[1] See Wackernagel, *Altind. Gramm.*, i, pp. lix ff.; Oldenberg, *Vorwissensch. Wissenschaft*, pp. 79 f., 238 ff.

[2] See Lakshman Sarup, *The Nighaṇṭu and the Nirukta*, pp. 54 ff. Cf. Prabhatchandra Chakrabarti, *Linguistic Speculations of the Hindus* (1924–5); S. Varma, JRAS. 1925, pp. 21 ff. (on analysis of meaning).

taining words which are derived from verbs by unusual affixes, and which in some form Pāṇini evidently knew.

This important period of studies was largely concerned with the preservation and interpretation of the Vedic texts; its work is seen in the preparation of the Padapāṭha of the *Ṛgveda* by Çākalya, who is known to Pāṇini, the similar work done on other Vedic texts, the Prātiçākhyas, which in their original form were probably older than Pāṇini, at any rate as far as concerns those on the *Ṛgveda*, *Taittirīya* and *Vājasaneyi Saṁhitās*,[1] and the Çikṣās, which as we have them are probably later than Pāṇini, but doubtless existed in his time, proving the care taken to secure due correctness of pronunciation of the scriptures. But the grammarians were clearly concerned also with the Bhāṣā, the spoken speech of the day, and it was in connexion with it, especially as it grew more distinct from the sacred texts on the one hand and the speeches of the lower classes on the other, that secular grammar grew up. Pāṇini knew and cites by name many predecessors, including Çākaṭāyana, Āpiçāli, and Çaunaka, as well as minor names, and his allusion to easterners and northerners, if it applies to forms of speech used in these parts, is also testimony to the existence of grammarians to note them, unless we are to assume[2] that he himself of the north lived in the east and noted the differences for himself, which is implausible in the extreme. What is clear from Pāṇini's own work is that he summarizes the efforts of many previous writers, from whom we may be sure he borrowed his form as well as many facts.

2. *Pāṇini and his Followers*

The *Aṣṭādhyāyī*[3] of Pāṇini consists of about 4,000 short Sūtras divided into eight books, treating of technical terms and rules of interpretation (i), nouns in composition and case relations (ii); the adding of suffixes to roots (iii) and to nouns (iv, v), accent and changes of sound in word formation (vi, vii) and the word in

[1] Cf. Liebich, *Einführung in die ind. einheim. Sprachwissenschaft*, ii. 35 ff., with Keith, HOS. xviii, pp. xxxix–xli, clxxi.

[2] Franke, GGA. 1891, pp. 957, 975 ff.

[3] Ed. and trans. O. Böhtlingk, Leipzig, 1887; Śrīśa Chandra Vasu, Allahabad, 1891–8.

the sentence (viii). But this scheme is constantly interrupted, rules being interpolated illogically because it was convenient to do, or because space could thus be saved, for the whole book is dominated by the aim to be as brief as possible. The, to us, illogical order and impracticability of learning Sanskrit by the use of the grammar are explained, if we remember that the book was to be learned by heart by those who were already accustomed to use Sanskrit in conversation, and had not to learn how to speak it, but to know what forms were correct, what vulgar. Of the incoherence, however, part is doubtless due to the fact that Pāṇini was only working up a mass of traditional matter, as may be seen not merely from certain irregularities in case usage,[1] but also from the employment to denote a Vedic use of three terms, *chandasi*, *nigame*, and *mantre*, of which the first prevails with his followers. The main object of the grammar is to deal with the Bhāṣā, the living speech of the day; an amount of Vedic matter is incorporated. This part is of uneven value, suggesting that it was based on a number of special studies, imperfectly co-ordinated; thus minute details from the *Kāṭhaka* or *Maitrāyaṇīya Saṁhitās* are noted; but at other times a vague reference is made to Vedic irregularities, Vedic words are cited without analysis, and causeless variations of form are permitted as Vedic.

The principle underlying the grammar is the derivation of nouns from verbs, Pāṇini avoiding dealing with the hard cases by alluding to the Uṇādi list existing in his time. All derivation is done by affixes, and, therefore, when the word agrees with the root form of a verb, or one nominal form is the same as that whence it is derived, it is necessary to assume suffixes which are invisible, e.g. *badara*, fruit of the *badara* tree. Phonetics do not receive investigation save incidentally as changes of words occur in processes of derivation. But in this field Pāṇini, or more correctly his predecessors, achieved very remarkable results, as in the postulate of Guṇa and Vṛddhi changes, of forms with long *ṝ* vowel, roots in *ai*, *masj* as the original of *majj*, dive, *s* as the ending of inflexions. The analysis of forms is normally carried out with great acumen; it is very rare to find such a phenomenon as the periphrastic future, e.g. *kartāsmi*, treated as a simple verbal

[1] Cf. Weber, IS. xviii. 508 ff.

form. In comparison with the work of Greek grammarians Pāṇini is on a totally different plane in this regard. The suggestion that he and his predecessors were creating a language, or that the forms which are not recorded in earlier literature are not to be accepted as prima facie valid, is now definitely disposed of.

To secure the brevity aimed at many devices are adopted; the cases are used pregnantly, verbs are omitted, leading rules are understood to govern others which follow; above all algebraic formulae replace real words; the rule that a vowel is changed into the corresponding semi-vowel when a vowel, not itself, follows is denoted by *iko yaṇ aci*; the last Sūtra *a a* denotes that *a* which has been treated in the grammar as an open letter, corresponding to which we have long *ā*, is really a closed letter pronounced like *u* in 'but'. Older than Pāṇini are probably some technical terms of ungrammatical make-up, such as *parasmaipada*, active, *ātmanepada*, middle, *napuṅsaka*, neuter; others are reduced forms of the original as *it* to denote a letter not pronounced, appended to a word to indicate some feature regarding its treatment, from *iti*, so. The use of such Anubandhas is doubtless before Pāṇini, as the term Uṇādi itself proves.

Pāṇini's date is unhappily uncertain.[1] He was later than Yāska and Çaunaka, probably he came after not only the Brāhmaṇas but also the older Upaniṣads and was alive during the Sūtra period of Vedic literature, but unhappily these facts give us nothing save a relative chronology. We know he was a native of Çalātura near the modern Atak, where Hiuen Tsang saw a statue to his memory; his mother was Dākṣī, and a legend ascribes his death to a lion. His connexion with the north-west is important, when we find in his work Yavanānī, meaning probably Greek (Ionian) writing. We may, of course, scent an interpolation, and, if so, the word is valueless. If not, it leaves us still in doubt, for the assumption that it is a proof that Pāṇini wrote after the invasion of Alexander the Great, though it has been supported[2] by the occurrence in the *Gaṇapāṭha* of the names

[1] Keith, HOS. xviii, pp. clxviii f.; *Aitareya Āraṇyaka*, pp. 21 ff.; Lüders, SBA. 1919, p. 744; Liebich, *Pāṇini* (1891); Kielhorn, GN. 1885, pp. 185 ff.; Wecker, *Bezz. Beitr.* xxx. 1 ff., 177 ff. A date *c.* 700–600 is claimed by Belvalkar (*Systems of Sanskrit Grammar*, p. 15; cf. Bhandarkar, JBRAS. xvi. 340 f.; Keith, IOC. ii. 242.

[2] Lévi, JA. 1890, i. 234 ff.

Āmbhi and Bhagala, Omphis and Phegelas, is clearly unfounded, seeing that India was in contact with Greece as early as the expedition of Xerxes. On the whole, however, it seems needless to carry back Pāṇini beyond the fourth century; if he flourished *c.* 350, then Kātyāyana, who may be placed *c.* 250–200, might easily have found sufficient divergence of speech to justify his corrections. There are, indeed, proofs that language had changed, as we have seen; but to assign Pāṇini to the sixth or seventh century B.C. on that score appears to lack any plausibility.

Kātyāyana probably lived in the third century B.C.,[1] though no strict proof is possible, and this date really depends on the fact that he apparently did not long precede Patañjali; the impression left by Kātyāyana's Vārttikas is certainly that sometimes, not by any means always, he is attacking or correcting Pāṇini on the score of differences in usage which had arisen between the time of the two, while with Patañjali it seems as if he and Kātyāyana were parted by no great interval of time. Kātyāyana was not a captious critic of Pāṇini; he was not the first to call in question his rules; what he did was to examine criticisms, rejecting some, accepting others, and therefore supplementing and limiting Pāṇini's rules. But, while we need not treat him as hostile, he seems not to have been sorry to find Pāṇini in error. Patañjali, whose *Mahābhāṣya* has preserved us Kātyāyana's Vārttikas of some 1,245 Sūtras, takes up Kātyāyana's criticisms, and in many cases defends Pāṇini, but by no means as a matter of course. Moreover, he carries out in great measure his predecessor's work by examining other Sūtras of Pāṇini and correcting or explaining them. It is clear that Patañjali had many criticisms and works before him beside that of Kātyāyana; there are Vārttikas in verse which need not all have been Kātyāyana's, and Kārikās, memorial verses which probably are by various hands, including Patañjali himself; the variety of metres used in these verses is remarkable, including some later quite rare, but complex, metres. Among others Patañjali mentions Vyāḍi, of whose work—the *Saṁgraha*—much has been conjectured but very little is known, Vājapyāyana, Pauṣkarasādi,

[1] Jayaswal's arguments for a period 248–200 (IA. xlvii. 138; xlviii. 12) from Vārttika, ii. 1. 60 are invalid. For his style see V. G. Paranjpe, *Le Vârtika de Kâtyâyana* (1922), who claims an earlier date; cf. Smith, EHI. p. 470.

Goṇikāputra, and Gonardīya, with whom he was formerly erroneously held to be identical.[1]

Our information regarding the personality of Kātyāyana and Patañjali is negligible. Kātyāyana, however, either bore the alternative name of Vararuci or was early confused with a person of that name, and to a Vararuci many works are ascribed, including the first extant Prākrit Grammar, *Prākṛtaprakāça* ; book iv of the *Kātantra* and the *Liṅgānuçāsana*[2]; the *Vārarucasaṁgraha*,[3] twenty-five Kārikās on case construction, compounds, verbs, and nominal formation ; a lexicon ; the Vedic *Puṣpasūtra* ; and stanzas of poetry. As Patañjali mentions a *Vāraruca kāvya* we may believe in a poet Vararuci of early date, but we need not identify him with the author of the Kārikās. His identity with the author of the *Prākṛtaprakāça* is most implausible, as the Prākrit of that work is very late in character, and we may assume that the other attributions are of no value. Late tradition makes Vararuci a contemporary of Pāṇini, and also a minister of the Nandas of Pāṭaliputra ; Kumāralāta[4] actually confirms this point, but even if this poet existed, it proves nothing for the grammarian, as Kumāralāta speaks only of a poet. Of more value is Patañjali's proof that Kātyāyana was a southerner.

Patañjali is regarded as an incorporation of the snake Çeṣa, Viṣṇu's resting-place during his slumber, and he is believed to be the author of the *Yoga Sūtra*, a view implausible on grounds of certain grammatical slips by the latter and slight deviations in philosophic terminology, apart from the fact that the tradition is very late and obviously due to likeness of name.[5] His date[6] is still disputed. The evidence for it is that statements in his grammar undoubtedly refer to a sacrifice for Puṣyamitra, whose reign began *c.* 185 or 178 B.C., and to a recent attack on Sāketa and Madhyamikā by a Yavana, who is very plausibly identified

[1] Kielhorn, IA. xv. 81 f. ; xvi. 101 f. ; GN. 1885, pp. 189 ff., who postulates a considerable period between Kātyāyana and Patañjali ; *Kātyāyana and Patañjali* (1876).

[2] Liebich, *Einführung in die ind. einheim. Sprachwissenschaft*, i. 11. See Winternitz, GIL. iii. 391.

[3] Ed. TSS. 33, 1913.

[4] *Sūtrālaṁkāra*, trans. E. Huber, p. 88.

[5] Cf. Woods, HOS. xvii, pp. xv ff. ; Jacobi, GGA. 1919, pp. 14 ff. ; DLZ. 1922, p. 271.

[6] Cf. Smith, EHI. pp. 227–9 ; Winternitz, GIL. iii. 389 ; Bühler, *Die indischen Inschriften*, p. 72 ; Keith, IOC. ii. 243 f.

with the Greek Menander (*c.* 156–153), dates which give *c.* 150–149 for the composition of the work, on the assumption probable, yet not conclusive, that the references are Patañjali's own. Some slight confirmation may be gained from the fact that Kātyāyana, but not Pāṇini, notes the title *devānām priya*, famed in Açoka's inscriptions, suggesting that he fell after 250 B.C., which would not suit ill with 150 B.C. for Patañjali. If this be rejected, we must content ourselves with noting that Kalhaṇa records a revival of the study of the *Mahābhāṣya* in Kashmir under Abhimanyu, whose date, however, we do not know, and that Bhartṛhari (*c.* 650) proves long study of the text before his time.

The *Mahābhāṣya* [1] is interesting stylistically as giving us a lively picture of the mode of discussion of the day. A question is posed; an Ācaryadeçīya deals with it, not altogether incompetently but not quite satisfactorily, and an Ācārya solves the issue. The style, therefore, is lively, simple, animated, and as in Açoka's inscriptions—possibly a confirmation of the date proposed—not rarely do we find the question 'Wherefore?', 'How?', or 'What?' put and then answered. Proverbial expressions and references to matters of everyday life are introduced and serve both to enliven the discussions and to give us valuable hints of the conditions of life and thought in the time of Patañjali, who thus is a source of information for religious and social history as well as for literature. A good example of his style is afforded by a famous reference [2] to the Mauryas: Pāṇini has a rule providing for the addition of the suffix *ka* to a name to denote an image of the person, but adds that it is dropped if the image is used to secure a livelihood (*jīvikārthe*) and is not vendible (*apaṇya*). Patañjali says: *apaṇya ity ucyate tatredaṁ na sidhyati Çivaḥ Skando Viçākha iti. kiṁ kāraṇam? Mauryair hiraṇyārthibhir arcāḥ prakalpitāḥ. bhavet tāsu na syāt. yās tv etāḥ samprati pūjārthās tāsu bhaviṣyati.* 'The difficulty is raised, with regard to Pāṇini's proviso that images are not to be vendible, that on this doctrine the forms Çiva, Skanda, Viçākha, are incorrect. Why is that? Because the Mauryas, in their greed for money, used as means images of the gods (i.e. they bartered them, so that the forms should be Çivaka, &c.). (Final answer.) Very well, granted that the rule for dropping *ka* does not apply to those images of

[1] Ed. Kielhorn, BSS. 1906 ff.

[2] Bhandarkar, JBRAS. xvi. 206 ff.

the Mauryas; still as regards images now used for purposes of worship it does apply.' It will be seen that the amount which must be understood to make such passages intelligible is rather a strain on the reader,[1] and in point of fact the *Mahābhāṣya* evidently gave serious trouble to later students. Bhartṛhari, who died *c.* 651, wrote a commentary on it which is all but lost, and also the *Vākyapadīya*,[2] in three books of verse, which mainly deals with questions of the philosophy of speech; a difficult work, it contains much evidence of thorough knowledge of contemporary philosophical disputes. Kaiyaṭa's[3] commentary on the *Mahābhāṣya*, which may belong to the twelfth century but which tradition places earlier, borrows largely from Bhartṛhari, and is itself commented on by the voluminous writer Nāgojī Bhaṭṭa (*c.* 1700). Both show that they often had as much trouble to understand Patañjali as have we.

Save for Bhartṛhari, Patañjali closes the line of great grammarians. We do not doubt that he drew on the speech of his day; his preface insists on the absurdity of learning words that are not used, and like Kātyāyana he views Pāṇini in the light of a living language. Thereafter use is made of the three great grammarians, efforts are made to explain them, or to re-expound their systems for purposes of more effective exposition, but nothing is done to restate the facts of language with reference to living speech. For reasons which we cannot certainly explain, the authority of Pāṇini and his immediate followers prevailed; deviations from his rules were even in great poets like Kālidāsa deemed to be errors.

One commentary of Pāṇini deserves praise for its extent of information, its comparative clearness, and its evidence of changes in Pāṇini's text, the *Kāçikā Vṛtti*[4] of Jayāditya and Vāmana, which was written before I-tsing visited India, when he found it regularly used by Chinese in order to study Sanskrit grammar, and when he records its school use by boys for five years after attaining fifteen years of age. Books i–v seem to have been

[1] Cf. B. Geiger, *Mahābhāṣya zu P. vi. 4. 22 und 132* (SWA. 1908).

[2] Ed. with Puṇyarāja's comm., BenSS. 1887–1907; Kielhorn, IA. xii. 226 ff.; Pathak, JBRAS. xviii. 341 ff.

[3] Bühler, *Report*, pp. 71 f.; Peterson, *Report*, i, p. 26.

[4] Ed. Benares, 1898; B. Liebich, *Zwei Kapitel der Kāçikā* (1892); on Pāṇini's text, Kielhorn, IA. xvi. 178 ff.

Jayāditya's; presumably Vāmana finished it by reason of his death. A comment on it was written *c.* 700 by the Buddhist Jinendrabuddhi, and the *Nyāsa* referred to by Māgha [1] appears to be this book. Another Buddhist, Çaraṇadeva, wrote in 1172 under the supervision of Sarvarakṣita a *Durghaṭavṛtti*,[2] dealing with the difficult passages of Pāṇini's text. Among his many citations are three verses of the *Jāmbavatīvijaya* of a Pāṇini, whose identity with the grammarian we may safely dismiss as unproved. But Pāṇini could not teach Sanskrit, for which end his grammar was not written. For such purpose re-writing and re-arrangement were essential, giving us (*c.* 1400) Rāmacandra's *Prakriyākaumudī*,[3] based on which is Bhaṭṭoji Dīkṣita's well-known and not unsatisfactory *Siddhāntakaumudī*,[4] on which he wrote a comment, the *Prauḍhamanoramā*. From it come two school grammars of Varadarāja, *Madhyasiddhāntakaumudī* and *Laghukaumudī*.[5]

As we have seen, Pāṇini presupposes an *Uṇādisūtra* [6]; our extant text contains late words like *dīnāra* or *mihira* and omits some, e. g. *pāntha* mentioned by Patañjali; Çākaṭāyana or Vararuci is given as author. The *Dhātupāṭha* goes back in substance to Pāṇini; it gives the roots according to classes, with indicatory letters containing information regarding their formation; on it are based the *Dhātupradīpa* of Maitreyarakṣita, the *Daiva* of Deva, and the *Puruṣakāra*, a joke on the name, by Kṛṣṇalīlāçuka,[7] who is later than Hemacandra, and the *Mādhavīya Dhātuvṛtti* [8] ascribed to Sāyaṇa's brother Mādhava in the fourteenth century. The *Gaṇapāṭha* has been interpolated, and Vardhamāna's *Gaṇaratnamahodadhi* [9] (1140) is not based on it but on some other grammar. Rules on accent, Vedic and classical, are dealt with in the *Phiṭsūtra* [10] of Çāntanava, who is later than Patañjali. The rules of interpretation which govern the construction of the

[1] ii. 112. Ed. by Srish Chandra Chakravarti (Rājshahi, 1914 ff.), see i. 47, 48 on the authorship of the *Kāçikā*. On it is based Puruṣottamadeva's *Bhāṣāvṛtti* (*c.* 1150); ed. 1918.

[2] Ed. TSS. 6, 1909. [3] S. C. Vidyabhusana, JPASB. 1908, pp. 593 ff.

[4] Ed. Bombay, 1882. Date seventeenth century.

[5] Ed. and trans. J. R. Ballantyne, Benares, 1867.

[6] Ed. Böhtlingk, St. Petersburg, 1844; Ujjvaladatta's comm., ed. London, 1859.

[7] Ed. TSS. 1, 1905.

[8] Ed. *Pandit*, iv–viii, xvii–xix. [9] Ed. J. Eggeling, London, 1879.

[10] Ed. F. Kielhorn, AKM. iv. 2, 1866.

grammar must have been early formulated, if not explicitly laid down by Pāṇini himself; of several collections, that commented on by Nāgojī Bhaṭṭa in his *Paribhāṣenduçekhara*[1] is best known.

3. *The Later Schools*

The later schools present no features of essential interest and may be reviewed briefly. The oldest was probably the *Kātantra*,[2] 'little treatise,' called also *Kaumāra* or *Kālāpa*, the latter names indicating acceptance of the legend that its author Çarvavarman wrote under Çiva's special favour. The legend which brings him into contact with Sātavāhana has been noted and its worth questioned.[3] What is certain is that in Kashmir and Bengal the work had much influence, and that it affected deeply the Pāli grammar of Kaccāyana and the Dravidian grammarians. Originally of four books, it appears with supplements both in the Tibetan translation and in Durgasiṅha's commentary; fragments have been found in Central Asia,[4] and the *Dhātupāṭha* is extant only in the Tibetan version. In addition to Durgasiṅha's *Vṛtti* on which he himself wrote a *Ṭīkā*, a sort of commentary is provided in Ugrabhūti's *Çiṣyahitānyāsa* (1000).[5] Tibetan tradition ascribes to Çarvavarman the use of the grammar of Indragomin, and this work seems to have been popular among the Buddhists of Nepal, but it is lost, though the reality of its author's existence is certain.

Use is made in the *Kāçikā Vṛtti*, without acknowledgement, of the *Cāndra Vyākaraṇa*,[6] the grammar of Candra, which was popular in the Buddhist countries, Kashmir, Tibet, and Nepal, and which reached Ceylon. The date is uncertain, for Bhartṛhari and Kalhaṇa ascribe to Candra study of the *Mahābhāṣya*, while south Indian tradition connects him with Vararuci and makes him condemn the *Mahābhāṣya* as much talk with few ideas. He alludes in his grammar to a victory of a Jarta over the Hūṇas,

[1] Ed. and trans. Kielhorn, BSS. 1868; ed. ĀnSS. 72.

[2] Ed., with Durgasiṅha's comm., J. Eggeling, BI. 1874–8. See B. Liebich, *Einführung in die ind. einheim. Sprachwissenschaft* (Heidelberg, 1919), who dismisses the work of Indragomin, now lost; cf. Kielhorn, IA. xv. 181 f.

[3] Winternitz (GIL. iii. 379) suggests the third century A. D.

[4] Cf. L. Finot, *Muséon*, 1911, p. 192.

[5] Sachau, *Alberuni*, i. 135; *Bodleian Catal.* ii. 129.

[6] Ed. B. Liebich, Leipzig, 1902; comm., 1918.

which points to A.D. 470 as an earliest date, and A.D. 600 seems at least as likely if we may trust Chinese sources. He wrote a comment on his own grammar, and has a distinct terminology from that of Pāṇini, though he is essentially dependent on him. A *Dhātupāṭha*, *Gaṇapāṭha*, *Uṇādisūtra*, and *Paribhāṣāsūtra* belong to the text, and *c.* 1200 the monk Kāçyapa wrote a *Bālāvabodhana* which became popular in Ceylon.

The Jains, in their turn, had grammars of their own. The *Jainendra Vyākaraṇa*,[1] ascribed to the Jinendra, really written by Pūjyapāda Devanandin, perhaps was composed *c.* 678. The *Çākaṭāyana Vyākaraṇa*[2] belongs to the reign of Amoghavarṣa (814–77), when Çākaṭāyana compiled it, using the terminology of Pāṇini, of Candra, and also of the *Jainendra*. The grammar has besides a full commentary, abridged by Yakṣavarman in his *Cintāmaṇi*, works on *Dhātu*, *Gaṇa*, *Uṇādi*, *Paribhāṣā*, and a *Liṅgānuçāsana*. Based on it is the *Siddhahemacandra* or *Haima Vyākaraṇa*,[3] written for Jayasiṅha Siddharāja who had eight older works brought from Kashmir for his use; the work is practical in arrangement and terminology, which is mainly that of the *Kātantra*, and omits, of course, Vedic grammar and accent. Hemacandra wrote two commentaries, an *Uṇādigaṇasūtra* and a *Dhātupāṭha*.[4]

Other grammars won local acceptance, most at a late date. The *Saṁkṣiptasāra*[5] of Kramadīçvara, its commentary revised by Jūmaranandin, deals in seven chapters with Sanskrit, in an eighth with Prākrit grammar; its popularity was in western Bengal, and it was written after 1150. Vopadeva's *Mugdhabodha*[6] and *Kavikalpadruma*, on roots, won greatest popularity in Bengal and were written after 1250 under Mahādeva of Devagiri. Eastern Bengal favoured Padmanābhadatta's *Supadmavyākaraṇa* (1375), Bihar and Benares the *Sārasvatī Prakriyā* with commentary by Anubhūtisvarūpa.

Of grammatical and lexical importance are the *Liṅgānuçāsanas*,[7] treatises on gender, similar to those appended to the lexica.

[1] Ed. *Pandit*, N.S. xxxi–xxxiv.
[2] Ed. London, 1913. Cf. Pathak, ABI. i. 7 ff.
[3] Kielhorn, WZKM. ii. 18 ff.
[4] Ed. J. Kirste, Vienna, 1895–9.
[5] See Zachariae, *Bezz. Beitr.*, v. 22 ff.; IOC. i. 218 ff.; ii. 278.
[6] Ed. Böhtlingk, St. Petersburg, 1847; IOC. i. 230 ff.
[7] Franke, *Die indischen Genusregeln* (Kiel, 1890).

That ascribed to Pāṇini cannot be so old; that in Āryā verses ascribed to Vararuci is known to the *Liṅgānuçāsana* of Harṣadeva (606–47) and Vāmana (*c.* 800). We have also texts ascribed to Çākaṭāyana and Hemacandra.[1]

4. *Grammars of Prākrit*

It is clear that the Prākrit grammars[2] which we have were written under the direct influence of Sanskrit grammars. The tradition which ascribes to Pāṇini a Prākrit grammar is doubtless a mere invention to honour Prākrit, and the further contention that Katyāyana produced the *Prākṛtaprakāça*[3] of Vararuci is equally absurd. That grammar handles Māhārāṣṭrī very fully, in nine chapters, then gives one each to Paiçācī, Māgadhī, and Çaurasenī, treating Māhārāṣṭrī as the highest form, but finding Sanskrit as the original of all Prākrits. The forms of these Prākrits are clearly later than those of Açvaghoṣa and reflect perhaps the works of the third century A. D. at earliest. What is certain is that Vararuci, if we give this name to the author, was commented on by Bhāmaha, the writer on poetics (*c.* 700). The relative age of Vararuci and Caṇḍa, author of the *Prākṛtalakṣaṇa*[4] is disputed; unhappily that work has come down in the two recensions, and, even if one is older than Vararuci, the other is younger, while its original views on many important points, as to retention of inter-vocalic consonants, depend on dubious readings; it may give us a stage not otherwise represented of Ārṣa or Ardhamāgadhī, the Prākrit of the Jains, it gives one Sūtra only each to Apabhrança, Paiçācikī, and Māgadhikā. As we have seen, another testimony as to a Prākrit is given by the chapter on Prākrits in the *Nāṭyaçāstra*.

Vararuci seems to have belonged to the east—which is another sign of distinction from Kātyāyana of the south. His tradition is alleged to have been followed by a mysterious Lañkeçvara or Rāvaṇa,[5] who wrote a *Prākṛtakāmadhenu* on which

[1] Ed. Göttingen, 1886.

[2] Pischel, *Grammatik der Prakrit-Sprachen* (1900).

[3] Ed. and trans. E. B. Cowell, Hertford, 1854.

[4] Ed. A. F. R. Hoernle, BI. 1880.

[5] Grierson, AMJV. III. i. 120 ff.; Mitra, *Notices*, ix, nos. 3157, 3158; these notices are quite inadequate foundations for any theory.

is based Rāma Tarkavāgīça's *Prākṛtakalpataru*, a work of the seventeenth century, which again was used by Mārkaṇḍeya's *Prākṛtasarvasva* in that century, while Kramadīçvara's section on Prākrit grammar represents the same school. Lankeçvara is also credited with a comment on Çeṣanāga's *Prākṛtavyākaraṇa-sūtra*—not, as stated by Grierson, on his own work—and, as the manuscripts alleged to contain his works have vanished, his existence is decidedly in the air.

The western school is held to be represented by the *Vālmīki-sūtras* which are lost in their original form, and are only preserved in a much expanded late version. In Hemacandra's grammar,[1] book viii deals with Prākrit; he adds Ārṣa to the list as a good Jain must, and takes note of Jain Māhārāṣṭrī as well as the ordinary Māhārāṣṭrī of the poets; besides Paiçācī he places Cūlikāpaiçācika, and handles Apabhrança, giving stanzas of unknown source. For Māhārāṣṭrī he cites Hāla and the *Setubandha*, for Paiçācī, it seems likely, the *Bṛhatkathā*, probably, however, not in the original version. He is followed by Trivikrama in his *Prākṛtaçabdānuçāsana*,[2] who uses the *Vālmīki Sūtra* terminology, by Sinharāja (14th cent.) in the *Prākṛtarūpāvatāra*,[3] by Lakṣmīdhara (16th cent.) in the *Ṣaḍbhāṣācandrikā* and others.

This account, however, of the schools is based on inadequate grounds, for Rāvaṇa is merely a name to us. In the case of the *Vālmīki Sūtra* we have more evidence, for the Sūtras are recognized in different forms by Trivikrama, Sinharāja, and Lakṣmīdhara. But the question arises whether it is correct to assume that they are older than Hemacandra. Trivedī,[4] from a comparison in detail with the Sūtra of that author, holds that the *Vālmīki Sūtra* is an improved version of the work of Hemacandra, basing his conclusion on the fact that the Sūtras are sometimes better expressed, sometimes abridged, Hemacandra. Against this has been set by Hultzsch[5] the fact that, as both the text of the *Vālmīki Sūtra*, when preserved alone, and Lakṣmīdhara, to whom we may add the *Çambhurahasya*, ascribe the Sūtra

[1] Ed. Pischel, Halle, 1877–80.
[2] T. Laddu, *Prolegomena zu Trivikrama's Prākrit-Grammatik* (1912).
[3] Ed. E. Hultzsch, London, 1909. Cf. Keith, IOC. ii. 299.
[4] *Shaḍbhāshāchandrikā*, pp. 6 ff.
[5] *Prākṛtarūpāvatāra*, p. vii.

to the author of the *Rāmāyaṇa*, the work can hardly have come into being after the date of Hemacandra. This, however, is decidedly conjectural, for we have no certainty of Trivikrama's date. All that is certain is that he wrote after Hemacandra and before Lakṣmīdhara and the *Ratnāpaṇa* of Kumārasvāmin, who was a son of Mallinātha. Now Lakṣmīdhara was, it seems, the protégé of Tirumalarāja[1] of the third dynasty of Vijayanagara, who flourished about the middle of the sixteenth century A. D., and Kumārasvāmin's father Mallinātha lived before A. D. 1532, when a verse of his appears in an inscription,[2] and after A. D. 1400, since he quotes the *Vasantarājīya* (*c.* 1400).[3] Kumārasvāmin also knows Lakṣmīdhara, so that there can be no real doubt of the latter's date. We, therefore, can hardly say that the *Vālmīki Sūtra* could not have been composed after Hemacandra, and at present this seems the most probable conclusion. Siṅharāja's date is also quite dubious; the reference[4] to the fourteenth century is conjectural, and it is possible that he is really later than Bhaṭṭoji Dīkṣita. Lakṣmīdhara and he agree in treating of Māhārāṣṭrī as the Prākrit *par excellence*, and then shortly giving the particular features of Çaurasenī, Māgadhī, Paiçācī, Cūlikāpaiçācī, and Apabhrança. Of other grammarians Mārkaṇḍeya is noteworthy for his treatment of a large number of forms of Prākrit as a result of his revising the tradition of varieties of dramatic Prākrit; he treats of five principal divisions, Māhārāṣṭrī, Çaurasenī, Prācyā, Āvantī with Bāhlīkī, and Māgadhī with Ardhamāgadhī, and also of Çākārī, Cāṇḍālī, Çābarī with Ābhīrī and Auḍhrī, Ṭākkī, Nāgara and Upanāgara Apabhrança, and Paiçācī. It would be interesting to know how far he based his work on earlier writers, how far on the study of texts; that the latter was the case in the seventeenth century, when Prākrit was far more of a dead language than Sanskrit, must, despite Grierson's assumption[5] that Mārkaṇḍeya was a predecessor of Pischel, be regarded as wholly implausible, and the fact that Rāma Tarkavāgīça by no means agrees with his statements suggests that both were more or less intelligent compilers, not original investigators.

[1] Hultzsch, *Report III*, p. viii; EI. iii. 238.
[2] IA. v. 20 *n*.
[3] EI. iv. 327; Hultzsch, p. iv, n. 4.
[4] Winternitz, GIL. iii. 406, n. 2.
[5] AMJV. III. i. 123.

The value of the Prākrit grammarians has been strongly depreciated by Bloch [1] and Gawroński,[2] while it has been defended by Pischel [3] among others. On the whole they do not make a very favourable impression; their rules are often obviously much too wide, a fault shared by them with the Sanskrit grammarians; moreover, they have clearly often generalized, while for many difficulties they afford no aid. On the other hand, recent investigations regarding Apabhrança [4] have proved that they had often real grounds for forms which they give, and it must be remembered that they are often poorly preserved and inadequately explained.

The Pāli grammarians, though they are deeply influenced by Sanskrit grammar, yet do not assume that Sanskrit is the source whence Pāli is derived, and they write in Pāli, not Sanskrit. Like the Prākrit grammarians, they draw from literature for their models, not from spoken languages. Kaccāyana, the most famous, is later than Buddhaghosa, not perhaps before the eleventh century; he uses freely the *Kātantra* as well as Pāṇini; Moggallāna, in the twelfth century, who started a rival grammar, shows the influence of Candra also. The Burmese monk Aggavaṅsa's *Saddanīti* (1154), which has won fame in Burma and even in Ceylon, depends on Kaccāyana.[5]

1 *Vararuci und Hemacandra* (1893), pp. 30 ff.

2 KZ. xliv. 247 ff.

3 *Gramm. der Prakrit-Sprachen*, pp. 45 f.

4 Jacobi, *Sanatkumāracarita*, pp. xxiv ff.

5 Franke, *Zur Geschichte und Kritik der einheimischen Pāli-Grammatik und Lexikographie*, and Geiger, *Pāli*. Sanskrit is used for a Kanarese grammar in Bhaṭṭākalañkadeva's *Karṇāṭakaçabdānuçāsana* (ed. Bangalore, 1923), written *c.* 1600 A. D.

XXII

CIVIL AND RELIGIOUS LAW (DHARMAÇĀSTRA)

1. *The Origin of the Dharmaçāstras*

IT was perfectly natural that when Sūtras began to be composed on matters of ritual there should be adopted the practice of including in these texts instructions on matters closely akin to ritual, the daily life of the people, their duties of all kinds, including matters which more advanced civilization would classify as questions of etiquette and social usage, moral, legal, or religious. Included of course in such rules must be regulation of all issues affecting caste, especially the vital one of marriage, and, as it was clearly customary for Brahmins to be approached to act as arbitrators in disputes or to advise as to the due custom, these books came to serve in some measure as rudimentary texts on law. Sūtras of this kind were distinguished as Dharmasūtras from those dealing with the more formal and the domestic ritual, the Çrautasūtras and Gṛhyasūtras, but we may assume that no very vital distinction was originally felt between the various parts, and the whole could rank as one Kalpasūtra. Like Sūtras in general, they were composed in prose, usually as briefly as possible, but with Çlokas or Triṣṭubh verses here and there interposed to justify a doctrine or sum it up effectively.

Of these old Dharmasūtras several are preserved but in different conditions. One of the oldest is the *Gautamīya Dharmaçāstra*[1]—the title Dharmasūtra is here as in other cases merged in the wider name; it seems to belong to the Rāṇāyanīya school of the *Sāmaveda*, and its text is not free from interpolation. Another old text is the *Hārīta Dharmaçāstra*[2] in thirty Adhyāyas, extant in one manuscript. Both these are mentioned by the *Vāsiṣṭha*

[1] Ed. London, 1876; ĀnSS. 61, 1910; BS. 50, 1917; trans. G. Bühler, SBE. ii. On all these texts see J. Jolly, *Recht und Sitte* (1896).

[2] Jolly, IA. xxv. 147 f.; OC. x, ii. 117 ff.

Dharmaçāstra,[1] which, however, is preserved either in fragmentary or interpolated manuscripts; it mentions Manu as an authority while it is quoted in the *Manu Smṛti.* Apparently we may believe Kumārila when he assigns it to a lost *Ṛgveda* school, the Vāsiṣṭhas. Yama and Prajāpati appear in it as authorities. The *Baudhāyana Dharmaçāstra*[2] and the *Āpastambīya Dharmasūtra*[3] are both parts of greater complexes, Sūtras of schools of the *Black Yajurveda*, but the former is interpolated, while the latter is well preserved. The school of Hiraṇyakeçin is as usual closely akin to the Āpastambīya. The dates of these works have often been determined[4] on the assumption that the Āpastambīya by reason of its incorrectnesses of speech, and its treatment of the Vedic Çvetaketu of the *Çatapatha Brāhmaṇa* among recent personages, cannot be placed later than the fourth or fifth century B. C., but this naturally depends on many assumptions including that of the date of Pāṇini, and it might be wiser to place the date as far down as the second or third century B. C.

The *Vaiṣṇava Dharmaçāstra*[5] is even more strikingly interpolated, for Vaiṣṇavas have turned it into the shape of a dialogue between Viṣṇu and the earth. In fact, however, it goes back to a Dharmasūtra of the Kāṭhaka school of the *Black Yajurveda*, just as the Hārīta, which as it stands is in prose with much verse intermingled, represents the Maitrāyaṇīya school. The writing up of the Vaiṣṇava shows knowledge of Greek terms of astronomy and astrology, and cannot be placed before the third century A. D. The *Vaikhānasa Dharmaçāstra*[6] in three chapters deals with the duties of the castes and of the different stages of the life of the Brahmin, but predominantly with the period of life when asceticism should be practised. It has the appearance of a late work drawn up in the Sūtra style, but it may contain some matter which was given in the older text known to Baudhāyana.[7] Grave doubt exists as to the antiquity of the alleged Dharmasūtras of

[1] Ed. BSS. 23, 1916; trans. SBE. xiv.

[2] Ed. AKM. 8, 1884 and 1922; trans. SBE. xiv.

[3] Ed. BSS. 1892–4; trans. SBE. ii.

[4] See Winternitz, GIL. iii. 480 f.

[5] Ed. BI. 1881; trans. SBE. vii.

[6] Ed. TSS. 28, 1913. Cf. Th. Bloch, *Über das Gṛhya- und Dharmasūtra der Vaikhānasa* (1896).

[7] ii. 6. 11. 14.

Paiṭhīnasi, attached to the *Atharvaveda*, of Çañkhalikhita [1] attached to the *White Yajurveda*, of Uçanas, Kāçyapa, Bṛhaspati, and others. We may reasonably suspect that the works passing under these names were later imitations of the older style of Sūtras; in the case of Çañkhalikhita it certainly seems that the sages Çañkha and Likhita owe their existence to a misunderstanding of the old idea of the fate or law written by the gods on men's foreheads.

The unsatisfactory state of the text of these works is a proof of what was inevitable, the decline in importance of the old Vedic schools, which had formerly preserved the text intact, so that for instance a Vaiṣṇava sect could appropriate to itself the old Kāṭhaka Dharmasūtra. There developed instead at an early date, it would seem, the tendency to study law, in the widest sense of that term, in special schools, which therefore were not content to adopt the practices of any single Vedic school. To the activities of these schools we doubtless owe the vast amount of didactic verse which we find in the *Mahābhārata* [2] and in the later law-books. These schools, however, were strictly Brahmanical, and they stood out in point of view from the schools of *Arthaçāstra* which we shall have to consider, and which dealt with politics and practical life from the standpoint, not of the old Brahmanical code, but of practical commonsense as engendered by actual contact with administration in all its branches. They represent in contrast to these schools the Brahmanical ideals in their widest sense as opposed to these ideals transmuted under the pressure of the functions arising from active participation in the direction of affairs; they represent in a sense the general Brahmanical feeling as contrasted with the narrow realism of the Purohitas, domestic priests, and their associates.

2. *The Smṛti of Manu*

This is the point of view from which we can best understand the origin of the *Mānava Dharmaçāstra* or *Manu Smṛti*, and the later Smṛtis. These works have the common characteristic that

[1] Ludwig, WZKM. xv. 307 ff.

[2] Cf. the German evidence of the close relation of epic poetry, legal poetry, and religious works; R. Koegel, *Gesch. der deutschen Litt.*, i. 1. 97, 242 ff.

they claim to be generally applicable to all orthodox Hindus and cover the duties of all the castes; though they differ from the Dharmasūtras proper by the much greater development which they accord to the duties of the king and the distinctly more advanced treatment of what we style civil and criminal law. Their compilers, it is clear, drew largely on the floating mass of popular principles, and they adopted the verse form in which this was couched, while they were under the influence of the epic with its practical illustration of principles of polity and its easy versification which presented comparative simplicity of imitation. Even later law-books acknowledge beside the Çruti, holy writ, and the Smṛtis themselves the usage of experts (*çiṣṭācāra*) and the customs of places, castes, and families as sources of law, and these naturally were exploited by the makers of the Smṛtis. Further, in order to secure acceptance for their works, they were only too anxious to ascribe them divine provenance and to pass them off as the utterances of old sages.

That one of these sages was Manu followed naturally from the fact that as the man who escaped the deluge,[1] accepted by some authorities at least, he was the renewer of sacrificial ordinances and the dispenser of maxims of justice. The *Taittirīya Saṁhitā*[2] declares that all he said was medicine, Yāska[3] cites him—not our text—for the law of succession, the Gṛhyasūtras, the Dharmasūtras, the epic repeatedly assert that Manu said so and so. Only in part do these assertions agree with the *Manu Smṛti*; even Açvaghoṣa's[4] citations of a *Mānava Dharma* agree only twice with that text. An investigation of the epic[5] reveals that, without any citation of Manu, there are especially in books iii, xii, and xvi, 260 verses, say a tenth of the Smṛti, in substance and largely even in form identical with verses of the Smṛti. As in some cases the epic, in others the Smṛti, shows the more original form, the priority of either may be excluded, and the verses be referred to a common source; this is supported by the recurrence of similar phenomena in other cases, the *Vāsiṣṭha Dharmaçāstra* having 39, the text of Viṣṇu 160 verses in common. On the other hand, especially in book xiii of the epic,

1 *Çatapatha Brāhmaṇa*, i. 5. 1. 7.
2 ii. 2. 10. 2.
3 iii. 4.
4 In the *Vajrasūcī*, if that be his.
5 See Bühler, SBE. xxv, whose trans. is most valuable.

we find real knowledge in the form of citations with Manu as the authority of the *Manu Smṛti*; the Nārāyaṇīya episode of xii undoubtedly used the Dharmaçāstra of Manu and texts ascribed to Uçanas and Bṛhaspati. Manu again recognizes the heroes and legends of the epic, so that it is clear that, while the older parts of the epic were composed before the *Manu Smṛti* and the didactic parts of the text often merely draw from the same sources as the Smṛti, yet the Smṛti was in existence much as it now is before the epic was finally redacted as we have it. Unluckily this gives us little help towards a genuine date, and the wide limits of 200 B.C. to A.D. 200 are still all that can be legitimately asserted. The former limit arises from the mention of Yavanas, Çakas, Kāmbojas, and Pahlavas, showing that the work was written when the frontiers were no longer safe from invasion, the latter by general probability, and priority to the other Smṛtis.

While we may readily believe that the kernel in some degree of the Smṛti was formed by an older Dharmasūtra, and, while it is natural to see in this the *Mānava Dharmasūtra* of a branch of the Maitrāyaṇīya school of the Black Yajurveda, it must be admitted that no strict proof is possible. The *Vāsiṣṭha Dharmaçāstra*[1] cites from the Mānava a long passage in prose and verse which agrees in part with the Smṛti, and some minor detailed similarities can be traced between the Smṛti and the fortunately extant Gṛhyasūtra of the Mānavas.[2] The difficulties in the text which here and there occur, and occasional incongruities, may best be accounted for by use of an old Sūtra. The Smṛti itself ascribes its origin to Brahman, whence it came to men via Manu and Bhṛgu; while the *Nārada Smṛti* tells of a Smṛti in 100,000 verses by Manu reduced to 12,000 by Nārada, 8,000 by Mārkaṇḍeya and 4,000 by Sumati, son of Bhṛgu. This might suggest that there was a successive series of redactions of the original Sūtra, and the inconsistencies in the Smṛti, as well as later allusions to a *Vṛddha-Manu* and *Bṛhan-Manu*,[3] have been adduced in support of this view. It seems, however, much more probable that the Smṛti is an early attempt at composition, whence

[1] iv. 5–8.

[2] P. von Bradke, ZDMG. xxxvi. 417 ff., 433 ff.; G. B. Beaman, *On the Sources of the Dharma-Śāstras of Manu und Yājñavalkya* (1895).

[3] G. Herberich, *Zitate aus Vṛddhamanu und Bṛhanmanu* (1893).

its defects, while the larger texts were writings up of a popular original. Unfortunately we cannot find any historical event to explain precisely why the new effort became specially appropriate ; there was a Brahmanical revival in the first century B.C.,[1] though on a small scale and no great duration, and the Gupta revival of the fourth century is probably rather late for the composition of the work. In what sense it was an individual production or the work of a group we cannot say.

Book i contains an interesting semi-philosophical account of creation in the popular Paurānic type of a realistic Vedānta combined with Sāṁkhya terms, including the essential doctrine of the three constituents of nature, which, however, is not independent but a creation, as also are the souls. In ii the sources of law are declared, and the duties of the student ; in iii–v the householder occupies attention; his marriage, daily rites, funeral offerings (iii), occupation and general rules of life (iv), lawful and forbidden food, impurity and purification, and rules as to women. Book vi deals with the two further stages of life, the hermit in the forest and the ascetic. In vii we come to the duties of the king, including general political maxims. In viii and ix we have civil and criminal law, including procedure and evidence, especially ordeals ; the topics are given as eighteen, a precision without any parallel in the Sūtras ; recovery of debts ; deposit and pledge ; sale without ownership ; partnership concerns ; subtraction of gifts ; non-payment of wages ; non-performance of agreement ; rescission of sale and purchase ; masters and herdsmen ; disputes as to boundaries ; defamation ; assault and hurt ; theft ; violence ; adultery ; duties of husband and wife ; inheritance and partition ; gambling and wagers. Book ix adds an account of the duties of kings and of those of Vaiçyas and Çūdras. In x are dealt with the mixed castes, the rules as to occupation affecting the castes, and occupation in time of distress when normal rules must yield. In xi we find rules for gifts, sacrifices and penances, while xii follows the sinner to his retribution in the next life by the rules of transmigration, and adds counsel regarding the means of

[1] Cf. the Vikramāditya epoch ; in the second century B.C. Puṣyamitra's rule was decidedly Brahmanical, and Wema Kadphises was a Māheçvara, devotee of Çiva ; Bhandarkar (*Early History of India*, pp. 63 ff.) would put *Manu* in the Gupta era.

attaining release. In this as in i we have the popular Vedānta with strong Sāṁkhya and Yoga influences.

The *Manu Smṛti*, however, is not merely important as a law-book; it is unquestionably rather to be compared with the great poem of Lucretius, beside which it ranks as the expression of a philosophy of life; in that case, however, the views presented were merely those of a school of wide but not commanding influence; in Manu we have the soul of a great section of a people. Characteristic also is the lack of individuality in the work, which causes so deep a contrast with the passionate utterances of Lucretius against the tyranny of superstition: *tantum religio potuit suadere malorum.* To the author instead all is perfectly ordered in a world created by the divine power, regulated according to the principle of absolute justice by that power. Heretics existed, but they are passed over with severe condemnation; the life of cities and affairs is little in the thoughts of the writer, who instead envisages a simple kingdom in which the Brahmins take the first place, and in close accord with them, enforcing their discipline, abides the king; Vaiçyas and Çūdras, the vast bulk of the people, are recognized, but disposed of with a curious brevity, and nothing better than the doctrine of mixed castes, into which even the Yavana and Çaka are pressed, is adduced to account for the vast numbers who had no claim to be even Vaiçyas or Çūdras. The hand of a narrow religion lies heavily over the work, and its pedantry is seen in the treatment of infinitely small transgressions of etiquette as crimes requiring grave penalties hereafter, if not in this world, but remediable by penances to be ordered by the Brahmins—a source of profitable employment. The failure to evolve any clear plan is obvious, but in complete agreement with Indian modes of thought. Some advance, too, is visible—doubtless derived from the law schools in the classification of the topics of law, for the five which are concerned with criminal law are grouped together even if they appear between sections on civil law; moreover, beside the old relentless cruelty of primitive law, there does appear recognition of the necessity of considering not the mere act, but also the motive of the doer. Law, however, appears not as the possession of the people, but as the privilege of the king, and the king has a sanctity only inferior to the Brahmin; he is a divine creation, doubtless a deliberate attack on the Buddhist doctrine of a social contract which made the king a mere wage-receiver, a doctrine which the more realistic *Arthaçāstra* actually enunciates. The king rewards his supporters by obeying their claims to exemption from punishment for all save the gravest crimes, and the work insists throughout on preferring the high to the low, in lieu of exacting from those in high place a nobler standard of conduct. In these demands for the Brahmins, and in a certain vagueness throughout in the legal sections, it is easy to recognize the hand of the theorist rather than of the practical lawyer. We are seeing law, indeed, but through a somewhat distorting medium in which ethical considerations obscure our vision; thus the use of torture which the *Arthaçāstra* urges is ignored in favour of the ordeal, which the Brahmins preferred both on ideal grounds and as involving their aid in administration. Rationalism, of course, is utterly foreign to the spirit of the writer, but his command of language, his earnestness, his happy similes, his carefully handled metre which almost approaches the standard of correctness of the classical poets, while it preserves some tinge of epic variety, combine to render the work a striking one, however ludicrous may seem to us Nietzsche's [1] preference of it to the Bible.

The work is rich in happy expressions of principle; the time for retirement to the forest is given as:

gṛhasthas tu yadā paçyed valipalitam ātmanaḥ
āpatyasyaiva cāpatyaṁ tadāraṇyaṁ samāçrayet.

'When he sees wrinkles on his face and gray in his hair, and a son born to his son, then should the householder fare to the forest.' The king's divinity is absolute:

bālo 'pi nāvamantavyo manuṣya iti bhūmipaḥ
mahatī devatā hy eṣā nararūpeṇa tiṣṭhati.

'Though a child, a king must not be despised on the score of mere humanity; in him a great deity is embodied in human shape.' The claims of righteousness to respect are effectively depicted:

[1] *Antichrist*, § 56; *Wille zur Macht*, § 194, cited by Winternitz, GIL. iii. 492, n. 1. On the metre see Oldenberg, ZDMG. xxxv. 181 ff.

ekaḥ prajāyate jantur eka eva pralīyate
eko 'nubhuṅkte sukṛtam eka eva ca duṣkṛtam.
mṛtaçarīram utsṛjya kāṣṭhaloṣṭasamam bhuvi
vimukhā bāndhavā yānti dharmas tam anugacchati.

'Alone man is born, alone he dies, alone he reaps the fruit of good and of evil done by him. Laying down on the ground the body of the dead as if it were a clod or a log, the kin depart with face averted; righteousness alone is his companion.' In the philosophical parts the tone often rises to a grave dignity, reminiscent of the *Bhagavadgītā*.

Comments on the Smṛti are many; that of Medhātithi is not later than the ninth century, Govindarāja belongs to the twelfth and the popular Kullūka, who follows him, to the fifteenth. The influence of the text is attested by its acceptance in Burma, Siam, and Java as authoritative, and the production of works based on it.

3. *The Later Smṛtis*

If we were to believe the *Nārada Smṛti*,[1] it would represent an older account of Manu's views than the *Manu Smṛti*, but the claim is disproved by the contents; it subdivides titles of law into 132, has 15 kinds of slaves, 21 ways of acquiring property, 5 ordeals, 11 classes of witnesses, and lays great stress on records in procedure and written proofs. The term *dīnāra* suggests a date not before the second century A.D.; Bāṇa in the seventh knows it, and Asahāya commented on it in the eighth. It is preserved in two recensions; a prose preface in one claims it as chapter ix of Nārada's recension of Manu, and an old Nepalese manuscript supports the claim, but its validity is dubious. The text cannot vie with Manu in importance, but it here and there contains passages of the same earnestness, as in the admonishments directed to witnesses warning them that 'truth is the one mode of winning purity, truth the ship that bears men to heaven, truth weighed against a thousand horse sacrifices outweighs them, truth is the highest oblation, the highest asceticism, the highest morality, truth the summit of

[1] Longer text ed. J. Jolly, BI. 1885; trans. SBE. xxxiii.

bliss, by telling truth man attains by himself the highest self which is itself truth.'

The *Bṛhaspati Smṛti*[1] is extant only in fragments, but its character is clear; it is almost a Vārttika on Manu whom it supplements. But it is distinctly more advanced in legal view even than Nārada; it develops further the treatment of records, and it approves, quite out of harmony with Manu, the practice of widow burning; its date may be assigned to the sixth or seventh century.

These texts are of minor importance compared with the *Yājñavalkya Smṛti*,[2] whose title recalls the great authority of the *White Yajurveda*; in point of fact some similarity has been traced to the *Pāraskara Gṛhyasūtra* of that Veda, though also to the *Mānava Gṛhyasūtra*. The Smṛti refers to the *Bṛhadāraṇyaka Upaniṣad*, so that the connexion may be accepted as valid. There can be no doubt of its importance or of its posteriority to Manu. It adds written documents to his means of proof, recognizes five in lieu of two ordeals, fire and water, it also knows Greek astrology, and has the term *nāṇaka* for coined gold, suggesting a date not before A.D. 300. The arrangement is better than in Manu; three chapters of about the same length handle rules of conduct, Ācāra, law, Vyavahāra, and penances; the eighteen topics of Manu which are not formally enumerated are in effect adhered to with the addition of one of relations of service and another on miscellaneous topics. Yājñavalkya shows many of the traits of Manu; his outlook is largely similar, and he indulges in philosophical remarks on the fate of the soul in much the same strain of Vedānta-Yoga-Sāṁkhya as appears in Manu. New is an embryology taken from some medical treatise.[3] In style there is much resemblance to Manu, but there is less elaboration. The whole duty of man is thus set forth:

> *satyam asteyam akrodho hrīḥ çaucaṁ dhīr dhṛtir damaḥ*
> *saṁyatendriyatā vidyā dharmaḥ sarva udāhṛtaḥ.*

'Truth, honesty, mildness, modesty, purity, wisdom, firmness,

[1] Trans. J. Jolly, SBE. xxxiii.; cf. WZKM. i. 275 ff.

[2] Ed. and trans. A. F. Stenzler, Berlin, 1849; with *Mitākṣarā*, Bombay, 1882; trans. SBH. 2, 1909.

[3] For his anatomy cf. Hoernle, *Osteology*, pp. 37 ff.

self-control, the restraint of the senses, learning, these make up the whole of righteousness.' Release is won by the knowledge of self: in the midst of the veins is a circle:

maṇḍalaṁ tasya madhyastha ātmā dīpa ivācalaḥ
sa jñeyas taṁ viditveha punar ājāyate na tu.

'In the midst of that circle abides the self as if a motionless light; it must be known, and knowing it no man is born again to life.' But a very much simpler duty is preached for kings:

nātaḥ parataro dharmo nṛpāṇāṁ yad raṇārjitam
viprebhyo dīyate dravyam prajābhyaç cābhayaṁ sadā.

'No higher duty is there than this for kings, to give to Brahmins wealth won in battle and ever to afford protection to their people.' In language and metre Yājñavalkya conforms closely to the style of Manu.

Yājñavalkya formed the subject of a very large number of important commentaries; the best known, the *Mitākṣarā* of Vijñāneçvara, was written in the south in the eleventh century, and constitutes an important treatise on law, which won acceptance in the Deccan and also in Benares and north India; Colebrooke's version [1] of the section on inheritance gave it currency in the English courts in India. The author used the work of Viçvarūpa; [2] Aparārka [3] wrote on the Smṛti in the twelfth century, while Bālambhaṭṭa Vaidyanātha and his wife Lakṣmīdevī [4] commented on the *Mitākṣarā* in an interesting manner, emphasizing the claims of women to property rights.

Other Smṛtis exist in indefinite numbers [5]—one list mentions 152; in many cases we have *Laghu*, *Bṛhat*, or *Vṛddha* forms of the same text, or the same name is given to quite different texts. A Parāçara appears as an authority in Yājñavalkya and is cited by Medhātithi, but the *Parāçara Smṛti* [6] on which Mādhava wrote in the fourteenth century an elaborate comment, adding a chapter on law to those on custom and penance of the original, is doubtless later than either of these authors. A *Bṛhat* version

[1] *Two Treatises on the Hindu Law of Inheritance* (1810).
[2] Jolly, GN. 1904, pp. 402 ff.; ed. TSS. 74 and 81.
[3] Ed. ĀnSS. 46, 1903–4. [4] Ed. BI. 1904 ff.
[5] 28 ed. Bombay, 1883; 27 in ĀnSS. 48. Cf. IOC. i. 372 ff.; ii. 367 ff.
[6] Ed. BI. 1890–2; BSS. 1893–1919; trans. BI. 1887.

of this text is five times as long. We have various texts ascribed to Atri, Uçanas, Āpastamba, Dakṣa, Çañkha, Likhita, Saṁvarta, and so on, but more interesting than these which hardly touch on law proper are certain authors of whom we have but fragments; Pitāmaha[1] appears already in Bṛhaspati as an authority on ordeals; Kātyāyana and Vyāsa agree often with Nārada and Bṛhaspati, and juristic verses by Hārīta are found which are not in the Dharmaçāstra preserved. The number of Smṛtis can be augmented from the epic and the Purāṇas which contain long sections which might as well be Smṛtis; thus in a manuscript of the epic is found a *Bṛhad Gautamasmṛti* which is quite different from the old text of Gautama.

4. *The Digests of Law*

It was a natural result of the number of these Smṛtis that the need was felt for compilations, and we find from the twelfth century onwards many of these digests, Dharmanibandha, prepared at the order of kings. One of the earliest is the *Smṛtikalpataru* of Lakṣmīdhara, foreign minister of Govindacandra of Kanauj (1105–43), who includes religious as well as civil and criminal law and the law of procedure. Halāyudha's *Brāhmaṇasarvasva*,[2] written for Lakṣmaṇasena of Bengal, deals with the whole duty of a Brahmin, and is only in minor degree a lawbook. The same remark applies to Devaṇṇa Bhaṭṭa's *Smṛticandrikā* (*c.* 1200), the work of a southern author, and to Hemādri's *Caturvargacintāmaṇi*,[3] in which, written between 1260 and 1309 for Yādava princes, he sets out in enormous detail rules of vows, offerings, pilgrimages, the attainment of release, and offerings to the dead. This text is exceptionally rich in Smṛti citations *in extenso*, as is also the *Madanapārijāta*[4] of Viçveçvara who wrote for Madanapāla (1360–70), mainly on religious duties, but also on the law of succession. Much more important for law are the *Smṛtiratnākara*[5] of Caṇḍeçvara, minister of Harasiṅhadeva (*c.* 1325), and the *Cintāmaṇis*[6] of Vācaspati, who wrote for

[1] K. Scriba, *Die Fragmente des Pitāmaha* (1902).
[2] Ed. Calcutta, 1893.
[3] Ed. BI. 1873–95.
[4] Ed. BI. 1893.
[5] *Vivādaratnākara*, ed. BI. 1887.
[6] *Vivādacintāmaṇi*, ed. Calcutta, 1837.

Harinārāyaṇa of Mithilā (*c.* 1510). Before the fifteenth century, in all probability, Jīmūtavāhana produced his legal work, *Dharmaratna*, containing the famous *Dāyabhāga* [1] which dominates the views of Bengal on inheritance. In the following century Raghunandana wrote his twenty-eight treatises, *Tattvas*, which won special acceptance as regards ordeals, procedure, and inheritance. The seventeenth century saw the *Nirṇayasindhu* of Kamalākara, which is still a religious authority in the Marāṭha country, the *Bhagavantabhāskara* of Nīlakaṇṭha, and the encyclopaedic *Vīramitrodaya* [2] of Mitra Miçra who also commented on the *Mitākṣarā*, and whose work touches on astrology and medicine as well as the doctrine of emancipation.

The works of these authors, meritorious in their own way, never exhibit the highest qualities of legal interpretation. They were bound to follow authority, and they fail to evolve any independence of attitude to that authority, or to do more than exhibit very considerable ability in reconciling the irreconcilable, and establishing the legitimacy of a custom of their district by torturing ancient texts which obviously meant something else. How far their citations were from really old authorities it is impossible to say; that verses were freely forged when it was impossible to check the process may be guessed, especially as the epic ranked as a high authority and no one then, or now, could assert definitely what was or was not contained therein.

[1] Ed. Calcutta, 1863–6; for date, see Keith, *Bodl. Cat.*, i, App., p. 89; for Vācaspati, p. 81

[2] Ed. ChSS. 1906 ff.

XXIII

THE SCIENCE OF POLITICS AND PRACTICAL LIFE (ARTHAÇĀSTRA, NĪTIÇĀSTRA)

1. *The Origin of the Arthaçāstra*

THE Vedic literature, permeated as it is with religion, affords a quite false impression of the Vedic Indian as a person given to reflection and religious practices without regard to practical life. Nothing, of course, can be farther from the truth; the East, in lieu of bowing low before the West in disdain or otherwise, confronted Alexander with an obstacle which he did not attempt to penetrate, and his garrisons had soon after his death to be withdrawn. If we are to judge India aright, we must add two other objects to the Dharma, religious, and moral duty which is dwelt on in the Vedic texts. Already the *Hiraṇyakeçi Gṛhyasūtra*[1] knows of the three objects in life, Dharma, Artha, politics and practical life in general, and Kāma, love. The epic[2] recognizes this set, the *Viṣṇu Smṛti*[3] and *Manu* accept it, it is found in Patañjali,[4] in Açvaghoṣa, and in the *Pañcatantra*. The older system, however, no doubt combined these subjects as parts of Dharma in the wider sense; the Dharmasūtras deal with royal duties, capitals and countries, officials, taxes, and military preparations as they do with justice, and the epic,[5] in a list of authorities of the science of kings (*rājaçāstra*) includes Bṛhaspati, Viçālākṣa, Uçanas, Manu, son of Pracetas, and Gauraçiras, who pass also for authorities on Dharma. The *Bṛhadāraṇyaka Upaniṣad*[6] incidentally shows that a wide knowledge of the arcana of love was prevalent in Brahmanical circles, the holy Çvetaketu becoming a recognized authority later on the topic. Gradually there must have sprung up schools[7] who studied Artha and

[1] ii. 19. 6. [2] i. 2. 381. [3] lix. 30.
[4] On Pāṇini, ii. 2. 34, Vārttika 9. [5] xii. 58. 1 ff. [6] vi. 3.
[7] *Contra*, Jacobi, SBA. 1912, pp. 838 ff.; cf. Hillebrandt, ZDMG. lxix. 360; Jolly, ZDMG. lxvii. 95.

Kāma in themselves, and this is attested to us by the Smṛtis and the epic.

Doctrines of Artha seem early to have found, like those on Dharma, expression in didactic verse. The *Mahābhārata*[1] assures us that Brahman, the creator, was the author of a work in 100,000 sections on the three topics, that Çiva as Viçālākṣa reduced it to 10,000 in consideration of the brevity of life, that Indra brought it down to 5,000, and that finally Indra's work, called *Bāhudantaka,* from an epithet of his, was reduced by Bṛhaspati to 3,000, and by Uçanas to 1,000, sections. The *Kauṭilīya Arthaçāstra* mentions Bṛhaspati, Bāhudantīputra, Viçālākṣa, and Uçanas as authorities, and the *Kāmasūtra* ascribes Dharma to Manu, Artha to Bṛhaspati, and Kāma to Nandin. The epic itself contains sections which deal with polity, such as Kaṇika's lecture to Dhṛtarāṣṭra[2] regarding the merciless destruction of enemies, several of Vidura's speeches,[3] and other scattered sections, while we may find traces[4] of actual use of a formal *Arthaçāstra* in one or two passages. There is no doubt that the Smṛtis of Manu,[5] Yājñavalkya,[6] and Viṣṇu[7] made use of texts of this sort in compiling their contents, and both Yājñavalkya[8] and Nārada[9] expressly provide that in case of divergence between Arthaçāstra and Dharmaçāstra the latter must prevail. That in fact it did is, of course, a very different question; as we have seen, the Dharma texts are ideal as compared with the Arthaçāstra; they deal after all with duty and morality as the basis of law; the Arthaçāstra is concerned with profit, and it is not concerned with religion or duty save in so far as it can use the former to advance the interest of the prince, or the latter is good policy to win popular affection, for instance, in a conquered state. But none the less the Arthaçāstra or, as it is equally called, Nītiçāstra, science of conduct, Rājanīti, conduct of kings, or Daṇḍanīti, policy of punishment, was respected by the poets who lived at royal courts; Bhāsa in his *Pratijñāyaugandharāyaṇa* and *Pratimānāṭaka*, Kālidāsa, Bhāravi, Māgha, and their followers show their skill in Nīti as they do in Kāma. It was left to the Buddhists to protest as does the *Jātakamālā*,[10] where

[1] xii. 59. 28 ff. [2] i. 140. [3] v. 33, 36 f., 39.
[4] xv. 5-7. [5] vii. 155 ff. [6] i. 344 ff.
[7] iii. 38 ff. [8] ii. 21. [9] i. 39. [10] ix. 10; xxxi. 52.

the royal doctrine that right should be followed only so far as it does not conflict with profit, is hotly denounced and the science of Nīti condemned. In this, however, Buddhism merely showed its incapacity for accommodating itself effectively to Indian conditions of life and thought.

Bṛhaspati, as we have seen, ranks in the epic as a founder of the science, and Bhāsa cites a *Bārhaspatya Arthaçāstra*[1] as an object of study by Brahmins. But the text, which has come down to us under that style, is a modern production of uncertain but late date, which contains little if anything of the old doctrines of the school even as we know them from the *Kauṭilīya Arthaçāstra.* By its condemnation of heretics it shows that it has advanced to the Dharma standard rather than that of Artha.

2. *The Content and Form of the Kauṭilīya Arthaçāstra*

As usual we find as the earliest preserved text a work exhibiting every sign of a long prior development, which, however, by reason of its completeness has deprived earlier treatises of the possibility of survival. The *Arthaçāstra* made known to us in 1909, is unquestionably one of the most interesting works in Sanskrit, because it affords a vast amount of detailed information about the practical side of Indian life as opposed to the spiritual, and, while in parts it covers ground touched on in the treatises on Dharma, it does so with a wealth and accuracy of detail which is completely other than the often vague generalities which are the stock-in-trade of these texts. As we have it, the book is divided into fifteen great sections, Adhikaraṇas, and 180 subdivisions, Prakaraṇas, but this division is crossed by one into chapters, Adhyāyas, which are marked off from the prose of the work by the insertion of verses summing up the doctrine expounded above. There is the possibility that this division is secondary, possibly also the verses which mark it out.

[1] Thomas, *Le Muséon*, 1916, i. no. 2.

[2] Ed. R. Shama Sastri, Mysore, 1909 (2nd ed. 1919); trans. Bangalore, 1915 (2nd ed. 1923). Also ed. T. Gaṇapati Śāstrī, TSS. 79, 80, and 82; J. Jolly and R. Schmidt, Lahore, 1923–5; trans. J. J. Meyer, Hanover, 1925 f. On the varied and often excellent treatises on it, see Jolly, *Zeit. f. vergl. Rechtswissenschaft*, xli. 305–18. See also G. B. Bottazzi, *Precursori di Niccolo Machiavelli in India ed in Grecia, Kauṭilya e Tucidide* (1914), who ignores the fact that Thucydides' own ideal is that of Perikles (ii. 34 ff.) differing *toto caelo* from Kauṭilya; cf. Grote, *Hist.*, ch. xlviii.

Adhikaraṇa i deals with the bringing up and education of a prince. He is to study philosophy including Sāṁkhya, Yoga, and the Lokāyata, religion including the Vedas and Vedāñgas—the *Arthaçāstra* accepts wholesale the Brahmanical theory of the castes and their duties,—economics, agriculture, pastoral pursuits, trade and industry, and polity, Daṇḍanīti. The ministers of the king, his council, are described, and above all his spies who serve him to secure a firm hold over all within the realm, high and low, from the princes of his house who aim at his death to the humblest people; his emissaries abroad are spies as well as ambassadors, and spies serve to keep him informed of all that happens to his neighbours. His duties are enumerated, a crushing burden in seeming. His harem receives elaborate attention and insistence is laid on the dangers to which he is exposed in it, historic examples being heaped up of kings slain there. But not only in the palace, but also in streets and all public places, elaborate precaution is necessary for the royal safety from assassination. In the following book we have given in detail the duties of a vast army of inspectors, showing the detailed control of administration exercised in an Indian state. In iii law is discussed, while in iv is taken up the topic of the repression of evil-doers by police action and heavy penalties; cheating doctors and tradesmen are among those denounced, while measures are taken to prevent artificial increase of prices, adulteration, use of false weights, &c. Book v is instructive; it explains how a king can rid himself of a minister of whom he is tired, either by sending him on an expedition and providing bravos to set on him and slay him at the front, or by procuring these ruffians to allow themselves to be captured with weapons on them in the royal presence, when they confess that they were agents of the obnoxious minister who is then promptly disposed of. But not less ingenious are the means of extorting taxes to fill the treasury. The peasantry and handworkers are to be cajoled or threatened into parting with their goods, spies are to induce rich men to offer benevolences, miraculous appearances of temples and statues are to bring crowds flocking and tolls from them,[1] or secret agents are to pretend that there are demons in trees and collect gold to ban

[1] The bartering of statues referred to by Patañjali is not here noticed; cf. chap. xxi, § 2.

them, or rich men can be accused of crime, and their goods and lives forfeited. Heretics also may be plundered. With excellent taste there follows a chapter on the remuneration of the royal entourage, ranging from 48,000 to 60 *paṇas* yearly. In vi we come to more serious things; the seven elements of politics are described, the king, minister, land, fort, treasure, army, and ally, and this is followed by a purely formal analysis of inter-state relations carried out in much detail, but without life or reality. Book vii deals with the six possible causes of action, peace, war, neutrality, preparation to march out, alliance, and doubtful attitude, while viii enumerates the evils that may arise from a king's addiction to hunting, gambling, women, and drink, and the misfortunes which fire, water, or other cause may bring on a land. Books ix and x deal with war; the king is given abundant ruses to avoid a fair fight; if he must do so, he encourages the soldiers by assuring them that he is a paid servant of the state like themselves, asks them to be true to their salt, and is aided by astrologers, priests, and bards in his efforts. But cunning is better, and in xi we are told how the king is to sow dissension in and destroy the cohesion of hostile aristocracies of warriors, for which purpose women will readily serve. In xii further means by which a weak king may aggrandize himself are adduced; spies, secret agents, bravos, poisoners, including women, can give aid, whether by murdering the enemy king, or poisoning food, or bringing about the fall of walls at places of pilgrimage. In xiii we are told how a king can capture a fortified city by spreading the view of his omniscience and enjoyment of divine favour. The former he can attain by stating things that he has learned secretly from spies, the latter by addressing and receiving replies from a statue in which an agent is concealed. Or an enemy king can be tempted to hold conversation with an alleged ascetic who is four hundred years old and is about to renew his life by entering into fire; the king is asked to attend with his family the miracle, and, when thus off his guard, is disposed of, as indeed he deserves to be. But we do hear also of a genuine capture by force of arms, followed by maxims for securing the affection and loyalty of a conquered people. He is to adopt their dress and customs, respect and share in their religion, by land grants and immunity from taxation attract the favour of the upper classes, in all ways surpass the virtues, if any, of his defeated foe, because these means are the mode adapted to secure his end. With xiv we come to the Aupaniṣadika, or secret part, consisting of recipes to enable one to murder, to cause blindness or madness, and so on. A man is taught also how to make himself invisible, to see in the dark, to fast for a month, to walk unharmed through fire, to change his colour, to send men and beasts to sleep; the text is extremely obscure, but we cannot reject it on that ground or because of its—to us worthless—character. The last book gives a plan of the work, and sets forth with examples thirty-two methodological principles used in the discussion, a number contrasting remarkably with the five or six elsewhere known.

The *Arthaçāstra* has often been regarded as comparable to the works of Machiavelli,[1] but there is a certain misunderstanding in such a view. The work is in no sense intended as a treatise on political philosophy; the author remains throughout on the basis of Brahmanical belief. For discussions of fundamental issues such as the relation of right and might, of fate and human endeavour, even the origin of the kingship, we must go to the epic or Buddhist texts.[2] The *Arthaçāstra* accepts the existence of the three aims of life, Dharma, Artha, and Kāma; it holds Artha the most important, but makes no effort to determine the relation of the three or to derive them from any rational basis. It is content to hold that government is essential to them all; without it there would be the reign of anarchy in which fish eats fish; under the sceptre the four castes and their ordered ways of life prosper, Dharma, Artha, Kāma are fulfilled. The state, we may say with Machiavelli and Mussolini, is all in all, but the *Arthaçāstra* means something quite definite by the state, namely an order of society which the state does not create, but which it exists to secure. The ways of a king, for the text assumes that rule must be royal, are dictated by the necessity of preserving his power; as Hobbes logically and deliberately, so the *Arthaçāstra* implicitly argues, the king's duty of securing the welfare of the system of which he is protector gives to him a morality of

[1] C. Formichi, *Salus Populi, Saggio di scienza politica* (1908). Cf. Meinecke, *Die Idee der Staatsräson* (1924).

[2] See Hillebrandt, *Altindische Politik* (1923).

his own. It is not much use comparing with this such dicta as Spinoza's[1] *uniuscuiusque ius potentia eius definitur*, or the Hegelian theory of the state; these are philosophical doctrines based on reasonings which the *Arthaçāstra* does not touch. What we have instead is the carrying out quite consistently of the doctrine that the end, the maintenance of a firm rule, justifies the means, coupled with the assumption that a reign of peace between neighbouring states is not to be dreamed of, so that in addition to maintaining peace in the realm the king must always be prepared for foreign war. In the use of means to secure obedience and to defeat enemies the *Arthaçāstra* is as ruthless as Machiavelli: spies abound, the harem and the royal family are suspect, and princes are deliberately debauched to prevent their rending, like crabs, their parent; orthodox as is the work, it advocates the shameless use of religion as a cloak for baseness. Moreover, it lacks the redeeming quality of Machiavelli, his historical method which makes him turn at every hand to the facts of history; at best the *Arthaçāstra* gives us names of kings who came to grief by one fault or another. Nor have we anything to compare with Machiavelli's investigations as to the best form of government for a state, in which he reveals his preference for a measure of democratic rule. The *Arthaçāstra* recognizes the risks run by a king from court intrigues, military oligarchical factions, false ministers, unruly heads of gilds; it even seems to recognize him as no more than a servant of the state, but of control by the people or constitutional limitations it knows nothing.

The form of the work is said to be a prose Sūtra with Bhāṣya, commentary, both by the same hand, but we cannot with certainty say what was intended to be Sūtra, what comment; the headings of chapters are clearly too slight to form the Sūtra, and a collection of Sūtras ascribed to Cāṇakya is merely a list of maxims rather of the didactic moral type than suited to the *Arthaçāstra.* The work, therefore, is rather a blending into one of the two elements. Occasional verses, usually Çlokas, but sometimes Triṣṭubhs, are inserted, and each chapter as we have the text ends with a few verses summarizing its effect. The dryness of mere exposition in dogmatic form is broken here and

[1] Eth. iv. 37 sch.

there by the exposition of a series of views of authorities; thus, as regards choice of ministers the issue is developed by setting out the divergent opinions of Bhāradvāja, Viçālākṣa, Parāçara, Piçuna, Kauṇapadanta, Vātavyādhi, Bāhudantīputra, and Kauṭilya, who in this case accepts the conclusion of Bāhudantīputra. The view that this is a sober setting down of actual views may be regarded as implausible in the extreme; it is doubtless rather a device, introduced to lend liveliness and to set out conflicting views which might actually or more often conceivably be held. The same device is adopted in Buddhist texts, where possible philosophical opinions are asserted to be actually held.

The language of the text is as a rule correct, occasional irregularities being often probably due to the manuscript tradition rather than the author. It naturally abounds in rare words drawn from technical science, and hence the meaning is often obscure. There is much effective expression of shrewd and hard common sense, and as usual the author appears to best advantage in pithy verses:

prajāsukhe sukhaṁ rājñaḥ prajānāṁ ca hite hitam
nātmapriyaṁ hitaṁ rājñaḥ prajānāṁ tu priyaṁ hitam.

'In the happiness of his people lies the happiness of the king, in their well-being his well-being; his own pleasure is not the king's well-being, but the pleasure of his people is his well-being.'

yathā hy anāsvādayituṁ na çakyaṁ: jihvātalastham madhu vā viṣaṁ vā
arthas tathā hy arthacareṇa rājñaḥ: svalpo 'py anāsvādayituṁ na çakyaḥ.
matsyā yathāntas salile caranto: jñātuṁ na çakyās salilam pibantaḥ
yuktās tathā kāryavidhau niyuktā: jñātuṁ na çakyā dhanam ādadānāḥ.

'Even as what lies on the tongue, be it honey or poison, cannot but be tasted, so a little at least of the royal gold that a minister handles must be savoured by him. Even as when fish move within the water one cannot know if they drink water or not, so it is impossible to say of ministers entrusted with business whether or not they help themselves to the royal treasure.'

nakṣatram atipṛcchantam bālam artho 'tivartate
artho hy arthasya nakṣatraṁ kiṁ kariṣyanti tārakāḥ?

'The fool who ever asks fortune of the stars wealth passeth by; wealth is the star of wealth; what can the stars avail?'

sādhanāḥ prāpnuvanty arthān narā yatnaçatair api
arthair arthāḥ prabadhyante gajāḥ pratigajair iva.

'Men of action achieve their ends, even if it cost hundreds of efforts; wealth is won by wealth as elephants by decoy elephants.' In the last stanza we find an example of the figure Dīpaka:

yena çastraṁ ca çāstraṁ ca Nandarājagatā ca bhūḥ
amarṣeṇoddhṛtāny āçu tena çāstram idaṁ kṛtam.

'This book was composed by him who in impatience rescued the science of politics, the practice of arms, and the realm which had passed under the rule of Nanda.'

3. *The Authenticity of the Arthaçāstra*

The current belief[1] which ascribes the *Arthaçāstra* to Cāṇakya or Viṣṇugupta or Kauṭilya, minister of Candragupta, rests on the verse just cited, on statements at the end of i. 1 and ii. 10 where Kauṭilya—the variant Kauṭalya has no value, being obviously a correction—appears as the author, and in the latter of which he claims to have gone through all the sciences and to have had regard to practice (*prayoga*), while a verse added at the very end, after the last colophon, says that Viṣṇugupta composed both the text and the comment, apparently because he noticed that in other cases there was discrepancy between these two important elements of a scientific work. These statements are taken to offset the fact that, by using the phrase *iti Kauṭilyaḥ* to give normally the deciding opinion in discussions, one would conclude that the work was not by the author, but was the product of a school which followed his views, as in the case of Jaimini or Bādarāyaṇa in the philosophical Sūtras. It must, however, be

[1] Jacobi, SBA. 1911, pp. 732 ff., 954 ff.; 1912, pp. 832 ff.; ZDMG. lxxiv. 248 ff., 254, and the editors other than Jolly. Against this view see Winternitz, GIL. iii. 518 f.; Bhandarkar, POCP. 1919, i. 24 ff.; Keith, JRAS. 1916, pp. 130 ff.; 1920, p. 628; EHR. 1925, pp. 420 f.; JCL. vii. 275 f.

noted that under the explanation of Apadeça in the last book is cited one of Kauṭilya's sentences, from which the prima facie conclusion is that Kauṭilya is cited as an authority, not as the author. The case, therefore, must be solved by considerations of general probability based on what we know of Cāṇakya, and what we find in or are told about the work.

It is significant that, though we hear of Cāṇakya in the Purāṇas and later texts as the minister of Candragupta, and though the *Mudrārākṣasa* makes an interesting figure of him, we have not the slightest reference there or elsewhere to his literary activity. Doubt has even been cast on his historic character, for Megasthenes, the ambassador of Seleukos who spent a considerable time at the court of Candragupta, does not mention him; but, owing to our fragmentary knowledge of Megasthenes, this argument cannot be stressed. Nor can we make much progress by discussing the probability whether an Indian statesman would write memoirs like Bismarck, for, while the indifference to morality and the insistence on distrust as a quality of a wise king are common to both, there is all the difference in the world between the detailed accounts of real events in which he figured given in Bismarck's *Gedanken und Erinnerungen* [1] and the absolutely general and very pedantic utterances of the *Arthaçāstra*, which never anywhere hints that its author had any knowledge of the overthrow of the Nandas and the wars which brought Candragupta his empire and the cessions made by Seleukos. His sovereign's name, his family, what is still more amazing his country, his capital, are passed over in absolute silence by this alleged ancient statesman meditating in his days of retirement on the maxims of policy. The rules laid down are those which might be valuable for a moderate-sized state, and ignore entirely the issue of the government of an empire such as that of Candragupta. So complete does the impossibility of such silence appear to be that one critic,[2] accepting the genuineness of the ascription, explains the book as written before Candragupta acquired the empire. This is a candid admission but really serves to prove that the claim is absurd.

Efforts have naturally been made to find at least striking resemblances between the account given in the *Arthaçāstra* and

[1] Stuttgart, 1898. [2] Smith, EHI. p. 146.

the fragments of Megasthenes. The effort is a complete failure;[1] coincidences there are many in number, but on matters which hold good of India generally in the period before and after Christ. The vital resemblances of important detail are absolutely lacking, even when we put aside all those statements of the Greek author which rest doubtless on misunderstandings or are obscurely reported. The *Arthaçāstra* knows nothing of the wooden fortification of Pāṭaliputra but provides for stone work; it ignores the boards of town officials without any head of each, but engaged in co-operation which Megasthenes specifies; it knows nothing of the commander-in-chief of the fleet, and a regular navy such as Candragupta must have used, but which was probably of minor account in many states. The care of strangers, escorting them to the border, seeing after their effects if deceased, are unknown to the *Arthaçāstra*, which does not provide for the registration of births and deaths, while the work of Megasthenes' board in selling old and new manufactured articles contrasts strikingly with the highly developed commercial and industrial conditions envisaged by the *Arthaçāstra*. Megasthenes' statement as to the king's ownership of the land is supported by other Indian evidence; it is not the view of the *Arthaçāstra*; Megasthenes describes a knowledge of minerals far less advanced than that of the *Arthaçāstra* which knows much of alchemy; the taxes of Megasthenes are simple as compared with the numerous imposts of the text, and, while Megasthenes ignores writing, the *Arthaçāstra* is full of rules on registration, the preparation of royal documents, and recognizes passports.[2]

If we abandon the unhappy identification, the date becomes difficult to settle. We may, however, note that Patañjali does not know the work, that the knowledge of alchemy suggests acquaintance with Greek science,[3] and that the term *surungā*, mine, is doubtless borrowed from Greek syrinx, probably not until after the Christian era.[4] Moreover, it seems most probable that the *Arthaçāstra* knew and used the Smṛtis of Manu, Yājña-

[1] Stein, *Megasthenes und Kauṭilya*, SWA. 1921.

[2] The metre of the work is not early, and its grammatical irregularities are not primitive; Keith, JRAS. 1916, pp. 136 f.

[3] Jolly's ed., pp. 42 f., against Ray, *Hist. of Hindu Chemistry*, ii. 31; R. V. Patvardhan, POCP. 1919, i, p. clv.

[4] Stein, ZII. iii. 280 ff.; Winternitz, IHQ. i. 429 ff.

valkya, and Nārada at least; in the case of Yājñavalkya the case appears to be proved;[1] where that text penalizes operations on boils, the *Arthaçāstra* sensibly excludes operations on dangerous boils, and in other cases it takes up the language of the Smṛti. The identity of the exhortation to the soldiers with a verse of Bhāsa may denote borrowing, but, as Bhāsa's date is uncertain, this does not help much to a definite result. The text was doubtless known to Daṇḍin who mentions its length, 6,000 Çlokas (i. e. sets of thirty-two syllables), and considers it as recent, unless we put this down to dramatic propriety in his notice; Bāṇa recognizes it, and Kālidāsa's remarks on hunting were perhaps taken from it. This accords well with the fact that the *Kauṭilīya* and Cāṇakya are known to the *Nandīsūtra* and *Anuyogadvāra-sūtra* of the Jain canon in the middle of the fifth century A.D., and that Varāhamihira in his *Bṛhatsaṁhitā* has parallel matter, while Caraka's medical treatise enumerates thirty-six special devices as compared with thirty-two of the last book of the text. Further, the work is before the *Kāmasūtra*, whose date, as will be seen, may be the fourth century A.D., before Vātsyāyana's *Nyāyabhāṣya*, and before the *Tantrākhyāyika* or *Pañcatantra*, perhaps of the same period. That the work was a product of *c.* 300, written by an official attached to some court, is at least plausible, if it cannot be proved. Whether anything goes back to Cāṇakya is an insoluble question. The author may have lived in the south, since he refers to the pearls, diamonds, shells, and gems of that part, and South Indian and Ceylonese gems bulk largely in the chapter on the examination of gems, but this is conjecture, for the fact that manuscripts exist only in the south is not of much importance.

The literature known to the text included Vedas, Vedāñgas, epic, didactic and narrative, Purāṇas, Itivṛttas, Ākhyāyikās, and probably a large number of texts on special sciences such as examination of jewels, agriculture, military matters, architecture, alchemy, veterinary art, and other topics. The theory that the information given in the text was merely derived from fellow

[1] As shown by T. Gaṇapati Śāstrī, TSS. 79, pp. 8 ff. A defence of the antiquity of the work is given by Narendranath Law (*Calc. Review*, Sept. Dec. 1924) and K. P. Jayaswal (*Hindu Polity*, App. C), but neither of these authors explains why the author knows nothing of an empire or Pāṭaliputra. 'Credo quia impossibile' is still, it appears, not obsolete.

experts is contradicted by the express assertion of the text and all probability. The text also knew Jain legends, Jain gods and technical terms, while its version of epic legends is by no means always derived from the great epic, but may be paralleled in the Vedic and Buddhist literature. All this coincides with the date above suggested as likely.

4. *Later Treatises*

The later works are of minor importance. Based mainly on the *Arthaçāstra* is the *Nītisāra*[1] of Kāmandaki, who hails Cāṇakya as his master. But it is not merely a redaction of the *Arthaçāstra.* It is simplified by the omission of the details regarding administration in books ii–iv of that text, and of the subject-matter of the last two books. Moreover, in book iii and elsewhere it delights in didactic morality which is foreign to the *Arthaçāstra.* On the other hand, some parts of the original are taken up with special zest as in ix–xi; the theory of foreign policy is there developed into its fullness of theoretical elaboration, without any relation to history. In xvi–xx we find a repetition of the advice of the *Arthaçāstra* to engage in treacherous warfare wherever possible on the ground that, as that text says and the *Tantrākhyāyika* repeats:

ekaṁ hanyān na vā hanyād iṣuḥ kṣipto dhanuṣmatā
prājñena tu matiḥ kṣiptā hanyād garbhagatān api.

'The archer's arrow may slay one, or it may not; the cunning of the wise can slay foes ere they are even born.' The *Kāmandakīya* is written in easy verses, and not only is it divided into cantos like an epic, but its commentator ascribes to it the character of a great Kāvya.[2] The praise is naturally not deserved, and, since the discovery of its original, its importance, not very great, is much diminished.

Its date can be determined only very vaguely. It is not known to the *Pañcatantra* in its oldest form nor to Kālidāsa, who both rather use the *Arthaçāstra*; even Daṇḍin seems to be unaware of it, but Bhavabhūti's mention of a nun Kāmandakī may have significance, though that dramatist, like Viçākhadatta in his

[1] Ed. BI. 1849–84; TSS. 14, 1912.

[2] Jacobi, SBA. 1912, p. 836.

Mudrārākṣasa, used the *Arthaçāstra*. Vāmana[1] knows it (*c.* 800), so that the date may be *c.* 700, though others have put it contemporaneous with Varāhamihira. Its presence on the island of Bali in the Kawi literature is of no importance, as it was not till the tenth century that that literature flourished to the greatest extent.[2]

Much more interesting is the *Nītivākyāmṛta*[3] of Somadeva Sūri, the interesting author of the *Yaçastilaka*, who lets us know that he wrote that work before this treatise on royal duties. Deeply as he is indebted to the *Arthaçāstra*, his spirit is quite different. The details of administration and war interest him not at all, and he is definitely far more of a moral teacher, advising kings how to behave well and prudently rather than with cunning. Thus, like the Smṛtis, he enjoins the use of ordeal, not of torture, as does the *Arthaçāstra*. His attitude throughout is but slightly affected by his Jain views. He entirely accepts the rule of the castes, disapproves intermarriage, demands from each caste adherence to its own duties, and can find a place for a good Çūdra who observes purity and devotion to his work. He recommends the practice of not taking life, but without any special insistence, and for a king he recommends the Lokāyata, or materialistic philosophy, on the score that ascetic principles and practices are absurd in him.

Somadeva's style is his own ; it consists of short pithy sentences, quite unlike the abbreviated Sūtras, for he is always clear, and more lively than the smooth verses of Kāmandaki. He shows here as in his *Yaçastilaka* a remarkable depth of reading ; thus he alludes to the story of the *Pañcatantra* of the priest whom rogues cheated into believing the goat he was carrying a dog, and to the plot of Bhavabhūti's *Mālatīmādhava*. He tells also the famous tale of the ingratitude of man as contrasted with the gratitude of animals in the shape of the tale how an ape, a snake, a lion, and an archivist were rescued from a well by Kāñkāyana and how, while the former all proved their appreciation, the man brought about the death of his benefactor. It is, however, significant of the mode in which literary property was treated in

[1] iv. 1. 2.

[2] Kuhn, *Der Einfluss des arischen Indiens auf die Nachbarländer* (1903), p. 19.

[3] Ed. Bombay, 1887–8 ; Jolly, ZDMG. lxix. 369 ff.

India that he only indirectly alludes to Cāṇakya, whence his information was so largely derived.

Interesting also from the point of view of the complete dependence on Brahmanical science of Jain politicians is the *Laghu Arhannīti*[1] of Hemacandra (1088–1172), which is an abbreviation of his large work on this topic in Prākrit. Written in Çlokas it deals with war (i), with punishments (ii), law (*vyavahāra*) in iii, and penances (iv). Interesting as a sign of the Jain influence on Hemacandra is his insistence that war is in itself undesirable because of the loss of life it involves and his insistence on humanity in conducting hostilities; he condemns the use of poisoned or heated weapons, stones, or masses of earth, and demands quarter for ascetics, Brahmins, those who surrender, and all kinds of weaklings. In law he follows the eighteen heads of the Smṛti of Manu, and in penances he is quite orthodox, imposing them for taking meals with unsuitable persons.

Of Brahmanical texts there may be mentioned also the *Yuktikalpataru*[2] ascribed to Bhoja, and the *Nītiratnākara*[3] of Caṇḍeçvara, the jurist. Like the *Nītiprakāçikā*, the *Çukranīti*[4] is a work of quite late date which mentions the use of gunpowder and is of no value whatever as evidence for early Indian usage or philosophy.

5. *Ancillary Sciences*

The term Arthaçāstra at least in the later Indian view covers a number of minor sciences the results of which appear in part in the *Arthaçāstra*. In the case of practically all of these we have no certainly early works, and those extant are probably the results of long developments which, however, produced nothing of commanding influence. Archery, Dhanurveda, was naturally an old and respectable science among a warlike people, but none of the extant works can be assigned with any certainty to an early date; their authors include Vikramāditya, Sadāçiva, and Çārṅgadatta. Architecture, Çilpa- or Çilpi-çāstra, Vāstuvidyā, is represented by various anonymous works including the *Mayamata*, *Sanatkumāravāstuçāstra*, *Mānasāra*, and Çrīkumāra's *Çilparatna* (16th cent.); many of the texts are written in a mere

[1] Ed. Ahmedabad, 1906.
[2] Cf. Sarkar, *Hindu Sociology*, i. 12 f.
[3] Haraprasād, *Report I*, p. 12.
[4] Ed. Sarkar, New York, 1915.

pretence of Sanskrit and their verses are extremely rude.[1] Elephants have been more fortunate in that the *Hastyāyurveda* in the form of a dialogue between king Romapāda of Aṅga and the ancient sage Pālakāpya [2] has been preserved; the age of this curious compilation is quite uncertain. The *Mātaṅgalīlā* [3] of Nārāyaṇa on the other hand has a distinctly modern form, being written in part in elaborate metre; it recognizes Pālakāpya's claim to be the father of the science. The science of horses, Açvaçāstra, is ascribed to another sage Çālihotra, who sometimes figures in a more general way as a patron of learning in respect of elephants and other animals. It bears also, in its aspect as dealing with their diseases, the styles of Açvacikitsā, Açvavaidyaka, or Açvāyurveda. Of personal authors we have the *Açvāyurveda* of Gaṇa, the *Açvavaidyaka* of Jayadatta and of Dīpaṁkara, the *Yogamañjarī* of Vardhamāna, and the *Açvacikitsita* of Nakula.[4] Bhoja again is credited with a *Çālihotra*,[5] which treats in 138 verses of the care of horses and their diseases.

The importance of jewels rendered it natural that a science of them, Ratnaçāstra, Ratnaparīkṣā, should develop, and Varāhamihira shows himself familiar with the examination of jewels. The texts extant, which give very varied information regarding jewels as well as legends concerning them, are of unknown but very probably late date; they include the *Agastimata*, the *Ratnaparīkṣā* of Buddha Bhaṭṭa, the *Navaratnaparīkṣā* of Nārāyaṇa Paṇḍita and minor texts.[6] Not inappropriately may be mentioned here the counter science of stealing, for the *Mṛcchakaṭikā* reminds us, as do other texts, of the existence of a regular manual of practice for thieves. One text which is extant, *Ṣaṇmukhakalpa*,[7] insists in this connexion on a sound knowledge by a thief of magic, just as we have seen the *Arthaçāstra* stresses the value of that accomplishment to a politician.

On music we have, beside the important if obscure information given in the *Nāṭyaçāstra*, much late literature, which deals comprehensively with the whole topic, the kindred subject of singing,

[1] A *Vāstuvidyā* is ed. TSS. 30, 1913; cf. *Madras Catal.*, xxiii. 8755 ff.
[2] Ed. ĀnSS. 26.
[3] Ed. TSS. 10, 1910.
[4] Ed. BI. 1887. Cf. Haraprasād, *Report I*, p. 10.
[5] Jolly, *Munich Catal.*, p. 68; G. Mukherje, IHQ. i. 532 ff.
[6] Ed. L. Finot, *Les lapidaires indiens* (1896).
[7] Haraprasād, *Report I*, p. 8.

arrangements for concerts and so forth. These include the *Saṁgītaratnākara*[1] of Çārṅgadeva (13th cent.), and the *Saṁgītadarpaṇa*[2] of Dāmodara which follows it with additional matter derived from other sources. The late *Rāgavibodha*[3] of Somanātha (1609) deals with Rāgas, musical modes, and includes fifty pieces of the author's own composition for the lute with notation. Our knowledge, however, of Indian music in the earlier period is limited.[4]

On painting little that is early has survived; the *Viṣṇudharmottara*[5] of uncertain but not early date contains a section on this topic.

[1] Ed. ĀnSS. 35, with Kallinātha's comm. (1450).

[2] Simon, ZDMG. lvi. 129 ff.; comm. by Çiṅga (1330); P. R. Bhandarkar, POCP. 1919, ii. 421 f.

[3] Simon, SBayA. 1903, pp. 447 ff.; ZII. i. 153 ff. See also V. G. Paranjpe, POCP. 1919, ii. 427 ff.

[4] See E. Felber, *Die indische Musik der vedischen und der klassischen Zeit* (1912); H. A. Popley, *The Music of India*; R. Simon, ZDMG. lx. 520 ff.; WZKM. xxvii. 305 ff. On Bharata's *Nāṭyaçāstra*, xxviii cf. T. Grosset, *Contribution à l'étude de la musique hindoue* (1888); P. R. Bhandarkar, IA. xli. 157 ff. For late works see *Madras Catal.*, xxii. 8717 ff. See also A. B. F. Rahamin, *The Music of India* (1925).

[5] Trans. S. Kramrisch (Calcutta, 1925). The references to literature in P. Brown's *Indian Painting* are inaccurate. See also V. Smith, *History of Fine Art in India and Ceylon* (1911); Havell, *Indian Sculpture and Painting* (1908); Lady Herringham, *Ajanta Frescos* (1915); A. K. Coomaraswamy, *Arts and Crafts of India and Ceylon* (1913); *Rajput Painting* (1916); *Mediaeval Sinhalese Art* (cf. Kramrisch, IHQ. i. 111 ff.); *The Influence of Indian Art* (1925); G. Roerich, *Tibetan Painting* (1925); L. Binyon, *L'Art asiatique au British Museum* (1924). Cf. the *Sādhanamālā*, ed. Bhattacharya (1925), his *Buddhist Iconography*, &c.

XXIV

THE SCIENCE OF LOVE

THE third of the aims of man is Kāma, love, and this subject is taken quite as seriously by Indian writers as Dharma or Artha. As the Arthaçāstra is intended for kings and ministers, so the Kāmaçāstra is to be studied by men of taste, Nāgarakas, who desire to practice refinement and profit to the most by their knowledge of all that is meant by love; women may study it also if they are such as come into contact with gentlemen, that is, courtesans, princesses, and the daughters of high officers. It is not surprising that in the *Kāmasūtra*[1] of Vātsyāyana Mallanāga, our first great treatise on the topic, we should find a close imitation of the *Arthaçāstra*; as in that text we are introduced into the importance of the three ends of man; there is a section on the sciences as they existed at the author's time, and the book ends with a secret chapter as in the *Arthaçāstra*. Moreover, the author solemnly assures us that the study of the Çāstra will be to induce him who practises love to remember during it the claims of the other sides of man's activity, Dharma and Artha, so that he will observe due moderation. Moreover, the morality of the work is that of the *Arthaçāstra*; on the principle that 'all's fair in love and war,' the author complacently gives instruction in modes of deceiving maidens and of seducing the wives of others with as much *sang-froid* as the *Arthaçāstra* in inculcating the benefits of defeating an opponent by guile. The pious Madhusūdana Sarasvatī,[2] who assigns the Kāmaçāstra to the general head of medicine, assures us that the *Kāmasūtra* in five sections—a discrepancy from our text—teaches that nothing but sorrow results even from all the refinements taught in the text; but that is certainly not the impression

[1] Ed. Bombay, 1891; Benares, 1912; trans. R. Schmidt, Leipzig, 1897; cf. *Beiträge zur indischen Erotik* (1911).

[2] *Prasthānabheda.*

left by the *Kāmasūtra.* Even in style the resemblance to the *Arthaçāstra* is quite marked. The work is written in a dry didactic style which is in a sense midway between Sūtras and a Bhāṣya, and the sections are finished off by verses in the manner of the *Arthaçāstra.*[1]

The *Kāmasūtra* is divided into seven parts; the first deals with generalities, the purpose of the book, the three ends of man, the sciences, the character of an elegant, and the description of the friends and go-betweens who help him in his intrigues. Part ii discusses the modes of enjoying love; iii relations with maidens, giving hints for courtship which imply a state of society in which child marriages were by no means universal, and marriage ceremonials, supplementing the information of the Gṛhyasūtras; iv discusses relations with married women; v relations with the women of others; vi hetairai; and vii secret potions to secure love. The sociological and medical importance of the treatise is admittedly considerable, it is certain that it was very freely used by the poets to guide them in their descriptions of love scenes.

The work, however, makes it clear that it has no claim to be the first written. In the introduction we hear of Çvetaketu, the Vedic scholar, as having composed a treatise which Pāñcāla Bābhravya condensed in seven chapters. Of these Dattaka, at the bidding of the hetairai of Pāṭaliputra, chose the sixth for working up as a special subject and his example was followed by Cārāyaṇa, Suvarṇanābha, Ghoṭakamukha, Gonardīya, Goṇikāputra, Kucumāra, who each took up a section. Then, in view of the size of Bābhravya's work, it was reduced to reasonable dimensions by the author. In point of fact both he and his commentator cite these worthies and give verses from them, so that we may believe that books under their names were actually current. Of these names Cārāyaṇa and Ghoṭakamukha are found in the *Arthaçāstra*, Gonardīya and Goṇikāputra in Patañjali's *Mahābhāṣya*, Ghoṭakamukha beside Kauṭilya in the Jain lists, and that Bābhravya left a school is reasonably certain from the *Kāmasūtra*'s citation of the views of Bābhravīyas. The

[1] Jacobi, SBA. 1911, pp. 962 ff., 1912, p. 840. Cf. E. Müller-Hess, *Festschrift Kuhn*, pp. 162 ff.; Jolly, ZDMG. lxviii. 351 ff.

Buddhists also recognize the Kāmaçāstra as one of the arts in which the young Buddha was instructed, and Açvaghoṣa clearly knew some early work of this sort.

The actual dating of the text of Vātsyāyana is difficult. Kālidāsa, like Açvaghoṣa, knew an early Kāmaçāstra, and we cannot prove that he actually used Vātsyāyana for his descriptions in his dramas, in the last canto of the *Raghuvança*, or cantos vii and viii of the *Kumārasambhava*.[1] He is not in either of these two poems in perfect agreement with the rules of the science, as we have it in the *Kāmasūtra*. It is different with Subandhu, who actually refers to Mallanāga or Malanāga and his work, while his account of the hetairai of Kusumapura seems to follow the *Kāmasūtra*. It was certainly known to Māgha, to Bhavabhūti, and to Varāhamihira, whose *Bṛhatsaṁhitā* shows clear signs of using it. The effort[2] to use the mention of Andhras and Ābhīras as rulers to prove that the date must be later than A.D. 225, since before that the Andhras were paramount rulers, and not merely on the footing of the Ābhīras, may be dismissed as inconclusive, as is the reference to Kuntala Çātakarṇi Sātavāhana who accidentally killed his queen. The dating of the work in the fourth century A.D. is thus purely speculative, if it is perhaps not far from the truth. It may well be, however, that this is too high, and that A.D. 500 is a reasonable date, for the *Arthaçāstra* may not be earlier than *c.* A.D. 400, or even later.

The text would be very unintelligible but for the explanations of obscure terms given by Yaçodhara in his *Jayamaṅgalā*, who wrote under Vīsaladeva (1243–61). Of minor importance are all other works, besides being of late date. These include the *Pañcasāyaka* of Jyotirīçvara[3] who knows Kṣemendra; the *Ratirahasya* of Kokkoka, before 1200, who employs elaborate metres, and claims to have used Nandikeçvara and Goṇikāputra as well as Vātsyāyana in compiling his work; the short *Ratimañjari*[4] of Jayadeva,

[1] Contrast Peterson, JBRAS. xviii. 109 ff.; R. Narasimhachar, JRAS. 1911, p. 183, who compares *Raghuvança*, xix. 31 and *Çakuntalā*, iv. 17 with *Kāmasūtra*, pp. 328, 239. But *Kum.* iii. 68; vii. 77; *Ragh.* vi. 81 violate *Kāmasūtra*, p. 266.

[2] H. Chakladar, *Vātsyāyana* (1921); cf. Jolly, *Arthaśāstra*, i. 26 ff. Bhandarkar (POCP. 1919, i. 25) puts the date *c.* A.D. 100. Vātsyāyana used Āpastamba and the *Mahābhāṣya*, and was a westerner; ABI. vii. 129 ff; viii. 43 ff.; AMSJV. iii. 1. 327 ff.

[3] On these works see Schmidt, *Beiträge zur ind. Erotik*, pp. 35 ff.

[4] Ed. Pavolini, GSAI. xvii. 317 ff.

who is apparently not to be identified with the poet of the *Gīta-govinda*, and the *Anaṅgaraṅga*[1] of Kalyāṇamalla in the sixteenth century. A *Ratiçāstra*[2] is also attributed to a Nāgārjuna, but we need not identify its author with the famous Buddhist sage who has had the misfortune of becoming the reputed author of many treatises on dubious topics.

[1] Ed. Lahore, 1920; trans. London, 1885.

[2] Cf. Schmidt, WZKM. xxiii. 180 ff. and on the comm., *Smaratattvaprakāçikā* of Revaṇārādhya, WZKM. xviii. 261 ff.

XXV

PHILOSOPHY AND RELIGION

1. *The Beginnings of Indian Philosophy*

THE religious and philosophical spirit of India which appears already in marked development in the *Ṛgveda* found its most brilliant literary exposition in the Upaniṣads, but with them we are still distinctly before the time of formal systematization. On the other hand, we find at an unknown date Indian philosophy, so far as it is orthodox, framed in a number of Sūtras for which great antiquity is asserted by the schools, while the Jains and Buddhists alike assert the same of their texts, and even the materialists ascribe their doctrines to a mythical Bṛhaspati. These claims to antiquity we may justly dismiss, and assume that after the period of the Upaniṣads dates the time when ideas of earlier thinkers were gradually taken up and made into a definite system, Darçana,[1] taught in a philosophic school in the sense of a series of teachers who developed or at least expounded one definite body of doctrine. After this development had been in existence for some time, there ultimately came the desire to fix in definitive form the doctrines of the school, and this led to the composition of the Sūtras. These texts are based on the principle of short catchwords which must from the first have been accompanied by verbal expositions. These are naturally lost, and it appears clear that it was only in each case at some considerable distance after the Sūtra had been produced that the need of writing down a comment was devised. Our oldest surviving commentaries contain abundant signs that they do not represent an unbroken tradition, sure of itself, from the first teacher. Later we find independent works of the several schools, but these recognize the authority of the Sūtras, and make it clear that it was held that in them lay the essential doctrines of the school, which might be expanded and expounded but were not to be contradicted.

[1] The term occurs in *Vaiçeṣika Sūtra*, ix. 2. 13 and the late epic.

The Sūtras themselves were redacted at a time when the schools had been in contact, and for that reason we have no real chance of determining their dates even relatively, for it seems as if those of the Pūrvamīmāṅsā, the Vedānta, the Nyāya, and Vaiçeṣika cannot have been composed as they stand at any very great distance of time from one another. The investigations of Jacobi[1] resulted in the belief that the *Nyāya* and *Brahma Sūtras* were composed after the nihilistic school of Buddhism but before the appearance of the Vijñānavādin idealism, say between A. D. 200 and 450, while the *Pūrvamīmāṅsā* and *Vaiçeṣika* might be a little older. The *Yoga Sūtra*, on the other hand, he assigned to the period after the Vijñānavāda school and the *Sāṁkhya* to a late date. The last result is clearly sound, but the Vijñānavāda is dated too late, and must fall in the fourth century at latest, while the nihilistic school is also probably postdated by a century. Jacobi[2] also deduces from the mention in the *Arthaçāstra* under the style of Ānvīkṣikī of Lokāyata, Sāṁkhya and Yoga only, that these three branches of philosophy had definitely developed by 300 B. C., but not the others. This view, however, must be wrong, since the *Arthaçāstra*, as we have seen, is much later than the period proposed, and its groupings of philosophy must be explained by the tenets of that school. We must content ourselves with the belief that between the dates of the chief Upaniṣads and the third or fourth century A. D. there proceeded an active stream of investigation which we have only in its final form.

2. *The Pūrvamīmāṅsā*

Among the schools, Darçanas, the Pūrvamīmāṅsā can claim on the score of its character considerable age. Performers of Vedic rites found themselves in need of rules of interpretation, Nyāyas, to guide them through the maze of texts, and the *Āpastambīya Dharmasūtra*[3] already refers to those who know Nyāyas. The Sūtra of the school essentially aims at laying down principles

[1] JAOS. xxxi. 1 ff.; DLZ. 1922, p. 270. Dasgupta (*Indian Phil.* i. 370, 418 f., 280) puts the dates far too high, as does V. G. Paranjpe, *Le Vârtika du Kâtyâyana*, pp. 76 ff., who argues on the basis of styles, which involves the assumption that style in grammatical and philosophic texts is strictly comparable. The dates of the early forms of the Sūtras is another question which is unanswerable.

[2] SBA. 1911, pp. 732 ff.

[3] ii. 4. 8. 13; 6. 14. 3.

regarding interpretation of texts in their connexion with carrying out the sacrificial ritual; man's duty is the performance of sacrifice in due manner, and the Veda is the one authority. The relation of sound and meaning is thus a relevant problem, as is that of the personal existence of gods, but deeper philosophic issues were introduced only by the commentators who developed true systems of philosophy. The Sūtra, however, develops a method which is common to Indian science generally, and which was adopted by the writers on law; the subject is posed, the doubt is raised; the prima facie view is set out; then the correct decision is developed, and the matter brought into connexion with other relevant doctrines. From Medhātithi onwards use is made of Mīmāṅsā principles in deciding legal difficulties, such as arose from the recognition in the law schools of many conflicting texts as all having authority, just as the Vedic texts before the compilers of the Mīmāṅsā presented innumerable incongruities.

The twelve books of Sūtras[1] give often the impression of not very effective compilation. They were commented on by Upavarṣa and later by Çabarasvāmin, both of whom wrote also on the *Brahma Sūtra* of the Vedānta. Jacobi holds that from the first the Pūrvamīmāṅsā and the Vedānta, or Uttaramīmāṅsā were one school, and that it was only later through Kumārila and Çañkara that they were differentiated. This, of course, would give the Pūrvamīmāṇsā a very different aspect, as merely a part of a philosophy, not the whole, but the contention seems dubious, and the syncretism of the systems seems rather to be due to the commentators. Çabarasvāmin seems to have known the nihilistic school of Buddhism, perhaps also the idealistic, and he has a definite theory[2] of the soul which seems to regard it as produced from the absolute Brahman, but as thereafter existing independently for ever, a view which recurs in Rāmānuja; that this is really the doctrine of the *Bṛhadāraṇyaka Upaniṣad* ascribed to Yājnavalkya must be emphatically denied.

On the Bhāṣya of Çabarasvāmin we have two different systems founded, one by Prabhākara (*c.* 600) in his *Bṛhatī*,[3] great

[1] Ed. BI. 1873 ff.; trans. by Gangānāth Jhā, SBH. 10, 1910. See Keith, *The Karma-Mīmāṁsā* (1921); K. A. Nilakantha Sastri, IA. l. 211 ff., 340 ff.

[2] Jacobi, *Festschrift Windisch*, pp. 153 ff.

[3] Trans. G. Jhā, IT. ii and iii.

(commentary), the other by Kumārila who wrote perhaps about 700. His comment[1] falls into three parts, the *Çlokavārttika* on i. i, of the Sūtra, *Tantravārttika* on i. 2–iii, and *Ṭupṭīkā* on iv–xii. Kumārila is traditionally made out to have instigated persecution of the Buddhists, but the justification for this view seems merely to have been his bitterness against them as the chief enemies of the Veda. He derides the doctrine of the Buddha as omniscient, which none of his contemporaries was competent to know, derides also the followers of the Buddha, and declares empirical means of knowledge worthless; if right be judged by causing pleasure to others, then the violation of the chastity of the wife of the teacher as giving her pleasure would be right instead of a heinous crime. Kumārila was a native of southern India, who reveals his knowledge of Dravidian languages, and recommends that borrowed words should be given Sanskrit terminations; he refers both to literature and to current practices, and his ingenuity is very considerable. His differences in philosophy from Prabhākara are considerable, but both agree with Çabarasvāmin in holding that the individual soul in some sense is immortal; both again do not accept the doctrine of illusion. A pupil of Kumārila, on one theory, of Çañkara on another, was Maṇḍana Miçra who wrote a *Mīmāṇsānukramaṇī* and a *Vidhiviveka*;[2] on the latter Vācaspati Miçra (*c.* 850) writes a comment, the *Nyāyakaṇikā*; he also set forth Kumārila's views in his *Tattvabindu*.[3] Of late works the *Nyāyamālāvistara*[4] of Mādhava (14th cent.), the *Mīmāṅsānyāyaprakāça*[5] of Āpadeva, and the *Arthasaṁgraha*[6] of Laugākṣi Bhāskara are best known, but of more philosophic interest is Nārāyaṇa Bhaṭṭa's *Mānameyodaya*[7] (*c.* 1600) in which Kumārila's epistemology and metaphysics are interestingly summarized.

3. *The Vedānta*

While the Pūrvamīmāṅsā represents a very primitive need involving no great philosophical skill, the Uttaramīmāṅsā or Vedānta school represents a definite gathering up of the philo-

[1] Ed. ChSS. 1898–9; BenSS. 1890, 1903; trans. G. Jhā, BI. 1900 ff.

[2] Ed. *Pandit*, N.S. xxv–xxviii. His identity with Sureçvara is traditional, and is not disproved by Hiriyanna, JRAS. 1924, p. 96.

[3] Ed. *Pandit*, N.S. xiv.

[4] Ed. London, 1878.

[5] Ed. *Pandit*, N.S. xxvi, xxvii.

[6] Ed. BenSS. 1882.

[7] Ed. TSS. 19, 1912.

sophical doctrines of the Upaniṣads in an attempt to frame a system which will embrace them all. The contemporaneity of redaction of the Sūtras is suggested by the fact that while the *Pūrvamīmāṅsā* mentions Ātreya, Bādari, and Bādarāyaṇa, the *Brahma*,[1] also called *Vedānta*, *Uttaramīmāṅsā*, or *Çārīraka-mīmāṅsā*, *Sūtra* cites frequently Jaimini, as well as Ātreya, Āçmarathya, Auḍulomi, Kāçakṛtsna, Kārṣṇājini, and Bādarāyaṇa himself, an indication, as in the case of the *Pūrvamīmāṅsā Sūtra*, that the works were produced not by Bādarāyaṇa or Jaimini[2] themselves, but by schools expressing their views. The *Brahma Sūtra* deliberately leaves out points on which the Pūrvamīmāṅsā has sufficient matter, and it may be the case that the school regarded themselves as entitled to adopt what they wished of the Pūrvamīmāṅsa, while carrying the philosophical doctrine much further, and rejecting those views of Jaimini which they disliked.

The doctrine of Bādarāyaṇa evidently directed itself strongly against the Sāṁkhya system and the atomism of the Vaiçeṣikas, but its miserable presentation in catchwords leaves us guessing at its meaning. What does seem clear is that Bādarāyaṇa wás not a believer in the illusion doctrine of Çaṅkara's school, that he held that individual souls, if derived from the absolute, remained distinct from it and real, and that matter derived also from the absolute had a distinct reality of its own. But this, though probable, cannot be proved because we cannot now recover the verbal explanations which originally accompanied the text, but which were never written down, and so permitted the rise of different interpretations.

(a) *The Doctrine of Nonduality and Illusion*

Of these interpretations the most interesting is that which holds that all reality, as we know it, is a mere illusion. This view is preserved for us in a definite shape in the *Gauḍapādīya Kārikās*,[3] 215 memorial verses written by Gauḍapāda, whom tradition

[1] The apparent reference in the *Bhagavadgītā* (xiii. 4) is doubtless an interpolaticn.

[2] K. A. Nilakantha's effort (IA. l. 167 ff.) to distinguish various Jaimini's and Bādarāyaṇa's, is thus rather misplaced.

[3] Ed. ĀnSS. 10, 1911; trans. P. Deussen, *Sechzig Upanishad's des Veda*, pp. 537ff. Cp. Vidhusekhara Bhattacarya, IHQ. i. 119 ff., 295 ff., who contends that the Upanishad is based on the *Kārikās*. For the school see M. Sarkar, *System of Vedantic Thought and Culture*; Hiriyanna, POCM. 1924, pp. 439 ff., on Bhartṛ-Prapañca.

makes out to be the teacher of Govinda, teacher of Çaṅkara, and therefore of *c.* 700 A.D. There is no doubt that this work, of which the first part deals with the short *Māṇḍūkya Upaniṣad*, is strongly influenced by the nihilistic school of Buddhism. It shares with it a rich store of metaphors and similes, designed to make plausible the doctrine of illusion, such as the phenomena of dreams, the Fata Morgana, the rope mistaken in the dark for a stick, nacre mistaken for silver, the reflection in the mirror. In its last section, the Alātaçānti, it adds the brilliant picture of the circle of sparks which a boy makes when he swings a torch without altering the glowing end of the torch, giving a parallel to the manifestation of unreal phenomena from the real absolute. The idea is found in the Buddhist *Laṅkāvatāra* and the *Maitrāyaṇīya Upaniṣad*, but we need not accept the theory that in this doctrine of illusion we have a borrowing from the Buddhists. The idea is suggested strongly in certain passages of the Upaniṣads; it was probably developed by an Aupaniṣada school, affected the growth of Buddhism, and in turn was affected by the brilliant if rather wasted dialectic of Nāgārjuna. Gauḍapāda's existence has indeed been questioned and his Kārikās made out to be those of north-west Bengal (Gauḍapāda), the work being placed before the Sūtra, but this is clearly untenable.[1]

The full defence and exposition of the illusion theory with its insistence on Advaita, absence of any duality, is due to Çaṅkara, who may have been born in 788 and may have died or become a Sannyāsin in 820, and who, at any rate, worked *c.* A.D. 800. The biographies alleged, absurdly, to be by Ānandagiri, his pupil, the *Çaṅkaravijaya*,[2] and Mādhava's *Çaṅkaradigvijaya*[3] are worthless, and many works attributed to him are probably not his. But many commentaries on the Upaniṣads, one on the *Bhagavadgītā*,[4] and the *Bhāṣya*[5] on the *Brahma Sūtra* are genuine, nor need we doubt the ascription of the *Upadeçasāhasrī*,[6] three chapters in prose and nineteen in verse, or various shorter works, including lyrics of considerable power and the *Ātmabodha*[7]

[1] M. Walleser, *Der ältere Vedānta* (1910).

[2] Ed. BI. 1864-8.

[3] Ed. ĀnSS. 22.

[4] B. Faddegon, *Çaṃkara's Gītābhāṣya* (1906).

[5] Ed. ĀnSS. 21; trans. G. Thibaut, SBE. xxxiv and xxxviii; cf. Kokileswar Sastri, *Advaita Philosophy* (1924); ii. 1 and 2 ed. and trans. Belvalkar, Poona, 1923.

[6] Ed. *Pandit*, iii-v.

[7] Ed. Hall, Mirzapore, 1852.

in sixty-seven stanzas with commentary. Philosophically, Çaṅkara is remarkably ingenious in his key to the Upaniṣads, the finding of a higher and a lower knowledge, which similarly allows him to conform to the whole apparatus of Hindu belief on the lower plane, while on the higher he finds no true reality in anything; his logic, it has well been said, starts by denying the truth of the proposition A is either B or not B. His dialectical skill is very great, and, though he doubtless misrepresents Bādarāyaṇa, he does more justice to the Upaniṣads in so far at least as they seem to consider that at death the soul when released is merged in the absolute and does not continue to be distinct from it. In style Çaṅkara's *Bhāṣya* is unquestionably far advanced from the dialogue tone of the *Mahābhāṣya* or the *Bhāṣyas* of Vātsyāyana or Çabarasvāmin. It has taken on the style of a lecture, with longer sentences, longer and more compounds, more involved constructions, fewer verbal and more nominal forms. But it is still far removed from the formalism of the later philosophical texts, and the author is not unwilling to show his command over the more difficult and unusual grammatical usages.

Çaṅkara is credited with the authorship of the text or a comment on the *Hastāmalaka*[1] which in fourteen verses plays on the refrain which asserts that the self as the form of eternal apprehension is all in all. To pupils of his are attributed expositions of his system; thus Padmapāda wrote the *Pañcapādikā*[2] on the first five books, and was commented on by Prakāçātman; Sureçvara wrote in prose and memorial verses the *Naiṣkarmyasiddhi*[3] to prove that knowledge alone achieves release, and a paraphrase, the *Mānasollāsa*,[4] of the *Dakṣiṇāmūrtistotra* of his master. His pupil Sarvajñātman wrote the *Saṁkṣepaçārīraka*,[5] a summary of the *Bhāṣya*, while *c.* 850 Vācaspati Miçra wrote the *Bhāmatī*,[6] which is invaluable for its knowledge of Buddhist views *inter alia*. Mādhava again in his *Pañcadaçī*,[7] written in part with Bhāratītīrtha, and *Jīvanmuktiviveka*[8] definitely

[1] Ed. and trans. IA. ix. 25 ff.
[2] Ed. VizSS. 2, 1891–2.
[3] Ed. BSS. 38, 1891; 2nd ed. by Hiriyanna, 1925.
[4] Cf. JPASB. 1908, pp. 97 f.
[5] Bhandarkar, *Report*, 1882–3, pp. 14 f., 202.
[6] Ed. BI. 1876–80.
[7] Ed. *Pandit*, N.S. v, vi, and viii.
[8] Ed. ĀnSS. 20, 1889.

supports Çañkara's views. From a different standpoint Çrīharṣa, the poet, in his *Khaṇḍanakhaṇḍakhādya*,[1] sought, by proving all other views to be contradictory, to establish that all knowledge is vain and that the doctrine of Çañkara is therefore unassailable. Other treatises are innumerable, especially in the later Middle Ages, but the *Vedāntasāra*[2] of Sadānanda (*c.* 1500) is of importance because it shows the elaborate confusion of Sāṁkhya tenets with the Vedānta to form a complex and ingenious but quite unphilosophical whole. The *Vedāntaparibhāṣā*[3] of Dharmarāja is well known as a manual of the modern school.

(b) *Rāmānuja*

A very different view of the Upaniṣads and Sūtra is presented by Rāmānuja, who died about 1137. Son of Keçava and Kāntimatī, he studied at Kāñcī under the Advaita philosopher Yādavaprakāça, but abandoned his teaching for that of Yāmuna whom he succeeded as head of a Vaiṣṇava sect, and at whose request he wrote his *Çrībhāṣya*[4] on the *Brahma Sūtra*. Among other works he wrote a *Gītābhāṣya*,[5] attacked in the *Vedārthasaṁgraha*[6] the illusion theory, summarized his *Bhāṣya* in the *Vedāntadīpa*[7] and gave a convenient summary of his doctrine in the *Vedāntasāra*. His views were defended against those of Çañkara in the *Vedāntatattvasāra*[8] of Sudarçana Sūri, and expounded in the *Yatīndramatadīpikā*[9] of Çrīnivāsa. Rāmānuja claims to represent a long tradition, citing the Vākyakāra, the Vṛttikāra Bodhāyana, and Dramiḍācārya, who was known to Çañkara, and he relies on the *Çāṇḍilya Sūtra* as revealing the true doctrine of the Sutra. In essentials he differs from Çañkara; if in a sense there is an absolute whence all is derived, the individual souls and matter still have a reality of their own, and the end of life is not merger in the absolute but continued blissful existence. This state is to be won by Bhakti, faith in

[1] Trans. IT. i–v.
[2] Trans. G. A. Jacob, London, 1904.
[3] Ed. and trans. A. Venis, *Pandit*, N.S. iv–vii.
[4] Ed. BI. 1888 ff.; trans. G. Thibaut, SBE. xlviii; cf. xxxiv.
[5] Ed. Bombay, 1893.
[6] Ed. *Pandit*, N.S. xv–xvii.
[7] Ed. BenSS. 69–71.
[8] Ed. *Pandit*, N.S. ix–xii.
[9] Ed. ĀnSS. 50; trans. R. Otto, Tübingen, 1916.

and devotion to God. His view of matter permits him to adopt largely the Sāṁkhya principles.[1]

(c) *Other Commentators*

No other comment can be compared in importance with those of Çañkara and Rāmānuja, the former representing the most sustained intellectual effort of Indian thought, the latter presenting a theory of the world which has many similarities to popular Christian belief, and which may through the Nestorians actually have been affected by Christian thought. Nimbārka, who is reputed a pupil of Rāmānuja, wrote a *Vedāntapārijātasaurabha*, commenting on the Sūtra and a *Siddhāntaratna* in ten Çlokas summing up his system. Viṣṇusvāmin, in the thirteenth century, developed a new aspect of theory which was used by Vallabha (1376–1430) when he wrote his *Aṇubhāṣya*[2] on the Sūtra and propounded a doctrine of Bhakti in which the teacher on earth is regarded as divine and receives divine honours. More distinctive is the dualism of Madhva[3] or Ānandatirtha, who commented on seven of the important Upaniṣads, the *Bhagavadgītā*, the *Brahma Sūtra*, and the *Bhāgavata Purāṇa*, while a number of independent tracts, including the *Tattvasaṁkhyāna*,[4] set out his principles briefly. What he insists on is the existence of five fundamental dualisms, Dvaita, whence his system derives its name, as opposed to the Advaita of Çañkara and the Viçiṣṭādvaita, qualified nondualism or the nonduality of that which is qualified, of Rāmānuja. A summary of the views of Rāmānuja, Viṣṇusvāmin, Nimbārka, and Madhva is given in the *Sakalācāryamatasaṁgraha*[5] of Çrīnivāsa.

4. *Theology and Mysticism*

Often closely allied with Vedānta ideas, but, like the developments of that system, powerfully affected by the Sāṁkhya and with strong affinities to the conceptions of which the Yoga

[1] Cf. Keith, ERE. x. 572 ff.

[2] Ed. BI. 1888–97.

[3] Date perhaps 1197–1276; but cf. EI. vi. 260 (1238–1317). His works are ed. Kumbhakonam, 1911.

[4] Ed. and trans. H. von Glasenapp, *Festschrift Kuhn*, pp. 326 ff.; *Madhva's Philosophie* (1923).

[5] See R. Otto, *Visnu-Nārāyana*, pp. 57 ff.

philosophy is an ordered exposition, there exists a large mass of theological and mystical speculation. A comparatively early specimen not much distinguished from the Vedānta is the *Yogavāsiṣṭha*,[1] which is reputed an appendix to the *Rāmāyaṇa* and deals with all manner of topics, including final release; it is moderately old, as it was summarized in the ninth century by the Gauḍa Abhinanda in the *Yogavāsiṣṭhasāra*. An imitation of the *Mahābhārata*, the *Jaimini Bhārata*,[2] of which Book xiv, the Āçvamedhikaparvan, alone has come down to us, is intended rather as a text-book of a Vaiṣṇava sect.

The sectarian literature of the Pañcarātra school of Vaiṣṇavas, long best known from the late *Nārada Pāñcarātra*[3] (perhaps 16th cent.), is better represented by a large number of Saṁhitās which may be of considerable age; the *Ahirbudhnya*,[4] which has been claimed to belong to the period of the later epic, gives no very favourable impression of the literature which mixes Vedānta and Sāṁkhya ideas in a curious way. The *Īçvara Saṁhitā* is quoted in the tenth century, but others are at least worked over if they are really ancient in substance, the *Bṛhad Brahma Saṁhitā* alluding to doctrines of Rāmānuja. The *Bhakticāstra*, ascribed to Nārada, is a late production, and so are the *Bhaktisūtras*,[5] alleged to be by Çāṇḍilya, who appears as an authority on the Pañcarātra both in Çaṅkara and Rāmānuja. Quite modern is the Hindi *Bhaktamāla*[6] which is interesting, apart from its technical explanations of the doctrine of faith, for its legends. The effect of Christian influence in it may be readily admitted in view of the prolonged existence in India of a Christian church.[7]

The doctrine of Rāmānuja gave rise to divergent schools of thought, whose differences turned largely on minor points such as the position of Lakṣmī, wife of Viṣṇu, or the necessity or otherwise of activity by the soul which sought salvation. The literature induced by this split, partly local between north and

[1] Ed. Bombay, 1911; trans. Calcutta, 1909.

[2] Cf. Weber, *Monatsber. BA.* 1869, pp. 10 ff., 369 ff.

[3] Ed. BI. 1865.

[4] Ed. Madras, 1916. See F. O. Schrader, *Intr. to the Pāñcarātra* (1916); Govindācārya, JRAS. 1911, pp. 951 ff.

[5] Ed. BI. 1861; trans. BI. 1878.

[6] Grierson, JRAS. 1910, pp. 87 ff., 269 ff.

[7] Grierson, JRAS. 1907, pp. 314 ff.; cf. ERE. ii. 548 ff.

south, is in part only in Sanskrit and is not of the highest importance for religion or philosophy.

On the other hand, in Kashmir, where Çaivism was predominant, there developed two schools with close affinity in many regards to the Vedānta. The first and less important is represented in the ninth century by the *Çiva Sūtra*[1] of Vasugupta, on which in the eleventh century Kṣemarāja, pupil of Abhinavagupta, commented, and by Kallaṭa's *Spandakārikā*. God here appears as creator without material cause or the influence of past action, Karman; he creates by the mere effort of his will. The Pratyabhijñāçāstra owes its fame to Somānanda's *Çivadṛṣṭi* (*c.* 900), the *Īçvarapratyabhijñāsūtra* of Utpaladeva, his pupil, son of Udayākara, and to Abhinavagupta's comment[2] on that text (*c.* 1000), and his *Paramārthasāra*,[3] in 100 Āryā verses, in which he adapts to his peculiar view some popular Kārikās ascribed to Ādi Çeṣa or Patañjali. The special point of this system, which is also briefly summarized in the *Virūpākṣapañcāçikā*[4] of Virūpākṣanātha, is the insistence on the necessity, in order to enjoy the delight of identity with God, for man to realize that he has within him the perfections of God, just as a maiden can only enjoy her lover if she realizes that he possesses the perfections of which she has been told.

Other Çaiva systems existed; Çrīkaṇṭha Çivācārya, who wrote a *Çaivabhāṣya*[5] on the *Brahma Sūtra*, belonged to the Vīraçaiva or Liñgāyat school of southern India in which Bhakti towards Çiva is specially inculcated, and Appayya Dīkṣita, the polymath of the sixteenth century, was of the same persuasion.

Of no philosophical importance, but of great interest to the history of superstition, are the Tantras, the essence of which is to clothe in the garments of mysticism, the union of the soul with God or the absolute, the tenets of eroticism. That the Tantra literature is reasonably old is proved in all probability by the existence of manuscripts from 609 onwards, but the exact dates of the extant texts are hard in each case to determine; they

[1] Trans. IT. iii and iv.

[2] Ed. *Pandit*, ii and iii.

[3] Ed. Barnett, JRAS. 1910, pp. 707 ff.; 1912, p. 474; Sovani, pp. 257 ff.; Winternitz, GIL. iii. 446.

[4] Ed. TSS. 9, 1910. A *Tattvaprakāça* by Bhoja is ed. TSS. 68, 1920.

[5] Ed. *Pandit*, vi and vii. On all the sects, see Bhandarkar, *Vaiṣṇavism, Śaivism, &c.*; Carpenter, *Theism in Mediaeval India*.

include the *Kulacūḍāmaṇi Tantra*, the *Kulārṇava*, *Jñānārṇava*, *Tantrarāja*, *Mahānirvāṇa*, and so on. The Liṅgāyats of the south have a *Vīramaheçvara Tantra*. High claims have been raised for the cultural interest of these works, but there remains the essential fact that, so far as they contain philosophy, that is better given in other texts, and, so far as they are original, in addition to inculcating all sorts of magic practices they teach the doctrine of the eating of meat, the drinking of spirits, and promiscuous sexual intercourse, the deity being supposed to be present in the shape of the female devotee, as a means to the end of union with the highest principle of the system. In form also they lack attraction; the original texts seem to have been composed in rather barbarous Sanskrit, while the later are compilations badly arranged and collected. It is, however, true that the Tantric cult has had, and still possesses, an enormous power over the minds of Indians even in high ranks of society and of superior culture.[1]

5. *Logic and Atomism*

We may fairly find the impulse to logic[2] as given by the investigation of the Mīmāṅsā school; the term Nyāya suggests this conclusion, and it is entirely in accord with common sense, though of course it was a distinct act to advance to what may fairly be deemed logical science. Of the antiquity of logic we have no real knowledge; efforts to find it early in Buddhism are ruined by the lateness of Buddhist texts, and the attempts to ascribe the beginnings of the *Nyāya Sūtra*[3] to a Gotama (*c.* 500 B.C.), while the true Nyāya is ascribed to Akṣapāda (*c.* A.D. 150) rest on no adequate ground. Nor can we reach any result by the argument[4] that the commentator Vātsyāyana preceded the *Māṭhara Vṛtti* on the *Sāṁkhyakārikā*, and it the *Anuyogadvārasūtra* of the Jains, for, apart from the fact that

[1] See 'A. Avalon', *Principles of Tantra* (1914–16); *Mahānirvāṇa Tantra* (1913), and many other texts. Cf. Das Gupta, AMSJV. III. i. 253 ff.

[2] Keith, *Indian Logic and Atomism* (1921); S. C. Vidyabhusana, *History of Indian Logic* (1921); B. Faddegon, *The Vaiçeṣika System* (1918); G. Jhā in *Indian Thought* and POCP. 1919, ii. 281–5 (on original atheism of the Nyāya).

[3] Vidyabhusana, p. 47.

[4] A. B. Dhruva, POCP. 1919, ii. 264 ff. His argument is vitiated by reliance on the Jain texts as evidence for 300 B.C.

the Jain Sūtra is only as it stands authority for the fifth century at best, the *Māṭhara Vṛtti*, as we have it, is not an early text.[1] All that we really know is that the *Nyāya Sūtra* as it stands, a compilation no doubt representing earlier thought, takes cognizance of the nihilistic school of Buddhism, probably as it developed in the first century A.D. And even that result is uncertain. The *Vaiçeṣika Sūtra* is likewise of wholly uncertain date, though probably more or less contemporaneous with the *Nyāya*. If the Nyāya essentially gives us a logic, the Vaiçeṣika represents a naturalistic view which finds in atoms the basis of the material world, but both Sūtras accept in some measure the view of the other. Kaṇāda, the alleged author of the *Vaiçeṣika Sūtra*, is a mere nickname, and the Sūtra shows much unevenness of composition. The rise of the Vaiçeṣika has been ascribed to the second century B.C. on the score that it is attacked by Açvaghoṣa, and that it agrees in many points with the Jain philosophical views; thus it believes in the real activity of the soul, denied by the Vedānta of Çañkara, holds the effect to be different from the cause, the qualities from the substance, and accepts atoms. But this is quite inconclusive, and we cannot say even that the Vaiçeṣika ever was materialistic in the Lokāyata sense of deriving the soul from matter. The question of the original view of the two Sūtras as to God is disputed, but at least both say very little on the topic, and that little may be due to working over at the time when they had become definitely theistic schools.

The *Nyāya Sūtra* found an expositor in Pakṣilasvāmin Vātsyāyana, who wrote the *Nyāyabhāṣya*[2] before the Buddhist logical Dignāga. His work resembles in style the *Mahābhāṣya*, and he propounds modifications of the Sūtra in short sentences comparable to Vārttikas, but this is far from sufficient to justify us in assigning him to the second century B.C. The fourth century is more plausible, though a rather earlier date is not excluded. Uddyotakara Bhāradvāja, a fervent sectarian of the Pāçupata belief, in his *Nyāyavārttika*[3] defended Vātsyāyana and explained the Sūtra and Bhāṣya; his date falls *c.* A.D. 620. A further comment on this work was written by Vācaspati Miçra (*c.* 850) in

[1] See Keith, BSOS. iii. 551 ff.

[2] E. Windisch, *Uber das Nyâyabhâshya* (1888).

[3] Ed. BI. 1907.

the *Nyāyavārttikatātparyaṭīkā*,[1] on which Udayana in the tenth century wrote the *Tātparyapariçuddhi*.[2] Udayana, as a convinced theist, in his *Kusumāñjali*[3] in Kārikās with a prose explanation proved the existence of God, and in the *Bauddhadhikkāra*[4] assailed the Buddhists, who had developed an important school of thought which manifestly greatly influenced the Nyāya itself.

Dignāga, the chief of the early Buddhist logicians, lived probably before A.D. 400; writing the *Pramāṇasamuccaya*, *Nyāyapraveça*, and other texts, most of which are preserved only in translations.[5] Dharmakīrti attacked Uddyotakara in vindication of Dignāga in the seventh century, and his *Nyāyabindu*[6] has fortunately been preserved, with the comment of Dharmottara (*c.* 800) and the super-comment, *Nyāyabinduṭīkāṭippaṇī*,[7] of Mallavādin, probably written shortly afterwards. Much less important are the Jain works, of which Siddhasena Divākara's *Nyāyāvatāra*[8] is assigned dubiously to A.D. 533, while Māṇikya Nandin's *Parīkṣāmukhasūtra*,[9] on which Anantavīrya commented in the eleventh century, may be dated *c.* 800. Hemacandra (1088–1172) wrote a *Pramāṇamīmāṅsā* in Sūtra style. Polemical matter against these Buddhist, and in a minor degree Jain, comments is to be found in Jayanta's *Nyāyamañjarī*[10] (9th cent.), which comments on the Sūtras; Bhāsarvajña's *Nyāyasāra*[11] (*c.* 900), which shows a marked Çaiva tendency and embodies Vaiçeṣika doctrines; and Varadarāja's *Tārkikarakṣā*,[12] which knows Kumārila and was used in the *Sarvadarçanasaṁgraha* (*c.* 1350).

A definite step in the history of the Nyāya was marked by the appearance of Gañgeça's *Tattvacintāmaṇi*[13] (*c.* 1200) in four books, which expounds with much subtlety the means of proof permitted in the Nyāya, incidentally expounding the metaphysics of the school at the same time. Gañgeça was no mean philosopher, though it seems difficult to call his prose clear and

[1] Ed. VizSS. 12, 1898.
[2] Ed. BI. 1911–24.
[3] Ed. BI. 1888–95.
[4] Ed. Calcutta, 1849 and 1873, as *Ātmatattvaviveka*.
[5] S. C. Vidyabhusana, *Indian Logic*, pp. 27 ff. *Nyāyapraveça* is ed. Baroda, 1927.
[6] Ed. BI. 1889. On Dharmottara's date, Hultzsch, ZDMG. lxix. 278 f.
[7] Ed. BB. xi. 1909.
[8] Ed. Calcutta, 1908.
[9] Ed. BI. 1909.
[10] Ed. VizSS. 1895.
[11] Ed. BI. 1910.
[12] Ed. *Pandit*, N.S. xxi–xxv.
[13] Ed. BI. 1888–1901.

simple, though it is both compared to the diction of his commentators. These include his own son Vardhamāna, the dramatist Jayadeva, and, most famous of all, Raghunātha Çiromaṇi[1] (*c.* 1500), on whom Gadādhara commented (*c.* 1700), and Mathurānātha. This is scholasticism of the worst description, in which definitions alone were of interest, and it is regrettable that in the sixteenth century the Sanskrit schools of Navadvīpa formed the centre of intellectual life in the country, since but for their overloading of his doctrine Gañgeça's real merits might have been recognized more widely. In point of fact, from a rough system of argument from examples Indian logic rose to a developed and able scheme of inference based on universals, and the formation of universals it explained by a well-thought-out metaphysical theory. Buddhist logic, again, in the hands of Dignāga developed a doctrine of knowledge which certainly deserves careful study and which in certain aspects shows close affinity to the views of Kant, though the likeness has sometimes been exaggerated.

The *Vaiçeṣika Sūtra*[2] was far less fortunate; it was taken up and given new life by Praçastapāda in his *Padārthadharmasaṁgraha*,[3] which is not a comment on the Sūtra but a completely new exposition of the same subject-matter, with additions of importance. The date of the author depends on his relation to Dignāga, who seems to have influenced his logical views, so that he may be assigned to the fifth century A.D. A commentary on his work, the *Nyāyakandalī* of Çrīdhara, belongs to 991. We find in him the same view of theism and the addition of non-existence as a seventh to the six Vaiçeṣika categories—substance, quality, action, generality, particularity, Viçeṣa—whence the name of the system is usually derived, and inseparable relation. Udayana also wrote a comment, *Kiraṇāvalī*[4] on Praçastapāda's Bhāṣya, and an independent text, the *Lakṣaṇāvalī*.[5] It is clear that the Sūtra contains matter which was not before the commentators, and that they knew Sūtras which it does not notice. A formal comment on the Sūtra is that of Çañkara

[1] *Dīdhiti* ed. with the *Gādādharī*, ChSS. nos. 186, 187. For a specimen of scholasticism see S. Sen, *A Study on Mathurānātha's Tattvacintāmaṇirahasya* (1924).

[2] Ed. Candrakānta Tarkālaṁkāra, Calcutta, 1887; also BI. 1861; BenSS. 1885 ff.

[3] Ed. VizSS. 1895; trans. G. Jha, *Pandit*, N.S. xxv–xxxiv.

[4] Ed. in part BenSS.

[5] Ed. *Pandit*, N.S. xxi and xxii.

Miçra, the *Upaskāra*,[1] which dates from *c.* 1600 and is far from adequate.

As practical guides to the two schools serve a number of short handbooks which deal with the doctrines of both as a whole and present a fusion of the two traditions. One of the earliest of these is Çivāditya's *Saptapadārthī*,[2] which is earlier than Gaṅgeça; Keçava Miçra's *Tarkabhāṣā*[3] is variously assigned to the thirteenth or fourteenth century; Laugākṣi Bhāskara's *Tarkakaumudī*[4] is by the author of the *Arthasaṁgraha* on the Mīmāṅsā, and may be after 1400; Annam Bhaṭṭa, a native of southern India, wrote his *Tarkasaṁgraha*[5] with an important commentary before 1585, and the *Tarkāmṛta*[6] of Jagadīça falls *c.* 1700. The *Bhāṣāpariccheda*[7] of Viçvanātha is approximately dated by the fact that its author commented on the *Nyāya Sūtra* in 1634; the text is in 166 memorial verses, some of which are borrowed from older sources, as is seen from the fact that they are given also in Sureçvara's *Mānasollāsa*, where they doubtless represent borrowing from a contemporary text. In this period divergences of view between Vaiçeṣika and Nyāya had reduced themselves to very minor, not to say scholastic, points. The schools were now fully theistic, as had individual adherents been for a long time; Udayana, like Uddyotakara, was a Çaiva and identified God with Çiva, and the Buddhist writers Guṇaratna and Rājaçekhara report on the Çaiva affiliations of Nyāya and Vaiçeṣika sects in their time.

The interpretation of the physics of the Vaiçeṣika presents great difficulties, and it is extremely dubious if we are justified with modern scholars,[8] Indian and Western, in seeking to read recent results into the simple and rather rude concepts of the ancient text which the commentators did little to refine. Their interest was metaphysical, and it is not usual for science and philosophy to be effectively combined. The effort to show that the Vaiçeṣika system is at the base of Caraka's system of

[1] Ed. BI. 1861.
[2] Ed. A. Winter, Leipzig, 1893; trans. ZDMG. liii. 328 ff.
[3] Ed. S. M. Paranjape, Poona, 1909; trans. G. Jhā, IT. ii.
[4] Ed. M. N. Dvivedī, BSS. 32, 1886; trans. E. Hultzsch, ZDMG. lxi. 763 ff.
[5] Ed. BSS. 55, 1918; trans. E. Hultzsch, AGGW. ix. 5, 1907.
[6] Ed. Calcutta, 1880.
[7] Ed. BI. 1850; trans. E. Hultzsch, ZDMG. lxxiv. 145 ff.
[8] R. Stübe, *Ann. d. Naturphil.*, viii. 483 ff.

medicine, dating that system *c.* A. D. 80 and thence deducing the early date of the Vaiçeṣika, appears quite invalid, resting as it does on two errors, the belief that the system is vital to Caraka, and the assumption that the text of Caraka dates from the first century A. D. Still more absurd is the attempt to make out the school to be pre-Buddhist and to be derived from the Pūrvamīmāṅsā.

6. *The Sāṁkhya and Yoga Schools*

While the Vedānta is a direct descendant of the Upaniṣad discussions, and the systems of logic and atomism at least do not go out of their way to challenge orthodoxy, and ultimately adopt more and more the authority of scripture, the Sāṁkhya system in its original form unquestionably marks a break with tradition. But this is a very different thing from claiming that the philosophy is not derived by legitimate process of development from ideas found in the Upaniṣads. The issue eventually turns on the interpretation to be given to the fact that a number of Upaniṣads, in special the *Kaṭha,* present features which may either be regarded as a preliminary stage in the development to the Sāṁkhya or as the influence of an already existing Sāṁkhya on the Upaniṣads. The idea of an independent creation of thought, that of warriors as opposed to priests, is really fantastic, and there can be little doubt that the Sāṁkhya follows legitimately from certain Upaniṣad positions when they are fully developed. The absolute of the Upaniṣads tends to become meaningless, and the Sāṁkhya gets rid of it by postulating only an infinite number of spirits, while matter it similarly divorces from the absolute, ascribing to it the power of evolution; consciousness is explained by some form of contact between spirit and matter, and release is attained when the unreality of any connexion between the two is appreciated. This is undoubtedly an illogical and confused system, for in it spirit is meaningless, and its connexion with nature, being non-existent, cannot serve as the motive for bondage. Such confusion accords best with a derivative theory, not with original thought. The most important contribution to Indian thought made by the Sāṁkhya is the conception of three Guṇas, constituents rather than qualities, as pervading nature and man alike. Even for this view, however, we find a basis in the Upaniṣads, where water, fire, and earth appear as the three fundamental elements derived from the creator or pervaded by him.[1]

The date of the Sāṁkhya has been fixed by arguments based on the derivation of Buddhism from it, but we have rather to do with the derivation of Buddhism from the early doctrine of the Upaniṣads which ultimately gave also the Sāṁkhya, but in the case of Buddhism with far more conscious rejection of Vedic views. In any case, however, the date of the development of Buddhist doctrine is far too obscure to be of any real aid in fixing the date and the claim[2] that the Sāṁkhya represents a philosophy of 800–550 B.C. seems quite inadmissible.

All the early teachers of the Sāṁkhya appear in legendary guise; the reality of Kapila, the alleged founder of the system, has been abandoned by Jacobi; Āsuri is a mere name, and Pañcaçikha, of whom we have views, is quite uncertain in date. The epic presents us with some information as to the Sāṁkhya, though usually it gives a composite philosophy, but our first definite text is the *Sāṁkhyakārikā*[3] of Īçvarakṛṣṇa. From Buddhist sources we hear of an older contemporary of Vasubandhu (*c.* 320),[4] Vārṣagaṇya, who wrote a *Ṣaṣṭitantra* on the Sāṁkhya; his pupil Vindhyavāsa corrected his master's views in a set of seventy verses known as the Golden Seventy verses, which Vasubandhu criticized in his *Paramārthasaptati*. It is natural to identify Vindhyavāsa with Īçvarakṛṣṇa, and, though the identity is unproven, it is not improbable. Otherwise the only certain fact is that the Kārikā with a commentary was translated into Chinese by Paramārtha in A.D. 557–69, and therefore must have existed earlier. The view that the original of this comment exists in the recently discovered *Māṭhara Vṛtti* is certainly wrong.[5] We have, however, a derived version of this comment by Gauḍapāda, whose date is uncertain, as is his identity with the author of the *Gauḍapādīya Kārikā* on the Vedānta, who

[1] Keith, *The Sāṁkhya System* (2nd ed. 1924); *Religion and Philosophy of the Veda* (1925).

[2] Cf. Winternitz, GIL. iii. 450. The use of Caraka as an early Sāṁkhya source is quite unwarranted.

[3] Ed. BenSS. 1883; trans. J. Davies, London, 1881; P. Deussen, *Gesch. d. Phil.*, I. iii. 413 ff.

[4] N. Péri, BEFEO. xi. 311 ff.

[5] Keith, BSOS. iii. 551 f.

seems a man of much higher calibre. Of greater importance is Vācaspati Miçra's *Sāṁkhyatattvakaumudī*, in which he displays his usual impartiality and capacity of exposition. He cites a *Rājavārttika* of Raṇaraṅgamalla or Bhoja. The Kārikā itself is doubtless indebted to older works for its substance which is expressed in dry Āryā verses which exhibit, however, traces of the distinctive feature of Sāṁkhya exposition, the choice of happy illustrative examples, such as the similitude drawn between nature and the modest maiden who retires once she has been seen by spirit.

The *Sāṁkhya Sūtra*[1] is a late text; it is not used in the *Sarvadarçanasaṁgraha* and is commented on by Aniruddha (*c.* 1450). It may contain older matter, but the Sūtras given by Siddharṣi in the *Upamitibhavaprapañcā kathā* are not in it, and we do not know if he did not invent them, though that is not very likely. The system here is fully developed and scripture is invoked in support of it. Interesting is book iv in which we find brief references to illustrative stories; the comment explains these allusions; recognition of the distinction between spirit and matter comes by instruction as in the case of the king's son who, brought up by a Çabara, has the truth of his origin revealed to him and at once assumes the princely bearing and mien. So the forgetting of truth brings sorrow as in the case of the frog-maiden, who was married by a king on his promise never to let her see water; one day, unluckily, he forgot and let her have some when tired, with the result that he had to bear the pain of her return to her frog shape. In addition to Aniruddha's comment,[2] we have the curious work of Vijñānabhikṣu[3] in which, anticipating much modern opinion, he seeks to deal with the Sāṁkhya not as opposed to the Vedānta but as representing one aspect of the truth of that system. He also wrote the *Sāṁkhyasāra*,[4] a brief introduction to the topic, and his date is *c.* 1650. Before 1600 was written the catechism *Tattvasamāsa*,[5] which has been held to be an old text, but which at any rate is not of much philosophic importance.

[1] Ed. BI. 1865; trans. SHB. 11, 1912.
[2] Ed. and trans. R. Garbe, BI. 1888–92.
[3] Ed. R. Garbe, HOS. 2, 1895; trans. AKM. ix. 3, 1889.
[4] Ed. BI. 1865.
[5] Max Müller, *Six Systems*, pp. 224 ff.

Closely allied as a philosophy with the Sāṁkhya is the Yoga. In itself Yoga is merely the application of the will on the concentration of the mind, whence it denotes concentration, and, if the concentration aims at union with a deity as it may often have done, the sense may have come to be that of unity, the result being put for the effort. But primitively the object of Yoga was doubtless often to secure by practices of repression of the breath, sitting in certain postures and deep concentration, magic powers such as are believed throughout Indian thought to be the fruit of such exercises, for we find the same doctrine in Buddhism and Jainism. Yoga, therefore, in a sense can figure in all philosophies, but as a system it has been developed under Sāṁkhya influence, the only real difference being that the Yoga, as a result of the early connexion with the desire of finding union with a god, insists on finding a place for the deity as the twenty-sixth principle in addition to the twenty-five of the Sāṁkhya. This spirit is in constant connexion with subtle matter and possesses power, wisdom, and goodness. The Yoga thus figures as the theistic Sāṁkhya, while the Sāṁkhya appears as atheistic. Both systems in fusion with Vedānta ideas appear largely in the epic philosophy and again in the Purāṇas and the law-book of Manu.[1]

The *Yoga Sūtra*[2] is ascribed to Patañjali, and the similarity of name has led to the foolish identification of the philosopher with the author of the *Mahābhāṣya*. The Sūtra has been accused of being a mere patchwork of different treatises, and, though this is exaggerated, it is a confused text, which is only intelligible by the aid of the *Yogabhāṣya* ascribed to Vyāsa, who may or may not have accurately rendered the original sense, very probably moulding it to his own views. His date is probably before Māgha, but nothing certain can be said, save that the Bhāṣya is commented on by Vācaspati Miçra (*c.* 850) as well as by Vijñānabhikṣu,[3] while again the Bhāṣya mentions the mysterious

[1] P. Tuxen, *Yoga* (1911); J. W. Hauer, *Die Anfänge der Yogapraxis* (1922); Keith, *Religion and Philosophy of the Veda* (1925).

[2] Ed. with Vyāsa and Vācaspati, BSS. 46, 1892; trans. J. H. Woods, HOS. 17, 1914; Rāmaprasāda, SBH. 1910.

[3] Ed. *Pandit*, N.S. v and vi. His *Yogasārasaṁgraha* is ed. and trans. G. Jhā, Bombay, 1894.

Vārṣagaṇya. Bhoja is credited with the *Rājamārtaṇḍa*,[1] an important comment on the Sūtras. The work falls into four parts, dealing with the nature of concentration, the means towards it, the winning by it of supernormal powers, and the state of Kaivalya which results from complete concentration. The relation of the individual spirit to God is treated as part of the ethic of Yoga or Kriyāyoga. For information in detail regarding the practices followed to induce the trance condition desired we must refer to late works such as Svātmārāma Yogīndra's *Haṭhayogapradīpikā*[2] in which we find with some surprise the author, despite his style, indulging in *double entendres* of somewhat dubious character. Other texts are the *Gorakṣaçataka* and the *Gheraṇḍasaṁhitā*, of dubious age and authorship.

7. *Buddhism*

The use of Sanskrit in lieu of Prākrits or Pāli for texts defending Buddhist principles is of uncertain age. What is fairly clear is that the Mūlasarvāstivādins from the first period of their activity adopted Sanskrit as the language of the school, and we have fragments of their canon, from the *Udānavarga*, *Dharmapada*, *Ekottarāgama*, and *Madhyamāgama*, as well as the *Vinaya*, which point to derivation in some degree from texts similar to those represented in the Pāli canon. But the date of these Buddhist Sanskrit texts as extant is wholly uncertain, and has been placed as late as the third century A. D., which is probably too low.[3]

Much more important is the *Mahāvastu*,[4] a Vinaya text of the Lokottaravādin school of the Mahāsāñghikas, which presents us with a partial Buddha biography, combined with much miscellaneous matter, including many Jātaka stories of the Buddha in previous births. It reveals a new attitude in its account of the ten stages through which a Bodhisattva must move to achieve Buddhahood, in its insistence on the miraculous birth of

[1] Ed. and trans. R. Mitra, BI. 1883.

[2] Ed. and trans. Bombay, 1893.

[3] Cf. Oldenberg, ZDMG. lii. 654 ff.; and see Keith, *Buddhist Philosophy* (1923). Przyluski (*La légende de l'empereur Açoka*, pp. 166 ff.) holds that the literature began *c.* 150 B. C. contemporary with Menander and Patañjali in Mathurā.

[4] Ed E. Senart, Paris, 1882–97. See Oldenberg, GN. 1912, pp. 113 ff.

Bodhisattvas without parental intervention and on the great number of Buddhas, and in such episodes as the Buddhānusmṛti which is a panegyric of the Buddha in the usual Stotra form of the Kāvya literature. Its date is utterly uncertain, for its structure is complex, as is revealed by style and language; references to such late matters as Chinese speech and writing, a Horāpāṭhaka, and the Huns show that the final redaction need not have been before the fourth century A. D. The language is mixed Sanskrit, both in prose and verse, for verse frequently alternates with prose, versions of the same matter being given sometimes side by side in two accounts. The less good the Sanskrit, the older in many cases the passage, but no absolute criterion is possible. From the point of view of doctrine the work yields all but nothing of importance.

The *Lalitavistara*,[1] which also was originally of the Sarvāstivāda school, gives a biography of the Buddha which has been altered in the sense of the Mahāyāna development of Buddhism. The book is full of miracles, including the tales which have been asserted to have spread to the west of the falling down of the statues before the young child when he visited the temple, and of his explaining to the teacher the sixty-four kinds of writing, including those of the Chinese and the Huns. In style the work is as much of a patchwork as in substance. It is written in prose in Sanskrit with verse portions in mixed Sanskrit; these normally do not carry on the prose account, but run parallel with it, giving it in brief form. The ballads of this sort are often clearly old, as shown by comparison with the Pāli tradition as in the case of the Asita legend (vii), the Bimbisāra story (xvi), the dialogue between the Buddha and Māra (xviii), but the prose also is sometimes used in old matter, as in the version of the sermon at Benares (xxvi), while among the verse portions occur later work, where such elaborate metres as Çārdūlavikrīḍita and Vasantatilaka are used. The date of the text is quite uncertain; it was rendered into Tibetan in the ninth century and was well known to the artists of Boro Bodur in Java (850–900). Its spirit of reverence of the Buddha corresponds to the artistic revolution of the Gandhāran art which reveals the portrait of the Buddha,

[1] Ed. S. Lefmann, Halle, 1902–8; trans. F. Foucaux, AMG. vi and xix. See F. Weller, *Zum Lalitavistara* (1915).

whereas the older tradition of Sānchi and Bharhut showed symbols only of the blessed one, and the work may in the main belong to the period from the second century A. D.

Açvaghoṣa's works have already been considered in their aspects as epics and lyrics or as the application of the tale to moral and religious ends. The *Mahāyānaçraddhotpāda*,[1] if it be really his, is more simply philosophical and develops a very complex system of thought in which the influence of the Brahmanical absolute appears distinctly operative. Avadānas are numerous both individually and in collections; in addition to the *Avadānaçataka* and *Divyāvadāna*, already mentioned, there are the *Dvāviṅçatyavadāna*,[2] a collection of twenty-two tales in prose with verses inserted; the *Bhadrakalpāvadāna*,[3] thirty-four legends in verse; the *Vratāvadānamālā*,[4] a collection of legends to explain certain ritual vows; and in Kāvya style the *Avadānakalpalatā*[5] of the polymath Kṣemendra of Kashmir, the one hundred and eighth tale being added by his son Somendra, who also provides an introduction. As usual in Kṣemendra, his version is valuable for matter, not form.

Of the Mahāyāna Sūtras proper the *Saddharmapuṇḍarīka*[6] occupies the most prominent place. It displays throughout the ideal of the Bodhisattva and luxuriates in the glorification of the Buddha as a being of ineffable glory and might. It appears possible that originally it was written in mixed Sanskrit verses with short prose passages interspersed; but, as we have it, it is in prose with mixed Sanskrit verse sections in the older chapters, while in xxi–xxvi, in which the worship of Bodhisattvas is inculcated, we have prose only; the comparative lateness of these chapters is confirmed by the Chinese version made before 316, which has them out of place as appendices. The work as a whole need not date before A. D. 200 and is not likely to be much earlier. It contains, among other legends, the tale of the father[7] whose son lived as a beggar in his house but was enriched by his

[1] Trans. T. Suzuki, Chicago, 1900.

[2] Mitra, *Nep. Buddh. Lit.*, pp. 85 ff.; on the language, see Turner, JRAS. 1913, pp. 289 ff.

[3] Later than Kṣemendra acc. to S. d'Oldenburg, JRAS. 1893, pp. 331 ff.

[4] Mitra, *op. cit.*, pp. 102 ff., 221 ff., 275 ff.

[5] Ed. BI. 1888 ff.

[6] Ed. BB. x. 1908 ff.; trans. SBE. xxi.

[7] Cf. Poussin, *Bouddhisme*, pp. 317 ff.

father on his deathbed, a parable of how the Buddha gradually draws mankind to him, which has been unwisely compared with the biblical tale of the son who was lost and was found.

The Bodhisattva Avalokiteçvara, the subject of chapter xxiv of the *Saddharmapuṇḍarīka*, is also the hero of the *Avalokiteçvaraguṇakāraṇḍavyūha*, which exists in a prose version and a version in verse, which is, doubtless, the younger and which recognizes an Ādi Buddha or creator god. One form of the Sūtra was rendered into Chinese in A. D. 270, but the date of either of the extant texts is uncertain. It contains the story of the visit of Avalokiteçvara to the abode of the dead, which has been compared with the legend of Nikodemos whence it could, doubtless, have been derived. The paradise of Amitābha and himself are glorified in the *Sukhāvatīvyūha*,[1] which exists in a longer version and in a shorter, apparently derived from the longer text. The *Amitāyurdhyānasūtra*,[2] extant in a Chinese version, explains how by meditation on the god to attain this paradise; versions of the *Sukhāvatīvyūha* were made in China before A. D. 170 and the three texts are the foundation of two Japanese sects, the Jō-do-shū and Shin-shū. Another heaven, that of Padmottara, is described in the *Karuṇāpuṇḍarīka*,[3] rendered into Chinese before A. D. 6co. The worship of Mañjuçrī is recorded in the *Avataṅsakasūtra*[4] or *Gaṇḍavyūha*, rendered into Chinese by A. D. 420, and the chief work of the Ke-gon sect of Japan.

Of more philosophical content is the *Laṅkāvatārasūtra*[5] in which nihilistic and idealistic doctrines are found, but the work is useless for chronological conclusions, as it refers to the Guptas and to barbarians who succeed them, and so cannot have been composed as we have it before *c.* A. D. 600, though one version was made into Chinese in 443. The *Daçabhūmīçvara Mahāyānasūtra*[6] deals with the ten stages to Buddhahood, and was translated by 400. The *Samādhirāja*[7] deals with meditation. The *Suvarṇaprabhāsa*[8] again, though in high repute in Nepal, Tibet, and Mongolia, is a work of inferior type, including many

[1] Ed. Oxford, 1883; trans. SBE. xlix.
[2] Trans. SBE. xlix.
[3] Ed. Calcutta, 1898.
[4] Winternitz, GIL. ii. 242.
[5] Ed. Calcutta, 1900; London, 1925.
[6] Mitra, *Nep. Buddh. Lit.*, pp. 81 ff.
[7] Mitra, *op. cit.*, pp. 207–21.
[8] Ed. Calcutta, 1898.

Dhāraṇīs, spell formulae, and inclining to the nature of a Tantra; it was translated into Chinese in the sixth century. In the *Rāṣṭrapālaparipṛcchā*,[1] translated before 618, we find an interesting satire on the laxity of contemporary Buddhism, then waning in strength; the work is written in poor Sanskrit with verses in Prākrit and still worse Sanskrit.

The quintessence of the new doctrine is also given in the numerous *Prajñāpāramitās*, of which we have versions of from 700 to 100,000 Çlokas,[2] i. e. units of thirty-two syllables in length in prose. These merely assert that intelligence, the highest of the perfections, Pāramitās, of the Buddha consists in the recognition of the vacuity, Çūnyatā, of everything. The most famous is the *Vajracchedikā*,[3] diamond-cutter, which spread over Central Asia,[4] China, and Japan, in which it serves with the *Prajñāpāramitāhṛdaya* as the chief texts of the Shin-gon sect.

The views expressed in the *Prajñāpāramitās* are far better brought out in the *Mādhyamikasūtra*[5] of Nāgārjuna, who seems to have been a Brahmin, perhaps from southern India, who was converted to Buddhism. His nihilistic or negativistic doctrine accepts, as does the Vedanta, two truths, the higher which ends in the vacuity of all conceptions owing to self-contradiction, and the lower which allows for ordinary life. He may be placed as a later contemporary of Açvaghoṣa. His own comment exists in Tibetan, as do those of Buddhapālita and Bhāvaviveka; that of Candrakīrti of the seventh century A. D. is extant in Sanskrit. To Nāgārjuna are attributed also a *Dharmasaṁgraha*,[6] a collection of technical terms, and a *Suhṛllekha* extant in Tibet. Of Āryadeva we have already spoken.

The Vijñānavāda school is represented by Asaṅga's *Bodhisattvabhūmi*, part of the *Yogācārabhūmiçāstra*,[7] and the *Mahāyānasūtrālaṁkāra*[8] in verse with comment. His brother Vasubandhu wrote the *Gāthāsaṁgraha* and the *Abhidharmakoça*[9] of which

[1] Ed. L. Finot, BB. ii. 1901.
[2] Ed. BI. 1902 ff. Trans. before 405. *Aṣṭasāhasrikā*, BI. 1888.
[3] Ed. Oxford, 1881; trans. SBE. xlix.
[4] Leumann, *Zur nordarischen Sprache*, pp. 56 ff., 84 ff.
[5] Ed. de la Vallée Poussin, BB. iv. [6] Ed. Oxford, 1885.
[7] U. Wogihara, *Asaṅga's Bodhisattvabhūmi* (1908).
[8] Ed. and trans. S. Lévi, Paris, 1907–11.
[9] Trans. de la Vallée Poussin, 1918 ff.

we have Yaçomitra's Vyākhyā in Sanskrit, and which is one of the most important sources of our knowledge of the tenets of the Sarvāstivādin and other schools of the Hīnayāna. When converted to the Mahāyāna, he wrote many commentaries; one short poem in Kārikās has been rendered from Tibetan. His *Paramārthasaptati* is an attack on the Sāṁkhya system. Of Candragomin's many works we have only a poem, and Çāntideva is the author of a *Çikṣāsamuccaya*,[1] valuable for its large number of citations, written in prose, which shows none of the real ability of his *Bodhicaryāvatāra*.

The Stotras of Buddhism have already been mentioned; the Dhāraṇīs, spells of all kinds, appear to have been used early, for they occur in Chinese versions of the fourth century; sometimes they appear collected into groups as in the *Meghasūtra*. Even philosophic doctrines were condensed to this shape as in the *Prajñapāramitāhṛdayasūtra*[2] preserved since 609 in Japan. In such uses we are in full touch with ordinary Hinduism and still more is the case with the Tantras which either deal with ritual and ceremony or with Yoga. The former are innocuous, and are comparable with Hindu ritual treatises; of this kind is the *Ādikarmapradīpa*.[3] The latter include magic, eroticism, and mysticism in the usual Tantra manner; they include the *Kālacakra* which knows of Mecca; the *Mahākāla*, which teaches how to find hidden treasure, win a wife, make a foe mad, or kill him; the *Tathāgataguhyaka*, which enjoins even the eating of the flesh of elephants, horses, and dogs, and intercourse with Caṇḍāla girls; the *Mañjuçrīmūlatantra*, which prophesies the advent of Nāgārjuna, and the *Saṁvarodaya*, which is Çaiva in tone. To Nāgārjuna are actually attributed five of the six sections of the *Pañcakrama*,[4] but, as one is ascribed to Çākyamitra, who is probably to be dated *c.* A.D. 850, we may reject the identification with the great philosopher. The form of these works is as unsatisfactory as their contents, but it is idle to deny their influence; the Shin-gon sect in Japan rests on Tantras.

[1] Ed. C. Bendall, BB. i. 1902; trans. London, 1922.
[2] Ed. Oxford, 1884.
[3] de la Vallée Poussin, *Bouddhisme* (1898), pp. 177 ff.
[4] de la Vallée Poussin, *Études* (1896).

8. *Jainism*

Jaina philosophy, originally written in Prākrit, was driven by the advantage of Sanskrit to make use also of that language, and in the *Tattvārthādhigamasūtra*[1] of Umāsvāti we find in Sūtras and commentary a very careful summary of the system. His example was followed widely; Samantabhadra wrote in the seventh century the *Āptamīmāṅsā*[2] on which Akalaṅka commented; both were attacked by Kumārila and defended against him by Vidyānanda, in his comment on the *Āptamīmāṅsā*, and Prabhācandra, a Digambara whose tomb records his death by starvation, in his *Nyāyakumudacandrodaya* and *Prameyakamalamārtaṇḍa*. Çubhacandra's *Jñānārṇava*[3] belongs to *c.* 800. In the eighth century Haribhadra, a voluminous writer, produced his *Ṣaḍdarçanasamuccaya* and *Lokatattvanirṇaya*,[4] which are less specifically Jain than his *Yogadṛṣṭisamuccaya*, *Yogabindu*,[5] and *Dharmabindu*,[6] which gives a review of ethics for laymen, monks, and the blessings of Nirvāṇa. Hemacandra's *Yogaçāstra* and other works have already been recorded. To his *Vītarāgastuti* Malliṣeṇa in 1292 wrote a *Syādvādamañjarī*,[7] which is an important contribution to Jain philosophy. Āçādhara's *Dharmāmṛta* is ascribed to the thirteenth century; it is a full account of the whole subject, but his date precludes the assertion that he was a contemporary of the well-known poet Bilhaṇa. To Sakalakīrti in the fifteenth century we owe the *Tattvārthasāradīpikā*, which contains a full account of the Digambara sacred books, and the *Praçnottaropāsakācāra*, which, in the favourite form of question and answer, deals with the duties of laymen.

Other works are, though intended to inculcate the Jain faith, more vitally connected with branches of literature in the narrower sense of that term, and these, as in the case of Siddharṣi's *Upamitibhavaprapañcā kathā*, Amitagati's *Subhāṣitasaṁdoha* and

[1] Ed. BI. 1903–5; trans. H. Jacobi, ZDMG. lx. 287 ff., 372 ff., who places him before A. D. 600. The traditional date for this author in S. C. Vidyabhusana (*Indian Logic*, pp. 168 f.) is untenable. See H. von Glasenapp, *Der Jainismus* (1925).

[2] Cf. Fleet, EI. iv. 22 ff.

[3] Weber, *Berlin Catal.*, ii. 907 ff.

[4] Ed. and trans. L. Suali, GSAI. xviii. 263 ff.

[5] Ed. Bhavnagar, 1911.

[6] Ed. and trans. GSAI. xxi. 223 ff.

[7] Ed. Benares, 1900.

Dharmaparīkṣā, have been noted above. There must be mentioned numerous Caritras, legends of saints, some in Sanskrit, and even Purāṇas, including the *Harivañçapurāṇa* (784) of Jinasena, and the *Ādipurāṇa* of another Jinasena, whose pupil, Guṇabhadra, wrote the continuation, the *Uttarapurāṇa*, giving the lives of the Tīrthakaras after Ṛṣabha. A further continuation was made by Lokasena in 898. Much later is the *Çatruṁjayamāhātmya*, a panegyric of mount Çatruṁjaya, in fourteen cantos of epic style. The *Padmapurāṇa* of Raviṣeṇa is ascribed to *c.* A. D. 660.

The Jain contribution to philosophy, so far as it was original, lies in the effort to solve the contrast between what is abiding and what passes away by insisting that there is an abiding reality, which, however, is constantly enduring change, a doctrine which in logic is represented by the famous Syādvāda, which essentially consist of the assertion that in one sense something may be asserted, while in another it may be denied. But any serious development of metaphysics was prevented by the necessity of accepting as given the Jain traditional philosophy which could not be rationalized.

9. *Cārvākas or Lokāyatas*

Materialists existed, we need not doubt, in early India, though curiously enough efforts have been made [1] to explain away the Lokāyata philosophy, which is condemned by Buddhists and Brahmins alike, as simply in origin a popular philosophy of common sense. No books of these materialists have been allowed to come down to us, and we have merely summaries of their doctrines by their opponents, from which we learn that they endeavoured to prove the birth of spirit from matter by analogies from chemistry, and contended that as this was the origin of the body, so, when it dissolved in death, the spirit ceased to be. They, therefore, commended only the pleasures of the body, ridiculing the doctrine of the reward to be reaped in heaven by those who sacrifice and give presents to greedy and fraudulent priests whose Vedas and ceremonies they condemned as being merely tricky means of livelihood. We need not doubt that works were current, under the name of Bṛhaspati, who had an

[1] Jacobi, GGA. 1919, p. 22.

evil repute among the orthodox as the teacher of the Asuras, the demon foes of the gods, and from one or other of these may come the few phrases which can be ascribed more or less safely to the school.[1] The term Cārvāka applied to it may have been due to a teacher of that name, or be an abusive nickname from a famous infidel, not necessarily a member of the school. But the oblivion of its writings probably does not correspond at all to the actual importance it enjoyed.

10. *Historians of Philosophy*

A history of Indian philosophy was never attempted in India; the most that was achieved was the grouping of systems by reason of their similarities, and accounts of contending views based on the desire to prove by this means the superiority of some doctrine or other. The common view of six systems, grouped in pairs, Pūrvamīmāṅsā and Vedānta, Sāṁkhya and Yoga, and Nyāya and Vaiçeṣika, and treated as orthodox, because they accept the Veda as authoritative, is certainly not early, though a sketch of these six is found in Siddharṣi's *Upamitibhavaprapañcā kathā* (A.D. 906). Haribhadra's *Ṣaḍdarçanasamuccaya*,[2] of the eighth century, deals with Buddhist views, Nyāya, Sāṁkhya, Vaiçeṣika, and Pūrvamīmāṅsā as well as Jain metaphysics, and very shortly with the Cārvāka views; thus suggesting that the number six was traditional but not rigidly fixed in significance. In the *Sarvadarçanasiddhāntasaṁgraha*,[3] which is erroneously ascribed to Çaṅkara, we find accounts of the Lokāyatika, the Jain system, the Buddhist schools, Mādhyamikas, Yogācāras, Sautrāntikas, and Vaibhāṣikas, Vaiçeṣika, Nyāya, Pūrvamīmāṅsā—according to Prabhākara and Kumārila, Sāṁkhya, Patañjali, Vedavyāsa, that is the *Mahābhārata*, and Vedānta, which is the author's own view. The date is dubious, but the *Bhāgavata Purāṇa* is known while Rāmānuja is ignored, and the alleged[4] allusion to the Turks is uncertain. Later probably is the well-known *Sarvadarçanasaṁgraha*, which deals with

[1] Hillebrandt, *Festschrift Kuhn*, pp. 14 ff.; ERE. viii. 403 f.

[2] Ed. L. Suali, BI. 1905 ff.

[3] Ed. and trans. M. Raṅgācārya, Madras, 1910.

[4] Jacobi, DLZ. 1921, p. 724. Contrast Liebich, DLZ. 1922, pp. 100 f.

the systems arranged from the point of view of relative error. The Cārvākas are followed by the Buddhists, Jains, Rāmānuja—a very palpable hit at a rival school, various Çaiva schools, Vaiçeṣika, Nyāya, Pūrvamīmāṅsā, followed by a grammatical school ascribed to Pāṇini, Sāṁkhya, and Yoga. The chapter on Vedānta seems not to be part of the original work, but to have been added later, conceivably by the father of the author if we take him to be Mādhava,[1] son of Sāyaṇa, not his brother, though this view is only conjectural and to Sāyaṇa himself the work is sometimes attributed. The date is the fourteenth century, in the latter part. Of unknown author and date is the *Sarvamatasaṁgraha*,[2] which sets three Vedic schools against three non-Vedic, describes Jain, Buddhist, and materialist views, and then sets out Vaiçeṣika and Nyāya as Tarka; the theistic and atheistic Sāṁkhya; and Mīmāṅsā and Vedānta as Mīmāṅsā.

11. *Greece and Indian Philosophy*

Parallels between Indian and Greek philosophy are well worth drawing, but it may be doubted whether it is wise thence to proceed to deduce borrowing on either side. The parallelism of Vedānta and the Eleatics and Plato is worth notice, but it is no more than that, and the claim that Pythagoras learned his philosophic ideas from India though widely accepted rests on extremely weak foundations.[3] The attempt to prove a wide influence of the Sāṁkhya on Greece depends in part in the belief in the very early date of the Sāṁkhya, and if, as we have seen, this is dubious, it is impossible to assert that the possibility of influence on Herakleitos, Empedokles, Anaxagoras, Demokritos, and Epikuros is undeniable. But what is certain is that there is no such convincing similarity in any detail as to raise these speculations beyond the region of mere guesswork. An influence of Indian thought on the Gnostics[4] and Neoplatonists may be held to be more likely,

[1] Cf. R. Narasimhachar, IA. xlv. 1 ff., 17 ff. But this is not proved, and Sāyaṇa's son's name is Māyaṇa. The text is ed. Calcutta, 1908; ĀnSS. 51, 1906; Poona, 1924; trans. E. B. Cowell and A. E. Gough, London, 1894.

[2] Ed. TSS. 62, 1918.

[3] See Keith, *Religion and Philosophy of the Veda*, chap. xxix; JRAS. 1909, pp. 579 ff.

[4] Cf. Kennedy, JRAS. 1907, pp. 477 ff.; Legge, *Forerunners and Rivals of Christianity*, ii; I. Scheftelowitz, *Die Entstehung der manichäischen Religion* (1922);

and it would be unjust to rule it out of court. But it is essential to note that Neoplatonism is clearly a legitimate and natural development of Greek philosophy, and that what there is in it similar to Indian thought can be easily explained from Greek philosophy; striking similarity of detail is lacking, for what has been adduced is clearly far from convincing, and in part cannot be proved to have existed in India before it is found in Greece. The case of the Gnostics [1] is more obscure, and is complicated by the fact that in Persia Indian doctrine doubtless had considerable influence, but it is extremely difficult to assign to India views which may not have been originated in Persia or Asia Minor. It may be tempting to trace the doctrine of the Aion to the Brahmanical speculations regarding the year which is identified with Prajāpati, but ideas of this kind may just as well have been Iranian as Indian, and be part of the heritage of the Indians and Iranians. We reach, in fact, in such speculations a region in which really effective means of proof are wanting. Nor is it possible to say more in favour of the suggestions so often made to find in Greece the origin of Indian logic or strong influences on its development,[2] or again the source of the atomic doctrine which is accepted by the Jains and the Vaiçeṣika school. We may regard such influences as reasonable, but we must admit that real proof is wanting. If India borrowed, she had the power to give her indebtedness a distinctive character of its own, and a certain argument against indebtedness can be drawn from cases in which Indian borrowing is undoubted; the proof of it as regards astronomy and astrology is perfectly convincing, and we may doubt whether, if borrowing were real as regards philosophy, it would be so effectively concealed.

The effort, however, has been made with special emphasis in the case of Buddhist legends, as we find them both in Pāli and Sanskrit texts, to prove derivation of events in the gospels, including the apocryphal gospels from India. The argument is also supported by hagiographic legends, beyond all by the tale of Barlaam

Lévi, RHR. xxiii. 45 ff.; E. de Faye, *Gnostiques et Gnosticisme* (1925); Wesendonk, *Urmensch und Seele in d. iran. Überlieferung* (1925); L. Troja, *Die Dreizehn und die Zwölf im Traktat Pelliot* (1925); F. C. Burkitt, *The Religion of the Manichees* (1925); *Festgabe Garbe*, pp. 74-7.

[1] Cf. Weber, SBA. 1890, p. 925; on Basilides, Kennedy, JRAS. 1902, pp. 377 ff.

[2] Cf. S. C. Vidyabhusana, JRAS. 1918, pp. 469 ff.; *Indian Logic*, pp. 497 ff.

and Josaphat, for it is generally admitted that the Bodhisattva is the figure whence Josaphat is derived. But the parallel of the legends is clearly very small beyond the presence of this figure, and the late date of the story renders it extremely probable that India was only remotely concerned.[1] The figure of the Bodhisattva was most probably taken up by Persian thought in Mahomedan times, made into a typical Sufi, taken thence to Bagdad and Syria, where under Christian hands it was converted into a saint. Other cases are far less plausible;[2] the man-eating monster Christophoros cannot fairly be compared with the Bodhisattva-bearing Brahmadatta; the figures in their respective legends have little in common, and it becomes necessary to suppose that the idea was transferred through pictorial delineations misunderstood, while the Christophoros legend can be explained as a variant of the Märchen of the stronger—the effort to find out who is the strongest of all—and conjectural explanations of names. Similarly, the attempt to parallel the legend of Placidas who becomes the holy Eustachios as the outcome of pursuing a deer, loses and finds again his wife and children, by a combination of a Jātaka of a deer which brings about the conversion of a king, of a woman who lost her children, and the sufferings of the hero of the *Vessantara Jātaka* is clearly fallacious. The essential parts of the legends belong to the realm of myth or Märchen, and for borrowing there is no real evidence.

Nor is the case better with gospel narratives.[3] The birth of Christ from a virgin is not comparable with that of the Buddha, whose mother is never in early texts represented as a virgin, the miracles attending both his birth and death are commonplaces of the appearance of the great, be they divine or semihuman. Even the temptation by Māra is ethnic or Indo-European, as the temptation of Ahura by the evil spirit in Zoroastrianism shows.

[1] See Günter, *Buddha*, pp. 32 ff. Cf. Kuhn, *Barlaam and Joasaph* (1894).

[2] Günter, *op. cit.*, pp. 8 ff.; Kennedy, JRAS. 1917, pp. 213 ff., 504 ff.

[3] Günter, *op. cit.*, pp. 74 ff. Cf. Winternitz, GIL. ii. 277 ff.; Garbe, *Indien und das Christentum*; Kennedy, JRAS. 1917, pp. 508 ff., who argues for borrowing from the west, both as regards Buddha's youth and the young Kṛṣṇa, and makes out a plausible case, without proving it. For parallelism in the duration of gestation (ten months), the tree motif (Leto and Apollo), speech on birth (Zoroaster's laugh and Vergil's *Eclogue*), see Printz, ZDMG. lxxix. 119 ff. For the evidence of Art—Greek influence but later Indian reaction, see Foucher, *L'Art Gréco-Bouddhique*, ii. 564 ff., 787 ff.

The legend of the statues which in Egypt are broken before the young Christ is clearly a fulfilment of the prophecy of Isaiah; in the *Lalitavistara* they merely bow in respect, for the Buddha is not come to end the being of the gods, who are less than he, but not false. Similarly, the cleverness of the Child Christ and of the Buddha in explaining the alphabet is a common idea, and the treatment of the two by their teachers is quite unlike; that of the Buddha bows in respect before him, that of the Christ strikes him, and falls before him only because he is cursed by his charge. There is an equal discrepancy between the obedience of the beasts of the wild to the Christ Child and the Buddha's benevolence towards them; the distinction corresponds to a difference in psychology of the minds of the peoples. It is the parallelism of the human mind again that explains why the palm-tree bends on the journey to Egypt to feed Mary, and in the *Vessantara Jātaka* the hapless family is similarly nourished. The sleep of nature at the birth of the Buddha and of Christ is an old motif, that of the magic slumber which reappears in the whole cycle of tales of the sleeping beauty. Ethnic also are the seven steps of the young Buddha in the *Lalitavistara* and of the mother-to-be of Christ. The miracle of the loaves and fishes has been compared with the feeding of 500 monks by the Buddha, but these magic foods are commonplaces. The legend of Peter's walking on the water has a Buddhist parallel, but in this case the evidence in time is much in favour of the priority of the Christian tale. Similarly, the widow's mite is not paralleled until late in India, and there is very little real resemblance between the two versions of the son who was lost and was found. Great stress has been laid on the parallel between the legend of Simeon and that of Asita, but this seems quite unjustified; the divergences are great, and there seems something peculiarly natural in the conception in either case, testifying to the similarity of the human mind.[1] Still less can one take seriously the mere fact that the young Buddha was found in deep meditation while the young Christ stayed in the temple to talk to the teachers; the difference in the action is characteristic of the divergence of two civilizations.

[1] Cf. O. Wecker, *Christus und Buddha*, pp. 15 ff.; K. Beth, DLZ, 1915, p. 898. Kennedy (JRAS. 1917, pp. 523 ff.) holds that the Asita legend is later than the Christian.

Equally slight is the connexion between the declaration by a woman of Mary's blessedness and the similar assertion made of the mother of the Buddha, apart from the fact that the western tale is here far older, and, if an angel or spirit is to aid the Lord or the Buddha, it is purely natural that it should be when either is fasting. Similarly in the legends of Buddhist, Jain, and Brahmin saints and those of Christian holy men [1] there are constant parallelisms arising from the very nature of the ascetic life with its exaggerated virtues, its hatred of sin, and its constant absorption in the effort to avoid sin. We find thus instances of sudden and complete conversions; of evil men, like the robber Aṅgulimāla, who become most holy; of the efforts of women to seduce the saint; even of women who seek to lead as men the ascetic life; of selling oneself into slavery for the sake of others; of the sacrifice of an eye to stay the love of the flesh; of the conversion of a Brahmin by realization that the god to whom he was about to sacrifice could not even protect the destined victim, and so on. For coincidence in thought among different peoples great allowances must be made; between the Taoist Chuang Tse of the fourth century B. C. and Calderon and Shakespeare curious and illuminating coincidences have been pointed out, which cannot be accounted for by borrowing.[2]

[1] Cf. Günter, *op. cit.*, chap. ii.

[2] Cf. A. Forke, *Die indischen Märchen*, pp. 46 ff.; cf. Kennedy, JRAS. 1917, p. 216, n. 1.

XXVI

MEDICINE

1. *The Development of Indian Medicine*

WE have in the Vedic literature abundant evidence of the magic which precedes or accompanies in simple peoples the practice of medical art. The belief in demons of disease which dominates the *Atharvaveda* and the ritual text-books is preserved through Indian medicine, for one of its topics is the treatment of diseases derived from this source. Anatomy had begun to be studied,[1] possibly as a result of the constant slaughter of victims by the priests for the animal offering; we have also knowledge of Vedic ideas of embryology and hygiene. Late tradition recognizes the Āyurveda, also called Vaidyaçāstra, science of the doctor *par excellence*, as a Upāñga of the *Atharvaveda* and ascribes to it eight topics, major surgery, minor surgery, healing of disease, demonology, children's diseases, toxicology, elixirs, and aphrodisiacs. Patañjali proves the early cultivation of the science in Sanskrit by mentioning Vaidyaka along with the Añgas and Itihāsa, Purāṇa, and Vākovākya. Moreover, we have many names of ancient sages who gave instruction, Ātreya, Kāçyapa, Hārīta, Agniveça, and Bheḍa, but, though Saṁhitās occur attributed to these worthies, we can be reasonably certain that they are generally not original works. It is, indeed, probable, though not exactly proved, that in the earliest period of literary compositions on medicine works were styled Tantras or Kalpas and took the form of monographs on special topics and not of Saṁhitās, which are comprehensive treatises covering a wide range of topics. Ātreya is of these sages the one usually declared to have been the founder of the science, but Cāṇakya also is credited with writing on medicine.[2]

[1] *Çatapatha Brāhmaṇa*, x. 5. 4. 12; xii. 3. 2. 3 f.; *Atharvaveda*, x. 2. See J. Jolly, *Medicin* (1901); Girindranath Mukhopadhyay, *History of Indian Medicine and Surgical Instruments of the Hindus*, whose views are, however, often unacceptable.

[2] C. Zachariae, WZKM. xxviii. 206 f.; he is known to Arabic writers as Šānaq.

Buddhist tradition talks of Jīvaka, who studied under Ātreya and was an expert on children's diseases; the *Vinaya Piṭaka*[1] and other texts show a wide knowledge of elementary medicine, surgical instruments, the use of hot baths, and so forth. It was, of course, inevitable that living as they did in communities the Buddhists had early to consider the tendance of their sick members.[2]

2. *The Older Saṁhitās*

The oldest of the extant Saṁhitās is generally held to be that ascribed to Caraka, who according to tradition was the physician of Kaniṣka, whose wife he helped in a critical case. Unhappily we cannot tell the value of such stories when they come to us at a late date. Further, we know from the text itself[3] that it is not, as we have it, Caraka's work, for it was revised by one Dṛḍhabala, who admits to having added the last two chapters and to having written 17 out of 28 or 30 chapters of book vi. Dṛḍhabala, who was a Kashmirian, son of Kapilabala, is ascribed to the eighth or ninth century, and in addition to his more substantial work he revised and altered the text, which, moreover, has come down to us in a very unsatisfactory form. The work does not claim to be original; it appears to have been a revision of a number of Tantras on special topics written by Agniveça, pupil of Punarvasu Ātreya and fellow student of Bheḍa or Bhela, whose Saṁhitā is on that ground asserted by some to be older than that of Caraka. As we have it, part i, Sūtrasthāna, deals with remedies, diet, the duties of a doctor; ii, Nidānasthāna, is concerned with the eight chief diseases; iii, Vimānasthāna, with general pathology and medical studies; it contains a statement of the regulations laid down for the conduct of the newly fledged student: he is to give his whole energies to his work, even if his own life is at stake, never to do harm to a patient, never to entertain evil thoughts as to his wife or goods, to be grave and restrained in demeanour, to devote himself in word, thought, and deed to the healing of his charge, not to report outside affairs of the house, and to be careful to say nothing to a patient likely to

1 *Mahāvagga*, vi. 1–14; *Majjhimanikāya*, 101 and 105.

2 Cf. Takakusu, *I-tsing*, pp. 130 ff., 222 ff.; Jolly, ZDMG. lvi. 565 ff.

3 Trans. Calcutta, 1890–1911; often ed.

retard recovery. The Çārīrasthāna (iv) deals with anatomy and embryology; Indriyasthāna (v) with diagnosis and prognosis; Cikitsāsthāna (vi) with special therapy; and the Kalpa- and Siddhi-sthānas (vii and viii) with general therapy. Caraka, however, as we have him is more than an author on medicine; he gives us information of a considerable number of points of philosophy and develops a form of Sāṁkhya which has erroneously been regarded as old, whereas there is nothing to show that it is not a comparatively late addition to the text. He is familiar also with Nyāya and Vaiçeṣika views, which suggests no early date.[1] The form of the work is prose interspersed with verses, and it has no very ancient appearance, perhaps owing to the work of Dṛḍhabala. We know that it was rendered at a fairly early date into Persian, and that an Arabic translation was made *c.* 800.

Suçruta is equally famous with Caraka, and he is named with Atreya and Hārīta in the Bower Manuscript, while the *Mahābhārata*[2] represents him to be a son of Viçvāmitra, and Nāgārjuna[3] is credited with having worked over his text. Moreover, like Caraka, he won fame beyond India, for in the ninth and tenth centuries he was renowned both in Cambodia in the east and Arabia in the west. But his text also is not definitely assured until we have, as in the case of Caraka, the commentary of Cakrapāṇidatta in the eleventh century. We know of the older comments of Jaiyyaṭa and Gayadāsa, and Cakrapāṇidatta is supplemented by the comment of Ḍallana[4] of the thirteenth century. We have also a revised text of Suçruta prepared by Candraṭa on the basis of the commentary of Jaiyyata.[5]

The Saṁhitā begins with a Sūtrasthāna, which deals with general questions and makes out that Suçruta's teacher was king Divodāsa of Benares, an incorporation of Dhanvantari, physician of the gods. In Nidānasthāna (ii) pathology is developed;

[1] Dasgupta (*Ind. Phil.*, i. 280 ff.) seeks to prove Caraka early (*c.* A. D. 80), but, even if the contemporaneity with Kaniṣka asserted in China (Lévi, IA. xxxii. 282; WZKM. xi. 164) is real, the date of our text is dubious. On Dṛḍhabala see Hoernle, *Osteology*, p. 11; JRAS. 1908, pp. 997 ff.; 1909, pp. 857 ff.

[2] xiii. 4. 55.

[3] Cordier, *Récentes Découvertes*, p. 12.

[4] Ed. Calcutta, 1891. See Hoernle, JRAS. 1906, pp. 283 ff.; Jolly, ZDMG. lviii. 114 ff.; lx. 403 ff.

[5] Eggeling, IOC. i. 928. Trans. Calcutta, 1907–16.

Çārīrasthāna (iii) covers anatomy and embryology; Cikitsāsthāna (iv) therapeutics; Kalpasthāna (v), toxicology; and the Uttaratantra, which is clearly a later addition, supplements the work. The view of Hoernle[1] that even this later book is as old as Caraka and the *Bhela Saṁhitā* appears to be quite untenable, for it rests on his erroneous view that the anatomical views of Suçruta were known to the author of the *Çatapatha Brāhmaṇa*, a view which has been disproved.[2] It is of interest to note the high standard demanded from a doctor by Suçruta; the introduction of the student is based on the formal initiation of a youth as a member of the twice-born; he is made to circumambulate a fire, and a number of instructions are given to him, including purity of body and life; he is to wear a red garment—an idea with many parallels; his nails and hair are to be cut short; he is to treat as if they were his kith and kin, holy men, friends, neighbours, the widow and the orphan, the poor and travellers, but to deny his skill to hunters, bird-catchers, outcastes, and sinners.

The *Bhela Saṁhitā*[3] is preserved in a single, very defective manuscript. It contains the same divisions as the *Caraka Saṁhitā*, and what is preserved is mainly in Çlokas, with a limited amount of prose. Where comparison with the *Caraka Saṁhitā* is possible, there seems no doubt that the *Bhela*, which knows Suçruta, presents an inferior tradition. As regards osteology Hoernle[4] holds that a third version of the system of Ātreya, in addition to those of Caraka and Bhela, is to be found in the *Yājñavalkya* and *Viṣṇu Smṛtis* and the *Viṣṇudharmottara* and *Agni Purāṇas*, but the provenance of this list in *Yājñavalkya* must be regarded as uncertain in the extreme. Moreover, the conclusion drawn by Hoernle as to the original account of Ātreya and its relations to these later versions must be held to be vitiated by an excessive number of suggested corrections resting on modern knowledge of the true number and kinds of bones in the human body.[5]

[1] Hoernle, *Osteology*, pp. 8 ff.
[2] Keith, ZDMG. lxii. 136 ff.
[3] Ed. Calcutta, 1921; Hoernle, *op. cit.*, pp. 37 ff.; *Bower MS.*, pp. 54 ff.
[4] *Op. cit.*, pp. 40 ff.
[5] A *Kāçyapa Saṁhitā* is also known, of uncertain date; Haraprasād, *Report I*, p. 9. So there are *Hārīta* or *Ātreya*, and *Āçvīna* texts.

3. *The Medical Tracts in the Bower Manuscript*

We attain a certain measure of certainty as regards date in regard to the tracts on medicine which form part of the contents of the manuscript from Kashgar known by the name of its discoverer in 1890.[1] Palaeographically it can be referred with fair certainty to the fourth century A. D., and in the first of its seven[2] treatises one tract[3] deals with garlic (*laçuna*) and its valuable qualities for prolonging life; a second gives also a recipe for an elixir to secure a thousand years of life, and discusses eye-washes and eye-salves with many other topics. Another text (iii) gives fourteen recipes for external and internal application, while great importance attaches to the *Nāvanītaka* (ii), which by its title proclaims itself the cream of former treatises. Divided into sixteen sections it gives information regarding powders, decoctions, oils, elixirs, aphrodisiacs, and other recipes, including a treatise on children's diseases which often is cited and preserved in manuscript in varied forms. The treatises are written in verse, not seldom the more elaborate metres being used, and this peculiarity is preserved not rarely in later recipes. The advantage, it may be surmised, of this proceeding was that, as the syllables were fixed in number and length, it was possible to ensure in some measure the correctness of important recipes.

Among the authors cited are Ātreya, Kṣārapāṇi, Jātūkarṇa, Parāçara, Bheḍa, and Hārīta, all sons of Punarvasu Ātreya, but Caraka is not mentioned, though Suçruta's name occurs. This, however, is no evidence against use of the *Caraka Saṁhitā*, which may be regarded as certain, for Ātreya ranked as the teacher of Caraka, and the pupil, therefore, was covered by the teacher's name. The *Bhela Saṁhitā* is also used.

The language of the Bower Manuscript[4] is of a peculiar

[1] Hoernle, *The Bower Manuscript* (1914).

[2] Parts I–III are medical, IV and V on *Pāçakakevalī*, cubomancy, VI and VII *Mahāmāyurī Vidyārājñī*, a charm against snake-bite.

[3] Forty-three verses with eighteen or nineteen metres, including Aupacchandasika, Çārdūlavikrīḍita, Suvadanā, Pṛthvī, Vaṅçasthavila, Mandākrāntā, Pramāṇikā, Pramitākṣarā, Toṭaka, Sragdharā, Sudhā, Mālinī, Çālinī, Mattamayūra, Kusumitalatāvellitā. The other parts use few metres save the Çloka, Āryā, and Triṣṭubh forms.

[4] Prākritisms are rare in Parts I and III, very common in IV–VII.

character, being popular Sanskrit heavily affected by Prākritisms, suggesting comparison with the mixed dialect of Buddhist Sanskrit, which it may resemble in being an effort to write Sanskrit by persons used to writing in Prākrit. A barbarous Sanskrit is found also in medical formulae discovered in Eastern Turkestan, accompanied by a version in an Iranian dialect.[1] It must, of course, be remembered that doctors were often men of a restricted culture who could not be expected to be familiar with the niceties of Sanskrit, a phenomenon seen far more strongly in the works on architecture.

4. *Later Medical Works*

Indian tradition traces Vāgbhaṭa as the third of the great names of medical science, not without recognition that he is later than Suçruta. Two writers of this name must be distinguished, though both claim the same parentage in their works, the *Aṣṭāñgasaṁgraha*[2] and the *Aṣṭāñgahṛdayasaṁhitā*,[3] as we have them. The elder Vāgbhaṭa, Vṛddha Vāgbhaṭa, is son of Siṅhagupta, and grandson of Vāgbhaṭa, and his teacher was the Buddhist Avalokita. His work was clearly used by the younger writer, whose metrical form as contrasted with the prose mixed with verses of his predecessor confirms his later date. For the date of the elder writer we have a valuable hint in I-tsing's reference[4] to a man who shortly before had made a compendium of the eight topics of medicine; to identify him with Vāgbhaṭa, who was clearly a Buddhist, seems eminently reasonable. For Vāgbhaṭa we have also the Prākrit form Bāhaṭa, and for Siṅhagupta Sañghagupta. The younger writer was very possibly a descendant of the older, though we have no proof for such a conjecture beyond the fact that it might explain their confusion. His work was probably also that of a Buddhist; it was translated into Tibetan, and there seems no reason to put him more than a century after his elder namesake. Both agree in citing Caraka and Suçruta, including in his case the Uttaratantra.[5]

[1] Hoernle, *Bhandarkar Comm. Vol.*, pp. 416 ff.; cf. JRAS. 1925, pp. 110 f., 623 ff.

[2] Ed. Bombay, 1880.

[3] Ed. Bombay, 1891.

[4] Hoernle, JRAS. 1907, pp. 413 ff.; Keith, IOC. ii. 740.

[5] Cordier (JA. 1901, ii. 147 ff.) treats the two works as recensions of one original.

Of the eighth or ninth century is the *Rugviniçcaya*[1] of Mādhavakara, son of Indukara, which is an important treatise on pathology, of decisive importance on later Indian medicine. It is probable, if not proved, that Mādhava is older than Dṛḍhabala. The *Siddhiyoga*[2] or *Vṛndamādhava* of Vṛnda follows in its order of diseases that of the *Rugviniçcaya*, and provides prescriptions for curing a large number of ailments from fever to poisoning. The suggestion that Vṛnda is the true name of the author of the *Rugviniçcaya* is plausible, but unproved. Vṛnda is used largely in Cakrapāṇidatta's treatise on therapeutics, the *Cikitsāsārasaṁgraha* (*c.* 1060), and Mādhava and Suçruta in the work of the same name by Vañgasena, son of Gadādhara, of the eleventh or twelfth century. In 1224 Milhaṇa wrote at Delhi the *Cikitsāmṛta* in 2,500 verses. To a Nāgārjuna are ascribed a *Yogasāra* and *Yogaçataka*.[3] The Saṁhitā of Çārñgadhara was commented on by Vopadeva, son of the physician Keçava, and protégé of Hemādri (*c.* 1300), who also wrote a *Çataçlokī* on powders, pills, &c. Çārñgadhara provides for the use of opium and quicksilver and the use of the pulse in diagnosis, methods which have been referred to Persian or Arabic sources. Later works are numerous and expansive; especially favoured are Tīsata's *Cikitsākalikā* (14th cent.), Bhāva Miçra's *Bhāvaprakāça* (16th cent.), Lolimbarāja's *Vaidyajīvana* (17th cent.).[4] Numerous monographs on different kinds of diseases, including Surapāla's *Vṛkṣāyurveda* on plant diseases, are recorded, but none are early.

Historically important is the branch of Indian literature dealing with the merits of metallic preparations of which quicksilver (*raseçvara*) ranks first in importance. Quicksilver is attributed equal power over the body as over metals, and it serves as the philosopher's stone to transmute base metals while enormously increasing their bulk, an idea expressed in the *koṭivedhin rasa* of the *Rājataranginī*. Elixirs of this sort are deemed to give perpetual youth, life for a thousand years, invisibility, invulnerability, and other good things. The date of the earliest writings is

[1] Cf. Hoernle, *Osteology*, p. 14; JRAS. 1906, pp. 288 f.; 1908, p. 998; Vallauri, GSAI. xxvi. 253 ff.

[2] Ed. ĀnSS. 27, 1894.

[3] Cf. Haraprasād, *Report I*, pp. 9 f.; *Nepal Catal.*, p. xxii.

[4] An *Āyurvedasūtra* (*Bibl. Sansk.*, 61, Mysore) is a late revival of the old style; the 'considerable antiquity' of JRAS. 1925, p. 355, is clearly a mistake.

uncertain; the *Rasaratnākara*[1] of Nāgārjuna is assigned by Ray, but not on completely convincing grounds, to the seventh or eighth century. Alberūnī[2] (1030) derides the whole science of elixirs, Rasāyana, as worthless. The *Rasārṇava*[3] is assigned by its editor to *c.* 1200, and we have in the *Sarvadarçanasaṁgraha*[4] a fairly early proof of the love of alchemy in the account of the Raseçvaradarçana, the system of quicksilver. These adepts were Çaivas, but they were also convinced of the high importance attaching to the preservation of the body as a means to obtaining release in life, and the text cites passages from the *Rasārṇava*, *Rasahṛdaya*, and *Raseçvarasiddhānta*. The *Rasaratnasamuccaya*[5] is ascribed to Vāgbhaṭa in some texts, in others to Açvinīkumāra or Nityanātha; it has been assigned conjecturally to 1300. Nityanātha is author of the *Rasaratnākara*, while a *Rasendracintāmaṇi* by Rāmacandra is extant, and the Jain Merutuñga wrote a comment on a *Rasādhyāya*. The interest of these works is, however, entirely dependent on substance.

Medical dictionaries may be ancient; none of those preserved is old. The *Dhanvantari Nighaṇṭu*[6] may in principle be older than Amara, but it refers to quicksilver and, therefore, presumably is later than his—dubious—date, which indeed has been placed after Vāgbhaṭa on the score of his use of the term *jatru*.[7] The *Çabdapradīpa* was written for Bhīmapāla of Bengal by Sureçvara in 1075, while Narahari's *Rājanighaṇṭu*[8] dates from 1235–50, and Madanapāla's *Madanavinodanighaṇṭu*,[9] a comprehensive dictionary of materia medica, is as late as 1374. Works on terms of dietetics and cookery are also recorded, such as the *Pathyāpathyanighaṇṭu*.[10]

1 Ray, *History of Hindu Chemistry*, ii, Sanskrit Texts, p. 14. On the question of origin cf. chap. xxiii, § 3. The lateness of Arabic alchemy is proved by J. Ruska, *Arabische Alchemisten* (1924).

2 Sachau, *Alberuni's India*, i. 188 ff.

3 Ed. BI. 1908–10.

4 Chap. ix. On Govinda's *Rasahṛdaya*, in twenty-one chapters, see Haraprasād, *Nepal Catal.*, pp. xxii, 239 ff.

5 Ed. ĀnSS. 19, 1910; on the date cf. Jolly, *Festschrift Windisch*, p. 192, n. 1.

6 Ed. ĀnSS. 33. The *Sārottaranirghaṇṭa* of a Buddhist exists in a MS. of 1080; Haraprasād, *Report I*, p. 6.

7 Hoernle, JRAS. 1906, pp. 929 ff.

8 Ed. ĀnSS. 33.

9 Ed. Benares, 1875.

10 For descriptions of many later works cf. *Madras Catal.*, xxiii (1918) and the *I. O. Catal.* i. 973 ff.; ii. 750 ff.

5. *Greece and Indian Medicine*

The striking similarity in many points between the Greek and the Indian medical systems[1] has long been well known. We find in both such things as the doctrine of humours, whose derangement explains disease, the three stages of fever and other disorders which correspond to the Greek triad of ἀπεψία, πέψις, and κρίσις; the division of means of healing into hot and cold, or dry and oily; the healing of diseases by remedies of opposing character; the insistence in the manner of Hippokrates on prognosis; the oath exacted from doctors and the rules of etiquette and professional conduct declared to be incumbent on healers. There are also many detailed correspondences; both systems emphasize the influence of the seasons on health, and contrary to Indian feeling we have in some cases insistence on the use of strong drink as a remedy. Quotidian, tertian, and quartan fevers are noted, consumption is prominently dealt with, while little account comparatively is taken of affections of the heart. There are also similarities in regard to embryology; the doctrine of the simultaneous development of the members is held, the connexion of the male sex with the right side is noted, and a like cause is given for the production of twins; the viability of an eighth-month foetus is asserted, that of a seventh-month is denied; there is similarity in regard to the removal of a dead foetus. In surgery there is similarity in the operation for stone, in modes of dealing with haemorrhoids, in blood-letting, in the use of leeches, including according to Suçruta[2] those from Greece, cauteries, many surgical instruments, and the use of the left hand to deal with the right eye in ophthalmology. It must, however, be confessed that it is very difficult to determine how much is due to Greek influence and how much is merely parallel development. The doctrine of the three humours, which at first sight might be held to be definitely Greek, is in close connexion with the Sāṁkhya

[1] See Jolly, *Medicin*, pp. 17 f. with references. He deals also with Indian relations to Persia, China, &c. Cf. G. N. Banerjee, *Hellenism in Ancient India*, pp. 220 ff. For parallels in beliefs as to birth see Printz, ZDMG. lxxix. 119 ff.

[2] i. 13. The oath of the doctor in Caraka (ZDMG. xxvi. 448 f.) has often been compared with that in Hippokrates (iv. 629 ff.); Jones, *The Doctor's Oath* (1924).

system of the three Guṇas or constituents; moreover, one of the humours, wind, is already known in the *Atharvaveda*, and the *Kauçika Sūtra*[1] is alleged by the comment, perhaps with justification, to have recognized the doctrine of three, wind, bile, and phlegm.

On the other hand,[2] we must recognize that we have certain information that both Ktesias (*c.* 400 B.C.) and Megasthenes (*c.* 300 B.C.) visited or lived in northern India, and other facts can be adduced to suggest derivation, especially of surgical doctrine, from Greece. Whatever was the case with Hippokrates, there is no doubt of the prevalence of dissection of the human body in the Alexandrian schools of Herophilos and Erasistratos in the third century B.C., while in India we have no original passage in Caraka which admits of this, though Suçruta has two chapters on surgical instruments and one on the mode of operation. But there is difficulty in postulating Indian borrowing, because the Alexandrians developed such accurate knowledge, comparatively speaking, of the muscular and vascular systems that it is difficult to suppose that India, if it had borrowed its anatomy from Greece, would have been content to remain indifferent to the other advances made in Greece. The definite evidence of relation is rendered almost impracticable of attainment by the absence of any early Greek lists of the bones of the human body as reckoned in Greek surgery. Celsus, it has been noted, giving the Greek osteology of the first century B.C. speaks of the carpus and tarsus as consisting of many minute bones, the number of which is uncertain, but says that they present the appearance of a single, interiorly concave, bone, and in Suçruta and Caraka respectively we have the opposed views of a number of small bones and a single bone. Again, the Greek and the Indian views correspond in regarding the fingers and the toes as consisting each of three joints springing from the metacarpals. Against these facts Hoernle points out that, if a Talmudic summary can be regarded as representing Greek views, which is possible, there must have been a profound difference between the Greek and the Indian enumeration of bones in the body. Greece, of course, borrowed from India the use of several medicinal plants, but

[1] Bloomfield, SBE. xlii. 246, 483, 516 f.

[2] Cf. Hoernle, *Osteology*, pp. iii ff.

there is clearly no ground for the assumption of Indian influence in early days on Greek medicine. The disrepute of anatomy[1] acted as a fatal barrier to the progress of India in the field of surgery and hampered its success in the field of medicine.[2]

[1] In Vāgbhaṭa this is already clearly evident.

[2] On Greek medicine cf. R. O. Moon, *Hippocrates and his Successors* (1923); T. C. Albutt, *Greek Medicine in Rome* (1921); C. Singer, *Greek Biology and Greek Medicine* (1924). See also H. Fichner, *Die Medizin im Avesta* (1925); D. Campbell, *Arabian Medicine* (1926); E. G. Browne, *Arabian Medicine* (1921); Neuburger, *History of Medicine*, i. (1910).

XXVII

ASTRONOMY, ASTROLOGY, AND MATHEMATICS

1. *The Pre-scientific Period*

THERE is a definite breach of continuity in Indian thought on astronomy, with which astrology and mathematics are ever closely connected.[1] In the Vedic period we find extremely little sign of astronomical study; the year is vaguely reckoned, and the twenty-seven or twenty-eight Nakṣatras, moon stations, are of dubious origin. At the close of the Vedic period we have more elaborate works on the calendar evinced in Sūtra notices and summed up in the *Jyotiṣa Vedāñga*,[2] preserved in two versions, for the *Yajurveda* and the *Ṛgveda*; we find here a calendar arranged on the basis of a five-year Yuga, with a 366-day year, notices of the position of the sun and moon at the solstices, and at new and full moon with regard to the Nakṣatras. Some further development of a purely Indian type is found in the case of works like the *Gārgī Saṁhitā*, of which we have fragments, the astronomical hints of the *Vṛddha Gargasaṁhitā*, the fragment of Pauṣkarasādin preserved in the Weber MS., the *Nakṣatra* and other Pariçiṣṭas of the *Atharvaveda*, and the *Paitāmaha Siddhānta* recorded by Varāhamihira. The Jain texts, chiefly the *Sūryaprajñapti*,[3] though they develop a fantastic view of their own, are essentially of this type. The epic, the Purāṇas, the Smṛtis, and old writers such as Parāçara known from fragments are of the same type.

The characteristics of this period are a general ignorance of the mean motions of the sun and moon, resulting in faulty appreciation of the length of years and months; a total ignorance of the true motion as opposed to mean motion; the teaching of an equal daily increase or decrease of the length of the day; dividing

[1] See G. Thibaut, *Astronomie, Astrologie und Mathematik* (1899); Kaye, *Hindu Astronomy* (1924).

[2] Ed. A. Weber, ABA. 1862; *Pandit*, N.S. xxix.

[3] See Thibaut, JASB. xlix. 108 ff.

the sphere into twenty-seven or twenty-eight Nakṣatras; entertaining fantastic ideas of the constitution of the earth and the universe, and a determination on false premisses to work out large numerical calculations. All save the Jain texts assume that the winter solstice fell at the beginning of the Nakṣatra Dhaniṣṭhā, but this datum is quite insufficient to enable us to fix in any way the date of the works. They contribute to the scientific period two ideas of great importance, if of no value: the conception of great Yugas, during which a complete change of the heavenly bodies is carried out, so that a new Yuga begins with all of them in the same places as the preceding Yuga; and the conception of the lunar day, Tithi, which is a thirtieth part of a synodical month, a strange and not convenient unit.

In one sphere, however, distinctly interesting results were attained in geometry as a result of the care taken in the measurement of altars. These results are enshrined in the Çulbasūtras, works which are of the late Sūtra period, possibly of *c.* 200 B.C., though this is mere guesswork. They are concerned with the construction of squares and rectangles; the relation of the diagonal to the sides; the equivalence of rectangles and squares; and the construction of equivalent squares and circles. We find the Pythagorean problem stated generally, but there is nothing to show how far it was fully understood and what exactly was the Indian conception of the irrational. The question of influence on Pythagoras or influence of Greece or Egypt on India has been much discussed [1] without proving any dependence in either case. But in any event the theories of the Çulbasūtras for whatever reason had apparently no effect on the later progress of geometry.

2. *The Period of the Siddhāntas*

Varāhamihira, who is asserted to have died in A. D. 587, and who wrote perhaps *c.* 550, has preserved in his *Pañcasiddhāntikā* [2] information of the contents of five Siddhāntas of an earlier

[1] Cf. Keith, JRAS. 1910, pp. 519–21; Kaye, JRAS. 1910, pp. 749–60; Thibaut, *op. cit.*, p. 78.

[2] Ed. G. Thibaut and Sudhākara Dvivedī, Benares, 1889. See also M. P. Kharegat JBRAS. xix. 109 ff.; V. B. Ketkar, POCP. 1919, ii. 457 f., who argues that the *Sūrya Siddhānta's* fixation of the initial point of the ecliptic points to *c.* A. D. 290; cf. Bhandarkar, *Early History of India*, p. 69.

date. Of these the *Paitāmaha* belonged to the pre-scientific period, but the other four in various degrees showed a new spirit, which it is impossible not to ascribe to Greek influence, which displayed itself also indelibly in the case of astrology. It is significant in the extreme that two of these Siddhāntas bear non-Indian names, the *Romaka*, which must be connected with Rome, and the *Pauliça*, which reminds us of the name of Paulus Alexandrinus, of whom, however, we have preserved only an astrological treatise. The *Sūrya Siddhānta*, in the form in which we have it, asserts that it was revealed by Sūrya to Asura Maya in Romaka, which is significant. The *Romaka* adopts not the Indian Yuga system, but one of its own, namely the Metonic period of nineteen years multiplied by 150 which gives the smallest Yuga exactly divisible into integral numbers of lunar months and civil days. Further, it makes calculations for the meridian[1] of Yavanapura, city of the Greeks; and the *Pauliça*, which does not adopt a constant Yuga, but operates with specially constructed short periods of time, gives the difference in longitude between Yavanapura and Ujjain. The *Romaka* again alone of Indian works operates with the tropical revolutions of the sun and moon, while the *Sūrya Siddhānta* and probably even the *Pauliça* deal with sidereal revolutions. The *Sūrya*, it seems, shows us the process of adaptation of the new science to Indian ideas in its most pronounced state; thus it accepts the Kalpa system, while, on the other hand, it is more precise in doctrine than its rivals; it alone gives a general rule for the equation of the centre, and its full treatment of eclipses contrasts with the meagre rules of the *Romaka* and the rough formulae of the *Pauliça*. The mention of Romaka, of course, need not be interpreted as an allusion to Rome; it is due to the fame of the Roman Empire when the knowledge which came probably from Alexandria came to be associated with the name of the great metropolis.

The evidences of Greek derivation in the Siddhāntas, and still more plainly in later works, may be summed up as follows.[2] The division of the ecliptic into the Nakṣatras yields to that into the signs of the zodiac, with names borrowed from the Greek; the motions of the planets, hitherto neglected, come to be

[1] No doubt Alexandria. Kern, *Bṛhatsaṁhitā*, p. 54.

[2] Kaye, *Hindu Astronomy*, pp. 39 ff.

explained by the doctrine of epicycles; the notion of parallax and methods of calculating it were introduced; new methods of calculating eclipses appear; the heliacal rising and setting of heavenly bodies was studied, especially with astrological reference; correct measurements of day and night were achieved; the length of the year was revised; and the names of the planetary week-days were introduced. We find already in the *Pauliça*—perhaps also in the other Siddhāntas—an important contribution to Indian trigonometry, in the shape of a table of sines, which seems clearly to have been borrowed from Ptolemy's table of chords, the device being adopted of dividing the radius not into sixty parts with Ptolemy but into 120 parts, thus enabling the value given for the chords to be taken over bodily for the sines of half the angles. It is only in Āryabhaṭa that we find the radius as 3438′ with the necessary change of sine values.

The exact mode and date of the introduction of these Greek elements has been disputed, and Whitney [1] suggested that it fell in a period before the *Syntaxis* of Ptolemy, a view supported by the constant difference in detail as in the figures of the epicycles of the planets. The question is rendered specially obscure by the fact that we do not know how Greek astronomy progressed between Hipparchos and Ptolemy. It is true that Hipparchos already settled the theory of the sun and the moon and had discovered the mean periods of the revolutions of the planets, and it is conceivable that the *Romaka Siddhānta* may have contented itself with treating of sun and moon only, in accordance with the necessities of the calendar and the practice of the earlier Indian period. But Ptolemy claims to have been the first to take into account the anomalies in planetary motions dependent on the distance of the planet from the sun and its distance from the apsis. The *Vāsiṣṭha* and *Pauliça Siddhāntas* seem to have taken some note of planetary anomalies, though exactly what is uncertain. But apart from the similarity as regards sine values noted above, which is strongly in favour of use of Ptolemy's results, the position may best be explained on the basis of Thibaut's suggestion as to the means by which Ptolemy's views reached India. It is indeed incredible that Indian astronomers should

[1] JAOS. vi. 470 ff. Cf. Thibaut, *Pañchasiddhântikâ*, pp. li ff.; *Astronomie*, pp. 47 ff.

have deviated so largely and needlessly from his work, if they had real knowledge of it. But they probably learned their views from books of a very inferior type, the sort of manual used by astrologers and calendar makers, works which troubled not at all about the basis of their *résumés*, but simply gave results convenient for practical purposes. The Indian Siddhāntas, then, of the *Sūrya* type would represent not a mere borrowing nor an adaptation, but a combination and development on independent lines of elements borrowed in the shape of practical rules and vague hints of theory from mere manuals. The date of the borrowing cannot be determined with certainty. If, as is probable, the year 505 marks the date of Lāṭa, who commented on the *Romaka Siddhānta*, it is natural to place that text about A.D. 400 at latest, and, if we place the period of reception somewhere in the time between A.D. 300–500, we reach a plausible result, though not one admitting of strict proof. This accords with the period when the Gupta Empire was showing many signs of contact with the Roman Empire in other spheres of activity, and the Sassanian dynasty's rule may have promoted intercourse. But the old *Sūrya Siddhānta* shows us a specifically Indian reaction; it accepts where it thinks fit the new matter, but it fits it in as far as may be with the old; it revels in the theory of Kalpas, restores the pre-eminence of mount Meru at the north pole, finds room for the Nakṣatras, and so forth.

None of the Siddhāntas which Varāhamihira had before him has come down to us in its original form. We know that Bhaṭṭotpala had before him a *Pauliça* so changed as to render the retention of the same name anomalous. The *Paitāmaha Siddhānta* of Varāhamihira differed little from the pre-scientific period; it commenced, however, a Yuga in the third year of the Çaka epoch, which may give its date. It differed from the *Brahma Siddhānta* forming part of the *Viṣṇudharmottara Purāṇa* on which Brahmagupta's *Sphuṭa Brāhmasiddhānta* is on one view based, and from the *Brahma Siddhānta* or *Çākalya Siddhānta*,[1] all of which present the orthodox modern doctrines. The *Romaka Siddhānta* was perhaps touched up by Lāṭa *c.* A.D. 505, and certainly later was revised drastically in the modern sense by Çrīṣeṇa, who wrote after Lāṭa and before Brahmagupta. The

[1] Eggeling, IOC. i. 998 ff.

Vāsiṣṭha Siddhānta appears before Brahmagupta's time to have been revised by Vijayanandin and then by Viṣṇucandra, but the *Laghu Vāsiṣṭha Siddhānta*[1] which we have is clearly not connected with the original or the revision, and the *Vṛddha Vāsiṣṭha Siddhānta*,[2] which exists in manuscripts, seems equally far removed. The *Sūrya Siddhānta*[3] which we have in fourteen chapters of Çlokas, is clearly in many respects modernized from the original; possibly Lāṭa had a hand in this, as Alberūnī ascribes the work to him, and he commented on the *Romaka* and *Pauliça* texts.

3. *Āryabhaṭa and Later Astronomers*

Before the discovery of the *Pañcasiddhāntikā* the credit of introducing the new ideas into Indian astronomy was usually given to Āryabhaṭa of Kusumapura, who was born in A.D. 476 and wrote in 499. We have of him only the *Āryabhaṭīya*,[4] in the shape of 10 stanzas in Āryā verses; the *Daçagītikāsūtra*, in which he gives his numerical notation; and the *Āryāṣṭaçata*, 108 Āryās, divided into the *Gaṇita*, 33 stanzas on mathematics; *Kālakriyā*, 25 stanzas on measurement of time; and *Gola*, 50 stanzas on the sphere. His other works are lost; Alberūnī already could judge of him only by Brahmagupta's attacks. His fame in the light of our larger knowledge seems overdone, as he does not advance much beyond the old *Sūrya Siddhānta* and his views often agree with those of *Pauliça*, but he may have earned commendation by the brevity and elegance of his composition; moreover, his is the first work to show a distinct chapter on mathematics in relation to astronomy, and the division of astronomical topics may have seemed effective. It is, however, of very real interest that he held that the earth was a sphere and rotated on its axis; the idea was not approved by either Varāhamihira or Brahmagupta; if it were so, why can falcons return from the sky to their nests, and why are not flags always blown in one direction as a result of the motion? It is tempting to see here a borrowing by Āryabhaṭa from Greece, but obviously

[1] Ed. Benares, 1881.

[2] Eggeling, IOC. i. 991.

[3] Ed. BI. 1854-8 and 1909 ff.; trans. W. D. Whitney, JAOS. vi. 141 ff.; cf. S. B. Dīkshit, IA. xix. 45 ff.; for comm. IOC. i. 996 ff.; ii. 765 ff.

[4] Ed. H. Kern, Leiden, 1874. Cf. Kaye, JPASB. 1908, pp. 111 ff.

that is a mere guess. He did not believe, we learn, in the height of Meru, he equated the four Yugas despite traditional difference of length, and he ascribed eclipses not to the operation of Rāhu, but to the moon and the shadow of the earth, for which Brahmagupta severely censures him. From Āryabhaṭa a second writer of that name must be distinguished; he was known to Albērūnī and we have a work of considerable size, the *Ārya Siddhānta*,[1] which has been ascribed to *c.* 950, and which in its numerical notation differs entirely from Āryabhaṭa.

In addition to Lāṭa and Āryabhaṭa, Varāhamihira mentions Siṅha, Pradyumna, and Vijayanandin. His own work lay mainly in the field of astrology, but his *Pañcasiddhāntikā* is of very high historical importance, despite its obscurity through the corruption of the text and lack of old commentaries. Albērūnī thought well of him, and he shows common sense, as when he declines to accept conjunctions of planets as explaining eclipses. Much more important was Brahmagupta, born A.D. 598, son of Jiṣṇu of Bhillamalla near Multan, who wrote his *Brāhma Siddhānta*[2] or *Sphuṭa Siddhānta* in 628; as has been said, this is believed traditionally to be based on a section of the *Viṣṇudharmottara*, but it may be rather that that version is borrowed from Brahmagupta. In 665 he wrote the *Khaṇḍakhādyaka*,[3] a Karaṇa, that is, a practical treatise giving material in a convenient shape for astronomical calculations, but this was based on a lost work of Āryabhaṭa, who again agreed with the *Sūrya Siddhānta*. Brahmagupta is essentially on the same level as that text, but he is far more systematic and complete, and in chapter xi of the *Siddhānta* he attacks very severely Āryabhaṭa in a tone which called down upon him the just censure of Albērūnī. It is clear also that he was under the control of orthodoxy more than his predecessor, while, like him, he excelled in mathematics. One chapter of the *Siddhānta* he devotes to solving astronomical problems.

Later than Brahmagupta probably must be put Lalla, author of the *Çiṣyadhīvṛddhitantra*,[4] treatise to increase the pupil's

[1] Ed. Benares, 1910. Cf. Fleet, JRAS. 1911, pp. 788 ff.; 1912, pp. 459 ff.

[2] Ed. *Pandit*, N.S. xxiii and xxiv.

[3] Ed. Babuya Misra, Calcutta, 1925.

[4] Cf. Kern, *Ārvabhaṭīya*, p. vi.

intelligence, which was commented on by Bhāskara, though tradition makes him a pupil of Āryabhaṭa. To Bhōja is ascribed the *Rājamṛgāṅka*, a Karaṇa of 1042, and the *Bhāsvatī*,[1] a Karaṇa by Çatānanda, begins its reckoning from A.D. 1099. Far more important is the *Siddhāntaçiromaṇi*[2] of Bhāskarācārya, written in 1150. It falls into four parts, the *Līlāvatī* and *Bījagaṇita*, containing the mathematical part of his work, and the *Grahagaṇita* and *Gola*, chapters giving astronomy proper. In the *Gola* there is a section on astronomical problems, a treatise on astronomical instruments, and a description of the seasons. His *Karaṇakutūhala*[3] dates from 1178. His attitude is that of the *Sūrya Siddhānta* and Brahmagupta, but he is clear and precise, while his commentary on his Āryā stanzas has the merit of making his ambiguous phrases intelligible. After Bhāskara no progress can be recorded in Indian astronomy, though there were written popular works like the tables of Makaranda (1478), *Tithyādipattra*, or the *Grahalāghava* of Gaṇeça, son of Keçava, who wrote in 1520. The advent of Persian and Arabic influences has left Indian astronomy unchanged, nor has it ever been extinguished by western science.

4. *Āryabhaṭa and later Mathematicians*

Āryabhaṭa, as we have seen, was the first to insert a definitely mathematical[4] section in his astronomy. He deals in it with evolution and involution, area and volumes; then, after a semi-astronomical section dealing with the circle, shadow problems, &c., he proceeds to progressions and algebraic identities. The rest of the *Gaṇita* deals with examples, save at the close when indeterminate equations of the first degree are taken up ($ax + by = c$). We find also a remarkably accurate value[5] of π, viz. 3·1416, and the rule known as the epanthem,[6] and the type of definition not otherwise in use in India, 'The product of three equal numbers is a cube and it also has twelve edges.' On the other hand, we must set clear errors in the volume of

[1] Ed. Benares, 1883. [2] Ed. Benares, 1866; M. Jhā, *Pandit*, N.S. xxx–xxxiii.

[3] Ed. Benares, 1881.

[4] See Kaye, *Indian Mathematics* (1915); *Scientia*, xxv. 1 ff.

[5] The epic value is 3·5; Hopkins, JAOS. xxiii. 154 f.

[6] It is known to Thymaridas (A. D. 380) and Iamblichos (350).

a pyramid and a sphere. His notation[1] is unique; it uses the consonants *k* to *m* for 1 to 25, the rest, *y* to *h*, for 30 to 100, while the vowels denote multiplication by powers of 100, *a* being 100^0 and *au* 100^{16}.

Brahmagupta's work covers very briefly the ordinary arithmetical operations, square and cube roots, rule of three, interest, progressions, geometry, including treatment of the rational right-angled triangle and the elements of the circle, elementary mensuration of solids, shadow problems, negative and positive quantities, cipher, surds, simple algebraic identities, indeterminate equations of the first and second degrees, in considerable detail, and simple equations of the first and second degrees which are briefly treated. Special attention is given to cyclic quadrilaterals. Later, in the ninth century under the Rāṣṭrakūṭa king Amoghavarṣa, we have the *Gaṇitasārasaṁgraha*[2] of Mahāvīrācarya, which insists on the importance of its subject for every kind of science from cooking to logic, and adapts in its exposition the elegance which is later still further affected by Bhāskara. The work is fuller but rather more elementary than that of Brahmagupta; it gives many examples of solutions of indeterminates, but not the 'cyclic method' of Brahmagupta; it introduces geometrical progressions and alone deals, inaccurately, with ellipses, but has no formal algebra. Çrīdhara, born 991, in his *Triçatī*[3] is much on the same level as Mahāvīra, but is cited as having dealt with quadratic equations. On Çrīdhara's work and those of Brahmagupta and a certain Padmanābha was based the *Līlāvatī*[4] of Bhāskara, in which a lovely maiden is addressed, and problems set to her; it includes combinations, while the *Bījagaṇita*, which agrees largely with Brahmagupta, is the fullest and most systematic account of Indian algebra. With Bhāskara ends the active period of Indian mathematics; a school to study his work was founded in 1205 by Cañgadeva, his grandson,[5] but its interest seems to have been given to astrology. Of dubious age is the mathematical manuscript known as the Bakhshālī

[1] Cf. Fleet, JRAS. 1911, pp. 109 ff.; IHQ. iii. 116.

[2] Ed. and trans. M. Rañgācārya, Madras, 1912.

[3] See N. Rāmānujācārya, *Bibl. Math.*, 1913, pp. 203 ff.

[4] See H. T. Colebrooke, *Algebra* (1817); his trans. is ed. H. Ch. Banerji, Calcutta, 1893. Cf. Brockhaus, BSGW. 1852, pp. 1–46.

[5] See EI. i. 338 ff.

manuscript,[1] from its place of discovery in Peshāwar. It is written in Sūtra style with examples in Çlokas, taken from daily life, and explanations in prose. The mixed Sanskrit in which it is written induced Hoernle to ascribe the work to the third or fourth century A.D., and the manuscript on palaeographic grounds was ascribed by him to the eighth or ninth century, but these conclusions are far from being certain, and the work may date much later.

5. *Greece and Indian Mathematics*

The relation of India to Greek mathematics in this period is one of complexity and difficulty, and it cannot be disposed of by insisting on the indebtedness of India to Greece in respect either of astronomy or astrology, for in both cases the exact extent of that influence is obscure.[2] The question is obscured also by the fact that we have lost the works of Hypatia, murdered in 415 by the Alexandrian mob, and therefore cannot trace the progress of mathematics after Diophantos (*c.* 260). The visit of the philosophers expelled from the schools of Philosophy in Athens in 530 to the court of Chosrau of Persia in 532 was brief, and it is not much use speculating on its possibilities, though Damaskios and Simplikios, who had some repute in mathematics, were among those involved. The facts are that, as regards indeterminate equations, the Greeks by the fourth century had achieved rational solutions, not necessarily integral, of equations of the first and second degree and of some cases of the third degree. The Indian records go distinctly beyond this. Brahmagupta shows a complete grasp of the integral solution of $ax \pm by = c$, and he indicates one method, called by Bhāskara the method by composition, of the solution of $Du^2 + 1 = t^2$. Bhāskara adds the cyclic method, as he calls it, and the combination of these two methods, which gives integral solutions, has been styled by

[1] Hoernle, OC. VII, i. 128 ff.; IA. xvii. 33 ff. Contrast Kaye, JPASB. 1907, pp. 498 ff.; 1912, pp. 349 ff.

[2] Kaye (*Hindu Mathematics*) goes rather far in his claims for Greece. Contrast D. E. Smith in Raṅgācārya's *Gaṇitasārasaṁgraha*, pp. xxi ff. For older views see Hankel, *Gesch. der Math.* (1874), pp. 172 ff.; Cantor, *Gesch. der Math.*, i. 505 ff.; M. Simon, *Gesch. der Math.* (1909). See also J. L. Heiberg, *Mathematics and Physical Science in Classical Antiquity* (1922); D. E. Smith, *Hist. of Mathematics* (1925); Peet, *The Rhind Mathematical Papyrus* (1923); Heath, *Hist.* (1921).

Hankel the finest thing achieved in the theory of numbers before Lagrange. To find an ultimate Greek origin for these discoveries seems due rather to a *parti pris* than to justice.

Another point on which special interest in India was centred was the question of obtaining integral solutions in the case of the rational right-angled triangle. The results achieved there are interesting and may be compared with similar work, not by any means identical, of Euclid and Diophantos, as well as solutions ascribed to Plato by Proclus. Brahmagupta, Mahāvīra, and Bhāskara all contribute to the topic, and the former first states certain historically interesting problems; the sum of the sides is 40 and area 60; the sum of the sides is 56 and the product 7×600; the area is numerically equal to the hypotenuse; or to the product of the sides. Brahmagupta further did important work on cyclic quadrilaterals, achieving as one of his results his theorem: $x^2 = (ad+bc)\ (ac+bd) / (ab+cd)$, and $y^2 = (ab+cd)\ (ac+bd) / (ad+bc)$, where x and y are the diagonals of the cyclic quadrilateral, a, b, c, d. Mahāvīra and Çrīdhara repeat some of his matter, but their commentators show ignorance of the principle, and Bhāskara severely condemns both him who puts such a question and him who answers it. It is interesting, but by no means a proof of borrowing, that a commentator on Brahmagupta constructs from triangles new triangles and actually uses the same examples as Diophantos. Nor can we draw any definite conclusion from the fact that Indian mathematics in regard to geometry shows an absence of definitions, does not deal with angles nor mention parallels, nor give a theory of proportion, while traditional inaccuracies are common and knowledge is in the later period steadily declining. The same facts are seen in Greek geometry from A.D. 300, and possibly we can best understand Indian facts as indicating borrowings from such a decadent school, but there is no cogency in the contention.

The independence and originality of Indian mathematics have been defended on the score that the love of dealing with large numbers and making calculations is recorded early for India, where it is alleged the abacus[1] was invented, and that the numerals of the west are borrowed from India, where the place

[1] *Contra*, Kaye, JPASB. 1908, pp. 293 ff., but see Fleet, JRAS. 1911, pp. 121, 518 ff. Cf. IHQ. iii. 357 ff.

value system[1] was introduced. The abacus, on the other hand, is asserted to be of comparatively modern date, and it has been suggested that India borrowed it from Greece. The question of numbers is very dubious; the figures of the Brāhmī or Kharoṣṭhī notation have not place value, but their origin is uncertain. India knows, beside the unique system of Āryabhaṭa, the use of words for numbers, and place value is actually found in inscriptions from the ninth century onwards, but its earliest occurrence on an inscription of 595 is doubted, though the *Yogabhāṣya* clearly knows it, as did Āryabhaṭa and Varāhamihira.[2] But there is considerable antiquity for the tradition of the borrowing; the Indian figures were known in Syria in A. D. 662, and Mascūdi ascribes the origin to a congress of sages gathered together by king Brahma. The probability still remains that India did render a great service in this regard, and in any case excelled Greece. It is, of course, perfectly possible, and in view of the facts as regards astronomy and astrology not at all unlikely, that India borrowed its impulse to mathematics from Greece in the shape of those manuals whence she borrowed her astronomy, and this is certainly supported by the fact of Āryabhaṭa's evaluation of π, which is also ascribed to Puliça, and it was known to Apollonios and Ptolemy.

Recently the claim of India to have inspired Arabic mathematics has also been attacked, on the score that Muhammad ibn Mūsā (782) in his Algebra is not, as was long believed, really under Indian but under Greek influence, and a good case seems to have been made against any substantial importance of India in this regard; but there seems equally slight ground for the counterclaim that India borrowed after Brahmagupta from Arab mathematics at least in the period up to Bhāskara. But it must be remembered that Arabian science from A.D. 771 borrowed freely from Indian astronomy,[3] translating and adapting both Āryabhaṭa and Brahmagupta, so that, if we hold that Arabia was independent in mathematics of India, we must recognize that

[1] See Kaye, JPASB. 1907, pp. 475 ff.; Bubnow, *Arithmetische Selbständigkeit der europäischen Kultur* (1914); *contra*, D. E. Smith and L. C. Karpinski, *The Hindu Arabic Numerals* (1911); Nau, JA. sér. 10, xvi. 225-7; C. de Vaux, *Scientia*, 1917, pp. 273 f.; Sukumar Ranjan Das, IHQ. iii. 100 ff., 356 ff.

[2] Woods, HOS. xvii. 216.

[3] Nallino, ERE. xii. 95.

borrowing of astronomy or astrology must not be adduced as conclusive for borrowing of mathematics. Coincidences with Chinese[1] mathematics are numerous and interesting, and it has, of course, long been urged that China invented the system of Nakṣatras found in early Indian astronomy,[2] but at present at least the case for dependence on China is not made out, and Indian influence on China is proved sufficiently by the history of Chinese Buddhism and the discoveries in Central Asia.

6. *Varāhamihira and early Astrologers*

That the celestial bodies exercise influence on the fate of men, and that the future can be foretold from their aspect, is a very early belief in India, whether we believe it appeared there independently or was borrowed from Babylon. In the Brāhmaṇas and the Sūtras we find recognition of the idea of a lucky star, and the Dharmasūtras demand that the king shall have an astrologer just as he has a house chaplain, while the *Arthaçāstra* ranks court bards, the servants of the chaplain, and astrologers among the lower court functionaries. In war an astrologer is essential to foretell the result from the signs, and to encourage the army and terrify the foe. On the other side, we have the fact that, like a magician, an astrologer may be ritually impure, and the Buddhists denounce the occupation as they do many others.

We need not doubt that text-books of astrology were numerous, and in fact Varāhamihira, whose great work caused all the older texts to disappear, mentions Asita Devala, Garga, Vṛddha Garga, Nārada, and Parāçara among authorities. We have possibly genuine fragments of these works, but the most considerable are those of the *Vṛddha Garga Saṁhitā*, or *Gārgī Saṁhitā*,[3] which is well known for containing in pseudo-prophetic form some allusions to Greek rule in India. That it existed as early as the first century B.C. is a mere guess. It is important,

[1] See Yoshio Mikami, *Development of Mathematics in China and Japan* (1913); Kaye, *Indian Mathematics*, pp. 37-41; Smith, *Hist.*, i. 22 ff., 138 ff., 148 ff.

[2] Cf. Oldenberg, GN. 1909, pp. 544 ff.

[3] The relation of these texts is uncertain; Kern, *Bṛhatsaṁhitā*, pp. 33 ff. The astronomical data of the *Gārgī* are given by Weber, ABA. 1862, pp. 33 ff., 40 ff.; IS. ix. 460 ff. Garga is reputed the author of the Atharvan Pariçiṣṭas, li, lxii, lxiv. In the Weber MS. (JASB. lxii. 9) is a fragment of Pauṣkarasādin on astronomy.

however, for its definite assertion that the Greeks are barbarians,[1] yet among them the science of astrology was well established and those who knew it were honoured like seers; how much more so then a Brahman skilled in it?

Varāhamihira himself divides the science of Jyotis into three branches. The first, the astronomical and mathematical foundations, is called Tantra; the next, Horā, deals with horoscopes, and its name is obviously Greek; the third, Saṁhitā, covers the sphere of natural astrology. His own work on astronomy has been mentioned, but, valuable as it is, it is much less important than his *Bṛhatsaṁhitā*,[2] in which he shows himself a master of the learning of his day in wide fields of knowledge, and thoroughly skilled in language and metre, not at times without a real touch of poetic ability. The scope of the text is ample. After insisting on the importance of knowledge of astrology, he deals with the effects of the movements of the sun, of the changes of the moon, its conjunction with the planets and eclipses. Then he takes up the several constellations and describes their powers over the fate of man. Incidentally we have in chapter xiv an interesting sketch of Indian geography, and we learn what lands, people, and things stand under the aegis of each planet; the planetary movements also determine the wars of kings, and each year owes its fortune or mishap to the planet which presides over it. We are told also of the signs of weather, and how to foretell not merely the crop but the rise and fall of prices. The festival of the raising of Indra's banner (xliii) is poetically described and is followed by further religious matter. The importance of the astrologer in connexion with architecture, the digging of tanks, the laying out of gardens, and the making of images leads to valuable chapters on these topics (liii-lx). Then comes a description of the specific characteristics of oxen, dogs, cocks, tortoises, horses, elephants, man, woman, parasols, &c. (lxi-lxxiii). A praise of women, which is worthy of an anthology, occupies chapter lxxiv, and is followed by a section on the life of the harem, which shows affinity with the *Kāmasūtra* and *Arthaçāstra*. Couches and seats come next (lxxix), then jewels[3]

[1] Cf. *Bṛhatsaṁhitā*, ii. 15.

[2] Ed. H. Kern, BI. 1865; VizSS. 1895-7; trans. C. Iyer, Madura, 1884.

[3] Ed. and trans. L. Finot, *Les lapidaires indiens*, pp. 59 ff.

(lxxx–lxxxiii); short chapters deal with lamps and tooth sticks; then a long Çākuna, on augury, fills eleven chapters; of the rest, two chapters (c and ciii) deal with marriage, while cvi is a finale, followed by an index. The question of marriage is also taken up in the *Bṛhad Vivāhapaṭala* and the *Svalpa Vivāhapaṭala* of the author, while he deals with the wars of kings in his *Yogayātrā*,[1] marching out under favouring combinations, which exists also in two forms, in the first part of it he resumes the question of the relation of king and astrologer touched on in the *Bṛhatsaṁhitā*, insisting that the king has a part to play as well as the astrologer. In these works, as in the *Bṛhatsaṁhitā*, we have no reason to see anything but a development of the ideas prevalent in India itself.

7. *Greece and Indian Astrology*

The case, however, is clearly different with the *Horā* section of astrology on which Varāhamihira has left us a *Bṛhaj*[2] and a *Laghu Jātaka*. The borrowing of the name and of other terms from Greece is flagrant and it is only interesting to note the efforts made to give the words an Indian tinge; the names of the Houses prove dependence beyond a peradventure: Horā, Paṇaphara, Āpoklima, Hibukạ, Trikoṇa, Jāmitra, Meṣūraṇa; the signs of the zodiac include Kriya, Tāvuri, Jituma, Leya, Pāthona, Juka, Kaurpya, Taukṣika, Ānokero, Hṛdroga, and Itthya, as well as translations. Moreover, among his authorities, Maya, Satyācārya, Viṣṇugupta, Devasvāmin, Jīvaçarman, Piṇḍāyu, Pṛthu, Çaktipūrva, and Siddhasena, occur Maṇittha and Yavanācārya. The only difficulty is the period when the borrowing took place. Jacobi[3] held that it fell not before the fourth century, as the stage reached seems to be that attained in the works of Firmicus Maternus (*c.* 350), but it is by no means certain that this view can any longer be accepted. A Nepalese manuscript[4] of a

[1] Ed. and trans. H. Kern, IS. x. 161 ff.; xiv. 312 ff. There are variant texts; IOC. i. 1057; *Nepal Catal.*, p. xxx.

[2] Trans. N. Ch. Aiyar, Madras, 1905; SBH. 12, 1912. Cf. Haraprasād, *Nepal Catal.*, p. xxxi.

[3] *De astrologiae Indicae 'Horā' appellatae originibus* (1872). Cf. Fleet, JRAS. 1912, pp. 1039 ff.

[4] Haraprasād, *Report I*, p. 8; *II*, p. 6; *Magadhan Literature*, p. 129; *Nepal Catal.*, p. xxx.

Yavana Jātaka contains a very obscure and mutilated statement which appears to mean that a Yavaneçvara translated the work from his own speech in the year 91 of an unspecified era, while another person, a king Sphūrjidhvaja, brought out the work in the shape of 4,000 Indravajrā verses in 191. Now Bhaṭṭotpala, the commentator on Varāhamihira, tells us of one Yavaneçvara Sphujidhvaja who used the Çaka era, and who, therefore, may be a somewhat confused reminiscence of this set of two people—unless our fragmentary text has obscured the true facts. Kern's suggestion [1] that Yavaneçvara was younger than Varāhamihira ignores the fact that Varāhamihira cites a Yavanācārya who may well be meant for this writer, whose date then would be A.D. 169. We have later texts of the *Yavana Jātaka*, a *Vṛddha* of 8,000 verses, and another text ascribed to Mīnarāja Yavanācārya,[2] which need not be before Varāhamihira, but the evidence clearly renders it difficult to rely implicitly on Jacobi's dating. Maṇittha has been compared with Manetho, author of the *Apotelesmata*, and this view is strongly supported by the fact that he is given as agreeing with the ancient Greeks and disagreeing with Varāhamihira and Satya. The date of Jacobi is supported by Fleet, who lays stress on the order of the planets in Varāhamihira, beginning with the sun, as showing that India adopted a Jewish-Christian week, Jewish in respect of order and Christian in respect of the names. We know that, according to Dio Cassius, the calendrical use of the names of the planets was regular in his time, and in 321 Constantine gave the seven days' week its definite sanction by appointing Sunday as a day of rest. It is fair, however, to note that the use of planet names is to be traced much farther back than Dio Cassius, and that the argument is not altogether conclusive. But it is supported to some extent by the fact that the first case of the use of a name of this kind in an inscription is in A.D. 484, after which it is still rare down to A.D. 800.

[1] *Bṛhatsaṁhitā*, p. 51.

[2] Eggeling, IOC. i. 1096. Mīnas as Minos is suggested by Brockhaus, BSGW. 1852, p. 18.

8. *Varāhamihira's Poetry*

Varāhamihira is often effective and spirited in style and the existence of his work proves the long period of cultivation of the Kāvya prior to his time. Whether his own or Garga's, the plight of the king who has no guide is well phrased:

apradīpā yathā rātrir anādityaṁ yathā nabhaḥ
tathāsāṁvatsaro rājā bhramaty andha ivādhvani.

'Like the night without a light, like the sky without the sun, even so the king without an astrologer wanders blindly on his way.' Misfortunes are effectively portrayed:

vātoddhataç carati vahnir atipracaṇḍo: grāmān vanāni nagarāṇi ca saṁdidhakṣuḥ
hā heti dasyugaṇapātahatā raṭanti: niḥsvīkṛtā vipaçavo bhuvi martyasaṅghāḥ.

'A fire, fanned by the breeze, rages, seeking to devour villages, forests, cities; robbed of their all, without cattle, overwhelmed by the onslaught of hordes of robbers, the people wail miserably.'

abhyunnatā viyati saṁhatamūrtayo 'pi: muñcanti na kvacid apaḥ pracuram payodāḥ
sīmni prajātam api çoṣam upaiti sasyaṁ: niṣpannam apy avinayād apare haranti.

'The clouds aloft in the sky, though teeming, will not yield their abundant water; the grain that springs up in the fields withers away, or if it ripens is stolen by evil strangers.' Very different is the case in happier times:

kṣatraṁ kṣitau kṣapitabhūtibalāripakṣam: udghuṣṭanaikajayaçabdavirāvitāçam
saṁhṛṣṭaçiṣṭajanaduṣṭavinaṣṭavargāṁ: gām pālayanty avanipā nagarākarāḍhyām.

'The kingly power destroys on earth the vast power of the foe; the sky rings with many an echoing shout of victory; joyful the good, destroyed the wicked, and kings rule a land where cities and treasures abound.' The sound effect of the first line is perfectly obvious, and it is very clear in the following line, where the intensives indicate the poet's grammatical knowledge:

pepīyate madhu madhau saha kāminībhir: jegīyate çravaṇahāri saveṇuvīṇam
bobhujyate 'tithisuhṛtsvajanaiḥ sahānnam: abde sitasya madanasya jayāvaghoṣaḥ.

'In the spring month honey drink is drunk with loving maidens, to flute and lute many a sweet song is sung; with guests, friends, kindred, food is freely shared, and love reigns triumphant in the year of Sita.' A stanza cited in an anthology is effective and pointed:

lokaḥ çubhas tiṣṭhatu tāvad anyaḥ: parāñmukhānāṁ samareṣu puṅsām
patnyo 'pi teṣāṁ na hriyā mukhāni: puraḥ sakhīnām iha darçayanti.

'However fair a face the world may turn to those who flee in battle, their wives in shame cannot bear to show their faces before their friends.'

Still more interesting is the number of metres[1] used by Varāhamihira. In the *Bṛhatsaṁhitā* some sixty-four occur, eleven of which are of extreme rarity and of dubious form. The Āryā predominates; then come verses of Indravajrā type, then the Çloka, Vasantatilaka, Rathoddhatā, Çārdūlavikrīḍita, Çālinī, Vaitālīya, and Aupacchandasika: all else are sporadic, many occurring only in civ. They include Anavasitā, Aparavaktra, Kusumavicitrā, Kokilaka or Narkuṭaka, Tāmarasa, Toṭaka, Daṇḍaka, Dodhaka, Drutavilambita, Dhiralalitā, Puṣpitāgrā, Pṛthvī, Prabhāvatī, Pramāṇikā, Pramitākṣarā, Praharṣiṇī, Bhadrikā, Bhujaṅgaprayāta, Bhujaṅgavijṛmbhita, Bhramaravilasita, Maṇiguṇanikara, Mattamayūra, Mattā, Mandākrāntā, Mālatī or Varatanu, Mālinī, Meghavitāna, Meghavisphūrjita, Moṭanaka, Rukmavatī, Rucirā, Vaṅçapattrapatita, Vaṅçasthā, Vātormī, Vidyunmālā, Vaiçvadevī, Çikhariṇī, Çuddhavirāj, Çrīpuṭa, Suvadanā, Sragdharā, Svāgatā, Hariṇapluta, Hariṇī, and Udgatā, Drutapada, Vilāsinī, Sumānikā, Tūṇaka, and varieties of Vidyunmālā. The *Bṛhaj Jātaka* uses thirty-three metres, of which eight have irregularities. The skill of Varāhamihira is thus equal to that of the most accomplished Kāvya writers.

[1] Stenzler, ZDMG. xliv. 4 ff.

9. *Later Works on Astrology*

Little need be said of later exponents of this dubious science. Pṛthuyaças, son of Varāhamihira, wrote a *Horāṣaṭpañcāçikā*,[1] on nativities, on which Bhaṭṭotpala commented, as he did on all Varāhamihira's works, the comment on the *Bṛhaj Jātaka* being dated in 966; he himself wrote a *Horāçāstra* in seventy-five verses. Bhaṭṭotpala is historically interesting for the citations he makes from lost works. The *Vidyāmādhavīya* (before 1350) claims to put in correct language as opposed to barbarisms (*apaçabda*) the precepts of Vasiṣṭha, Bṛhaspati, Gārgya, and others.

Other texts of dubious antiquity are not rare, including a *Vṛddha Vāsiṣṭha Saṁhitā* and the Jain *Jyotiṣasāroddhāra* of Harṣakīrti Sūri. The *Jyotirvidābharaṇa*[2] may be mentioned, because it is the source whence was derived the current doctrine of the nine jewels of the court of Vikramāditya; it is quite late, shows Arabic influence, and need not date before the sixteenth century; it was commented on in 1661. Many works were written also on the auspicious moments for ceremonies, marriages, journeys, and so forth, under the style of Muhūrta as the first part of the title; and, when Arabic and Persian influences became marked under the Mahomedan régime, Tājikas appeared, the name being derived from Persian Taiji, 'Arabic'. Nīlakaṇṭha's *Tājika*, in two parts, *Saṁjñā-* and *Varṣa- tantra*, was written in 1587 and exists in numerous manuscripts and editions.

On omens and prognostications there are also many late treatises; the *Adbhutasāgara*[3] was begun in 1168 by Ballālasena of Bengal and finished by Lakṣmaṇasena, while the *Samudratilaka*, begun in 1160 under Kumārapala of Gujarāt by Durlabharāja, son of Narasiṅha, was finished by his son Jagaddeva, who also wrote the *Svapnacintāmaṇi*,[4] explaining dreams; the similarity of dream motifs to Märchen is noteworthy. The *Narapatijayacaryā Svarodaya*[5] was written at Aṇahillapattana

[1] Ed. Calcutta, 1875.

[2] Weber, ZDMG. xxii. 708 ff.; xxiv. 393 ff.

[3] Bhandarkar, *Report*, 1887–91, pp. lxxxii ff. Cf. IHQ. iii. 186–9.

[4] J. von Negelein, *Der Traumschlüssel des Jagaddeva* (1912); cf. WZKM. xxvi. 403 ff.

[5] Eggeling, IOC. i. 1110 ff. For Jagajjyotirmalla's comm. (1614) see Haraprasād, *Nepal Catal.*, p. lxiii. Cf. Keith, IOC. ii. 836 ff.

under Ajayapāla of Gujarāt (1174–7) by Narahari, son of Āmradeva of Dhārā; it deals with the use of magic diagrams, marked with mystic letters or syllables, as a means of prognostication in respect of warlike operations and adventurous undertakings. From Persia appears to have been borrowed the art of geomancy, which is represented by the *Ramalarahasya*[1] of Bhayabhañjanaçarman and many other treatises of late date. Of much earlier date are two treatises on cubomancy under the style of *Pāçakakevalī* preserved as parts iv and v of the Bower manuscript[2] in bad Sanskrit with many signs of Prākritic influence; later tracts are known, ascribed to Garga,[3] which show knowledge of the term Horā, and therefore postulate the period of Greek influence.

[1] *Ibid.*, i. 1121 ff.

[2] Hoernle, *Bower MS.*, pp. 84 ff

[3] J. E. Schröter, *Pāśakakevalī* (1900); Weber, *Ind. Streif.*, i. 274 ff. For astrology in general see also *Madras Catal.*, xxiv (1918).

ENGLISH INDEX

Abacus, invented in India, 526, 527.
Abdallah ibn al-Moqaffa', translator of Pahlavi *Pañcatantra*, 357.
Abhimanyu, king of Kashmir, revives study of *Mahābhāṣya*, 428.
Abhinanda, son of Jayanta, 135; *Yogavāsiṣṭhasāra*, 480.
Abhinanda, son of Çatānanda, 135.
Abhinavagupta, philosopher and writer on poetics, xvii, 214, 387, 388, 392, 395, 481.
Ābhīras, 33, 34, 223, 370, 469; speech of, 32.
Ablative, with words denoting near or far, 18.
Abnormal causation (*vibhāvanā*), 374, 380.
Abu'l-Maālī Naṣrallāh ibn Muhammad ibn 'Abd al-Ḥamīd, *Kitāb Kalīla wa Dimna*, 358.
Accent, in Vedic and Classical Sanskrit, 7.
Accusative with adjectives in *uka*, 18.
Achievement of Sanskrit poetry, 344–51.
Achilles Tatius, tale of Kleitophon and Leukippe, 363, 368.
Act of truth, *motif*, 343.
Ādarça, western boundary of Āryāvarta, 11.
Ādi Buddha, 494.
Ādi Çeṣa, alleged author of Kārikās, 481.
Āḍhyarāja, i.e. Harṣavardhana, 316.
Aelian, 371.
Aeneid, unevenness of, 97, n. 1.
Aerial car, 96.
Aesthetic pleasure, 388, 389.
Agatharchos, contemporary of Alexander the Great, 357.
Aggavaṅsa, *Saddanīti*, 436.
Agnivarman, king, 97.
Agniveça, authority on medicine, 505, 566.
Āhavamalla, Cālukya, 154, 155, 156, 157.
Ahirs, descendants of the Ābhīras, 33.
Aihole inscription, of Ravikīrti, xvii, 97, n. 1.
Aims and training of the poet, 338–44.
Airships, Greek, 369.
Aischylos, Greek tragedian (525–457 B.C.), 195.
Aisopos (*c.* 550 B.C.), 352; fables of, 245.
Aithiopika, 367.
Aja, prince, husband of Indumatī, 91, 94, 95.
Ajaṇṭā frescoes, 68.
Ajātaçatru, parricide, 65.
Ajayapāla, of Gujarāt, 535.
Akalaṅka, comm. on *Āptamīmāṅsā*, 497.
Akbar, Emperor of India, 415.
Akṣapāda, *Nyāya Sūtra*, 482–4.
Alakā, 85.
Alaṁkāra, brother of Maṅkha, 136; patron of poets, 161.
Alaṭa (Alaka, Allaṭa), joint author of *Kāvyaprakāça*, xvii, n. 4, 394.
Alberūnī, Arabian geographer, 512, 521, 522.
Alchemy, 460.
Alexander the Great, 33, n. 3.
Alexandrian poetry, compared with Sanskrit, 347, 361.
'Alī bin Ṣāliḥ, *Humāyūn Nāmeh*, 358.
Alliteration, 45, n. 1, 49, 79, 97, 105, 130, 212, 218, 232, 311, 313, 333, 341, 343, 369, 373, 378, 384, 386–8.
Amaracandra, *Bālabhārata*, 137; *Kāvyakalpalatā*, 397, 398.
Amaraçakti, of Mahilāropya or Mihilāropya, 248, 250.
Amarasiṅha, lexicographer and poet, 76, 308, 339, 413, 512.
Amaru, 183–7.
Amitābha, heaven of, 494.
Amitagati, *Dharmaparīkṣā* and *Subhāṣitaratnasaṁdoha*, 240, 241, 497.
Amoghavarṣa, Rāṣṭrakūṭa king, 53, n. 2, 524.
Amṛtānanda, work of, on the *Buddhacarita*, 58.
Āmradeva, of Dhārā, 535.
Amrakūṭa, hill, 85.
Ānanda, brother of Bilhaṇa, 153.
Ānanda, *Mādhavānalakathā*, 293.
Ānandajñāna, commentator on Çaṅkara, xxi, n. 4.
Ānandatīrtha, *Yamakabhārata*, 197, n. 2.
Ānandavardhana, writer on poetics, x, 33, 43, 87, 105, 218, 232, 313, 341, 373, 386–8, 411.
Ananta, *Bhāratacampū*, 336.
Ananta, *Vīracaritra*, 292.
Ananta, king of Kashmir, 281.
Anantavīrya, comm. on *Parīkṣāmukhasūtra*, 484.
Anatomy, study of, 505.
Andhaka, legend of, 134, 135.
Andhrabhṛtyas, 33.
Andhras, 469.
Androclus, and the lion, 356.

Añgulimāla, legend of, 504.
Aniruddha, comm. on *Sāṁkhya Sūtra*, 489.
Annam Bhaṭṭa, *Tarkasaṁgraha*, 486.
Anthologies, 222, 223.
Anthonius von Pforr, *Das buch der byspel der alten wysen* (*sine loco et anno*, about 1480), 358.
Antonius Diogenes, Greek writer of Romance, xi.
Anubhūtī, *Sarasvatīprakriyā*, 432.
Anwāri Suhailī, by Husain ibn 'Alī al-Wā'iẓ, 358.
Aorists, use of, 19, 20, 63, 115, 258, 307.
Āpadeva, *Mīmāṅsānyāyaprakāça*, 474.
Aparārka, commentator on *Yājñavalkya Smṛti*, 447.
Āpastamba, 469, n. 2; see *Āpastamba Dharmasūtra*.
Aphrodisiacs, 505.
Āpiçāli, ancient grammarian, 423.
Apollonius of Tyana, xxii, n. 8.
Apollonius of Perga, Greek mathematician (*c.* 225 B.C.; Heath, *Hist.* ii. 126; *Apollonius of Perga*, 1896), 527.
Apollonios Rhodios, Alexandrian poet (3rd cent. B.C.), author of *Argonautika*, 325, n. 1, 348, 349, 350.
Appayya Dīkṣita, polymath, 481; *Kuvalayānanda*, 396.
Apsarases, as types of beauty, 57.
Āptas, perfect men of Jainism, 240.
Apuleius, xi; *Metamorphoses*, 367.
Arab rule, mediates between civilizations of west and east, 360.
Arabians, connexion with India, 507, 511, 523, 527, 528, 534.
Arabian Nights, 360, 361.
Arabic alchemy, 512, n. 1.
Arabic numerals, xxiii, xxiv.
Arabic terms in Sanskrit, 25.
Archery, treatises on, 464.
Archilochos, 352, 355.
Architecture, treatises on, xx, 464, 465.
Ārdradeva, father of Haricandra, 143, n. 2.
Ares and Aphrodite, amour of, 337.
Arhaddāsa, 295.
Arhat, ideal of an, 61.
Arikesarin, Cālukya king, 333.
Arisiṅha, *Kāvyakalpalatā*, 397, 398; *Sukṛtasaṁkīrtana*, 173.
Aristeides, *Milesiaka* (not *Ephesiaka*), xi, 367, 368.
Aristotle, xxi, 194, 361; *Politics* of, xviii.
Arjuna, hero, 109.
Arjuna Kārtavīrya, and Rāvaṇa, strife of, 133.
Ārjunarāvaṇīya, by Bhaumaka, 133.
Arjunavarman, king, 53, n. 2; comments on *Amaruçataka*, 183.
Arnold, Matthew, 348, n. 2.
Ars amatoria, of Ovid, 350.
Artistic parallels of Açvaghoṣa's epics, 63, n. 3.
Āryabhaṭa I, astronomer, 75, 411, 519, 521, 522, 523, 527.
Āryabhaṭa II, *Ārya Siddhānta*, 522.
Ārya Deva, *Catuḥçatikā*, 71.
Ārya Çūra, ix, 67–70.
Ārya Sañghasena, teacher of Guṇavṛddhi, 283.
Aryan speeches, 3.
Āryāvarta, region of, defined, 11.
Āçādhara, *Dharmāmṛta*, 497.
Āçmarathya, authority on ritual (MS. vi. 5. 16), and on philosophy (BS. i. 2. 29; 4. 20), 475.
Açoka, emperor, xxv, xxvi, 162, 163.
Açoka, tree, 343.
Açokan dialects, xxv, 11.
Açokan inscriptions, 27, 28.
Açvaghoṣa, poet, viii, ix, xvi, xxiii, 12, 18, 31, 39, n. 3, 45, 51, 54, 55–64, 80, 91, 126, 224, 433, 440, 450, 469, 483, 493, 495.
Açvaghoṣarāja, king, not identical with Açvaghoṣa, 55.
Açvinīkumāra, *Kasaratnasamuccaya*, 512.
Asahāya, commentary on *Nārada Smṛti*, 445.
Asañga, Buddhist philosopher, *Mahāyānasūtrālaṁkāra*, viii, 73, 77, 495.
Ascetic life, Buddhist and Christian legends of, 504.
Ass in lion's skin, *motif*, 355.
Ass without heart and ears, *motif*, 357.
Assam, king of, pays homage to Harṣa, 318.
Assamese, source of, 32.
Assonance (*yamaka*), 135, 141, 197, 198, 201, 212, 313, 369, 373, 378, 384, 385.
Astrologers, satire of, 238.
Astrology, 75, 528–35.
Astronomy, 75, 516–23.
Asuras, Bṛhaspati as teacher of the, 499.
Āsuri, Sāṁkhya teacher, 488.
Athens, role of hetairai in, 52.
Atomism, 483–7.
Ātreya, authority on medicine, xxiii, 505, 506, 507.
Ātreya, ritual authority, 475.
Aucassin et Nicolette, style of, 70, n. 2.
Auḍulomi, philosopher, 475.
Austroasiatic influences on Indian culture, Przyluski's theory of, 4, n. 2.
Austroasiatic origin of the Svayaṁvara, xi, 361, n. 1.
Autumn, description of, 84, 110, 120.
Avalokita, teacher of Vāgbhaṭa I, 510.
Avalokiteçvara (from *Avalokita-svara* contaminated with *lokeçvara* acc. to Mironov, JRAS. 1927, pp. 241–52), 222.

Avantī, Bhūtabhāṣā in, 386.
Avantivarman, king of Kashmir, 133, 134, 164.
Avantisundarī, wife of Rājaçekhara, and authority on poetics, 205, n. 1, 342.
Ayodhyā, city, 96, 120; forlorn condition of, described by Vālmīki, 43.
Azulis, 369.

Babrios, Greek fable writer, 352.
Babylonian influence on Indian astrology, 528.
Bādarāyaṇa, author of *Brahma Sūtra*, xxi, 458, 475, 477.
Bāhaṭa, variant of Vāgbhaṭa, 510.
Bāhudantīputra, authority on Arthaçāstra, 451, 457.
Bakhshālī MS., mathematics in, 524, 525.
Bakchai, by Euripides, religious feeling in the, 194.
Balabhadra, brother of Govardhana, 202.
Balabhadra, brother of Kṛṣṇa, 162.
Bālāditya, Gupta of Magadha, 74.
Bālāditya, king of Kashmir, 163.
Bālambhaṭṭa Vaidyanātha, commentator on *Yājñavalkya Smṛti*, 447.
Balarāma, hero, 85.
Bald-headed man and fly, *motif*, 355.
Baldo, *Novus Esopus*, 359.
Ballālasena, *Adbhutasāgara*, 534.
Ballālasena, *Bhojaprabandha*, 293, 344, n. 3.
Bali, binding of, by Viṣṇu, 45.
Bāli (Vāla, Vālin), foe of Rāma, 120.
Bāṇa, poet, xiii, xxii, 19, 50, 53, 60, 77, 97, n. 3, 132, 135, 138, 139, n. 3, 150, 152, 159, 165, 169, 173, 201, 202, 205, 210, 213, 214, 225, 266, 267, 297, 299, 307, 331, 333, 336, 339, 343, 345, 347, 349, 365, 369, 376, 381, 412, 445, 461.
Barlaam and Josaphat, legend of, 501, 502.
Bartering of statues, by the Mauryas, 428, 453, n. 1.
Beast fable, 39, 242–65.
Bell-Māgha, 130.
Bellerophon, Homeric hero, 362, n. 4.
Bengālī, source of, 32.
Betel and coco-palms of Kaliṅga, 80.
Bhādānakas, speech of, 386.
Bhagala, Phegelas, 426.
Bhallaṭa, *Çataka*, 231, 232.
Bhāmaha, xvi, 14, 32, 101, n. 1, 116, 297, 309, n. 1, 338, 340, 373, 374, 375, 376, 378, 381, 382, 383, 385, 389, 392, 411, n. 1, 416, 433.
Bhaṇḍi, Harṣa's friend, 317.
Bhānudatta, *Rasamañjarī* and *Rasataraṅgiṇī*, 398.
Bhāradvāja, alleged authority on Arthaçāstra, 457.
Bhāradvāja, *see* Uddyotakara.
Bharata, 132; see *Nāṭyaçāstra*.
Bhāratacandra, *Vidyāsundara*, 188.
Bhāratan epic, known to Kumāralāta, 56.
Bhāratītīrtha, part author of *Pañcadaçī*, 477.
Bhāravi, *Kirātārjunīya*, xvi, xvii, 9, 39, 87, n. 2, 89, 90, 97, n. 1, 101, n. 1, 108, n. 1, 109–16, 121, n. 1, 122, 126, 127, 128, 130, 131, 132, 133, 140, 141, 165, 208, 209, 262, 307, 339, 345, 347, 416, 451.
Bharhut, monumental evidence of fable, 243; sculptures, 352, 364.
Bhartṛhari, 116, 117, 183, 184, 232, 347, 428, 429, 431.
Bhartṛmeṇṭha, 132, 133.
Bhartṛ-Prapañca, philosopher, 475, n. 3.
Bharvu, preceptor of Bāṇa, 330.
Bhāsa, dramatist, xii–xvi, 11, 80, 173, 268, 271, 307, 316, 336, 372, 386, n. 2, 451, 461.
Bhāskara, astronomer, 409, 525, 527.
Bhaṭṭākalaṅkadeva, *Karṇāṭakaçabdānuçāsana*, 436, n. 5.
Bhaṭṭāra Haricandra, 300.
Bhaṭṭi, poet, 18, 87, n. 2, 116–19, 123, 128, 178, 373, 375, 398.
Bhaṭṭiprolu inscriptions, 27.
Bhaṭṭoji Dīkṣita, *Prakriyākaumudī*, 430.
Bhaṭṭotpala, comm. on Varāhamihira, 416, 531, 534.
Bhaumaka, poet, 18, 133.
Bhāva, protégé of Nāgarāja, 234.
Bhavabhūti, 53, n. 2, 132, 381, 416, 462, 463, 469.
Bhāva Miçra, *Bhāvaprakāça*, 511.
Bhāvaviveka, comm. on Nāgārjuna, 495.
Bhayabhañjanaçarman, *Ramalarahasya*, 535.
Bheḍa, Bhela, authority on medicine, 505, 508, 509.
Bhikṣācara, grandson of Harṣa, 159.
Bhillamalla, 522.
Bhillas, 285.
Bhīma, poet, 133.
Bhīmapāla of Bengal, patron of Sureçvara, 512.
Bhīmaratha, legend of, 46.
Bhīṣma, hero, 125.
Bhoja, king and polymath or patron, xiv, xvi, n. 5, 53, 153, 292, 297, 336, 393, 395, 464, 465, 481, n. 4, 489, 491, 527; *see also* Bhojarāja.
Bhoja, prince of Kashmir, 160, 169.
Bhojadeva, of Kindubilva, 190.
Bhojarāja, recension of *Cāṇakyanīti*, 228.
Bhūma, Bhūmaka, Bhaumaka, *Rāvaṇārjunīya*, 133.
Bhūṣaṇa Bhaṭṭa, rather Pulina, son of Bāṇa, 314.
Bihārī, source of, 32.

Bihārī Lāl, *Sat'saī*, 202.
Bilhaṇa, poet, xxvii, 14, 51, 108, n. 1, 131, 153–8, 165, 169, 173, 188–90, 232.
Bion, 370.
Bismarck, German statesman, 459.
Black Yajurveda, 438.
Boccaccio, *L'Ameto*, style of, 70, n. 2.
Bodhāyana, philosopher, 478.
Bodhisattva ideal, 72, 491, 492.
Boethius, style of, 70, n. 2.
Bombast, of Gauḍa style, 212.
Boro Bodur artists, 492.
Borrowing, by poets, 341, 342.
Bower MS., 507, 509, 510, 535; language of, 23.
Bṛhaspati Cippaṭa, 134, 164.
Brahmagupta, astrologer, 411, 521, 522, 524, 526, 527.
Brahman, god, 99, 154, 301.
Brahmanical gods, attacked, 240.
Brahmāvarta, country, 85.
Brahmin, kinds of, 228.
Bran, Irish king, legend of, 354.
Brother's life *versus* husband's, *motif*, 355.
Būd, Syriac *Kalila und Dimna* (ed. and trs. F. Schulthess, Berlin, 1911), 357.
Buddha, 159, 222.
Buddha Bhaṭṭa, *Ratnaparīkṣā*, 465.
Buddha biography, 492.
Buddhaghoṣa, Buddhist philosopher, 362, 436.
Buddhaghoṣācārya, *Padyacūḍāmaṇi*, 143.
Buddhapālita, comm. on Nāgārjuna, 495.
Buddhism, Buddhists, 63, 64, 148, 159, 243, 249, 270, 285, 301, 315, 346, 443, 450, 471, 474, 488, 490, 491–6, 499, 500.
Buddhist Tantras, 496.
Budhasvāmin, *Bṛhatkathāçlokasaṁgraha*, 271, 272–5.
Burns, Robert, refashions popular songs, 224.
Burzōe, Pahlavi translation of the *Pañcatantra*, xxvii, n. 1, 357.

Caesuras, 90, 108, 417.
Caitanya, 219.
Cakora, bird, 341, 343.
Cakrapāṇi, continues *Daçakumāracarita*, 297, n. 3.
Cakrapāṇidatta, comm. on Suçruta, 507.
Cakravāka, bird, 343.
Calderón, Chinese parallels to, 504.
Cambodia, 507; Sanskrit inscriptions of, 16.
Campā, Sanskrit inscriptions in, 16.
Cāṇakya (possibly Cāṇikya), xvii, 461, 462, 505; see also *Kauṭilīya Arthaçāstra.*
Caṇḍa, *Prākṛtalakṣaṇa*, 433.
Caṇḍāla maidens, intercourse with, in Buddhist Tantric ritual, 496.
Candaladevī, Rājput princess, 155.
Caṇḍālas, depressed condition of the, in Gupta times, 75, 99.
Caṇḍamāri-devatā, 333.
Caṇḍeçvara, *Smṛtiratnākara*, 448.
Caṇḍī, goddess, 135.
Candra, *Cāndra Vyākaraṇa*, 431, 432.
Candrāditya, king, 205, n. 1.
Candrakirti, commentator on Nāgārjuna, 493.
Candragomin, *Çiṣyalekhadharmakāvya*, 71, 72.
Candragopin, 72.
Candragupta I, 74, 78.
Candragupta II, 74, 75, 76, 77, 80, 81.
Candragupta Maurya, 228, 294, 459.
Candragupta, poet, 339.
Candralekhā, princess, 188.
Candrāpīḍa, hero of the *Kādambarī*, 321.
Candraṭa, revises text of Suçruta, 507.
Cañgadeva, grandson of Bhāskara, 524.
Canpaka, father of Kalhaṇa, 158.
Capalā, form of Āryā, 418.
Caraka, medical authority, xxiii, 13, 461, 486, 488, n. 2, 506, 507, 508, 509, 510, 513, n. 2, 514.
Cārāyaṇa, authority on erotics, 468.
Cardonne, translation of Turkish *Humāyūn Nāmeh*, 358.
Cāritrasundara Gaṇin, 143.
Cariyāpiṭaka, 68.
Carmaṇvatī, river, 85.
Cārvākas, 499.
Cases, use of, 21.
Caṣṭana, Kṣatrapa, of Ujjayinī, 49.
Castles in the air, 362.
Cat and the candle, legend of, 364.
Cat and mice, fable of, 242.
Cātaka, bird, 343.
Catullus, 194, 345; *Attis*, 26, n. 1.
Caura, Cora, poet, 188.
Celsus, osteology of, 514.
Cerebralization, 27; perhaps due to Dravidian influence, 5.
Cetasiñha, oppressed by Warren Hastings, 337.
Character and extent of the use of Sanskrit, 8–17.
Characteristics and development of Sanskrit in literature, 17–26.
Characteristics of Old Prākrits, 29, 30.
Characteristics of the Çāstras, 406–11.
Characterization, 325.
Charadrios, legend of, 356.
Chares of Mytilene, 366.
Charioteer, discusses etymology with a grammarian, 10.
Charition, farce as to adventures of, x.
Chavillākara, Kashmirian historian, 162.
Children's diseases, treatise on, 509.

China, Chinese, 75, 492, 493, 494, 495, 527, 528.
Christian influence on religion, 480.
Christian Fathers, xxi.
Christian legends, and Buddhist, 502–4.
Christophoros, legend of, 502.
Chronology, lack of, 155.
Chuang Tse, parallel of his thoughts with Calderón's, 504.
Cidambara, *Rāghavapāṇḍavīyayādavīya*, 138.
Cintāmaṇi Bhaṭṭa, *Çukasaptati*, 291.
Citrakūṭa, mountain, 43.
Clearness of sense (*prasāda*), 50, 374, 377.
Cippaṭa Jayāpīḍa, 134, 164.
Circe, Indian parallel to, 363.
Classification of figures of speech, 398.
Claudian, Roman poet, 169, n. 2.
Coin, legends in Prākrit, 16.
Colas, 154, 155.
Colonies of Indians, 386.
Compounds, case of, 97, 311, 313, 326, 327, 331, 379, 381, 384, 390, 391.
Confusion of gender, 23.
Confusion of similars (*parivṛtti*), 380.
Consonants, as affecting style, 390.
Constant du Hamel, legend of, 364.
Constantine, makes Sunday a day of rest, 531.
Contrast by dissimilitude (*vyatireka*), 213, 374, 380, 399.
Cookery, 512.
Cool season, description of, 84.
Corroboration (*arthāntaranyāsa*), 106, 374, 380.
Crusades, effect of, 360.
Cubomancy, treatises on, 535.
Cyclic quadrilaterals, 526.

Dākṣī, mother of Pāṇini, 425.
Dakṣiṇāvartanātha, commentator, 81, 87.
Dallana, comm. on Suçruba, 507.
Damaskios, neo-Platonist and director of the Athenian school (A.D. 510), 525.
Damayantī and Nala, tale of, 140, 141.
Ḍāmaras, of Kashmir, 159, 160.
Dāmodara, great-grandfather of Daṇḍin, xvi.
Dāmodara, of Dīrghaghoṣa family, *Vāṇībhūṣaṇa*, 417.
Dāmodara, son of Lakṣmīdhara, *Saṁgītadarpaṇa*, 466.
Dāmodaragupta, *Kuṭṭanīmata*, 236, 237.
Damanaka, 249, 250.
Danae, *motif*, 284.
Daṇḍin, xvi, xvii, n. 6, 19, 31, n. 1, 32, 49, 59, 60, 92, 101, 116, 266, 268, 271, 296–330, 308, 326, 338, 340, 362, 375, 376, 377, 378, 379, 380, 381, 382, 383, 384, 389, 461, 462.
Dardic branch of Indian race, 33.
Dardura hills, 94.
Daçapura, city, 85; panegyric of, 79; *Bhūtabhāṣā* in, 386.
Daçārṇa, country, 85.
Dative, usages with, 18.
Dattaka, of Pāṭaliputra, authority on erotics, 468.
Dattaka Sarvāçraya, father of Māgha, 124.
Defects in poetry (*doṣa*), 374.
Deinias and Kymbas, 369.
Demokritos, Greek philosopher, 356.
Deodars of the Himālayas, 80.
Derivative forms of the *Pañcatantra*, 259–63.
Deva, *Daiva*, 430.
Devadatta, version of *Çukasaptati*, 292.
Devāditya, father of Trivikrama Bhaṭṭa, 332.
Devaṇṇa Bhaṭṭa, *Smṛticandrikā*, 448.
Devaprabha Sūri, 143.
Devasmitā, legend of, 284, 364.
Devasvāmin, astrologer, 530.
Dhanaṁjaya, *Daçarūpa*, 266.
Dhanaṁjaya, *Nāmamālā*, 414.
Dhanaṁjaya Çrutakīrti, 137.
Dhanapāla, *Tilakamañjarī*, 272, 331; *Pāiyalacchī*, 415.
Dhanurveda, works on, 364.
Dhanvantari, author of a medical glossary, 96, 414.
Dharmadāsa, imitates Bāṇa, 327.
Dharmakīrti, philosopher, xxii, 308.
Dharmanātha, a Tīrthakara, 143.
Dharmarāja, *Vedāntaparibhāṣā*, 478.
Dhavalacandra, patron of Nārāyaṇa, 263.
Dhoī, poet, *Pavanadūta*, 53, 86, 190, 219, n. 1, 220.
Dhvanikāra, 393, 396.
Dialects in Sanskrit, 4.
Dialects of the Açokan inscriptions, 27, 28.
Dialogue in Kalhaṇa, 169.
Didactic fable, 242–65.
Didactic tale, 293–5.
Digambara Jain monk, 301.
Digambaras, 28.
Dignāga, philosopher, xxi, xxii, 81, 107, 484, 485.
Digvijaya, of Raghu, 93.
Dilīpa, father of Raghu, 93.
Dio Cassius, 531.
Dio Chrysostomos, 370, 371.
Diophantos, astronomer, (*c.* A.D. 250–75; Heath, *Diophantus of Alexandria*, 2nd. ed. 1910), 525.
Dīpaṁkara, *Açvavaidyaka*, 465.
Directorium vitae humanae, see *Liber Kelilae et Dimnae*, 358.
Direct speech, love of, 244, 245.
Disadvantages of poetic form in Çāstras 411.
Divākaramitra, a Buddhist sage, 318.
Divodāsa, king of Benares, 507.

Doctors, satire against, 238.
Dog flesh, eating of, in Buddhist Tantra ritual, 496.
Doni, *La Moral Filosophia del Doni* and *Trattati diversi di Sendebar Indiano filosopho morale* (Venice, 1552), 358.
Double entendre, 7, 8, 21, 97, 127, 141, 152, 211, 215, 216, 257, 311, 316, 326, 345, 491.
Doubling of consonants, forbidden in passionate speech, 9.
Dṛḍhabala, reponsible for recension of *Caraka Saṁhitā*, xxiii, n. 3, 506.
Drama, 10, 11, 376, 416.
Dramiḍācārya, philosopher, 478.
Draviḍas, musical recitation of, 386.
Dravidian influence on Sanskrit, 4, 22.
Dravidian words borrowed, 474.
Dubois, Abbé, *Le Pantchatantra ou les cinq ruses*, 262.
Duration of gestation, 502, n. 3.
Durgasiṅha, *Vṛtti* on *Kātantra*, 431.
Durlabharāja, *Samudratilaka*, 534.
Durlabhavardhana, king of Kashmir, 163.
Durvinīta, of Koṅgaṇi, alleged commentary on *Kirātārjunīya*, xvii.
Dyā Dviveda, *Nītimañjarī*, 239.

Eagle and tortoise, fable of, 355.
Eastern Hindī, source of, 32.
Eastern Prākrit, 27, 28.
Eastern school of Prākrit grammarians, 33, 433, 434.
Egypt, possible influence on India, 367, n. 1, 517; account-keeping in, xxiv, n. 1.
Elephant flesh, eating of, in Buddhist Tantric ritual, 496.
Elevation (*udārata, udāratva*), 374, 377, 390.
Elixirs, 511.
Elks in Black Forest (Caesar, *De Bello Gallico*, vi. 27), 356.
Emboxing of stories within stories, 244, 245, 255, 258, 319, 320, 367, n. 1.
Emotion (*bhāva*), 63, n. 3, 92, 373.
Encyclopaedic learning, characteristic of Kāvya writers, 348.
English, as a vernacular, xxvi.
Entering another's body, *motif*, 343.
Epanthem, 523.
Ephesos, story-tellers of, 367.
Epic, 12, 13, 46, 47, 93; see also *Mahābhārata* and *Rāmāyaṇa*.
Epics, as aristocratic literature, 13.
Epigrammatic style, characteristic of Flavians and Kāvya, 348, 349.
Epigrams, 208, 209.
Equal pairing (*tulyayogitā*), 213, 380, 399.
Erasistratos, Greek physician, 514.
Étienne of Bourbon, 362.
Etymology, 212.
Euphues, by Lyly, 370.
Euripides, Greek tragedian (480-406 B.C.), 195.
Exaggeration, 97, 212.
Exhaustive statement (*parisaṁkhyā*), 313.
Explicitness of sense (*arthavyakti*), 50, 374, 390.
Expression of pleasure (*preyas*), 380, 382, 389.
Extempore verse, 80, 344.
Eye-washes and salves, treatise on, 509.

Fables, x, xi, 242-65.
Fa-hien, Chinese traveller, 75, 99.
Fairy tales, 39, 40, 266-93.
False ascetics, *motif*, 343.
Farce, Charition's adventures, x.
Fate, 167.
Feminine forms of certain words, 10.
Figures (*alaṁkāra*), 105, 106, 351, 379, 380, 381, 382, 385, 389, 390, 391, 392, 393, 394, 395, 396.
Firdausī, 366.
Firenzuola, Agnolo, *Discorsi degli animali ragionanti tra loro* (1568), 358.
Firmicus Maternus, astrologer, 530.
Flying birds, *motif*, 363.
Flying machines, Yavanas experts in, 279.
Fools, tales of, 283.
Force (*ojas*), quality of style, 50, 327, 374, 378, 379, 381, 390.
Foreign invasions, alleged effect of, on development of the Kāvya, 39, 48, 49.
Fox and eagle, fable of, 355.
Fox and raven, fable of, 354.
Frog hymn of *Ṛgveda*, 242.
Frog maiden, legend of, 489.
Future middle, in Classical Sanskrit, 6.

Gadādhara, comm. on Raghunātha Çiromaṇi's *Dīdhiti*, 485.
Gadādhara, father of Vaṅgasena, 511.
Galland, *Les contes et fables indiennes de Bidpaï et de Lokman* (Paris, 1774), 358.
Gaṇa, *Açvāyurveda*, 465.
Gaṇeça, *Grahalāghava*, 523.
Gandhāra, 369, n. 1, 370, 371.
Gandharva, 94, 95, 110, 219, n. 1.
Gaṅgādatta, poet, 221.
Gaṅgādhara, poet, defeated by Bilhaṇa, 153.
Gaṅgeça, *Tattvacintāmaṇī*, 408, 484, 485.
Garga, astrologer, 528, 532, 535.
Gargacandra, of Lahara, 159.
Gārgya, ancient grammarian, 422.
Garlic, treatise on, in Bower MS. of, 509.
Gauraçiras, authority on Rājaçāstra, 450.
Gauḍa, Gauḍīyā, style (*mārga, rīti*), 59,

60, 121, n. 1, 131, n. 2, 150, 212, 310, 316, 377, 378, 379, 381, 384, 395.
Gauḍapāda, author of *Kārikās*, 475, 476.
Gauḍapāda, comm. on *Sāṁkhya Kārikā*, 488, 489.
Gauḍas, defective in Prākrit, 385.
Gaurī, Tantric worship of, 263.
Gayadāsa, comm. on Suçruta, 507.
Genitive, uses of, 18.
Geography, 529.
Geomancy, borrowed by India from Persia, 535.
Gerund, forms mixed in epic and Kāvya, 20; simplified in Classical Sanskrit, 6; uses of, 258.
Gerundives, extended use of, in classical Sanskrit, 6.
Gesta Romanorum, 363.
Ghaṭakarpara, 76.
Ghoṭamukha, authority on erotics, 468.
Gipsies, as intermediaries of tales, 360.
Girnar Inscription of Rudradāman, 48, 50.
Gnomic verse, 46, 47, 225, 227–36.
Gnostics, Indian influence on, 500, 501.
God, in Nyāya-Vaiçeṣika, 482, n. 2, 483, 484, 485.
Goethe, appreciates Indian poetry, 82, 191.
Golden Seventy verses, by Vindhyavāsa, 488.
Goldsmiths, satire of, 240.
Gomukha, minister of Naravāhanadatta, 271.
Gonanda, name of kings of Kashmir, 162, 163.
Gonardīya, authority on erotics, 468.
Gonardīya, grammarian, 427.
Goṇikāputra, authority on erotics, 468, 469.
Goṇikāputra, grammarian, 427.
Gopāla, legend of, 272.
Gopīnātha, revises *Daçakumāracarita*, 297, n. 3.
Gospel narratives, Buddhist parallels, 502–4.
Gottfried of Strassburg, *Tristan und Isolde*, 359.
Govardhana, poet, 53, 190, 192, 202, 223, 266, 327.
Govinda, teacher of Çaṅkara, 476.
Govindacandra, of Kanauj, 448.
Govindarāja, commentary on *Manu*, 445.
Grahavarman, Maukhari king, 317.
Grammarians, influence of, on development of language, 4, 5.
Grammatical Kāvya, 63, 64.
Grateful dolphin, *motif*, 357.
Greedy jackal, tale of, 362.
Greek fable literature, 352–7.
Greek influence, 47, 75, 80, 145, 438, 460, 513–15, 518, 519, 520, 525–8, 530, 531.
Greek medicine, influence on India, 513–15.
Greek renderings of Indian names, 16.
Greeks, 39.
Grierson, Sir George, theory of Māhārāṣṭra Apabhraṅça, 35.
Guha, destroyer of Tāraka, 213.
Guhasena, of Valabhī (A. D. 559–69), uses Apabhraṅça, 32.
Guhyakas, mountain sprites, 110.
Gujarātī, 261.
Gūjars, in United Provinces, 33.
Gulistān, style of, 70, n. 2.
Gumāni, *Upadeçaçataka*, 234.
Guṇabhadra, *Uttarapurāṇa*, 336.
Guṇacandra, *Nāṭyadarpaṇa*, xv.
Guṇāḍhya, *Bṛhatkathā*, 28, 40, 246, 262, 266–87, 300, 307, 319, 320.
Guṇaratna, Buddhist philosopher, 486.
Guṇavṛddhi, translator, 283.
Gupta dynasty, Sanskrit flourishes under, 15, 74–7, 520.
Gurjara, Gūrjara, 24, 32, 33, 34, 151, 152, 223.

Hāla, *Sattasaī*, 25, nn. 4, 5, 40, 54, 187, 202, 223–5, 226, 434.
Halāyudha, *Brāhmaṇasarvasva*, 448; poet, 207.
Halāyudha, poet and grammarian, 18, 133; *Abhidhānaratnamālā*, 414; comm. on *Chandassūtra*, 416, n. 1.
Haṅsa, bird, 343.
Haradatta, a merchant, 291.
Haradatta, *Padamañjarī*, 209.
Haradatta Sūri, *Rāghavanaiṣadhīya*, 138.
Harasiṅhadeva, patron of Caṇḍeçvara, 448.
Haribhadra, Jain philosopher, 497, 499; date of, xxi, xxii.
Haricandra Bhaṭṭāra, prose author, 300, 339.
Haricandra, *Dharmaçarmābhyudaya*, 143, 336.
Haricandra, *Jīvandharacampū*, 336.
Harihara, patron of Irugapa, 414.
Harinārāyaṇa, of Mithilā, 449.
Hariṣeṇa, panegyrist of Samudragupta, 76, 77, 78, 98, 300, 332.
Hārīta, authority on medicine, 505, 509.
Harṣa, king of Kanauj, xxviii, 53, 77, 124, 134, 150, n. 2, 201, 211, 214, 215, 232, 237, 297, 308, 314, 316–19, 339, 342, 347, 395.
Harṣa, king of Kashmir, 233, 234.
Harṣadeva, *Liṅgānuçāsana*, 433; *see* Harṣa, king of Kanauj.
Harṣakīrti Sūri, *Jyotiṣasāroddhāra*, 534.
Harsh sounds, 311, 312.
Hastipaka, 132.
Hāthigumphā inscription of Khāravela, 41.
Hegelian theory of the State, 456.

Heinrich Seuse, *Büchlein der Ewigen Weisheit*, 363.
Hekataios of Miletos, 145, n. 1.
Helārāja, Kashmirian historian, 162.
Helen, legend of, xi, n. 4.
Heliodoros, 368.
Hemacandra, Jain polymath, 32, 34, 35, 131, 142, 143, 172, 208, 226, 241, 269, 290, 294, 361, 384, 414, 415, 416, 430, 434, 435, 464, 484, 497.
Hemādri, *Caturvargacintāmaṇi*, 448; *Çataçlokī*, 511.
Hemavijaya, *Kathāratnākara*, 295, n. 5.
Hepa, goddess in Mitanni, xxiv.
Herodotos, Greek historian, 145, 352, 355, 356.
Herophilos, Greek physician, 514.
Hesiod, 352.
Hetairai, 32, 52, 239, 300.
Hexameter, 370, 371.
Himālaya, mountain, 80, 88, 94.
Hīnayāna school of Buddhism, 72.
Hindī, language, 25; literature, 36.
Hippokleides' marriage, 355.
Hippokrates, Greek physician, 513.
Hīra, father of Çrīharṣa, 139.
Historia Apollonii Tyrii, 70, n. 2.
Historians of philosophy, 499, 500.
Historical method, lacking in Çāstras, 410.
History, causes of weakness of Indians in scientific, 145–7.
Hiuen Tsang, 14, 164, 315, 319, 425.
Hobbes, 451.
Hochsprache, xxv, xxvi.
Homer, 352, 362, 368, 370.
Homoioteleuton, 369.
Horse-flesh, eating of, 496.
Horse sacrifice, as sign of paramount power, 76.
Human sacrifice, 151, 285, 289, 367.
Humours, medical dictum of, 514.
Huns, 74, 80, 81, 166, 223, 317, 492.
Husain ibn 'Alī al Wā'iẓ, *Anwāri Suhailī*, 358.
Huṣka, king of Kashmir, 163.
Huviṣka, inscription of, 15, n. 1.
Hypatia, astronomer, (A.D. 370–415; Heath, *Hist. of Greek Math.*, ii, 528), 525.
Hyperbole (*atiçayokti*), 378, 399.
Hyper-Sandhi, 23.

Ideal of feminine beauty, continuity of, from Vedic times, 42, n. 1.
Ikṣvāku, 93.
Iliad, 13, 61, 366.
Illustration, (*nidarçana*), 380, 399.
Imperative mood, 115.
Imperfect tense, 20, 115, 307.
Impersonal passive, favourite construction, 90.
Incest, as a *motif*, 294.
India, known in Egypt, x.
Indirect expression (*paryāyokta*), 380, 382, 396.
Indra, god, 110, 111.
Indra III, 332.
Indragomin, grammarian, 431.
Indrakīla, place of Arjuna's penance, 110.
Indrāyudha, horse of Candrāpīḍa, 321.
Indukara, father of Mādhavakara, 511.
Indumatī, wife of Aja, 91, 94, 95.
Inference, as opposed to suggestion, in poetry, 393.
Infinitive, loss of varieties of, in Classical Sanskrit, 6.
Inscription, use of Sanskrit in, 14, 15.
Inscriptions, 311, 320, n. 1.
Inspiration in poetry, 340.
Instrumental, old usages with, 18.
Inter-state relations, 454.
Iron-eating mice, *motif*, 251, 352.
Irugapa, *Nānārtharatnamālā*, 414.
Īçvara, creator, 99, 100.
Īçvarakṛṣṇa, philosopher, 77, 488, 489.
Iṣṭarāma, brother of Bilhaṇa, 153.
Īsāpur inscription, 15, n. 1.
Isis, goddess worshipped in India, x.
Isolde, 356.
I-tsing, Chinese pilgrim, 55, 72, 176, 177, 429.

Jābāli, narrator of part of the *Kādambarī*, 320.
Jackal and indigo vat, story of, 257.
Jacob ben Eleazar, Hebrew version of the *Pañcatantra*, 358.
Jagaddeva, *Svapnacintāmaṇi*, 534.
Jagadīça, *Tarkāmṛta*, 486.
Jagajjyotirmalla, comm. on *Narapatijayacaryā*, 534, n. 5.
Jagannātha, *Bhāminīvilāsa*, 234; *Rasagañgādhara*, 396, 397.
Jaimini, alleged author of *Mīmāṅsā Sūtra*, xxi, 458.
Jains, 15, 148, 240, 241, 246, 261, 292, 294, 295, 301, 490, 499, 500, 501.
Jain Stotras, 214, 215.
Jaiyyaṭa, comm. on Suçruta, 507.
Jalauka, son of Açoka, 163.
Jalhaṇa, *Mugdhopadeça*, 239; *Subhāṣitamuktāvalī*, 222; *Somapālavilāsa*, 172.
Jambhaladatta, version of *Vetālapañcaviṅçatikā*, 288.
James of Vitry, 362.
Janaka, king, 95, 120.
Jātūkarṇa, authority on medicine, 509.
Java, Kavi literature in, 16.
Jayacandra, of Kanauj, 139.
Jayadatta, *Açvavaidyaka*, 465.
Jayadeva, *Gītagovinda*, 53, 190–8, 219, 327, 469.
Jayadeva, dramatist, comm. on Gañgeça, 485; *Candrāloka*, 396.

Jayadeva, *Ratimañjarī*, 469.
Jayāditya, author of *Kāçikā Vṛtti*, 429, 430.
Jayanta Bhaṭṭa, father of Abhinanda, 135; *Nyāyamañjarī*, 221, 484.
Jayāpīḍa, king, 169, 236.
Jayaratha, *Alaṁkāravimarçinī*, 173; *Haracaritacintāmaṇi*, 137, 266.
Jayasiṅha, Cālukya prince, 154.
Jayasiṅha, king of Kashmir, 136, 159, 160, 168.
Jayasiṅha Siddharāja, patron of Hemacandra, 432.
Jewish-Christian week, adopted in India, 531.
Jews, intermediaries in civilization, 360.
Jīmūtavāhana, hero, 285.
Jīmūtavāhana (perhaps 12th. cent.), *Dāyabhāga*, 449.
Jinakīrti, stories by, 295.
Jinasena, *Harivaṅçapurāṇa*, 498.
Jinasena, *Ādipurāṇa*, 498; *Pārçvābhyudaya*, 86.
Jinendrabuddhi, *Nyāsa*, 124, 376, 413, 430.
Jiṣṇu, of Bhillamalla, father of Brahmagupta, 522.
Jīvaka, expert on children's disease, 506.
Jīvaçarman, astrologer, 530
Jō-do-shū, sect, 494.
Joel, Rabbi, Hebrew version of the *Pañcatantra*, 358.
Jogīmārā inscription, 40.
John of Capua, *Liber Kelilae et Dimnae*, 358.
Jonarāja, of Kashmir, 173, 174, 223.
Joseph and Potiphar, *motif*, 343.
Julian, emperor, 356.
Julius Valerius, style of, 70, n. 2.
Jūmaranandin, revises comm. on *Saṁkṣiptasāra*, 432.
Juṣka, king of Kashmir, 163.
Juvenal, 351.
Jyeṣṭhakalaça, father of Bilhaṇa, 153.
Jyotirīçvara, *Pañcasāyaka*, 469.

Kaccāyana, Pāli grammar, 436.
Kādamba king, Kāmadeva, 137
Kadiri, version of the *Çukasaptati*, 359.
Kaikeyī, wife of Daçaratha, 95.
Kālakavana, eastern boundary of Āryāvarta, 11.
Kālarātri, demon, 279.
Kalaça, son of Sūryamatī, 281.
Kalhaṇa, historian of Kashmir, 132, 152, 158–72, 223, 237, 281, 285, 339, 347, 349, 428, 431.
Kālidāsa, x, xii, xiii, xiv, xv, xvi, xvii, 8, 20, 21, 30, 39, 43, 51, 54, 60, 76, 79–108, 109, 115, 116, 119, 123, 126, 131, 132, 135, 136, 140, 145, 149, 194, 199, 201, 205, n. 1, 209, 210, 218, 262, 307, 310, 316, 339, 340, 341, 344, 347, 372, 380, n. 1, 392, 413, 416, 429, 451, 462, 469.
Kaliṅga, country, 93; betel and cocopalms of, 80.
Kaliṅgasenā, hetaira, 271.
Kallaṭa, *Spandakārikā*, 481.
Kallimachos, Greek poet, 197, 348, 349, 353.
Kalyāṇamalla, *Anaṅgaraṅga*, 470.
Kāma, love god, 88, 92.
Kāmadeva, Kādamba king, 137.
Kāmadeva, king of Jaintia, patron of Kavirāja, xvii, n. 5.
Kamalākara, *Nirṇayasindhu*, 449.
Kamalavardhana, bad policy of, 168.
Kāmandakī, nun, 263.
Kāmandaki, *Nītisāra*, 462.
Kāmapāla, king in *Daçakumāracarita*, 297.
Kāmarūpa, elephants of, 94.
Kāmbojas, Kambojas, people, 81, 441; their special speech uses, 10.
Kamikioi, by Sophokles, 355.
Kampana, (possibly from Latin campus), 170.
Kāmyaka, forest, 109, 110.
Kāṇabhūti, a Yakṣa, 266, 267.
Kaṇāda, *Vaiçeṣika Sūtra*, 483, 485.
Kanaka, uncle of Kalhaṇa, 158.
Kanakamañjarī, Jain legend of, 361.
Kanakasena Vādirāja, 142.
Kanakhala, mount, 85.
Kanarese, alleged use of, in Greek farce, x.
Kaṇika, (? conn. with Cāṇikya, older form of Cāṇakya), lectures Dhṛtarāṣṭra, 451.
Kaniṣka, Emperor, xxvii, xxviii, 18, 39, n. 2, 74, 163, 506, 507, n. 1.
Kandarpaketu, hero of the *Vāsavadattā*, 309, 310.
Kaṅsa, slaying of by Kṛṣṇa, 45.
Kāntimatī, mother of Rāmānuja, 478.
Kapila, legendary founder of the Sāṁkhya, 488.
Kapilabala, father of Dṛḍhabala, 506.
Kapiñjala, friend of Puṇḍarīka, 321, 322, 323.
Karaṭaka, 249, 250.
Kārkoṭa dynasty, 163, 164.
Karṇa, of Ḍāhala, 153.
Karṇadeva Trailokyamalla, of Aṇhilvāḍ, 153.
Karṇāṭas, speech of, 386.
Karṇīsuta, authority on thieving, 303.
Kārṣṇājini, authority on ritual, 475.
Kāçakṛtsna, philosopher, 475.
Kāçyapa, authority on *Alaṁkāra*, 372.
Kāçyapa, authority on medicine, 505.
Kāçyapa, *Bālāvabodhana*, 432.
Kāçyapa, *Dharmasūtra*, 439.
Kashgar, MS. from, 509.

Kashmir, 133, 134, 248, 284, 285; not home of Sanskrit, 17; sandal of, 80.
Kashmirian *Bṛhatkathā*, 275, 276.
Kashmirian pronunciation, 386.
Kāṭhaka school, 438.
Kātyāyana, grammarian, author of *Vārttikas*, xxvi, n. 1, 10, 17, 40, 308, 426, 427.
Kātyāyana, lexicographer, *Nāmamālā*, 413.
Kauṭalya, Kauṭilya, xvii; see *Kauṭilīya Arthaçāstra*.
Kāverī, river, 94.
Kavi, Kawi, speech and literature in Bali, 16, 463.
Kavirāja, title, 76, 138, 139, n. 3, 307, 386.
Kavirāja Sūri, *Rāghavapāṇḍavīya*, xvii, n. 5, 137, 138, 139.
Kedāra Bhaṭṭa, *Vṛttaratnākara*, 417.
Ke-gon, Buddhist sect, 494.
Kerala, ladies of, 94.
Keçava, father of Gaṇeça, 523.
Keçava, father of Rāmānuja, 478.
Keçava, father of Vopadeva, 511.
Keçava Miçra, *Tarkabhāṣā*, 486.
Keçavasvāmin, *Nānārthārṇavasaṁkṣepa*, 414.
Khañkha, Kashmirian minister, 163.
Khāravela, king, 40, n. 1, 41.
Khazars, alleged identity with Gurjaras, 33, n. 3.
King, position of the, 444, 447, 453, 454.
Kings as poets and patrons, 52–4.
Kinnaras, 321.
Kirāta, Çiva as a, 111.
Kiṣkindhā, forest, 90.
Kitāb el Sindbād, 360.
Kauṇapadanta, alleged authority on Arthaçāstra, 457.
Kauravas, destroy Pāṇḍava army, 256, 257.
Kauçāmbī, town, 29, n. 2, 268, 270.
Kautsa, a Brahmin, 94.
Koine, Prākrit, assumed, 35, n. 3.
Kokkoka, *Ratirahasya*, 469.
Kṛṣṇa, brother of Harṣavardhana, 314
Kṛṣṇa, god, 125, 126, 162, 191, 192, 210–17.
Kṛṣṇa, king (A.D. 1247), 222.
Kṛṣṇa III, Rāṣṭrakūṭa king, 133, 333.
Kṛṣṇalīlāçuka, *Puruṣakāra*, 430.
Kṛttikās, Pleiades, 89.
Kramadiçvara, *Saṁkṣiptasāra*, 33, 432.
Krauñca, mountain, 85.
Kṣapaṇaka, lexicographer, 76.
Kṣārapāṇi, authority on medicine, 509.
Kṣatrapas, 268.
Kṣatriyas, speech of, 8.
Kṣemaṁkara, version of *Siṅhāsanadvātriṅçikā*, 292.
Kṣemarāja, comm. on *Çiva Sūtra*, 481.
Kṣemendra, Kashmir polymath, x, 33, 135, 136, 159, 161, 208, 209, 237, 240, 262, 276–80, 281, 321, 397, 416, 469, 493.
Kṣīrasvāmin, comm. on *Amarakoça*, 414.
Kubera, god, 94.
Kucumāra, authority on erotics, 468.
Kulaçekhara, xiv, n. 1.
Kulaçekhara, patron of Vāsudeva, 98.
Kulaçekhara, *Mukundamālā*, 218.
Kullūka, comm. on *Manu*, 445.
Kumāra, war god, 89, 90.
Kumāradāsa, king of Ceylon, 80.
Kumāradāsa, *Jānakīharaṇa*, 89, 108, n. 1, 119–24, 209, 336.
Kumāragupta, emperor, 74, 76, 80, 81, 94, n. 1.
Kumāralāta, *Kalpanāmaṇḍitikā* or *Sūtrālaṁkāra*, viii–x, 55, 56, 69.
Kumārapāla, king of Gujarāt, 143, 172.
Kumārasvāmin, *Ratnāpaṇa*, 435.
Kumārila, philosopher, xxi, 24, n. 2, 25, 438, 473, 474, 484, 497, 499.
Kumbhakarṇa, a Rākṣasa, 117.
Kuntala (*v. l.* Kuntaka), *Vakroktijīvita*, 392, 393.
Kuntala Çātakarṇi Sātavāhana, kills his queen, 469.
Kuntala, Sātavāhana of, 341.
Kurukṣetra, Abhīras in, 33.
Kurus, tribe, 3.
Kuçāvatī, city, 96.
Kuṣaṇas (Kuṣanas), 145, 163, 166.
Kusumadeva, *Dṛṣṭāntaçataka*, 234.
Kusumapura, Pāṭaliputra, 521, 522.
Kuvinda, of Çūrasena, 341.

Laḍahacandra, poet, 204, 205.
La Fontaine, *Fables*, 359.
Lagrange, J. L., Comte, astronomer (1736–1813), 526.
Lahndā (Lahndī), speech of the western Panjāb, 32, 33.
Lakṣmaṇa, brother of Rāma, 96, 120.
Lakṣmaṇa Ācārya, *Caṇḍīkucapañcāçikā*, 221.
Lakṣmaṇa Bhaṭṭa, father of Rāmacandra, 139.
Lakṣmaṇa Bhaṭṭa, *Rāmāyaṇacampū*, 336.
Lakṣmaṇasena, king, 53, 190, 219, 222, 448.
Lakṣmīdeva, father of Jalhaṇa, 222.
Lakṣmīdevī, wife of Bālambhaṭṭa Vaidyanātha, 447.
Lakṣmīdhara, *Ṣaḍbhāṣācandrikā*, 434, 435.
Lakṣmīdhara, *Smṛtikalpataru*, 448.
Lalitāditya, king, 54, 150, 168.
Lalitasuradeva, poet, 150.
Lalla, *Çiṣyadhīvṛddhitantra*, 522.
Lañkā, not Ceylon, 95, n. 1, 97.

Lañkeçvara or Rāvaṇa, as a Prākrit grammarian, 433, 434.
Lāṭa, astronomer, 520.
Lāṭa, description of, 79.
Lāṭas, dislike Sanskrit, 385.
Latin of Middle Ages, not a precise parallel to Sanskrit, 11, 13.
Laugākṣi Bhāskara, *Arthasaṁgraha*, 474; *Tarkakaumudī*, 486.
Laugh and cry *motif*, 343.
Lauhityā, river, 94.
Laukika era of Kashmir, 164.
Lavaṇaprasāda, of Gujarāt, 173.
Law, origin of works on, 404.
Leon of Medina, 139.
Lexicography, 406, 413–15.
Liber de Dina et Kalila, by Raimundus de Biterris, 359.
Liber Kelilae et Dimnae, Directorium vitae humanae, by John of Capua, 358.
Licchavi princess, marries Candragupta, 74.
Līlāvatī, capital of Kapphaṇa, 133.
Līlāçuka, *Kṛṣṇakarṇāmṛta*, 218.
Liñga worship, 285.
Lingual letters, as affecting style, 390.
Lion and woodpecker, fable of, 355.
Lively fancy (*utprekṣā*), 106, 312, 316, 375, 399.
Livy, Roman historian (B.C. 59–17 A.D.), most unmilitary of historians, 169.
Llewelyn and Gelert, legend of, 354.
Loaves and fishes, Buddhist parallel to miracle of, 503.
Logic, 482–7.
Lohara dynasty of Kashmir, 164.
Lokasena, continues *Uttarapurāṇa*, 498.
Lokāyata, philosophy, 453, 472, 483, 498, 499, 500.
Lokottaravādins, Buddhist school, 491.
Lolimbarāja, *Harivilāsa*, 137; *Vaidyajīvana*, 511.
Lollaṭa, writer on poetics, 387, n. 3.
Longus, *Poimenika*, 370.
Loṭhana, pretender in Kashmir, 160.
Love, 324, 325.
Loveliness, of style (*kānti*), 374, 377, 381, 390.
Lucan, Roman poet (A.D. 39–65), 145, n. 3, 346, 347, 348, 349.
Lucretius, Roman poet (*c.* 99–58 B.C.), 194, 345.
Lukianos (*c.* A.D. 125–190), Λύκιος ἢ ὄνος, 368, n. 2.
Lydia, as intermediary in transmission of fables, 353.
Lykophron, Greek poet, 26.
Lyly, *Euphues*, 370.
Lyric poetry, 39, 40, 41, 42, 47, 48.

Machiavelli, N., 455, 456.
Madana, king of Ujjain, 267.
Madanābhirāma, of Pañcāla, 188.
Madanamañcukā, Madanamañjukā, 271.
Madanapāla, *Madanavinodanighaṇṭu*, 512.
Madanasena, son of Haradatta, 291.
Mādhava, brother of Sāyaṇa, part author of, *Jīvanmuktiviveka*, 477; *Dhātuvṛtti*, 430; *Nyāyamālāvistara*, 474; *Pañcadaçī*, 477; *Parāçarasmṛtivyākhyā*, 447.
Mādhava, *Çañkaradigvijaya*, 476.
Mādhava, *Sarvadarçanasaṁgraha*, 499, 500.
Mādhavakara, *Rugviniçcaya*, 511.
Mādhava Bhaṭṭa, perhaps name of Kavirāja, 137.
Madhusūdana Sarasvatī, *Prasthānabheda*, 467.
Madhva, Ānandatīrtha, school of, 479.
Madhyadeça, speech of, 386.
Madhyamikā, city, 427.
Märchen, 245, 246, 249, 257, 263.
Magadhas, like Sanskrit, 385.
Māgha, *Çiçupālavadha*, 18, 39, 87, n. 2, 89, 108, n. 1, 109, 115, 116, 119, 121, n. 1, 124–31, 133, 140, 141, 165, 208, 260, 263, 294, 336, 340, 345, 378, 384, 385, 430, 451, 469, 490.
Magic powers, obtained by Yoga, 490, 491.
Mahādeva, of Devagiri, patron of Vopadeva, 432.
Mahākāla, shrine of, 85.
Mahānāman, *Mahāvaṅsa*, 148.
Mahārāṣṭra, lyric of, 60.
Mahāsāñghikas, school of Buddhism, 491.
Mahāvīra, Jain sage, 143.
Mahāvīra, mathematician, 524, 526.
Mahāyāna, Buddhist philosophy, 55, 72, 73, 413, 492, 493.
Mahāçvetā, lover of Puṇḍarīka, 321, 322, 323.
Mahendra, 94.
Mahendravikramavarman, dramatist, 53, n. 2.
Maheçvara, *Viçvaprakāça*, 414.
Mahiman Bhaṭṭa, *Vyaktiviveka*, 393.
Mahiṣa, demon, 210.
Maḥmūd Ghaznī, 164.
Mahomedans, 164.
Maitrakanyaka, legend of, 65, 66.
Maitrāyaṇīya school, 438, 441.
Maitreyarakṣita, *Dhātupradīpa*, 430.
Makaranda, *Tithyādipattra*, 523.
Māla, 85.
Mālava, king of, defeated by Harṣa, 317, 319.
Malaya hills, 94.
Mallanāga, Malanāga, *see* Vātsyāyana.
Mallārjuna, pretender in Kashmir, 160.
Mallavādin, *Nyāyabinduṭīkāṭippaṇī*, 484.

Mallinātha, commentator, 81, 83, 87, 417, n. 2, 435.
Malliṣeṇa, *Syādvādamañjarī*, 497.
Mālyavant, 266, 267.
Mamma, battle of, with Utpala, 152.
Mammaṭa, *Kāvyaprakāça*, xvii, 87, n. 5, 140, 141, 237, 373, 384, 387, 388, 390, 393, 394, 395, 396, 398.
Man about town, characteristics of the, 51, 52.
Mānasa, lake, 85.
Mānatuñga, *Bhaktāmarastotra*, 214.
Mandākinī, river, described by Vālmīki, 43.
Maṇḍana Miçra, works by, 474.
Mandaradeva, a Vidyādhara, 279.
Manetho, *Apotelesmata*, 531.
Man-eating monster, Buddhist and Christian legend of, 502.
Māṇikya Nandin, *Parīkṣāmukhasūtra*, 484.
Māṇikya Sūri, *Yaçodharacaritra*, 142, 334, n. 1.
Maṇittha (cf. Manetho), 530.
Mañkha, poet, 136, 137, 161, 172, 307, 339, 396, 414.
Manners (*rīti*), of diction, 383, 384, 389, 391.
Māra, legend of, 66, 502, 503.
Marāṭhī literature, 36; language, 24, 90.
Marco Polo, on devilries of Kashmir, 166.
Maria Stuart, by Schiller, 86.
Marīci, legend of, 302.
Māridatta, legend of, 333, 334.
Marie of France, 362.
Mārkaṇḍeya, *Prākṛtasarvasva*, 33, 269, 434, 435.
Martial, 127, n. 1, 310, 313, n. 1, 348; exiled from Rome, 56.
Martianus Capella, style of, 70, n. 2.
Marwar, Apabhrañça loved in, 386.
Mary, mother of Jesus, legends of, 502, 503, 504.
Mas'ūdi, Arab geographer and historian (died Cairo, A. D. 956), 360, 527.
Mātañga Divākara, poet, 201, 214.
Mathematics, 75, 404, 408, 523–8.
Mathurā school, uses Sanskrit, 15, n. 3.
Mathurānātha, *Tattvacintāmaṇirahasya*, 485.
Mātṛceṭa, perhaps identical with Açvaghoṣa, 64.
Mātṛgupta, 132, 133, 163.
Mauryas, use of images for profit, 428.
Maya, astrologer, 530.
Māyā, alleged Indian representative of Isis, x.
Māyaṇa, son of Sāyaṇa, 500.
Mayūra, poet, 152, 201, 202, 211, 315, 412.
Māyurāja, royal dramatist, 53, n. 2.
Mayūraka, a snake doctor, 315.
Max Müller, theory of renaissance of Sanskrit, 35.
Meat, eating of, in Tantric ritual, 482, 496.
Mecca, known to *Kālacakra Tantra*, 496.
Medhātithi, commentary on *Manu*, 445, 473.
Medhātithi, i.e. Gautama, *Nyāyaçāstra*, xiii.
Medhāvirudra, blind author, 119, n. 2.
Medical dictionaries, 512.
Medicine, 404, 408, 505–15.
Medinīkara, *Anekārthaçabdakoça*, 414.
Megasthenes, 459.
Meghavāhana, king of Kashmir, 163.
Meghavijaya, *Pañcākhyānoddhāra*, xii, 261.
Menander, Greek comedian, 428.
Meṇṭha, poet, 132, 133, 307, 339.
Meru, mount, in astronomy, 520.
Merutuñga, comm. on *Rasādhyāya*, 512.
Merutuñga, *Prabandhacintāmaṇi*, 293, 344, n. 3.
Mestra, legend of, 365.
Metaphors, 43, 44, 61, 62, 78, 79, 106, 212, 350.
Metamorphoses, by Apuleius, 367.
Metamorphoses, by Ovid, 368.
Methodological principles, recognized by Kauṭilya and Caraka, 461.
Metonic period, adopted in *Romaka Siddhānta*, 518.
Metre, 47, 48, 64, 92, 107, 108, 115, 118, 123, 124, 130, 131, 137, 141; forms of, 417–21; writers on, 415–17.
Metrics, 405, 407, 415–17.
Mihirakula, Hūṇa king, 163; *see the next*.
Mihiragula, leader of the Hūṇas, 74.
Milesiaka, by Aristeides, xi.
Milhaṇa, *Cikitsāmṛta*, 511.
Mīmalladevī, mother of Çrīharṣa, 139.
Mimes, by Sophron, 367.
Mīnarāja Yavanācārya, astrologer, 531.
Mitanni influence on Aryans, xxiv.
Mitra Miçra, *Vīramitrodaya*, 449.
Mixed Sanskrit, 482, 492, 493, 495, 510.
Mixture of languages, 398.
Moggallāna, *Saddalakkhaṇa*, 436.
Mongols, influence of, on transmission of tales, 360.
Moriyas, identity of, 22, n. 2.
Morphology, changes in, 5, 6.
Moschos, Greek pastoral poet, 370.
Moses Bassola, 139.
Mothers, goddesses, 285.
Mountains, Kālidāsa's love of, 88.
Muhammad ibn Mūsā ab-Khowārizmī, mathematician at the court of al-Māmūn, died *c.* A.D. 840 (L. C. Karpinski, *Robert of Chester's Latin*

Translation of the Algebra of al-Khowarizmi, 1915), 527.
Mūka, demon in boar form, 111.
Mūka, *Pañcaçatī*, 218.
Mukta, servant of Harṣa, 158.
Muktāphalaketu, Vidyādhara emperor, 278.
Muktikalaça, great-grandfather of Bilhaṇa, 153.
Mukula, father of Pratīhārendurāja, 383.
Mūladeva, typical rogue, 238, 291.
Mūlasarvāstivādins, Buddhist school, 491.
Mummuṇirāja, of the Konkan, 336.
Muṇḍā tribes, linguistic influence of, 4.
Muñja, king, 53, n. 2.
Muralā (*v. l.* Marulā), river, 94.
Murāri, *Koça* ascribed to, 412.
Music, works on (cf. also Nārada's *Saṁgītamakaranda*, GOS. 16), 465, 466.
Mussolini, Italian dictator, 455.

Nachshabī, *Tūtīnāmeh*, 359.
Nāgadevī, mother of Bilhaṇa, 153.
Nāgarāja, *Bhāvaçataka*, 234.
Nāgarakas, 467.
Nāgārjuna, Buddhist philosopher, 71, 72, 476.
Nāgārjuna, *Yogaçataka* and *Yogasāra*, 511.
Nāgārjuna, *Ratiçāstra*, 470.
Nāgārjuna, *Rasaratnākara*, 512.
Nāgas, mythical creatures, 134.
Naghuṣa, for Nahuṣa, 25.
Nāgojī Bhaṭṭa, comm. on Kaiyaṭa, 429; *Paribhāṣenduçekhara*, 431.
Nairuktas, etymologists or expositors, 403.
Nakṣatras, alleged Chinese origin of, 528.
Nakula, *Açvacikitsita*, 465.
Nala, hero, 295.
Namisādhu, commentator on Rudraṭa, 384, n. 1.
Nanda, legend of, 56, 57.
Nandas, dynasty, 427, 458, 459.
Nandikeçvara, authority on erotics, 469.
Nandin, authority on *Kāmaçāstra*, 451.
Nārada, as astrologer, 528.
Nārada, *Bhaktiçāstra*, 480.
Narahari, *Rājanighaṇṭu*, 512.
Narahari, *Narapatijayacaryā Svarodaya*, 535.
Narasiṅha, of Orissa, patron of Vidyādhara, 395.
Naravāhanadatta, hero of *Bṛhatkathā*, 270, 271.
Nārāyaṇa, *Hitopadeça*, 263–5.
Nārāyaṇa, *Mātañgalīlā*, 465.
Nārāyaṇa, *Svāhāsudhākaracampū*, 336.
Nārāyaṇa, *Vṛttaratnākara*, 417, n. 4.
Nārāyaṇa Bhaṭṭa, writes introduction to *Daçakumāracarita*, 297, n. 3.
Nārāyaṇa Bhaṭṭa, *Mānameyodaya*, 474.
Nārāyaṇa Paṇḍita, *Navaratnaparīkṣā*, 465.
Navadvīpa, logical school of, 483, 485.
Nāyaka Bhaṭṭa, 390, 391, 392.
Negative with finite verb, 19.
Nemāditya, father of Trivikrama, possibly = Devāditya, 332, n. 3.
Neo-Platonists, Indian influence on, 500, 501.
Nepalese *Pañcatantra*, 246, 262.
Nestorian Christians, possible influence of, 479.
Nicula, alleged poet and friend of Kālidāsa, 107.
Nigel of Canterbury, 362.
Nihilism, 472, 473.
Nikodemos, legend of, 494.
Nīlakaṇṭha, *Bhagavantabhāskara*, 449.
Nīlakaṇṭha, *Tājika*, 534.
Nīlanāga, 163.
Nine Jewels of Vikramāditya, 76.
Nirvindhyā, river, 85.
Niçcayadatta, tale of, 363.
Nityanātha, *Rasaratnākara*, 512.
Nominal style, 20, 21, 258.
Nominal use of gerundive, 265.
North, taste of poets in the, 316.
North, Thomas, *The Morall Philosophie of Doni*, 358.
Northerners, uses of the, 10.
North-western Prākrit, 27, 28.
Novus Esopus, by Baldo, 359.
Numerals, xxiii, xxiv, 527, 528.
Numerical formulae, 228.
Nuti, Giulio, *Del Governo de' regni* (Ferrara, 1583), 358.
Nyāya philosophy, 499, 500, 507.

Oath, of doctors, 513.
Obedience of the wild creatures to the Christ Child, 503.
Oḍayadeva, *Gadyacintāmaṇi*, 331.
Odo of Sheriton, 362.
Odyssey, 13, 61, 337, 367.
Oknos and his ass, 354.
Old Ardhamāgadhī, 28.
Old Gujarātī, resembles Apabhrañça, 35.
Old Māgadhī, 28.
Old Çaurasenī, 28.
Old Syrian *Pañcatantra*, 246.
Opium, medicinal use of, 511.
Optative forms, reduced in classical Sanskrit, 6.
Ordeal, fabricated in Tristan and Isolde, 291.
Origin of Sanskrit, 3–7.
Origin of the fable literature, 242–6.
Origin of the Çāstras, 403–5.
Oṛiyā, source of, 32.

Ovid, Augustan poet, 194, 347, 350, 365, 368.
Oxyrhynchus Papyri, x.

Pādalipta, *Taraṅgavatī*, 34.
Padmagupta, 201, n. 4.
Padmanābhadatta, *Supadmavyākaraṇa*, 432.
Padmamihira, Kashmirian historian, 161, 162.
Padmapāda, *Pañcapādikā*, 477.
Painting, Greek influence on Indian, 371.
Painting, works on, 466.
Pahlavas, 441.
Pahlavi version of *Pañcatantra*, 246, 259.
Paiṭhīnasi, *Dharmasūtra*, 439.
Pakṣilasvāmin, *see* Vātsyāyana.
Pālaka, legend of, 272.
Pālakāpya, authority on veterinary science, 465.
Palatal sibilant, as affecting style, 390.
Pāli, language, 29, 69.
Palms, mating of, 365.
Palm-tree, homage of, to Mary, 503.
Pāmpaka, 290, n. 1.
Pañcāla, speech of, 386.
Pāñcāla Bābhravya, authority on erotics, 468.
Pañcarātra school of Vaiṣṇavism, 480.
Pañcaçikha, Sāṁkhya authority, 488.
Pāṇḍavas, 243, 257.
Pāṇḍyas, pearls of, 94.
Pāṇini, grammarian, xxv, 5, 7, 9, 10, 13, 17, 18, 20, 21, 40, 45, 339, 372, 406, 423, 500.
Pāṇini, poet, 203, 204, 416, 430.
Panegyrics, 149, 150.
Paraleipsis (*ākṣepa*), 378, 380.
Paramānanda, *Çṛṅgārasaptaçatikā*, 202.
Paramārtha, renders *Sāṁkhyakārikā* into Chinese, 488.
Parāçara, alleged authority on *Arthaçāstra*, 457.
Parāçara, astrologer, 528.
Parāçara, authority on medicine, 509.
Paraçurāma, sage, 85, 95.
Pārasīkas, 81.
Parasol-Bhāravi, 114.
Parihāsapura, home of Kalhaṇa, 158.
Parimala, *see* Padmagupta.
Parisoi, 369.
Pāriyātra, southern boundary of Āryāvarta, 11, 97; *Bhūtabhāṣā* in, 386.
Paronomasia (*çleṣa*), 50, 106, 107, 212, 310, 312, 351, 378, 380, 381, 384, 390, 396.
Parrot, as narrator of the *Kādambarī*, 321, 324.
Parthians, 39, 145.
Participles, 115, 258, 307.
Particles, use of, 63, 64, 123.
Pārvatī, goddess, 110, 285.
Pāṭaliputra, town, 76, 461, n. 1; fortifications of, 460.
Patañjali, *Mahābhāṣya*, xx, xxvi, 5, 7, 10, 15, 45–8, 199, 227, 241, 308, 339, 426, 453, n. 1, 460, 505.
Patañjali, philosopher, 490, 499.
Patent remedies, satire of, 238.
Pathos, 63, 68, 69.
Patriotism, not evident in Sanskrit poetry, 345, 346.
Pattralekhā, form of Rohiṇī, 321.
Paulus, of Alexandria, xxiv.
Pauṣkarasādi, grammarian, 426.
Pauṣkarasādin, medical fragment by, 516.
Pausanias, 354.
Pearl fisheries of the Tāmraparṇī, 80.
Perceforest, legend of, 364.
Perfect passive, 123, 138.
Perfect tense, 20, 115, 307.
Perikles, ideas of, 452, n. 2.
Periphrases, use of, 90.
Periphrastic perfect, in classical Sanskrit, 6.
Persian tale, 366.
Persia, Persians, 423, 511, 534, 535.
Peter Alfonsi, 362.
Petronius, author of *Satira* or *Satirae*, xi, 310, 368, n. 2, 370; style of, 70, n. 2.
Phaedrus, fable writer, 352, 355.
Phaidra and Hippolytos, *motif*, 356.
Philemon and Baukis, Indian legend of, 284.
Philosopher's stone, 511.
Philosophy, 404, 405, 471–504.
Phokylides, maxims of, 227.
Phonetics, change in, 4, 5.
Physiologos, alleged borrowing from India in, 356.
Pilpay, Vidyāpati, 359.
Pindar, Greek lyric poet, 26, 349, n. 3.
Piṇḍāyu, astrologer, 530.
Piṅgala, *Chandas*, 48, 416.
Piçācas, 269.
Piçuna, alleged authority on Arthaçāstra, 457.
Pīṭhamarda, as companion of the man about town, 52.
Place value system, 526, 527.
Placidus, legend of, Buddhist parallel to, 502.
Plagiarism, 385.
Plant diseases, 511.
Plato, xxi, 367, 500; *Republic* of, xviii.
Poetesses, 205.
Poetic conventions, 343.
Poetics, 372–400, 407.
Poets, power of, 165, 170.
Poimenika, by Longus, 370.
Poison, accepted as cause of death by Roman writers, 166.
Poison maiden, 361, n. 3.

Politics, of Aristotle, xviii.
Polybios, Greek historian, 164.
Polygnotos, painting of Oknos, 354.
Polykrates' ring, *motif*, 355, n. 3.
Popular speech, influence of, on literary dialect, 6, 7.
Portraiture of the Buddha, in Gandhāran art, 490, 491.
Post-Augustan poetry, compared with Sanskrit, 347-51.
Pṛthu, astrologer, 530.
Pṛthuyaças, *Horāṣaṭpañcāçikā*, 534.
Pṛthvīrāja, king of Ajmir and Delhi, 173.
Prabhācandra, 497; *Prabhāvakacaritra*, 294, n. 5.
Prabhākara, philosopher, xxi, 473, 474, 499.
Prabhākaravardhana, father of Harṣa, 317.
Prabhudevī Lāṭī, poetess, 205, n. 1.
Prācyamadhyas, uses of the, 10.
Pradyota, king, 364.
Pradyumna, astronomer, 522.
Pradyumna Sūri, *Prabhāvakacaritra*, 294, n. 5.
Prāgjyotiṣa, 94.
Prājya Bhaṭṭa, *Rājāvalipatākā*, 174.
Prakāçātman, comments on *Pañcapādikā*, 477.
Prākrits, xxv-xxvii, 26–31, 49, 80, 224, 261, 295, 341, 376, 385, 386.
Prākrit grammarian, 433-6.
Prākrit literature, 245.
Prākrit lyrics, 223–6.
Prākrit originals, alleged for Sanskrit poetry, 39-42.
Prakṛti, legend of, 65.
Praçastapāda, *Padārthadharmasaṁgraha*, xxi, 485.
Pratāparudra, of Warangal, patron of Vidyānātha, 395.
Pratāparudradeva, king (A.D. 1499), 191.
Pratīhārendurāja, commentator on Udbhaṭa, 383.
Pratiṣṭhāna, on the Godāvarī, 50, 267, 268.
Pravarasena, king (of Kashmir or Vākāṭaka), 97, 132, 133, 168, 316.
Prepositional compounds, 90, 213.
Present participle in *antī* or *atī*, 20.
Primary Prākrits, 27.
Prītikūṭa, home of Bāṇa, 314.
Priyañgu, legend of, 46.
Prolongation of vowels, 9.
Propertius, Roman poet, 26, 194, 348, 356.
Prose, in Kāvya, 300.
Prose and verse, use of, ix, 69, 70, 244, 255, 256, 311, 330, 332, 408, 409.
Ptolemy, 50; *Syntaxis* of, 519.
Pulakeçin, king, defeats Harṣa, xvii, 315, n. 1.
Pulastya, a seer, 267.
Pulindas, tribe, 285.
Puliça, xxiv; see *Pauliça Siddhānta*.
Pulse, used in diagnosis, 511.
Punarvasu Ātreya, authority on medicine, 509.
Puṇḍarīka, beloved of Mahāçvetā, 321, 322.
Pūrṇabhadra, *Pañcatantra*, 246, 261, 262, 291.
Purohitas, of Kashmir, 161.
Puruṣottamadeva, *Bhāṣāvṛtti*, 430.
Puruṣottamadeva, father of Devadatta, 292.
Puruṣottamadeva, *Trikāṇḍaçeṣa*, 414; *Hārāvalī*, 414.
Pūrvamīmāṅsā philosophy, 472–4, 499, 500, 507.
Puṣpadanta, legend of, 266, 267.
Puṣpadanta, *Mahimnaḥstava*, 220, 221.
Puṣpaketu, a Vidyādhara, 309.
Puṣpasena, teacher of Oḍayadeva, 331.
Puṣyamitra, king, 39, n. 2, 427, 442, n. 1.
Pygmalion and Galatea, legend of, 366.
Pythagorean problem, 517.

Quicksilver, used in medicine, 511, 512.

Ṛṣabha, Jain saint, 214.
Ṛṣyamūka, mountain, 248.
Ṛṣyaçṛñga, legend of, 294, n. 4.
Raḍḍa, Kashmir official, 159.
Rādhā, beloved of Kṛṣṇa, 191.
Raghu, son of Dilīpa, 93, 94.
Raghunandana, *Tattvas*, 449.
Raghunātha Çiromaṇi, *Dīdhiti*, 485.
Raimundus de Biterris, Raimond de Béziers, *Liber de Dina et Kalila*, 359.
Rainy season, description of, 84, 120.
Raivataka, mountain, 125.
Rājakalaça, grandfather of Bilhaṇa, 153.
Rājaçekhara, Buddhist, 486.
Rājaçekhara, *Antarākathāsaṁgraha*, 295, n. 5; *Prabandhakoça*, 293.
Rājaçekhara, dramatist and critic, xiii, xiv, xxvii, 45, 53, n. 1, 119, 132, 135, 205, n. 1, 214, 270, 319, 334, 339, 340, 341, 342, 343, 345, 395.
Rājasthānī, connected with Nāgara Apabhrañça, 32.
Rājavadana, Kashmirian pretender, 161.
Rājiga, Cola prince, 154.
Rājputs, national vices of, 156.
Rājyavardhana, brother of Harṣa, 317.
Rājyaçrī, sister of Harṣa, 317, 318.
Rāma, father of Somadeva, 281.
Rāma, hero, (on his killing of Çambūka, see Printz, ZII. v. 241–6), 96, 97, 120, 135, 210, 271.
Rāma, patron of Vāsudeva, 98.
Rāmacandra, *Nāṭyadarpaṇa*, xv.
Rāmacandra, *Prakriyākaumudī*, 430.

Rāmacandra, *Rasendracintāmaṇi*, 512.
Rāmacandra, son of Lakṣmaṇa Bhaṭṭa, 139.
Rāmagiri, 85.
Rāma Kavīçvara, poet, 149, 150.
Rāmānuja, philosopher, 473, 478, 479, 480, 499.
Rāmapāla, king of Bengal, 174.
Rāmarudra, commentator on Amaru, 183, n. 2.
Rāma Tarkavāgīça, commentator and grammarian, 33, 188, 434, 435.
Raṇāditya, king of Kashmir, 163.
Raṇaraṅgamalla or Bhoja, *Rājavārttika*, 489.
Rāṣṭrakūṭa, 133.
Rati, wife of Kāma, 90, 91.
Ratnākara Rājānaka Vāgīçvara, 134, 135, 164, 215, 216.
Ratnaçekhara, *Chandaḥkoça* (*Chandakosa*), 416, n. 3.
Rāvaṇa, as a Prākrit grammarian, 433, 434.
Rāvaṇa, foe of Rāma, 95, 96, 97, 117, 120, 133, 157, 295.
Rāvaṇārjunīya, by Bhaumaka, 133.
Ravicandra, commentator on Amaru, 183, n. 2, 184.
Ravideva, *Rākṣasakāvya*, 98.
Ravikīrti, poet, 97, n. 1.
Raviṣeṇa, *Padmapurāṇa*, 498.
Rāyamukuṭa, *Padacandrikā* on *Amarakoça*, 209, 414.
Recitations, effect of, on Roman literature, 347, n. 1.
Reconstruction of the *Pañcatantra*, 246–8.
Red garment, of physicians, 508.
Renaissance of Sanskrit literature, alleged, 39.
Repetition (*punarukta*), 106.
Republic, of Plato, xviii.
Resignation, as dominant sentiment of Kalhaṇa's history, 165.
Revaṇārādhya, *Smaratattvaprakāçikā*, 470, n. 2.
Rhampsinitos, legend of, 356.
Riddles, 381.
Right-angled triangles, 526.
Rilhaṇa, minister in Kashmir, 161.
Rime, 97, 141.
Rohaka, tale of, 364.
Romaka, 518.
Rotation of earth on axis, 521.
Rudra Bhaṭṭa, writer on poetics, 184, 260, 384, n. 1, 394.
Rudradāman, king, 15, 16, 49, 300.
Rudradeva, *Çyainikaçāstra*, xx.
Rudramadeva, commentator on Amaru, 183, n. 2.
Rudraṭa, writer on poetics, 32, 33, 34, 330, n. 1, 339, 373, 384, 391, 398.
Rūpa, poet (before 900 A.D.), 339.
Rūpagosvāmin, 202, 219, 220, 223.
Rūpavatī, legend of, 66.
Ruyyaka, *Alaṁkārasarvasva*, 237, 396, 411.

Çabarasvāmin, commentator on the Pūrvamīmāṅsā, 24, n. 2, 473, 474.
Çaka epoch, theories of the, 55, n. 3.
Çakas, 39, 145, 441, 443.
Çākaṭāyana, ancient grammarian, 422, 423.
Çaktibhadra, *Āçcaryacūḍāmaṇi*, xii, n. 3, xiii.
Çaktipūrva, astrologer, 530.
Çākyamitra, *Pañcakrama* in part by, 496.
Çalātura, home of Pāṇini, 425.
Çālihotra, authority on veterinary science, 465.
Çālivāhana, 292.
Çambhu, *Anyoktimuktālatāçataka*, 233; *Rājendrakarṇapūra*, 174, 233, 234.
Šānaq, 505.
Çaṅkara, philosopher, xix, 19, 184, 216, 217, 218, 236, 406, 473, 476, 477, 478, 479, 480, 483.
Çaṅkara, *Sarvasiddhāntasaṁgraha*, 499.
Çaṅkara, *Çaṅkaracetovilāsacampū*, 337.
Çaṅkara Miçra, *Upaskāra*, 486.
Çaṅkaravarman, king of Kashmir, 231.
Çaṅkarasvāmin, *Nyāyapraveça* ascribed to, xxii.
Çaṅku, one of Nine Jewels of Vikramāditya, 78, 152.
Çaṅkuka, poet, 152.
Çaṅkhalikhita, *Dharmasūtra*, 439; *Smṛti*, 448.
Çāntanava, *Phiṭsūtra*, 430.
Çāntideva, Buddhist philosopher and poet, 72, 73, 236, 346.
Çāradātanaya, *Bhāvaprakāça*, xv.
Çaraṇa, poet, 190, 219, 220.
Çaraṇadeva, *Durghaṭavṛtti*, 220, n. 1, 430.
Çārṅgadatta, on Dhanurveda, 464.
Çārṅgadeva, *Saṁgītaratnākara*, 466.
Çārṅgadhara, *Çārṅgadharapaddhati*, 222.
Çārṅgadhara, *Saṁhitā* on medicine, 511.
Çarvavarman, *Kātantra*, 267, 431.
Çaçāṅka of Gauḍa, 317, 318.
Çaçiprabhā, princess, 151.
Çāçvata, *Anekārthasamuccaya*, 414.
Çāçvata, poet, 208.
Çatānanda, *Bhāsvatī*, 523.
Çatānanda, father of Abhinanda, 135.
Çatānanda, father of Rudraṭa, 384, n. 1.
Çātavāhana, 30: *see* Kuntala *and* Hāla.
Çaunaka, grammarian, 423, 425.
Çeṣanāga, *Prākṛtavyākaraṇasūtra*, 434.
Çobhana, brother of Dhanapāla, 331.
Çīlābhaṭṭārikā, poetess, 205, 331.
Çīlāditya, 163.

Çilhaṇa, *Çāntiçataka*, 232, 233.
Çiçunāga, of Magadha, 341.
Çiçupāla, king of Cedi, 125, 126.
Çiva, god, 83, 89, 90, 99, 109, 110, 111, 134, 135, 136, 154, 158, 176, 210, 285, 302, 349, 451.
Çivadāsa, *Kathārṇava*, 293; recension of *Vetālapañcaviṅçatikā*, xi, 262, 263, 288; *Bhikṣāṭanakāvya*, 221; *Çālivāhanakathā*, 292.
Çivarāma, commentator on *Vāsavadattā*, 308.
Çivasvāmin, 133, 134.
Çrāvastī, Prasenajit of, 133, 134.
Çrīdhara, *Nyāyakandalī*, 485.
Çrīdhara, *Triçatī*, 526.
Çrīdharadāsa, *Saduktikarṇāmṛta*, 222.
Çrīharṣa, poet and philosopher, 18, 20, 108, n. 1, 336, n. 2, 412, 478.
Çrīkaṇṭha Çivācārya, *Çaivabhāṣya*, 481.
Çrīkumāra, *Çilparatna*, 464.
Çrīmāla, home of Māgha, 131, n. 2.
Çrīmatī, wife of Bimbisāra, legend of, 65.
Çrīnivāsa, *Yatīndramatadīpikā*, 478; *Sakalācāryamatasaṁgraha*, 479.
Çrīṣeṇa, astronomer, 520.
Çrīvara, *Kathākautuka*, 361; *Jaina Rājataraṅgiṇī*, 174; *Subhāṣitāvalī*, 223.
Çrīvatsāṅka, *Yamakaratnākara*, 197, n. 2.
Çrīvijaya, 142.
Çrutadhara or Çrutidhara, epithet of Dhoī, 220.
Çubhacandra, *Jñānārṇava*, 497.
Çuddhodana, and Daçaratha, 61.
Çuddhodana, legend of, 59.
Çūdra, Brahmanic contempt for, 99.
Çūdraka, alleged royal author, 53, n. 1; rewards poets, 339.
Çūdraka, of Vidiçā, hero of the *Kādambarī*, 321.
Çūdraka, hero of *Vīracaritra*, 292.
Çuka, pupil of Prājya Bhaṭṭa, 174.
Çukanāsa, father of Vaiçampāyana, 321, 322, 323.
Çvetadvīpa, legend of visit to, 279.
Çvetaketu, authority on erotics, 99, 468.
Çvetaketu, husband of Lakṣmī, 322, 323.

Sadānanda, *Vedāntasāra*, 478.
Sadāçiva, on Dhanurveda, 464.
Sa'dī, *Gulistān*, style of, 70, n. 2.
Sāgaranandin, *Nāṭakalakṣaṇaratnakoça*, xv.
Sāhasāṅka, royal patron, 53, n. 1; rewards poets, 339.
Sahid, David, and Gaulmin, *Livre des lumières ou la Conduite des roys* (Paris, 1644), 358.
Sahṛdaya, perhaps name of author of Kārikās on Dhvani, 387.
Sahya, mountain, 94.
St. Elizabeth of Portugal, 362, n. 4.
St. Guinefort, legend of, 363.
St. Martin, bird of, 362.
Sakalakīrti, *Tattvārthasāradīpikā*, 497.
Samantabhadra, *Āptamīmāṅsā*, 497.
Sāṁkhya philosophy, 56, 77, 99, 391, n. 1, 453, 472, 478, 479, 487–9, 499, 500, 507.
Samudrabandhu, commentator on *Alaṁkārasarvasva*, 396.
Samudragupta, emperor, 53, 75, 76, 77, 78, 80, 94.
Sand of the Indus, 80.
Sandabar, Hebrew, 360.
Sandal of Kashmir, 80.
Sandhimati, resurrection of, 167.
Sandhyākara Nandin, poet, 137, 174.
Saṅghagupta, father of Vāgbhaṭa, 510.
Sanskrit, xxv–xxvii; Part I; *see also* Mixed Sanskrit; use of, 244, 268, 295, 341, 385, 386, 484, 492, 493, 495; barbarisms in technical texts, 407, n. 3.
Sappho, Greek poetess, 34.
Sarasvatī, festival of, encourages poetic talent, 53; sacrifice to, in expiation of errors in speech, 5.
Sarasvatī, river, 85.
Sarvajñamitra, *Sragdharāstotra*, 215.
Sarvajñātman, *Saṁkṣepaçārīraka*, 477.
Sarvāṇanda (Sarvānanda), *Jagaḍūcarita*, 173.
Sarvarakṣita, grammarian, 430.
Sarvāstivāda, Sarvāstivādin, Buddhist school (fragments from Turkestan of the *Bhikṣuṇīprātimokṣa*, ed. Waldschmidt, 1926), 55, 64, n. 4, 496; uses Sanskrit, 15, n. 3.
Sassanian dynasty, 520; cf. Burzōe.
Sātavāhana, 40, 53, n. 1, 54, 70, n. 1, 223, 224, 267, 268, 316, 339, 341, 469.
Saturae Menippeae, style of, 70, n. 2.
Satyācārya, astrologer, 530.
Sātyaki, hero, 126.
Sāyaṇa, (for his work *see* A.M.J.V. III, iii. 467 ff.), *Ṛgvedabhāṣya*, 239; *Subhāṣitasudhānidhi*, 223, n. 4.
Saxo Grammaticus, 362.
Schiller, *Maria Stuart*, 86.
Sculpture, Hellenistic influence on Indian, 371.
Sea, as impure, 94.
Seasons, description of, 136, 137.
Second person plural perfect, disused in Patañjali's time, 10.
Secondary Prākrits, 27.
Seleukos, Greek king of Syria, 459.
Sentiment (*rasa*), 92, 372, 373, 383, 388, 389, 390, 391, 393, 394.
Seven-league boots, *motif*, 363.
Seven Seers, as wooers, 89.
Seven steps of the young Buddha, 503

Sexual intercourse, in Tantric ritual, 482, 496.
Shahriar and Shahzeman, 361.
Shakespeare, xvi.
Shin-gon, Buddhist sect, 495, 496.
Shin-shū, Buddhist sect, 494.
Sibilants, 27, 28.
Siddhāntakaumudī, by Bhaṭṭoji Dīkṣita, 430.
Siddharṣi, *Upamitibhavaprapañcā kathā*, 14, 294, 489, 497, 499.
Siddhasena, astrologer, 530.
Siddhasena Divākara, *Kalyāṇamandirastotra*, 215; *Nyāyāvatāra*, 484.
Simeon and Asita, comparison of legends of, 503, 504.
Simeon, son of Seth, *Stephanites kai Ichnelates*, 358.
Similes, 49, 61, 62, 78, 79, 89, 90, 105, 106, 212, 350, 372, 380, 384, 399.
Similitudes, used in illustration of scientific theories, 409.
Simplicior text of *Pañcatantra*, 246, 247, 260, 261, 264.
Sindhī, alleged origin of, 32.
Sindhurāja Navasāhasāñka of Mālava, 151.
Sindhu, river, 85.
Sindhudeça, Peshāwar district, 33.
Sindibādnāmeh, 360.
Singers, demerits of popular, 240.
Single consonants, in lieu of double, alleged to exist in North-West Prākrit, 35, n. 2.
Siṅha, astronomer, 522.
Siṅhagupta, father of Vāgbhaṭa I, 510.
Sinhalese, Sanskrit influence on (W. Geiger, *Litteratur und Sprache der Singalesen*, pp. 90 f.), 16.
Sins of the gods, 301.
Sirenes, 363, n. 3.
Siri Puḷumāyi, Nāsik inscription of, 50.
Sisenna, translator of *Milesiaka*, 367, 368.
Sītā, wife of Rāma, xi, n. 4, 61, 90, 96, 118, 120, 135, 271; Vālmīki's picture of her woes, 43.
Sītābengā inscription, 40, n. 1.
Sīyaka, of Dhāvā, 331.
Siṅharāja, *Prākṛtarūpāvatāra*, 434.
Skanda, god, 111.
Skandagupta, advises Harṣa, 317.
Skandagupta, emperor, 74, 81.
Sleep of nature, at birth of the Buddha and of Christ, 503.
Social contract theory, in Buddhism, 443.
Soḍḍhala, *Udayasundarīkathā*, 336.
Solomon, judgement of, 362.
Soma, *Rāgavibodha*, 192, n. 1.
Somadeva, *Nītivākyāmṛta*, 463, 464; *Yaçastilaka*, 144, 266, 272, 333–6.
Somadeva, Kashmirian poet, 54, 246, 262, 281–7, 288, 321, 347.
Somānanda, *Çivadṛṣṭi*, 481.
Somanātha, *Rāgavibodha*, 466.
Somendra, son of Kṣemendra, 493.
Someçvara, Cālukya prince, 154.
Someçvaradatta, poet, 173.
Son lost and found, parable of, 494.
Sophokles, 98, 195, 354.
Sophron, *Mimes*, 367.
Sotadean verses, 127.
Sound effects, 350.
Sound variation, 212.
Sources of the Kāvya, 39–42.
South, taste of poets in the, 316.
Southern *Pañcatantra*, 246, 247, 262.
South-western dialect of Prākrit, 29.
Spanish translation of the *Pañcatantra*, *Exemplario contra los engaños y peligros del mundo* (Saragossa, 1493), 358.
Spherical nature of earth, 521.
Sphujidhvaja, Sphūrjidhvaja, astrologer, 531.
Spies, used by kings (Vallauri, RSO. vi. 1381 f.), 453.
Spinoza, B., 456.
Spirits, drinking of, in Tantric ritual, 482.
Spring, description of, 84, 95, 120.
Statius, Roman poet (born *c.* A.D. 60), 348, 349, 350.
Stem formations, confused, 23.
Sthāṇvīçvara, Harṣavardhana's family seat, 317.
Style, of Açvaghoṣa, 60–4; *Divyāvadāna*, 66, 67; Ārya Çūra, 68, 69; Hariṣeṇa, 77, 78; Vatsabhaṭṭi, 79; Kālidāsa, 101–7; Bhāravi, 112–15; Bhaṭṭi, 117, 118; Kumāradāsa, 120–3; Māgha, 127–30; Kavirāja, 138, 139; Çrīharṣa, 140–2; Padmagupta, 151, 152; Bilhaṇa, 156, 157, 189, 190; Kalhaṇa, 169–72; Bhartṛhari, 178–82; Amaru, 184–7; Jayadeva, 192–7; Bāṇa, 210, 211, 213, 326–30; Mayūra, 211–13; Mātañga Divākara, 214; Çañkara, 216, 217; Līlāçuka, 218, 219; Çaraṇa, 219, 220; *Cāṇakyanīti*, 229–31; Bhallaṭa, 232; Çilhaṇa, 232, 233; Dāmodaragupta, 237; Kṣemendra, 239, 240; *Pañcatantra*, 256–9; *Hitopadeça*, 264, 265; Somadeva, 286, 287; Daṇḍin, 304–7; Subandhu, 310–13; Somadeva Sūri, 335, 336; *Manu Smṛti*, 444, 445; *Yājñavalkya*, 446, 447; *Arthaçāstra*, 457, 458; Varāhamihira, 532, 533.
Style (*rīti*), 381, 384, 389, 391, 394, 395.
Subandhu, poet, viii, xxii, 19, 21, 50, 77, 132, 138, 139, n. 3, 266, 275, n. 2, 297, 299, 345, 347, 349, 365, 370, 376, 381, 469.
Subhadrā, poetess, 205, n. 1.
Subjunctive forms, in the main disused in classical Sanskrit, 6.
Sugrīva, ally of Rāma, 92, 120.

Suhmas, people, 93.
Sukhavarman, son of Utpala, 164.
Sumanas, tale of, as prototype of the *Kādambarī*, 321.
Sumanottarā, legend of, 46.
Sumati, *Subhāṣitāvalī*, 223, n. 1.
Sumerians, accounts kept by, xxiv, n. 1.
Summer, description of, 84, 96.
Sunandā, confidante of Indumatī, 94, 95.
Sunandana Bhaṭṭa, poet, 221.
Sundara, of Caurapallī, 188.
Sundarī, legend of, 57.
Sundarī, mother of Dhanapāla, 415.
Sunday, as day of rest (recognized in *Hitopadeça*), 531.
Superstition, played on by kings, 453, 454.
Superstitions, in history, 146.
Suprabhadeva, grandfather of Māgha, 124.
Sūra, poet, 339.
Surapāla, *Vṛkṣāyurveda*, 511.
Surāṣṭras, speech of, 10, 386.
Sureçvara, *Mānasollāsa*, 477, 484.
Sureçvara, *Çabdapradīpa*, 512.
Sūryamatī, princess of Jalandhara, suicide of, 168, 169; *Kathāsaritsāgara* written for, 281.
Suçruta, medical authority, xxiii, n. 3, 507, 508, 509, 510, 511, 513, 514.
Sussala, king of Kashmir, 159, 167, 168, 169.
Suvarṇākṣī, mother of Açvaghoṣa, 55.
Suvarṇanābha, authority on erotics, 468.
Suvrata, Kashmirian chronicler, 161.
Suyodhana, name of Duryodhana in the *Kirātārjunīya*, 110, 112.
Svāhā, wife of Agni, amour with the moon, 337.
Svātmārāma Yogīndra, *Haṭhayogapradīpikā*, 491.
Sweetness of style (*mādhurya*), 50, 374, 378, 381, 382.
Sybaris, story-tellers of, 367.
Syntipas, Greek, 360.

Tacitus, Roman historian, 349.
Tāḍakā, demoness, 95.
Ṭakkas, speech of, 386.
Tailapa, Cālukya, 154.
Talking birds, *motif*, 343.
Tāmraparṇī, pearl fisheries of the, 80, 343.
Tāntrikas, rites of Bengal, 263.
Tārā, goddess, 215.
Tārā, her lament for Vālin, 91.
Tāraka, demon foe of the gods, 90; destroyed by Guha, 213.
Tārāpīḍa, of Ujjain, 321.
Technopaignia, 127.
Temptation of the Buddha, and of the Christ, 502.
Tennyson, Alfred, Lord, 82, 348.
Tertiary Prākrits, 27.
Tertiary verbal forms, developed in classical Sanskrit, 6.
Tešup, god of Mitanni, xxiv.
Theagenes and Chariklea, 367.
Theft of poetry, 342.
Theokritos, Greek poet, 349, 370.
Theories of poetry, chap. xviii.
Thousand and One Nights, 360, 361.
Thucydides, ideals of, 164, 452, n. 2.
Tiastenes of Ozene, 49.
Tirumalarāja, of Vijayanagara, 435.
Toramāṇa, leader of the Hūṇas, 74, 163.
Translations of the *Pañcatantra*, 357–9.
Transmutation of base metals, 511.
Travaṇas, speech of, 386.
Trikūṭa hill, 94.
Trilocanapāla, Çāhi king, 164.
Trimalla, *Pathyāpathyanighaṇṭu*, 512.
Tripura, demon destroyed by Çiva, 136.
Tristan und Isolde, by Gottfried, 359.
Trivikrama Bhaṭṭa, *Nalacampū*, 266, 332, 333.
Trivikrama, *Prākṛtaçabdānuçāsana*, 434.
Trivikramasena, hero of *Vetālapañcaviṅçatikā*, 288, 289.
Trojan horse, *motif*, 355.
Tuṅga, Kashmirian general, 164.
Tuñjina, Kashmirian hero, 168.
Turks, conquer Hun kingdom on the Oxus, 74; alleged reference to, 499.
Turkish terms in Sanskrit, 25.
Twenty-five, and twenty-six, principles of Sāṁkhya, and Yoga, 490.

Uccala, king of Kashmir, 159.
Udaya, Kashmirian soldier, 161.
Udayākara, father of Udayadeva, 481.
Udayana, brother of Govardhana, 202.
Udayana, hero, 270.
Udayana, philosopher, 408, 484, 486.
Udbhaṭa, writer on poetics, 383, 384, 385, 389, 391, 396.
Uddhava, counsellor of Kṛṣṇa, 126.
Uddyotakara, logician, xxii, 308, 376, 483.
Ugrabhūti, *Çiṣyahitānyāsa*, 431.
Ujjayinī, town, 31, 76, 81, 85, 268, 270.
Umā, wins Çiva in marriage, 88, 89.
Umāpatidhara, poet, 53, 190, 219.
Umāsvāti, *Tattvārthādhigamasūtra*, 497.
Ungrateful snake, fable of, 355.
Unwinking eyes of gods, 366.
Upakoçā, legend of, 364.
Upavarṣa, commentator on the *Pūrvamīmāṅsā*, 339, 473.
Uçanas, authority on Rājaçāstra, 450, 451.
Uçanas, *Dharmasūtra*, 439; *Smṛti*, 448.
Utpala, king of Kashmir, 164, 166.

Utpaladeva, *Īçvarapratyabhijñāsūtra*, 481; *Stotrāvalī*, 218.
Utprekṣāvallabha, *Bhikṣāṭanakāvya*, 221.
Utsavas, tribe, 94.
Ūrvīdhara Bhaṭṭa, poet, 235.

Vācaspati, *Cintāmaṇis* on law, 448.
Vācaspati, *Çabdārṇava*, 413.
Vācaspati Miçra, philosopher, xxi, 474, 477, 483, 484, 489, 490.
Vādībhasinha, *see* Oḍayadeva.
Vādirāja Sūri, 334, n. 1.
Vāgbhaṭa I, *Aṣṭāñgasaṁgraha* (on relation to *Aṣṭāñgahṛdayasaṁhitā*, cf. Kirfel, *Festgabe Garbe*, pp. 107 f.), 510, 515, n. 1.
Vāgbhaṭa II, *Aṣṭāñgahṛdayasaṁhitā*, 510.
Vāgbhaṭa, *Alaṁkāra*, 395.
Vāgbhaṭa, *Kāvyānuçāsana*, 395.
Vāgbhaṭa, *Neminirvāṇa*, 143.
Vaidya Bhānu Paṇḍita, alleged author of *Saduktikarṇāmṛta*, 222, n. 3.
Vainateya, poet, 235, 236.
Vaiçampāyana, 322.
Vaiçeṣika, philosophy, 408, 484, 485–7, 498, 499, 500, 501, 507.
Vaiçyas, speech of, 8.
Vaiyākaraṇas, grammarians, 403.
Vājapyāyana, grammarian, 426.
Vākāṭaka, family, x, 97, n. 4.
Vākkūṭa, poet, 204.
Vākpati, of Dhārā, 331.
Vākpatirāja, poet, 54, 150, 307, 336.
Vākyakāra, 478.
Valerius Flaccus, Roman poet, 348, 349.
Vāli, Vālin, husband of Tārā, 91.
Valkalacīrin, legend of, 294, n. 4.
Vallabhadāsa, version of *Vetālapañcaviñçatikā*, 288.
Vallabhadeva, *Subhāṣitāvali*, 222, 223.
Vālmīki, poet, 43, 61, 96, 97, 111.
Vālmīki, *Sūtra*, 35, 434.
Vāmadeva, sage, 279.
Vāmana, author of *Kāçikā Vṛtti*, 429, 430.
Vāmana, authority on poetics, 119, 220, n. 1, 340, 373, 381, 382, 383, 384, 385, 389, 390, 391, 463; *Liñgānuçāsana*, 433.
Vāmana Bhaṭṭa Bāṇa, *Pārvatīpariṇaya*, 315.
Vāmuka, father of Rudraṭa, 384, n. 1.
Vandāru Bhaṭṭa, 141, n. 1.
Vandyaghaṭīya Sarvānanda, *Ṭīkāsarvasva* on *Amarakoça*, 414.
Vañgasena, *Cikitsāsārasaṁgraha*, 511.
Vañkṣū, Oxus, referred to by Kālidāsa, 81.
Varadarāja, *Madhyasiddhāntakaumudī* and *Laghusiddhāntakaumudī*, 430.
Varadarāja, *Tārkikarakṣā*, 484.
Varāhamihira, astronomer, astrologer, and mathematician, 75, 76, 159, 409, 411, 416, 461, 463, 465, 469, 516, 517, 520, 521, 527, 528–33, 534.
Vararuci, authority on *Alaṁkāra*, 372.
Vararuci, *Liñgānuçāsana*, 433.
Vararuci, one of Nine Jewels, 76, 307.
Vararuci, *Nītiratna*, 231.
Vararuci, *Prākṛtaprakāça*, 40, 433, 434, cf. 339.
Vararuci, *Sinhāsanadvātriñçikā*, 292.
Vardhamāna, comm. on Gañgeça, 485.
Vardhamāna, *Gaṇaratnamahodadhi*, 430.
Vardhamāna, *Yogamañjarī*, 465.
Varmalākhya, Varmalāta, king, 124.
Varro, *Saturae Menippeae*, style of, 70, n. 2.
Varṣa, writer of a Çāstra, 339.
Vārṣagaṇya, *Ṣaṣṭitantra*, 488.
Vāsavadattā, legend of, 46.
Vāsiṣka, inscription of time of, 15, n. 1.
Vastupāla, minister of Gujarāt, 173.
Vasubandhu, Buddhist philosopher, xxii, 73, 75, 77, 488, 495, 496.
Vāsudeva, king (Kāṇva or Kuṣaṇa), patron of poets, 53, n. 1, 339.
Vāsudeva, poet, 97, n. 5.
Vasugupta, *Çiva Sūtra*, 481.
Vātavyādhi, alleged authority on Arthaçāstra, 457.
Vatsabhaṭṭi, Mandasor Praçasti of, x, 77, 79, 81, 82, 90, 116.
Vātsyāyana, *Kāmasūtra*, 13, 51, 52.
Vātsyāyana, *Nyāyabhāṣya*, xxii, 406, 461, 477, 482, 483.
Vaṭudāsa, father of Çrīdharadāsa, 222.
Vedāñgarāya, *Pārasīprakāça*, 415.
Vedānta, philosophy, 387, 391, n. 1, 483, 495, 499, 500.
Vedic lyric, 41, 42.
Vemabhūpāla, commentator on Amaru, 183, n. 2, 184.
Veṅkaṭādhvarin, poet, 138, n. 1.
Vergil, Virgil, 82, 100, 101, 345, 349, 350, 502, n. 3.
Vernacular (*deçabhāṣā*), 56, 416.
Verse-fillers (*pādapūraṇa*), 90, 123.
Verse mixed with prose; *see* prose.
Vetāla Bhaṭṭa, one of Nine Jewels, 76.
Vetāla Bhaṭṭa, *Nītipradīpa*, 231.
Vetravatī, river, 85.
Vidiçā, city, 85.
Vidura, speeches on Arthaçāstra, 451.
Vidūṣaka, as companion of the man about town, 52.
Vidyā, princess, 188.
Vidyādhara, *Ekāvalī*, 87, n. 2, 395.
Vidyādhara Bhaṭṭa, father of Ānanda, 293.
Vidyādharas, spirits, 270, 271.
Vidyānanda, comm. on *Āptamīmāṅsā*, 497.

Vidyānātha, *Pratāparudrayaçobhūṣaṇa*, 395.
Vidyāmādhava, 139, n. 3.
Vidyāpati, *Puruṣaparīkṣā*, 293.
Vidyāpati, Pilpay, 359.
Vigour (*ūrjasvin*), 380, 382, 389.
Vigraharājadeva, royal dramatist, 53, n. 2.
Vijayabhaṭṭārikā, queen, 205, n. 1.
Vijayacandra, of Kanauj, 139.
Vijayanandin, astronomer, 521.
Vijayāñkā, poetess, 205, n. 1.
Vijjakā, poetess, 205, n. 1.
Vijñānabhikṣu, comm. on *Sāṁkhya Sūtra*, 489; on *Yogabhāṣya*, 490.
Vijñānavādin, Buddhist school, xxiii, 472, 473.
Vijñāneçvara, *Mitākṣarā*, 411, 447.
Vikaṭanitambā, poetess, 205, n. 1.
Vikrama, *Nemidūta*, 86, n. 2.
Vikramāditya, on Dhanurveda, 464.
Vikramāditya, legendary king, 163, 178, 201, 275, n. 2, 288, 289, 292, 293, 307, 364, 413, 442; Nine Jewels of, 76.
Vikramāditya, poet, 221.
Vikramāditya, *Saṁsārāvarta*, 413.
Vikramāditya VI, Cālukya of Kalyāṇa, 153.
Vināyaka, writes introduction to *Daçakumāracarita*, 297, n. 3.
Vindhya, 269, 270.
Vindhyavāsa, authority on Sāṁkhya, 488.
Vīradhavala, of Gujarāt, 173.
Vīrasiṅha, of Mahilapattana, 188.
Vīrasena Kautsa Çāba, minister of Candragupta, 76.
Virgin birth, 502, 503.
Virūpākṣanātha, *Virūpākṣapañcāçikā*, 481.
Viçākhadatta, dramatist, 175, 462.
Viçālākṣa, authority on *Arthaçāstra*, 450, 451, 457.
Viçvāmitra, father of Suçruta, 507.
Viçvāmitra, sage, 95, 120.
Viçvanātha, *Bhāṣāpariccheda*, 486.
Viçvanātha, *Sāhityadarpaṇa*, 388, 390, 391, 394, 395.
Viçvarūpa, commentator on *Yājñavalkya Smṛti*, 447.
Viçveçvara, *Madanapārijāta*, 448.
Viṣṇu, god, 98, 99, 260, 261, 285, 349.
Viṣṇucandra, astronomer, 521.
Viṣṇugupta, xvii, 458; *see* Kauṭilya.
Viṣṇugupta, astrologer, 530.
Viṣṇu Kamalāvilāsin, temple of, 155.
Viṣṇuçarman, alleged author of *Pañcatantra*, 248, 250.
Viṣṇusvāmin, philosopher, 479.
Viṣṇuvardhana, prince, xvii.
Viṭas, as companions of the man about town, 52.
Vitruvius, xx.
Vocative, neuter of *an* stems, 10.
Voices, confusion of, 20.
Vopadeva, *Mugdhabodha*, 432; *Kavikalpadruma*, 432; *Çataçlokī*, 511.
Vṛddha Garga, astrologer, 528.
Vṛnda, *Siddhiyoga*, 511.
Vyāḍi, writer of a Çāstra, 339; *Saṁgraha* on Pāṇini, 426.
Vyāsa, sage, 109, 110.
Vyāsa, *Yogabhāṣya*, 490.

Walking on the water, Buddhist and Christian miracle of, 503.
Walter Mapes, 362.
Warriors, alleged creators of Upaniṣads, 487.
Weber MS., treatises in, 413, 528, n. 3.
Wema Kadphises, a Māheçvara, 442, n. 1.
West, taste of poets in the, 316.
Western Hindī, origin of, 32.
Western Kṣatrapas, use Sanskrit for their inscriptions, 16.
Western Prākrit, 27, 28.
Western school of Prākrit grammar, 434, 435.
White Island or Continent, 279.
White Yajurveda, 439, 446.
Widow's mite, legend of, 503.
Winter, description of, 84.
Witchcraft, as cause of death, 166, 285.
Wolf and lamb, fable of, 355.
Woman, jeremiad against, 240.
Writing, 386, n. 1; sixty-four kinds of, 492.
Wright's Chaste Wife, 364.

Xenophon, 368.

Yādavaprakāça, Advaita philosopher, 478; *Vaijayantī*, 414.
Yakṣa, hero of the *Meghadūta*, 85, 86.
Yakṣavarman, *Cintāmaṇi* on *Çākaṭāyana Vyākaraṇa*, 432.
Yāminīpūrṇatilakā, princess, 188.
Yāmuna, philosopher, 478.
Yaçodā, mother of Kṛṣṇa, 219.
Yaçodhara, *Jayamañgalā* on *Kāmasūtra*, 469.
Yaçodharā, and Sītā, 59.
Yaçodharman, of central India, 74, 80.
Yaçomitra, *Abhidharmakoçavyākhyā*, 496.
Yaçovarman, king of Kanauj, 53, n. 2, 54, 150.
Yāska, *Nirukta*, xxv, xxvi, 10, 15, 372, 403, 412, 422, 425, 440.
Yātrās, in Bengal, 191, 192.
Yaugandharāyaṇa, minister of Udayana, 271.
Yavakrīta, legend of, 46.
Yavanas, 94, 279, 369, 441, 445.

Yavanācārya, astrologer, 530, 531.
Yavanapura, Alexandria, 518.
Yavaneçvara, astrologer, 531.
Yayāti, legend of, 46.
Yudhiṣṭhira, hero, 109, 110, 125, 126, 162.
Yoga, philosophy, 99, 100, 453, 472 479, 490, 491, 499, 500.
Yueh-chi, people, 39.
Yusuf and Zuleikha, 361.

Zainul-'Abidīn, 361.
Zariadres and Odatis, tale of, 366.
Zodiac, signs of, 518.
Zoroaster, date of, xxiv; laughs on birth, 502, n. 3.

SANSKRIT INDEX

A stems, disappearance of certain forms of, in classical Sanskrit, 5, 6.
a vowel, xxv.
akar, Vedic form, 7.
Akṣaracchandas, metres, 418–20.
Agastimata, 465.
Agni Purāṇa, 373, 416; on poetics, 393; on medicine, 508.
Aghaṭakumārakathā, xii.
aghaṭate, 130.
aṁgāraavāra, 223, n. 6.
Añguttara Nikāya, 228, 340, n. 1.
Acaladhṛti, metre, 141, 418.
ajarya, friendship, 123.
ajākṛpāṇīya, story of the goat and the razor, 48.
Aṇubhāṣya, by Vallabha, 479.
Atiçayokti, hyperbole, 330, 378, 399.
Atyukti, exaggeration, 377.
Atri Smṛti, 448.
Atharva Prātiçākhya, xxv.
Atharvaveda, 42, n. 1, 199, 404, 439, 505, 514, 516.
Adbhutasāgara, by Ballālasena, and Lakṣmaṇasena, xxiv, n. 4, 534.
Advaita, theory, 476, 477.
adhijaladhi, 213.
adhyayana, 92.
an stems, locative of, 6; vocative of neuter stems in, 10.
Anañgarañga, by Kalyāṇamalla, 470.
Ananvaya, self-comparison as figure, 399.
Anavasitā, metre, 418, 533.
anīya, gerunds in, developed in classical Sanskrit, 6.
Anukramaṇīs, by Kātyāyana, 415.
anugiram, on the mountain, 18.
anujīvisātkṛta, handed over to a servant, 115.
Anuprāsa, 313, 369, 378; *see* Alliteration.
Anubandha, indicatory letter, 425.
Anuyogadvārasūtra, 34, 461, 482.
Anuçāsana, form of literature, 9.
anekārtha, homonymous (dictionaries), 412.
Anekārthakoça, by Mañkha, 414.
Anekārthaçabdakoça, by Medinīkara, 414.
Anekārthasaṁgraha, by Hemacandra, 414.
Anekārthasamuccaya, by Çāçvata, 414.
anta, as verse-filler, 90.
Antarakathāsaṁgraha, by Rājaçekhara, 295, n. 5.
Anvitābhidhānavādin, school, 388, n. 1.
anyatara, *anyatama*, anyone, 67.
anyatra, with locative, 49.
Anyoktimuktālatāçataka, by Çambhu, 233.
anvavasarga, allowing one his own way, 18.
anvāje-kṛ, strengthen, 17.
apacasi, comic form, not Vedic (Keith, JRAS. 1906, p. 722), 10.
apadeça, citation, 459.
Apabhrança, form of language, 197, 198, 223, 226, 341, 370, 371, 376, 386, 433, 434, 435.
Aparavaktra, metre, 115, 308, 330, 418, 533.
apaçabda, 11.
Apahnuti, denial, 399.
api . . . api, use of, 64, 69.
apy eva, perhaps, 67.
Aprastutapraçansā, *Aprastutastotra*, incidental praise, 380, 399.
Abhidharmakoça, by Vasubandhu, 495, 496.
Abhidhā, denotation of words, 387.
Abhidhānacintāmaṇi, by Hemacandra, 414.
Abhidhānaratnamālā, by Halāyudha, 414.
abhividhi, including, 18.
Abhihitānvayavādin, school, 387, n. 4.
abhyāsa, practice, 340.
abhreṣa, equitableness, 18.
acakamata, aorist, 123.
Amitāyurdhyānasūtra, 494.
Ambāṣṭaka, 218.
argala, false form, 24, n. 4.
Artha, prose exposition, ix; science, 450, 451, 455.
Arthavyakti, explicitness of sense, 50, 374, 390.
Arthaçāstra, 408, 409, 410.
Arthaçāstra, Kauṭilīya, xvii–xx, 243, 249, 439, 443, 467, 468, 469, 472.
Arthasaṁgraha, by Laugākṣi Bhāskara, 474, 486.
Arthāntaranyāsa, corroboration, 106, 374, 380.
Arthālaṁkāra, figures of sense, 49, 92, 101, 116, 373.
Ardhamāgadhī, a Prākrit, 14, 28, 29, 433, 434, 445.
Ardhamāgadha Apabhrança, supposed source of Eastern Hindī, 32.

Alaṁkāra, a work, referred to by Subandhu, vii, 308.
Alaṁkāra, *see* Figures.
Alaṁkāravatī, book xv of *Bṛhatkathāmañjarī*, 279; ix of *Kathāsaritsāgara*, 282.
Alaṁkāravimarçinī, by Jayaratha, 173.
Alaṁkārasaṁgraha, by Udbhaṭa, 383.
Alaṁkārasarvasva, by Ruyyaka, 396.
alam, verse-filler, 90.
Alaukika, transcendental, 389.
Avataṅsakasūtra or *Gaṇḍavyūha*, 494.
avatapte nakulasthitam, maxim, 409.
Avadāna, type of literature, 64–7.
Avadānakalpalatā, by Kṣemendra, 493.
Avadānaçataka, 65, 133.
Avantisundarīkathā, ascribed to a Daṇḍin, xiii, xvi, xvii, 296, n. 2.
Avantisundarīkathāsāra, xvi.
avarṇa, shame, 123.
Avalokiteçvaraguṇakāraṇḍavyūha, 494.
Avahaṭṭhā, form of Apabhrañça, 35.
Avitatha, metre, 124, 419.
avivakṣita-vācya, form of suggestion, 388.
Açvacikitsita, by Nakula, 465.
Açvamedha, horse sacrifice, 94, n. 1.
Açvalalita, metre, 48, 118, 418.
Açvavaidyaka, by Jayadatta, 465.
Açvāyurveda, by Gaṇa, 465.
Aṣṭamahāçrīcaityastotra, by Harṣavardhana, 215.
Aṣṭāñgasaṁgraha, by Vāgbhaṭa, xix, n. 7, 510.
Aṣṭāñgahṛdayasaṁhitā, by Vāgbhaṭa, xix, n. 7, 510.
Aṣṭādhyāyī, by Pāṇini, xxvi, 5, 423–6.
asaṁlakṣya-krama, form of apprehension, 388.
asti, as a particle, 63.
asme, dropped in classical Sanskrit, 7.
Ahiṅsā, principle of, 241.
Ahirbudhnya Saṁhitā, 480.
Ākṣepa, paraleipsis, 378, 380.
Ākhyāna, narrative verses, 244.
Ākhyāyikā, form of narrative, 245, 308, 313, 319, 320, 375, 376, 383, 391, 411, n. 1, 461.
ājaghne, irregular form, 115.
āṇapayati, *ājñāpayati*, 11.
Ātmatattvaviveka, by Udayana, 454, n. 4.
Ātmabodha, by Çañkara, 476, 477.
Ātreya Saṁhitā (Jolly, *Munich Catal.*, p. 50), 508, n. 5.
Ādikarmapradīpa, 496.
Ādi Granth, 191.
Ādipurāṇa, by Jinasena, 498.
āna, perfect participle middle in, 18.
Ānandalaharī, ascribed to Çañkara, 218.
Ānokero (with variants), name of sign of Zodiac, Aigokeros, borrowed from Greek, 530.
āpatti, sin, 67.
Āpastamba Dharmasūtra, xix, 472, n. 1.
Āpastamba Smṛti, 448.
Āpoklima (Apoklima, star's declination), astrological term borrowed from Greek, 530.
Āptamīmāṅsā, by Samantabhadra, 497.
Ābhīrī, a Prākrit, 435.
āmūlataḥ, 83.
āmekhalam, 83.
āyaḥçūlikatā, violence, 123.
Āyurvedasūtra, 406, n. 1, 407, n. 3, 511, n. 4.
Āryabhaṭīya, 521.
Āryasaptaçatī, by Govardhana, 202.
Ārya Siddhānta, by Āryabhaṭa II, 522.
Āryā, or *Āryāṇī*, feminine form, 10.
Āryā, metre, ix, 118, 131, 182, 224, 311, n. 3, 330, 384, 409, 412, 418, 509, n. 3, 523, 533; Prākrit, ix.
Āryāgīti, metre, 418.
Āryāṣṭaçata, by Āryabhaṭa, 521.
Āvantī, a Prākrit, 435.
Āvantī, a Vibhāṣā, 3.
Āvantikā, style, 394.
Āçis, benediction, 380.
Āvaçyaka, 261.
Āçcaryacūḍāmaṇi, by Çaktibhadra, xii, n. 3, xiii.
Āçvalāyana Gṛhyasūtra, 9.
Āsāra, Apabhrañça metre, 376.

ikṣuçākaṭa, field of sugar cane, 123.
iñjita, Buddhist term, 64.
Itivṛttas, 461.
Itihāsa, form of literature, 9.
ito vyāghra itas taṭī, maxim, 409.
Itthya, or *Ittha*, or *Ithusi*, fish (from Greek, Ichthys), 530.
Indravajrā, metre, 47, 107, 115, 118, 124, 130, 141, 157, 183, 231, 419, 533.
Indriyasthāna, diagnosis and prognosis, 507.
iya, gerund in Çaurasenī, 31.
iva, as first word, 123.
Ī stems, confusion of root and derivate, in classical Sanskrit, 6.
Īçvarapratyabhijñāsūtra, by Utpaladeva, 481.
Īçvara Saṁhitā, 480.

uka, adjectives in, with accusative, 18.
Uṇādisūtra, claimed for Pāṇini (Pathak, ABI. iv. 111 ff.), 422, 423.
Uttaranaiṣadhīya, 141, n. 1.
Uttarapīṭhikā, of the *Daçakumāracarita*, 298.
Uttarapurāṇa, by Guṇabhadra, pupil of Jinasena, 336, 498.
Uttararāmacarita, by Bhavabhūti, xv, n. 2.

ut-tr, from *ava-tr*, 24.
Utprekṣā, lively fancy, 106, 312, 316, 375, 399.
utsañjana, throwing up, 18.
Utsara, metre, 419.
Utsāha, alleged work of Āḍhyarāja, 316, n. 3.
utsuka, with instrumental, 18.
Udayasundarīkathā, by Soḍḍhala, 336.
Udātta, elevation, 382.
Udānavarga, 491.
Udāra, *Udāratā*, *Udāratva*, elevation, 374, 377, 390.
Udgatā, metre, 64, 115, 137, n. 2, 151, n. 1, 418, 533.
Udgīti, metre, 418.
udgr, used metaphorically, 378.
Uddhava, cheerfulness, 67.
Upagīti, metre, 418.
Upajāti, metre, ix, 47, 90, 92, 115, 118, 124, 130, 141, 416, 419, 420.
Upadeçaçataka, by Gumāni, 234.
Upadeçasāhasrī, by Çañkara, 476.
Upanāgara Apabhrañça, 35, 435.
Upanāgarikā, elegant manner (*vṛtti*), 383, 399.
Upaniṣads, 41, 71, 227, 242; Sāṁkhya derived from, 487, 488.
upapadyetarām, in Çañkara, 19.
Upamā, simile, 372, 380, 384, 399.
Upamitibhavaprapañcā kathā, by Siddharṣi, 14, 294, 489, 497, 499.
Upameyopamā, form of simile, 399.
Upaskāra, by Çañkara Miçra, 486.
Upasthitapracupita, metre, 64.
upāje-kr, strengthen, 17.
upādhyāyī, or *upādhyāyānī*, 10.
Upendravajrā, metre, 419.
ubhayatas, with accusative, 123.
ubhayataḥpāçā rajjuḥ, maxim, 409.
Ullekha, figure of speech, 399.
ūṇa, gerund in *Māhārāṣṭrī*, 31.
Ūrjasvin, vigour, figure of speech, 380, 382, 389.

Ṛk-Prātiçākhya, xxvi, n. 1, 415, 423.
Ṛgveda, xxiv, 3, 4, 5, 41, 70, 93, 105, 199, 227, 239, 242, 301, 415, 438, 471, 516.
Ṛtusaṁhāra, by Kālidāsa, xiii, 82–4, 99, 107.
Ṛṣabhapañcāçikā, by Dhanapāla, 331.

e, for *az*, in eastern dialects, 28.
e, short vowel, xxv.
e, termination of third singular middle, dropped in classical Sanskrit, 6.
Ekākṣarakoça, 414.
Ekāvalī, by Vidyādhara, 87, n. 2, 395.
Ekottarāgama, 491.
ebhis, form in Vedic and Prākrit, 7.

Aitareya Brāhmaṇa, 42, 227, 244.

Ojas, force, 50, 327, 374, 378, 379, 381, 390.

Aucityavicāra, by Kṣemendra, 397.
Auḍhrī, a Prākrit, 435.
Aupacchandasaka (*Aupacchandasika*), metre, 47, 115, 118, 130, 158, 418, 509, n. 3, 533.
Aupaniṣadika, section of *Arthaçāstra*, 455.

kaṭa, Prākritic form, 4.
Kaṭha Upaniṣad, 100.
kaṇe-han, fulfil one's longing, 17.
Kathā, type of literature, 24, 25, 68, 308, 313, 319, 320, 375, 376, 383, 391.
Kathānaka, Jain form of literature, 295.
Kathākoça, 295.
Kathākautuka, by Çrīvara, 361.
Kathāpīṭha, book i of *Bṛhatkathāmañjarī* and *Kathāsaritsāgara*, 277, 281.
Kathāmukha, book ii of *Bṛhatkathāmañjarī* and *Kathāsaritsāgara*, 277, 281.
Kathāratnākara, by Hemavijaya, 295, n. 5.
Kathārṇava, by Çivadāsa, 293.
Kathāsaṁgrahaçloka, recapitulatory verses, 244.
Kathāsaritsāgara, by Somadeva, xi, 54, 261, 266, 281–7, 300, n. 1, 324, 361, 363.
Kapphaṇābhyudaya, by Çivasvāmin, 133, 134.
kamāra, not = *karmakāra*, 30, n. 1.
kampana, loan-word, xxvii, n. 1.
Karaṇakutūhala, by Bhāskarācārya, 523.
Karuṇāpuṇḍarīka, 494.
Karṇasundarī, by Bilhaṇa, 151.
Karṇāṭakaçabdānuçāsana, by Bhaṭṭākalañkadeva, 436, n. 5.
kartāsmi, misunderstood by Pāṇini, 424.
Karman, action, 146, 167, 378, 385.
kalama, Greek loan-word, 25, n. 5.
Kalahañsa, metre, 131, 419.
Kalāvilāsa, by Kṣemendra, 238.
Kalās, arts, 51, n. 1.
Kalpanāmaṇḍitikā, by Kumāralāta, viii–x, 56.
Kalpasthāna, toxicology, 507, 508.
Kalyāṇamandirastotra, by Siddhasena Divākara, 215.
Kavikaṇṭhābharaṇa, by Kṣemendra, 397.
Kavikalpadruma, by Vopadeva, 432.
Kavirahasya, by Halāyudha, 133.
Kavīndravacanasamuccaya, 222.
kasi, for *kṛçi*, 11.
kākatālīya, story of the crow and the palm fruit, 48.
Kāku, intonation, 384.

Kāṭa, Prākritic form, 4.
Kāṭhaka Dharmasūtra, 409.
Kātantra, by Çarvavarman, 267, 431.
Kātyāyana Smṛti, 448.
Kādambarī, by Bāṇa, 136, 309, 314, 331.
Kādambarīkathāsāra, by Abhinanda, 135.
Kānti, loveliness of style, 374, 377, 381, 390.
Kāntotpīḍā, metre, 48.
Kāma, love as end of man, 450, 451, 455.
Kāmavilāpa Jātaka, 85, n. 1.
Kāmaçāstra, 134, 135, 405.
Kāmasūtra, xxvii, 13, 32, 51, 52, 237, 299, 407, 410, 461, 467–70, 529.
Kārikās, in *Mahābhāṣya*, metre of, 47.
Kālacakra Tantra, 496.
Kāvyakalpalatā, by Arisiṅha and Amaracandra, 397, 398.
kāvyagoṣṭhī, 341.
kāvyatraya, of Kālidāsa, xvii.
Kāvyapuruṣa, spirit of poetry, 385.
Kāvyaprakāça, by Mammaṭa and Alaṭa, xvii, 140, 394, 395.
Kāvyamīmāṅsā, by Rājaçekhara, xxvii, 385.
Kāvyaliñga, figure of speech, 384.
Kāvyādarça, by Daṇḍin, 266, 296, 381.
Kāvyānuçāsana, by Vāgbhaṭa, 395.
Kāvyānuçāsana, by Hemacandra, 395.
Kāvyālaṁkāra, by Rudraṭa, 384.
Kāvyālaṁkāra, with *Vṛtti*, by Vāmana, 381, 382, 384.
Kāçikā Vṛtti, by Jayāditya and Vāmana, 71, 72, 119, 124, 209, 429, 430.
Kāçyapa Saṁhitā, 508, n. 5.
kim bata, how much more, 64.
Kiraṇāvalī, by Udayana, 485.
Kirātārjunīya, by Bhāravi, xvii, 64, 109–16, 125, 133.
Kīrtikaumudī, by Someçvaradatta, 173.
Kuṭila, metre, 115; and see *Madhyakṣamā*.
Kuṭilagati, metre, 48.
Kuṭṭanīmata, by Dāmodaragupta, 236, 237.
Kuṇāla Jātaka, 70.
Kunteçvaradautya, ascribed to Kālidāsa, x.
Kumārapālacarita, by Hemacandra, 172.
Kumārasambhava, by Kālidāsa, 13, 80, 87–92, 99, 106, 108, 122, 194.
Kulaka, groups of verses, 376.
Kulacūḍāmaṇi Tantra, 482.
Kulārṇava Tantra, 482.
Kuvalayānanda, by Appayya Dīkṣita, 396.
Kusumavicitrā, metre, 419, 533.
Kusumasārakathā, xii.
Kusumāñjali, by Udayana, 484.
Kusumitalatāvellitā, metre, 509, n. 3.
kṛchra, for *kṛpsra*, 4.
Kṛt, suffixes, 422.
Kṛṣṇakarṇāmṛta, or *Kṛṣṇalīlāmṛta*, by Bilvamañgala, 218, 219.
ketus, influence on man, xxiv, n. 4.
Kaikeya Apabhraṅça, conjectural source of Lahndā, 32.
Kaivalya, result of *Yoga*, 491.
Kokilaka, metre, 48, 419, 533.
kola, raft, 67.
Koça, unconnected verses, 376.
Koças, dictionaries, 404, 412–15.
Kauṭilīya Arthaçāstra, xvii–xx, 168, 249, 256, 452–62, 528, 529.
Kaurpya, name of sign of Zodiac, Scorpios, borrowed from Greek, 530.
Kauçika Sūtra, 404, 405, 514.
kramela, Greek loan-word, 25.
Kriya, Ram as sign of Zodiac (from Greek Krios), 530.
Kriyāyoga, forms of concentration, 491.
krīḍāsāras, as ornamental epithet, 377.
klam, as finite verb, 18.
klamathu, dubious form, 123, n. 2.
kṣ, treatment of, in Açokan dialects, 28.
kṣatrapa, Persian loan-word, 25.
kṣatriyā, or *kṣatriyāṇī*, 10.
Kṣapaṇaka, 261.
Kṣamā, metre, 419.

Khaṇḍanakhaṇḍakhādya, by Çrīharṣa, 140, 478.
Khaṇḍakhādyaka, by Brahmagupta, 522.
khalu, with gerund, 18; as first word in sentence, 123.

g, long syllable, 416.
Gaüḍavaha, by Vākpati, ix, 54, 150, 307.
Gaṇacchandas, 198, 418.
Gaṇapāṭha, Pāṇini's system, 24, 425, 430.
Gaṇaratnamahodadhi, by Vardhamāna, 430.
Gaṇita, by Bhāskarācārya, 523.
Gaṇitasārasaṁgraha, by Mahāvīrācārya, 524.
Gaṇḍīstotragāthā, by Açvaghoṣa, 56.
Gadyacintāmaṇi, by Oḍayadeva, 331.
Garuḍa Purāṇa, xix.
Galitaka, Prākrit metre, 198.
Gāthā, type of Buddhist literature, 12.
Gāthās, 9, 22, 58.
Gāthāsaṁgraha, by Vasubandhu, 495.
Gārgī Saṁhitā, 516.
gāvī, for *gaus*, 11.
Gītagovinda, by Jayadeva, 190–8, 469.
Gītābhāṣya, by Rāmānuja, 478.
Gītābhāṣya, by Çañkara, 476.
Gīti, metre, 118, 131, 182, 418.
guccha, for *gutsa*, 24.
Gucchas, title of subdivisions of *Kathāsaritsāgara*, 281.
guṇībhūta-vyañgya, type of poetry, 389.
gṛhya, irregular form, 63.

Gṛhyasūtra, xx, 437, 440, 468.
gotā, *gopotālikā*, for *gaus*, 11.
gonām, dropped in classical Sanskrit, 7.
Gomūtrikā, figure, 127.
Gorakṣaçataka, 491.
Gola, by Āryabhaṭa, 521.
Gola, by Bhāskarācārya, 523.
Govinda, for *Gopendra*, 24.
Gauḍapādīya Kārikās, 475, 476.
Gauḍī Prākrit, in Daṇḍin, 31, n. 1.
Gautamīya Dharmaçāstra, xix, 437.
Grahagaṇita, by Bhāskarācārya, 523.
Grahalāghava, by Gaṇeça, 523.
Grahaçānti, in *Yājñavalkya Smṛti*, xx.
Grāmyā, manner, 383.

Ghaṭakarparakāvya, 87, 197, n. 2, 200, 201, 227; 373.
Gheraṇḍasaṁhitā, 491.

Cakra, figure, 127.
Cakravartin, ideal of, 270.
Cañcalākṣikā, metre, 48.
Caṇḍīkucapañcāçikā, by Lakṣmaṇa Ācārya, 221.
Caṇḍīçataka, by Bāṇa, 210, 213, 214, 315.
caturarcam, 213.
Caturdārikā, book v of *Bṛhatkathāmañjarī* and *Kathāsaritsāgara*, 277, 281.
Caturvargacintāmaṇi, by Hemādri, 448.
Caturvargasaṁgraha (ed. KM. v. 75 ff.), by Kṣemendra, 239.
Catuḥçatikā, by Ārya Deva, 71.
Candrāloka, by Jayadeva, 396.
Candrikā, metre (27 + 29 *morae*), 115.
Camatkāratva, characteristic of pleasure, 397.
Campakaçreṣṭhikathānaka, by Jinakīrti, 295.
Campū, form of literature, 266, 332–7, 376.
Carpaṭapañjarikāstotra, 198, n. 2.
Cāṇakyanīti, 177, 228.
Cāṇakyarājanīti, 228.
Cāṇakyasūtrāṇi (second edition of *Arthaçāstra*, by Shama Sastri, App.), 456.
Cāṇḍālī, a Vibhāṣā, 31.
Cāṭakāṣṭaka, 234, 235.
Cārucaryāçataka, by Kṣemendra, 239.
Cārudatta, by Bhāsa, 271.
Cāruhāsinī, metre, 48.
Cikitsākalikā, by Tīsaṭa, 511.
Cikitsāmṛta, by Milhaṇa, 511.
Cikitsāsārasaṁgraha, by Cakrapāṇidatta, 511.
Cikitsāsthāna, or *Cikitsitasthāna*, therapeutics, 507, 508.
Citra, picture-like kind of poetry, 384, 389, 391.
Citralekhā, metre, 131, 419.
Cintāmaṇi, on *Çākaṭāyana Vyākaraṇa*, by Yakṣavarman, 432.
Cūlikā Paiçācikā, a Prākrit, 434, 435.
celaknopam, until the clothes were wet, 18.
Caurapañcāçikā, or *Caurīsuratapañcāçikā*, by Bilhaṇa, 188–90, 233.

Chandasi, 'in the Veda', 424.
Chandassūtra, by Piṅgala, xxiv, 48, 415, 416.
Chando'nuçāsana, by Hemacandra, 416, 417.
Chandomañjarī, by Gaṅgādāsa, 417.
Chandoviciti, 296, 307.

Jagaḍūcarita, by Sarvāṇanda, 173.
Jagatī, metre, 417.
jatru, sense of, 512.
Janmabhāṣā, mother tongue, 14.
jampatī, variant of *dampatī*, 123.
Jayamaṅgalā, comm. on *Kāmasūtra*, by Yaçodhara, 469.
jayamānam, irregular middle, 123, n. 2.
Jaladharamālā, metre, 131, 419.
Jaloddhatagati, metre, 115, 131, 419.
jas, with genitive, 18.
Jātakas, 8, 41, 68, 69, 70, 245, 249, 320, 352, 353, 354, 355.
Jātakamālā, by Ārya Çūra (on relation to Jātakas, see Oldenberg, GN. 1918, p. 464), ix, 67–70, 255, 268, 332, 451.
Jānakīharaṇa, by Kumāradāsa, 119–24.
jāmitra, diameter, Greek loan-word, 25, 80, 530.
Jāmbavatīvijaya, by Pāṇini, 45, 430.
Jituma (Didymos), name of sign of Zodiac (the Heavenly Twins), borrowed from Greek, 530.
Jīvandharacampū, perhaps by Haricandra, 143, n. 2, 331.
Jīvanmuktiviveka, by Mādhava, 477.
Juka (Zugon), name of sign of Zodiac (the Wain), borrowed from Greek, 530.
Jaina Māhārāṣṭrī, a Prākrit, 28, 31, 34, 434.
Jaina Çaurasenī, a Prākrit, 28, 29, 31.
Jainendra Vyākaraṇa, by Pūjyapada Devanandin, 432.
Jaimini Bhārata, 480.
joṣam abhūyata, curious use, 123.
jjh, for Aryan *gzh*, 4.
Jñānārṇava, by Çubhacandra, 497.
Jñānārṇava Tantra, 482.
Jyotirvidābharaṇa, 534.
Jyotiṣa, 404.
Jyotiṣa Vedāṅga, 516.
Jyotiṣasāroddhāra, by Harṣakīrti Sūri, 534.
jyotis, for *dyotis*, 4.

Ṭākkī, a Prākrit, 435.
Ṭākkī, a Vibhāṣā, 31.

Ṭupṭīkā, by Kumārila, 474.

ḍ and *ḍh*, as *ḷ* and *ḷh*, 3, 5.
Ḍhākkī, a *Vibhāṣā*, 31.

Tattvacintāmaṇi, by Gañgeça, 484, 485.
Tattvabindu, by Vācaspati Miçra, 474.
Tattvas, by Raghunandana, 449.
Tattvasaṁkhyāna, by Madhva, 479.
Tattvasamāsa, 489.
Tattvārthasāradīpikā, by Sakalakīrti, 497.
tatprathamataḥ, as a conjunction, 67.
Tatsamas, words, xxvii, 415.
Tathāgataguhyaka, 496.
Taddhita, suffixes, 422.
Tadbhavas, words, 415.
tan, free use of, introduced by Bhāravi, 121, n. 1.
Tanucchada, feather, 123.
Tanumadhyā, metre, 48, 118, 419.
Tantrayukti, list of, xxiii, n. 3.
Tantravārttika, by Kumārila, 474.
Tantrarāja Tantra, 482.
Tantras, 481, 482.
Tantrākhyāyika, version of *Pañcatantra*, 70, 175, 245, 246, 247, 259, 260, 261, 461, 462.
tapasyadbhavanam, dubious form, 123, n. 2.
Tarañgavatī, by Pādalipta, 34.
Tarañgas, divisions of *Kathāsaritsāgara*, 281.
Tarkakaumudī, by Laugākṣi Bhāskara, 486.
Tarkabhāṣā, by Keçava Miçra, 486.
Tarkasaṁgraha, by Annam Bhaṭṭa, 486.
Tarkāmṛta, by Jagadīça, 486.
tavant, participle in, freely used in classical Sanskrit, 6.
tave, infinitive in, dropped in classical Sanskrit, 7.
tavai, infinitive, 18.
Tājika, by Nīlakaṇṭha, 532.
tāt, imperative in, 213.
Tātparya, doctrine of, 387, 388.
Tātparyapariçuddhi, by Udayana, 484.
Tāmarasa, metre, 419, 533.
Tārkikarakṣā, by Varadarāja, 484.
tāvanta, for *tāvant*, 67.
Tāvuri, or *Taururi* (Tauros), name of sign of Zodiac (the Bull), borrowed from Greek, 530.
Tithi, doctrine of, 517.
Tithyādipattra, by Makaranda, 523.
Tilakamañjarī, by Dhanapāla, 272, 331.
tum, infinitive in, prevails in classical Sanskrit, 6.
Tulyayogitā, equal pairing, 213, 380, 399.
Tūṇaka, metre, 419, 523.
Tūtīnāmeh, by Nachshabī, 359.
tṛṇabhakṣaṇanyāya, maxim, 409.
tṛtīya, pronominal forms of, 10.
Taittirīya Prātiçākhya, xxv, 423.
Taittirīya Saṁhitā, 440.
Toṭaka, metre, 47, 107, 118, 131, 141, 419, 509, n. 3, 533.
Tol-kāppiyam, date of, 22, n. 2.
Taukṣika, name of sign of Zodiac (the Archer), borrowed from Greek, 530.
ty, treatment of, in Açokan dialects, 28.
tya, pronominal base, 18.
Trikāṇḍaçeṣa, by Puruṣottamadeva, 414.
Trikoṇa, triangle, term borrowed from Greece, 530.
Tripuradahana, by Vāsudeva, 97, n. 5.
Trirūpakoça, 414.
Triṣaṣṭiçalākāpuruṣacarita, by Hemacandra, 143, 294.
Triṣṭubh, metre, 417, 437, 455, 509, n. 3.
Theragāthās, 199.
Therīgāthās, 199, 225.

Dakṣa Smṛti, 448.
Dakṣiṇāmūrtistotra, by Çañkara, 198, n. 2, 477; comm. on, by Sureçvara, 477.
daṇḍa, not = *dandra*, 30, n. 1.
Daṇḍaka, metre, 419, 533.
Daṇḍanīti, 453.
Damayantīkathā, by Trivikrama Bhaṭṭa, 332.
Darpadalana, by Kṣemendra, 238, 239.
Darçana, philosophic system, 471.
darçayate, with double accusative, 115.
darçayitāhe, in Çrīharṣa, 18.
Daçakumāracarita, by Daṇḍin, xvi, 296–300, 319, 320, 370, 381.
Daçagītikāsūtra, by Āryabhaṭa, 521.
Daçabhūmīçvara Mahāyānasūtra, 494.
Daçarūpa, by Dhanaṁjaya, 266.
Daçāvatāracarita, by Kṣemendra (cf. Meyer, *Altind. Schelmenbücher*, i, pp. xxxiii f.; Foucher, JA. 1892, ii. 167 ff.), 136.
Dākṣiṇātyā, a Vibhāṣā, 31.
Dānastutis, 41.
Dāmakaprahasana, xiii.
Dāyabhāga, by Jīmūtavāhana, 449.
Digambara, 261.
divira, Persian loan-word, 25.
Divyāvadāna, 15, 22, 62, n. 4, 65–7, 210, 289, 301.
diçā, epic form, 20.
disi, for *dṛçi*, 11.
dīnāra, 63, 248, 283, 445.
Dīpaka, illuminator, figure, 213, 373, 380, 399.
Dīrghavyāpāravādin, school, 387, n. 3.
duruttara, for *duṣṭara*, 24.
durūhadruta, doubtful sense of, 220, n. 1.

Durghaṭavṛtti, by Çaraṇadeva, 220, n. 1, 430.
duhitā, as dissyllabic in Vedic, 7; epic form, 20.
duhutuya, southern form of *duhitṛ*, 29.
Dṛṣṭānta, exemplification, 383, 399; parable, ix.
Dṛṣṭāntaçataka, by Kusumadeva, 234.
Devajanavidyā, 8.
devatrā, form obsolete, 18.
devānām priya, title, 428.
Devīçataka, by Ānandavardhana, 33, 218.
Devyaparādhakṣamāpaṇastotra, ascribed to Çaṅkara, 217.
deçabhāṣā, vernacular, 14, 32.
deçī, words, 415.
Deçīnāmamālā, by Hemacandra, 415.
deçīçabda, 34.
Daiva, by Deva, 430.
Dodhaka, metre, 47, 131, 141, 183, 370, 419, 533.
Doṣas, of poetry, 391.
doṣā, incorrect form, 123.
Dohada, *motif*, 343.
Dohā, metre, 370, 371.
Drutapada, metre, 419.
Drutavilambita, metre, 107, 118, 124, 130, 141, 183, 187, 419, 533.
Druti, of mind, relation to *Mādhurya* of style, 390.
Dvādaçapañjarikāstotra, ascribed to Çaṅkara, 217, 236.
dvāra, frontier watch station, 170.
Dvāvinçatyavadāna, 493.
dvitīya, pronominal forms of, 10.
Dvirūpakoça, 414.
Dvisaṁdhānakāvya, by Daṇḍin, xvi, n. 5.
Dvaita, dualism, 479.
Dvyāçrayakāvya, by Hemacandra, 172.

dh, reduced to *h*, 3, 7.
Dhanvantari Nighaṇṭu, 512.
Dhammapada, Dutreuil de Rhyns MS., 29, n. 4, 227.
Dharma, custom, law, righteous conduct, 92, 450, 451, 455, 467.
dharmadeçanā, 261.
Dharmapada, 491.
Dharmaparīkṣā, by Amitagati, 240.
Dharmabindu, by Haribhadra, 497.
Dharmaratna, by Jīmūtavāhana, 449.
Dharmaçarmābhyudaya, by Haricandra, 143, 336.
Dharmaçāstra, 243, 405, 408, 437–9, 451, 456.
Dharmasaṁgraha, by Nāgārjuna, 495.
Dharmasūtra, 50, 71, 408, 440.
Dharmāmṛta, by Āçādhara, 497.
Dhātukāvya, by Vāsudeva, 133, n. 3.
Dhātupāṭha, 24, 412.
Dhātupradīpa, by Maitreyarakṣita, 430.
dhāraṇā, concentration, 99.
Dhāraṇīs, spells, 495.
dhi, termination disused in imperative in classical Sanskrit, 6.
dhitā, *dhītā* forms of *duhitṛ* (*dhītā* from *dhe* is not plausible), 29.
dhītā, Pāli, 7.
Dhīralalitā, metre, 419, 533.
dhūyā, Ardhamāgadhī form, 29.
Dhṛtaçrī, metre, 131, 419.
dhva, termination dropped in classical Sanskrit, 6.
Dhvani, doctrine of, 386–94.
Dhvanyāloka, by Ānandavardhana, 386–8.
Dhvanyālokalocana, by Abhinavagupta, 387.
dhvāt, imperative termination disappears in classical Sanskrit, 6.

na cāpi ca, 64.
Nakṣatra Pariçiṣṭa, 516.
Nagnaka, 261.
Naṭasūtras, mentioned by Pāṇini, 372.
nanivṛtam, compounded, 115.
Nandana, metre, 118, 419.
Nandīsūtra, 461.
Narapatijayacaryā Svarodaya, by Narahari, 534, 535.
Naravāhanaḍ(datta)janman, book iv of *Bṛhatkathāmañjarī* and *Kathāsaritsāgara*, 277, 281.
Narkuṭaka, metre, 118, 419, 533.
Nala, 140.
Nalacampū, by Trivikrama Bhaṭṭa, 332, 333.
Nalābhyudaya, by Vāmana Bhaṭṭa Bāṇa, 315, n. 2.
Nalodaya, by Vāsudeva, 87, n. 2, 97, 98, 197, n. 2.
Navaratnaparīkṣā, by Nārāyaṇa Paṇḍita, 465.
Navasāhasāṅkacarita, by Padmagupta, 151, 152, 201, n. 4.
Navasāhasāṅkacarita, by Śrīharṣa, 147, 336.
Nāgara Apabhraṅça, 35, 435; supposed source of Rājasthānī and Gujarātī (Chatterji, *Bengali*, i. 6 f.), 32.
Nāgaraka, character of the, 51, 52.
Nāgānanda, play by Harṣa, xiv, 124, 134, 232.
Nāṭakalakṣaṇaratnakoça, by Sāgaranandin, xv.
Nāṭyadarpaṇa, by Rāmacandra and Guṇacandra, xv.
Nāṭyaçāstra, 12, 31, 60, 132, 308, 372, 373, 381, 383, 392, 407, 416, 433, 465.
Nāṇaka, a coin, 446.
nāth, with genitive, 18.
Nānārtha, homonymous dictionaries, 412.
Nānārtharatnamālā, by Irugapa, 414.

Nānārthārṇavasaṁkṣepa, by Keçavasvāmin, 414.
Nāmamālā, by Kātyāyana, 413.
Nāmamālā, by Dhanaṁjaya, 414.
Nāmaliṅgānuçāsana, by Amarasiṅha, 413, 414.
Nārada Pāñcarātra, 480.
Nārada Smṛti, xix, 441, 445, 446, 451, 461.
Nārāçaṅsīs, type of literature, 9, 41.
Nāvanītaka (on date cf. Keith, IOC. ii. 740), 509.
nigame, 'in the Veda', 424.
Nighaṇṭavas, 412.
Nighaṇṭuçeṣa, by Hemacandra, 414.
Nidarçana, illustration, figure of speech, 380, 399.
Nidānakathā, 57.
Nidāna Sūtra, 415.
Nidānasthāna, pathology, 506, 507.
niravasita, excommunicated, 18.
Nirukta, by Yāska, 412.
Nirṇayasindhu, by Kamalākara, 449.
Nirvāṇadaçaka, ascribed to Çaṅkara, 198, n. 2.
niçāmya, irregular use, 63.
niṣedivān, 130.
ni-ṣṭhīv, metaphorical use of, 378.
Nītiprakāçikā, 464.
Nītimañjarī, by Dyā Dviveda, 239.
Nītiratna, by Vararuci, 231.
Nītiratnākara, by Caṇḍeçvara, 464.
Nītivākyāmṛta, by Somadeva, 464.
Nītiçataka, 175, 177.
Nītiçāstra, 243, 405, 451.
Nītisāra, by Kāmandaki, 462.
Nītisāra, ascribed to Ghaṭakarpara, 201, 231.
Nīlamatapurāṇa, 161.
nīçāra, covering, 123.
Nṛpāvalī, by Kṣemendra, 161.
Nepālamāhātmya, 267.
Nemidūta, by Vikrama, 86, n. 2.
Nemināhacariu, in Apabhrañça, 35.
Neminirvāṇa, by Vāgbhaṭa, 143, n. 3.
Naiṣadhīya, by Çrīharṣa, 18, 139–42, 147.
Naiṣkarmyasiddhi, by Sureçvara, 477.
nyadhāyiṣātām, 130.
Nyāyakaṇikā, by Vācaspati Miçra (cf. Th. Stcherbatsky, *Festgabe Jacobi*, pp. 369–80), 474.
Nyāyakandalī, by Çrīdhara, 485.
Nyāyakumudacandrodaya, by Prabhācandra, 497.
Nyāyapraveça, by Dignāga or Çaṅkarasvāmin, xxi, n. 3, xxii, 484.
Nyāyabindu, by Dharmakīrti, 484.
Nyāyabinduṭīkā, by Dharmottara, 484.
Nyāyabinduṭīkāṭippaṇī, by Mallavādin, 484.
Nyāyabhāṣya, by Vātsyāyana, 461, 483, 484.
Nyāyamañjarī, by Jayanta Bhaṭṭa, 221, 484.
Nyāyamālāvistara, by Mādhava, 474.
Nyāyavārttikatātparyaṭīkā, by Vācaspati Miçra, 484.
Nyāyas, maxims, 409, 410.
Nyāyas, rules of interpretation, 472.
Nyāyasāra, by Bhāsarvajña, 484.
Nyāya Sūtra, xxii, 406, 407, 472, 482–4.
Nyāyāvatāra, by Siddhasena, 484.
Nyāsa, by Jinendrabuddhi, 124, 376, 413, 430.

Paumacariya, by Vimala Sūri, 34.
Pañca, book xiii of *Bṛhatkathāmañjarī*, 278; xiv of *Kathāsaritsāgara*, 282.
Pañcakrama, by several hands, 496.
Pañcatantra, xxvii, n. 1, 48, 70, 243, 245, 246, 247, 263, 275, 283, 285, 291, 319, 320, 332, 347, 356, 360, 361, 362, 450, 461, 462, 463.
Pañcadaṇḍacchatraprabandha, 293.
Pañcadaçī, by Mādhava, 479.
Pañcapādikā, by Padmapāda, 477.
Pañcaçatī, by Mūka, 218.
Pañcasāyaka, by Jyotirīçvara, 469.
Pañcasiddhāntikā, by Varāhamihira, 75, 517.
Pañcastavī, 218.
Pañcākhyānaka, 261.
Pañcākhyānoddhāra, by Meghavijaya, xii, 261.
Paṭṭāvalis, Jain lists of teachers, &c., 148.
Paṇaphara (Epanaphora), astrological term borrowed from Greek, 530.
Pathyāpathyanighaṇṭu, 512.
Padamañjarī, by Haradatta, 209.
Padārthadharmasaṁgraha, by Praçastapāda, 485.
Padma Purāṇa, alleged but improbable use of, by Kālidāsa, x, 97, n. 2.
Padmapurāṇa, by Raviṣeṇa, 498.
Padmāvatī, book xii of *Bṛhatkathāmañjarī*, 278; xvii of *Kathāsaritsāgara*, 282.
Padya-Kādambarī, by Kṣemendra, 136.
Padyacūḍāmaṇi, by Buddhaghoṣācārya, 143.
Padyāvalī, by Rūpagosvāmin, 219, 223.
pabbhāra, from *prahvāra*, 25.
Paramārthasaptati, by Vasubandhu, 488.
Paramārthasāra, by Abhinavagupta, 481.
Parāçara Smṛti, 447, 448.
Pariṇāma, commutation as figure, 399.
pari-bhāṣ, abuse, 67.
Paribhāṣāsūtra, on Pāṇini's grammar, 430, 431; on *Cāndra Vyākaraṇa*, 432; on *Çākaṭāyana Vyākaraṇa*, 432.
Paribhāṣenduçekhara, by Nāgojī Bhaṭṭa, 431.
Parivṛtti, confusion of similars, 380.

Pariçiṣṭaparvan, by Hemacandra, 294.
Parisaṁkhyā, exhaustive statement, 313.
Parīkṣāmukhasūtra, by Māṇikya Nandin, 484.
parut, goes out of use, 18.
Paruṣā, harsh manner (*vṛtti*), 383, 391.
parokṣe, past tenses used of, 115.
Paryāyokta, indirect expression, 380, 382, 396.
Parṣad, corporation of Purohitas, 170.
palāṣa, for *palāça*, 11.
Pavanadūta (best ed. by Chintaharan Chakravarti), by Dhoī, 86, 219, n. 1.
paçyatohara, robber in broad daylight, 123.
Pāiyalacchī, by Dhanapāla, 331, 415.
Pāñcāla, *Pāñcālī*, style, 205, 331, 381, 384, 394, 395.
Pāṇḍavacaritra, by Devaprabha Sūri, 143.
Pātālavijaya, by Pāṇini, 45.
Pāthona (with variants, *Pāthena*, &c.), name of sign of Zodiac (the Virgin), Parthenos, borrowed from Greek, 530.
pādāgra, high revenue office, 170.
Pāramitās, perfections, 68.
Pārasīprakāça, 415.
pārejalam, 130.
Pārvatīpariṇaya, authorship of, xiii, 315.
Pārvatīrukmiṇīya, by Vidyāmādhava, 139, n. 3.
Pārçvābhyudaya, by Jinasena, 86.
Pālagopālakathānaka, by Jinakīrti, 295.
Pāçakakevalī, 535.
Pitāmaha Smṛti, 448.
putrādinī, as term of abuse, 9.
Punarukta, repetition, 106.
Purāṇa, form of literature, 9.
Purāṇas, 93, 147, 148, 461.
Puruṣakāra, by Kṛṣṇalīlāçuka, 430.
Puruṣaparīkṣā, by Vidyāpati, 293.
Puṣpasūtra, 427.
Puṣpitāgrā, metre, 107, 115, 118, 124, 130, 141, 157, 183, 418, n. 2, 419, 533.
Pūrvapīṭhikā, of the *Daçakumāracarita*, 298.
Pūrvamīmāṅsā Sūtra, xxi, 472.
pūṣāṇaṃ, epic form, 19.
Pṛthvī, metre, 78, 118, 131, 141, 158, 183, 419, 509, n. 3, 533.
Pṛthvīrājavijaya, 172, 173.
Paitāmaha Siddhānta, 516, 518.
Paiçācikā, a Prākrit, 434, 435.
Paiçācī, a Prākrit, 28, 29, 31, 267, 269, 270, 276, 433, 434, 435.
Poruḷadhikāraṁsūtra, 22.
Pauliça Siddhānta, xxiv, 518, 519, 520, 521.
Prakriyākaumudī, by Rāmacandra, 430.
pragraha, equivalent to *pragṛhya*, xxv.
pra-ghaṭ, ooze forth, 67.
Prajñāpāramitās, 495.
Prajñāpāramitāhṛdaya, 495.
Pratāparudrayaçobhūṣaṇa, by Vidyānātha, 395.
Pratijñāyaugandharāyaṇa, by Bhāsa, xv, 101, n. 1, 451.
Pratibhā, genius, 340.
Pratimānāṭaka, by Bhāsa, xxiii, 451.
Prativastūpamā, typical comparison, 399, 400.
prativedha, Buddhist term, 64.
Pratīpa, converse, figure of speech, 399.
Prabandhakoça, by Rājaçekhara, 293.
Prabandhacintāmaṇi, by Merutuñga, 293, 339.
Prabhā, metre, 115, 131, 419.
Prabhāvakacaritra, by Prabhācandra and Pradyumna Sūri, 294, n. 5.
Prabhāvatī, metre, 419, 533.
Pramadā, metre, 131, 419.
Pramāṇamīmāṅsā, by Hemacandra, 484.
Pramāṇasamuccaya, by Dignāga, 484.
Pramāṇikā, metre, 419, 509, n. 3, 533.
Pramitākṣarā, metre, 47, 115, 118, 124, 130, 419, 509, n. 3, 533.
Prameyakamalamārtaṇḍa, by Prabhācandra, 497.
pravara, covering, 123.
praverita, Buddhist term, 64.
Praçastis, characteristics of, 149, 150.
Praçnottaropāsakācāra, by Sakalakīrti, 497.
praçrabdhi, Buddhist term, 64.
prasabham, from *sah*, 25.
Prasāda, clearness of style, 50, 374, 377.
prasita, with instrumental, 18.
Praharaṇakalitā (v.l. *Praharaṇakalikā*), metre, 118, 419.
Praharṣiṇī, metre, 47, 107, 115, 118, 124, 419, 533.
Prākṛtakalpataru, by Rāma Tarkavāgīça, 434.
Prākṛtakāmadhenu, by Rāvaṇa, 433, 434.
Prākṛta Piñgala, 33, 35.
Prākṛtaprakāça, by Vararuci, 40, 433, 434.
Prākṛtarūpāvatāra, by Siṅharāja, 434.
Prākṛtalakṣaṇa, by Caṇḍa, 433.
Prākṛtavyākaraṇasūtra, by Çeṣanāga, 434.
Prākṛtaçabdānuçāsana, by Trivikrama, 434.
Prākṛtasarvasva, by Mārkaṇḍeya, 434.
prāg eva, how much more, 64.
Prācyā, a Prākrit, 435.
Prācyā, a Vibhāṣā, 31.
prājitṛ, driver, 10.
Prātiçākhyas, xxv, 423.
Priyadarçikā, by Harṣa, xiv.
priyākhya, irregular epic form, 20.
Preyas, expression of pleasure, 380, 382, 389.
protha, Prākritic, xxvi.

Prauḍhamanoramā, by Bhaṭṭoji Dīkṣita, 430.

Phiṭsūtra, by Çāntanava, 430.

bahādura, Persian loan-word, 25.
Bālabhārata, by Amaracandra, 137.
Bālāvabodhana, by Kāçyapa, 432.
Bāhudantaka, 451.
Bāhlīkī, a Prākrit, 435.
Bārhaspatya Arthaçāstra, 452.
bibharāmbabhūve, 130.
Biruda, form of literature, 149, n. 1.
Bilhaṇakāvya, 188.
Bījagaṇita, by Bhāskarācārya, 523.
Buddhacarita, by Açvaghoṣa, 56, 58, 59, 91.
busa, for *bṛça*, 4.
Bṛhaj Jātaka, by Varāhamihira, 530.
Bṛhatī, by Prabhākara, 473, 474.
Bṛhatkathā, by Guṇāḍhya, 28, 31, 40, 157, 246, 262, 266–87, 307, 316, 319, 320, 364, 368, 369, 434.
Bṛhatkathāmañjarī, by Kṣemendra, 246, 261, 276–80.
Bṛhatkathāçlokasaṁgraha, by Budhasvāmin, 271, 272–5.
Bṛhatsaṁhitā, by Varāhamihira, 159, 416, 461, 529, 532, 533.
Bṛhadāraṇyaka Upaniṣad, 98, 450, 473.
Bṛhad Gautama Smṛti, 448.
Bṛhad Brahma Saṁhitā, 480.
Bṛhad Vivāhapaṭala, by Varāhamihira, 530.
Bṛhan Manu, 441.
Bṛhaspati Smṛti, 450, 451, 452.
Bodhicaryāvatāra, by Çāntideva, 72, 73.
Bodhisattvabhūmi, by Asañga, 495.
Bauddhadhikkāra, by Udayana, 484.
Bauddhasaṁgati (or *saṁgīti*), viii, 308.
Baudhāyana Dharmasūtra, xix.
Brahmasabhās, 339.
Brahma Siddhānta, 520.
Brahma Sūtra, 406, 472.
Brāhmaṇas, 70, 71, 422.
Brāhmaṇasarvasva, by Halāyudha, 448.
Brāhma Siddhānta, by Brahmagupta, 522.

bh, reduced to *h*, 3, 7.
Bhaktamāla, 480; *see* the next.
Bhakt Mālā, 191.
Bhaktāmarastotra, by Mānatuñga, 214.
Bhaktiçāstra, ascribed to Nārada, (later than *Çāṇḍilya Sūtra*; P. K. Gode, ABI. iv. 63–95), 480.
Bhaktisūtras, ascribed to Çāṇḍilya, 480.
Bhagavadgītā, 445.
Bhagavantabhāskara, by Nīlakaṇṭha, 449.
bhañgī-bhaṇiti, imaginative speech, 392.
Bhaṭṭārakavāra, as sign of date, 263.
Bhadrakalpāvadāna, 493.
Bhadanta, origin of, 24.
Bhadrikā, metre, 419, 533.
Bharaṭakadvātriṅçikā, 293.
Bhavānyaṣṭaka, ascribed to Çañkara, 218.
Bhavisattakaha, 35.
Bhāgavata Purāṇa, 138, 199.
Bhāmatī, by Vācaspati Miçra, 477.
Bhāmahavivaraṇa, by Udbhaṭa, 383.
Bhāminīvilāsa, by Jagannātha, 234.
Bhāratacampū, by Ananta, 336.
Bhāratamañjarī, by Kṣemendra, 136.
Bhāva, emotion, 63, n. 3, 92, 373.
Bhāvakatva, generalizing power of words, 392.
Bhāvaprakāça, by Bhāvamiçra, 511.
Bhāvaprakāça, by Çāradātanaya, xv.
Bhāvaçataka, by Nāgarāja, 234.
Bhāvika, quality of style, 378, 380, 382.
Bhāṣā, of Pāṇini, xxvi, 7, 424.
Bhāṣāpariccheda, by Viçvanātha, 486.
Bhāṣāvṛtti, by Puruṣottamadeva, 430.
Bhāṣya, on *Brahma Sūtra*, by Çañkara, 476, 477.
Bhāṣya, 407, 456.
Bhāsvatī, by Çatānanda, 523.
Bhikṣāṭanakāvya, by Çivadāsa, 221.
bhidelima, fit to be broken, 123.
Bhujañgaprayāta, metre, 419, 533.
Bhujañgavijṛmbhita, metre, 419, 533.
Bhūtabhāṣā, 386.
bhūyasyā mātrayā, still more, 67.
Bheḍa (*Bheḷa*, *Bhela*) *Saṁhitā*, xxiii, 508.
Bhojakatva, cause of enjoyment of poetry, 392.
Bhojaprabandha, by Ballālasena, 293.
Bhramaravilasita, metre, 131, 420, 533.
Bhrāntimat, confusion as figure of speech, 399.

m, molossus, 416.
Mañgalāṣṭaka, 218.
mañjaka, for *mañcaka*, 11.
Mañjarī, metre, 48, 420.
Mañjubhāṣiṇī, metre, 107, 130, 420.
Mañjuçrīmūlatantra, 496.
Maṇiguṇanikara, metre, 420, 533.
Maṇimekhalai, Tamil work, xxii.
Mattamayūra, metre, 107, 115, 131, 420, 509, n. 3, 533.
Mattā, metre, 420, 533.
Madanapārijāta, by Viçveçvara, 448.
Madanamañcukā, book vii of *Bṛhatkathā*, 277, 278; vi of *Kathāsaritsāgara*, 282.
Madanarekhākathā, xii.
Madanavinodanighaṇṭu, by Madanapāla, 512.
Madālasācampū, by Trivikrama Bhaṭṭa, 332.
Madirāvatī, book xi of *Bṛhatkathāmañ-*

jarī, 278; xiii of *Kathāsaritsāgara*, 282.
Madhyamakakārikās, by Nāgārjuna, 71.
Madhyamāgama, 491.
Madhyasiddhāntakaumudī, by Varadarāja, 430.
madhyesamudram, 130.
Manu Smṛti, xix, 404, 411, 424, 438, 439–45, 450, 460, 464.
mano-han, fulfil one's longing, 17.
mantre, 'in the Veda', 424.
Mandākrāntā, metre, 78, 84, 105, 118, 124, 131, 141, 157, 183, 187, 416, 509, n. 3, 533.
manye, parenthetical use of, 10.
Mayamata, 464.
Mayūrāṣṭaka, by Mayūra, 201, 202.
maragaa, Greek loan-word, 25, n. 5.
maruta, by-form of *marut*, 123.
marmāvidh, piercing the vitals, 123.
masi, termination dropped in classical Sanskrit, 6.
masiṇa, for *mṛtsna*, 24.
Mahākavi, title, 386.
Mahākāla Tantra, 496.
Mahākāvya, 92, 101, 376.
Mahānirvāṇa Tantra, 482.
Mahābhārata, 9, 12, 13, 41, 43, 45, 70, 109, 137, 159, 165, 227, 242, 248, 256, 261, 264, 276, 279, 362, 371, 439, 451, 480, 489.
Mahābhāṣya, by Patañjali, xx, 5, 9, 19, 20, 45–7, 71, 153, 406, 407, n. 1, 427–9, 431, 469, n. 2, 477, 483, 490.
Mahābhiṣeka, book xvii of *Bṛhatkathāmañjarī*, 279; xv of *Kathāsaritsāgara*, 282.
Mahāmāyūrī Vidyārājñī, 509, n. 2.
Mahāmālikā, metre, 107, 131, 420.
Mahāyānaçraddhotpāda, 56, 493.
Mahāyānasūtrālaṁkāra, by Asaṅga, viii, 73, 495.
Mahārṇavayugacchidrakūrmagrīvārpaṇanyāya, maxim, 410.
Mahāvagga, 57.
Mahāvastu, 15, 22, 491, 492.
Mahāvyutpatti, 415.
Mahimnaḥstava, by Puṣpadanta, 220, 221, 386.
Mahīpālacaritra, by Cāritrasundara Gaṇin, 143.
Mahosadha Jātaka, 363.
mā, with present participle, 18.
Māgadha Apabhraṅça, supposed source of Māgadhī, 32.
Māgadhī, a Prākrit, 28, 29, 30, 31, 35, 341, 433, 435.
Māgadhī, style, 394.
Māṭhara Vṛtti, on *Sāṁkhyakārikā*, 482.
Mātaṅgalīlā, by Nārāyaṇa, 465.
mātulī, or *mātulānī*, 10.
Mātrāchandas, 418.
Mātrāsamaka, type of metre, 183.
Mādhavānalakathā, by Ananda, 293.
Mādhavīya Dhātuvṛtti, by Mādhava, 430.
Mādhurya, sweetness of style, 50, 374, 378, 381, 382.
Mādhyamikasūtra, by Nāgārjuna, 495.
Mānameyodaya, by Nārāyaṇa Bhaṭṭa, 474.
Mānava Gṛhyasūtra, 441.
Mānava Dharmaçāstra, see *Manu Smṛti*.
Mānasāra, xx, 464.
Mānasollāsa, by Sureçvara, 477.
mārisa, origin of, 24.
Mārga, school of poetry, 376, 377.
Mālatī metre, 47, 420, 533.
Mālatīmādhava, by Bhavabhūti, 285.
Mālavikāgnimitra, by Kālidāsa, 80.
Mālā, metre, 48.
Mālinī, metre, 107, 115, 118, 124, 130, 141, 158, 183, 187, 420, 509, n. 3, 533.
Māhārāṣṭra Apabhraṅça, supposed source of Marāṭhī, 32, 35.
Māhārāṣṭrī, a Prākrit, 28, 29, 30, 34, 40, 48, 150, 224, 226, 268, 292, 433, 434, 435.
Mitākṣarā, by Vijñāneçvara, 447.
Mittavindaka Jātaka, 285.
mihira, Persian loan-word, 25.
Mīmāṅsānukramaṇī, by Maṇḍana Miçra, 474.
Mīmāṅsānyāyaprakāça, by Āpadeva, 474.
Mīmāṅsā Sūtra, 407, n. 1, and see *Pūrvamīmāṅsā Sūtra*.
Mukundamālā, by Kulaçekhara, 218.
Muktaka, single verses, 376.
Mugdhabodha, by Vopadeva, 432.
Mugdhopadeça, by Jalhaṇa, 239.
mudrā, Persian loan-word, 25.
Mudrārākṣasa, by Viçākhadatta, 175, 258, 459, 460, 463.
muṣṭiṁdhaya, baby, 123.
Muhūrta, works on, 534.
Mṛgāvatīcaritra, by Devaprabha Sūri, 143.
Mṛcchakaṭikā, xii, 52, 271, 296, 465.
Meghadūta, by Kālidāsa, 81, 82, 84–7, 99, 107, 159, 189, 191, 380, n. 1.
Meghavitāna, metre, 420, 533.
Meghavisphūrjita, metre, 420, 533.
Meghasūtra, 496.
Meṣūraṇa (Mesouranios), astrological term borrowed from Greece, 530.
maitrā, based on *mettā*, 64.
Maitrāyaṇīya Upaniṣad, 476.
Mokṣa, release, 92.
Moṭanaka, metre, 533.
Mohamudgara, ascribed to Çaṅkara, 236.

Yajurveda, 403, 415, 516.
Yajñagāthās, 71.
yat khalu, as a conjunction, 67.

Yathāsaṁkhya, observance of relative order in statement, 63, n. 3, 375, 398.
yadbhūyasā, as a conjunction, 67.
yaṁ, for *yat*, 67.
Yamaka, assonance, chiming, 45, n. 1, 63, 105, 121, 135, 141, 197, 198, 201, 212, 313, 369, 373, 378, 384, 385.
Yamakabhārata, by Ānandatīrtha, 197, n. 2.
Yamakaratnākara, by Çrīvatsāñka, 197, n. 2.
Yavana Jātaka, 531.
Yavanānī, Greek writing, 425.
Yaçastilaka, by Somadeva Sūri, 142, 266, 272, 333–6, 463.
Yaçodharacarita, by Kanakasena, 140.
Yaçodharacaritra, by Māṇikya Sūri, 142.
Yājñavalkya Smṛti, xviii, xix, 446, 447, 451, 460, 461, 508.
yāmaki, odd form in KB., 10.
yāvat, quippe, 67.
Yuktikalpataru, by Bhoja, 464.
Yugas, doctrine of, 517.
Yudhiṣṭhiravijaya, by Vāsudeva, 97, n. 5, 133, n. 2.
yuvam, *yuvat*, dropped in classical Sanskrit, 6.
yuṣme, dropped in classical Sanskrit, 7.
Yogadṛṣṭisamuccaya, by Haribhadra, 497.
Yogabindu, by Haribhadra, 497.
Yogabhāṣya, by Vyāsa, 490.
Yogamañjarī, by Vardhamāna, 465.
Yogavāsiṣṭha, 480.
Yogavāsiṣṭhasāra, by Abhinanda, 480.
Yogaçataka, by Nāgārjuna, 511.
Yogaçāstra, by Hemacandra, 241.
Yogasāra, by Nāgārjuna, 511.
Yogasārasaṁgraha, by Vijñānabhikṣu, 490.
Yoga Sūtra, 427, 472, 490, 491.
Yogācārabhūmiçāstra, by Asañga, 495.

r, in Vedic and classical Sanskrit, 4, 5.
r terminations dropped in classical Sanskrit, 6.
Raghuvaṅça, by Kālidāsa, 42, 80, 81, 98, 99, 100, 108, 119, 159.
Ratirahasya, (R. Schmidt, ZII. v. 185 ff.), by Kokkoka, 469.
Ratiçāstra, ascribed to Nāgārjuna, 470.
Ratnaparīkṣā, by Buddha Bhaṭṭa (cf. *Garuḍa Purāṇa*, lxviii–lxxx; Kirfel, *Festgabe Garbe*, p. 108), 465.
Ratnaprabhā, book xiv of *Bṛhatkathāmañjarī*, 279; vii of *Kathāsaritsāgara*, 282.
Ratnaçāstra, 465.
Ratnāvalī, by Harṣa, xiv, 237, 315.
Rathoddhatā, metre, 107, 115, 130, 141, 157, 183, 420, 533.
Rasa, sentiment, 92, 372, 373, 383, 388, 389, 390, 391, 393, 394.
Rasagaṅgādhara, by Jagannātha, 396, 397.
Rasataraṅgiṇī, by Bhānudatta, 398.
Rasamañjarī, by Bhānudatta, 398.
Rasaratnasamuccaya, by Vāgbhaṭa, 512.
Rasaratnākara, by Nāgārjuna, 512.
Rasaratnākara, by Nityanātha, 512.
Rasavat, rich in sentiment, as figure, 380, 382, 389.
Rasahṛdaya, 512.
Rasādhyāya, 512.
Rasārṇava, 512.
Rasika, man of taste, 339.
Rasendracintāmaṇi, by Rāmacandra, 512.
Raseçvaradarçana, 512.
Raseçvarasiddhānta, 512.
Rahasyas, literary works, 9.
Rākṣasakāvya, by Ravideva, 98.
Rāgavibodha, by Somanātha, 192, n. 1, 466.
Rāghavanaiṣadhīya, by Haradatta Sūri, 138.
Rāghavapāṇḍavīya, by Dhanaṁjaya, 137; by Kavirāja, 137, 307.
Rāghavapāṇḍavīyayādavīya, by Cidambara, 138.
Rājataraṅgiṇī, by Kalhaṇa, 223, 511.
Rājanighaṇṭu, by Narahari, 512.
Rājanīti, 451.
Rājanītisamuccaya, 228.
Rājamārtaṇḍa, by Bhoja, 491.
Rājamṛgāñka, by Bhoja, 523.
Rājavārttika, by Raṇaraṅgamalla, or Bhoja, 489.
Rājāvalipatākā, by Prājya Bhaṭṭa, 174.
Rājendrakarṇapūra, by Çambhu, 174, 233, 234.
Rāmacarita, by Abhinanda, 135.
Rāmapālacarita, by Sandhyākara Nandin, 137.
Rāmāyaṇa, 12, 13, 17, 20, 42–5, 56, 59, 63, 70, 85, 90, 91, 99, 133, 137, 159, 266, 270, 276, 480.
Rāmāyaṇacampū, by Bhoja and Lakṣmaṇa Bhaṭṭa, 336.
Rāmāyaṇamañjarī, by Kṣemendra, 136.
Rāvaṇārjunīya, by Bhauma, 18.
Rāṣṭrapālaparipṛcchā, 495.
Rīti, style 381, 384, 389, 391, 394, 395.
rukkha, for *vṛkṣa*, 24.
Rukmavatī, metre, 420, 533.
Rugviniçcaya, by Mādhavakara, 511.
Rucirā, metre, 118, 130, 420, 533.
ruj, with genitive, 18.
rūkṣa, origin of, 24.
Rūpakṛtin, epithet of Candragupta, 77.
Romaka Siddhānta, 518, 519, 520, 521.

ḷ and *ḷh* in *Ṛgveda*, 3.
l, south Indian, 25.
l, eastern usage, 4.
l, denotes *laghu*, short syllable, 416.
Lakṣaṇā, transferred sense of words, 387.

Lakṣaṇāvalī, by Udayana, 485.
Laghu Arhannīti, by Hemacandra, 464.
Laghu-Cāṇakya, 228.
Laghu Jātaka, by Varāhamihira, 530.
Laghu Vāsiṣṭha Siddhānta, 521.
Laghusiddhāntakaumudī, by Varadarāja, 430.
Laṅkāvatārasūtra, xxiii, 476, 494.
Lambhakas, divisions of *Bṛhatkathāmañjarī*, and *Kathāsaritsāgara*, 281.
Lalitavistara, xxiv, 15, 58, 492, 493, 503.
Lalitā, metre, 137, n. 2, 420.
Laçuna, garlic, treatise on, 509.
Lāṭī, Prākrit, in Daṇḍin, 31, n. 1.
Lāṭīyā, style, 384, 395.
Lāvānaka, book iii of *Bṛhatkathāmañjarī* and *Kathāsaritsāgara*, 277, 281.
Liṅgānuçāsana, texts by various authors, 432, 433.
lipi, Persian loan-word, 25.
līlāmbuja, as ornamental epithet, 377.
Līlāvatī, by Bhāskarācārya, 523.
Leya, name of sign of the Zodiac (the Lion), borrowed from Greek, 530.
Leça, figure, 375, 380.
Lokatattvanirṇaya, by Haribhadra, 497.
lokapakti, duty of Brahmins, 8.
loke, 'in ordinary life', 10.
lopāka, *lopāça*, Greek loan-word, 25, n. 5.

Vaṅçapattrapatita, metre, 115, 131, 420, 533.
Vaṅçasthā, metre, 47, 107, 118, 130, 141, 157, 183, 231, 416, 420, 533.
Vaṅçasthavila, metre, 509, n. 3.
Vaktra, metre, 47, 308, 330; see also *Çloka*.
Vakrokti, various uses in poetics, 381, 382, 384, 392.
Vakroktijīvita, by Kuntala, 392, 393.
Vakroktipañcāçikā, by Ratnākara, 215, 216.
Vajjālagga, by Jayavallabha, 226.
Vajracchedikā, 495.
vaṭṭati, *vartate*, 11.
vaḍḍhati, for *vardhate*, 11.
Vanamālā, metre, 420.
vandī, captive, 25, n. 4.
vam, used metaphorically, 378.
Varṇakas, cf Jain texts, 70, n. 1.
Varṇanārhavarṇana, by Mātṛceṭa, 64, n. 3.
varṇaniyama, 208, n. 1.
Vardhamāna, metre, 64.
varṣābhū, for *varṣāhū*, 25.
vas, voc. of *vant* stems, dropped in classical Sanskrit, 6.
Vasantatilaka (*Vasantatilakā*), metre, ix, 47, 48, 115, 124, 130, 135, 141, 158, 182, 187, 231, 330, 420, 533.
Vasantarājīya, 435.
Vākovākya, form of literature, 8, n. 4, 9, 505.
Vākyapadīya, by Bhartṛhari, 429.
Vājasaneyi Prātiçākhya, xxv, 423.
Vāṇībhūṣaṇa, by Dāmodara, 417, n. 4.
Vātormī, metre, 420, 533.
Vāraruca kāvya, 46, 427.
Vārttā, figure of speech, 374.
Vārttikas, 407.
Vāsavadattā, by Subandhu, viii, 124, 308–13, 315, 316, 368, 369.
Vāsiṣṭha Dharmaçāstra or *Dharmasūtra*, xix, 437, 438, 440, 441.
Vāsiṣṭha Siddhānta, 519, 521.
vikāsa, of mind, relation to *Prasāda* of style, 390.
vi-kurv, origin of, 24.
Vikramāñkadevacarita, by Bilhaṇa, 153–8, 233.
Vikramodaya, 293.
Vikramorvaçī, by Kālidāsa, 80, 167.
vicchitti, for *vikṣipti*, 24, meaning of, 392.
vijāmātṛ, southern use of, 15.
vi-jjhai, for *vi-kṣai*, 24.
vitaratitarām, 213.
vitūst-, comb one's top knot, 123.
Vidyāmādhavīya, by Vidyāmādhava, 534.
Vidyās, 9.
Vidyāsundara, by Bhāratacandra, 188.
Vidyunmālā, metre, 47, 420, 533.
Vidhiviveka, by Maṇḍana Miçra, 474.
Vibhāvanā, abnormal causation, 374, 380.
Vibhāṣās, 31.
vibhu, active, 213.
Vinaya, of the Sarvāstivādins, viii, 64, n. 4, 65.
Vinaya Piṭaka, 506.
Vināyakaçānti, in *Yājñavalkya Smṛti*, xx.
Vipulās, 108, 115, 116, 130, n. 3, 131, 157, n. 1, 421; of Āryā, 418.
Viyoginī, metre (⏑ ⏑ — ⏑ ⏑ — ⏑ — ⏑ — *a* and *c*; ⏑ ⏑ — — ⏑ ⏑ — ⏑ — ⏑ — *b* and *d*), 92.
Virūpākṣapañcāçikā, by Virūpākṣanātha, 481.
Virodha, *Virodhābhāsa*, seeming incongruity, 213, 310.
Vilāsinī, metre, 420, 533.
vivakṣitānyaparavācya, type of suggestion, 388.
vivardhayitvā, irregular form, 63.
viçāla, broad, 118.
Viçiṣṭādvaita, philosophic system, 479.
Viçeṣa, description of a special distinction, 380.
Viçvaprakāça, by Maheçvara, 414.
Viṣamaçīla, book x of *Bṛhatkathāmañjarī*, 278; xviii of *Kathāsaritsāgara*, 282.

Viṣṇudharmottara, on painting, 466.
Viṣṇudharmottara Purāṇa, 520.
Viṣṇu Purāṇa, 33.
Viṣṇu Smṛti, 450, 451, 508.
vi-ṣvan, eat noisily, 18.
vi-svan, howl, 18.
Vistara, or *Vistāra*, of mind, related to *Ojas* of style, 390.
Vītarāgastuti, by Hemacandra, 497.
Vīracaritra, by Ananta, 292.
Vīramaheçvara Tantra, 482.
Vīramitrodaya, by Mitra Miçra, 449.
vīçaduttarāṇi, Prākritism, 49.
Vṛkṣāyurveda, by Surapāla, 511.
Vṛttaratnākara, by Kedāra Bhaṭṭa, 417.
Vṛttaratnākara, by Nārāyaṇa, 417, n. 4.
Vṛtti, manner, 383, 384, 389, 391.
Vṛddha Gargasaṁhitā, 516.
Vṛddha Cāṇakya, 228.
Vṛddha Manu, 441.
Vṛddha Vāsiṣṭha Siddhānta, 521.
Vṛndamādhava, by Vṛnda, 511.
Vetālapañcaviṅçatikā, xi, 263, 264, 285, 288, 292, 320.
Vedāṅga, 405, 453, 461.
Vedāntatattvasāra, by Rāmānuja, 478.
Vedāntadīpa, by Rāmānuja, 478.
Vedāntaparibhāṣā, by Dharmarāja, 478.
Vedāntapārijātasaurabha, by Nimbārka, 479.
Vedāntasāra, by Sadānanda, 478.
Vedānta Sūtra, xxi, and see *Brahma Sūtra*.
Vedārthasaṁgraha, by Rāmānuja, 478.
Vemabhūpālacarita, by Vāmana Bhaṭṭa Bāṇa, 315, n. 2.
Velā, book viii of *Bṛhatkathāmañjarī*, 278; xi of *Kathāsaritsāgara*, 282.
Vessantara Jātaka, 503.
Vaikhānasa Dharmaçāstra, 438.
Vaijayantī, by Yādavaprakāça, 414.
Vaitālīya, metre, 107, 115, 118, 124, 130, 141, 158, 183, 418, 533.
Vaidarbha, *Vaidarbhī*, style (*mārga*, *rīti*), 49, 59, 60, 101, 121, 131, n. 2, 205, n. 1, 304, 378, 379, 381, 382, 384, 394, 395.
Vaidyajīvana, by Lolimbarāja, 511.
Vairāgyaçataka, by Bhartṛhari, 175, 177.
vairāyitāras, 130.
Vaiçeṣika Sūtra, 471, n. 1, 472.
Vaiçvadevī, metre, 131, 420, 533.
Vaiṣṇava Dharmaçāstra, 438.
Vyaktiviveka, by Mahiman Bhaṭṭa, 393, n. 1.
Vyañjanā, suggestion implicit in words, 387.
Vyatireka, contrast by dissimilitude, 213, 374, 380, 399.
vyatisārayati kathām, converse, 67.
Vyantara, Jain spirit, 261.
Vyājastuti, praise concealed as censure, 380.
Vyāḍi-saṁgraha, 339, 426.
Vyāsa Smṛti, 448.
vyutpatti, culture, 340.
vraṇasaṁrohaṇī, plant, 366.
Vratāvadānamālā, 493.
Vrācaṭa, *Vrājaḍa*, *Apabhrançа*, 32, 34, 35.

Çakuntalā, by Kālidāsa, xv, 175, 191, 348.
Çaktiyaças, book xvi of *Bṛhatkathāmañjarī*, 279; x of *Kathāsaritsāgara*, 282.
Çaṅkaracetovilāsacampū, by Çaṅkara, 337.
Çaṅkaradigvijaya, by Mādhava, 476.
Çaṅkaravijaya, ascribed to Ānandagiri, 476.
Çataka, by Bhallaṭa, 231, 232.
Çatapañcāçatikastotra, by Mātṛceṭa, 64.
Çatapatha Brāhmaṇa, 8, 9, 438, 508.
Çataçlokī, ascribed to Çaṅkara, 236.
Çataçlokī, by Hemādri, 511.
Çatruṁjayamāhātmya, 498.
Çabdapradīpa, by Sureçvara, 512.
Çabdārṇava, by Vācaspati, 413.
Çabdālaṁkāra, figures of sound, 49, 373.
çam, Vedic root, 213.
Çambhurahasya, 434.
Çaçāṅkavatī, book ix of *Bṛhatkathāmañjarī*, 278; xii of *Kathāsaritsāgara*, 282.
Çākaṭāyana Vyākaraṇa, 432.
Çākalya Siddhānta, 520.
Çākārī, a Prākrit, 435.
Çākārī, a Vibhāṣā, 31.
Çāṅkhāyana Çrautasūtra, 415.
Çāṇḍilya Sūtra, 478, 480.
Çāntiçataka, by Bhallaṭa, 232, 233.
Çābarī, a Prākrit, 435.
çāyikā, sloth, 123.
Çārīrasthāna, anatomy, &c., 507, 508.
Çārṅgadharapaddhati, by Çārṅgadhara, 222.
Çārdūlakarṇāvadāna, 65, 66.
Çārdūlavikrīḍita, metre, ix, 48, 78, 107, 118, 124, 131, 158, 182, 187, 231, 311, n. 3, 330, 420, 509, n. 3, 533.
Çālinī, metre, 47, 107, 115, 131, 183, 420, 509, n. 3, 533.
Çālivāhanakathā, by Çivadāsa, 292.
Çālihotra, by Bhoja, 465.
çās, with double accusative, 114.
Çāstra, 385.
Çikṣās, 423.
Çikṣāsamuccaya, by Çāntideva, 72, 73, 496.
Çikhariṇī, metre, 115, 124, 131, 141, 158, 182, 187, 311, n. 3, 416, 420, 533.
çithira, for *çṛthira*, 4.

çibikodyacchannaravat, maxim, 410.
Çilparatna, by Çrīkumāra, 464.
Çilpa-, *Çilpi-çāstra*, *Vāstuvidyā*, 464, 465.
Çivadṛṣṭi, by Somānanda, 481.
Çiva Sūtra, by Vasugupta, 481.
Çivāparādhakṣamāpaṇastotra, by Çaṅkara, 216.
Çiçupālavadha, by Māgha, 64, 124–31, 133.
Çiṣṭas, meaning of term, 10, 11.
Çiṣṭācāra, usage of experts, 440.
Çiṣyadhīvṛddhitantra, by Lalla, 522.
Çiṣyahitānyāsa, by Ugrabhūti, 431.
Çīghrakavi, 344.
Çukasaptati, xii, 263, 264, 290–2, 359, 362.
Çukranīti, 464.
çuklīsyāt, usage of type which becomes obsolete, 18.
Çuddhavirāj, metre, 420, 533.
çune man or *çvānaṁ man*, 18.
Çulbasūtras, 404.
Çūnya, zero, xxiv.
Çṛṅgārajñānanirṇaya, 236.
Çṛṅgāratilaka, 87, 184, 199.
Çṛṅgāratilaka, by Rudra Bhaṭṭa, 384, n. 1.
Çṛṅgāraprakāça, by Bhoja, xiv, xvi, n. 5, 394.
Çṛṅgārarasāṣṭaka, ascribed to Kālidāsa, 199, n. 2.
Çṛṅgāravairāgyataraṅgiṇī (trs. R. Schmidt, *Liebe und Ehe in alten und modernen Indien*, pp. 36 ff.), by Somaprabha, 241.
Çṛṅgāraçataka, by Bhartṛhari, 175, 177.
Çṛṅgārasaptaçatikā, by Paramānanda, 202.
Çaivabhāṣya, by Çrīkaṇṭha Çivācārya, 481.
Çaurasena Apabhraṅça, source of Western Hindī, 32.
Çaurasenī, a Prākrit, 28, 29, 30, 34, 433, 435.
Çaurikathodaya, by Vāsudeva, 97, n. 5.
Çyāmalādaṇḍaka, 218.
Çyainikaçāstra, by Rudradeva, xx.
Çrīkaṇṭhacarita, by Maṅkha, 136, 137, 307.
Çrīpuṭa, metre, 420, 533.
Çrībhāṣya, by Rāmānuja, 478, 479.
Çrutabodha, by Kālidāsa, 416.
Çrautasūtras, 437.
çlāgh, with dative, 18.
Çleṣa, paronomasia, 50, 106, 107, 212, 310, 312, 378, 380, 381, 384, 390, 396.
Çleṣārthapadasaṁgraha, by Çrīharṣa, 412.
Çloka, metre, ix, 42, n. 3, 90, 92, 107, 108, 115, 116, 118, 124, 130, 131, 141, 157, 182, 231, 233, 407, 408, 409, 417, 420, 421, 437, 457, 461, 509, n. 3, 533.
Çlokavārttika, by Kumārila, 474.
çvapucchonnamana, maxim, 410.

Ṣaḍdarçanasamuccaya, by Haribhadra, 497, 499.
Ṣaḍbhāṣācandrikā, by Lakṣmīdhara, 434, 435.
Ṣaṇmukhakalpa, 465.
ṣaṣa, for *çaça*, 11.
Ṣaṣṭitantra, by Vārṣagaṇya, 488.

saṁlakṣya-krama, form of apprehension, 388.
Saṁvarta Smṛti, 448.
Saṁsārāvarta, by Vikramāditya, 413.
Saṁsṛṣṭi, mingling of figures, 384.
Saṁhāra, 83.
Sakalācāryamatasaṁgraha, by Çrīnivāsa, 479.
sakāmam, to please, 67.
Saṁkara, mixing of figures, 384.
Saṁkīrṇa, mixing of figures, 380.
Saṁkṣiptasāra, by Kramadīçvara, 432.
Saṁkṣepaçārīraka, by Sarvajñātman, 477.
Saṁkhyāna, reckoning, xxiv.
Saṁgītadarpaṇa, by Dāmodara, 466.
Saṁgītaratnākara, by Çārṅgadeva, 466.
Saṁgraha, by Vyāḍi, 426.
Saṁghāta, collected verses, 376.
saṁ-jñā, with instrumental, 18.
Sattasaī, by Hāla, 202, 223–5.
Sat'saī, by Bihārī Lāl, 202.
satyāp-, declare truth, 123.
Saduktikarṇāmṛta, by Çrīdharadāsa, 69, n. 1, 222, 232.
Saddanīti, by Aggavaṅsa, 436.
Saddharmapuṇḍarīka, 493, 494.
sadyaḥ, as verse-filler, 90.
Sanatkumāravāstuçāstra, 464.
Saṁdeha, doubt, 399.
Sandhi, 92.
Saptapadārthī, by Çivāditya, 486.
Saptaçatī, 223, 266.
Sabhā, darbar, 136, 137, 386, 407, 408.
Samatā, evenness of sound, 378, 390.
Samayamātṛkā, by Kṣemendra, 238.
Samarāṅgaṇasūtradhāra, by Bhoja, xx.
Samasyāpūraṇa, 46, 86, 344.
Samādhi, metaphorical expression, 374, 378, 390.
Samādhirāja, 494.
Samānī, metre, 47.
Samāsokti, suggestion by metaphorical expression, 44, 328, 374, 380, 383.
Samāhita, figure of speech, 380.
Samudratilaka, by Durlabharāja, 534.
saṁpra-yam, with instrumental, 18.
Saṁbhāvana, figure, 312.
samyaktva, 295.
Samyaktvakaumudī, 295.

sarati, for *dhāvati*, 20.
sarasī, large pond, 15.
Sarasvatīkaṇṭhābharaṇa, by Bhoja, 333, 393, 394.
Sarasvatīprakriyā, by Anubhūti Svarūpācārya, 432.
Sarasvatīstotra, 218.
Sargabandha, literary type, 376, 383.
Sarpajanavidyā, 8.
sarpi, for *sarpis*, 67.
sarvatas, with accusative, 123.
Sarvatobhadra, figure, 127.
Sarvadarçanasaṁgraha, by Mādhava, 484, 489, 499, 500.
Sarvadarçanasiddhāntasaṁgraha, ascribed to Çañkara, 499.
Sarvamatasaṁgraha, 500.
sarvānte, after, 67.
sahṛdaya, connoisseur, 389.
Sahokti, mentioning two events as simultaneous, 312, 380.
Sāṁkhyakārikā, by Īçvarakṛṣṇa, xx, 77, 409, 488, 489.
Sāṁkhyatattvakaumudī, by Vācaspati Miçra, 489.
Sāṁkhya Sūtra, 472, 489.
Sārottaranirghaṇṭa, 512, n. 6.
sāha, *sāhi*, Persian loan-word, 25.
Sāhityadarpaṇa, by Viçvanātha, 335, 394, 395.
Sāhityavidyā, science of poetics, 385.
Siṅhāsanadvātriṅçikā, 292, 293.
Siṅhonnata, metre, 48.
Siddhahemacandra, by Hemacandra, 432.
Siddhāntaratna, by Nimbārka, 479.
Siddhāntaçiromaṇi, by Bhāskarācārya, 523.
Siddhiyoga, by Vṛnda, 511.
su, verse-filler, 90.
Sukumāratā, smoothness of sound, 378.
Sukṛtasaṁkīrtana, by Arisiṅha, 173.
Sukhāvatīvyūha, 494.
sudeçika, irregular form, 63.
Sudhā, metre, 509, n. 3.
Supadmavyākaraṇa, by Padmanābhadatta, 432.
Suprabhātastotra, by Harṣavardhana, 215.
Subhāṣitanīvi, by Vedāntadeçika, 223, n. 4.
Subhāṣitamuktāvalī, by Jalhaṇa, 222.
Subhāṣitaratnasaṁdoha, by Amitagati, 240, 497.
Subhāṣitasudhānidhi, by Sāyaṇa, 223, n. 4.
Subhāṣitāvali, by Vallabhadeva, xvii, n. 5, 72, 222, 223.
Subhāṣitāvalī, by Çrīvara, 223.
Sumānikā, metre, 420, 533.
Suratamañjarī, book xviii of *Bṛhatkathāmañjarī*, 279, 288; xvi of *Kathāsaritsāgara*, 282.
Surathotsava, by Someçvaradatta, 173.
suruñgā, *suruñga*, Greek syrinx, 25, 460.
Suvadanā, metre, 64, 420, 533.
Suvarṇaprabhāsa, 494.
Suvṛttatilaka, by Kṣemendra, 416.
Suhṛllekha, by Nāgārjuna, 72, 495.
Sūktikarṇāmṛta, by Çrīdharadāsa, 222.
Sūkṣma, figure of speech, 375, 380, 382.
Sūtra, style, 406, 407.
Sūtras, philosophical, 471, 472.
Sūtrasthāna, in Caraka, 506; in Suçruta, 507.
Sūtrālaṁkāra, rather *Kalpanāmaṇḍitikā*, by Kumāralāta (ed. H. Lüders, Leipzig, 1926), viii, ix, 55, 56.
sūre, for *sūraz* (*sūras*), 4.
Sūryaprajñapti, 517.
Sūryaprabha, book vi of *Bṛhatkathāmañjarī*, 277; viii of *Kathāsaritsāgara*, 282.
Sūryaçataka, by Mayūra, 201, 211–13.
Sūrya Siddhānta, 517, 518, 520, 521.
Setubandha, by Pravarasena, 97, 133, 316, 434.
Sevyasevakopadeça, by Kṣemendra, 239.
Somapālavilāsa, by Jalhaṇa, 172.
Saukumārya, smoothness of sound, 374, 381, 390.
saukharātrika, unusual compound, 123.
Saundarananda, by Açvaghoṣa, 56, 57, 59.
sausnātaka, asking if one has bathed well, 18.
Skandhaka, Prākrit metre, 376.
Stotras, 210–21.
Stotrāvalī (ed. Chowkhambā Sanskrit Series, No. 15, Benares, 1902), by Utpaladeva, 218.
sthā, with dative, 18.
Sthānāñga Sūtra, 228.
sthāpayitvā, except, 67.
Spandakārikā, by Kallaṭa, 481.
Sphuṭa Brāhmasiddhānta, by Brahmagupta, 520, 522.
Sphoṭa, doctrine of, 387.
Smaraṇa, remembrance as figure, 399.
Smaratattvaprakāçikā, by Revaṇārādhya, 470, n. 2.
smṛ, with genitive, 18.
Smṛtikalpataru, by Lakṣmīdhara, 448.
Smṛticandrikā, by Devaṇṇa Bhaṭṭa, 448.
Smṛtiratnākara, by Caṇḍeçvara, 448.
Syādvāda, 498.
Syādvādamañjarī (ed. Chowkhambā Sanskrit Series, 1900), by Malliṣeṇa, 497.
Sragdharā, metre, 78, 118, 124, 131, 141, 158, 182, 187, 311, n. 3, 330, 420, 509, n. 3, 533.
Sragdharāstotra, by Sarvajñamitra, 215.
Sragviṇī, metre, 420.
Svapnacintāmaṇi, by Jagaddeva, 534.
Svapnavāsavadattā (*Svapnavāsavadattanāṭaka*), by Bhāsa, xiii, xiv, xv.

Svabhāvokti, in style, 312, 375, 379, 382, 383.
Svayaṁvara, marriage ceremonial, 93, 94, 155, 156, 361, n. 1.
Svalpa Vivāhapaṭala, by Varāhamihira, 530.
Svāgatā, metre, 115, 131, 137, n. 2, 141, 420, 533.
Svāhāsudhākaracampū, by Nārāyaṇa, 336.

Haṭhayogapradīpikā, by Svātmārāma Yogīndra, 491.
Hayagrīvavadha, by Meṇṭha, 132.
Haracaritacintāmaṇi, by Jayaratha, 137, 266.
Haravijaya, by Ratnākara, 164.
Haravilāsa, by Rājaçekhara, 386, n. 2.
Hariṇapluta, metre, 420, 533.
Hariṇī, metre, 107, 131, 141, 158, 183, 187, 420, 533.
Harivaṅçapurāṇa, by Jinasena, 498.
Harivilāsa, by Lolimbarāja, 137.
Harṣacarita, by Bāṇa, 150, 159, 165, 173, 300, 307, 314, 316–19, 324, 325, 336, 343, 369.
halacarma, furrow, 123.
Hastavālaprakaraṇavṛtti, by Ārya Deva, 71.
Hastāmalakastotra, ascribed to Çaṅkara, 198, n. 2, 477.
Hastyāyurveda, 465.
Hārāvalī, by Puruṣottamadeva, 414.
Hārīta or *Ātreya Saṁhitā* (cf. Jolly, *Munich Catal.*, pp. 50 f.), 508, n. 5.
Hārīta Dharmaçāstra, 437.
hi and *tu* combined, 64.
Hitopadeça, by Nārāyaṇa, 246, 248, 262, 263–5.
Hibuka, astrological name, borrowed from Greek (Hypogeion), 530.
Hiraṇyakeçi Gṛhyasūtra, 450.
Hiraṇyakeçi Dharmasūtra, 438.
Hṛdayadarpaṇa, by Bhaṭṭa Nāyaka, 391, 392.
Hṛdroga, Greek loan-word, name of sign of Zodiac (Hydrochoos), 25, 530.
heṭṭhā, for *adhastāt*, 24.
Hetu, figure of speech, 375, 380.
Haima Vyākaraṇa, by Hemacandra, 432.
Horā, Greek loan-word, 223, n. 6, 530.
Horāpāṭhaka, 492.
Horāçāstra, by Bhaṭṭotpala, 534.
Horāṣaṭpañcāçikā, by Pṛthuyaças, 534.